OCR **RECOGNISING ACHIEVEMENT** **HODDER EDUCATION**

Official Publisher Partnership

OCR **BUSINESS STUDIES** for **A2**

Andy Mottershead
Alex Grant
Judith Kelt

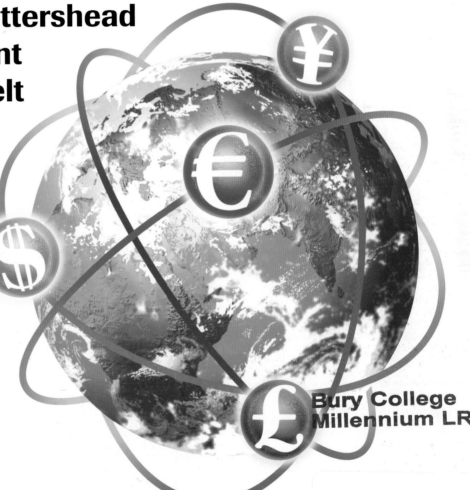

Bury College
Millennium LRC

HODDER EDUCATION
AN HACHETTE UK COMPANY

Orders: please contact Bookpoint Ltd, 130 Milton Park, Abingdon, Oxon OX14 4SB.
Telephone: (44) 01235 827720. Fax: (44) 01235 400454. Lines are open from 9.00 – 5.00,
Monday to Saturday, with a 24 hour message answering service. You can also order through
our website www.hoddereducation.co.uk

If you have any comments to make about this, or any of our other titles, please send them to
educationenquiries@hodder.co.uk

British Library Cataloguing in Publication Data
A catalogue record for this title is available from the British Library

ISBN: 978 0 340 982 082

This Edition Published 2009
Impression number   10 9 8 7 6 5 4 3 2
Year   2012, 2011, 2010, 2009

Hachette UK's policy is to use papers that are natural, renewable and recyclable products and
made from wood grown in sustainable forests. The logging and manufacturing processes are
expected to conform to the environmental regulations of the country of origin.

Cover illustration by Oxford Designers and Illustrators
Typeset by Pantek Arts Ltd
Printed in Great Britain for Hodder Education, An Hachette UK Company, 338 Euston Road,
London NW1 3BH

Contents

Introduction

This textbook has been written specifically to meet the needs of students taking OCR A2 Business Studies. It provides a comprehensive coverage of the new specifications, and uses a wide range of up-to-date examples. The order of units within the book reflects the 'Unit Content' of the OCR specification, which is available in hard copy or on the OCR website.

Special features

This book contains several special features designed to aid your understanding of the concepts and examination techniques required by OCR.

Examiner's Voice

All three authors are either Principal or Senior Examiners. They have many years' experience of examining for OCR, and use their experience to provide useful advice where appropriate. The advice concentrates on what students should do, and which common pitfalls should be avoided.

Your Turn (Questions and Case studies)

Questions

Each unit provides questions for the student to tackle, either in the form of short questions, which are intended for reinforcement and revision purposes, or longer questions requiring more detailed answers.
A mark scheme provides a guide as to the amount of time which should be spent on each question and the amount of detail required (see answer style). There are numerical questions where appropriate, in line with the type of questions set by OCR.

Case studies

At the end of most units is a case study which requires you to apply new concepts within the context of a business. The case study will also offer you an opportunity to practise your examination technique. The types of questions are similar to those in the examination modules. Marks are allocated as a guide, and are similar to those in the examination modules.

The case studies also meet the requirements as stated within OCR's introduction to the specifications:

> 'The fundamental philosophy of the specifications is that the study of Business Studies requires an integrated approach at all stages of the course.'

For this reason, some of the case studies include a wide range of material. Furthermore, they have been written to support OCR's statement:

> 'The specifications require an approach which views business behaviour from a variety of perspectives.'

Group tasks or Task

Some of the units feature tasks. These are intended to stimulate debate and encourage you to learn the technique of justifying your view, a skill necessary for evaluation.

Further sources

The majority of the 'further sources' are websites for you to view and find additional up-to-date material and examples. Obvious websites such as Bized have not been included.

Key Terms

These are included as a summary of the key concepts that you will need to know.

The examinations!

The examination format

You will have to take two modules to gain an A2 pass and an overall A-level pass grade.

Module code	Module Name	Length of exam	Type of examination
F293	Marketing (optional paper)	Two hours, partly synoptic	Unseen case study, six questions
F294	Accounting (optional paper)	Two hours, partly synoptic	Unseen case study, six questions
F295	People in organisations (optional paper)	Two hours, partly synoptic	Unseen case study, six questions
F 296	Production (optional paper)	Two hours, partly synoptic	Unseen case study, six questions
F297	Strategic management (compulsory paper)	Two hours, synoptic paper	Pre-issued case study, four questions

These modules can be taken in January or June to suit your needs. Your teacher will be best placed to help you decide when to take each module.

Examination advice

The 'Examiner's Voice' feature contains useful hints on certain issues and topics. Remember, the authors are highly experienced teachers and examiners! There are several other important factors for you to remember, which apply to all modules.

- For ALL modules, answering in the context of the case is very important.
- Read the case with care to ensure you are familiar with:
  - A. the type of business (its status, size, place in the market)
  - B. the product or service
  - C. the consumers
  - D. the objectives of the business.

- Read the question with care to ensure you have noted the trigger word: state, explain, outline, analyse, evaluate, to what extent. Questions beginning with these words require different types and lengths of answers. Writing too much for a 'state' question could lose time and therefore many marks. A 'state' question requires you to write perhaps no more than a couple of words, and in some cases just one word.
- Mark allocation: noting the number of marks will help you write an appropriate amount.
- A question beginning with 'outline' is often a four-mark question, especially in the first module, An introduction to business. It is asking you to show an understanding of a concept, which can be done easily by offering a link. For example: 'Outline why the government uses regional policy.' You could answer: 'The government uses regional policy in order to encourage employment opportunities. In Scotland, there are areas of high unemployment and therefore grants will provide jobs.'
- Be careful when phrases such as 'other than' are used. Many candidates miss the opportunity to gain marks by ignoring this instruction. For example: 'Other than by taxation, suggest how a business may be affected by the government.' Any references to taxation will not gain marks!
- The quality of language IS important. Examiners are aware of the pressure under which students write their answers. Nevertheless, using paragraphs and spelling certain words incorrectly such as 'business', 'interest' and 'their' (belonging to someone), are likely to mean that full marks are not awarded!
- Always try to write specific points related to the case, rather than general points, which could apply to any business.
- Answer the actual question, rather than the one you prepared for or hoped would be there!
- It is essential that you take careful note of your time allocation. Many of the large mark questions are at the end of the papers! Remember, you must give yourself enough time to read the case properly to ensure that you answer in the context of the case.

Levels of response

Level	Key Word	Definition	Trigger words
L1	Knowledge	Business knowledge/ facts	State, List
L2	Explanation or application	Knowledge of the issues and or concepts. An explanation of the knowledge.	Explain, Outline, Describe, How?
L3	Analysis	The implication for the business	Analyse
		How the business will be affected	
		How the business reacts	
		For L3, your point MUST be in the context of the business	
L4	Evaluation	Supported judgements and/or, weighting of arguments and/or consideration of long- and short-term issues	Evaluate, To what extent? Discuss, Assess, Recommend

Ensuring you reach the highest levels (L3 and L4) as quickly as possible will ensure higher marks.

Analysis

There is not a magic number of points that need to be analysed before you have reached level 3. As long as you have shown how a particular point has affected the business or how the business is likely to react, you will gain level 3 marks.

Example
Analyse how a building company will be affected by demographic changes.

Answer
If there were changes in the demographics of a country, this may mean that the building company would have to change the type of housing that it built. As a result the business may have higher costs, as it would need to design different types of houses to meet the changes. As the population increased and there were more elderly people, land would become more expensive and therefore the builder's costs would rise, which in turn would affect its profits. If it wanted to keep its profits at the previous level, it may have to increase its prices.

This answer shows how the business would be affected and how it would react (including both is not essential; it depends upon the question) and therefore a level 3 mark would be gained.

Evaluation

The key element for evaluative comments is to ensure that you offer a 'justified judgement'. Questions where evaluation is required are asking you to suggest which factor is:

• the most important to that particular business
• most likely to benefit the business
• most likely to occur
• likely to damage the business the most.

To be evaluative, you will need to compare and weigh the evidence, having considered the positives and the negatives for the business in the case. It is always advisable to think about a balanced view.

Example
Evaluate how a change in technology might affect the business.

Answer
A change in technology may affect the business in several ways. If the new technology has to be bought in order to remain competitive, then the business will have to find the money and this may lead to an increase in its

costs in the short term. However, once the new technology is bought, it may help to give the business a competitive edge and therefore increase its sales and its market share.

Depending upon the type of technology bought, there may be an additional opportunity cost, as employees may be made redundant if the technology requires fewer units of labour. This may mean that in the short term the business will have to pay out a significant amount of money in redundancy payments, reducing its profits for that year. However, in the long term, the technology will bring savings in labour and unit costs, which will yield higher profits in the following years.

In this answer, there is a clear judgement that has been justified and an attempt has been made to consider the short and long term. Consequently, this would gain a level 4 mark.

The order of the units reflects the order of the topics within the specification.

The authors would like to express their thanks to numerous individuals who have contributed to the completion of this book.

Acknowledgements

Andy would like to thank, yet again, Sheila for her understanding during the writing period. It really will help with the retirement fund! Thanks also to the pupils of Tettenhall College, who have tested some of the case studies and questions within the book.

Alex would like to thank his wife Kate and sons James and Ben for putting up with his long absences in the study. Thanks also to MK Dons for being an inspiration in demonstrating that you do not give up when things become difficult and don't go as planned.

Judith would like to thank Tom for his help and encouragement while writing the book. His comments, constructive criticisms and IT support were invaluable, if not always well received.

Every effort has been made to trace the copyright holders of material reproduced here. The authors and publishers would like to thank the following for permission to reproduce copyright illustrations:

5.1, NDP/Alamy; 5.02, Advertising Archives/Dove; 9.05, Realimage/Alamy; 10.02, Rex Features; 10.04, Jaegermeiste; 11.02, courtesy of Period Features; 15.01, NBCUPHOTOBANK/Rex Features; 25.01, Antony Nettle/Alamy; 27.02, Bettmann/Corbis; 28.01, University of Adelaide; 28.03, University of Utah; 32.2, courtesy of Sainsbury's; 33.01, Chabruken/Gettyimages; 36.01, Getty Images; 36.02, John MacDougall/AFP/ Getty Images; 36.03, Courtesy of Sweetart Cakes; 39.01, Jeff J Mitchell/Getty Images; 39.04a, E. M. Welch/Rex Features; 39.04b, Cate Gillon/Getty Images; 43.02, Clynt Garnham/Alamy; 45.05, Kitemark; 47.01, Kromekat Digital Media Design/Adam Benton; 47.02 Getty Images/John McGrail; 49.06, Andy Mottershead; 53.01, Stuart Clarke/Rex Features; 58.03, Peter Macdiarmid/Getty Images; 60.02, Shaun Curry/AFP/Getty Images; 64.01, Jason Hawkes/Getty Images; 65.03, Jenny Matthews/Alamy; 66.01, Vario Images GmbH & Co.KG/Alamy; 67.01, Geoff Caddick/epa/Corbis; 68.01, BL Images Ltd/Alamy; 68.02, LH Images/Alamy; 70.01, Bettmann/Corbis; 70.2, courtesy of Trade Union Congress (TUC); 70.3, courtesy of Confederation of British Industry (CBI)

Crown copyright material is reproduced with the permission of the Controller of HMSO and the Queen's Printer for Scotland.

MARKETING

Unit 1

MARKETING SEGMENTATION AND GROWTH

Introduction

The success of a business in being able to achieve its objectives may be greatly influenced by the ability of the marketing function to perform its task effectively. However, the marketing function cannot be undertaken in isolation. It is governed by budgetary constraints, as are all the other functions within the business. The finance function is crucial to the well-being of the business, but marketing can improve the success of the business if it is successful in persuading potential customers to buy the product.

Employee performance also has a significant effect on the effectiveness of the marketing function. Employee morale and their level of motivation may affect the ability of the marketing function to achieve the objectives of the business.

Marketing also relies on the production function of the business. It is of little value to the business if the marketing department is able to attract customers without sufficient products being available. Therefore it is essential that all the functions of the business liaise with each other to achieve the common goal.

The chapters within this section cover the requirements as stated within the specification. To avoid duplication, certain marketing topics that also appear within other options may be located elsewhere.

Market segmentation

Once a business has used market research to find out about its customer base, it can begin to split its market into different groups with different characteristics and needs. This process is called market segmentation. Knowledge of different groups within a potential customer base can help the business target those consumers by a variety of methods:

- differentiated products
- special offers
- targeted advertising
- the range of goods stocked.

For example, Marks & Spencer stock different ranges of clothes in its smaller stores to reflect the characteristics of its customers. In its store in the City of London, most of the clothes are smart suits and accessories for both men and women; in a seaside resort like Llandudno, a section of the clothes are aimed at the older age group who are likely to visit the town on day trips and coach tours.

The market can be segmented in many different ways. A business may use different types of market segmentation in different situations.

Types of market segmentation

Age

This is one of the most obvious methods of segmentation, separating the potential market into different groups that can be targeted by a particular range of the business's goods or services. The age distribution of the UK population has changed dramatically over the past century. In 2008 there were more retired people in the UK population than children under the age of 16, for the first time in the UK's history. This means that there is a growing market aimed at the older sector of the population (see Unit 65). Holiday companies like Kuoni now target pensioners who have plenty of time and high levels of disposable income with holidays such as educational, historic cruises or guided holidays to long haul destinations like New Zealand.

Geography

This involves splitting the population according to the area in which they live within the UK, within the EU or within the world economy. In some markets there are significant regional differences in the characteristics of consumers. Segmenting the market makes it possible for a business to target these regional markets more effectively. For example, the sales of alcoholic drinks through off-licences and supermarkets vary from region to region. In areas where there is a large proportion of elderly people there will usually be higher then average sales of sherries, ports and spirits.

Gender

Many products are aimed either at men or women. A business may produce or adapt its products to ensure that they can be marketed effectively to one or other of the sexes. For example, Gillette, the shaving equipment manufacturer, produces a range of shaving equipment aimed specifically at female users. The razors are produced in colours such as pink or pale blue, and have features that make them suitable for shaving legs rather than faces!

Social class

Social class segmentation categorises individuals according to their occupation. Several different systems are used to define social class. An example of one such system is given in Figure 1.1.

- **A**   Upper class/upper-middle class – professional, higher managerial (e.g. company directors, lawyers, accountants)
- **B**   Middle class – other professional, middle management, senior administrative (e.g. teachers, nurses)
- **C1** Lower-middle class – Junior management, skilled non-manual workers (e.g. police, clerical staff)
- **C2** Skilled working class – trained (trade) skilled workers (e.g. technicians, plumbers, electricians)
- **D**   Working class – unskilled manual workers, semi-skilled workers (e.g. labourers, farm workers)
- **E**   Unskilled/unemployed – those on state benefit (e.g. pensioners, unemployed)

Figure 1.1 Social class groupings A–E

Residence

The ACORN (A Classification of Residential Neighbourhoods) system of classification allows businesses to target people living in a particular type of accommodation. This system categorises different types of housing such as flats, terrace housing, large detached housing etc. This system might be used by an independent school that wanted to send a mailshot to parents who are likely to consider private schooling for their children.

Type of Housing	Percentage of UK population
A. Agricultural areas	3%
B. Modern family housing, higher incomes	18%
C. Older housing of intermediate status	17%
D. Poor quality older terraced housing	4%
E. Better-off council estates	13%
F. Less well-off council estates	9%
G. Poorest council estates	7%
H. Multi-racial areas	4%
I. High status non-family areas	4%
J. Affluent surburban housing	16%
K. Better-off retirement areas	4%
U. Unclassified	1%

Table 1.1 Classification of housing

Religion or ethnic grouping

Some firms may produce ranges of products for specific ethnic or religious groups in societies. Food manufacturers, for example, may produce ranges of ingredients for Indian or Chinese customers, although there will obviously be others outside those groups who will also buy these products. Similarly, specialist butchers (such as halal) provide for the requirements of certain groups in the type of meat they sell.

Disadvantages of market segmentation

Although there are obvious advantages for a business in segmenting the market, it is also important for a business to ensure that it is not excluding other customers by taking segmentation too far. Increasingly, consumers are prepared to move over boundaries in their purchasing patterns, and it is becoming increasingly difficult to categorise consumers and their behaviour.

Market share

Market share is the proportion of the total market that a particular firm has achieved. The market share can be measured in different ways; the main methods are by sales volume or by sales value. In some cases however, a business may look at the number of customers it has or the number of retail outlets. A high street bank may be interested in the number of customer accounts it holds or in the number of branches it has in comparison to its competitors.

Measuring market share by sales volume or sales value may give different results. It is useful and valuable to compare these values and to account for any differences.

The formula for calculating market share is:

$$\text{Market share} = \frac{\text{sales value or volume for the individual business}}{\text{sales value or volume for the whole market}} \times 100$$

For example, if a local bakery sells £2,000 of bread each week in a small town and the total bread sales in the town are £10,000, its market share will be as follows:

$$\text{Market share} = \frac{2000}{10000} \times 100$$
$$= 20\%$$

The calculation of market share allows a business to assess its success, both in comparison with its competitors and with past performance. Increasing market share may also be used as a target or objective for the business in the future. Businesses like the major supermarkets are often as concerned with their share of the market as they are with profitability (see Unit 21).

To be able to use the calculation of market share in a sensible way, the business needs to be able to identify accurately which market it is in, and who and what is its competition. A business like Boots the Chemist is selling in a number of different markets such as pharmaceuticals, beauty products, small electrical goods and baby products. Market share calculations need to take each of these markets separately because it is unlikely that there is a similar business among Boots' competitors, selling exactly the same range of goods, with which it could make comparisons.

In 2000 British Airways introduced 'Club World' which offered a horizontal bed in business class. Market research had identified that customers wanted the opportunity to sleep when they were travelling in business class. Following product development, the new flat bed seat was introduced on the London to New York Route in April 2000. British Airways then monitored changes in market share over the period Jan 2000 to Jan 2001 as shown below.

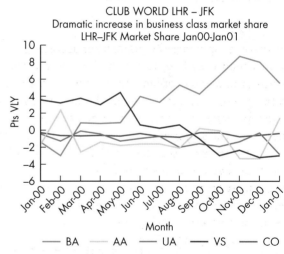

Figure 1.2 Market share for Club World

Following the introduction of the 'Club World' bed in April 2000, British Airways share of the market steadily increased. In March 2001 the Marketing Director of British Airways presented the above market share data as evidence of the success of this particular strategy.

Market growth

As well as knowing about its share of the market, the business also needs to know what is happening to the market in terms of its overall size. Market growth and its impact on the sales of a business can have a dramatic impact on the success of the firm.

If a business knows that the market it is in is growing, it would hope to maintain or increase its share of the market. Businesses will always want to target markets where sales are growing if possible. Market growth may be affected by any of the following factors.

- The nature of the product. Products such as mobile phones and games consoles face volatile markets that have periods of rapid growth in sales when a new product is launched.
- Changes in fashion and tastes. The market for women's clothes changes very rapidly through the seasons.
- Population changes. Changes in birth and death rates or in immigration can cause the market to grow rapidly (see Unit 65). For example, recent increases in the birth rate in the UK increased the market for baby-related products.
- Standard of living. Increases in income and employment mean that people have more disposable income. The result may be an increase in the market for DIY products and home improvements.

Market growth can also be calculated, either using value or volume figures. For example, if the market for baby clothes increases from £2 million to £2.5 million, the market growth is calculated as follows:

$$\text{Market growth} = \frac{\text{Increase (or decrease) in total sales by value or volume}}{\text{Original sales value or volume}} \times 100$$

$$= \frac{(2.5 - 2)}{2} \times 100$$

$$= 25\%$$

Factors affecting buyer behaviour

When looking at its share of the market and its performance in a growing market, a business will want to understand the way in which buyers behave. Marketing departments and analysts now spend large amounts of time and money trying to assess and predict buyer behaviour; sometimes they will be successful in doing this, but sometimes buyers will behave in ways that seem unpredictable and irrational. The following factors are likely to be the most important in influencing buyer behaviour.

- Income, standard of living and employment. In general as the state of these economic factors improves, customers are likely to increase their spending in most areas. The exception may be items such as economy brands from supermarkets which usually experience higher sales when economic times are difficult.
- Consumer confidence. Sometimes, even when the economy is doing well, consumers may lack confidence about the future. This will reduce spending, particularly on non-necessities.
- Advertising or publicity campaigns can have an impact on buyer behaviour. Similarly, bad publicity for business will put buyers off (such as the bird flu outbreak at Bernard Matthew's turkey farms in 2007).
- Supermarkets make sure that the layout of their shops encourages the consumer to spend more and to take their time wandering around the store. Common purchases such as bread, milk and tea are usually positioned in different parts of the store to encourage consumers to walk along all the aisles.
- Many consumers (particularly young people) are very influenced by fashion trends, media coverage and celebrities. They may feel that they need the latest 'must-have' handbag or pair of trainers.

In all these cases it is important for the business to have an awareness of the market in which it is operating, and a thorough knowledge of its customer base. It will usually find this information through the use of market research (see Units 3 and 4).

Further Sources

www.marketsegmentation.co.uk

www.businessbureau-uk.co.uk

www.telegraph.co.uk – Article 'They have ways of making you spend'

Questions Time allowed 20 minutes

1. A business is in a market where weekly sales are £50,000. If Business A has sales of £7,500 each week, what share of the market does it have?

(4 marks)

2. Sales in the market in question 1 increase to £55,000.

   A. What is the percentage market growth?

(4 marks)

   B. If Business A maintains its market share, what are its sales in the new situation? (4 marks)

   C. If Business A continues to sell £7,500 of goods each week, what is its new market share of the increased market? (4 marks)

(16 marks)

Case Study Time allowed 45 minutes

Sport England market segmentation

Sport England has developed nineteen sporting segments to help us understand the nations' attitudes and motivations – why they play sport and why they don't.

The segments provide the knowledge to influence people to take part. This work is part of our divide to get two million people doing more sport by 2012.

Each segment can be explored at differing geographic levels. It is possible to find out what people's sporting habits are in a particular street, community, local authority or region.

For example – Leanne is a Supportive Single.

She is the least active segment amongst 18–25 year olds. We know that she is likely to be single, living in private/council rented accommodation and will have a number of children. We now also know what motivates her, what brands she aspires to, how we can overcome things that stop her taking part in sport and how to get her involved in sports she likes – such as the gym and keep-fit. From this we can work out which sporting interventions are likely to be more successful for Leanne.

The 19 segments:	Paula – a stretched single mum
Ben – a competitive male urbanite	Philip – a comfortable mid-life male
Jamie – a sports team drinker	Elaine – an empty-nest careerist
Chloe – a fitness class friend	Roger and Joy – an early retirement couple
Leanne – a supportive single	Brenda – an older working woman
Helena – a career focussed female	Terry – a local old boy
Tim – a settling down male	Norma – a later life lady
Alison – a stay-at-home mum	Ralph and Phyllis – a comfortable, retired couple
Jackie – a Middle England mum	Frank – a twilight year gent
Kev – a pub league teammate	Elsie and Arnold – retirement home singles

Source: www.sportsengland.org

1. Explain two ways in which Sport England have segmented the population. (5 marks)

2. Analyse the ways in which market segmentation may help Sport England to use available funds more effectively. (10 marks)

3. Take one of the segments identified and discuss ways in which you think Sport England should target this segment to involve them in sporting activities. (15 marks)

(30 marks)

Over the past 50 years, there has been a rapid increase in the amount of protection given to consumers by the law. As the business world has become increasingly competitive, successive governments have recognised that consumers sometimes need to be protected from the actions of businesses. The following factors have contributed to this situation:

- monopoly control of the industry (see Unit 63)
- health and safety concerns
- new products and services
- the growth of internet and mail-order buying
- the globalisation of markets (see Unit 68).

Laws governing consumer protection

Sale of Goods Act (1979)

This was an important Act when it was introduced, and remains important today. As with the Health and Safety Act of 1974 it has since been extended, particularly by the Consumer Protection Act (1987).

Under the Sale of Goods Act, all goods must be:

- of 'satisfactory quality' (i.e. the product must not be damaged or defective)
- 'as described' – this applies not only to advertisements but also to any explanations given by a shop assistant
- 'fit for the purpose for which they were intended'.

If any of these conditions is not met, a business must provide consumers with a replacement or their money back. A business cannot avoid the law by saying that it has a policy not to accept returned goods. The Act also imposes a duty on businesses to ensure that their products are safe to use.

In addition to these civil laws, there are a number of criminal laws.

Trade Descriptions Act (1968)

A consumer cannot be expected to understand everything about a product. The purpose of this Act is to prevent consumers from being intentionally misled when they buy goods. It states that any description of the goods on sale must not be false or misleading. The Act refers to all types of description – sign, advertisement or verbal.

Weights and Measures Act (1985)

It is an offence to give 'short measures' or an incorrect indication of the amount of a product on sale. If a product is labelled as containing 1 litre, that is what it should contain.

Unsolicited Goods Act (1971)

It is illegal to demand payment for services that have not been ordered. If a publishing business delivers a quantity of books that have not been ordered to someone's house, and then demands payment for them, the business is breaking the law.

The Trading Standards Authority is a public body that investigates breaches of consumer laws. It also assists consumers in taking a business to court if the business refuses to comply with its legal obligations.

European Union laws

Some laws affecting UK businesses originate in the European Union (EU). Many of these come from the EU's Social Charter, which is a charter of rights for employees concerning areas such as working conditions, wages and consultation of the workforce. UK businesses have to adhere to these EU laws just as if they had originated from the UK parliament. There are two types of EU law:

- Regulations, which have to be adopted and applied in a certain way.
- Directives, which must also be applied as law, but the individual member country can decide how to implement them.

Working Time Directive

The Working Time Directive is an example of EU legislation. It became law in the UK in 1998, and states that a business must not allow an employee to work more than 48 hours per week on average. The directive is partly aimed at reducing the UK's culture of long working hours. There are also provisions relating to an employee's entitlement to rest breaks and the pattern of shifts that can be worked. Employees can sign away their legal rights to these if they wish, but if a business dismisses a person for refusing to do so, this constitutes unfair dismissal. Some employees (such as the police) are exempt from the directive.

The effects of increased legislation on businesses

Changes in legislation and increased consumer protection affect businesses in a variety of ways.

- The need to ensure health and safety concerns are addressed at every stage of production and beyond imposes costs on businesses. For example, a business that manufactures toys must be aware of the paint finishes and components that are used in production, even if these toys are made abroad. Lead in paint or easily detachable components that can be swallowed by a child are prohibited. Not only will the business run the risk of prosecution by ignoring these rules, it may also cause widespread bad publicity for the business.

- Increasingly, businesses need to become market-orientated rather than product-orientated (see Unit 5). They need to ensure that they are producing goods and services that the consumer wants to buy. This involves extra costs in undertaking market research before new products are introduced, and follow-up research when they reach the market.
- Customer service is an increasingly important part of the operation of businesses, particularly in the service sector. Businesses need to have staff who can deal with customer complaints and questions in a sympathetic and calm manner, and who are then empowered to deal with the problems. The department store John Lewis has built up a reputation for dealing promptly with customer complaints without the need to refer the problem to senior managers. This results in customer satisfaction and confidence in the business.

What happens if a business breaks the law?

Alleged breaches of employment law are heard in an **employment tribunal**. If the tribunal rules in favour of the employee, it will order the business to pay the employee compensation for what has occurred.

> ## Key Terms
>
> **Employment tribunal:** a special sort of court that only deals with employment-related issues (e.g. victimisation by an employer, breach of contract, unfair dismissal and discrimination).

For alleged breaches of criminal law, the business will be prosecuted in the criminal courts, either a magistrates' court for minor offences or the Crown Court, where the penalties are more severe, for serious offences. If found guilty, a business can be fined and/or those responsible for the breach may be imprisoned. Any alleged breach of the civil law will be heard in the County Court, where the business can be sued for damages.

If a business fails or refuses to pay damages or compensation, the business or person that is owed the money can apply to the County Court for payment to be enforced. County Court judgements against a business can generate bad publicity and the hearing will be expensive. Furthermore, an adverse County Court judgement can affect a business's ability to obtain credit.

The Office of Fair Trading (OFT)

The OFT is a government department responsible for making markets work well for consumers. 'This is achieved by promoting consumer interests throughout the UK, while ensuring that businesses are fair and competitive.' (OFT website) The OFT investigates situations where businesses are operating unlawfully in any area of UK trade.

In 2008 a new piece of legislation was introduced called the Unfair Trading Regulations 2008.

> ## Office of Fair Trading: Consumer Protection from Unfair Trading Regulations 2008
>
> The Consumer Protection from Unfair Trading Regulations 2008 came into force on 26 May 2008. They implement the Unfair Commercial Practices Directives (UCPD) in the UK, and replace several pieces of consumer protection legislation that were in force prior to 26 May 2008. The Regulations introduce a general duty not to trade unfairly and seek to ensure that traders act honestly and fairly towards their customers. They apply primarily to business to consumer practices (but elements of business to business practices are also covered where they affects, or are likely to affect, consumers).
>
> The vast majority of UK businesses are fair dealing and should not have needed to change their business practices to comply with regulations, which aim to tackle those businesses who don't always treat their customers well.

The new act covers unfair trading in many areas which include:

- Giving incorrect pricing and product information to mislead the consumer; for example, falsely claiming that a product can cure illness.
- Using promotional information that misleads; for example, packaging shampoo so that it resembles that of a well-known competitor.
- Aggressive sales practices that put the consumer under undue pressure; for example, pressurising an

elderly or confused person to sign a contract immediately for roof repairs.
- Falsely claiming accreditation; for example, claiming to have signed up to an industry code of conduct when this is not true.

Trading Standards

The Trading Standards Organisation offers advice both to businesses and consumers on the application of the laws for buying and selling. Its work covers retail sales and internet buying and selling. If a consumer has a problem with a retailer, Trading Standards will investigate the issue for them and discuss the legal situation with the business concerned. For example, suppose a consumer purchases a handbag which falls apart after two weeks. This situation will be covered by the Sale of Goods Act because the bag was 'not fit for purpose'. In these circumstances the consumer is entitled to her money back. If the retailer refuses to do this, the consumer can take the issue to the local Trading Standards Office. An officer will be appointed to take up the case and investigate on behalf of the consumer.

Advertising

The use of advertising in the UK is under the control of the Advertising Standards Authority (ASA).

> ## About the ASA: what we do
>
> The Advertising Standards Authority regulates the contents of advertisements, sales promotions and direct marketing in the UK.
>
> We make sure standards are kept by applying the advertising standards codes.
>
> We can stop misleading, harmful or offensive advertising. We can ensure sales promotions are run fairly. We can help reduce unwanted commercial mail – either sent through the post, by e-mail or by text message – and we can resolve problems with mail order purchases.

Anyone who is unhappy with an advertisement can make a complaint to the ASA who will then investigate the situation. The ASA has codes of conduct for advertising on television, radio and all other areas. In general, the ASA works on the understanding that advertising should not mislead, cause harm or offend. In addition there is a separate set of rules for the advertising of products like alcoholic drinks, children's items and gambling. The advertising of cigarettes and tobacco is now prohibited in the UK.

For example, in a recent case that was investigated by the ASA, the retail store Halfords was prohibited from running a series of advertisements because the ASA felt that customers had been misled about some of the price reductions they were offering, and also because the advertisement seemed to suggest that bicycle safety checks were only available through them.

After a judgment has been made, most businesses agree to follow ASA recommendations by changing or removing advertisements. Those who ignore the rulings will be reported to the Office of Fair Trading who will take up the issue.

Data protection

The Data Protection Act 1998 was introduced to protect individuals where information about them was held by any business or organisation. Businesses or organisations that hold any information about customers or employees are bound by this legislation. For example, a bank or building society must ensure that customer information is held securely.

The Act works in two ways. Firstly, anyone who processes personal information must insure that the information is:

- fairly and lawfully processed
- processed for limited purposes
- relevant and not excessive
- accurate and up-to-date
- not kept longer than is necessary
- processed in line with the individual's rights
- secure
- not transferred to other countries without adequate protection.

The second part of the Act covers the rights of the individual to know what information is being held about them by any organisation. (Source: Information Commissioner's Office.)

Monopoly and the Competition Commission

One particular area where the consumer may be at risk from unfair treatment is where a monopoly exists, or there is some sort of monopoly control over the market. In monopoly situations the seller has the ability either to force up the price of the good or service, or to restrict the quantity sold on the market. In the UK, monopoly is not prohibited by law but its operation in the market is controlled through legislation. This legislation applies particularly to the use of restrictive practices (see Unit 64).

Examples of restrictive practices operated by firms with large market shares include:

- Ownership or control of a basic raw material that results in the price to the consumer being increased.
- Fixing prices either with other producers or with retail suppliers.
- Limiting the number or type of business that can stock particular products.
- Insisting that a retailer does not stock the products of competitors.

In the UK, a legal monopoly is a firm with a market share of 25 per cent or more. Perhaps the best example of such a company is the software giant Microsoft which controls a much larger percentage of the worldwide market for computer systems.

If such a monopoly is acquired naturally over time by a business, UK legislation will operate to stop the use of restrictive practices by the business.

If a business will acquire a market share of 25 per cent or more by taking over another business or merging with it, the takeover or merger is likely to be investigated by the Competition Commission. As a result of investigation, the Competition Commission can stop the takeover going ahead if it is felt that the new business will not operate within the interests of consumers. For example, if the Competition Commission feels that a takeover will create a business that will be a dominant supplier with the power to drive out competition, it will not allow the takeover to go ahead. When the supermarket Safeway was put onto the market for sale, all its major competitors were interested in buying it. After lengthy investigation, Morrisons were allowed to buy the chain, but the Competition Commission insisted that not all Safeway stores could be included in the sale. As a result, smaller supermarkets like Waitrose and The Co-op were allowed to buy stores in areas where it was felt that extra competition was needed.

Benefits of monopoly

The UK government allows monopolies to continue to exist because it recognises that in some cases there may be advantages to a monopoly rather than a large number of smaller firms. Some of the advantages are:

- Economies of scale from large scale production; for example, in electricity generation.
- Removing unnecessary duplication of services; for example, in the delivery of domestic mail.
- Willingness to undertake expensive research and development into new products; for example, in the pharmaceutical industry.

Further Sources

www.direct.gov.uk
www.bbc.co.uk/consumer/guides_to/
www.lawsociety.org.uk
www.competition-commission.org.uk
www.oft.gov.uk
Wikipedia Consumer Protection section

Your Turn

Activity   Time allowed 40 minutes

In groups of two or three, look at the website of the Competition Commission (www.competition-commission.org.uk). Find the details of a case that has been investigated recently. This might be a proposed takeover, merger or an investigation into unfair competition. Prepare a five-minute report on the case to present to the rest of your class.

Case Study   Time allowed 1 hour

Ragdolly Anna

Kathryn Ford owns and runs a small business making rag dolls from a unit on a trading estate. She started the business in 2000 and has gradually expanded it until she now employs 20 workers. She sells mainly through mail order, but some of her dolls also go into gift shops within the UK.

The dolls can be customised to specific requests from customers. A customer can look at the samples on Kathryn's website and order different sorts of clothes in a range of colours. For example, it is possible to have a rag doll dressed as a horse-rider or a ballerina. When gift shops order from the firm they usually have a theme in mind. Kathryn sells a range of dolls dressed in Welsh or Scottish costume.

Recently, Kathryn has run into one or two problems with customers. The first complaint was from an internet customer who said that the doll she had received was not dressed as had been requested. This complaint had been handled by the administrative assistant, who had been fairly unsympathetic when the customer had asked for the doll to be changed to the design and colours requested.

Another more serious complaint had come from a retail customer. There had been a problem with one of the dolls he had sold. One of the eyes of the doll had become detached, and the child who was playing with it had pushed the eye into her ear. This had required a visit to hospital and, although there was no serious injury to the little girl, the shop owner was worried about the risk of being sued by the customer. The shop-owner was awaiting a visit from a Trading Standards officer.

Kathryn is beginning to realise that she needs to take her legal obligations to her customers far more seriously. She obviously needs to put processes into place to ensure that problems like these do not happen in future, and that when complaints do arise they are dealt with properly.

1. Explain one piece of UK legislation that might affect Kathryn's business.   (5 marks)

2. Analyse how the complaint about the incorrect doll should have been handled by Ragdolly Anna's staff.   (10 marks)

3. Evaluate the actions that Kathryn should take to improve her customer service throughout the business.   (15 marks)

(30 marks)

MARKET RESEARCH

Keeping up with the pace of change, not only in the general economy but also within any given market, requires a constant updating of the information that a business collects.

Most businesses want to ensure that they are well informed on what is happening in the market for their particular products or services. In addition, they want to know about anything that may affect their particular markets, both at the present time and in the future. In order to achieve this, market research is essential.

Market research is a systematic, objective collection and analysis of data about a particular target market. It always involves some form of data collection, whether primary or secondary (see below). Market research concentrates on recognising a consumer need and exploring how best to satisfy that need.

The purpose of any market research project is to achieve an increased understanding of the subject matter. With markets throughout the world becoming increasingly more competitive and complex, market research is now essential for most organisations, large or small. Knowing the market may help a business keep in touch with market trends and therefore avoid being left behind by competitors.

Market research is undertaken in order to:

- describe the market
- explain the market
- predict changes in the market
- investigate the reaction of consumers in the future.

Describing the market

1. The business must be able to identify the customers or consumers. This information can be used to ensure that customers are targeted in an appropriate manner. If the market is for young female clothes, then advertising can be positioned carefully in order to reach the target market.

2. Identifying trends within the market is also vital. If sales are declining, it may be appropriate to increase the marketing budget to counter the fall in sales. Alternatively, sales may be in permanent decline and therefore an alternative product may be required. The business may be advised not to join a market with a declining trend; equally, if there is an upward trend, the business may be well advised to join the market. Regardless of which strategy is adopted, knowing the trends is essential.

3. The market also refers to the actual market share. Information about the percentage of the market which a business holds is valuable, as it can help a business to decide what it ought to do next. The business can attempt to increase or maintain its market share (see Unit 2 for more information on this topic).

$$\text{Market share} = \frac{\text{sales} \times 100}{\text{total market share}}$$

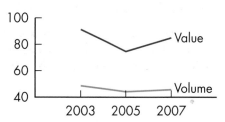

Figure 3.1 Vital signs for Kleenex market share
Source: Marketing, 10 September 2008

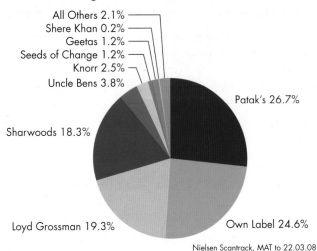

Indian sauces in glass – % value share at 22.03.08

- All Others 2.1%
- Shere Khan 0.2%
- Geetas 1.2%
- Seeds of Change 1.2%
- Knorr 2.5%
- Uncle Bens 3.8%
- Sharwoods 18.3%
- Patak's 26.7%
- Own Label 24.6%
- Loyd Grossman 19.3%

Nielsen Scantrack, MAT to 22.03.08

- The total ambient Indian category is worth £159m, up 6% year-on-year
- Sauces in Glass represents nearly half of the category by value and in this important sector Patak's is outperforming both the market, with year-on-year growth of 13% vs 2%, and other leading brands
- Patak's also dominates the £11m pastes market, with an 89% market share and growth of 22% year-on-year

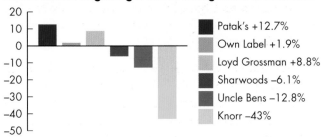

Indian sauces in glass growth % change MAT to 22.03.08

- Patak's +12.7%
- Own Label +1.9%
- Loyd Grossman +8.8%
- Sharwoods −6.1%
- Uncle Bens −12.8%
- Knorr −43%

Figure 3.2 Breakdown of the market in Indian sauces

	Previous week	Brand	Agency/TV Buyer	%
1	(2)	Asda	Fallon London/Carat	66
2	(–)	Gillete Fusion	BBDO New York/MediaCom	56
3	(–)	McDonald's	Leo Burnett/OMD UK	53
4	(–)	Moonpig	Space City/MNC	52
5=	(10)	Flora pro.activ	Krow Communications/ MindShare	49
5=	(15=)	Tesco	The Red Brick Road/Initiative	49
7	(14)	Argos	CHI & Partners/ MindShare	48
8	(–)	Andrex	JWT London/ MindShare	47
9=	(8)	Morrisons	DLWK/ Mediaedge:cia	44
9=	(–)	Magners Original	Young Euro RSCG/ MPG	44
11	(–)	Norwich Union Direct	Abbot Mead Vickers BBDO/OMD UK	42
12	(–)	118 118	WCRS/OMD UK	41
13	(–)	Clairol Herbal Essences	Leo Burnett/Starcom	40
14	(–)	British Gas	CHI & Partners/ Carat	38
15	(–)	Carphone Warehouse	CHI & Partners/ CHIP Partners & Media	35

Table 3.1 Which of the following television commercials do you remember seeing recently? Adwatch figures for the week ending 3 September 2008

Explaining the market

1. The business must understand why changes in the market have taken place, and more importantly why one particular business has increased or decreased its market share (see Figure 3.2).

2. It is also important to identify the reasons for the success or failure of a change in the marketing strategy of a business. Did the recent changes in prices or sales promotion work? Did the consumers see the adverts on the television? Market research can answer such questions. In the magazine Marketing, a weekly analysis is made of consumers' ability to recall particular adverts.

3. Market research makes it possible to find out why consumers prefer to purchase one brand as opposed to another. Eurostar, having discovered that some customers are concerned about the carbon footprints of different modes of transport, have built an advertising campaign highlighting the fact that Eurostar is an acceptable green alternative to air travel.

4. Businesses need to know whether there are differences in consumer reactions on a regional basis.

A. The Loyalty Management Group (which operates the Nectar card) has an online research tool for some of its clients such as Sainsbury's, Nestle and Unilever.

B. Dunnhumby holds grocery expenditure details of the 13 million Tesco club cardholders. The service enables managers to analyse and respond to consumer spending patterns, identifying the products which customers are buying in different areas.

It is also about to launch an attitudinal panel, allowing its clients to link consumer-buying behaviour with their media purchases. This will enable the research company's clients to match their promotion in the right media to suit consumer spending patterns.

Predicting the market

1. Knowing how consumers will react to changes in the prices of products provides a valuable insight which can then be exploited.

   Verdict Consulting issued a report in 2008 into the shopping habits of consumers hit by the 'credit crunch'. Its report argued that a growing number of consumers were switching to an alternative store where prices were considered to be lower. Over a third of consumers said they would switch supermarkets.

2. Research can be used to highlight the consequences of introducing a new model. After introducing the new Fiesta in September 2008, Ford would be interested to note what happened to the sales of its other existing brands.

3. If competitors introduce new products or reduce prices, research is helpful in gauging the reaction of its existing customers. Have they been tempted to switch to the competitors' brand, will they do so in the future, and if so, why?

4. Being aware of changes in lifestyles is also significantly important. Marketing departments in many businesses have taken notice of the trend for a healthier lifestyle, and have responded to a market in which consumers are aware of the latest health issues surrounding sugar, salt, e-numbers, chocolate, wine, low fat foods and the need for exercise.

The market research process

In order to conduct market research, businesses may decide to undertake the project themselves (perhaps by a marketing research department) or they may choose to hire a market research agency or consultancy. Regardless of which approach is taken, it is crucial to define the research objectives before undertaking any research project, listing what the business needs to find out.

Once the objectives of the research have been established, the researchers can use many types of research techniques and methodologies to find the required information. The research collected will either be quantitative or qualitative information. Which type of information is used and what order it is collected (if both are used) depends on the research objectives. It is generally accepted that results are most useful when the two methods are combined.

Quantitative research

This type of research is regarded as being objective as it involves the collection of facts. It concentrates on what consumers actually purchase or use, such as how many consumers eat cereals.

Quantitative research concentrates on numerical data. It requires significant attention to the measurement of market trends and often involves statistical analysis. For example, a hotel might collect data on the number of people taking holidays in the area of the hotel. This will provide quantitative information that can be analysed statistically.

The main rule with quantitative research is that every respondent is asked the same series of questions. The approach is very structured and normally involves large numbers of interviews, questionnaires or simply looking at records.

Quantitative research is often used initially to establish the trends within a particular market. Undertaking this type of research can help the business to decide whether it is worthwhile continuing with a more detailed level of research, which may involve qualitative research.

Often quantitative research will be seen as secondary research. Market research surveys are a popular method of collecting quantitative data. These quantitative surveys can be conducted face-to-face (in-street or in-home), by using post, telephone, email or the internet, or using past records and journals. The questionnaire is one of the more common methods for collecting data from a survey, but it is only one of a wide-ranging set of tools.

Examiner's voice

Be careful not to confuse primary research where opinions are sought and secondary data that tends to concentrate on numbers and trends.

Qualitative research

This type of research is often regarded as being subjective because opinions are sought.

Qualitative research provides an understanding of how or why things are as they are. For example, a market researcher may stop a consumer who has purchased a particular type of bread and ask him or her why that type of bread was chosen. Unlike quantitative research there are no fixed set of questions, but instead a topic guide (or discussion guide) is used to explore various issues in more depth. The discussion between the interviewer (or moderator) and the respondent is largely determined by the respondent's own thoughts and feelings.

As with quantitative techniques, there are also various types of qualitative methodologies. Research of this sort is mostly conducted face-to-face, and one of the best-known techniques is market research group discussions (or focus groups). These are usually made up of six to eight targeted respondents; a research moderator whose role is to ask the required questions, draw out answers, and encourage discussion; an observation area usually behind one-way mirrors; and video and/or audio taping facilities.

Qualitative research often involves primary research, which concentrates on the opinions of consumers. Secondary research will inform a business as to the numbers within a market for a product, whereas primary research starts to establish why products are bought.

Conducting the research

Primary (field research)

Primary research can be carried out in a number of ways, such as interviews, questionnaires, observation,

consumer panels and focus groups. A marketing plan will consider the most appropriate way in which to collect the information required. Deciding which method to use will depend upon a variety of factors:

1. cost and budget constraints
2. marketing objectives
3. information required
4. information already available
5. number of persons to be questioned
6. location of respondents.

Interviews

Interviews allow for a great amount of detail to be extracted from the consumer, whose opinions can be clarified immediately. However, it is a time-consuming and therefore expensive method of research. Interviewers need to be well trained to ensure that the questions are asked without bias and that the responses are recorded appropriately.

Today many interviews take place using CAPI (computer assisted personal interviewing.) Interviews are conducted face-to-face and the replies recorded onto a laptop computer. Once a reply has been recorded, the next question automatically pops up on the screen. This ensures a consistent approach where all respondents are asked the same questions in the same order.

In addition CATI (computer assisted telephone interviewing) and CAWI (computer assisted web interviewing) are used.

Surveys/questionnaires

One of the most widely used methods of collecting research material is the questionnaire. It is a quick and economical method of gaining the opinions of consumers and potential consumers. If the questionnaires need to be posted, the usual procedure is to enclose a business reply card. The more replies gained, the more reliable is the information.

Effective questionnaires are brief to ensure that potential respondents are not put off answering due to the amount of time that would be taken to complete them. Many effective questionnaires offer incentives to encourage respondents.

Observation

Watching consumers and users of products can offer a good insight for the researchers. When interviewing and

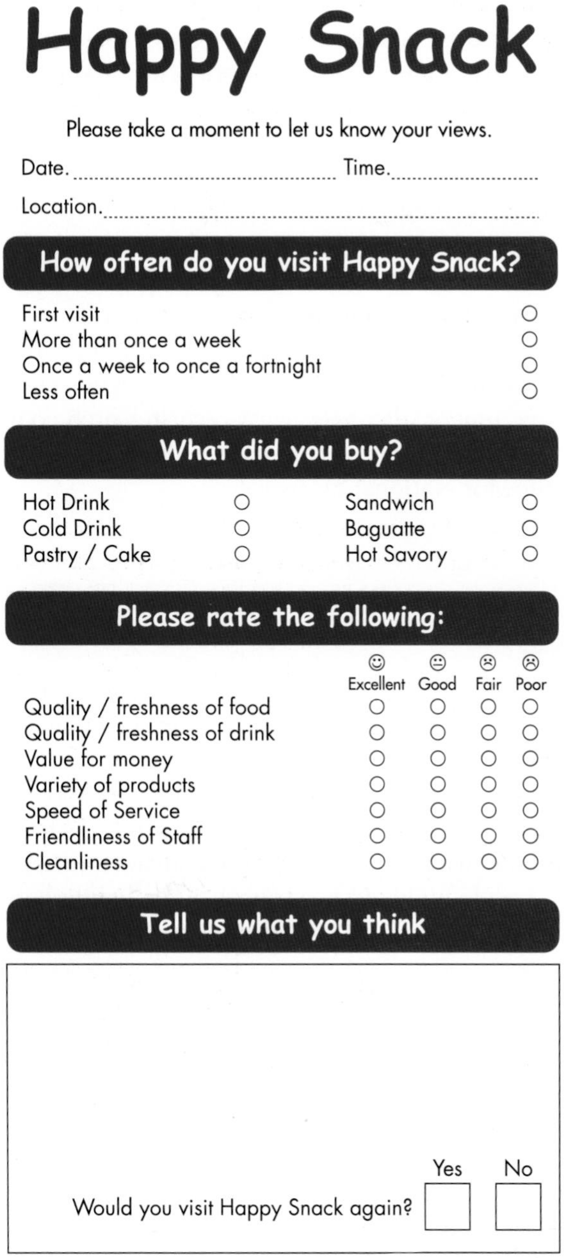

Happy Snack

Please take a moment to let us know your views.

Date. _____ Time. _____

Location. _____

How often do you visit Happy Snack?

First visit ○
More than once a week ○
Once a week to once a fortnight ○
Less often ○

What did you buy?

Hot Drink	○	Sandwich	○
Cold Drink	○	Baguatte	○
Pastry / Cake	○	Hot Savory	○

Please rate the following:

	☺ Excellent	☺ Good	☹ Fair	☹ Poor
Quality / freshness of food	○	○	○	○
Quality / freshness of drink	○	○	○	○
Value for money	○	○	○	○
Variety of products	○	○	○	○
Speed of Service	○	○	○	○
Friendliness of Staff	○	○	○	○
Cleanliness	○	○	○	○

Tell us what you think

Would you visit Happy Snack again? Yes ☐ No ☐

Figure 3.3 An example of a questionnaire

questionnaires may prove difficult, observation is a viable alternative. For example, when testing how young children play with particular toys, it is not always possible to ask them, and therefore observation provides the necessary information.

Consumer panels

Testing products is often done by the use of consumer panels. Such panels frequently test washing powders and liquids. Samples of new products are sent to panel members who fill in forms to gauge their responses to the products.

Similarly, perfume and aftershave products are often tested in this manner.

Focus groups

These usually consist of about eight to ten people who are offered various stimuli and their responses gauged and recorded.

Sometimes Monadic rating is used: the respondent is asked to rate a product on a scale, but without comparisons to another product.

Secondary (Desk research)

This is data that already exists. There are two main sources: internal and external sources.

Internal sources

- **Sales data/figures:** assuming that the information recorded is accurate, trends can be established to help in the decision-making process for future marketing and production schedules.
- **Previous survey results:** although these can be used as a basis for comparison, the reliability of such data is questionable. This will depend upon the nature of the product and its market. For some goods that change rapidly in terms of technology, data for sales of an old model may not be very useful.
- **Customer information:** (often from loyalty card details) knowing who buys what, when and where can be invaluable data. When planning at whom or where to target a particular sales promotion, or deciding which advertising media to use, knowing the details of its consumers allows a business to be more effective in its marketing spend.
- **Company reports:** the business may have undertaken its own marketing reports and summaries of past performances. There may be occasions when such information is useful.

External sources

- **Market research companies:** although the collection and collation of secondary data may be expensive, it can be good value for money, especially to the smaller businesses that cannot afford to generate their own research. Mintel is one of the largest market research businesses. Other market research companies such as TNS, Mori, Millard Brown and Nielson, all provide research material for a wide range of clients.
- **The internet:** the internet now plays a much larger role in providing secondary data. Market research

businesses have their own websites and some reports are available online for a fee. Small firms can access information more cheaply than hiring a market research company to do the research for them.

- **Trade publications:** reading trade publications (such as *Marketing, The Grocer*) is a cheap method of keeping up to date on any particular market. Information is available not only on the latest developments but also on competing businesses. Because such journals tend to specialise in a particular market, the information is easier to extract than from a more general business magazine.
- **Newspapers and magazines:** some newspapers carry particular features on certain sectors of industry that may provide valuable secondary information. *The Times, Guardian* and *The Daily Telegraph*, along with the Sunday press, carry such features. *The Economist, Business Today, Marketing* and *Marketing Weekly*, all provide useful material on a wide range of topics. *Marketing*, a weekly trade journal, often includes features on various markets. Although such research is often conducted by market research companies, being collated into one article makes the information more accessible and convenient.
- **Competitors:** see the section on trade journals above.

In addition, it is of course possible to purchase competitors' products and see exactly what is being offered. It is clear that when Ford first introduced ABS braking systems, other car manufacturers were quick to follow suit! This was also the case with the Dyson vacuum cleaner; other manufacturers were quick to introduce their own versions, without breaking any patent laws, as soon as they were legally entitled.

- **Government statistics and reports:** government statistics are available in abundance! Each government department has its own website and issues documents and statistics regularly. The Government database www.oscar-research.co.uk is an extensive source for market research, as is the Office for National Statistics.

Conclusion

It is important to understand that market research is not an exact science. Bias is often a problem and may influence the answers gained from respondents. To gain a reliable response, the number of respondents is important. However, the cost of collecting the data also must be considered. Consequently, market research is often a trade-off between accuracy and reliability on the one hand, and cost-effectiveness on the other.

To add to the dilemma facing those who collect data, the time factor is crucial. Collecting sufficient information may contradict the need to have up-to-date information. Time spent collecting information may improve its reliability in terms of asking a sufficient number of people, but the information may quickly become out of date!

Drinks consumed by 11- to 25-year-olds once a week, March 2008 (%)

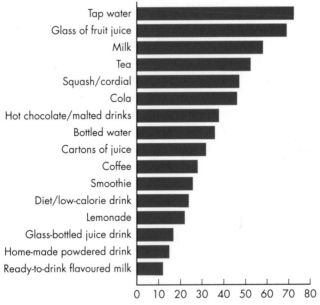

(Source: Q-Research/Mintel   Base: 815 11- to 25-year-olds)

Figure 3.4 Drinks consumed by 11–25-year-olds once a week, March 2008 (%)

Further Sources

www.marketresearchontheweb.com
www.marketresearchworld.net
www.researchinfo.com
www.buzzle.com
info@aqr.org.uk
info@cim.co.uk
www.mintel.com
www.marketingmagazine.co.uk/adwatch
Marketing Pocket Book, The Advertising Association, 2008.

Your Turn

Questions Time allowed 20 minutes

1. State two reasons why market research is undertaken. (2 marks)

2. State four methods of undertaking primary research. (4 marks)

3. Explain the difference between quantitative and qualitative research. (4 marks)

4. Analyse two factors that will affect the choice of research sources used. (6 marks)

(16 marks)

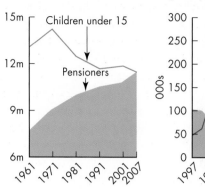

Figure 3.6 Changing face of the UK

Case Study Time allowed 30 minutes

The population pyramid

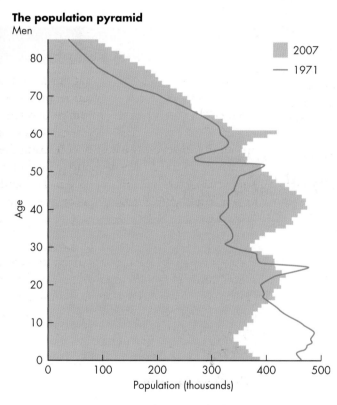

1. State what type of data the graphs represent. (1 mark)

2. Using the information in the population pyramid, suggest how a business of your choice may find this useful. (4 marks)

3. Recommend and justify a market research plan that would need to be implemented in order for a house builder to decide the most appropriate type of accommodation to build. (13 marks)

(18 marks)

MARKET RESEARCH (ANALYSIS)

Once the initial market research plan on how the information is to be collected is in place, consideration needs to be given to the sampling techniques employed. Insufficient data will not be reliable, and therefore any analysis will be flawed.

In order to improve the likelihood of gaining reliable data, there are several sampling techniques that can be applied.

Sampling methods

For most surveys, access to the entire population is almost impossible. However, the results from a survey with a carefully selected sample should closely resemble results that would have been obtained had the whole population provided the data.

Sampling therefore is a very important part of the market research process. If you have undertaken a survey using an appropriate sampling technique, you can be confident that your results will be 'generalised' to the population in question. If the sample were biased in any way, for example, if the selection technique gave older people more of a chance of selection than younger people, it would be inadvisable to make generalisations from the findings.

There are essentially two types of sampling: probability and non-probability sampling.

Probability sampling methods

Probability or random sampling gives all members of the population a known chance of being selected for inclusion in the sample. This does not depend upon previous events in the selection process. In other words, the selection of individuals does not affect the chance of anyone else in the population being selected.

Many statistical techniques assume that a sample was selected on a random basis. There are four basic types of random sampling techniques:

Simple random sampling

This is the ideal choice as it is a 'perfect' random method. Using this method, individuals are randomly selected from a list of the population, and every single individual has an equal chance of selection.

This method is ideal, but if it cannot be adopted, one of the following alternatives may be chosen.

Systematic sampling

Systematic sampling is a frequently used variant of simple random sampling. When performing systematic sampling, every 'nth' element from the list is selected (this is referred to as the **sample interval**) from a randomly selected starting point. For example, if we have a listed population of 6,000 members and wish to draw a sample of 2,000, we would select every 30th (6,000 divided by 200) person from the list. In practice, we would randomly select a number between 1 and 30 to act as our starting point.

A potential problem with this method of sampling concerns the arrangement of elements in the list. If the list is arranged in any kind of order, e.g. if every 30th house is smaller than the others from which the sample is being recruited, there is a possibility that the sample produced could be seriously biased.

Stratified sampling

Stratified sampling is a variant on simple random and systematic methods, and is used when there are a number of distinct subgroups, within each of which it is required that there is full representation. A stratified sample is constructed by classifying the population in sub-populations (or strata), based on some well-known characteristics of the population, such as age, gender or socio-economic status. The selection of elements is then made separately from within each stratum, usually by random or systematic sampling methods.

Stratified sampling methods also come in two types – proportionate and disproportionate.

- **Proportionate sampling:** In proportionate sampling, the strata sample sizes are in proportion to the strata population sizes. For example, if the first stratum is made up of males, then as there are around 50% of males in the UK population, the male strata will need to represent around 50% of the total sample.
- **Disproportionate sampling:** In disproportionate methods, the strata are not sampled according to the population sizes, but higher proportions are selected from some groups and not others. This technique is typically used in a number of distinct situations:

Cluster or multi-stage sampling

Cluster sampling is a practical and frequently used random sampling method. It is particularly useful in situations for which no list of the elements within a population is available and therefore the elements cannot be selected directly. As this form of sampling is conducted by randomly selecting subgroups of the population, possibly in several stages, it should produce results equivalent to a simple random sample.

Reasons for errors

Regardless of the sampling technique used, errors occur for a variety of reasons.

Non-sampling errors

- A respondent (person being interviewed) may give what he or she thinks should be said. This is often a politically or socially correct answer, rather than an honest answer that reflects what the respondent really thinks.
- There are occasions when respondents give an answer to please the interviewer.
- Sometimes if the respondent is in a hurry, they may give the first answer that comes into their head.
- Infrequently, there are occasions when a deliberate false answer is given. This sometimes occurs when respondents are asked how they voted. Voting is considered a private matter and therefore some people will not say how they actually voted.

All of the above may be classed as non-sampling errors and need to be noted when analysing research results.

Sampling errors

A sampling error is the difference between the mean value of the sample and the actual or true mean value of the population. (See below the calculation for arriving at the mean value.) If the mean value of a sample is 25 and the actual mean of the population is 26, the sampling error is 1.

Normally as the sample size increases, the sampling error falls.

Mean or average value

When research is undertaken, those responsible for its interpretation need to be aware of the significance of the data and its reliability. Ensuring that the data is used properly will depend upon how it is interpreted. Therefore it is important to find the average or mean for a selection of data. This average or mean, is also referred to as the central tendency.

To calculate the mean, the aggregate of all the results is divided by the number of results.

For example: add together 6, 7, 8, 9, 11, 14, 15 = 70, divide by 7 = 10

When looking at the results of any research, the data can be considered in terms of how it is distributed. A normal distribution is bell-shaped (see Figure 4.1).

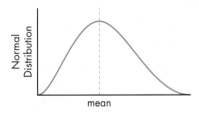

Figure 4.1 Normal distribution

To consider the distribution of the data still further, it can be compared to the mean (average).

Standard deviation

This is a measure of how spread out your data is, compared to the mean.

The standard deviation measures how far from the mean any finding, observation or response is, and can therefore be used to assess whether the result is roughly in line, more than or less than the average or mean.

It is important to realise that the closer the results are to the mean, the narrower is the spread of data; a large standard deviation suggests there is a wider spread around the mean.

Calculation of the standard deviation

For example: a market research survey collected the following data:

- 32, 34, 35, 35, 37, 37, 37, 38, 39

First, it is necessary to calculate the mean or average (aggregate of results divided by number of results).

- $32 + 34 + 35 + 35 + 37 + 37 + 37 + 38 + 39 = \dfrac{324}{9} = 36$

To find out how far each value deviates from the mean, each number is compared to the mean of 36. If less than the mean, it will be a minus number and if above the mean, it will be a positive number.

Therefore 32 = –4, 34 = –2 and so on:

Data result	32	34	35	35	37	37	37	38	39
Amount of deviation from the mean	–4	–2	–1	–1	+1	+1	+1	+2	+3

The next step is to ensure all the numbers are positive, and therefore each number is squared.

Examiner's voice

Squaring the numbers is part of a formula to gain an end result which can be used and judged for its reliability. You do not need to know why the numbers are squared; if you clearly state how you gained your figures, that will suffice.

Data result	32	34	35	35	37	37	37	38	39
Amount of deviation from the mean	–4	–2	–1	–1	+1	+1	+1	+2	+3
Square the deviation	16	4	1	1	1	1	1	4	9

Once the square of the deviations has been calculated, these numbers are then added and divided by the number of units of data (9).

- $\dfrac{16 + 4 + 1 + 1 + 1 + 1 + 1 + 4 + 9}{9}$ (38)

$= 4.22$ (the variance)

The square root of this number is calculated = 2.055. This number represents the standard deviation; 2.055 is a small standard deviation, and therefore the spread around the mean is small.

The actual formula to find the standard deviation is seen below.

Standard Deviation $= \sqrt{\dfrac{\Sigma(x - y)^2}{n}}$

x = each piece (unit) of date (the result)

y = the mean

n = the total number of pieces/units of data/results

x = 32, 34, 35, 35, etc

$\text{mean} = \dfrac{\text{total of pieces of data}}{\text{number of pieces of data}} \quad \dfrac{(324)}{(9)} = 36$

$(x - y) = 32 - 36 = -4$

The standard deviation shows how far away from the mean any results may be. Using a normal distribution curve, the standard deviation can be shown and the corresponding percentages of the distribution of the data.

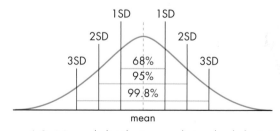

Figure 4.2 Normal distribution and standard deviation

Figure 4.2 shows that one standard deviation away from the mean will cover 65% of the data, two standard deviations from the mean will cover 95% of the data and three standard deviations from the mean will cover 99.8% of the data.

Scatter graphs

An alternative method for analysing data is to plot the relationship between two variables to see if there is any correlation. **Correlation** is a term used to show how closely two factors or variables are linked to each other.

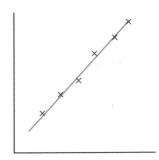

Figure 4.3 There is a strong correlation between the two variables

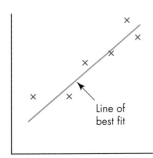

Figure 4.4 There is a weak correlation between the two variables

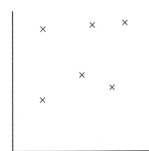

Figure 4.5 There is no correlation between the two variables

A scatter graph could look at the link between the amount of rainfall and flooding. For business studies, it could be used to look at the relationship (if any) between the level of expenditure on marketing and the level of consumption of a product. By plotting the figures onto a graph, it is possible to see if there is any correlation, once a line of best fit has been drawn.

Although the graph may show a strong correlation, it does not prove that there is a definite link in terms of cause and effect. It is plotting just two variables, and of course, there may be other variables that explain what appears to be a strong correlation.

Graphs can also be used to predict the likely trends that are based on previous data.

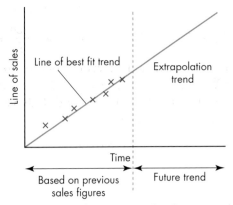

Figure 4.6 Extrapolating to predict future trends

Once the figures (for example sales figures) have been plotted, it is possible to continue the line. The data is extrapolated (continuing the line of best fit), and a future trend can be seen.

It is however, dangerous to assume that this is an inevitable trend; once again, there are many factors that may affect the sales of products in the future. Nevertheless this information is of some value and may help the other functions within the business to be able to respond accordingly.

Looking for trends

This is dealt with in Unit 54 where time series analysis (moving averages) is considered.

Further Sources

http://marketresearchworld.net
www.mintel.com

Your Turn

Questions Time allowed 25 minutes

1. Explain the difference between a stratified sample and random sampling. (4 marks)

2. State two examples of non-sampling errors. (2 marks)

3. In a recent survey, a market research team collected the following data on how many people had seen various adverts on television in a particular week.

   The results were: 20, 25, 28, 30, 36, 42, 44, 47, 52.

A. Calculate the mean number of people who had seen the adverts. (2 marks)

B. Calculate the standard deviation. (4 marks)

4. Explain how it could be possible to predict the level of future sales based on previous sales figures.

   (4 marks)

5. Draw a scatter graph diagram to show a weak correlation. Include a line of best fit. (4 marks)

   (20 marks)

MARKETING PLANNING AND STRATEGY

In any business it is important to take into account the situation in the market, the needs of the consumer and the action of competitors. The use of marketing planning is vital to ensure that all of these factors are taken into account in the application of the marketing mix. For example, a business like Unilever might want to introduce a new range of skin products. Before doing this, it will need to have identified its target market and undertaken some initial market research to investigate this market. This analysis of the market should help Unilever in the production of the product range and its subsequent marketing to consumers. Knowledge of the market, the consumer and the competition will help to show the best ways to price and promote the product when it is launched.

The marketing plan

Creating the marketing plan involves the business asking and answering a series of questions about the present and the future. One of the main uses of the plan is to help employees identify the marketing strategy for the business. The plan will help to explain necessary actions, set a budget and identify goals that are to be met. In small firms, the marketing plan may often be a series of discussions among the staff; in larger businesses the marketing plan will need to be a more formal document that can be viewed by all concerned.

The marketing plan will need to answer these questions:

- Where are we now?
- Where do we want to be?
- How will we get there?

Where are we now?

This is sometimes called a marketing audit. To answer this question the business will need to look at the internal and external factors that affect it. This will involve doing a SWOT analysis (see Unit 7). The strengths and weaknesses are internal factors that are within the business control; the opportunities and threats are external factors that are likely to be outside the business's control. There are economic, social, political and technological factors, as well as the actions of competitors. This audit will analyse the product portfolio in the current business climate, ensuring that the business matches its product range to the needs of the consumer.

Where do we want to be?

The answer to this question will involve the setting of objectives for the future (see Unit 50). This might be a strategic objective for the whole business, such as growth or diversification, or it could be a marketing objective, such as increasing market share or becoming market leader.

How will we get there?

To answer this question, a strategy for the future of the business needs to be developed. For example, the business could set itself an objective of becoming market leader. This will then require the use of the marketing mix to formulate a strategy by which this might be achieved within a particular timeframe.

Advantages and disadvantages of market planning

Advantages

1. The exercise of marketing planning helps the business to identify what it hopes to achieve through any spending on marketing. Marketing planning and marketing are both costly exercises. Too often a business will spend money in these areas without having a clear idea of what it hopes to achieve.

2. Setting clear objectives as a result of planning is a good way of motivating workers and setting targets for goals like market share, market growth or market leadership.

3. Marketing planning helps the business to rank projects so that money can be targeted and used where it will be most effective in improving performance from marketing spending.

4. A marketing plan should make it possible for the business to assess performance against expectations. Businesses can often undertake promotional campaigns with no clear idea of a result in terms of improved sales, for example. Marketing planning, if used correctly, should help to avoid this.

Disadvantages

1. It can be the case that marketing planning looks at every aspect of marketing, except the consumer. Businesses need to remember that the consumer is vital to success in any plan.

2. Marketing departments need to ensure that their plans include other departments in the firm. There is no point in having a promotional drive to increase sales if the production department has not been involved in the planning. Marketing departments cannot operate in isolation.

3. The marketing plan needs to be specific and focused rather than vague or wide-ranging. The plan should set a limited number of goals and concentrate on specific targets.

4. The plan must also take the external situation into account. A business selling luxury holidays is unlikely to achieve a large growth in sales from a new promotion at a time of economic recession.

Assessing success

Once the marketing plan has been put into operation, the business needs to measure its success. Marketing work is completed in order to achieve a goal such as increasing sales; it is important for the business to evaluate its success in achieving the goal. For example, a business might undertake an advertising campaign in order to launch a new product with a view to taking 5% of the market within six months of the launch. Throughout the six months the business should monitor the situation to see if the target is likely to be achieved. If sales are slower than expected, it may be possible to switch the advertising to a different media or time so that it is more effective in increasing demand.

The business can use any of the following measures to assess the success of putting a marketing plan into operation.

Sales

The business can look at the increase in sales generated by the implementation of the marketing plan. This type of analysis is probably the most commonly used. However, it is important to look at sales in the context of the wider picture of the total market, and whether the total market is rising or falling.

Market share

For some businesses, the market share they control is as important as the level of sales. These businesses will monitor the effect of the marketing campaign on their share of the market. This may be the case for supermarkets, who are interested in their share of the market compared with competitors.

Number of enquiries/hits

Internet and mail-order businesses will be particularly interested in the number of enquiries generated by a marketing campaign. For example, following a new advertising campaign, a car insurance company will be able to monitor success by looking at the number of requests for quotes that it receives.

Satisfaction surveys

These will involve sampling a selection of customers to see if they are happy with the good or service. Satisfaction surveys are frequently undertaken by banks, building societies and travel firms. They can be done by telephone or post, but, increasingly they are being done on the internet when the customer logs onto the site of the business.

Marketing strategy

Strategic planning is a vital element of the marketing process. To be able to develop and use a marketing strategy effectively, the business must have an in-depth knowledge of its market, its competition and its consumers. The process of market planning is the first part in the process of formulating a marketing strategy. The business will need to prepare a review of its current internal and external performance using a SWOT analysis. Alongside this the business will need to look at the budget that is available and the productive capacity. Marketing cannot be carried out in isolation from the production and financial departments of the business.

Once all these things have been done, the business will then be ready to put a marketing strategy in place, taking account of the following factors:

The business objectives
If the business wants to increase market share, it will need to look closely at the needs of the consumer and the actions of competitors.

The size of the business
Small businesses may find it difficult to market aggressively, particularly if they face competition from large businesses with more money in their marketing budgets.

The nature of the market
Businesses in markets like mobile phones and games consoles will need to change their strategy frequently to take account of new products and to respond to threats from competitors.

Management changes
New management in a business will often mean new ideas about marketing. New managers will usually be more willing to take risks in an effort to show that their appointment has been successful for the business.

Competitive strategies

The twenty-first century has seen a huge increase in the level of competition faced by businesses of all sizes. Much of this is as a result of the globalisation of world trade (see Unit 68). Today, most businesses compete in markets with producers from all over the world, so it is vitally important for each business to develop a marketing strategy that takes account of these competitors.

In these circumstances, the first thing that the business needs to do is to identify the competition and investigate all aspects of competing businesses. It will usually be easy to identify competitors in the same line of business, but many businesses face competition from outside their own segment. For example, a theme park like Alton Towers might be in competition for its visitors with a stately home like Chatsworth House or Warwick Castle, an attraction like Chester Zoo or even a visit to a shopping mall. All of these businesses are in the leisure market, trying to attract the same consumers to visit them.

Once the competition is identified, it is then necessary to look at all aspects of the way such a business is operating. For example:

- How does it market itself?
- Who are its customers?
- What are its strengths and weaknesses?
- What are its objectives for the future?
- How well is it placed to succeed compared with us?

Having investigated the competition, a business can then start to develop strategies for competing within the market. This strategy may be confined to one product or range within the business; it may be a range of strategies for different parts of the business; it may also be directed to increasing profit or market share, or to allowing the business to grow.

Types of strategy

Market leader strategies
The majority of markets have one dominant business that has control over the largest share of the market. Market leaders use a variety of strategies to retain that position and improve on it in the long term. They may try to improve their market share by the use of aggressive marketing, or they may try to achieve market growth and at the same time improve their market share. Tesco is an example of a business that has used all these tactics to achieve and maintain its market dominance. For example, Tesco has moved into many new areas of activity, like banking and insurance; at the same time it has tried to ensure that it has at least one retail outlet in every postcode area of the UK, to give it as wide a market coverage as possible.

Market challenger strategies
In this situation, a business with a smaller market share may try to attack the dominance of the market leader. In order to be able to do this, the business will need a

substantial marketing budget at its disposal. The attack may be made directly by trying to take market share through the use of promotion. More commonly, however, the challenge will be made in an area where the dominant firm is relatively weak.

Market follower strategies

Market leaders will normally respond to market challenger strategies with some form of retaliatory action. For example, if one supermarket starts a cut-price campaign, others are likely to follow and the market leader will be well-placed to cut prices most aggressively to win the price war. In many ways this is a 'no-win' situation. All that happens is that profit for all competitors is reduced. As a consequence, many businesses are happy to follow the market leader in whatever actions it takes. For example, the market follower may introduce new products or services to match those of the market leader.

Niche market strategies

Niche markets are small corners of a bigger market where businesses may choose to specialise. The market segments are usually quite small and customers have very specific demands. The Morgan car company operates in a niche market, selling handmade touring sports cars.

Figure 5.1 The sports car market is a niche market

Differentiation

Companies in many areas of the economy will try to differentiate their product from that of competitors, to try to attract business. For example, the National Westminster Bank uses advertising to inform consumers that it operates a 24-hour call centre within the UK and that many of its branches are open on Saturday mornings. This sets it apart from its main competitors.

Low cost strategies

Some large firms may try to maintain their dominance in the market through their ability to buy in bulk from suppliers at low cost per unit. This reduces their production costs, making it possible for them to pass these savings on to the consumer in terms of lower prices. Smaller businesses will be unable to match these prices because they will not have the power to command such low prices from their suppliers.

Market growth policies

If the firm wants to use marketing strategy to achieve growth in its markets, there are four options open to it. These are market penetration, product development, market development and diversification. The use of the marketing mix in these situations is explained by Ansoff's Matrix (see Unit 7).

Once the business has decided on its marketing strategy, its performance needs to be monitored and reviewed at regular intervals. The market situation will be changing constantly; businesses cannot afford to set policies in place and then leave them to run; nor should marketing strategies be left to operate without ongoing assessment of their effectiveness. Unfortunately, the market is subject to constant change, some of which can be anticipated and some which cannot. Marketing strategies will always be operating in a climate of uncertainty.

Further Sources

www.businesslink.gov.uk
www.ppamarketing.net
www.marketing.about.com
www.wikipedia.com

Case study Time allowed 1 hour

Dove

Since the launch of its moisturising soap in 1992, Dove's brand growth has been phenomenal, with a product portfolio now including 50 products. Dove has recently been voted as UK women's favourite personal care brand, with over a third of women using its products. Throughout this growth, Dove has used magazines as a key partner in its marketing strategy, recognising that consumer magazines have the ability to set the national agenda and enrich the Dove brand.

Dove regularly uses magazine advertising to place itself at the heart of the beauty arena, highlighted by a £2.8million spend in 2004. With the launch of its 'Campaign for Real Beauty', Dove recognised that magazines were the best medium to spearhead a national debate on what constitutes 'beauty'. In its advertising campaigns Dove has used ordinary women of different sizes and ages to try to dispel the myth that only models are beautiful. The campaign has been an overwhelming success since it was first introduced.

By the end of the campaign, Dove had become a national talking point and was ranked number three in the body lotions market. This success was then replicated in all the short-term brand campaigns that followed it.

Throughout all of this activity and brand-building, the use of magazines as a central marketing channel made it possible to promote dialogue with the customer and fashion journalists. Phil Cutts of Direct Marketing PPA commented:

'Dove's sustained commitment to magazines has proven how creative thinking and thorough understanding of magazines' unique strengths can be used to enhance a brand profile. It fully exploits the strengths of the magazine medium, developing powerful and engaging campaigns which really stand out.'

(Adapted from *PPA Marketing Case Studies*)

☐ fat?
☐ fit?

Does true beauty only squeeze into size 8?

campaignforrealbeauty.co.uk ◆ *Dove*

Figure 5.2 An advertisement from Dove's 'Campaign for Real Beauty'

1. Explain what is meant by 'product portfolio'. Give two examples of products in the Dove portfolio.
   (4 marks)

2. Explain two advantages for Dove in using magazine advertising as their main marketing medium. (6 marks)

3. Analyse the methods used by Dove to set itself apart from the competition. (10 marks)

4. Evaluate the ways in which market planning will have helped Dove establish its strong market position. (14 marks)

(34 marks)

INTERNATIONAL MARKETING

Recent years have witnessed the increasing globalisation of trade and a growth in the number of businesses that now trade across international boundaries (see Unit 69 on Change).

In the past, only the largest and most successful businesses were willing to consider selling overseas; today, overseas markets, particularly in the emerging and developing countries, are seen as markets that can be targeted by businesses of any size. The growth of electronic communication, such as emails, and improved transport has made trading much quicker and easier. It is now possible to make contact within seconds with anyone who has internet access, regardless of wherever they are in the world.

For UK businesses, opening up trade in the European Union and the expansion of membership (with the entry of Eastern European countries) meant that this is a market that cannot be ignored. Within the EU there are no tariffs or trading barriers, so in this respect, selling in Warsaw or Paris is the same as selling in Edinburgh, Cardiff or Newcastle. This gives businesses the opportunity to access huge markets throughout the EU. There are, however, marketing issues that businesses need to consider before starting to trade in other countries.

Reasons for international marketing

Population and the size of the market

For some businesses, the attraction of selling overseas is the access to a large market when compared to the UK market. Larger sales mean increased economies of scale for the business (see Unit 36). A business like Nestle sells its product range throughout Europe and beyond, achieving economies of scale in marketing and management. Multinational firms like Nestle can employ specialist sales staff and negotiate preferential distribution and advertising rates for its products.

Economic cycles

If a business is active in a number of different markets, it will have the opportunity to spread the risks of trading. If one market is moving into recession, it is likely that there will be other markets where trading prospects will be more promising.

Consumer law

In advanced economies, businesses have to be careful to adhere to trading laws. In the developing world, the rules are often much less rigorous. For example, tobacco firms have found that their sales have been badly affected by public smoking bans and advertising restrictions in many Western European countries. The trading conditions in Eastern Europe are not subject to these rules and regulations, and the opportunities for sales and profit are therefore much greater.

Differences in marketing overseas

Although moving into international markets may seem attractive, there are also problems and pitfalls that businesses need to be careful to avoid. This can only be done through the use of careful planning and a thorough awareness of trading and other conditions in the overseas market.

1. Even within the EU there are different rules for business and trading behaviour. Businesses moving into overseas markets need to make themselves aware of the laws of those countries so that they do not run into problems. Examples of these differences would be those applying to the labelling of cigarettes with health warnings, or the rules applying to the safety of toys.

2. The HSBC advertisements on television explain some of the many cultural differences between countries. These differences can lead to misunderstanding at best or hostility at worst if a business gets it wrong. For example, colours have different significance in other cultures; this can have an impact when businesses make decisions about packaging.

3. Businesses need to be aware of the political climate in other countries. In the West we are used to democratic political systems and the freedom of individuals to speak. Western Europe businesses operate relatively independently of control and government intervention. These circumstances are often different in other countries. For example, the advertising of alcohol is very strictly controlled or prohibited in some countries in the Middle East and Asia.

4. Religious and cultural differences also need to be considered. There may be particular implications for advertising, where it can be very easy to give offence in a country with a strong religious background. The role of women in society may also be different. This factor must therefore be considered in advertisements and in the range of products being sold.

5. In some countries, even in Europe, a payment that would be regarded as a bribe in the UK can be expected before a deal is achieved. In some instances this payment might have to be made to a government official. Businesses may find that they have to overcome their resistance to this sort of business practice if they are to succeed.

6. It may be necessary to take advice from within a country about ways to appeal to the market, particularly if there are large cultural differences from the domestic market. Very often, a business moving into a new country will use an agent to help ensure that all the important issues of marketing in the new country are appreciated and addressed.

7. Language difficulties can also present problems. Translations need to be made by someone who speaks the language fluently. It is always better to use a resident who is not only fluent, but aware of current language usage and styles of speaking. The use of names for products it also important. A word that is acceptable in one country could be offensive in another.

Differences between markets

The following factors need to be considered before moving into a market in another country. These factors should be investigated thoroughly before anything else is done, through the use of market research. Knowledge of all aspects of the market is essential if a venture into an international market is going to be successful. This research may be costly, but it is likely to alert the business to any possible problems and it may result in substantial savings in the long term. In some cases, the result of market research may be to persuade the business not to proceed.

Political factors

- Is the country politically stable?
- Are the trade unions active? Is there industrial unrest? Will these issues cause problems?
- Is it necessary to offer bribes to government officials or others? If this is the case, the business needs to think about whether it will prepared to be involved in bribery to attract business.

Economic factors

- Is there buoyant demand in the market?
- Is it a free market economy or is it centrally planned?
- Is the economy growing?
- What is the age distribution of the population?
- Is the population growing?
- What is the level and distribution of income in the population?

Legal factors

- How much legislation is there affecting business and trade?
- What are the laws on advertising?
- Do the courts operate freely and fairly?

Cultural factors

- What are the religious and cultural influences in the country?
- What is the attitude to women in society?

- How do people spend their leisure time?
- Will the business be able to advertise its product freely?

A move into an overseas market, however familiar a country may seem, is something that needs to be investigated carefully. Businesses must proceed cautiously and use local advisers wherever possible. The alternative may be a costly mistake that ends in failure.

Further Sources

www.thetimes100.co.uk
www.marketingteacher.com

Your Turn

Case study   Time allowed 1 hour

Commemorative Ceramics

Gill Dunn started Commemorative Ceramics (CC) in 1990, working by herself in a small unit in her garden. The business buys readymade ceramic pieces like mugs, plates and small dishes and then decorates them for special events and occasions. For example, Gill does some work for schools, colleges and universities who want to make presentations to leavers.

When Gill first started the business, most of her work was commissioned either by companies who wanted corporate gifts for clients or by private individuals for weddings. From the start, Gill decided that she did not want to be involved in commemorative ware for events like royal weddings, jubilees etc. because the large ceramic firms like Wedgwood and Royal Doulton dominated that market. Instead Gill liked to work on relatively small runs of up to 200 units per order.

Over the intervening years, Gill's business has gradually built up so that she has moved into a small unit on a local business park. Gill now employs ten workers in decoration, one designer who works part-time and two office staff who job-share. Most of the work that CC now handles is for the wedding market. Gill does some limited advertising in wedding magazines and in addition she distributes flyers at wedding fairs and with local photographers and florists. Despite its growth, CC is still a small-scale business.

Gill has recently been approached by an organisation involved in the wedding market in Poland. It would like Gill to start producing commemorative ware for the Polish market. The business would display Gill's gifts in the brochure they give to all prospective clients, and provide her website details for anyone who is interested in placing an order. Gill has been told that the wedding market in Poland is huge and that increased prosperity from Poland's entry into the European Union has meant that families now have more disposable income to spend on all aspects of weddings. She feels that this would be a good opportunity for her business to grow.

Gill is very tempted to try to move into this market, but she feels worried about the problems that she might encounter by moving into the unknown. She knows that she will need to investigate the situation carefully before she proceeds.

1. Explain two difficulties that Gill might encounter in trading in Poland.   (6 marks)

2. How has new technology made it easier to trade in overseas markets?   (6 marks)

3. Analyse the main factors that Gill should consider in deciding whether to start selling in Poland.   (10 marks)

4. The UK economy appears to be heading towards a recession. Advise Gill on whether she should move into the Polish market.   (18 marks)

(40 marks)

MARKETING MODELS

Promotion is an important part of the marketing mix and a feature that has increased in prominence as the impact of the media has grown in modern society. The object of promotion is to persuade the consumer to buy the goods or services of an individual business. Its other purpose is to inform the individual so that they can make a rational choice.

When promotion is successful, it will increase demand and encourage brand loyalty. This is made by altering the elasticity of demand through the use of advertising. For example, a large number of people will always buy the same bar of chocolate, whatever its price. Kit Kat has a high brand loyalty meaning that for some consumers it will always be the chocolate bar they purchase. This means that its elasticity of demand is low and that a change in price is likely to result in a proportionately smaller change in demand. In using promotion, Nestle want to attract new customers, but they also want the advertising to make its existing customers loyal to the brand.

DAGMAR

DAGMAR is a model aimed at promotion. One of the purposes of promotion is to help the consumer to become aware of the characteristics of the good or service, and to stress the ways in which it differs from competing products in the market. The acronym DAGMAR stands for:

- **D**efining
- **A**dvertising
- **G**oals
- **M**easuring
- **A**dvertising
- **R**esults.

In using DAGMAR, therefore, the business should be able to formulate a strategy for any new promotional campaign. In the first instance, the business should make decisions about what is to be achieved through the promotion in terms of customer awareness, explanation of the product and image. This is the first part of DAGMAR.

The second part is to measure the success in terms of some previously agreed criterion. This may be increased sales or market share. For example, a business like Muller Yoghurts may have an advertising campaign to launch a new range of chilled desserts on to the market. The promotion will need to differentiate the range from competitors and stress any special features. In launching the product, Muller will have set itself targets for sales over a period of time, and it will collect data from the supermarkets and other outlets to be able to monitor the success of the advertising campaign.

AIDA

AIDA is also a promotional model applied specifically to advertising. The application of AIDA will help a business to judge whether an advertisement is likely to succeed.

- **Attention:** the first thing that an advertisement needs to do is to grab the attention of the prospective customer. For example, some producers may use a particular jingle or music throughout all their advertisements so that consumers begin to associate its use with the product.
- **Interest:** having caught the attention in the first instance, the advertisement must retain the customer's attention so that the information about the product and its qualities can be delivered. The hope then is that, once consumers have listened to the advertisement, they will want to purchase the product.

- **Desire:** the result of all this must be a desire on the part of the consumer to buy the product, resulting in demand for the good or service.
- **Action:** this desire must then lead the consumer to act and actually purchase the product.

If the cycle is broken at any point, the advertisement will not result in a successful purchase. There are a number of ways in which this might happen.

- The consumer may watch the advertisement and be interested in the product but have no desire to buy. This can happen with advertisements that are artistically excellent and interesting or amusing to watch, regardless of whether the individual might buy the product or not. Guinness advertisements often win awards and are impressive to watch, although a large proportion of those who watch and admire the advertisements are unlikely to be interested in buying the product.
- The consumer may be unable to act on the desire to buy because of lack of availability of the product. For example, it is sometimes the case at Christmas that advertisements for toys or new electronic games are followed by shortages of supplies. The advertisement may be successful in encouraging a desire to buy, but the action will not be possible.
- The consumer may go through each stage up to the point of action and then be attracted to a competing product or be discouraged from purchase by the price.

SWOT analysis

Any business making a decision about its future strategy needs to consider the business situation, both internally and externally. A SWOT analysis can help the business to look objectively at its competitive situation and to decide on the best strategy for the future. SWOT stands for:

- Strengths
- Weaknesses
- Opportunities
- Threats.

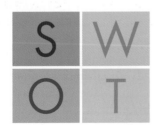

Figure 7.1 SWOT

The strengths and weaknesses of the business are internal factors, whereas the opportunities and threats will be part of the external market in which the business is trading. For example, for a large business like Unilever, one of its main strengths is likely to be the well-known brand names it produces such as Persil and Comfort. A possible weakness may be that the customer starts to view these brands as old and out-of-date if Unilever does not keep relaunching the products in different packaging or with new properties. Opportunities for a global company like Unilever will lie in the newly developing areas of the world economy. The threat of competition in this oligopolistic market is very high, and is likely to influence much of the company's strategic planning.

Uses of SWOT analysis

A SWOT analysis can be carried out by an individual department within a business or by a business as a whole. For example, a marketing department might assess the current market conditions and the quality of its current marketing strategies. These can then be considered in relation to the future. What might happen? How might the competition react? What is happening in the wider market?

The whole analysis can be used as a forward-looking tool. The managers can consider how effective the business is in respect of the environment in which it operates, and adjust their strategies and tactics as appropriate (see Unit 53).

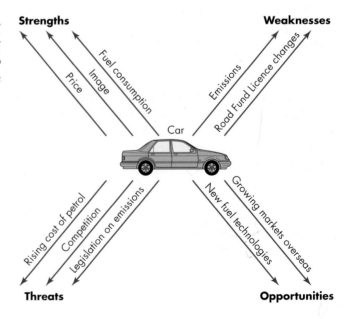

Figure 7.2 SWOT analysis of a car

Any business beginning a strategic planning process for the future will probably begin by completing a SWOT analysis. The analysis will be a useful beginning to discussion and planning, and will help the business to identify the best way to proceed for future success.

Ansoff's Matrix

Ansoff's Matrix is a strategic tool to help a business that wishes to grow. Igor Ansoff worked for Lockheed Electronics before leaving to become a university professor. He was interested in ways by which businesses could identify their competitive advantage in existing and new markets.

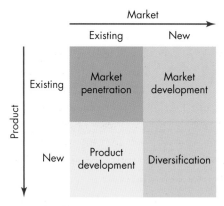

Figure 7.3 Ansoff's Matrix

The matrix looks at the business's markets in terms of existing and new products, and existing and new market opportunities. It identifies four possible strategies for growth: market penetration, market development, product development and diversification. Each of them will require the use of different elements of the marketing mix, together with market research.

Market penetration

This is a situation where the firm tries to sell more of its existing product in its existing market. To achieve this, the business may need to use more aggressive promotion, or it may need to price its product more competitively.

Market development

This involves selling the existing product to a new market segment. Careful market research will be required in the first instance to identify possible markets. The business then needs to ensure that it prices and promotes the product with the new market in mind.

Product development

Changes are made to the existing product, but it continues to sell in the same market. This might involve new packaging, new flavours or new formulation for the product.

Diversification

This entails selling a new product in a new market, and it is a high risk strategy for any business. Thorough market research will be needed so that the firm is aware of any threats that might exist, particularly in the form of competition.

Advantages of Ansoff's Matrix

Using Ansoff's Matrix makes it possible for the business to identify how it wants its market to grow and to formulate a strategy. For example, suppose that a business producing personalised, office stationery decides it wants to grow. Having looked at the alternatives and completed market research, managers make a decision to move into the market for wedding stationery where opportunities exist because there are few competitors. This is an example of diversification in the matrix; the business will be selling a new product in a new market. The business will need to ensure that the new product range meets the needs of the market at a price that consumers are willing to pay. Promotion will also be needed to create awareness of the new range among potential customers. The strategy will therefore be based around price, promotion and product. In all growth strategies, businesses will need to use elements of the marketing mix to ensure that success is achieved.

Examiner's voice

The advantage of using Ansoff's Matrix in a question on business strategy is that it encourages concentration on a combination of one or two factors from the marketing mix. This makes it less likely that the answer is a list of possibilities with little or no analysis or evaluation.

Further Sources

www.ezinearticles.com
www.businessstudiesonline.co.uk
www.marketingteacher.com
www.learnmarketing.net

Your Turn

Group task Time allowed 40 minutes

1. In groups of two or more, prepare a SWOT analysis for an organisation you know well, or a well-known product from the list below:

   - your school or college
   - a sports club
   - a chocolate bar
   - a mobile phone.

2. Using Ansoff's Matrix suggest the best way for this business to grow in the future. Justify your answer.

PRODUCT

Making the product distinctive is a marketing task which is very important to the success or failure of the product. Finding a unique selling point (USP) helps the product to stand out. If the product is one of many in a highly competitive market, any form of uniqueness will be valuable.

Choosing the correct product

- Branding is one way of establishing distinctness. A logo or distinct way of writing the name helps to make a brand recognisable.
- Branding may help consumers to recognise a product, but if the product is poor, any distinctive branding will be wasted. (See Unit 49 for further examples of branding.)
- Producing the 'right' type of product ought to be based on effective research. A market-orientated approach is more likely to lead to a successful product.

Value analysis

Using value analysis to consider the nature of the product enables the business to assess its priorities. Value analysis helps focus the manufacturer's mind on the main characteristics of the product.

It is important to achieve the right balance is achieved between:

- the function of the product,
- the aesthetics of the product, and
- the economic cost of the product.

The purpose of the product dictates whether the shape and colour are more important than the functional qualities. An i-pod needs to have the functional qualities to meet the expectations of the consumers in terms of its ability to 'play' music. However, it needs to look good and therefore the aesthetics are also important.

The economic cost is less important if the first two are of a high standard. The cost's significance will depend on the competitiveness of the market. Producing a product at a low economic cost will ensure a profit for the business. It would be of little value to produce a well-designed product that performs its function extremely well, but a loss is made.

For other goods, the most important aspect will be the aesthetics. The look of a fashion dress is essential; alternatively, the aesthetics of a plastic cup is of little importance when compared to the cost and its functional qualities.

The product life cycle

Regardless of the value analysis mix, all products progress through a life cycle. They are launched, hopefully increase in popularity, and eventually are

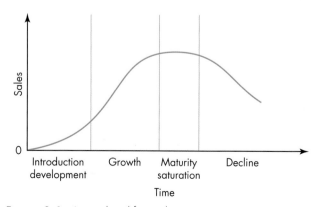

Figure 8.1 A product life cycle

replaced by new improved products or naturally decline. The soft drink Coca Cola has been sold since Dr John Pemberton invented it in 1886, and it is still selling well! However, some of the differently flavoured Coca Cola drinks have not lasted so long.

There are four stages to the product life cycle:

- introduction/development stage
- growth stage
- maturity/saturation stage
- decline stage.

Each stage of the product life cycle requires a different marketing mix.

Introduction/development stage

During this stage, the research and development will have been undertaken to discover what the consumer needs. The launch of the product will take place either in one particular region of the country or nationally. Initial sales may be slow until the consumer has tried the product and any marketing activity has had time to build interest. There is often reluctance on behalf of consumers to try anything new or change from the brand they are used to. It is at this stage of the life cycle that a product may fail.

Marketing mix?

- Sufficient market research to ensure the product meets its consumers' needs.
- Depending on the nature of the product, the pricing will include introductory offers to encourage consumers to try the product.
- Occasionally, research costs are very high and therefore the price of the product will initially be high until sales increase.
- The advertising will be informative to increase consumer awareness.
- Distribution channels will be low, though increasing sales outlets will be a priority.

Examiner's voice

The marketing mix ideas are only suggestions, because every product may need a distinct marketing strategy for its mix. Nevertheless this is an attempt to emphasise that the mix will change in line with the stage of the life cycle.

Growth stage

Once consumers are fully aware of the new product, the sales are likely to grow more quickly. Word-of-mouth and continued promotion may enhance sales still further. If products can reach this stage and achieve growth, the product is more likely to be a success. The rate of growth in sales will depend upon the nature of the product and the amount of alternatives (competition) in the market.

Marketing mix?

- Modifications may be made after initial feedback market research.
- If in a competitive market, pricing will have to reflect the market price unless a highly distinctive edge allows for a premium price.
- Informative advertising may continue but a move to competitive and persuasive styles is likely.
- Distribution is now much wider and therefore additional channels may be required.

Maturity/saturation stage

If this stage can be reached, it is likely that the product will be profitable. Depending upon the nature of the product and the level of development costs, by this stage all such costs should have been covered. Maintaining the product in this stage of the life cycle becomes the next issue. Sales are likely to flatten out, the nature of any marketing will have changed and competition from newer products becomes a concern.

Saturation implies that all the consumers who wanted to purchase the product have now done so and therefore, any additional sales will be difficult. The Mars Bar is still in its maturity stage, as are Kit Kats and Cadbury's Dairy Milk bars. Hovis bread has managed to remain in the maturity stage by promoting itself as a traditional loaf, with a recent advertising campaign stating: 'Hovis, as good as it's always been'. These products however are the exceptions!

The marketing of products in the maturity stage is concentrated on keeping sales within this stage and therefore avoiding sales falling. The promotion often reminds consumers of the existence of the product. There are several ways in which the business can encourage consumers to continue buying its product in the maturity stage. The strategies used are called extension strategies (see below).

Marketing mix?

- Product established although there may be slight variations to maintain sales.

- Depending upon the actual product, pricing will reflect the amount of competition in the market. However, price reductions may be used as extension strategies (see below).
- With an established product, any advertising will be used just to remind consumers of its existence. Such advertising will increase if newer products enter the market. Similarly, advertising and sales promotions could be used as extension strategies.
- There is the possibility of seeking new markets for the product and therefore establishing new outlets in which it can be made available.

Decline stage

Sales are now falling. Consumers may have lost interest in the product as newer and better alternatives enter the market. Sales may be so low that there is no reason to continue to make the product available.

In this stage a business has to decide if it wants to offer the product at heavily discounted prices to boost sales, or simply allow sales to decline. Much will depend upon whether the business has a replacement product that is soon to be launched into the market. The business does not want consumers to think that its product is outdated and may therefore allow sales to decline, ready for an improved version!

Marketing mix?

- There is little point in spending money on a product in decline.
- Prices may be drastically reduced in order to sell off any stock that is left before the new model/product is launched.
- Sales promotions may be heavily used to help sell off final stock.

Extension strategies

In order to maintain sales, extension strategies are used. Within the car industry, extension strategies are

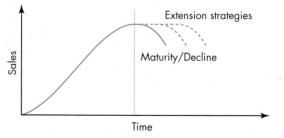

Figure 8.2 Extension strategies

commonplace. They are often used to help sell a model that will soon be replaced. Consumers may be aware of the new model that is soon to be launched, and are therefore reluctant to purchase an old model. However, the manufacturer is able to sell the old model by offering 'special editions'. Incurring only low additional costs, a model can be temporally revived with this technique. A special edition colour or go-faster stripe may be added.

Figure 8.2 shows how an extension strategy extends the life of the product but does not actually prevent the inevitable decline stage.

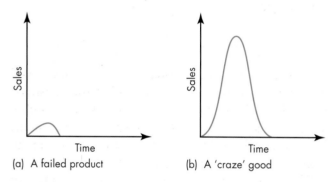

(a) A failed product   (b) A 'craze' good

Figure 8.3 Product life cycle variation

Product life cycle variations

The length and 'shape' of the product life cycle may vary considerably. Figure 8.3 shows two completely different life cycles. Figure 8.3a represents a failed product: sales are minimal and the life of the product is very short. In Figure 8.3b, the life of the product is short: sales quickly rise, but just as quickly fall. This is typical of a craze product. Its popularity is intense for a very short period of time before it quickly 'dies' as the next craze enters the market. Examples of craze products include merchandise associated with successful film, or a toy such as a Tamagochi in the 1990s.

Cash inflows and outflows

Although the product life cycle clearly shows the level of sales over time, it does not show what is happening to the level of cash inflows and outflows. Figure 8.4 shows these cashflows for each stage of the life cycle.

It is worth noting that for all of the first stage of the product life cycle, there is a negative cashflow for this product. The cost of the research and development, the cost of marketing the launch and subsequent promotion, means that more money is going out of the business than is coming in. Even when sales revenue starts to flow in,

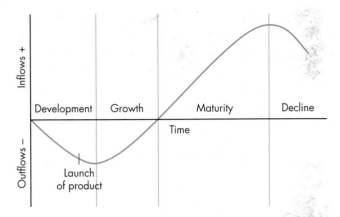

Figure 8.4 Product life cycle cash inflows and outflows

Figure 8.5 Product positioning for supermarkets

it may be some considerable time before there is a positive cashflow for this product.

The pricing strategy for the product will affect how quickly the cashflow becomes positive. The problem facing the business is what price to charge for the product. It may decide to set its price at a low level in an attempt to attract consumers. However, by charging a lower price, more sales will be needed before the initial costs are covered. Similarly, if a high price is set, sales may be harder to achieve but if achieved, the initial costs will be covered more quickly. There is no 'right' approach to this and the business will need to be mindful of the type of product and the market in which it is to be sold.

Once the cashflow is positive, the product may have moved into the maturity stage, although there is no set time when this occurs.

Any additional marketing expenditure will have to be considered in terms of its costs set against any likely increased revenue from additional sales.

Product positioning and the product portfolio

Product positioning

Selling the 'right' product in the 'right' segment of the market is a decision that a business will have to take. It is sometimes helpful to undertake research to ascertain what other products are in the market, and where each of them is positioned. Once the information has been collected it can be plotted to show the positioning. This can be done for the whole market, or a business can do this for its own product portfolio. Figure 8.5 shows a typical product-positioning chart.

Examiner's voice

There is no correct way in which to plot the products within a given market. What is used to mark the axis and help distinguish the various products is often arbitrary.

Product portfolio

Having considered one product, it is important to realise that many businesses produce a range of products. This collection of products is often referred to as the product portfolio. Deciding what products ought to be in a portfolio will depend upon a variety of factors.

The information on a product positioning chart such as Figure 8.5 can be used to help a business to decide if it wants to produce a product that will fill a gap in the market. However, the business needs to be careful because there may be a very good reason that gap in the market exists; it may simply be that there is no demand for that type of product. The product positioning chart can be used to see where the majority of the products are positioned. A business may then decide that it too should launch a product where all the others are concentrated in, even though it will mean entering a highly competitive sector of the market.

The product positioning chart can also help a business to see any obvious gaps in its own product portfolio. Many car manufacturers have a range of cars in their portfolio, each model ensuring that the name of the manufacturer is represented in most segments of the market. For example, Ford produces a wide range of cars, ranging from the Ford Ka, Ford Focus, Ford Galaxy to the Ford Transit Van. Each model is designed to satisfy a demand in the market, whether it is for a small family saloon car (the Fiesta), a people carrier (Ford Galaxy) or the 4×4 market (Ford Kuga). Ford has a very comprehensive product portfolio, with a model for almost every single type of car and commercial vehicle.

Boston Matrix

Another tool that a business can use when deciding what products to produce is the Boston Matrix. This is a different way of categorising the products within the portfolio of a business. This matrix considers products in terms of their market share and potential for market growth.

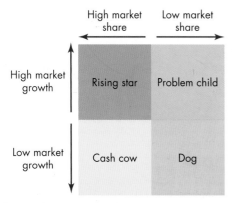

Figure 8.6 Boston Matrix

Figure 8.7 shows the four categories of products.

- Star
- Cash cow
- Problem child
- Dog.

Star

This is the category where the product has a high market share and it is in a market which has potential to grow. (It is sometimes referred to as a rising star.) Although this may appear the best category to be in, this is slightly misleading. In order to gain and maintain a high market share, the business may have had to advertise heavily in order to establish itself fully, and maintain a high advertising spend. Such products have the potential to be future cash cows.

Cash cow

The cash cow is the category that ensures high revenues. It is an established product that has a high share of the market. Although the market has low growth, the

product generates large amounts of cash. The cash cow is normally a mature product that does not need heavy marketing expenditure, and therefore sales revenues are profitable. Being sold in large quantities allows for low unit cost and therefore high profits. The large profits gained from cash cow products can be used to support problem child products, which do need the investment.

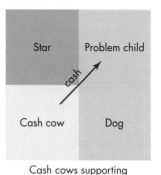

Figure 8.7 Boston Matrix – a marketing strategy to support the product portfolio

Problem child (or question marks)

The problem child has a low market share within a market that is rapidly growing. The aim is for a problem child to become a star or a cash cow. In order for this to be achieved, the business will need to invest heavily to help increase the market share of the product. A problem child product is normally a new product that has yet to establish itself in the market, and consequently is not profitable yet. Investment in marketing is needed in order to raise the profile of the product within the expanding market.

Dog

Dogs have a low market share and low market growth; consequently they have no real future. Unless the dog is a vital addition to the range of products offered by the business, it ought to be dropped as quickly as possible.

Advantages of using the Boston matrix

By looking at its range of products within the Boston matrix, a business can see if it has a balanced portfolio, and whether it has sufficient cash cows to feed the problem child. A business does not need dogs, but does need cash cows in order to convert problem child products into stars or cash cows. Too many stars may be a drain on financial resources, as they require large funds to maintain their position in the growth market.

Product differentiation

Finally, in order to make the products of a business stand out, they will need some form of product differentiation. In a mass market, any form of differentiation will help to make the product distinctive when compared to the rest of the market. Careful branding or having a unique selling point can achieve this. Even the best established brands occasionally need to relaunch or reposition their brands to help maintain its market share.

Heinz rebranded in 2008, moving away from Heinz Baked Beans to Heinz Beans, to link with its slogan of 'Beanz Meanz Heinz'. The product positioning uses an established brand name and an association with quality; if you are thinking about beans, it must be Heinz beans. Product positioning can be achieved by:

1. the price;

2. having a beneficial quality, such as durability, when compared to others in the market, or by being a niche product;

3. satisfying a small segment of the market;

4. being something completely different, as was the Dyson hoover when it first entered the market.

Wherever a product is positioned, it aims to increase revenues, either directly (as a result of higher sales of a specific product in a specific position within the market), or indirectly (by being in the market and therefore enhancing the recognition of the brand name without increasing revenues).

Further Sources

www.marketingteacher.com/boston
www.ford.co.uk

Your Turn

Questions Time allowed 40 minutes

1. State the three elements for value analysis.
   (3 marks)

2. Draw a diagram to show the different elements of the Boston Matrix. (4 marks)

3. How does a cash cow benefit a business?
   (4 marks)

4. Explain how an extension strategy may help extend the life of a product. (4 marks)

5. Draw a product life cycle for Kellogg's cornflakes.
   (4 marks)

(19 marks)

Group task   Time allowed 1 hour

1. Select a good or service. Undertaking the appropriate research, construct a product positioning chart for the brands within the market.

   OR

2. For a business you know, construct a Boston Matrix from its range of products. Ensure that you state which of its products/models are the cash cows, problem child, dogs and stars. Justify your selections.

PRICE

The price of a product or service indicates both its value and its quality. A consumer can use the price of a product to make a comparison with other goods and services.

The price that a business fixes for its products will determine the level of revenue that is earned. The price must also fit with the rest of the marketing mix implemented by the business, as the image of a product is influenced by its price. A product that has a high price ought not to be sold at discount shops or local markets, as this would not be compatible with its image.

Pricing can be viewed from different perspectives. Within the business, different departments and stakeholders will have differing views on the ideal price of a good or service.

- The finance department may want a price that yields a high profit.
- The marketing department will want a price that helps gain a foothold in the market, especially if it is a competitive market.
- The consumers will want value for money, and therefore usually a lower price.
- Shareholders will want a return on their investment.

All these stakeholders have some input on the eventual price of a product.

Factors affecting the price

There are also a wide range of factors that affect the price charged for a good or service:

- the objectives of the business, and its objectives for the given product or service
- the consumers, their income and tastes

- the cost of producing the good
- the level of demand within the market
- the level of competition within the market
- the actual nature of the product or service
- its stage in the product life cycle
- the rest of the marketing mix
- the scale of production
- the economic environment (boom or recession)
- the value of the pound (exchange rates)
- legislation
- weather conditions.

From another viewpoint, market forces normally determine the price of any good or service. Market forces consist of demand and supply.

Examiner's voice

This is a topic that you should have covered at AS level and therefore the level of detail shown here assumes that you already have a working knowledge of the issues.

As prices rise, the demand for goods and services fall because consumers can no longer afford to pay for the goods. On the other hand, suppliers are usually willing to supply more goods if prices are rising. The actual price that is charged for a good or service is a combination of the two.

The place that demand and supply intersect represents the equilibrium price. However, it is not easy for a business to know what this particular price is. There may be a certain amount of guessing or an attempt to gauge the right price by using market research; with so many factors affecting the setting of the price, it is not a

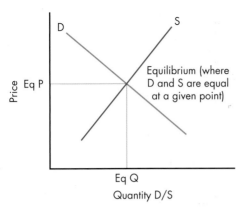

Figure 9.1 Demand and supply (price determinants)

straightforward process. Setting the price of petrol during 2008 and 2009 was not easy! The petrol companies had to consider:

- the cost of a barrel of oil
- the level of tax (excise duty and VAT on the product)
- what the competitors were charging
- the objectives of the business
- the area in which the petrol was sold
- what was happening in the economy.

Price elasticity

Elasticity measures the response of demand to a change in price (price elasticity of demand) or income (income elasticity of demand).

Price elasticity of demand (PED)

Whenever the price of a good or service is changed, the level of demand will also change. How much it will change will depend upon a number of factors:

- the nature of the product (whether it is a necessity or a luxury good)
- the level of the price change
- the income of the consumer
- the number of previous price increases
- how high the product is on a consumer's preference scale
- whether the purchase can be postponed.

A business will want to know the likely consequences if it decides to change the price of its product or service. As a consequence, the business will have to consider all of the listed factors above in an attempt to assess what will happen to the demand.

The combination of the above factors determines by how much demand changes. Looking at the characteristics of the product and the consumer will help to decide the likely elasticity.

Elastic Characteristics	Inelastic Characteristics
Large price increase	Small price increase
Large proportion of income	Small proportion of income
Purchase can be postponed	Purchase cannot be postponed
Large number of substitutes	Very few if any substitutes
Low on preference list	High on preference list
Low level of income	High level of income
Luxury good	Necessity

Table 9.1 Characteristics of elastic and inelastic demand

The rate of change is referred to as the elasticity of the product.

Apart from using the characteristics of the product and the consumer to judge the elasticity, it is possible to calculate a value for both price and income elasticity.

Once the elasticity is established, it is easier to gauge the likely consequences of any changes in the prices charged.

A business is able to see that if it increased its prices for product A by 10% (inelastic), demand will not fall very much (2%); consequently, the revenue will actually increase. However, an increase in the price of product B of 10% (elastic) will lead to a greater fall in demand (30%) and a fall in revenue.

Whether the marketing department will consider a loss in revenue acceptable will depend upon the reasons for the increase in price.

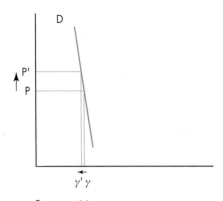

Revenue rising
10% increase in price – 2% fall in demand

Figure 9.2 Inelastic demand

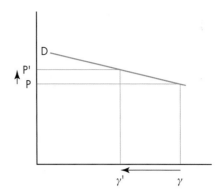

Revenue falling
10% increase in price – 30% fall in demand

Figure 9.3 Elastic demand

The marketing department will want to know the likely price elasticity of demand to help decide whether to increase or decrease its prices. An inelastic product can withstand price increases, as demand will not change by very much. However, if the product is more price sensitive (elastic), even small changes in the price could affect demand significantly.

Formula for determining the price elasticity of demand (PED)

This measures the response of demand to a change in price:

$$\frac{\text{Percentage change in demand}}{\text{Percentage change in price}}$$

Examiner's voice

As always, remember to state the formula, as you will be rewarded for showing your working. For A2 modules, to gain level 3 (analysis), it is important that you are able to comment on the significance of the answer in the context of the business and its products.

Income elasticity of demand

This measures the response of demand to a change in income.

Usually, when incomes increase, the level of demand increases as consumers have more spending power. What the extra income is spent on depends upon a wide range of factors.

The key characteristics that will help determine the level of income elasticity of demand are shown in Table 9.2.

Elastic Characteristics	Inelastic Characteristics
Inferior goods	
Luxury goods	Necessities
Large increase in income	Small increase in income
Consumer's income is low	Consumer's income is high

Table 9.2 Income elasticity of demand

The formula for determining the income elasticity of demand is:

$$\frac{\text{Percentage change in demand}}{\text{Percentage change in income}}$$

Examiner's voice

One of the major limitations of using the formula to gauge the elasticity is that it assumes you know the price or income changes **and** what happens to demand. This is highly unlikely when bringing out a new product. It is also unlikely that the use of previous changes in prices or incomes and demand will guarantee the same response.

Pricing strategies/methods

As we have seen above, deciding on the prices for the goods and services is not straightforward. However, the objectives of the business are crucial. Once it has decided what it wants to achieve for the business as a whole and for any individual product, the business can decide which pricing strategy or strategies to use.

Examiner's voice

When answering a question on pricing, it is worth remembering that there is no right strategy! It is important to use the information in the case study. This information will probably help you to eliminate several options as being inappropriate for the particular business selling a product in a particular market to a given segment of the market.

Skimming

Skimming describes the process in which the business sets a high price for its goods or services in an attempt to gain profits quickly; often when there are high research costs.

This pricing strategy is used for products that have a short life cycle because it is necessary to gain maximum benefits while possible. If other businesses note the high returns made by a specific business, they may also enter the market, which forces the price of the goods down.

In summary, skimming starts with a high price which it may eventually have to reduce.

Penetration pricing

This is a strategy that is used to help establish a new product in the market and subsequently gain a share of the market. To establish itself in the market, the business sets a low price initially, hoping to attract consumers. The product may also be heavily advertised, highlighting the introductory low price. Once a reasonable share of the market has been achieved or loyal consumers gained, the price may be increased. The level and rate of price increases will depend upon the desired price level when compared with the introductory price.

Premium pricing or prestige pricing

A high price is set for a product or service in an attempt to create an image and indicate a high level of quality. Initially, BMW took this approach in terms of its pricing. Stella Artois has tried to position itself as a premium product by selling its lager at a higher price. However, as competition has increased, it has reduced its prices using various promotional pricing campaigns.

Psychological pricing

This involves setting a price that sounds less than it really is. Charging 99 pence sounds substantially cheaper than one pound; similarly, charging £9.99 sounds much less than £10.

It is a practice that is used by many retailers and manufacturers.

- The clothing industry prices the majority of its clothes using this strategy, e.g. £10.99, £29.99, £69.99.
- The car industry prefers to price models at a pound below its ideal price, e.g. £6,999 rather that £7,000.
- The selling price for a house may be £199,950 rather than £200,000.

The difference in the actual price is minute but if it appears less, it may encourage consumers to purchase.

Psychological pricing is often used by the sellers of petrol, where the price per litre may be expressed as 99p. The difference of 0.1p is meaningless in terms of expenditure, and yet consumers will refer to the price as 99p and not almost £1. For this reason, it is a worthwhile practice.

Loss leaders

This pricing strategy is often used in order to entice consumers into a particular retail outlet. It is heavily used by supermarkets, which usually reduce the price of essential products such as sugar, milk, soups, beans and bread, to below cost.

Careful consideration is given to the placement within the shop of the loss leader so that, once consumers are enticed into the shop, they will have to pass a wide range of products that it is hoped they will purchase, often on impulse. These sales will more than compensate for the losses made on the loss leaders.

Competition-based price

There are occasions when a business will set the price of its goods below its competitors with the intention of gaining additional sales and 'beating' its competitors. This is a short-term pricing policy to gain additional sales until the competition respond! Predatory pricing (see below) is a similar pricing policy but on a more drastic level.

Predatory pricing (destroyer pricing)

Whichever name is used, the Office of Fair Trading often sees this type of pricing as anti-competitive. Predatory pricing is used when an established business responds to a new business entering the market by reducing its prices (often even to incur a loss in the short term.) With such low prices, the new entrant will find it impossible or very difficult to compete, and even if it did try to match the prices of the established business, it would also incur a loss. As a new entrant into the market, it would not be able to make cost savings due to a lack of economies of scale (still selling in small quantities) and may therefore find it impossible to sustain such low prices. The established business is then able to 'force' the new entrant out of the market.

This type of pricing is occasionally attempted with established rivals, but such price wars are often only short-lived or used as a form of promotional campaign or even loss leaders. Supermarkets at the end of 2008 used alcohol as a loss leader to entice consumers into the shop and thereby buy other products as well.

Market-based pricing (going-rate pricing)

Where products are very similar or even identical (homogeneous), a business will take its price from the market. Milk and petrol are classic examples. Oil companies tend to follow each other when prices fluctuate due to the changing price of a barrel of oil. In 2008, when a barrel of oil reached over $140, the price of a litre of petrol rose to 125p. However, as the barrel of oil price fell to below $60, petrol prices fell to 95p a litre and all petrol stations were charging very similar prices.

Promotional pricing

There are several forms of promotional pricing.

- BOGOF (buy one get one free)
- price reductions (10% off)
- '3 for 2' offers as used extensively at Boots the Chemist
- Loss leaders (see above).

These can be used at any stage of the product life cycle, and are useful strategies to maintain a high level of sales.

Cost plus

This is a way of actually setting the price to be charged to the consumer. The costs refer to the expenses of producing the product, namely the materials, labour and other costs such as marketing. In order to ensure that a profit is made, costs must be less than the selling price. The process of finding this price involves calculating the actual costs for the product and then adding an amount or percentage to the costs. For example:

- A restaurant has costs of £2.50 for a steak meal and adds a mark-up of 300%.
- The price will therefore be:
- costs of £2.50 + 300% (£7.50) = £10

There is often some confusion between mark-up and margin. The mark-up is when an amount (usually a percentage) is added to the total costs to gain the selling price. The margin (or profit margin) is the level of profit expressed as a percentage of the selling price.

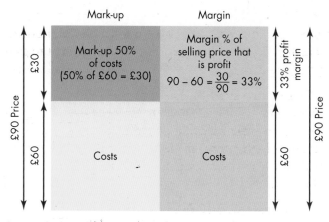

Figure 9.4 Mark-up and margin

In Figure 9.4, the mark-up is simply a percentage (50%) of the costs that is **added** to the costs to give a price of £90.

The margin is calculated as a percentage of the **selling price**, therefore is:

£90 – costs (£60) = £30 $\frac{£30}{£90} \times = 33\%$

Price discrimination

Price discrimination means charging different prices for the same product or service within different markets. Price discrimination is operated in several forms.

Area

A different price is charged for the same product in different parts of the world or country.

Time

A different price is charged for the same product or service at different times of the day. Prices for train tickets or rates for the telephone, gas and electricity vary according to the time of day. These are usually denoted by the terms 'peak charges' and 'off-peak charges'. The ability to charge different prices at different times of the day is related to the elasticity of the products or services. If a businessperson needs to be in London for a meeting at 9am, it will mean catching an early train. The train company knows that such travel is essential (inelastic) and therefore is able to charge a much higher price.

Age

Reductions for rail cards, buses and admission to various entertainment complexes are available to women and men over the age of 60. Similarly, lower prices are charged for children of varying ages, depending upon the service being used.

Figure 9.5 Different prices may be changed for the same product at different times of the day

Examiner's voice

This chapter concentrates on the strategies for pricing, and not how to actually calculate prices. The methods for calculating prices are to be found in other chapters as stated: absorption (Unit 40), marginal costing (contribution) (Unit 41), cost-based or full cost, standard pricing (Unit 40).

Examination questions tend to ask about strategies; in other words what it is hoped to achieve and therefore how to price the products, or how to calculate actual prices.

Further Sources

www.marketingteacher.com

Questions Time allowed 20 minutes

1. State the formula for price elasticity of demand.

(2 marks)

2. State two examples of promotional pricing.

(2 marks)

3. Explain price discrimination. (4 marks)

4. Explain how predatory pricing attempts to eliminate competitors. (4 marks)

5. If incomes increase by 10% and demand for a given product increases from 120 to 150, calculate the income elasticity of demand.

(4 marks)

6. If a product has costs of £120 and a mark-up of 15%, calculate the selling price. (4 marks)

(20 marks)

Task

(Group or individual work) 15 minutes

Using the list of factors affecting the price (page 41), select three and explain how each one will influence the price set.

Case study Time allowed 35 minutes

The hotel industry

The hotel industry started to suffer during 2008, as the 'credit-crunch' and economic recession started to affect consumer spending. Unemployment was also rising, with daily announcements of businesses making employees redundant.

Hotels that relied on business clients noticed a reduction in conference bookings and requests for accommodation.

Hotels that relied on the tourist trade were equally affected, as the number of 'extra' weekend breaks booked started to diminish significantly.

As a consequence, hotels had to think of appropriate pricing strategies in order to attract a falling number of potential consumers.

Location	B&B price per night	D B&B price per night
Leicester	£50	£65
Liverpool	£60	£70
Luton	£60	£70
Manchester	£55	£75

Special offer! Book online and save 10% off the price quoted!

	Price for 2 nights bed breakfast and dinner per person	Extra night rates per person
Taunton	£60	£35
Telford	£55	£30
Tonbridge	£75	£35

Figure 9.6 Adverts for holiday accommodation

1. State which type of pricing strategy is being used by both hotel chains. (1 mark)

2. With reference to the Eastern Hotel advert: if you booked a room for one night, bed and breakfast in Luton, calculate the price you would pay if you booked online. (3 marks)

3. With reference to the Traveller's Inn advert: if the hotel's costs at Telford for two nights bed, breakfast and dinner are £30, calculate the mark-up used by the hotel if the price charged by the hotel to consumers is, as stated, £55. (3 marks)

4. Explain how the hotels could use a price discrimination strategy for their hotel room rates.

(4 marks)

5. Analyse the consequences if a hotel chain decided to offer rooms as a 'loss leader' for two weeks.

(9 marks)

(20 marks)

PROMOTION

What is promotion?

Promotion is a collection of techniques used to inform and persuade potential consumers to buy a product or service that meets their needs. It is an integral part of the marketing process.

Promotion can fulfil a diverse range of functions. Through careful marketing and excellent use of promotion, Boots the Chemist managed to entice customers in 2007 to buy water (their Expert Sensitive Refreshing Facial Spritz) at a cost that is equivalent to £32.92 a litre! The information on the can informs the consumer that its contents are hypoallergenic and fragrance free, lanolin free and formulated to refresh and hydrate. It also claims to protect the skin from 'dryness'. The only content listed is 'aqua'; in other words water! The 125ml can was sold for £3.99.

The purpose of promotion is to:

- inform consumers or raise awareness
- increase sales
- decrease sales (for example, cigarettes)
- encourage brand loyalty
- enhance the reputation/image of the business.

Promotion includes various marketing tools such as advertising and sales promotion.

DAGMAR

Promotion is used as a method to complete the 'DAGMAR' stages (Defining Advertising Goals Measuring Advertising Results, see Unit 7). 'DAGMAR' highlights the stages which a successful promotion campaign should cover. The stages are:

- unaware
- aware
- comprehension
- conviction
- action.

AIDA

AIDA is another way of judging effective promotion. It is a useful way to remember the key stages, which any promotion should cover in order to be effective.

- **A** = Attraction/attention. It is essential before any message can be imparted to potential consumers that their attention is gained. Using an appropriate method of attraction is vital and needs to be matched to the targeted consumer.
- **I** = Interest. Ensuring the promotion is interesting allows the promotion to give the message about the product or service.

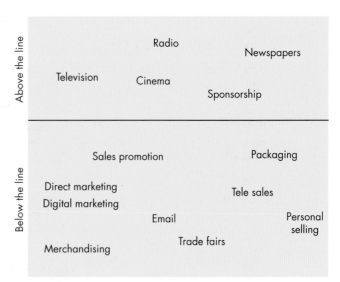

Figure 10.1 'Above the line' and 'below the line' promotion

- **D** = Desire. A good promotion will create a desire in the consumer to want to buy the product.
- **A** = Action. This is the hardest part of the promotional process. An interest in the product may have been generated, but persuading the consumer to go out and actually buy it needs a very effective campaign.

Advertising can be used for the first three stages of AIDA, whereas sales promotion is used to help achieve the 'action' stage by offering incentives at the point of sale.

There are different ways to achieve the promotion of a product or service. The various methods can be classified into 'above' and 'below the line' promotions.

'Above the line' promotion

'Above the line' promotion uses media where there is no direct contact with the potential consumer. The business has no control over the media involved. The media used is often referred to as mass media.

Television

Television remains a powerful media for promoting a product. The visual aspect of an advert is easier to remember than the spoken or written word.

An Adwatch survey found that 60% of people remembered seeing the advertisement for Sky+ (see Table 10.1 below). Perhaps the combination of a famous

	Previous week	Brand	Agency/TV Buyer	%
1	(–)	Sky+	Digital & Direct/ MediaCom	60
2	(–)	Kellogg's Coco Pops	Leo Burnett/MindShare	54
3	(–)	Foxy Bingo	Biscuit, in-house/Walker Media	47
4	(–)	Sainsbury's	Abbot Mead Vickers BBDO/PHD	46
5	(–)	Admiral	In-house/MindShare	44
6	(–)	L'Oréal Elvive	McCann Erickson/ ZenithOptimedia	41
7	(–)	Heat	Quiet Storm/OMD UK	38
8	(–)	The Sun Online Bingo	EHS Brann/MindShare	37
9=	(7)	Match.com	Hanft Raboy & Partner/Initiave	36
9=	(15)	Somerfield	WWAV Rapp Collins/WWAV Collins Media	36
9=	(–)	Avon – U fragrance	Soho Square/Starcom	36
12	(–)	O$_2$ – Apple iPhone	TBWA\Media Arts Lab/Manning Gottlieb OMD	35
13	(–)	Kinder Bueno	Audacity/Mediaedge:cia	34
14	(–)	Ariel	Saatchi & Saatchi/Starcom	29
15	(–)	Dell Inspiron 1525	Enfatico/MediaCom	28
16=	(–)	OK! Magazine	Portland Enterprise/MediaCom	27
16=	(–)	Harveys	Proximity London/MediaVest	27
18	(–)	Dreams	Robson Brown/Robson Brown	26
19=	(–)	MFI	McCann Erickson Birmingham/University McCann Birmingham	24
19=	(–)	Boots	Mother/MediaCom	24

Table 10.1 Which of the following television commercials do you remember seeing recently? Adwatch figures for the week ending 1 Octiober 2008

face (Kelly Brook) and the demonstration of the Sky+ attributes helped the advert to be successful.

Commercial radio

Radio advertising is common, especially for local radio stations. In the Midlands, BRMB and Beacon are examples that concentrate on providing an advertising media for local businesses. There are adverts for national chains, but less frequently used.

Magazines

Although there are many specialist magazines that can target consumers, it is still an 'above the line' media because there is no direct contact with the selected consumer. Although issued weekly or monthly, magazines do not date as long as they remain in circulation; someone will read the adverts within.

Cinema

Cinemas have experienced an increase in audiences over recent years, and consequently have become more popular as a media for adverts. The cinema has the advantage of appealing to both national and local advertisers, and is considerably cheaper than television advertising rates.

Newspapers

Newspapers are both national and local, and therefore appeal to a wide range of advertisers. The type of adverts that can be placed in newspapers varies considerably, from a full-page colour advert to a classified advert, depending upon the needs and budget of the advertiser. Because there is such a wide range of newspapers, it is possible to target a particular segment of the market.

Billboards, posters and video/plasma screens

Although these are static adverts and therefore only able to target a limited audience, they are nevertheless a cheap and effective form of advert. With a limited amount of space to put across the message, this form of advertising needs to be eye-catching and visual. The location of their placement is crucial if a sufficient number of people are to see them. The benefit of such adverts is that they can be used on a national basis or a local basis, even down to advertising the local village jumble sale.

Electronic adverts

As usage of the internet continues to grow, so does the number of 'pop-up' adverts. Such adverts appear with annoying regularity on certain websites. Nevertheless, it is a media that continues to grow in popularity.

'Below the line' promotion

'Below the line' promotion using the type of media where the business can directly contact the potential consumer. It can also have some influence and control of the media used.

Sponsorship

Some people would argue that sponsorship became popular when it was no longer possible to advertise cigarettes on television, and that sponsoring televised sporting events was a way around the law for the tobacco companies. However, sponsorship is an effective media to increase product awareness. Businesses are quick to have their name or brand name associated with a particular sporting or cultural activity. The Emirates airline, one of the fastest growing airlines in the world, has spent significant amounts of money on sponsoring cricket, Arsenal Football Club and other sporting events to help raise its profile. Local businesses help local sports teams in an attempt to establish their brands or names. Some people consider sponsorship at local level as an ethical gesture, by helping others as well as themselves.

Direct mail

Direct mail or the usage of mailshots is often referred to as 'junk mail' – much of what is received through the post has not been requested and is therefore placed straight in the bin! Its effectiveness is therefore in doubt, but nevertheless there is a place for this method if targets are carefully selected.

The economic downturn in 2008 and the increase in environmental lobbies have since led to a fall in the amount of money spent on direct mailing. It has however encouraged businesses to spend their money efficiently and target consumers more carefully.

Direct mail has also suffered from alternative direct channels such as email, which is significantly cheaper. As broadband becomes more widespread in the UK, direct mail will be used less and less.

Rank	Advertiser	Amount of spend (rounded) £million	Quantity of mailings (rounded) £million	% change in amount spent	Total of budget %
1	MBNA Europe	35	77.8	−22	86
3	Halifax	25.2	55.8	+11	48
5	Direct Wines	24	28.3	−11	96
8	RIAS (insurance)	17.6	38.4	+18	97
11	The Book People	15	20.5	−14	99
15	Saga Holidays	13.5	22.5	+18	96

Table 10.2 The top direct mail advertisers in 2008 (table adapted from Top 100 direct mail advertisers, Marketing, 1 October 2008

According to the experts, direct mail is now most effective when targeted at existing customers rather than potential or 'cold target' customers. The latter regard direct mail as junk mail, much of which is thrown away unopened and is therefore ineffective.

Sales promotion

Sales promotion is an incentive at the point of sale (at the retail outlet). The types of sales promotion used include:

- BOGOF (buy one get one free).
- Free: consumers are always interested in something for nothing!
- Win a competition: often the competition will encourage more than one purchase.
- 10% more: often used for food and drink products where adding to the normal quantity is practically possible.
- Buy 3 pay for 2: a favoured strategy of Boots the Chemist chain.
- Donations to charity: an ethical approach to sales promotion. The business hopes that the consumer will be pleased that they have indirectly helped donate something to charity by buying the product. Some schemes have vouchers to collect, to encourage brand loyalty.
- Loyalty points: many of the hotel chains offer points as a reward for staying at their hotels. Once sufficient points have been gained it is possible to exchange them for a free night at one of the hotels within a chain. This type of sales promotion encourages brand loyalty.
- Credit: for expensive items such as cars, furniture, kitchens and houses offering credit facilities with low interest payments or even free credit at 0% finance are huge incentives to consumers to purchase.
- Buy now pay later: in an attempt to encourage impulse buying, offering a consumer the opportunity to take a product away but not have to pay for it for a period of time, is another huge incentive to buy.
- Merchandising material: this is an area of considerable growth as businesses think of more ways to remind consumers of a particular business or product.

Packaging

Packaging still has a large role to play in the promoting of products. Not only does it protect and preserve the product, it can advertise and promote the product by the careful display of the brand name or its selling features. The packaging can enhance the display of the product on the shelves and can add value to entice the customer to purchase.

Public relations

The image of the product or service and its reputation can be a sales asset, and therefore it is important to maintain this positive image. Public relations play a vital role in either strengthening the image of the business by the issuing of a press release or defending/repairing an image if the business has to deal with a problem. For example, if a company has to recall a product due to a fault, the image of the product may be damaged in the view of its customers, and therefore the public relations department will be working hard to counter any adverse publicity.

Cadbury suffered a loss of reputation after it had to withdraw a huge number of chocolate bars from shops after a health scare at one of its production plants. The public relations department worked hard to restore the image of the business.

Personal selling and telesales

Personal selling or direct selling occurs when there is a direct link or communication between the salesperson and the customer. Sales assistants can encourage a sale by 'persuading' customers to buy. Personal selling can be achieved not only through face-to-face contact but via a phone (telesales.) This can be seen as an intrusion however, as the customer has not asked the salesperson to phone them and therefore may resent the call.

Trade fairs

Trade fairs and exhibitions are a popular method of encouraging interested parties (businesses and consumers) to visit a wide selection of fairs and exhibitions. The Car Show, The Clothes Show and the Good Food Show are good examples of trade fairs. At the business stands, customers will be able to meet staff, who can achieve face-to-face sales.

Customer publications (magazines)

This media is not to be confused with ordinary magazines, which are classified as 'above the line' media. Because customer magazines are specifically targeted and deal direct with the customer, they are classed as 'below the line' media.

There is a growing trend for businesses to strengthen the recognition of their brands by publishing their own

Figure 10.2 Trade magazines

magazine. According to ABC, seven out of the top ten magazines by circulation are customer publications.

The agency Seven Squared publishes customer magazines for British Airways, Marks & Spencer, Coutts, Waterstone's and Sainsbury's.

The best-selling magazine is a customer magazine issued to Sky subscribers called Skymag, which has a circulation of 7.4 million according to ABC. This type of magazine has become very popular, with 79% of the population reading a customer magazine.

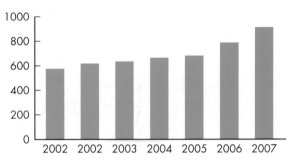

Figure 10.3 Total spend on customer publishing (£m)
Source: Association of Publishing Agencies

Businesses are spending increasing amounts of money on such magazines. It is suggested by Millard Brown/APA that brand sales increase by about 8% as a result of people reading a customer magazine.

Digital magazines

Taking advantage of consumers' greater usage of the computer as a source of information, businesses have grasped the opportunity to promote their products via the digital media.

Some customer magazines have now transferred into digital format. Ford has used this format to target specific segments of the market. It has also been to be able to claim that such a media is meeting its environmental promises by reducing the need to print on paper and using less fuel, as no distribution is required. This type of media is able to use the written word, pictures, video clips and even flash imagery in an attempt to engage its targeted audience.

Car manufacturers Seat launched its own digital campaign in 2008 in an attempt to encourage consumers to test-drive its cars. Seat, owned by Volkswagen, used a website to target 18–44-year-olds who were looking to buy a new car.

Email promotions

- EasyJet launched a digital marketing campaign in 2008, aimed at increasing its online bookings to counter the economic downturn. EasyJet has also formed a partnership with the internet site MySpace to launch an online community where consumers can post their photos of holidays from around the world.
- Range Rover used direct and digital marketing in an attempt to promote its Range Rover Sport model. The digital aspects included emails targeted at potential consumers to book test drives. It also had a microsite, which was used to show video footage of the car in action.

Selecting the appropriate promotional method(s)

Choosing which type of sales promotion to use will depend upon the type of product or service. In addition, the business and its budget will also affect which sale promotions are selected.

However, the most important issue is the consumer. The type of sales promotion must be something that will actually appeal to the consumer. It must also fit with the rest of the marketing mix and help achieve the marketing strategy of the business. The important factors affecting the method of promotion are:

- the business, its size, location and its budget
- the actual product or service to be promoted
- the customer
- the marketing strategy to be used (the marketing mix)
- external factors (legislation, economy and technology)
- time factor
- the product's stage in its life cycle.

Examiner's voice

Selecting the most appropriate promotion must be done in the context of the case information, taking careful note of the bullet points shown here.

Further Sources

www.marketingteacher.com

Your Turn

Questions Time allowed 20 minutes

1. State the DAGMAR stages

2. Explain the difference between 'above' and 'below the line' promotions. (4 marks)

3. Explain the difference between magazines and customer publications. (4 marks)

4. Comment upon the factors that would be considered in selecting the right type of sales promotion to use.

   (4 marks)

5. Explain why there has been a decline in the amount of money spent on direct mail. (4 marks)

   (16 marks)

Case Study Time allowed 45 minutes

The JagerTruck

Jagermeister is a unique German herbal spirit that is made from a blend of over 50 herbs, roots and fruits.

In an attempt to find a unique way to attract its target customers, a distinctively coloured truck parks, unravels its sound system, its mixers, its 10-metre bar and its plasma screens. Bands are able to pay on its fold-out stage, while the sales team give away key ring patches and lanyards. Drinks are served super chilled form the truck's 3 fridges and freezer. To

Figure 10.4 The JagerTruck

emphasise the product, a self- inflating, 5-metre high Jagermeister bottle stands on the roof like a statute.

The JagerTruck was originally an East German army vehicle, which has been converted beyond recognition from its original function to this highly unusual promotional tool.

The JagerTruck visits different events where the target market will be attending. 'Download festival' at Donnington Park and 'Rip Curl Boardmasters' at Newquay in Cornwall were examples of the events at which the truck would be present. Jagermeister also operates the Jagermusic programme that supports signed and unsigned bands in the UK as a form of sponsorship.

1. State three examples of sales promotion techniques the business could use. (3 marks)

2. Is the use of the JagerTruck an example of 'above' or 'below the line' promotion?

   (Justify your answer) (4 marks)

3. Analyse two methods of 'above the line' promotion that Jagermeister could use. (6 marks)

4. Evaluate the reasons why attending pop festivals and sporting events is an appropriate promotional strategy for Jagermeister. (16 marks)

(29 marks)

DISTRIBUTION

The final P of the four Ps in the marketing mix is 'place'. This refers to the methods by which the business delivers its good or service to the right place at the right time.

Examiner's voice

It is important to remember that 'place' refers to distribution and not the location of the business. Under exam conditions candidates often write about the wrong concept for this part of the marketing mix.

Channels of distribution

This is the method by which the good travels from the producer to the consumer. The main five channels of distribution are shown in Figure 11.1.

Some of the channels of distribution involve the use of intermediaries: these are wholesalers, retailers and agents.

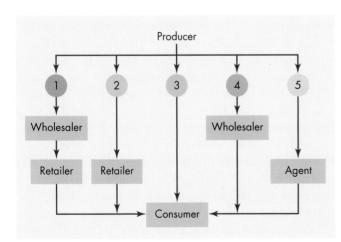

Figure 11.1 Channels of distribution

Wholesalers

The job of wholesalers in the distribution chain is to 'break bulk'. This means that wholesalers buy from manufacturers in large volume, and then break down what they buy into smaller units. This is particularly important for businesses such as corner shops or public houses whose owners may wish to buy in small volume and require mixed lots. For example, if a small shopkeeper was buying from a yoghurt producer directly, he might have to take large volume packs of the same yoghurt. The wholesaler will receive the larger packs in a variety of flavours and types, and put together a selection of mixed packs to be sold to a number of similar small businesses.

Wholesalers are able to use specialist knowledge of their part of the distribution network to benefit producers and retailers.

- They move goods around the country using their own network, reducing costs and valuable time for other businesses.
- They have purpose-built warehouses and storage facilities for the range of products they supply.
- The manufacturer and retailer are able to concentrate their efforts on the areas in where they specialise.
- They offer choice to the retailer.

Retailers

Retailers are responsible for the final part of the distribution chain; selling the final product to the consumer. Retailers vary from the tiny shop in a rural village, to huge businesses like Tesco and Marks & Spencer. In between these two extremes lie chain stores (e.g. Next and PC World), department stores (e.g. John Lewis and House of Fraser), and voluntary (independent) retail chains such as Londis. Increasingly in recent years, large retailers such as Sainsbury's and Argos have begun to use regional distribution centres. These centres are sited near motorway links (for example, the M6/M1 junction), to make distribution quicker, cheaper and more effective.

Agents

Agents work in several sectors of the distribution network. Their role is to negotiate between buyers and sellers. In doing this, they will never have ownership of the good or service they are selling. They are usually paid on a commission basis, and often work in such sectors as travel and ticket sales. When you buy a holiday in a travel agency, the agent is acting on behalf of the travel business or airline. If the sale is completed, the travel business will pay the agent a percentage as commission.

In some countries (e.g. Japan), it is necessary for exporters to sell their goods through an agent, rather than directly to the retailer or customer. For businesses about to break into a new market, this process can be very useful as the agent will have specialist knowledge of the market, the law and customs, and will speak the language. All this is helpful to prospective exporters moving into a new market (see Unit 6, International Marketing).

Changes in distribution

In the past, the most common channel of distribution in the retail trade was the first one shown in Figure 11.1. Most large retailers such as supermarkets, department stores and chains, bought from wholesalers who held stock that they had purchased from producers. The growth of the supermarket sector in particular has led to the increasing use of channel 2. As the supermarkets grew, they realised that they would be able to reduce their costs if they bought direct from the producer. In addition, as they grew, the size of their orders made it possible for them to negotiate huge discounts that could be passed on to the consumer.

Channel 3, where the producer sells direct to the customer, has also become much more popular with the growth of mail order and internet sales. This channel of distribution, called direct marketing, has benefits both for the producer and the consumer. For the producer, it cuts out the middleman and gives all the profit from the sale directly to the seller. For the consumer, it means that there is no need to visit a retail outlet; goods can be bought at home and delivered to home. As the cost of driving rises and congestion on the roads worsens, this is an important advantage for the customer.

The fourth channel in Figure 11.1 involves the public buying direct from a wholesaler. This channel is most commonly used by groups such as sports associations or scout groups, where food for catering is being bought for catering. The purchaser often needs a special card to be able to buy from the wholesaler to show that they belong to such a group. In some cases, warehouses may sell directly to the public to clear surplus stocks.

Channel 5 in Figure 11.1, together with any channel using an agent, is used in very specific cases like that of a travel agent or estate agent. Some businesses (e.g. Avon and catalogue companies) use agents to sell their products direct to the consumer. The agent will usually have a catalogue to display the range of goods and place customer orders with the producer. The 'Avon lady' is paid commission by Avon on any goods that she sells.

Reasons for changes in distribution channels

In the past 20 years, the retail sector has probably experienced more changes than any other sector of the economy. In order to meet the new needs of this sector, it has been necessary to change distribution methods.

- The size of supermarkets has risen sharply, as has the number of outlets they have. Tesco is now represented in almost every postcode area of the UK. This means that Tesco has strong bargaining power with producers and can make demands on them, in terms of price and delivery. Seven-day and twenty-four-hour opening means that supermarkets want deliveries throughout the week to ensure that their shelves are full.
- Many retail businesses have now moved to out-of-town retail parks. This makes physical distribution easier. Instead of having to deliver to congested town and city centres where the road network is often poor, deliveries can be made to retail parks that are served by good road systems.
- Improvements in telecommunications have meant that customers can contact producers directly or through call centres to place orders. This is often a more convenient way of shopping for busy people. Deliveries will then be made direct to the customer, either by post or courier service. The use of courier businesses as a means of physical distribution has grown alongside mail order and internet sales.
- The introduction of the internet and the growth of broadband access have made buying online one of the biggest changes in retail sales in recent years. Even traditional retailers, like Marks & Spencer and John Lewis now achieve a major part of their business through online sales.

- At one time, supermarkets only sold food items. They now sell clothing, electrical goods and services like banking and insurance. This has put them into competition with many other areas of the economy, where their size and power is a considerable threat to smaller businesses.
- The retail sector is increasingly customer-orientated, and a great deal of time and effort is spent improving the shopping experience and giving customers what they want. Customer service in all areas of retailing, whatever the distribution channel, is more important now than it has ever been. Customers are aware of the law and their rights as a consequence of television programmes like 'Watchdog', and they will take action if they feel that their rights are being abused. Getting the delivery system right is an important part of achieving customer satisfaction.

Physical distribution

This refers to the physical method of distribution which a business uses. For the UK economy, road transport is the most common method of moving goods from one place to another. Road transport of goods began to replace rail transport in the second half of the twentieth century. However, environmental concerns together with the high price of oil have encouraged businesses to look again at the viability of rail and canal transport.

Air transport is also more widely used now. This is obviously an important method of physical distribution for firms who have export markets. It is also important in situations where it is vital to deliver a perishable product to its market in as fresh a condition as possible. Fresh flowers and vegetables such as mange-tout peas and asparagus are air-freighted into the UK from Kenya and South America on a daily basis.

The means of physical distribution selected will depend on the following factors:

- the need for freshness for perishable items (e.g. fish)
- the price which the consumer is prepared to pay for fresh rather than frozen produce
- the bulkiness of the product
- the need to make regular deliveries (e.g. to a 24-hour supermarket)
- the price of the product (low value products need cheaper distribution systems)
- the size of the product: heavy or awkward items such as bricks or trampolines would usually be moved by road or rail
- the nature of the consumer: if internet-based Amazon is delivering books to an internet shopper, the postal service will be used: larger orders to commercial customers are likely to be sent by road
- the method of production: using just-in-time (JIT) production and stock control has meant that businesses have looked for suppliers who can meet their needs efficiently. If a manufacturer of washing machines is using JIT production, they will need to be confident that their suppliers will ensure that they always have the components to maintain production (see Unit 44)
- the sunk cost of the capital investment in equipment: e.g. docks in the UK are largely equipped with machines for lifting containers from lorries. This means that it would be very difficult for an exporting business to distribute its products through the docks by rail.

Further Sources

www.doleeurope.com
www.businesslink.gov.uk
www.emeraldinsight.com

Your Turn

Case Study   Time allowed 1 hour

Period Features

Lucie Storr set up her business, Period Features, selling homeware items, when illness forced her to give up her job as a translator.

She had identified a niche in the market for a business supplying good quality items for period homes, and so she started her shop in a small way in Leek in the Staffordshire Moorlands. At first the shop concentrated on selling hardware products and period paints, but the range of goods expanded gradually as the business grew. She now stocks a range of garden products, candles and period tiles, glass and lighting. The latter is a fast-growing market as a result of the current interest in house renovation.

Lucie quickly realised that there was a demand for her products beyond the local area, and within a year she had launched her own website offering a more limited range than that available in the shop. Lucie knew that the internet would be an ideal place to sell the type of non-branded products she stocks, such as door knobs and period light fittings. She could set her prices at a reasonable profit margin, because she does not face close competition. (By comparison, branded items such as electrical goods are offered by a wide range of firms through shops and on the internet; consequently the price competition is fierce and the profit margins are lower in that type of business.)

In setting up the website, Lucie recognised that there were certain features that she had to get right if she was going to be successful:

1. The website had to be designed appropriately to give an old-fashioned impression – a bit of a contradiction for such an up-to-date distribution channel, but an important marketing tool for a business selling period items. She asked the website designers to use a Victorian-style logo throughout the site, and she uses photographs of her products which reflect this old-fashioned theme.

2. The site had to appear as early as possible on the pages thrown up by a search engine. In the early months Lucie was prepared to have her site prioritised to achieve this. Although this added to her costs it was worthwhile in those initial stages, because it made the site easy to find and helped to build up a customer base. More recently Lucie has started to use a blog to keep her site at the top of searches.

3. The navigation of the site had to be straightforward and uncomplicated, otherwise customers would give up in frustration without buying.

4. There must be as few stages as possible between a decision to buy and a purchase being made. If there are too many stages, potential buyers sometimes start to have second thoughts about the purchase.

In the past year Lucie's internet sales have risen by 130%, and already they make up 25% of her sales. She hopes that they will rise to 75%, given the worldwide potential of the internet. She already has customers throughout Europe, USA and Japan. The costs of setting up this website and keeping it running are relatively small in comparison with the overheads of running the shop. This is one of the internet's attractions for Lucie in terms of the future profitability of the business.

In addition the website now acts as a promotional tool for all of the business. Lucie no longer buys advertising space in magazines, but instead she tries to persuade magazine and newspaper editors to run features on her business. This type of promotion costs her nothing and has the added advantage of being seen as a recommendation for her business from the publication.

Much of Lucie's success with internet sales, however, is a direct result of making the shopping experience on her website a personal and enjoyable experience. The site has pictures and details of all her staff for customers to see, so that they know who they are speaking to if they need to telephone. But the best-selling point of all is that each parcel is individually wrapped in brown paper and string, with a hand written address label. This creates a unique shopping experience for Lucie's customers.

Lucie knows that the potential for internet sales for her business is enormous, and she has developed her niche in the market to take full advantage of this.

(Adapted from 'Marketing on the Web', Judith Kelt in *Business Active*, January 2007)

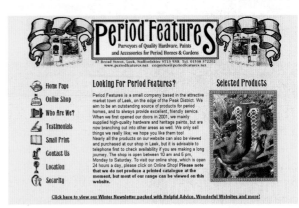

Figure 11.2 An image from the Period Features website

1. Look at Lucie's site (www.periodfeatures.net) and see if you can see why customers like using it. Try to find an example of a site which does not have so many of this one's good points. Analyse the difference between the two sites.　(10 marks)

2. What types of costs will be included in the overheads for the running of the shop? (5 marks)

3. Lucie has recently begun to write a monthly newsletter which is available on the site, but which is also emailed to customers and magazine and newspaper homepage editors. In what ways will this help her business?

　(5 marks)

4. Evaluate the reasons for Period Features's success on the internet.　(15 marks)

(35 marks)

Unit 12

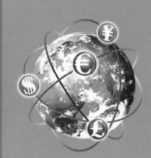

ACCOUNTING PERSPECTIVE

Introduction

Although some may suggest that the finance function of the business 'controls' all others, it would be more accurate to argue that, as with all the functions of the business, finance is dependent on the other functions. Budget constraints are important, but equally important is the ability to generate finance. The marketing of a business can stimulate demand for products, the production is there to meet the demand that has been generated and the human resource area employs people for all the functions within the business. All play a vital role in the generation of income, which is then used to ensure that the business survives and prospers.

The chapters within this section cover the requirements as stated within the specification. To avoid unnecessary duplication, certain topics that also appear within other options may be located elsewhere.

Examiner's voice

A variety of terms will be used within the next few chapters. It is important use the appropriate term whenever possible. However, there will be several instances when there is more than one term that can be used to explain or name a particular concept. It is therefore important to be aware of this to avoid being confused by an examination question if a slightly different term is used.

Bearing this in mind, reference will be made to financial data/information, which is the same as referring to the accounts of a business.

Financial information

A vital part of all businesses is the financial information. Any stakeholder of the business will find information from the financial function useful.

- Members of the board of directors or managers of the business will use financial information to make important decisions and to be able to plan for the future.
- Prospective shareholders will look at the financial information contained in the accounts to decide whether to invest in the business.
- Banks will look at the accounts of a business to check if the business is able to afford the repayments if money is borrowed, or even whether the business ought to be lent money in the first instance.
- Potential or existing suppliers may use financial information about a business to assess whether it is

'safe' to trade with, in terms of judging its ability to pay for any supplies provided.

- Directors or managers may use the accounts as a measure of success (or failure), in terms of the profitability of the business.
- Financial information can be used to set targets/objectives for a business.
- Companies may issue cashflow forecasts to aid planning and enhance any loan applications.
- Financial information can be used to examine the amount of cash flowing in and out of the business.
- There is a legal requirement to provide accounts (profit and loss accounts, and a balance sheet). Issuing such accounts is often referred to as the 'disclosure requirement'.
- Financial information is often looked at by competitors in an attempt to assess how a particular business is performing in comparison to itself.
- The state of the accounts may even be used by other businesses within the same industry as a benchmark.

Given the large number of uses for the accounts, it is essential that such information is accurate. To ensure that this is so, several principles are used when formulating the accounts (see Unit 13).

Like all other information that is collected or used by a business, such information is not used in isolation. The accounts department will need to liaise with other departments within the business in order to collect all the required data. Similarly, the production department will need the help of the accounts department, in order to check that the necessary funds are available to fund any additional production or pay rises.

Presenting financial information

As the accounts of a business are used by so many stakeholders, there are occasions when the figures are presented in a 'favourable' light. Some people may suggest that the figures presented are massaged in order to show the business in the best possible manner. However, such window-dressing must be undertaken within the principles and regulations related to accounts. This process of window-dressing may occur in order to:

- encourage shareholders to continue to buy its shares
- encourage potential shareholders to buy its shares

- suggest that the business is able to borrow money
- indicate that the business is able to repay any potential loans
- deter or attract potential takeover bids
- prevent employees from being concerned about long-term job security.

All of the above are legitimate reasons for wanting to create a favourable impression. Such an impression can be achieved in a variety of ways.

Revaluation of assets

On the balance sheet, the fixed assets may consist of land and buildings that have increased in value. Consequently, such assets are revalued. Within the restrictions of the principle of prudence, the business may attempt to put a value at the top end of any valuations gained.

Selling of fixed assets

By selling its assets, the business will gain cash which in turn will improve its liquidity. Having more cash may reduce the need to borrow money and ensure that it is more likely to meet any of its liabilities.

However, this approach to window-dressing is a very short-term 'fix', as once these assets have been sold they are no longer on the balance sheet, and may reduce the value of the business and its ability to offer security for loans in the future.

Leasing (sale and leaseback)

Although this process also means that the business will sell some of its assets, the business has an agreement to rent such assets back. In this process, the business has gained cash which may be needed to improve its liquidity, but will incur rental charges which is an added expenditure under current liabilities.

Although in the short term the working capital of the business may improve due to the injection of cash from the proceeds of the sale, in the long term its liabilities will increase.

However, depending upon the level of the rent to be paid to use the assets sold, this leasing process may be cheaper than borrowing money.

It is worth noting that financial analysts will probably see through any window-dressing!

Your Turn

Questions Time allowed 20 minutes

1. Outline how four stakeholders may find the financial information of a business useful.

(8 marks)

2. Explain two reasons why a business may be tempted to 'window-dress' its accounts. (4 marks)

3. Analyse the consequences of selling assets to improve the financial position of a business.

(8 marks)

(20 marks)

ACCOUNTING CONCEPTS AND CONVENTIONS

Accounting is a process of control on the expenditure of a business, and is a vehicle for the publication of figures for profit, value and cash.

Categories of accounting

The two main categories of accounting are financial accounting and management accounting.

- **Financial accounting:** the main purpose of this type of accounting is to satisfy the external stakeholders of a business such as the shareholders and financial institutions. This information will be issued in the annual report of the business. It concentrates on the assets, profits and levels of cash within the business.
- **Management accounting:** concentrates on the internal accounts, allowing the business to monitor and evaluate its performance. It also enables the business to set targets and therefore achieve its objectives.

Principles of accounting

Accounts are constructed in line with seven principles. These principles are used to ensure that the figures are produced in a standardised manner so that the accounts can be analysed, knowing they have been constructed in a recognised manner. All of these principles are 'guides', which exist in order for stakeholders to view accounts with some degree of confidence.

Consistency

The principle of consistency operates on the basis that all accounts will be produced in the same way. It is expected that a business will have a policy for the formulation of its accounts, and will apply this policy consistently.

By having a principle of consistency, any person using the accounts can be confident that the information within the accounts is accurate.

Going concern

This principle assumes that the business is operating as normal and that there is no reason not to expect it to operate as normal in the foreseeable future.
This is important, because if the business was about to close, be put into administration or liquidated, then a different set of rules would apply on the way in which the accounts are prepared and presented.

Matching (accruals)

The timing of information put into the accounts is another important principle. The dates used to record financial transactions are the ones when the transaction occurred and NOT when the actual payment is made. This may appear slightly strange but is more realistic. If thought is given to the balance sheet (a method of recording the value of a business at a given point in time), it is therefore important to record which sales have been made or which materials have been sold, regardless of when they are actually paid for.

Similarly, with a cashflow statement, recording the date of the transactions and not the payments is more realistic for the level of liquidity within the business at that moment in time. For example, a business sells a product to a customer in January but is not paid until March. The transaction (what is owed to the business) is recorded in January and not March.

This is a more realistic approach and allows comparisons of trading to be made from year to year. This comparison will be more realistic because payment periods may alter (e.g. offering extended credit terms as a promotional tool) and therefore distort the level of actual trading within a given period of time.

There is a 'match' between the date of the transaction, not when the payment is made.

Materiality

Accounting is concerned with the big picture. Calculating the value of the business requires a realistic figure to be reached, but not at the expense of calculating every single asset if it is of little or no value, and would therefore make no real (material) difference either to its balance sheet or profit and loss account. For example, counting the number of paper cups that a business such as BP has, will make no material difference to the value of the business. However, for a manufacturer of paper cups, their value would be important (material).

Objectivity

This principle is based on the idea that the accounts must be realistic and therefore based on facts, not opinions or guesses. It is very important to avoid any false statements or values. Similarly, bias must be avoided even if such bias would improve the figures. To ensure that this realistic picture is given, it is important to state the real value of the assets listed. Being optimistic is not the appropriate approach! For example, valuing a piece of machinery or factory highly because it is estimated that inflation would increase their value within a couple of months, is not being objective.

Prudence (conservatism)

This principle of prudence is similar to that of objectivity, in terms of not overstating the financial situation. Where there are any uncertainties as to the levels of profits or losses or valuations, then this principle suggests that it is right to understate the level of profits and overstate the level of losses. In other words, it is appropriate to take a pessimistic view. Being prudent is to be cautious and therefore the business will not be affected by figures that are less than expected.

The principle of prudence can compensate for the over-optimism of directors or managers within the business.

It could also be argued that prudence involves being realistic with valuations of assets within the business. Refusing to take the value of fixed assets at their purchase price but considering their depreciation, is considered a prudent measure.

Realisation

Realisation is similar to matching, in that realisation takes place when the legal ownership changes hands, and not when payment is made. Goods or services are 'realised' (become the property of the buyer) when any legal entitlement is exchanged. The seller has passed the legal title to the buyer; this process may take place several weeks before the buyer actually pays for the goods or services. Nevertheless, the article bought would now appear as an asset of the buyer's business, even if payment has not been made. For example, a buyer sells a product to the seller on 11 July; and consequently the buyer becomes the legal owner of the good (as legal title is transferred). Payment is not made until 5 August, but the product for accounting purposes is now owned by the buyer.

Examiner's voice

Examination questions may well ask you to consider the principles in the context of a given business and expect you to be able to discuss and evaluate such accounting procedures. Such questions may or may not have numerical data alongside.

Being able to have some critical awareness of these conventions or principles is essential.

Questions Time allowed 10 minutes

1. Explain the principle of materiality. (4 marks)

2. State one example of a business that would not be classed as a going concern, and therefore different accountancy rules would be applied.
(1 mark)

3. Which principle best describes:

   A. the concept of avoiding bias or over optimism?
(1 mark)

   B. the concept of conservatism? (1 mark)

   (7 marks)

Case Study Time allowed 25 minutes

Country Retreats Ltd (CRL)

This spa retreat business has been in operation for over 15 years and has seen consistent growth for the last few years. The main shareholders of CRL have been its owners from the start, when it was only a partnership. The business was quickly turned into a limited company as the demand for its services grew at a staggering rate. Now there are nine such spas, all offering weekend retreats for the cash-rich socio-economic groups A and B, who still have the money to pamper themselves and their partners.

After a recent board meeting it was decided the time was right to move the business forward and become a plc. This would allow the business to gain a valuable cash injection to facilitate its plans for further expansion.

Tom (the managing director who had previously bought a small specialist food chain which had been successfully sold within four years, and had the marketing skills to sell anything to anyone) was keen to ensure that the business looked good on paper. He was determined to ensure that the allocation of shares would be bought and at a high price. This would require the business to be presented in the best possible manner.

Sales at CRL had been increasing steadily, but Tom's projections for the next couple of years were quite dramatic, suggesting the business would increase sales by more than 30%, something that had not been previously achieved.

Even the economy looked favourable, despite official forecasts to the contrary. This was too much for Stuart, the accountant, who pointed out to Tom that there were certain conventions that should be applied when presenting the financial information about the business.

An argument started as Tom had also valued all the assets of the business. He had included stock that had not sold and probably would never be sold as new models had now been produced. He had even valued all the materials in the administration department, including the envelopes!

There was also some confusion as to what was to be counted and how it was to be counted. Tom suggested that a new policy should be introduced, allowing the business to produce accounts that would be seen in a more favourable manner by prospective shareholders.

Stuart was determined to keep to the appropriate principles of accounting, regardless of how such accounts would be seen by the public.

To what extent has Tom adhered to the accounting principles? (18 marks)

SOURCES OF FINANCE

Finance as a business resource must be carefully considered when determining strategy. For example, imagine that a private limited company operating from an old factory has developed some powerful and unique anti-virus software, that can be used with mobile phones as well as computers. It wants to raise £500,000 for a major product launch and for future research and development. The board of directors considers how to raise it. If it takes out a ten-year loan, it is committing itself to repayments over a substantial period of time and there is obviously an opportunity cost to these payments (e.g. the amounts involved could be spent on refurbishing the factory). If the board is considering the issue of more shares, then there will be reduced control over future decisions since shareholders have a vote. This issue (unlike the interest payments) will not simply last for ten years but will exist for as long as the company continues to trade – as will the expectation of dividend payments. If there is a discussion about 'going public' then there are other issues as well as control to discuss; not least that if the shares are bought by financial institutions, these will tend to have a short-term focus on share value and dividends rather than long-term growth. As shareholders, these organisations will vote for the directors most likely to achieve these short-term objectives and therefore will have a major influence on company strategy.

The different types of finance have varied implications for a business, and the short-term finance needed for the day-to-day running of the business (working capital) will not be raised in the same way as the finance required for growth. Finance for growth will be needed for several years, so how a business decides to finance each stage of its development makes a great deal of difference.

Key Term

working capital: short-term finance required for the day-to-day running of a business.

Examiner's voice

At A2 level it is essential not only to know and understand the different sources of finance, but to be able to analyse and evaluate their strategic implications as well.

A business might originally have been started using the owners' own capital. Apart from the owners' own funds, there is a variety of sources of finance available. These sources can be short-term, medium-term or long-term.

Short-term finance

Short-term finance (working capital) is needed for the day-to-day running of a business, and is usually for a period of up to three years. In order to understand short-term finance, it is necessary to understand the concept of **cashflow** (see Unit 18). There must be a sufficient inflow of cash (revenue) to meet cash outflows (expenditure). If this is not the case, it has a cashflow problem and so needs short-term finance to overcome this.

> ## Key Term
>
> **Cashflow:** a business needs sufficient inflows of cash to finance its day-to-day outgoings (e.g. wages and interest repayments); if cash receipts are insufficient, the business is said to have a cashflow problem.

When considering the sources of short-term finance, an obvious source is a bank. All of the commercial (high-street) banks offer various methods of finance for businesses.

Overdraft

There are two types of bank account: deposit accounts (also known as savings accounts), in which money deposited earns interest; and current accounts, which are used to make and receive payments. A cheque book is used with a current account.

A deposit account usually requires a period of notice before funds can be withdrawn, and is therefore not suitable for a business to use to make payments. With a current account, funds can be 'drawn' (i.e. taken out) whenever it is necessary. Current accounts therefore tend to earn less interest than savings accounts, and some pay no interest at all. When an overdraft is granted, no money is actually credited to the current account, but the business is allowed to run the account down to zero and then a further pre-arranged amount can be withdrawn, hence the term 'overdrawn'.

It is usual for a bank to permit a certain level of overdraft when a current account is opened. If a business wants a larger overdraft, it has to negotiate one, for which it may be charged an arrangement fee. If it fails to do this and simply tries to overdraw more than allowed, the bank may refuse to release the money and any cheques written will 'bounce' (i.e. not be paid). The business will then not be able to make its payments, which could damage its reputation as a customer.

Interest on an overdraft is only paid on the amount actually overdrawn. If the overdraft that has been granted by the bank is for £2,000 and the business only uses £1,500 of it, the interest is only charged on this lower amount and not on the full amount of the overdraft. If a business quickly returns its current account to a credit balance, it will not have to pay much interest.

An overdraft is therefore a safety net for a business; it should not be used for the purchase of capital items such as computers or photocopiers.

Loan

Another source of finance available from a bank is a loan. Short-term loans tend to be used to buy specific pieces of equipment or to purchase a particular consignment of raw materials in order to fulfil a contract.

A separate account (for the amount of the loan) is opened and the full amount is credited to the business's current account. When repayments are made, they are taken from the business's current account and paid into the loan account. This reduces the amount of the loan that is outstanding, and this continues until the balance owing on the loan account falls to zero (i.e. the loan is repaid).

A loan is not a safety net in the same way as an overdraft. There is little point in a business borrowing money in the form of a loan and keeping it in its current account 'just in case anything happens', because this would mean paying interest on funds that it was not using.

There is another important difference between an overdraft and a loan. If a business exceeds its overdraft limit, the bank has the right to demand the whole amount back at once. This cannot happen with a loan. The loan is granted for a particular period of time and can only be demanded back by the bank if the business fails to pay the interest due.

If the business defaults on (fails to pay) its interest, the loan will take longer to pay off, and the amount on which interest is charged will be higher. It is usually possible for a business to arrange a reduction in the amount of interest payable (or even a 'payment holiday' when no payments are made) for a certain period of time. However, this does not mean that the business has been let off the money it owes; the interest payment is simply being deferred until a later date.

It is sometimes asked why a business would want to take out a loan and pay the full amount of interest when it could negotiate an overdraft and only pay for the amount of money actually used. The answer lies in the concept of an overdraft as a safety net.

An overdraft should not be used for the purchase of capital items such as vehicles or office equipment. Suppose a business plans to expand. It is granted an overdraft and uses it for these types of purchase. Assume that it does indeed sell a lot of extra products. If these are sold on credit, it will promptly run into a cashflow problem and have to ask for an even greater overdraft. The bank will not regard this as financially responsible. If this extra overdraft is granted, it will be at a high rate of interest.

It is also likely that the amount of interest payable on an overdraft will be higher than the amount charged on a loan. A business therefore needs to use its short-term finance in the proper manner.

Factors influencing a bank's decision to lend

When deciding whether or not to lend, a bank will consider the following factors:

- what the finance is to be used for
- the company's past trading record, or the business proposal if it is a new business
- the type of product being sold – is it a luxury purchase or one that consumers will always require?
- the business's current financial position, including existing debts. What does it already owe? Who has 'first call' on the business's revenue?
- financial projections – revenue, profit, cashflow etc. The preparation of a business plan is essential.
- the nature of the market and forecasts of sales. Is the market growing or shrinking? At what rate?
- the role and experience of the business's managers. Are they steering the firm in the right way, so that it will be profitable and generate the returns to repay any money borrowed?

In addition to these considerations, the bank will want to know what sort of **security** will be offered by the business: i.e. what can be offered if the business becomes unable to pay back the money borrowed. This may not be so important with a small overdraft or a loan, but it becomes important when large sums of money are lent for long periods of time. The bank may want to take possession of the title deeds to the business's factory or office as security. These deeds are the documents that give legal ownership to a particular piece of land, perhaps the land that the factory or office is built upon. If the business fails to repay the loan, the bank (as holder of the deeds) is legally entitled to sell the factory or office in order to recover any amount outstanding on the loan.

Key Term

Security: something that acts as assurance to a lender that it will receive its money if a business is unable to pay back money it has borrowed.

Trade credit

This means making use of an opportunity offered to defer payment to a supplier. For example, a business called Soundrive makes high-quality audio equipment

for luxury cars, some of which it sells to a company called Maximotors. It receives the majority of its components from a firm called Wireright. It assembles these components immediately into finished products, delivers them and receives payment one month later.

Wireright allows a six-week period of trade credit to all its customers. Soundrive would therefore be foolish to pay for the components as soon as they are delivered. If it does not have to pay immediately, this means that it can wait until it receives payment from Maximotors, and so use the funds it would have used to pay Wireright for other purposes in the meantime. Thus, Soundrive's use of trade credit is a form of short-term finance, one that does not incur any interest charges.

Why would Wireright offer this sort of credit period? Surely it wants its money as soon as possible; after all, it has its own debts to pay. The answer is that it is common business practice, and any business not offering trade credit and insisting on immediate payment is likely to find itself at a considerable disadvantage when marketing its products. If trade credit is offered, a business should use it.

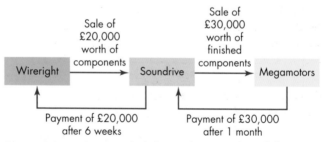

Figure 14.1 The use of trade credit means that Soundrive has £20,000 worth of finance to use, as necessary, for two weeks

Factoring

This means a business selling its debts to raise finance. Debt often takes the form of an 'IOU'. With regard to the example above, assume that Soundrive is holding a signed invoice (bill) from one of its large customers called Megacars. In this document, Megacars agrees to pay £100,000 in one month's time for the audio equipment it has received. The problem is that Soundrive needs the money immediately to pay its employees and the interest on its bank loan. This debt can be sold to a factoring company. Specialist companies exist for this, although most banks offer factoring services.

The factoring company (factor) will offer a certain percentage of the debt to Soundrive (say, 90%) and will then legally own the debt. When the payment becomes due, Megacars will pay the factor and not Soundrive. The factoring of the debt makes little, if any, difference to Megacars, which will only pay what it owed anyway.

The advantage to Soundrive is that it receives most of the finance at once, instead of having to wait until the end of the month for it. On the other hand, the drawback is that it has lost a percentage of the money it is owed. Whether this is worth it depends on Soundrive's circumstances. It is not beneficial to lose 10% of revenue in this way every month, and Soundrive should try to find some way of improving cashflow so that this is not necessary. However, if a financial problem has arisen that is only expected to last for a short while, or, at worst, the need for cash means the difference between survival and closure, Soundrive's use of a factor is sensible.

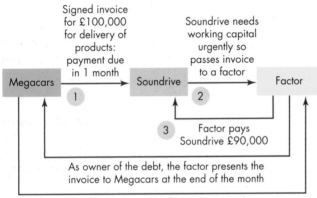

Figure 14.2 Factoring

Hire purchase

Hire purchase is a method of paying for an item in instalments over a period of months or years. As the name implies, the item is being hired by the business while the payments are being made, and does not actually become the business's property (i.e. is not actually 'purchased') until the last payment is made. Like all forms of credit, hire purchase has the advantage that a large sum of money does not have to be found all at once, and the repayments can be spread over a period of time.

This method of finance can certainly help improve cashflow, but it means that at the end of the contract, more money will have been paid out than if the business had paid cash in the first place.

Medium-term finance

Medium-term finance is normally for a period of between three and ten years. The most likely purposes for obtaining medium-term finance are to:

- replace expensive pieces of equipment that have broken down or become out of date
- expand; if a business decides on the objective of growth, it will need larger premises, more equipment or more modern machinery
- convert a business's persistent overdraft into a formal medium-term loan; the overdraft will then be cleared and, although a loan will have been created, this means that the overdraft can then achieve its proper purpose, as a safety net for cash-flow problems.

Various different forms of medium-term finance are available to a business.

Medium-term loan

As is the case with a short-term loan, an agreed amount is credited to the business's current account. For a medium-term loan (and indeed a long-term loan), the rate of interest charged by the bank is particularly important. Suppose that Soundrive wants a loan to finance some new technology in order to expand. The amount of interest payable on a medium-term loan depends on several factors:

- how much is borrowed
- how long the money is wanted for
- the security that is provided.

Soundrive has the option to choose either a variable rate or a fixed-rate loan. The former means that the amount of interest which Soundrive pays varies, according to the Bank of England's decisions on interest rates. A fixed-rate loan has the advantage of certainty: if Soundrive takes out a fixed-rate loan, then those running the business will know what the repayment costs are going to be. This will make financial planning easier. Soundrive will not be financially disrupted by a rise in interest rates.

The disadvantage of a fixed-rate loan is that, if rates fall, Soundrive still has to pay the rate that it has agreed. It will therefore be paying more than if it were on a variable rate loan. It is usually possible to end the fixed-rate agreement with the bank, but there is a penalty clause that could amount to several months' interest payments.

What happens if a business does not repay the interest due on a loan?

Organisations who lend money (typically a bank) in the form of a loan to a business, are creditors not owners and as such are not entitled to any voice in the business's decisions. However, the lender is entitled to the repayment of the loan with interest. Imagine that a business takes out a loan for £50,000 for a five-year period, and that it defaults (i.e. fails to pay) on its monthly loan payment after three years. Technically the bank is entitled to call in the whole of the remaining balance on the loan at once. In practice, it is unlikely to do so as this might cause the business to cease trading. At best, this would mean the loss of a customer that might well become profitable to the bank again in the future. Alternatively, at worst, it might mean that the business is liquidated (i.e. sells off its assets), and there are insufficient funds from this for the bank to receive all of its outstanding money.

It is usually possible for a business to negotiate a 'payment holiday' to ease its cashflow problems. This means that no interest is paid for a specified number of months; this of course does not mean that the interest is 'written off' – exactly the opposite! It is being added to the amount outstanding on the loan.

Also, it may be possible to renegotiate the loan and agree to repay it back over a longer period of time. In this case, instead of repaying it at the end of the agreed term in two years' time, the bank might agree to allow the remaining balance to be repaid over the next four years. The monthly payments will therefore be reduced, and so financial life will be easier for the business. It will, of course, mean that more interest will have to be paid in the long run than was originally the case.

It is much more likely that the bank will agree to these new conditions if the person responsible for finance at the business informs the bank of the impending problem in advance of the default. It may be difficult and embarrassing to admit to this, but it shows that the business is prepared to face up to its financial responsibilities. The bank will not be impressed with a business which has taken few or no steps to sort out its financial problems ahead of a 'crash'.

Hire purchase and leasing

Hire purchase, which has already been mentioned as a source of short-term finance, can also be considered as a method of medium-term finance. **Leasing** is similar in that it also allows payment to be made in instalments, thus spreading the cost over a number of years. However, as with hire purchase, this means that the total amount eventually paid will be (perhaps considerably) in excess of the cash price.

Leasing, however, differs from hire purchase in two important aspects. First, leasing an item is basically the same as renting it. This means that a business that leases something never actually owns it, unless the leasing company offers to sell it to the business when the agreement comes to an end.

If Soundrive wants a new network with specific facilities for computer-aided design and computer-aided manufacture, but cannot afford to pay for it all at once, it could contact a leasing company with the proposal to lease the equipment for six years. If the leasing company agrees, the equipment will be installed. Payments are made monthly but, unlike with hire purchase, the items leased do not become the property of Soundrive at the end of the six years.

The second way in which leasing differs from hire purchase is that, as the equipment is leased and not owned, if it breaks down, the leasing company must fix it at its own expense.

It may be part of the agreement that the leasing company updates Soundrive's computers and/or software. This would reduce the risk of the business getting left behind in technological terms. If this is the case, the lease will be more expensive.

Long-term finance

Long-term finance is usually for periods in excess of ten years. This finance is for securing the resources for long-term growth. For the long term, a business essentially has the choice of raising finance by borrowing or through the issue of shares.

Long-term loans

Long-term loans are used for expensive pieces of machinery, the cost of which needs to be spread over a lengthy period of time, perhaps as long as 20 years.

Loans for buildings are known as mortgages and can vary in duration of between 20 years and 30 years, although they usually run for 25 years. The amount of finance involved is large and the bank will certainly require the title deeds of the land as security. As with the medium-term loan, it is possible for a business to opt either for a variable or a fixed-rate mortgage. However, in the latter case, the rate would not be fixed for the whole length of the loan. Twenty years is too far ahead for either the bank or the business to judge whether the rate fixed at the beginning would be beneficial or not. It is much more likely that the option to renew on a fixed rate basis will be offered every few years.

Debentures

These are a special type of long-term loan that are only available to a public limited company. There are two differences between debentures and other types of loan. First, the company does not borrow money from a bank in the usual way, but sells debentures to investors in order to raise finance. The debentures carry a fixed rate of interest which the company must pay to the debenture holders every year. Second, the debentures can be resold to someone else if the investor needs his/her money back before the debenture matures (is paid back). Debentures are sometimes called 'loan stocks' or just 'stocks', as in the term 'stocks and shares'. Like other long-term loans, debentures are almost certainly secured on a specific asset of the company, so that if there are financial problems the debenture holders can force the company to sell the asset in order to get their money back.

The issue of shares

Share issue is also known as **equity finance**. When investors use the term 'equities', they are talking about shares. This type of finance is only available to a company.

In the case of a private company, there may be restrictions on the transfer of shares, and their value is not readily obvious because they are not traded in a market. With a public company, once shares are issued they are then traded on the **stock market**, the place where debentures and shares are bought and sold. Public companies are able to raise more capital than private limited companies, but in either case the shares are issued for ever; they are not like debentures or loans, which are paid back.

> ### Key Term
>
> **Stock market:** a market where shares and debentures are bought and sold; only public companies have their shares traded on the stock market.

Shareholders are entitled to a dividend (a share of the company's profits), but it is not a legal requirement that a dividend is paid every year; theoretically, a company could retain all its profit. The shareholders cannot demand their money back in the way that a bank can if interest on a loan is not paid. However, this would not be very popular and would result in some interesting scenes with the directors at the annual general meeting. Moreover, once knowledge of the company's action became public, the share price would be bound to fall.

When a company wants to issue more shares, this is known as a **rights issue**. Existing shareholders are offered the opportunity ('right') to buy more shares at a price that is lower than the current market value. This makes the shares tempting to buy, and the shareholders know that control over the company is being kept among the same group of people as before.

Examiner's voice

A common mistake is to assume that when shares are resold they are sold back to the company. This is not the case; they are sold to other investors. It should be apparent why. A company issues shares to raise large amounts of finance in order to purchase expensive buildings and equipment. If investors were entitled to sell their shares back to the company, it would either need to have a huge amount of cash constantly ready to hand (which would be earning no return) or have to sell the very equipment it has bought in order to pay them back.

Sale and leaseback

A business can raise finance by selling off an asset such as a building or a piece of land. This can raise a considerable amount of finance and is a sensible course of action if the asset is no longer needed.

Sale and leaseback is where the asset is sold but then leased back, usually for a long period of time. Soundrive, the audio business mentioned above, could sell off one of its factories and then agree to lease it back for 20 years. If it needs finance in order to fund an expansion, it can raise a large amount of finance in this way in the knowledge that it can operate from exactly the same site as before for many years.

There are disadvantages. Soundrive no longer owns the asset it is leasing. When the lease expires, there is no guarantee that it will be renewed; the business that owns the factory might want to sell it. Soundrive would then have to vacate the premises and go elsewhere. Furthermore, as is the case with all leasing, Soundrive must pay the leasing company for the next 20 years for using the very asset it owned previously.

Retained profit

Once a business has been operating profitably for several years, it is likely that some of the profit will be retained for the purpose of using it in the future. When this has happened, the retained profit can be a useful source of finance which does not incur debt on the business. As these retained profits have been used to finance the business and not distributed to the owners, there will be an entry on the liabilities section of the business's balance sheet (see Unit 17) under the heading 'retained profit', or alternatively 'profit and loss account', since this is where the profit was originally recorded in the accounts.

Examiner's voice

Do not suggest that a business's retained profit can be used as a source of finance; it has already been used!

Short-term	Medium-term	Long-term
Overdraft	Loan	Loan
Loan	Hire purchase	Sale of assets
Trade credit	Leasing	Sale and leaseback
Factoring	Retained profit	Retained profit
Hire purchase		Shares (if the business is a company)
		Debentures (if the business is a plc)

Table 14.1 Sources of finance: a summary

Other sources of finance

Government assistance

Government assistance does not come in the form of a 'no-strings-attached' bag of cash. It falls into two categories: assistance with obtaining a loan, and regional aid.

The Small Firms Loan Guarantee scheme (SFLG)

A lender requires security to ensure that it will get its money back. But what happens if, despite the fact that there is a sound business proposal, a business has little security to offer? In the past, this could have made it hard to obtain finance. The idea behind the SFLG scheme which began in 2003, is to enable small firms with little security to offer to obtain finance.

As the name implies, the SFLG is targeted at smaller businesses rather than established ones that are already financially secure. The finance is a loan *not* from the government but from a bank. The bank will need to see the usual documents (e.g. cashflow forecasts and business plans), and the actual decision whether to lend or not is left to the bank.

If the bank is satisfied with the proposal, the guarantee (security) for 75% of the loan comes from the government via the **Department of Trade and Industry (DTI)**.

Key Term

Department of Trade and Industry (DTI): a government department that exists to help businesses improve their competitiveness and productivity.

Regional Development Assistance (RDA)

Government financial assistance is also available if the business is located in, or is prepared to relocate to, certain areas of the UK (see Figure 14.3). These are usually the areas where traditional industries (e.g. coal mining, steel making) have been in decline for a number of years. This decline often means that the skills of the workforce are out of date and/or the infrastructure (e.g. transport links) is poor.

This aid is known as Regional Development Assistance. RDA is available for a business if it can demonstrate that, on receiving assistance, it will safeguard and create jobs or be helped to grow so that it can compete more effectively at home or abroad.

The assistance on offer includes **incentives** to locate in a particular area. These include:

- tax incentives, which lower the amount of tax a business has to pay
- sale of land or property to businesses at a discounted rate
- reduced rents for buildings and factories.

In addition, there are **grants** to businesses for:

- investment in equipment, to improve competitiveness
- training or retraining their employees, to improve skills and productivity
- research and development into new products, to keep ahead of foreign competition

Whereas the SFLG is intended for small businesses, RDA assistance is available to larger, more established businesses.

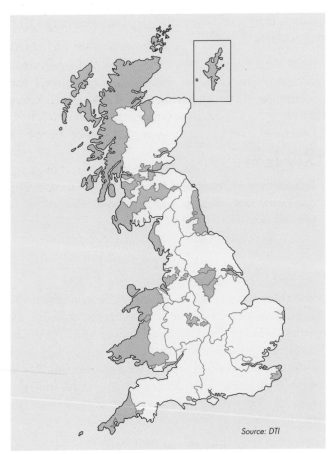

Source: DTI

Figure 14.3 Areas receiving Regional Development Assistance

Source: DTI

Depreciation

Over a period of time some of a business's assets (e.g. a removal company's vans) will wear out. They become worth less each year; that is, they depreciate. Eventually, new ones will have to be bought. The Inland Revenue permits the business to claim an allowance for this depreciation each year and to treat it as a cost to the business. Since profit equals revenue minus cost, any increase in cost will lower the business's (pre-tax) profit. This seems a rather odd thing for a business to want to do, but a lower profit will lower the amount of tax which it has to pay. It can therefore retain the amount 'saved' as a result of the depreciation allowance in order to purchase new equipment.

This is shown in Table 14.2. For simplicity, assume that the business only pays two costs, wages and raw materials, and that the rate of tax is 25%. In example 1, it can be seen that with no allowance for depreciation, the profit after tax is £75,000.

Example 1		Example 2	
Revenue	£200,000	Revenue	£200,000
Wages	£70,000	Wages	£70,000
Raw materials	£30,000	Raw materials	£30,000
		Depreciation	£10,000
Profit before tax	£100,000	Profit before tax	£90,000
Tax at 25%	£25,000	Tax at 25%	£22,500
Profit after tax	**£75,000**	Profit after tax	**£77,500**

Table 14.2 Depreciation

Assume that the allowance for depreciation is £10,000. In example 2, when depreciation is included, the profit after tax rises to £77,500.

It is important to understand that depreciation is not a source of finance like most other methods detailed in this chapter. Loans, overdrafts and funds from business angels all mean that the finance is available, and can be accessed, as soon as the paperwork and any other formalities are completed. With depreciation, the finance is *not* a sum of money that becomes available to spend; it is a reduction in the business's tax bill at the end of the financial year. It means that in the following year, the business has more funds available because it has not had to pay so much tax, but this does not become apparent until the business submits its tax return to the tax authorities and the figures are accepted.

Venture capital and business angels

Venture capitalists are individuals or firms who lend money, known as **venture capital**, to small and medium-sized businesses that require finance for starting up or expansion. Venture capitalists often take a gamble in doing this because it is quite likely that the business requiring the funds has been refused finance by other lenders as the risk of failure is high. However, a high risk is associated with the expectation of a high reward. A venture capitalist might agree to provide a certain amount of finance in exchange for 20% of a new company's shares and might adopt a 'take it or leave it' approach. If the company accepts and does well, then in a few years the venture capitalist will look forward to large dividend payments and a substantial capital gain from the shares if it chooses to sell them.

> ### Key Term
>
> **Venture capital:** finance from individuals or firms who lend money to, or buy shares in, small and medium-sized businesses that require finance for starting up or expansion.

Business angels are similar to venture capitalists, but they usually offer management advice as well. They can also bring knowledge of useful contacts, such as suppliers and potential customers, to a business.

The owner(s) of a small business need to evaluate carefully the use of this source of finance. An angel will require a financial return for its capital and time, and may insist on becoming actively involved in the running of the business in order to safeguard its investment. This may cause problems and conflict.

Internal and external sources of finance

Finance can also be classified according to whether it is internal or external.

If finance is raised internally, it does not increase the debts of the business. Internal sources include the funds available from the sale of any unwanted assets, from retained profit and from the use of trade credit. Internal sources are more likely to be available when a business is well-established.

External finance is provided by people or institutions outside the business in the form of loans, overdrafts, shares and debentures. The use of external sources of funding creates a debt that will require payment.

A business's choice of finance

There are advantages and disadvantages to every method of finance. The actual choice depends on several factors, as shown in Figure 14.4:

- **The type of business.** Sole traders and partnerships cannot issue shares and so are restricted in the types of finance available for growth.
- **The amount of control desired.** Becoming a partnership (or taking on a new partner if the business is already a partnership) will increase the capital available but reduce the control over decisions. In the case of a company, all shareholders have a vote (one per share), so becoming a company or issuing more shares will weaken control. If the company is a plc and it pays a dividend which is out of line with stock market expectations, the share price will fall which may leave the business open to a hostile takeover.
- **Security.** A lack of security may mean that banks are unwilling to grant a loan, in which case some other form of finance must be found.

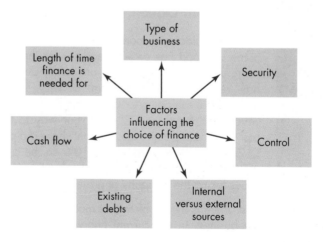

Figure 14.4 Factors influencing the choice of finance

- **Internal funds**. If the business has reserves of cash, should it use them for finance? On one hand, there will be no interest to pay; but on the other, once these funds are used, the business has no financial cushion to fall back on. Another issue is whether a company should hold back some of the funds available for dividend payments in order to finance a project. If it is a public limited company, it needs to consider how the stock market is likely to react to such a decision; the share price will probably fall. A fall of a few pence does not matter, but a large drop would be a sign of concern that the wrong decision had been made, and might tempt another firm into making a takeover bid.

- **The length of time involved**. If equipment is purchased in order to expand the business, how long will it take to generate the funds to pay back the investment? If the answer is several years, short-term finance is not appropriate.

- **The current methods being used to finance the business**. Inappropriate financial management, such as poor cashflow management or using an overdraft in the wrong way, will not impress a bank and will discourage it from lending.

- **Existing levels of debt**. If a business has already been granted several bank loans and then applies for another, the bank will think twice about authorising it because of the amount of interest that the business already has to pay. If yet another loan is allowed, the bank may wonder if the business will be able to repay all of them. If a company decides to try to raise the finance it wants via the issue of shares, it will find this difficult to do if it already has several loans. Potential investors will know that interest payments on the existing loans have to be met before any dividends are paid. If a lot of revenue is 'disappearing' into interest payments, this will reduce the amount of profit, and dividends might be low as a result. This will make the proposed issue of shares unattractive to investors. Furthermore, a business with a high proportion of its finance raised in the form of debt compared to the amount raised by equity is said to be 'highly geared'. A highly geared business is clearly going to be susceptible to the effects of a rise in the rate of interest.

- For these reasons, a business has to be careful about obtaining too much finance in the way of loans.

Further Sources

www.barclays.co.uk/business – a website giving examples of the sort of banking services available to business customers (e.g. financial advice and 'start up packs' for new businesses).

www.londonstockexchange.com – the London Stock Exchange is at the heart of the UK's financial markets. This site contains lots of information about the stock exchange and the companies whose shares are traded on it.

www.moneymadeclear.fsa.gov.uk/tools.aspx?Tool=loan_calculator – the Financial Service Authority's loan calculator. It will work out monthly repayments for various loan amounts, repayment periods and annual interest rates.

www.smallbusiness.co.uk – a useful site with guidance on start-up, and ongoing finance, for the small business.

Your Turn

Case study Time allowed 55 minutes

Wibraham Gallen Ltd (WGL)

WGL manufactures sports equipment for gym and home use, and has grown steadily over the past 25 years. Many of its employees are family members. It has recently benefited from a very successful promotional campaign for a new range of trampolines which used the slogan 'Bounce your way to health'. Last year the profit and loss account showed a profit of £127,000, which is up almost 10% on the previous year. There are nevertheless a number of important issues facing the company at present.

First, there is the problem that much of the growth of the business in the current financial year has been generated by allowing extended credit periods to its distributors. Rhys Wilbraham (the son of one of the original founders of the firm) is the finance director and has been trying to improve WGL's cashflow by factoring some of its debts, but he feels that this is only a short-term solution. The marketing director Jean O'Hanlon is in the process of negotiating a large order with a major national chain of sports shops, and she insists that WGL hold a large quantity of stock so that it is ready to make immediate deliveries and thereby create a good impression. Rhys is less keen on this policy, especially as the negotiations have been ongoing for almost six months. He vividly remembers the time three years ago when the firm's liquidity position was in a disastrous state. He does not want to see WGL with such a large overdraft ever again.

The board have recently discussed the possibility of an expansion. Even if Jean's negotiations with the national chain comes to nothing, the existing factory will not be able to cope with the growing volume of business for much longer; WGL has been operating close to capacity for the 18 months. There is scope on the current site for an extension to be built, although this would mean some disruption to the existing operations.

The estimated sum for the extension is £1.5 million. There has been considerable discussion of how this amount of finance might be raised. The majority shareholder (with 30% of the issued shares) is Nigel Gallen. Nigel was one of the original founders of the company and although he no longer takes an active part in the running of the business, he clearly stated at the last AGM that he does not want WGL to expand very much. He said that he did not want the business to take on a vast amount of debt, and stated that as a 'family business', one of its core objectives had always been to look after its stakeholders properly. Rhys argued that growing larger would enable WGL to do precisely that, and added that the finance for any expansion need not necessarily be raised by borrowing. He pointed out that there are other options such as leasing and hire purchase that could be explored.

There is a board meeting in one month's time and Rhys is keen to discuss the matter again. He has prepared some rough calculations for the board's consideration. These are based on raising the whole £1.5 million in the form of a loan at WGL's bank.

	Interest rate 7% 10-year term	Interest rate 7% 25-year term	Interest rate 8% 10-year term	Interest rate 8% 25-year term
Monthly repayment	£17,416	£10,602	£18,199	£11,577
Total repayment over term of loan	£2,089,953	£3,180,506	£2,183196	£3,473,172
Total interest paid during term of loan	£589,953	£1,680,506	£683,697	£1,973,173

Table 14.3 Calculations for the board to consider

	£000
Fixed Assets	1,200
Current Assets	
Stock	220
Debtors	237
Cash	45
	502
Current Liabilities	
Trade Creditors	301
Net current Assets	201
Net Assets	**1401**
Share capital*	700
Profit and loss account	701
Equity shareholders' funds	**1401**

*WGL has an authorised share capital of 100,000 £1 ordinary shares of which 70,000 have been issued.

Figure 14.5 Extract from WGL's balance sheet for last year

1. State the difference between 'debt' and 'equity' finance. (2 marks)

2. State the purpose of WGL having an overdraft facility at the bank. (1 mark)

3. Outline one advantage and one disadvantage of WGL factoring debt. (4 marks)

4. State two differences between hire purchase and leasing. (4 marks)

5. Evaluate the sources of finance that WGL could use for the proposed expansion. (18 marks)

(29 marks)

Unit 15

MEASURES OF PERFORMANCE: BUDGETS

Any attempt to make strategic plans for the future of a business should include the use of budgets. A budget is a plan for the future that takes into account the resources that are available to the business. In most cases it will apply monetary values to different aspects of business activity, such as revenue, output and costs. Managers can then monitor the performance of the business with respect to the budgeted figures. Budgets are normally used in those parts of the business where it is possible to exercise some control. Therefore, the main areas for budgeting involve the costs and revenues of a business. It is possible for a business to operate effectively in terms of production, communication, and efficiency, but unless all of these things are measured effectively the business will not know how successful it is or, in some cases, whether its future is viable. This is all part of the ongoing strategic planning process for a business.

All businesses need to set objectives in a quantifiable form for the coming time period. For example, an improvement of productivity for labour of 10% and a return on capital employed of 20% for the coming year might be the target. Similarly the marketing department might set a target for an improvement in sales as the result of an advertising campaign. To make all of this possible, the business must put a system in place for the collection of the data that it needs. This information needs to be used in assessing performance and setting targets for the next time period. The setting of budgets is the first part of a process that will enable a firm to review and monitor its progress and consider the need for change in the future.

The process and reasons for budgeting in a business are similar to those of a family working out a budget for the coming month or year. The act of budgeting requires the producing of inflows and outflows and encourages the organisation to confront problems and act on them. It will also show which areas of the business are likely to

be successful, and those that need extra attention or which may need to be changed or dropped. Therefore, there are many reasons for undertaking budgeting in the firm. These include:

- measuring the money entering and leaving the business in all areas, using this information to indicate the level of efficiency and effectiveness of the business's activities
- giving information on the productivity levels of staff and providing one possible means of appraising and rewarding workers
- providing information for current and prospective shareholders and investors
- ensuring that the cashflow is adequate to meet the day-to-day needs of the business
- providing managers with the information they need to manage their departments and monitor their performance
- giving the whole business a strategic perspective and target that focuses on where it is now and where it would like to be after a specific period of time
- providing the basis of control and meeting objectives.

Budgeting for cashflow

The use of cashflow information is one of the most important budgeting exercises for a business. Many businesses exist for relatively long periods of time while making losses. A situation where insufficient cash is entering the business to make it possible for it to meet its payment commitments is the one that most often forces a business to cease trading. The need to pay workers, either at the end of each week or month, makes it essential for the business to ensure adequate cashflow. It may be possible to delay demands from suppliers for payment without difficulty, but if wages payments are missed, the plight of the business will immediately become obvious to the outside world.

Examiner's voice

Be careful not to confuse cashflow with profit. Cash is the money entering and leaving the business. Profit is the difference between revenue and costs.

For many businesses, cashflow varies greatly from month to month, making it necessary to have overdraft facilities with the bank or cash reserves to call on. Chester Zoo is open to the public all year round, except for Christmas Day. Whatever the number of people who pass through the turnstile each day, it still has to pay to feed the animals and the wages of keepers and administrative staff. The variation between cashflow in the school summer holidays and the cold dark days of January is enormous. This has to be budgeted so that plans are in place to ensure that sufficient cash is available during the winter months.

Key Term

Overdraft facility: an agreement with a bank to be able to overdraw on an account up to a stated limit. This overdraft facility will usually have an agreed rate of interest (in relation to the Bank of England base rate) charged upon it.

Examiner's voice

The terms shown in accounts may vary. Terms such as sales revenue and receipts can be used interchangeably.

The uses of cashflow information

Example: Sally's Sweets
Sally Fordham runs an old-fashioned sweet shop in a holiday resort on the North Wales coast. She is often busy in the period running up to Christmas, but the main part of her business comes from holiday-makers and her busy time begins around the Easter holidays and runs through to the

(£000s)	Sept	Oct	Nov	Dec	Jan	Feb
Opening balance	11	11	10	6	4	(1)
Receipts (sales revenue)	7	5	4	10	2	2
Total (inflows)	18	16	14	16	6	1
Payments (expenses)	7	6	8	12	7	3
Closing balance	11	10	6	4	(1)	(2)

Table 15.1 Cashflow forecast for Sally's Sweets

end of October. Since opening the shop, Sally has made a point of calculating her cashflow monthly to ensure that she can meet all her payments. Sally's payments are relatively high in October, November and December because she has to order and pay her suppliers for special Christmas stock well in advance of the Christmas period. She also has to pay for extra staff during the Christmas period. Sally knows that February will be her worst month of the year, with fewest sales and the need for an overdraft at the bank. Business will then begin to pick up as Easter approaches. Preparing the cashflow forecast will help Sally in a number of ways. It will help her to see what her cash requirements are in any month, so that she can pay the part-time worker who helps her out during her busiest periods. She will also take this statement to her small business adviser at the bank to discuss her overdraft facilities with her. Sally knows that if she has shown that she is organised and planning ahead for all eventualities, this will reassure the bank that she is running the business effectively and that she is aware of problems that might arise in the future. The bank will also realise that over the summer months, Sally's account with them will have a substantial credit deposit.

Decision-making and strategic planning

As the example in Table 15.1 shows, the calculation of cashflow is an important tool for the business to use in preparing for the future and making strategic decisions about policy. Cashflow information can be useful in all the following situations.

The need for liquidity

The first thing a business needs to assess from a cashflow forecast is what the demand for cash is likely to be at any time, to allow the business to meet the demands for payments. Once these figures have been calculated, the manager/owner can start to think about how that cash might be generated. This will be one of the most important aspects of running a new business, when the outgoings are likely to be large and immediate but the revenue generated is small and takes time to arrive.

Improving liquidity

The most obvious source of cash for a business may be a loan, but this is not necessarily the best option. Cashflow can be improved significantly by delaying payments to suppliers and demanding payment from customers. Unfortunately, this option is often not available to new businesses because of their weak bargaining position with larger and more established firms. The larger business will know that it can delay payment and the small business will have to wait. This sort of business is often vital to the survival of the small business, and they cannot afford to do anything that puts future business at risk. Businesses can also limit outgoings by hiring or leasing equipment rather than buying it (see Unit 18).

Dealing with the bank or other lenders

The preparation of a cashflow chart will highlight the need for borrowing, and will ensure that the business takes action before the event rather than when forced to react to unforeseen circumstances. Borrowing from a bank is never easy because they are effectively lending their customers' money and they must, therefore, be cautious. The bank will require other information such as accounts and projected sales figures, but much of this information will be historic. The advantage of cashflow from the bank's point of view is that it looks into the future and assesses need. A realistic estimation of future needs will also show the bank that the owner of the business is aware of fluctuations in movements of money and will therefore take a realistic and honest view of the business's performance.

Making changes

Sometimes the cashflow forecast may highlight the fact that changes need to be made. For example, a theme park may decide that it is not worth opening at certain times of the year because the revenue generated is insufficient. In another situation a business might find that introducing longer opening hours solves some of its cashflow problems, because it will bring in larger revenue without the need for an equivalent increase in costs.

In all of these situations, the business needs to take account of the costs and benefits of its actions. For example, reducing the credit period given to customers might seem like a good way of improving cashflow, and it may work in the short term. It will reduce the debtor days ratio for the business (see Unit 22). There is always the risk however that the customer will find another supplier willing to give better credit terms, and that the order is lost for the long term. The need to ensure adequate cashflow is vital to the organisation, but decisions about generating cash need to be taken within the context of the whole commercial situation.

Budgeting in other areas

Budgeting is used in all areas of an effective business to ensure that spending is controlled and to provide forecasts of likely costs and returns. Budgeting by department makes it possible to split the business into smaller units and to pass responsibility to departmental

> **Key Term**
>
> **Delegation:** the passing on of responsibility, usually to someone at a lower level in the organisation.

heads for their own performance. This delegation of responsibility will be useful in a number of ways. Individual managers are likely to have a better immediate knowledge of their department, and should be able to ensure that their budgets are realistic and achievable. In addition, the responsibility for budgeting may be a motivator, showing that senior management trust the judgment of their more junior managers (see Unit 28 for information on motivation theory).

The success or otherwise of the budget may also be used to judge the performance of a particular department, its employees and its managers. It may be necessary however to use caution and common sense in the use of this information. Sometimes departments will fail to meet budgets for reasons outside their individual control. The figures should not be used in isolation from the performance of the rest of the firm, the market and the economy. For example, the terrorist attack on 11

Figure 15.1 The airline industry was deeply affected by the attacks on the World Trade Centre in 2001

September 2001 in the USA had a huge effect on airlines and travel businesses. This event, that could not have been predicted, meant that prepared budgets were no longer valid. Far less serious events may also make it impossible to meet budgeted targets. Management need to use common sense in these situations.

Zero budgeting

An alternative to traditional methods of budgeting is zero budgeting. This involves setting all budgets at zero, requiring managers to justify any requirement for funds. The advantage of this system is that it prevents a situation where the same money is given each year, or allowed to increase with inflation linking, without any consideration of actual need.

For example, the Head of the Business Studies department might have an annual budget this year of £500. This will be increased by 3% to £515 because of the current rate of inflation. The department has had very few outgoings this year because there were sufficient books and equipment for all its students, so there will be money left at the end of the year, unless the Head of Department can find a way to spend it. Next year, however, there will be a problem because £515 will not be sufficient to buy all the books required for the new specification. It is easy to see that this system is inefficient and wasteful, particularly if the first year's money is used to buy non-essential supplies. That money could have been better used elsewhere. In this situation, zero budgeting would have worked well.

A business might use zero budgeting where it has a number of potential developments planned but is only prepared to proceed with those that are cost-justified. In this situation, it would be wrong to budget for all alternatives because of the amount of management time that would be taken in preparing the budgets.

The main problem with zero budgeting is the amount of time it takes for budget holders and financial coordinators. The need to review items of expenditure and decide whether to pass them will be ongoing and may become tiresome for the person responsible. It may also mean that the business has a short-term perspective of the situation.

Flexible budgets

Flexible budgets allow a business to make allowances for changes in the level of sales volume so that adverse variances (see below) are avoided. If a business's sales rise by 5% in a particular time period, the business will expect some of its costs such as raw materials and direct labour to rise. This can be taken into account immediately by increasing the budget to take account of the higher figures in these areas. For example, if a cake manufacturer finds that sales have increased by 10% in the last month, the budgeted figures for ingredients would have to be adjusted to take account of this.

Variance analysis

The variance is the amount by which the actual results for an item differ from the amount in the budget. Variance can be adverse or favourable. For revenue, if actual sales exceed the budgeted figures the variance will be favourable, whereas for cost if actual costs exceed the budgeted figure the variance will be negative. A positive variance improves profit and a negative variance reduces actual profit.

Depart-ment	Budgeted figure (forecast)	Actual figure	Variance
Sales	£20,000	£22,000	(+)£2,000 Favourable
Sales	£20,000	£17,000	(–)£3,000 Adverse
Labour	£7,000	£7,500	(+)£500 Adverse
Raw materials	£3,000	£2,900	(–)£100 Favourable

Table 15.2 Variance analysis

Examiner's voice

Great care needs to be taken when deciding whether a variance is favourable or unfavourable and in putting a sign in front of the number. With an inflow like sales, an increase in the figure will result in a favourable variance and a positive sign. With an outgoing like labour costs, an increase in the number will mean there is more money leaving the business than has been budgeted for. This means that there will be a negative variance, but a positive sign. In each case it is important to think about whether the change will make the business's circumstances better or worse for determining whether the variance is favourable or unfavourable.

Variance analysis is useful because it allows managers to see where there are problems in meeting budgets and where departments are doing particularly well, but the business needs to exercise caution in using it and should also view it alongside other relevant data. Budget targets may not be reached for a variety of reasons: some of these might be the responsibility of workers or management, like poor productivity or a breakdown in the production process. On other occasions, failure to meet the budget may be because of circumstances outside the business's control. The heavy flooding in the south west of England during the summer of 2007 meant that many businesses in the tourist sector were hit by falling demand.

When variance analysis has been completed it will be necessary to assess the situation in the light of the business's situation. Managers will want to know what has happened to make variance adverse so that they can stop the problem arising again, and they will want to look at favourable variances to see if there are lessons that can be applied to other departments. Managers need to bear in mind that the variances might have occurred because the budget was unrealistic to start with. It is possible for forecasts to be too optimistic or pessimistic about future trends or for managers to have unreasonable expectations of what employees can achieve.

In large businesses, it will not be possible for senior managers to analyse and review every budget for the business. In these situations, a system called 'management by exception' will be used. Senior managers will only become involved if the variance analysis shows a particularly serious adverse variance or a particularly good favourable variance. This means that the rest of the business can be left to run without the need for intervention as long as the variances are within defined limits. This passing of responsibility for day-to-day managers helps in encouraging responsibility and motivation as well as a responsibility for outcomes. When further action is required, it is vitally important that the manager who is dealing with the problem is in full possession of all the facts. Attributing blame to workers for failure to meet a budget target when the circumstances were outside his or her control is likely to lead to a feeling of grievance at best, or industrial action at worst.

Summary

This chapter has shown that the use of budgets is important in any business and particularly the preparation of cashflow information. As with all financial information however, the figures are historic and managers need to remember that past experience is not always a good indicator of the future. If anything, it is the actual preparation of the budget that is important in the way it encourages a group of people to sit down and plan for the future. The alternative of leaving things to chance and good fortune is likely to cause problems at some point. In addition, the budgeting process can help in making managers responsible for their departments, encouraging discussion and delegation of authority and preventing overspending.

Key Term

Historic information: information that already exists from past years. For example, any figures included in a balance sheet will be historic figures, recorded at the point at which the account was dated.

Budgets cannot be used in isolation. Each business will need to consider the impact of the UK and world economy; it should look at its markets, its consumers and its competitors, and it should have contingency plans for difficult or disastrous situations. The budget should be used alongside information on sales, customer satisfaction and customer loyalty for the business to have a good idea of its future prospects.

Further Sources

www.bytestart.co.uk
www.businesslink.gov.uk
www.businessstudiesonline.co.uk
www.briefgroup.co.uk

Task

See if you can find the owner of a small business to speak to and ask about the following things. You will not need to know about actual figures.

- If the business was set up recently, ask about the problems that were faced in the first few months with the bank, suppliers, financing the operation and survival.
- Find out whether budgets and cashflow forecasts are prepared and how useful they are.
- Ask about sources of liquidity like trade credit, personal credit cards, leasing, loans and overdrafts.
- Find out what is the most difficult problem to resolve when it comes to planning for the future.
- Ask what advice they would give to someone about to set up in their line of business.
- Ask if they drew up a business plan.

Case study   Time allowed 1 hour

The Working Lunch Company (WLC)

Sarah Evans started The Working Lunch Company in a small Midlands town five years ago. The business makes a wide variety of sandwiches that are delivered to local businesses within a 30-mile radius of its production unit. These orders are generally phoned in on a daily basis. Sarah started the operation in a small unit on a business park, but has since had to move to a much bigger unit that includes space for the production of the food and office space.

Two years after starting the business, a local competitor closed down when its owner became seriously ill. This gave Sarah the opportunity to take over many of the competitor's contracts. One of these contracts, which is very lucrative, involves delivering to local garages and service stations, making sure that their supply of sandwiches are topped up throughout the day. This means that the business now has to work for seven days a week and Sarah has had to appoint a weekend manager to oversee the production and distribution of sandwiches on Saturday and Sunday.

As a consequence of this situation, Sarah had to expand her business very quickly and take on a number of extra staff. She soon found that, unlike the early years, she could no longer control the whole business herself. Sarah had to appoint a production manager who had specialist knowledge of large-scale food preparation; he now has 10 full-time operatives working for him in the week and 12 part-time weekend employees who are mainly students. She also had to appoint an office manager who has three employees working with her. They deal with orders, invoicing and staffing requirements.

In the last six months Sarah has expanded the business again after a request from several local firms for business and conference lunches. She now provides a service where food and serving staff are supplied for lunches within a 10-mile radius. This has proved to be a very popular service and this side of the business is expanding rapidly.

When Sarah started her business she planned out everything carefully with help from her bank's small business adviser. She completed cashflow forecasts and set herself targets for sales. As the business has expanded however, she has found it more difficult to keep control over what is happening and she is aware that the business could run into difficulties if she is not careful. The need to keep reliable staff is one of her main problems, so she has to juggle pay rates to keep costs as low as possible while retaining employees by paying reasonable rates of pay.

Sarah has been reluctant to hand over the planning and budgeting aspects of the business to her two managers, thinking it should be her own responsibility. The problem is that she no longer has the time to do it properly, and she is not sufficiently involved in the day-to-day business to realise when things are going wrong. Labour turnover has been increasing for some time and is at a high level. There is also a problem with the level of production over the weekend. Sarah feels that this comes from a lack of control by the weekend manager and poor productivity amongst the part-time staff.

In addition, the latest contracts for business lunches are causing serious cashflow problems for Sarah. Many of the businesses who order lunches from WLC are branches of larger organisations such as financial institutions and banks. Sarah's initial customers were individuals working in offices, who paid for their lunch when it was delivered. She now finds that she may have to wait up to two months for payment from these corporate clients, but she has to pay her suppliers much more quickly than this, and her workers on the production side expect to be paid weekly in cash.

WLC is a profitable business, but Sarah is aware that she may be heading for disaster if she does not get the situation under control quickly. She knows that she needs to set production targets, to improve labour turnover and, above all, to improve her cashflow situation to guarantee the business's long-term viability.

She is not sure how to do this or to what extent she should involve her production and office managers.

1. Give five examples of items that would be included in Sarah's cashflow forecast. (5 marks)

2. Discuss the importance of cashflow forecasting for WLC. (15 marks)

3. Evaluate the ways in which Sarah could improve cashflow. (15 marks)

4. Analyse the usefulness of cashflow forecasts for WLC. (10 marks)

(45 marks)

16 Unit PROFIT AND LOSS ACCOUNTS (P&L)

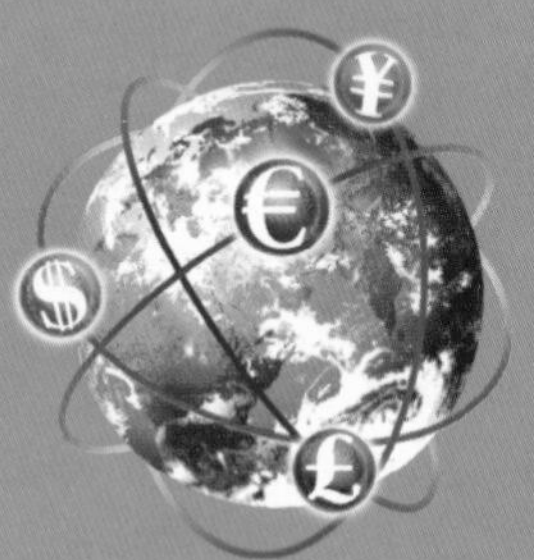

The profit and loss (P&L) account reports the level of profit or loss that a business has made in a given period of time (usually one year), often known as the trading or accounting period.

The P&L is a measure of the performance of the business, and is used to inform shareholders and other interested stakeholders of how well the business has performed. The layout of the P&L is important as the reader is able to see quickly the levels of revenues and costs within the business. This may be helpful when it comes to assessing the level of performance or considering how such performance can be improved.

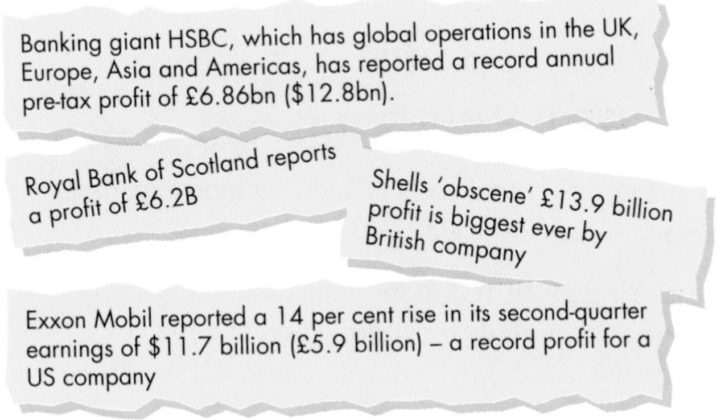

Banking giant HSBC, which has global operations in the UK, Europe, Asia and Americas, has reported a record annual pre-tax profit of £6.86bn ($12.8bn).

Royal Bank of Scotland reports a profit of £6.2B

Shells 'obscene' £13.9 billion profit is biggest ever by British company

Exxon Mobil reported a 14 per cent rise in its second-quarter earnings of $11.7 billion (£5.9 billion) – a record profit for a US company

Figure 16.1 Newspapers report the profits of large companies

Profit

It is important to establish exactly what is meant by the term 'profit'. Profit is:

- the difference between the level of income generated and the costs incurred by the business. In its most simplistic form, profit is calculated by subtracting the total costs from the total revenue.

- the return on an investment.
- the reward for taking risks.
- a source of income for the business.
- a measure of performance and noted by stakeholders such as the shareholders, employees and suppliers.

The profit and loss account

The profit and loss account always states the trading period (e.g. 'Profit and Loss Account for the year ending December 2008') so that stakeholders know that this

	Expenditure in £000	Income in £000
Sales revenue (or Turnover)		300,000
Minus cost of sales	120,000	
Gross profit		180,000
Minus expenses	100,000	
Operating profit		80,000
Minus interest payable	7,500	
Net profit		72,500
Minus tax	15,000	
Minus dividends	30,000	
Retained profit		27,500

Table 16.1 Profit and Loss account year ending December 2008

information will tell them how the business has performed in a given time period. Profits for public limited companies are normally declared every six months. Some of the larger companies declare their profits quarterly. The half-year profits are known as the 'interim results'.

The financial year can start at any time but the majority of businesses use either the tax year, which runs from April to April, or the calendar year, January to December.

Table 16.1 shows that the figures for income start off as high, but become smaller as deductions are made. The first deduction is for the cost of the sales, which is calculated in a special way.

Sales revenue (turnover)

This is a simple calculation based on the level of sales and their value:

price × sales.

It is important to ensure that the figures used are realistic, as in many instances the price of the goods or services will include VAT and possibly excise duties. The taxes included in the price of the good will have to be deducted to gain an appropriate figure.

Examiner's voice

It is not likely that any question would ask you to deal with this (taxes included in the price), but an awareness of this may be useful when commenting on such figures.

It is also important to note when the actual sale of the goods took place, to ensure that the figures are counted within the right year.

Cost of sales

The cost of sales describes the direct cost of producing the goods. Only direct or variable costs are counted and subtracted. Once the cost of sales has been calculated and subtracted from the sales revenue, the residue is the gross profit.

Knowing how much stock has actually been sold and therefore needs to be costed must be calculated with care.

To calculate the cost of sales:

Opening stock (from previous year) + stock purchased in this year – closing stock (what stock is left) = Cost of sales

Only the cost of the stock that was actually sold in the financial year must be counted. For example: if the business started with stock worth £95,000, bought £45,000 and at the end of the year had £20,000 left, the cost of sales would be:

Opening stock	£95,000
+ stock bought	£45,000
– closing stock	£20,000
Cost of sales =	£120,000

In the year, the actual amount of stock sold cost £120,000. That is the amount that has to be taken off the sales revenue of £300,000, to calculate the gross profit for 2008.

Gross profit

This is calculated as shown here:

Sales revenue – cost of sales
300,000 – 120,000 = 180,000

Gross profit only considers the direct costs of production.

Operating profit

This is calculated thus:

Gross profit – fixed costs (which include expenses)
180,000 – 100,000 = 80,000

Operating profit is a more realistic measure of profit as it has accounted for both direct costs (VC) and overheads (FC).

Net profit

This is calculated as shown here:

Operating profit – interest paid
80,000 – 7,500 = 72,500

An additional 'cost' to the business is interest on loans; these are treated separately as they are not related to the actual costs incurred with the production of the goods.

Retained profit

Retained profit is calculated as shown here:

Net profit – tax and dividends
72,500 – 45,000 = 27,500

Finally, the shareholders may be paid a dividend (their reward for holding shares in the business), and the government will want to deduct tax on the profits (corporation tax).

The retained profit is the money which the business can use after all deductions have been made. The business can decide how best to use this retained profit. It may be invested into the business in the form of new capital equipment, or it may be used to pay off some of the debts of the business.

Non-operating income/expenses

On some P&L accounts there may be reference to 'interest received or earned'. This is an additional source of income that has been generated within the period of time for that particular P&L account period. The figure is simply added to the accounts, usually after operating profit and before net profit. Another source of income could be rents or dividends which the business has earned from its investments in other businesses.

Similarly, money may have to be subtracted from the accounts due to interest payable on loans which the business has taken out.

Examiner's voice

- Amounts to be deducted can be put in brackets to signify it is a negative quantity, but in a P&L this is not essential. Again, the layout of your work is crucial to help both yourself and the examiner to see what you have done! It is not essential to have two columns for the figures; however, by doing so it is easier for you to know what is a deduction and which is a running total.
- It is NOT likely that you will be asked to undertake any calculations under examination conditions for the A2 strategy module; you will merely be asked to use the figures. Nevertheless, you should understand how the figures are deduced as this will make it easier for you to analyse the P&L. However, for the A2 accounting module, such calculations can be expected.

Divisions of the P&L account

The P&L can be divided into three divisions or sections:

- trading account
- profit and loss account
- appropriation account.

The trading account

This part of the P&L concentrates on the figures that are used to calculate the gross profit. The trading account considers just the sales revenue and the cost of sales.

This part can be used to judge the efficiency of the business in terms of its ability to convert its factors of production into finished goods; in other words, its ability to change the raw material into saleable goods.

The profit and loss account

This account concentrates on the calculation of the operating profit for the business. It considers not only the sales revenue and the cost of sales, but also the overheads of the business such as machinery, salaries, and expenditure of the accounting and marketing departments. This account is a more accurate reflection of the success of the business. This account will enable the business to assess its efficiency in ensuring that overheads (expenses) are kept under control.

Examiner's voice

There is often some confusion between operating profit and net profit. The latter takes into consideration ALL deductions from the business. There may be one-off payments that would not usually appear (extraordinary items) as they would offer a misleading picture of the business. Operating profit only takes into consideration direct and indirect costs, before dividends and tax is paid. Taxes and dividend payments are included in the profit and loss section/division.

The appropriation account

This part of the accounts concentrates on what actually happens to the profits (if any) that are made. In some texts there are references to 'profit utilisation', which is also how the profits are used.

The appropriation of accounts looks at how much is distributed to the shareholders in the form of dividends, and what proportion is retained by the business for future investment.

Examiner's voice

Care needs to be taken when assessing what amount of the profit goes to the shareholders. It may appear obvious in the short term that shareholders would want as much of the profits to be distributed to them in the form of dividends. However, limiting the distributed profits to the shareholders in order to have more retained profits to aid investment, may mean higher profits in the long term.

Interpretation of P&L accounts

	Figures for 2008 (in £000)	**Figures for 2007 (in £000)**
Sales revenue	130	140
Cost of sales	85	83
Gross profit	45	57
Expenses	27	35
Operating profit	18	22
Interest payable	6	9
Net profit	12	13
Tax and dividends	8	9
Retained profit	4	4

Table 16.2 Profit and Loss account for E&T Ltd 2007 and 2008

Examiner's voice

Be careful when commenting upon any form of financial statement. Ensure that you refer to the correct amount involved. In table 16.2, the values are for thousands of pounds.

A P&L account will often refer to at least two years of accounts. This will enable a comparison to be made. Analysing how the two years (2007 and 2008) differ is of interest. Although the amount of retained profit is the same (£4,000), the activities between the two years are different.

- The sales revenue has decreased by £10,000 while the cost of sales has only increased by £2,000; therefore the gross profit has decreased by only £8,000.
- The cost of sales has not fallen even though sales revenue has fallen. This may be due to a loss of the benefits from economies of scale; or perhaps the actual costs have risen because of increased cost of raw materials or direct labour. It may also be due to an increase in the number of goods sold, albeit at a reduced price.
- The operating profit has also decreased by £4,000 (although expenses decreased by £8,000).
- The fall in expenses may be because fewer machines were bought, as sales may have been expected to rise in 2008, and therefore additional overheads were incurred in 2007.
- Interest payable may support the point above. The need to borrow may have fallen, or some of the previous loans have been paid in full. Alternatively, the rate of interest may have fallen, but it is less likely that the amount paid in interest would fall if on a fixed-interest loan repayment.
- The retained profit is the same, possibly because the dividend paid has decreased (although the amount of tax paid could have decreased).

Be careful when assessing what has happened without the actual facts. Although tax and dividends are down, it is impossible to state clearly why this is the case. It is a good idea to offer possible reasons for the changes, which may include:

- less profit made and therefore less tax to be paid
- a fall in the rate of corporation tax
- a reduction in the amount of dividend paid to shareholders as a result of falling profits.

Examiner's voice

- It is important to ensure that you comment on P&L accounts in the context of the case information. Is the business new or well-established? The level of profit could vary according to the age of the business. Similarly, the level of profit could be affected by the nature of the product or service, and how competitive is the market in which the business is operating. A new business is more likely to want purely to survive, rather than expect to make a huge profit.

- A good student will try to evaluate and suggest the most likely reasons for the changes in the figures, with justification from the case study.

- If the case study states that the business is hoping to expand, then it is quite possible that the level of profit in the short term may be low, due to the cost of expansion. In the long run, profits will be higher, once the benefits of the expansion (assuming it is successful) have managed to increase production and therefore profits.

- For a pre-issued case study that includes a P&L account, much information can be gained from the figures. Ratios can be calculated, or trends established and measured against the objectives set by the business.

The value of P&L accounts

1. The P&L enables the business to make decisions. Being able to see the amount of profit made may affect any decisions on future expenditure.

2. Management can use the P&L to monitor the progress of the business in terms of targets. It allows comparisons to be made between financial years.

3. The figures can be used to calculate particular ratios to help assess the performance of the business.

4. It can help the business in formulating its objectives for the future.

5. A healthy profit may encourage a business to buy back shares from the shareholders. It may also encourage expansion plans.

6. It provides other stakeholders with valuable information. A bank may be interested to note the amount of profit a business has made in order to assess the amount of risk involved, and therefore help it decide whether to lend money to the business.

7. Investors will look to see whether they should invest their money in the business. A profitable business is more likely to attract further investors.

8. The Inland Revenue will be able to see that the correct amount of tax is paid.

9. The employees are able to see how much profit the business made, and therefore note whether the business is in a strong position to increase their wages and salaries.

10. It is a legal requirement to maintain and publish financial records for certain types of business (the Companies Act).

11. Suppliers may want to see the P&L as evidence of an ability to pay for materials supplied.

Key Terms

Gross profit: Sales revenue – cost of sales
Operating profit: Gross profit – fixed costs
Net profit: Operating profit – interest paid
Retained profit: Net profit – tax and dividends

Further Sources

Company Reports, which are available from the FT www.ftannualreports.com

Your Turn

Questions Time allowed 20 minutes

1. If the sales revenue for 'Shirts 4 all' in 2008 was £158,000 and the costs of sales was £69,000, calculate the gross profit. (2 marks)

2. What is the difference between gross profit and operating profit? (4 marks)

3. Outline three ways in which the P&L may be useful to external stakeholders. (6 marks)

4. Explain two ways in which internal stakeholders would be affected by a fall in the level of profit made by a company. (4 marks)

(16 marks)

Case Study Time allowed 45 minutes

Comfort Cruises

The P&L account for Comfort Cruises showed that revenues were up over 20% to nearly £10.3m. Felix

Wang, the Chairman of Comfort Cruises, stated, 'These results show the continuing success of our cruise business. Our ships are delivering the service which our customers crave.'

	Oct 2008 in £s	Sept 2007 in £s
Revenue	10,290,000	8,432,954
Cost of sales	5,890,875	4,150,746
Gross profit	4,399,125	4,282,208
Operating expenses	2,225,600	2,855,669
Other expenses*	55,000	84,029
Operating profit	2,118,525	1,342,510
Interest payable	55,724	64,334
Interest received	2,623	1,975
Profit before tax	2,065,424	1,280,151
Tax	717,921	496,689
Net profit	1,347,503	783,462

*additional expenses to include retraining programme to comply with maritime legislation

Table 16.3 Profit and Loss account for Comfort Cruises, year ended 31 October 2008

1. Using Table 16.3, calculate the percentage increase in net profit from 2007 to 2008.
   (3 marks)

2. Explain which stakeholders will benefit from the results in the P&L account shown in Table 16.3.
   (5 marks)

3. To what extent should Felix Wang be pleased with the results shown in the P&L account? (12 marks)

   (20 marks)

BALANCE SHEETS

A balance sheet is a statement about the value of a business at a given point in time, showing what it owns (assets) and what it owes (liabilities). All private and public companies issue balance sheets for their shareholders.

The balance sheet is normally headed: 'Balance sheet for (the name of the business/company), year ending (or 'as at') (insert date).'

Assets

Assets are what the business owns. Assets are a positive number on the balance sheet.

Fixed assets

A fixed asset may be the factory or buildings owned by the business. It also includes the fixtures and fittings of the business, such as the machines and equipment used. These are the assets that are necessary to enable the business to function. It is important to realise that the business can only count what it actually owns; rented facilities are not owned and therefore would not be counted.

Tangible assets

These are assets which can be seen. The factory and machines will be both fixed and a tangible fixed assets.

Intangible assets

These assets are not visible, such as a patent or the good will of the business, a value for its reputation or a good brand name.

It is very difficult to put an accurate value on intangible assets. The better known a business, the more likely that its intangible assets (good will) will be higher.

It will of course depend upon the 'health' of the business, as a business may be well-known for negative reasons!

Goodwill may only be specifically mentioned if the business is involved in a takeover or merger.

Prudence

This is an accounting phrase, to indicate that there is a need to be cautious when valuing a business. Overestimating the value of a business is inappropriate, and hence to gain a realistic value of the fixed assets, depreciation needs to be considered.

Depreciation

Depreciation is an allowance for the wear and tear on the fixed tangible assets. As the factory and machines age, their value decreases. Depreciation reflects this, usually as a percentage of the assets, to give a realistic value of the business.

Financial fixed assets

Occasionally the balance sheet refers to investments that are made by the business in government bonds. Investing in long-term bonds or shares is considered as a fixed asset.

Current assets

Current assets describe everything owned by the business which is not a fixed asset. These assets are capable of being converted into cash within the accounting period. The easier these assets can be converted into cash, the better. (This ability to convert assets into cash is known as liquidity).

Cash

Money is obviously the most liquid of the current assets, as it is already cash.

Stock

Stock can be in the form of materials, unfinished goods (work in progress) and finished goods. The liquidity of stock very much depends upon the type of stock.

- Finished goods are usually easier to convert into cash.
- However, raw materials may also be converted into cash if there is a market for such materials.
- The least liquid type of stock is unfinished goods, which are neither raw materials nor finished goods and therefore of little value to anyone until finished.
- Finished goods themselves will vary in terms of their liquidity. Perishable goods with a short shelf-life will be less liquid than goods with a longer shelf-life. The latter has a better chance of being sold and subsequently generating cash.
- FMCGs (fast moving consumer goods) are more liquid than other goods as there is a frequent and regular demand for such products.

Debtors

This category includes money that is owed to the business. Assuming that the debts owed to the business are due for payment within one year, they are counted as a current asset.

As for the stock, the liquidity of debtors will depend upon how quickly the debt is due to be paid, and the likelihood of the debt actually being paid.

The business may offer a period of credit, either 30 or 60 days, in which goods have to be paid for. (Any period can be offered. Offering a business time to pay is often used as a marketing incentive in order to gain business.)

Examiner's voice

It is important not to become confused between debtors (those that owe the business) and when a business offers credit. If a business offers credit to another business, the latter will become a debtor of the former. For example: Business A offers a credit facility to business B to pay for goods in 30 days time. Business A will have debtors (business B).

Liabilities

Liabilities are what the business owes. They are a negative on the balance sheet.

Current liabilities

Current liabilities are negatives on the balance sheet. They describe what is owed by the business and due for repayment within one year. They may consist of overdrafts and short-term loans.

Overdraft

An overdraft is an agreement with the bank to borrow money to avoid cashflow problems. Overdrafts may be used when a payment needs to be made and sufficient funds are not available until days or months later. An overdraft may be for anything from one day to just under a year.

The amount to be borrowed will vary according to the needs of the business. There is usually an agreement to borrow up to an agreed amount.

Short-term loan

This is a loan for a fixed amount over a fixed period of time, less than one year.

Creditors

Creditors are the opposite of debtors. They refer to other businesses (suppliers) who have not yet been paid. The business has received raw materials or components but does not have to pay until an agreed time.

Net current assets (working capital)

To calculate the net current assets, or working capital, subtract current liabilities from current assets.

Long-term liabilities

These are loans for more than one year. They can be in various forms.

1. Mortgage: associated with the buying of property.

2. Debenture: only issued by a company that is a plc. A debenture is a long-term loan with a fixed rate of interest.

3. Bank loan: a loan of more than one year.

Net assets

To calculate the net assets, add the value of the net current assets to the fixed assets, minus long-term liabilities. This figure reflects the value of the business at a given point in time.

Capital employed or shareholders' funds

This is the value of funds tied up in the business, in the form of shares and retained profits. The shareholders' funds may have arisen from different types of shares issued.

Ordinary shares

These are the shares that show an ownership of the business. Each share allows the holder a vote at the annual general meeting (AGM) of the business. The value of these shares may change, reflecting the well-being of the business. (However, the amount is fixed in the balance sheet).

Preference shares

Preference shares have priority (preference) over ordinary shares when the profits are distributed. The share of the profit is usually based on a fixed percentage rather than the size of the dividend declared, as is the case for ordinary shares.

Reserves

This refers to money that has been retained in the business in order to help it grow, rather than being distributed to the shareholders. It represents money that has been ploughed back into the business.

It is NOT cash, as cash appears as an asset under current assets.

Reserves are a balancing item to show that when a business increases its assets, some of the profit that did not go to shareholders has been invested in the business.

Examiner's voice

The presentation of your figures is vital; the use of columns should help you make the right additions and subtractions, and therefore gain the right answer.

Reading the balance sheet

The balance sheet will balance in terms of the calculations.

- Net assets (what the business owns) will always be equal to (balanced by) the shareholders' funds (which are sometimes written as 'financed by'), also referred to as the source of funds.
- For negative amounts (money that is owed), the figure is often shown in brackets. This makes it easier for you to remember that the figure is negative and needs to be subtracted to gain a realistic value of the business.

Looking at the balance sheet for Pods Galore Ltd, much information can be gained about the value of the business.

- The owner may want to state that he or she owns a shop, which is worth £120,000. However, because the shop is quite old and some of the fixtures are in need of replacing, the true value is less than this. Depreciation takes into account this ageing factor.
- The current assets of the business total £47,000. This does not mean that the owners spend this amount of money, even though this represents assets.
- Some of the £47,000 is tied up in stock (£30,000), which may or may not be sold soon. (A business selling food may have a lot of current assets tied up in stock that will not sell, perhaps due to the sell-by-date being reached.) In this business, the stock of i-pods may be out of date in terms of the latest versions/technology.
- Debtors represent some of the current assets. This is money that is owed to the business. However, it is not certain that this money will be paid to Pods Galore.
- Even after noting these points, there are current liabilities to be taken into account. Liabilities represent money that is owed by the business, in this case, £9,000.

As a consequence, the true value of Pods Galore's net current assets is £38,000 (assuming stock can be sold and that debtors will pay.)

To gain a more realistic value of the business, any long-term liabilities (money that is owed for more than one year) has to be taken into consideration. For Pods Galore Ltd, the actual value of the business is £71,000.

	Values and calculations in £	Running totals, in £	Comments/calculations
Fixed assets	120,000		
Less depreciation (10%)	12,000		(10% of 120,000 = 12,000) 120,000 – 12,000 = 108,000
		108,000	
Current assets			
Debtors	15,000		
Stock	30,000		
Cash	2,000		
Total current assets		47,000	(Adding cash, stock and debtors)
Current liabilities			
Overdraft	9,000		Overdraft is the only current liability stated
Total current liabilities		9,000	
Net current assets		38,000	(Current assets – current liabilities) 47,000 – 9,000
Long-term liabilities	75,000		
Net assets		71,000	(Fixed assets + net current assets – long-term liabilities) 108,000 + 38,000 – 75,000 = 71,000
Shareholders' funds*			
Ordinary share capital	50,000		
Retained profit	21,000		These amounts should balance (be equal to) the net assets.
		71,000	

Table 17.1 Balance sheet for Pods Galore Ltd, year ending 31 December 2008

This is calculated by adding the assets and deducting the liabilities:

Fixed assets (after depreciation)	108,000
Net current assets	38,000
(Current assets – current liabilities)	47,000 – 9,000
Minus long-term liabilities	75,000
Net assets	**71,000**

How useful is a balance sheet?

It is important to be able to look at a balance sheet and understand what is being stated. Do the figures make sense for this type of business selling this particular product? As the business is Pods Galore Ltd, a small retail outlet selling i-pods and similar equipment, the figures appear realistic. However, the make-up of the assets may vary depending on the type of business. A large supermarket chain store such as Tesco would have a high proportion of its current assets in stock and cash, whereas a furniture chain store such as DFS, which is often promoting its products with tempting offers of 'buy now pay later with three years' interest free credit', will have much less in stock (products are made to order) and a high proportion of debtors.

The balance sheet will be helpful if a business wanted to obtain a loan from a bank. By looking at the balance sheet, the bank would be able to assess if the business had sufficient assets that could be used for security against the loan.

The balance sheet is also helpful to a business, as it can assess if it has enough cash to keep itself afloat. By looking at the current assets and liabilities, it can calculate its net current assets to see if it has enough cash (working capital) to keep the business going. All businesses need money on a day-to-day basis to be able to buy raw materials, and pay bills and wages.

The balance sheet also provides a lot of information which can be used to calculate several ratios (see Units 20–24).

Interpretation of the balance sheet

In summary, it is always important to avoid just looking at the figures! Although it is necessary to look at the components of a balance sheet in the first place, to interpret an actual balance sheet requires an overview. It is tempting to look at the figures and reach a conclusion as to the value of the business at a particular moment in time. However, it ought to be looked at in the context of the business, its objectives and its business environment.

Key Terms

Balance sheet: A method of recording the value or wealth of a business at a given moment in time.
Assets: What the business owns.
Liabilities: What the business owes.
Current liabilities: Debts due for payment in less than one year.
Long-term liabilities: Money that is owed for more than one year.
Liquidity: The ability to convert assets into cash.

Further Sources

Company reports from the Financial Times.

Questions

Your Turn

Time allowed 20 minutes

1. From the list below, state whether each item is an asset or a liability. (You may want to say which category it belongs to, e.g. cash = asset (current asset).)

   A. debtors

   B. overdraft

   C. loan for three years

   D. machines. (4 marks)

2. State how to calculate net current assets (2 marks)

3. The figures in Table 17.2 are part of a balance sheet for two retail outlets. Comment on the figures. (6 marks)

Current assets (£000)	Business A	Business B
Cash	130	15
Stock	580	110
Debtors	15	600

Table 17.2 Balance sheet for two retail outlets

4. Using the information in Table 17.3, calculate the following:

   A. net current assets

   B. net assets

   State how you know that your answer for b) is correct. (8 marks)

Fixed assets			275
Current assets			
Debtors			45
Stock			120
Cash			15
Current liabilities			
Creditors			65
Net current assets			
Net assets			
Shareholders funds			390

Table 17.3 Balance sheet for Juicy Fruit Lollies Ltd, as at 31 March 2009 (£000)

(20 marks)

Case Study

Time allowed 40 minutes

Hudsons Ltd

The Staffordshire garage, Hudsons Ltd, has decided to expand its sales rooms in order to display more cars, both new and second-hand. At present it has only a small indoor showroom area, which can house three cars. There are many second-hand cars on display on the extensive forecourt of the garage. The planned extension would allow Hudsons to display three times as many cars and provide room for a comfortable sales office with a seating area and drinks facilities for prospective customers.

The cost of the extension is about £150,000. The shareholders of the company are unwilling to finance this extension plan, having recently financed a very successful new workshop for the repair and servicing of cars.

In order to gain the necessary finance, Hudsons' finance director has provided the bank with its most recent balance sheet (Table 17.4). 'We need to remain competitive,' said Ian, the managing director, 'The bank manager will take one look at our balance sheet and lend us the money without hesitation.'

Fixed assets	700
Less depreciation (10%)	70
Current assets	
Debtors	25
Stock	315
Cash	40
Current liabilities	75
Net current assets	
Long-term liabilities	110
Net assets	

Table 17.4 Balance for Hudsons Ltd as at 31 March 2009, in £000s

1. Calculate net assets. (4 marks)

2. Using the balance sheet, suggest whether the bank manager will be prepared to lend Hudsons the money it requires for the extension. (9 marks)

3. Other than the balance sheet, evaluate factors that are likely to affect whether Hudsons should borrow the £120,000 to build the proposed extension. (18 marks)

(31 marks)

CASHFLOW

The significance of cashflow

Cashflow is the blood of the business, and is essential if the business is to survive. Cash is constantly moving through and around the business. It comes into the business as a result of sales and borrowing (inflows), and leaves the business to pay for materials, labour, marketing, interest payments on loans (outflows).

Without cash, wages cannot be paid, loans cannot be repaid and raw materials cannot be bought. Without all of these inputs, there will be no business!

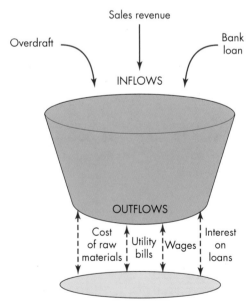

Figure 18.1 Cashflows

Unfortunately, for many businesses, the outflows occur before the inflows are received and consequently the business fails. Both large and small businesses can run out of cash and subsequently go into liquidation. For example:

- **Car manufacturers running out of cash:** In 2008 some of the largest car manufacturers suffered severe cashflow problems as the demand for cars fell drastically. General Motors of the United States and its UK Vauxhall plants at Luton and Ellesmere Port were in serious danger of collapse as cash was running out.
- **Woolworths' cash crisis:** The business announced it was to go into administration with debts of £385 millon in 2008. As early as January 2007, Woolworths had a cash crisis, when it asked its 700 suppliers for cash! The suggestion was that a small percentage of the suppliers' contract money would be deducted to help Woolworths to fund its previous investments.
- **MFI:** At the same time as Woolworths's problems, MFI was heading for administration. It too had run into a cash crisis. MFI had asked its landlords for a rent-free period in order to reduce its cash crisis. However, with falling sales, such action on its costs was not enough to avoid administration.

Cashflow forecasts

Cashflow forecasts are estimates of the likely inflows and outflows of cash into and out of the business, over a given period of time. The forecast shows the amounts of cash that will flow in and out, and in addition, the likely timing of such inflows and outflows. The timings of cash movements are just as important as the actual amounts.

For many businesses, it is not the amount of cash that creates the problems but the timings of the movements of cash. In many instances, the outflows will not only occur before the inflows, but there may be a significant period of time between the two that has to be managed and covered.

Reasons for cashflow forecasts

1. Preparing a cashflow forecast is a valuable planning procedure. It allows the business to put into place strategies to deal with any forecasted negative cashflow, such as organising a loan or an extension to its overdraft facilities.

2. Similarly, the forecast is useful for helping the business to set its prices.

3. The level of payment terms can be assessed or fixed to take account of any forecasted problems. A business will often alter its payment periods to its suppliers and the discount rate it offers to its customers, for prompt payment in order to help alleviate any cashflow problems.

4. If the forecasted sales revenue is low, the marketing team may consider promotional pricing in order to boost sales revenue.

5. Cashflow forecasts are looked at by potential investors. Venture capitalists and potential shareholders will be interested in the figures in order to assess its likelihood of success.

6. Suppliers may want to see such figures to assess if the business will be able to pay for the supplies on time.

7. The managers of the business will use the cashflow information to monitor the business and react accordingly.

The figures for the cashflow forecasts and statements are usually shown for each month of the year. This is because it will allow the business to see its cashflows throughout all the trading period. There may be seasonal variations in sales, and certain costs are paid quarterly and not monthly. It is therefore more accurate and reliable to show forecasts for all months.

Examiner's voice

This chapter assumes that you will draw on your knowledge of cashflow from the AS modules.

Item		January	February	March	April	May	June
Opening balance	**A**	0 **H**	(1,500)	(22,700)	(21,600)	2,000	28,600
Sales revenue		500 **J**	1,200	15,000	36,000	44,000	48,000 **M**
Bank loan	**B**	20,000	0	0	0	0	0
Total inflows	**C**	**20,500**	**(300)**	**(7,700)**	**14,400**	**46,000**	**76,600**
Raw materials		20,000 **K**	20,000	10,000	10,000	15,000	20,000
Wages		2,000	2,000	2,000	2,000	2,000	2,000
Utilities	**D**	0	0	1,500	0		1,700
Interest + repayments on loan			400	400	400	400	400
Total outflows	**E**	22,000	22,400	13,900	12,400	17,400	24,100
Net cash inflow	**F**	(1,500) **L**	(22,700)	(21,600)	2,000	28,600	52,500
Closing balance	**G**	(1,500)	(22,700)	(21,600)	2,000	28,600	52,500 **N**

Table 18.1 Cashflow forecast for ABC Ltd 2008, in £s

Examiner's voice

The presentation of cashflow forecasts will vary, but the fundamental elements of inflows, outflows and net cash inflows remain the same.

As for all calculations, as long as what you have done is clear to the examiner, marks can be allocated even if you make mistakes with the actual calculations.

Notes for guidance

- **A** Opening balance: there is a need to ascertain if the January figure is the first ever month of the business trading, or if it is just the first month of a new forecast. If it is the latter, it is more likely to be a more accurate forecast. The opening balance may include a positive cashflow for the previous month's closing balance, or it may take account of a loan.
- **B** Bank loan: there may also be a separate entry for an overdraft. Whatever is stated, it is important to remember that although the loan is a positive flow (an inflow), there will need to be outflows to pay back the loan with interest payments.
- **C** Total inflows: this is simply the addition of all inflows into the business (positive).
- **D** Utilities: this includes costs for gas, electricity, telephones and water. It is important to note that in some instances such bills are paid quarterly (every three months).
- **E** Total outflows: this is simply the aggregate of all the outflows (negative).
- **F** Net cash inflow: cash inflows – cash outflows.
- **G** Closing balance: the final figure (net cashflow + or –) that will be carried forward as the opening balance for the next month.
- **H** As the figure is 0, this shows that the business started with nothing and then gained a bank loan.
- **J** To gain sales revenue in the first month may be noteworthy; is it likely? Consideration of the actual product would be needed to comment on this.
- **K** It could be argued that the stock purchases are excessive. Too much money is tied up in stock, which will contribute to the negative cashflow.
- **L** The brackets indicate a negative cashflow, which could allow the business to cover the shortfall with an overdraft. The negative cashflow is set to continue into March and therefore will need to be addressed if wages are to be paid.

- **M** Sales revenue is set to continue growing throughout the first six months, but the rate of increase starts to decrease.
- **N** The comparatively large positive cashflow in June may suggest that there is more than enough cash in the business, and that some of it could be used to pay off the loan early or pay for further marketing or expansion.

Interpreting the data

Using Table 18.1:

1. Only the first six months of the year have been given. If the product or service is seasonal, these particular months will not necessarily show a true picture of the cashflows of the business.

2. It does not give any indication of how long the business has been trading, though the opening balance clearly suggests it has just started. The level of sales revenue compounds this.

3. The source of the sales revenue is just a total and gives no indication of whether it is from one or several products.

4. It is important to note although sales may be agreed, they should not be counted until payment is received.

5. The type of business is not given and therefore it may be difficult to judge the significance of the cashflow forecast.

6. There is no indication of what is happening to prices (inflation) within the period for the forecast. (In 2008 the rapid increase and decrease in oil process would have had a significant effect upon the accuracy of the forecast.)

Examiner's voice

Interpretation of cashflow forecasts and cashflow statements is a useful skill. Evidence of trends will be helpful, but the interpretation needs to be undertaken with care.

Extracts from cashflow statements

Example 1

	January	February	March	April	May	June
Sales revenue in £	200,000	180,000	130,000	80,000	30,000	10,000

Example 1 shows a falling level of sales revenue. It may be tempting to suggest that the business ought to think of ways to increase its cash inflows or reduce its outflows to compensate for the falling inflows. However, it would be more sensible to find out the reason for the apparent fall in revenues. If the sales were for ski holidays, then a fall would be expected as the table shows a change in the seasons.

Example 2 Extract from a cashflow statement

	January	February	March	April	May	June
Sales revenue in £	200,000	180,000	130,000	80,000	30,000	10,000

Example 2 also shows declining sales revenue. However, reasons for the declining cash inflows are different and therefore will need a different interpretation and response. In this example, the business is faced with the recession and therefore the declining sales revenue is due to a lack of demand and not necessarily because of a fault within the business. If the business is involved with the selling of a luxury product, it will be more likely to feel the effects of a recession than if it was selling a necessity product. In this instance, the business may need to address the problem and take action to improve the revenue, which will in turn improve the cash inflow for the business.

Example 3 Extract from a cashflow statement

	January	February	March	April	May	June
Sales revenue in £	200,000	180,000	130,000	80,000	30,000	10,000

Example 3 again shows a declining level of sales revenue (cash inflow). In this instance, the business is actually in decline and may have genuine liquidity problems as a result of the declining sales. The competition has superior products and therefore drastic action may need to be taken.

Examiner's voice

It is important to realise that only the sales revenue has been shown in these three examples. The outflows would need to be considered before any action could be decided upon.

Limitations of cashflow forecasts

Changes to the interest rate

Circumstances within the business environment can change very quickly. Not many people would have been able to forecast the fall in interest rates that took place at the latter end of 2008. The Bank of England had previously changed interest rates modestly, usually by only half of one per cent at any one time. However, in November 2008, in response to the effects of the credit crunch and in an attempt to stimulate the economy, rates were cut by 1.5%. This was followed by a further 1% cut in December, bringing interest rates to a 59-year low of just 2%. No cashflow forecast would be able to assume that such cuts would be made, or assume the likely outcomes of such drastic cuts.

The consequences of such low interest rates for businesses could mean a much lower level of costs in terms of repayments on overdrafts and loans. However, it is quite likely that the interest on loans will have been fixed when the loan was taken out.

Changes in economic policy

Being able to predict economic policy has always been difficult for businesses. What the government decides to introduce in its annual budget can have a significant effect on cashflow forecasts. Increases in taxation and national insurance contributions all affect the disposable income of consumers and therefore their ability to purchase products. Consequently, sales revenue forecasts can swiftly appear too optimistic or pessimistic.

It was not expected that the government would reduce VAT by 2.5% to 15% in December 2008 in order to help stimulate the economy.

Changes in the economic climate

The economic climate can affect a business very quickly. The massive fall in the FTSE during 2008 meant that the value of many businesses fell significantly overnight. Although such changes in the value of shares may not affect the cashflow of a business immediately, in time the effects may show when sales fall, or a business may have to pay a higher rate of interest because its asset values have fallen, making a loan more of a risk.

- The housing slump meant that home furniture businesses such as MFI suffered huge falls in sales, as there were fewer people moving home.
- As a result of the economic slowdown, car manufacturers Honda announced in November 2008 that its Swindon factory was to shut for two months in 2009. No cars were to be made in February and March 2009, to avoid excess production. In addition to the poor economic climate in the UK, Honda was hit badly by the downturn in Russia. The Swindon factory exports a high percentage of its output and has suffered from a change in demand at home and abroad. Any cashflow forecast could not have gauged the severity of the fall in demand for its cars.
- Huge fluctuations in the price of a barrel of oil made forecasting costs for businesses using large amounts of fuel almost impossible. In 2008, a barrel of oil rose to nearly $150. By the end of 2008, it was selling at less than $50 a barrel. The knock-on effect on the cost of petrol, gas and electricity made cashflow forecasts very difficult.

Forecasts are estimates

If a new business is putting together its first cashflow forecast, much of the forecast will be based on assumptions, guesswork and objectives, but with no certainty as to how potential consumers will respond in purchasing its products. The sales revenue forecasts are therefore at best 'guestimates!' The time of the year in which the business is launched will influence the forecast. The main sales period for many businesses is linked to Christmas and therefore the forecast for sales may be higher for this period.

Forecasting seasonal demand

Gauging demand for seasonal products is difficult. The sales of ice cream, soft drinks, alcohol and barbecues are all examples of goods that are dependent upon the weather in the UK. The summer weather of 2008 was poor and subsequently sales revenue for many drinks businesses was much lower than their predictions.

World events

World events can have a dramatic effect on cashflow forecasts: e.g. earthquakes, floods, plane crashes, terrorist attacks (such as on the World Trade Centre on 11 September 2001). All of these events can and have greatly affected sales revenues. In 2001, additional expenditure was necessary to restore consumer confidence in travelling by aeroplane, and therefore costs forecasts were inaccurate as well as the expected revenues.

Competitors' behaviour

How competitors act and react can also have an effect on the accuracy of any cashflow forecast. If competitors reduce their prices, this may affect the sales revenue of another business. A business may respond to competitor price changes with its own price changes, which in turn affect its sales revenue. To what extent sales revenue will be affected will depend upon the elasticity of the product or service and the degree of competition within the market.

Changes in technology

Changes in technology may affect sales revenue and costs. Competitors may launch a technologically superior product which makes the business's products inferior and therefore leads to a rapid fall in sales revenue. The business may need to respond by launching its own updated product in order to compete, resulting in higher investment costs and marketing costs to compete in the market place.

Given the large number of variables, the accuracy of any cashflow forecast is always in doubt. However, that does not mean that it is worthless as a decision-making tool or a planning tool. On the contrary, planning can help alleviate problems in the future.

Cashflow statements

To have a positive cashflow immediately is unusual but certainly not impossible, especially if the cashflow forecast has been considered carefully. It should be noted that the level of raw materials purchased has been reduced (when compared to the forecast), to avoid having a negative cashflow. However, gaining payment for goods sold in the first month should indicate that there was no 'debtor allowance' to its customers. This may also indicate the type of business and products that are being sold.

Item	January	February	March	April	May	June
Opening balance	0	3,000	(13,000)	(4,600)	14,900	32,200
Sales revenue	500	1,000	12,000	32,000	40,000	43,000
Bank loan	20,000	0	0	0	0	0
Short-term loan			10,000	0	0	0
Total inflows	20,500	4,000	9,000	27,400	54,900	75,200
Raw materials	15,000	15,000	10,000	10,000	15,000	16,000
Wages	2,000	2,000	2,000	2,000	2,000	2,200
Utilities	500	0	1,600	0		1,900
Interest + repayments				500	700	700
Total outflows	17,500	17,000	13,600	12,500	17,700	20,800
Net cash inflow	3,000	(13,000)	(4,600)	14,900	32,200	54,400
Closing balance	**3,000**	**(13,000)**	**(4,600)**	**14,900**	**32,200**	**54,400**

Table 18.2 Cashflow statement for ABC Ltd 2008

By February, there is a negative cashflow which requires an overdraft to cover the cost of purchases. There is some overestimation of sales, but nevertheless a positive cashflow soon follows in April.

For many businesses, the likelihood of a negative cashflow is more likely, and can be a serious issue.

Causes of cashflow problems

Level of sales

If a sudden fall in the level of sales revenue coincides with a heavy period of payments that are due, a negative cashflow may be inevitable.

Business environment

A change in the business environment caused by a range of factors such as ethical issues or new legislation, may lead to a fall in sales and an increase in costs. In December 2008, Stansted airport was 'invaded' by environmental protesters who chained themselves to the perimeter fences of the airport. As a result, over 50 flights were cancelled. This caused a huge loss of revenue for the airlines and the airport itself, as planes were not landing or taking off. Costs were incurred by the airlines that had to arrange accommodation for some of its passengers, reschedule flights and move aircrews to new rotas.

Changes in health and safety legislation may lead to additional costs for businesses, who have to implement the new laws and may face additional costs of safety equipment and further training for its employees.

Excess stock

Holding too much stock is a cost burden. If a large amount of stock in the form of raw materials, work-in-progress or finished goods are held in the factory, costs have been incurred without revenue being received. This in itself is a negative cashflow. The raw materials may have been paid for, wages will have been paid and the finished goods are costing money to be stored. All of these costs mean that the outflows will be considerable, but as yet, there are no inflows. This is one of the reasons why many businesses have adopted the just-in-time system of production (JIT), in order to reduce stock levels and therefore the amount of cash outflows.

Late payments from debtors

Any delay in payments by the debtors of a business will have a negative effect on the cashflow. Sales revenue is the lifeblood of the business and therefore debtors should be encouraged to pay on time. Unfortunately, offering delays to such payments is often used as a marketing ploy by businesses to gain trade. This is a classic example of where different departments of a business will have differing views on required strategies.

The marketing department will regard offering late payments to its creditors as a viable incentive, while the finance department will require payment as soon as possible.

Paying creditors too quickly

In some ways it is better to delay payment to the creditors of the business. However, there may be a delay in receiving attention to problems with supplies if payment to the suppliers (creditors) is delayed. It is therefore a balancing act between not paying immediately and keeping cash within the business, and ensuring that the relationship between the business and its suppliers is not damaged. If additional materials are required at short notice to satisfy an additional order, the business will want the supplier to help immediately. Being a 'prompt payer' may mean the business will be viewed as a preferential customer and gain an efficient service.

This is another example of a possible confrontation between departments within a business. The accounts department will want to delay payment, while the production department will want suppliers to be paid promptly to maintain a punctual supply of materials.

Over-trading

When a business grows very quickly, its need to buy materials and increase its productive capacity puts a strain on the cashflow of the business. The cost of such expansion is often greater than the present level of sales, and therefore there is a negative cashflow.

Holding the right amount of cash

There is no right amount of cash that should be held by a business. It will depend upon the nature of the business.

For example:

- Business A (a supermarket) will receive large amounts of cash because it is selling food, and a large

number of customers pay by cash. (It is not intended to suggest that 'cash' can only be notes and coins, but the use of debit and credit cards delays the actual flow of money into the business.)
- Business B (a restaurant) will have less cash than a supermarket, but after an evening's takings may have a large amount of cash. It is also likely that many of its staff will be paid in cash.
- Business C (a local garage repairing cars) may have little cash, as the number of customers may not be high.
- Business D (a money lender) will of course have a very high level of cash, as this is the 'product' of the business!

Examiner's voice

It is essential that all cashflow forecasts and statements are viewed with care and the type of business noted.

Liquidity ratios

(See Unit 20.) The use of liquidity ratios such as current ratio and acid test are simple ways to assess the level of cash within a business.

Too little cash

1. This creates an inability to meet creditor's requests for payment. Terms of purchase may be less favourable in the future. It may also mean that it becomes difficult to buy stock or raw materials. For some creditors, such as the bank, the consequences of not paying could be much more serious, as any loans may then be foreclosed.

2. A lack of cash may mean that additional funds will need to be borrowed from the bank, possibly at higher rates of interest.

Too much cash

1. There is a wasted opportunity to purchase more stock.

2. There may be a loss of interest if the excess cash was put into an account.

3. Any borrowing costs are being paid unnecessarily as the excess cash could be used to reduce debts.

Improving the cashflow of the business

Increase sales

This is easier said than done, especially in periods of an economic downturn. There may also be financial implications of gaining increased sales.

In the short term, there will be additional cash outflows to pay for the marketing needed to increase sales. The increased sales may only be achieved by reducing the price and therefore, although inflows will increase, the aggregate amount of revenue will not.

Reduce stock levels by selling off stock or buying less stock

The utilisation of JIT will reduce the level of stock held, though the same amount of stock has to be paid for at some stage. By holding less stock, the cost of storage and the time gap between the usage of stock and the sales revenue may be reduced.

Factoring

Factoring is the 'selling' of the debts of a business. It allows for revenue from debtors to be received earlier, although there is a 'price to pay'. The factoring company will take a proportion of the value of the debt as payment.

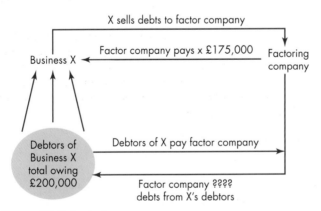

Figure 18.2 Factoring

In Figure 18.2, Business X has several debtors. If there is likely to be a delay in these debts being paid, X can sell the collective debt to a factor company.

The factor company will pay X a proportion of the total debt (£175,000 of the £200,000) immediately. X is satisfied as it will gain an injection of cash (£175,000) although it has had to 'lose' £25,000 of the debt in the form of a fee.

The factor or factoring company will now own the debt and be entitled to collect the money from the debtors.

Business X has to decide if the greater benefit is to have the majority of what it is owed immediately and pay a percentage of the debt to gain the cash now; or collect all of the outstanding debt (£200,000) at some time in the future.

The main criteria for deciding what to do will probably depend upon how much X needs the cash.

Leasing not buying

This is a form of borrowing. It is similar to renting in that ownership is not gained, but usage is exclusive during the period of the lease agreement.

The amount of cash required is obviously much less, and the cash paid out is spread over the period of the leasing agreement. Consequently, a large amount of cash is not needed, as it would be if payment for the machine was made immediately.

Loans

Although a loan allows a business to stagger the repayments over a given period of time, in the long run it is more costly because of the interest that has to be paid. However, a loan means that a large amount of capital is not required in one sum to pay for the required machine or building.

Changing creditor and debtor days

To improve the liquidity of a business, the number of debtors could be reduced. If the business no longer offered its customers time to pay for the products supplied, cash would flow into the business much sooner. However, the level of sales and therefore the amount of cash could fall, as the customers are reliant on a delayed payment.

Alternatively, the amount of time offered to customers could be reduced, to shorten the period between sales and the cash being paid. However, the marketing department may not be prepared to lose an effective promotional tool.

Creditor days could be increased. Delaying payment to creditors will allow cash to remain within the business for a longer period of time, and may mean that less cash is needed to cover any subsequent negative cashflow.

Examiner's voice

All of the ways to improve the cashflow of a business are appropriate, but some are better strategies than others. It depends upon the actual business involved, its circumstances, its performance over time, and the nature of the market in which it competes. In other words, the context of the case is essential when selecting a method to improve the cashflow of a business.

Cut operating costs

Expensive cash outflows in the short term can be alleviated by outsourcing. It may actually cost more to outsource, but on the other hand there may be an opportunity to reduce overheads and therefore reduce outflows.

Your Turn

Questions Time allowed 30 minutes

1. State three sources of cash inflows (3 marks)

2. State how to calculate net cash inflow (working capital). (2 marks)

3. Analyse two consequences on the cashflow forecast for a business if fuel costs increase and unemployment rises. (9 marks)

4. Explain how a negative cashflow could be improved by changing the creditor days. (4 marks)

5. Explain how factoring could improve the liquidity of a business. (4 marks)

(22 marks)

Case Study Time allowed 40 minutes

The wheel comes off at Wagon in Britain as orders for car parts dry up

The British division of Wagon, the car parts company, become the latest high-profile victim of the crisis gripping the global motor industry when it was put into administration yesterday.

The move puts 500 jobs at risk and there will be immediate cuts at the group's headquarters in Birmingham. However, Zolfe Cooper, the administrators, said they hoped to sell Wagon's factories in Coventry and Walsall as going concerns.

Wagon makes parts for many car makers worldwide, including General Motors, Ford, Honda, Nissan and Land Rover, and it intends to keep its operations outside the UK running as normal. The company, which is controlled by Wilbur Ross, the American billionaire, employs 6,300 people globally.

Wagon has been unable to secure extra funding for its global operation and has hit a liquidity crisis, its administrator said.

Alistair Beveridge, a partner with Zolfe Cooper, which specialises in interim management, blamed the direct state of the global car market for Wagon's demise. He said: "The global automotive sector is battling unprecedented market conditions, which have led many of the major car manufacturers significantly reducing their production schedules. This has had a major adverse impact on customers orders for Wagon and resulted in the liquidity crisis, which has led to the appointment of administrators."

All carmakers are imposing lengthy shutdowns to reduced production as sales plummet. Last week it revealed that UK car sales had slumped by 37 per cent in November, with some brands, such as Land Rover, suffering drops of more than 60 per cent.

Vauxhall, the British division of General Motors, the struggling American carmaker, is the latest to lengthen its Christmas shutdown, doubling it to a month. Mini the BMW-owned brand, is on a month-long closure and next year Honda will stop production for two months.

Wagon caused a sensation in Britain more than three years ago when it pulled the plug on MG Rover refusing to supply parts because it was not being paid. Its move led others to follow suit and the withdrawal of the supply chain hastened the collapse of the independent carmaker.

Source: www.timesonline.co.uk

1. Explain the term 'liquidity'. (4 marks)

2. Analyse two possible reasons why Wagon had cashflow problems. (6 marks)

3. Explain how a business such as Wagon could be making a profit, but would still be facing a liquidity problem. (4 marks)

4. Discuss the possible methods that Wagon could have used to improve its cashflow. (13 marks)

(27 marks)

19 Unit

DEPRECIATION

What is depreciation?

The concept of depreciation allows for the simple fact that a fixed asset will be of less value over time. Machines wear out due to usage, or are replaced by technologically improved versions. Consequently, it is important that the accounts of the business reflect this.

Fixed assets may have a 'life' of several years, but are not worth the same value throughout their lifetime. Depreciation takes this into consideration and spreads the cost of the assets over its lifetime.

Depreciation allows for an element of realism within the accounts of the business. If the business entered the cost of a fixed asset within just one year of its accounts, this expenditure would have a significant effect upon the profit in that year. The profit stated would be below its true figure. However, in the following years the profit of the business would appear inflated because no cost of the asset has been put against revenues. Therefore, spreading the cost of the fixed assets over the life of the asset allows for a more realistic statement of the financial status of the business, in terms of its profits and its value.

The value of fixed assets appears in the balance sheet as a fixed asset, from which is subtracted the depreciation (sometimes written as 'less depreciation'). Depreciation is a cost reduction in the profit and loss account.

Depreciation terminology

Net book value

The net book value of an asset is its cost minus the amounts that have been written off as it wears out (depreciates). By allowing for depreciation, the 'net book value' is calculated.

	2005	**2006**	**2007**	**2008**
Initial cost of machinery	£20,000			
Less depreciation	£5,000	£5,000	£5,000	£5,000
Accumulated depreciation	£5,000	£10,000	£15,000	£20,000
Net book value	£15,000	£10,000	£5,000	£0

Table 19.1 Calculating the net book value

Asset's life

The life of an asset will be affected by:

- the amount of 'wear and tear', which depends upon the level of its usage
- whether or not the product or machine becomes technologically obsolete
- the demand for the product or machine (market obsolescence).

The actual life of an asset will vary considerably, due to the reasons suggested above. The Channel Tunnel was built to last for many decades, while an office photocopier and computer will last for a much shorter period of time. Buildings tend to have a longer life than machines, but for each of these categories of assets there are large variations.

Accumulated depreciation

This is the addition of the depreciation for each year. In Table 19.1, the accumulated depreciation in 2007 is equal to £15,000 (following three years of depreciation of £5,000).

Residual value

The residual value represents the value of the asset at the end of its useful life. It is the estimate of what the asset could be sold at this time.

Historic cost

The initial cost of the asset is calculated as an historic cost, because the actual cost at the time of purchase is used.

Examiner's voice

Questions may refer to the historic cost or the initial cost.

Methods of measuring depreciation

Measuring the depreciating asset may vary. The two main depreciation methods are:

- straight-line, in which an equal amount is taken off the value of the asset on an annual basis; and
- declining balance, where the asset is reduced in value by a constant percentage on an annual basis.

Straight-line method

This is the simplest method of depreciation to calculate and apply. For this reason, it is the method that is used most frequently.

The cost of the asset is equally spread over its life. For example: if a machine that costs £120,000 has an expected or estimated life of 10 years, and a residual value of £20,000, the depreciation for each year would be:

$$\frac{\text{Initial cost} - \text{residual value}}{\text{Life of asset}} = \frac{£120,000 - £20,000}{10}$$

$$= \frac{£100,000}{10} = £10,000$$

As a consequence, the £10,000 would be written off the value of the asset for the ten years of its life. See Table 19.2 for a presentation of this rate of depreciation.

Year	Initial cost in £	Minus depreciation of £10,000 per year	Minus accumulated depreciation	Equals net book value
1	120,000	10,000	10,000	110,000
2		10,000	20,000	100,000
3		10,000	30,000	90,000
4		10,000	40,000	80,000
5		10,000	50,000	70,000
6		10,000	60,000	60,000
7		10,000	70,000	50,000
8		10,000	80,000	40,000
9		10,000	90,000	30,000
10		10,000	100,000	20,000

Table 19.2 Straight-line methods of depreciation

Table 19.2 shows the subtraction of the same amount of depreciation for each year of the asset's estimated life. After 10 years of depreciation, the book value is also the residual value.

Figure 19.1 shows the same information presented in a graph format.

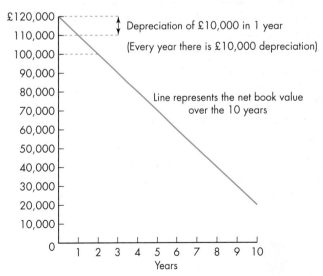

After 10 years, residual value (net book value for yr 10) = £20,000

Figure 19.1 Straight-line depreciation

In Figure 19.1, the rate of depreciation is constant at £10,000 per annum; this is why the depreciation line is a straight line. Each year the asset is depreciated by £10,000.

After one year, £10,000 is the amount of depreciation from the asset that had an initial cost of £120,000 and is therefore 'worth' after that one year, £110,000.

After 10 years, the asset is 'worth' £20,000. Using the straight-line graph it is easy to see the net book value at any time during the life of the asset.

Advantages of straight-line depreciation method

- The amount of depreciation is lower in the first few years.
- By having a lower level of depreciation, there is a higher valuation of the asset on the balance sheet, suggesting that the value of the business is higher.
- Because less is deducted for depreciation, the profit of the business will be higher in the early years of the asset.

Disadvantages of straight-line depreciation method

- An estimate of the residual value is required, which for many assets is difficult to gauge.
- It assumes that the life of the assets is known, which may not be the case.

- Having a lower amount of depreciation in the first few years can be misleading; the value of the business may appear inflated.

Declining balance

The declining balance method of depreciation applies a constant percentage rate of depreciation each year. This is NOT the same as a constant amount (see Table 19.3). Applying this method of depreciation means that a higher amount of depreciation is subtracted from the value of the asset in the early years of its life.

Although a higher amount is more realistic and allows for the fact that in the later years in the life of the asset, additional costs may be incurred to help maintain it and repair possible breakdowns, the declining balance allows the business to spread the costs throughout the life of the asset.

Note that, although the rate of depreciation is constant (20%), the actual amount taken off for depreciation is falling (unlike in the straight-line depreciation method).

It should be clear that the level of depreciation is significantly higher in the first few years when compared to the level of depreciation for the straight-line method

Year	Initial cost	Value after depreciation (net book value)	Minus depreciation of 20% per year	Minus accumulated depreciation	Equals net book value
1	£120,000		24,000	24,000	96,000
2		96,000	19,200	43,200	76,800
3		76,800	15,360	58,560	61,440
4		61,440	12,288	70,848	49,152
5		49,152	9,830	80,678	39,322
6		39,322	7,864	88,542	31,458
7		31,458	6,292	94,834	25,166
8		25,166	5,033	99,867	20,133
9		20,133	4,027	103,893	16,106
10		16,106	3,221	107,114	12,885

(N.B. Some of the figures have been rounded up for simplicity.)

Table 19.3 The declining balance method of depreciation

(£80,678 compared to £50,000 after five years). Figure 19.2 converts the information from Table 19.3 into a graph.

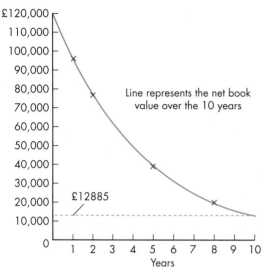

Figure 19.2 Declining balance

The difference between the two methods is demonstrated in Figure 19.2, in the gradient of the graph line which shows the net book value throughout the life of the asset (10 years). For the straight-line method it was literally a straight line because the amount of depreciation is the same. For the declining balance, the gradient is not constant and is much steeper in the early years.

Advantages of declining balance

- This method reflects more realistically the value of assets that lose value significantly in the early years (such as lorries, cars, aeroplanes).
- No estimate of the residual value is required.

Disadvantages of declining balance

- The level of depreciation is higher in the first few years.
- With a higher level of depreciation in the early years, the valuation of the assets is lower on the balance sheet.
- Lower valuation of assets may make it harder to borrow against assets.

Bury College Millennium LRC

Questions Time allowed 30 minutes

1. State two reasons why assets depreciate.
   (2 marks)

2. State which method of depreciation has a constant percentage of depreciation. (1 mark)

3. An asset is bought for £12,000 and has a residual value of 3,000. The life of the asset is expected to be three years. Calculate the rate of depreciation. (3 marks)

4. An asset is depreciated by £20,000 per year from £240,000 to £80,000. Calculate the expected life of the asset. (3 marks)

5. A hire-car business buys a new Ford Mondeo for £15,000. The business wants to keep the car for four years and has calculated a depreciation charge of £2,750 a year. Calculate the residual value of the hire car. (3 marks)

6. If an asset is depreciated at 15% per annum, having cost £50,000, calculate the net book value after four years. (3 marks)

(15 marks)

INTRODUCTION TO RATIOS AND LIQUIDITY RATIOS

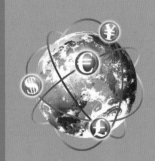

Introduction to ratio analysis

Ratio analysis is a method of measuring the performance of a business from various perspectives for the benefit of a range of stakeholders of the business, such as:

- directors and managers
- employees
- banks
- suppliers
- customers
- shareholders
- competitors
- government.

All stakeholders require information about a business, and can gain that information from some or all of the ratios.

The main sources of data for the calculation of the ratios usually come from the P&L account and the balance sheet of the business. Ratio analysis enables the business to:

- measure its performance over a given period of time
- make comparisons to be made over time and between other businesses (assuming they are of a similar size and nature)
- make comparisons between different departments within a business (intra-business).

Examiner's voice

It is vital that you are able to be selective in the ratios that you use. This will depend upon the wording of the question and the nature of the business.

Ratios are usually divided into various categories:

- liquidity
- profitability (performance)
- financial efficiency
- shareholder
- gearing.

Examiner's voice

Do not be too concerned about which category some of the ratios belong to. There is some overlapping between financial and profitability ratios. What is important is that you clearly:

A. state what a particular ratio shows

B. show the formula for the ratio

C. show the actual figures used (and where you found them)

D. comment (analyse) your answer in the context of the case

E. compare ratios for different years; it is dangerous to make conclusions based on just one year

F. offer reasons for the figures you have calculated.

Whether you cover all of the above will of course depend upon the actual question. Nevertheless, this provides you with a worthwhile list of possible areas to cover.

Type of ratio	Ratios included	Concerned with
Liquidity	1. current ratio 2. acid test	The ability of a business to cover its short-term (current) liabilities.
Profitability	1. gross profit margin 2. net profit margin 3. return on net assets 4. return on capital employed	Sometimes referred to as performance ratios, these consider the level of profit in relation to the actual business. The ratios simply consider how profitable the business is in relation to its sales, its assets, or the capital invested.
Financial efficiency	1. asset turnover 2. stock turnover 3. debtor days 4. creditor days	These ratios concentrate on the efficiency of the business in terms of its ability to move stock (1 and 2) or how efficient it is at collecting money it is owed or owes (3 and 4).
Shareholder	1. dividend per share 2. dividend yield 3. price earnings ratio	These ratios allow shareholders to judge how their investments in the shares of the business are performing, compared to alternative investment opportunities.
Gearing	1. gearing 2. interest cover	Gearing concentrates on the long-term liabilities of the business and its ability to borrow money (1), and its ability to cover the cost of borrowing (2).

Table 20.1 Ratio classification

Liquidity ratios

Type of ratio	Ratios included	Concerned with
Liquidity	1. Current ratio 2. acid test	The ability of a business to cover its short-term (current) liabilities.

Table 20.2 Liquidity ratios

Liquidity measures the ability to convert assets into cash. The most liquid asset is cash! However, other assets of a business vary in their ability to be converted into cash. Following the 'credit crunch' of 2008, selling assets such as houses was very difficult and therefore such an asset was viewed as very illiquid (because it was difficult to turn into cash).

Some debts and other current assets may be difficult to convert to cash. The debtor's ability to pay for goods will determine how liquid the business can regard that debtor. Stock, the other current asset, also varies in its ability to convert to cash. FMCGs (fast-moving consumer goods) are more likely to be able to be converted into cash quickly, whereas other luxury or expensive goods may be much harder to sell and therefore convert into cash.

Liquidity is all about having sufficient cash to keep the business working (working capital). The liquidity ratios focus on the ability of a business to have sufficient current assets in relation to the amount of current liabilities.

Cashflow problems are one of the main reasons for a business to fail, therefore the liquidity ratios are very important. There are two liquidity ratios: current ratio and acid test.

Current ratio

This ratio considers the current assets and the current liabilities. The ratio between the assets and the liabilities indicates the level of liquidity within the business. In other words, it considers the level of liabilities in relation to the level of assets, to ensure that there is sufficient working capital (enough cash to meet the short-term debts of the business).

This is a very important ratio as no business can survive without sufficient liquidity.

Formula

$$\text{Current ratio} = \frac{\text{Current assets}}{\text{Current liabilities}}$$

Source: the balance sheet.

Example
Current assets: £300
Current liabilities: £200

$$\text{Therefore the current ratio} = \frac{\text{current assets}}{\text{current liabilities}} = \frac{300}{200} = 1.5$$

The significance of the answer of 1.5 is that for every £1 of liabilities, the business holds £1.50 in assets. In other words, there are 1.5 times as many assets as there are liabilities. It implies that there are sufficient assets to cover the liabilities.

Examiner's voice

What is the ideal current ratio? It is often thought to be 1.5. However, it all depends upon the type of business, its circumstances and its objectives; therefore any such 'ideal' should be treated with caution.

Nevertheless, if the current ratio falls to 1 or even below 1, this can raise concerns because it indicates that there are insufficient assets to cover the liabilities.

It is difficult to rely on a current ratio to provide an accurate measure of a business's liquidity position: see Table 20.3.

$$\text{The current ratio} = \frac{\text{current assets}}{\text{current liabilities}}$$

$$= \frac{400}{200} = 2$$

This business has a current ratio of 2, which implies that for every £1 of liabilities there are £2 of assets. This may suggest that business X has a healthy liquidity ratio. However, the current ratio is a broad measure of liquidity. In this example, the assets include a large proportion of stock. There may be no certainty that the

Balance sheet	Value in £000
Current assets	
Cash	50
Stock	300
Debtors	50
Current liabilities	
Overdraft	200

Table 20.3 From the balance sheet of business X, year ending 31 December 2008

business will be able to sell this stock, and therefore the liquidity position is not as good as first appears. To alleviate such problems, there is a second ratio for liquidity. This second ratio is more stringent and ignores the stock as an asset. This ratio is the acid test.

Acid test

Because a business cannot be certain that it will be able to sell all of its stock, the acid test takes this fact into consideration. For certain businesses, this is a much more reliable test of liquidity. Selling perishable goods with a short shelf-life may mean that not all of the stock will be sold and therefore converted into cash (the most liquid asset).

Formula

$$\text{Acid test} = \frac{\text{current assets} - \text{stock}}{\text{current liabilities}}$$

Source: the balance sheet.

	Value in £000
Current assets	
Cash	25
Stock	150
Debtors	200
Current liabilities	
Overdraft	150

Table 20.4 Extract from balance sheet of business X, year ending December 31 2008

Example

$$\text{Acid test} = \frac{\text{current assets} - \text{stock}}{\text{current liabilities}} = \frac{375 - 150}{150} = \frac{225}{150} = 1.5$$

The answer shows that for every £1 of liabilities, the business has £1.50 in assets, sufficient to meet its liabilities. Some experts suggest that the ideal ratio for the acid test is 1, though this again depends upon the

Further Sources

www.timesonline.co.uk/business (for company results)
Company reports

type of business and the business environment in which it operates.

Examiner's voice

If the exam question asked you to comment on your answer, you would state the above and probably comment on the fact that although the acid test is positive (assets greater than liabilities), the level of debtors could be a problem depending on the type of goods being sold and the nature/standing of the debtors.

Your Turn Time allowed 35 minutes

Fixed assets	2007	2008
Current assets		
Cash	15	30
Stock	135	106
Debtors	67	94
Current liabilities		
Overdraft	55	39
Net current assets	162	191

Table 20.5 Balance sheet for T & M Ltd, in £000

1. Using the information in Table 20.5, calculate the current ratio and the acid test for 2007. (6 marks)

2. Using the information in Table 20.5, analyse the implications for the business when considering the changes in the current ratio and the acid test for 2008. (14 marks)

(20 marks)

Unit 21

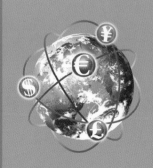

PROFITABILITY (PERFORMANCE) RATIOS

Type of ratio	Ratios included	Concerned with
Profitability	1. gross profit margin 2. net profit margin 3. return on net assets (primary efficiency) 4. return on capital employed (ROCE)	Sometimes referred to as performance ratios, these consider the level of profit in relation to the actual business. The ratios simply consider how profitable the business is in relation to its sales, its assets, or the capital invested.

Table 21.1 Profitability ratios

As the names of the ratios imply, they are concerned with the level of profit measured against various aspects of the business. Profitability ratios compare the profitability with the size of the business either by looking at the assets of the business, or at its level of sales.

Gross profit margin

This ratio looks at the level of profit as a percentage of the sales or turnover. The gross profit margin considers only the direct costs and not indirect costs (overheads). In other words, gross profit is the sales revenue minus the cost of sales (see Unit 16).

Formula

$$\text{Gross profit margin} = \frac{\text{gross profit}}{\text{sales}} \times 100$$

The answer will tell you how many pence (as a percentage) from every pound of sales is gross profit. If the answer is 40%, this means that for every £1 of sales, 40p is gross profit.
Source: P&L account

Example

Sales revenue	25
Less cost of sales	10
Gross profit	15
Expenses (overheads)	12
Operating profit	3

Table 21.2 P&L account year ending 2008 (£million)

$$\text{Gross profit margin} = \frac{\text{gross profit}}{\text{sales}} \times 100 = \frac{15}{25} \times 100 = 60\%$$

This means that for every £1 of sales, 60p is gross profit.

Net profit margin

This measures the net profit (or operating profit) as percentage of sales or turnover. This takes into consideration the direct and indirect costs, and is therefore a more realistic measure of the profitability against sales than gross profit margin.

Formula

Net profit margin = $\dfrac{\text{net profit}}{\text{sales}} \times 100$

Source: the P&L account

Example
Using Table 21.2 above:

Net profit margin = $\dfrac{\text{net profit}}{\text{sales}} \times 100 = \dfrac{3}{25} \times 100 = 12\%$

This means that for every £1 of sales, 12p is net profit.

Examiner's voice

It is important to note that a high percentage figure for this profit margin does not necessarily mean that the business is less successful; much will depend upon how many products are sold at this margin.

It is also important to note that the figure used for the net profit margin was operating profit, as this was the figure given. However, if in addition the P&L offers profit before tax (a more accurate net profit figure), then this should be used.

This again demonstrates the importance of showing your formula and figures.

Return on net assets

This ratio is also known as the primary efficiency ratio. It shows how efficiently a business uses its assets in order to generate a profit.

Formula

Return on net assets = $\dfrac{\text{operating profit}}{\text{net assets}}$

Source: the P&L account (for the operating profit) and the balance sheet (net assets)

Example

Return on net assets = $\dfrac{\text{operating profit}}{\text{net assets}} = \dfrac{£125m}{£500m} = 25\%$

This means that for every £1 of assets, the business has earned 25p in profits. Obviously, the higher the figure the better, as this suggests that the assets are being used in a more efficient manner.

Return on capital employed (ROCE)

This is a frequently used ratio for performance. The return on capital employed (ROCE) measures the net profit as a percentage of the capital employed.

Formula

Return on capital employed = $\dfrac{\text{net profit}}{\text{capital employed}} \times 100$

Source: the P&L account (profit) and balance sheet (capital employed).

Examiner's voice

There may be some debate as to which profit ought to be used for this ratio. Net profit or operating profit can be used as long as you state which you are using. It is usually profit before tax, to allow comparisons to be made within different countries that may have differing tax levels and to discount variations in UK tax rates.

Example

P&L account	£000s
Sales revenue	275
Cost of sales	95
Gross profit	180
Expenses	50
Operating profit	130
Interest payable	10
Profit before tax	120
Tax	4
Profit after tax Net profit	**116**

Table 21.3 Extract from P&L for year ending 2008

Balance sheet	£000
Fixed assets	800
Current assets	355
Current liabilities	295
Net current assets	60
Long-term liabilities	240
Net assets	**620**
Share capital	400
Reserves	220
Capital employed	620

Table 21.4 Balance sheet for year ending 2008

$$\text{Return on capital employed} = \frac{\text{profit}}{\text{capital employed}} \times 100$$

$$= \frac{116,000}{620,000} \times 100 = 18.7\%$$

Whether this is an efficient return depends upon the type of product and how competitive the market is. This ratio can compare different values:

- year-on-year
- the results of different investments
- departments or products (if capital not shared)

Further Sources

www.timesonline.co.uk/business (for company results)
Company Reports

Your Turn Time allowed 20 minutes

1. Using the information in Tables 21.5 and 21.6, calculate the ROCE for Judith's Garden Centres Ltd. (4 marks)

2. Suggest whether the ROCE indicates that this business is performing well. (10 marks)

(14 marks)

Balance sheet	£000
Fixed assets	800
Current assets	355
Current liabilities	235
Net current assets	120
Long-term liabilities	240
Net assets	**680**
Share capital	400
Reserves	280
Capital employed	**680**

Table 21.5 Balance sheet for year ending 2008

P&L account	£000's
Sales revenue	275
Cost of sales	95
Gross profit	180
Expenses	70
Operating profit	110
Interest payable	10
Profit before tax	100
Tax	4
Profit after tax Net profit	**96**

Table 21.6 P&L account for year ending 2008

Financial efficiency ratios measure the ability of a business to manage its assets and liabilities efficiently. The ratios include asset turnover, stock turnover, debtor days and creditor days.

Type of ratio	Ratios included	Concerned with
Financial efficiency	1. asset turnover 2. stock turnover 3. debtor days 4. creditor days	These ratios concentrate on the efficiency of the business in terms of its ability to move stock (1 and 2) or how efficient it is at collecting money it is owed or owes (3 and 4).

Table 22.1 Financial efficiency ratios

Asset turnover

This ratio measures how efficiently a business is able to use its assets to generate sales revenue.

The assets of a business are made up of fixed assets such as the factory and machines, which are used to make the products in order to generate sales. The current assets are needed for the working capital in order to keep the business going on a day-to-day basis. The current assets include stock that will be sold in order to generate the sales revenue. Having debtors allows the business to generate sales by offering credit facilities as a form of promotion.

The higher the ratio, the better, as it implies that the assets are being used in a more efficient manner to generate sales revenue. This ratio is heavily used to make intra-business comparisons, such as between different branches or shops or productive units.

Formula

$$\text{Asset turnover} = \frac{\text{sales revenue (turnover)}}{\text{net assets (or assets employed)}}$$

Source: the P&L account (for the sales revenue) and the balance sheet (for the assets, fixed assets and net current assets).

Example

Using Tables 21.3 and 21.4 (pages 113 and 114):

$$\text{Assets turnover} = \frac{\text{sales revenue}}{\text{net assets}} = \frac{275,000}{620,000} = .444$$

This suggests that the business is NOT very efficient in terms of the sales revenue generated from the assets of the business. For every £1 of assets, only 44p of sales is generated.

Examiner's voice

Such a comment as above could be misleading, as the result will very much depend upon the type of business. A capital-intensive business is less likely to have a high asset turnover, when compared with a business that does not possess many assets. It is, however, another ratio that can be used to help make a judgement about the efficiency of a business.

Stock turnover

This ratio measures how quickly the stock is turned over (sold).

Formula

Stock turnover = $\dfrac{\text{cost of stock (or sales)}}{\text{average stock}}$

(Average stock can be easily calculated by adding the opening stock to the closing stock and dividing by two.)

Source: sales figures and the P&L account for cost of sales.

Example

Stock turnover = $\dfrac{\text{cost of sales}}{\text{average stock}} = \dfrac{25,000}{10,000} = 2.5$

This means that the stock was sold 2.5 times within the trading period of one year. If the business needs to find out how many days it takes to turn the stock over, this can be calculated by:

$\dfrac{\text{stock}}{\text{cost of sales}} \times 365 = \dfrac{10,000}{25,000} \times 365 = 146 \text{ days}$

This means that if the stock turnover is 2.5, the stock is turned over (sold) in 146 days. This may be helpful in assessing re-order and delivery patterns.

There are many factors to note before passing judgements on the answer obtained. A high turnover may appear to be a good sign, but the business may be running stock levels down and therefore it is more likely to turn over a lower stock level more quickly. This may be due to poor sales and therefore holding less stock. However, a high stock turnover may be due to the usage of JIT (see Unit 46). If stock is delivered just-in-time, less stock is held, and therefore the stock will be turned over more quickly.

Alternatively, the rate of turnover may fall, which may be due to increased levels of stock in order to ensure that there is sufficient stock to meet a predicted increase in demand.

Debtor days

This ratio measures how quickly debts are turned into cash; in other words, how quickly the money owing to the business is paid.

It represents the average amount of time (days) which the debtors of the business, take to pay. Alternatively, the ratio can be used to measure how efficiently a business is at collecting its debts. Much will depend upon who owes the money. Often, the larger the business that owes the money, the longer it will take to pay.

Keeping debtor days as low as possible will help the cashflow of the business. However, it may be a deliberate strategy to extend the period before a customer has to pay. This may be part of a promotional campaign, but the consequences of such a strategy will be to increase the debtor days and subsequently damage the cashflow of the business.

Formula

Debtor days = $\dfrac{\text{debtors}}{\text{sales}} \times 365$

Source: Sales figures and sales agreements with its customers, the P&L account (sales) and the balance sheet (current assets).

Example

Debtor days = $\dfrac{\text{debtors}}{\text{sales}} = \dfrac{105,000}{£980,000} \times 365 = 39.1 \text{ days}$

Deciding if this is a satisfactory number of days will depend upon the normal trading (sales) agreements for the products involved. A business selling furniture may have a higher level of debtor days than a newsagent. There may be some businesses where debtor days do not exist at all. A fish and chip shop is unlikely to offer any form of credit sales.

Even when the number of debtor days is established, it will not necessarily be helpful information because the answer does not give any indication as to the distribution of the debtor days. One outstanding long-term debt may be hiding the fact that the majority are paid promptly.

Creditor days

This ratio measures how quickly a business pays its suppliers. It shows the number of days which a business takes, on average, to pay money it owes to its suppliers. This is a useful ratio because a business needs to be mindful of how long it is taking to pay its debts. If the business takes too long to pay its suppliers, they may restrict the level of credit available or even worse, cease to do business! By delaying payment, the credit rating of the business may be adversely affected.

However, being able to delay payment to its suppliers helps the cashflow of the business. It is therefore a careful balancing act between holding on to its cash and delaying payment without upsetting its suppliers; in other words, a careful balancing act between the debtor and creditor days.

Formula

$$\text{Creditor days} = \frac{\text{creditors}}{\text{purchases}} \times 365$$

Source: the balance sheet (creditors), P&L account (cost of sales) and sales agreements.

Example

$$\text{Creditor days} = \frac{\text{creditors}}{\text{purchases}} \times 365 = \frac{115,500}{890,850} \times 365$$

$$= 47.3 \text{ days}$$

This answer means that, on average, the business takes 47.3 days to pay its creditors. Whether this is acceptable or not will depend upon any agreement the business has with its suppliers. If the agreement is normally for a supplier to be paid within 30 days, then there are problems.

Examiner's voice

Again care needs to be taken before making any conclusions. The information in the case may offer a reason why the creditor days are longer than expected. Use the context of the case and consider any trends before commenting on your answer.

Your Turn Time allowed 20 minutes

1. Explain the difference between debtor days and creditor days. (3 marks)

2. Calculate the stock turnover for year 1 for the following business:

   - Year 1: sales of £45,000, average stock of £10,000
   - Year 2: sales of £35,000, average stock of £15,000. (3 marks)

3. Explain the likely reasons for the change in stock turnover in Year 2. (6 marks)

(12 marks)

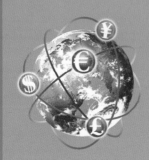

Unit 23

SHAREHOLDER RATIOS

Type of ratio	Ratios included	Concerned with
Shareholder	1. dividend per share 2. dividend yield 3. price earnings ratio	These ratios allow shareholders to judge how their investment in the shares of the business are performing, compared to alternative investment opportunities.

Table 23.1 Shareholder ratios

Shareholders buy shares for a variety of reasons. Some people buy shares for the perks attached to certain shares. Other companies offer discounts on their products or services for their shareholders; the building company Persimmon offers a 5% discount on the price of its new homes to its shareholders.

The majority of people buy shares as a form of investment. When deciding which shares to buy, a potential buyer will consider not only if the price of the shares will increase, but also if the shares will yield a dividend (share of the profits that are distributed to the shareholders).

Being able to measure the success or potential success of a business may lead a potential buyer to look at the ratios below.

Dividend per share

How much of the profits are distributed to the shareholders will depend on a range of factors. However, once the company has retained some of the profits for future investments, some may be distributed.

Formula

$$\text{Dividend per share} = \frac{\text{total dividend paid}}{\text{number of shares issued}}$$

Source: the P&L account (dividends to shareholders), balance sheet (number of shares issued) and company report (shares issued).

Example

A company declares a distributed profit of £70 million and has 800 million shares.

$$\text{Dividend per share} = \frac{\text{total dividend}}{\text{number of shares}} = \frac{£70m}{800m} = 8.75p$$

Although this shows the dividend per share, it does not show how much the shares cost to buy in order to receive this dividend. Knowing the share price will help to assess the value of the investment in the shares. It is also worth noting the trend in terms of the dividend payable.

Dividend yield

In order to resolve the problem of not knowing the price of the shares, the calculation of the dividend yield will provide a clearer picture for the potential shareholder.

The dividend yield measures the return (the dividend per share) on the investment (the cost of buying the share). It is similar to the ROCE (return on capital employed) in that the potential return of the investment can be compared to test its viability.

Formula

$$\text{Dividend yield} = \frac{\text{dividend per share}}{\text{market price of share}} \times 100$$

Source: Company report, press (*Financial Times*) and websites.

Example

Dividend yield = $\dfrac{8.75p}{655} \times 100 = 1.33\%$

This is not a high return on the price of buying the shares, especially when compared to the rate of interest that could be gained by depositing money into a savings account. However, potential investors may buy the shares because they will receive a dividend and possibly some perks for owning the shares, and because they are hoping for an increase in the price of the shares.

Any increase in the price of the shares will reduce the dividend yield for new shareholders, but may mean a shareholder can sell the shares for a capital gain. Similarly, any fall in the price of the shares will increase the dividend yield, but possibly discourage investors from wanting to buy the shares in the first place.

There are several variables that affect the purchasing of shares; the dividend yield is only one of those factors.

Although this ratio allows for a comparison to be made (the return on the investment of buying the share), it does not take into consideration other reasons why investors buy shares.

Examiner's voice

It is once again important to use the context of the case before passing judgment on the level of the yield.

Further sources

www.timesonline.co.uk/business (for company results)
Company reports

Price earnings ratio

This ratio is concerned with the expectations which potential investors hold. It is a measure of confidence about what the shares will earn. The ratio compares the current market price with the earnings for that share. If the price earnings ratio is 10, this means that the market price is 10 times the latest earnings per share. However, the earnings per share are NOT the same as the dividend per share.

- Dividends per share refer to the distributed profits in the form of dividends.
- Earnings per share represent the profit after tax. Not all of this profit will be distributed to the shareholders, as some of it could be retained by the company for investment purposes.

Formula

Price earnings ratio = $\dfrac{\text{market price of share}}{\text{earnings per share}}$

Source: the press, company reports, websites.

Example

Price earnings ratio = $\dfrac{\text{market price of share}}{\text{earnings per share}} = \dfrac{655p}{40}$
= 16.4

In this example, the market price is 16.4 times the earnings of the share. If earnings were constant, it would take 16.4 years to cover the cost of buying the shares!

An alternative way to consider this answer of 16.4 is in terms of the shareholder, who is willing to pay 16.4 times the earnings of the share in order to own such a share.

Your Turn

Question

Time allowed 20 minutes

Using the information in Table 23.2, analyse the possible reasons for the different figures.

(10 marks)

Year	Dividends per share (pence)
2004	10p
2005	12p
2006	20p
2007	25p
2008	13p

Table 23.2 Dividends per share for Country Club Hotels Ltd

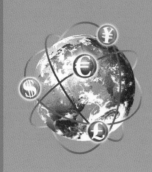

GEARING RATIOS

Type of ratio	Ratios included	Concerned with
Gearing	1. gearing 2. interest cover	Gearing concentrates on the long-term liabilities of the business and its ability to borrow money (1), and its ability to cover the cost of borrowing (2).

Table 24.1 Gearing ratios

This ratio considers the level of risk for a business. It measures the level of risk by comparing the levels of debt and the amount of equity (capital employed) within the business; in other words, the proportion of the business that is financed through long-term borrowing.

Gearing

Gearing is the percentage of long-term finance that is made up from loans, rather than shareholders funds and retained profits. The gearing ratio is deemed to be high if the long-term borrowing (liabilities) are more than 50% of the capital employed, and low if below 50%.

Examiner's voice

It is rather simplistic to talk about a business being highly geared because its long-term liabilities are above 50% of the capital employed. It will depend upon the circumstances facing the business.

If the proportion of borrowing (debt) is high, there is more interest to pay, and any fall in sales revenue and subsequently profit will make it harder for the business to finance this borrowing.

The higher the proportion of assets which is financed through long-term borrowing, the greater the risk for the business.

Similarly, if the business is highly geared (high proportion of debt), then a potential lender to the business is less likely to be willing to make further lending; the business is at greater risk of not being able to meet the interest charges and therefore the risk may be too high.

Banks are keen to know the level of gearing that already exists within a business before making any additional loans. If the business is already highly geared, the bank will be less likely to lend the money. If a high proportion of the capital within the business is borrowed, the business owns less capital to use as security on any additional loan.

Formula

Examiner's voice

There are several formulae for measuring the gearing of a business. Consequently, if you are making comparisons, ensure that you state the formula used and are consistent in its formula use.

The gearing ratio is used to judge if a loan should be granted

$$\text{Gearing ratio} = \frac{\text{long-term liabilities}}{\text{capital employed}} \times 100$$

Source: the balance sheet.

Example 1

Long-term liabilities	£000s
Creditors (more than one year)	5200
Capital	
Share capital	3,100
Retained profit/reserves	10,200
Total capital employed	18,500

Table 24.2 Extract from the balance sheet

$$\text{Gearing ratio} = \frac{\text{long-term liabilities}}{\text{capital employed}}$$

$$= \frac{5,200}{5,200 + 3,100 + 10,200} \times 100 = 28.3\%$$

This indicates that 28.3% of the total capital employed in the business is financed by long-term borrowing. This would be seen as a company with low gearing.

Example 2

Long term liabilities	£000s
Creditors (over one year)	215
Capital and reserves	
Shares	150
Retained profits/reserves	420
Capital employed	**785**

Table 24.3 Extract from the balance sheet

$$\text{Gearing ratio} = \frac{\text{long-term liabilities}}{\text{capital employed}} = \frac{215}{215 + 150 + 420}$$
$$\times 100 = 27.4\%$$

Debt to equity ratio

The difference between the gearing ratio and the debt to equity ratio (which is sometimes used for gearing) is interesting; remember to state your formula.

This ratio compares the long-term liabilities with the share capital and retained profits.

$$\text{Debt to equity} = \frac{\text{debt (215)}}{\text{equity (150 + 420)}} = 37.7{:}1$$

There are benefits to being highly geared (having a high proportion of long-term liabilities to shareholders funds and retained profits):

1. It may be a cheaper alternative source of funds when compared to shares, though much depends upon the level of interest rates and the level of profits.

2. If the gearing is high, perhaps there are fewer shareholders to be concerned about and therefore control of the company may be easier.

3. Being highly geared may be deliberate; some companies have bought back shares when profits are high to reduce dividend payments.

However, there are also benefits of having a low gearing ratio:

1. There are fewer funds that require repaying, helping to keep costs down. This could be significant if interest rates are high.

2. It is easier to gain future borrowing from banks.

Interest cover

Interest cover is used to help decide if a business can afford to repay any loan. This ratio measures the number of times in which a business can pay its interest charges with the operating profit it makes.

An answer of 3 means that there is sufficient profit generated to cover the cost of interest to be paid on a loan three times. The higher the number the better, as this indicates that the business can easily afford the interest payments.

Formula

$$\text{Interest cover} = \frac{\text{operating profit}}{\text{interest payable}}$$

Source: the P&L account.

Example

$$\text{Interest cover} = \frac{\text{operating profit}}{\text{interest payable}} = \frac{120,000}{30,000} = 4$$

An interest cover of 4 means that the business is generating sufficient profit to cover the cost of the interest on a loan four times over. Judging if four times is sufficient, or given other years' figures to compare with, can only be decided in the context of the given business.

Further Sources

www.timesonline.co.uk/business (for company results)
Company reports

Your Turn

Questions Time allowed 20 minutes

1. Explain the likely benefits of being highly geared.
(5 marks)

2. State the formula for interest cover. (2 marks)

3. Calculate the gearing ratio in Table 24.4.
(4 marks)

(11 marks)

Balance sheet	£millions
Long-term liabilities	90
Share capital	25
Reserves	35

Table 24.4 Extract from the balance sheet, accounts year ending 2008

Questions for Units 20–24

Time allowed 25 minutes

1. Using the information in Tables 24.5 and 24.6, calculate the following:

   A. current ratio

   B. acid test

   C. return on net assets

   D. gross profit margin. (16 marks)

Balance sheet	£000
Current assets	
Debtors	221
Stock	600
Cash	125
Current liabilities	
Overdraft	465

Table 24.5 Extract from balance sheet

P&L account	£000
Sales	100,240
Cost of sales	33,000
Gross profit	67240
Expenses	22,000
Operating profit	45240
Interest paid	2500
Net profit	42740

Table 24.6 Extract from the P&L account

2. State two limitations of the current ratio.(2 marks)

3. State the formula for the gearing ratio. (2 marks)

4. Which should be reduced if possible, debtor days or creditor days? Explain your answer. (4 marks)

(24 marks)

Task Time allowed 15 minutes

Prepare a table listing the stakeholders of a business and suggest which ratios will be of value to that particular stakeholder. For example:

Stakeholder	Which ratio is interesting?	Why is it interesting?
Bank	Gearing ratio	To ascertain proportion of loans to assets to help decide if able to lend money to the business. To assess risk involved.

Case Study

Time allowed 35 minutes

M & T's Bottles

M & T's is a small limited company that supplies designer bottles to the niche drinks market. Companies that sell drinks in 'shot' measures and miniatures for the airlines and special event companies are its main customers.

The business has only been operating for two years but has already made a profit (2008). Sales are increasing rapidly and things are looking good. Given its immediate success, Michael is keen to expand further as the business environment looks positive, especially in the local economy. He quickly writes out a new business plan to take to the bank, which he hopes will lend him some more money to finance his ideas for expansion. He has already had a loan for £20,000 from the bank to buy another bottling machine. He includes a copy of his P&L account and the balance sheet for the first two years, 2007 and 2008 (see Table 24.7).

His partner, Tom, suggests taking on more shareholders by issuing more shares, as an alternative method for raising additional funds. Michael does not agree with this suggestion, as he wants to keep the majority of the profit for himself and Tom; together, they hold 80% of the shares.

His fellow director, Felix, who is not an accountant, is worried when told that the business is having liquidity problems, judging from the accounts. Michael is not so concerned, suggesting that there is a good reason for the fall in the liquidity of the business.

Tom is keen to show that his marketing campaign has worked well. Offering an extended period of time to pay for their bottles has certainly helped, though, as Michael pointed out, there are drawbacks to the campaign.

Michael wants to increase his profit margin still further while improving the liquidity, but does not want to upset his main customers or put off new ones.

Balance sheet	2007	2008
Fixed assets	170	190
Current assets		
Debtors	67	94
Stock	135	106
Cash	15	30
Total current assets	217	230
Current liabilities		
Overdraft	55	39
Creditors	50	62
Net current assets	112	129
Long-term liabilities	110	130
Net assets	172	189
Shareholders funds		
Shares	120	120
Retained profit	52	69
Total	172	189

Table 24.7 M&T's balance sheet in £000s

Felix declares that expansion is bringing too many problems!

1. With the use of appropriate ratios, suggest whether the bank is likely to lend M&T's additional finance. (10 marks)

2. Analyse the impact on M&T's future plans, given its present liquidity situation. (10 marks)

3. Justifying your recommendation, advise M&T's whether to both increase its creditor days and reduce its debtor days. (14 marks)

(34 marks)

ACCOUNTING FOR DECISIONS

This chapter explores how a business can decide whether to undertake a particular capital investment (such as building a new factory or buying an additional machine). The business needs to establish whether the investment is appropriate or worthwhile. The business will have to consider the level of risk involved, how quickly the investment will pay for itself, and whether the investment will be profitable. Investments can include a range of activities or products such as:

- the purchase of machines
- building extensions or new factories
- buying another business (acquisitions)
- undertaking a large marketing campaign.

Figure 25.1 Before the new Airbus 380 airbus was built, investment appraisal techniques would have been applied.

Investment appraisal techniques are a quantifiable method of deciding if an investment should go ahead. The three methods of investment appraisal are:

1. payback

2. accounting rate of return (annual average rate of return)

3. net present value.

Examiner's voice

Although you may be asked to use one, two or all three investment appraisal techniques, there are also qualitative factors to consider, which will be looked at within this chapter.

Payback

This technique measures how quickly the cost of the investment can be paid back. The faster the payback, the better the investment. Payback is sometimes seen as a way of measuring the amount of risk involved. The longer the payback period, the greater the degree of risk involved.

This technique is often the first to be applied, because the length of time for the investment costs to be covered (paid back) is regarded as a more important factor at this stage, than the level of profit it may yield in the longer term.

Payback can be used to assess the viability of a given investment and to compare alternative investments. Both examples will be covered within this chapter. It is not a technique to ascertain whether a business is able to borrow the money needed for any investment, nor is it a technique to help decide if the business can afford to pay back interest on a loan used to pay for such an investment.

Payback terminology

1. EOY = end of year.

2. EOY 0 = a nought is added when the investment takes place.

3. EOY 1 = one year after the investment.

4. Net cash inflow = the likely return on an investment in a given year

5. To calculate net cash inflow = revenue – direct costs.

6. Cumulative cash inflow = the net amount of cash taking into consideration the initial investment and the net cash inflows (see Table 25.1).

Examiner's voice

It is important to understand that the net cash inflow does NOT take into consideration the cost of the investment or any of the overheads within the business, nor is depreciation considered.

Example 1

Year	Net cash inflows	Cumulative cash inflows
EOY 0	0	(100,000) (cost of the investment)
EOY 1	20,000	(80,000)
EOY 2	30,000	(50,000)
EOY 3	30,000	(20,000)
EOY 4	20,000	0

Table 25.1 Example of payback

Examiner's voice

The layout of an answer when using an investment appraisal technique is important. You will be credited for any formula used and clearly showing how you did any calculations. This is vital because if you make a mistake in any of the calculations, the 'own figure rule' will be used, which is to your advantage!

Similarly a clear layout, preferably within a table, will make it easier for the examiner to see what you have done. It may also help you to see what you have done! It does not matter if you use brackets or a minus sign for the negative values, as long as you are consistent.

With reference to Table 25.1:

- EOY 0: there is no net cash inflow; only the actual cost of the investment will appear in the cumulative cash flow column.
- EOY 1: the net cash inflow was £20,000 (revenue – direct costs); this is then subtracted from the cost of the investment (£100,000), leaving £80,000 still to be paid back.
- EOY 2: the net cash inflow is now £30,000 and again is subtracted from the last cumulative cash inflow figure (£80,000), to leave £50,000.
- EOY 3: the net cash inflow is another £30,000, which is subtracted from the previous year's cumulative cash inflow (£50,000), which leaves only £20,000 still to be paid back.
- EOY 4: the net cash inflow is £20,000 and this covers the remaining outstanding cumulative cash inflow.

The payback is therefore at the end of the fourth year. There has been a sufficient amount of net cash inflows to cover (pay back) the cost of the investment of £100,000. Sadly, not all payback calculations work out so easily!

Example 2

Year	Net cash inflow	Cumulative cash inflow
EOY 0		(150,000)
EOY 1	50,000	(100,000)
EOY 2	40,000	(60,000)
EOY 3	40,000	(20,000)
EOY 4	30,000	10,000

Table 25.2 Example of payback

In order to calculate the payback when it is within a given year, it is necessary to look at the year in which the payback occurs. Table 25.2 shows that the payback occurs within year 4. In order to calculate exactly when the payback occurs, it is necessary to look at how much is still to be paid back in the cumulative cash inflow column (£20,000) and the amount of the net cash inflow for the next year (£30,000). Dividing the amount still to be paid back (£20,000) by the net cash inflow for the following year (year 4, £30,000) will tell you exactly when within this year payback occurs:

$$\frac{20,000}{30,000} = \frac{2}{3} = 0.66 = \text{two-thirds of a year} = 8 \text{ months}$$

Therefore the payback in example 2 is 3 years and 8 months.

The payback can be calculated in days if you prefer (depending upon what you are asked to do in the question):

$$\frac{20,000}{30,000} = \frac{2}{3} = \times 365 = \text{payback of 3 years and 243.3 days}$$

Example 3

There are two possible investments:

1. investment A which will cost £50,000
2. investment B which will cost £35,000.

Year	Net cash inflow A	Cumulative cash inflow A	Net cash inflow B	Cumulative cash flow B
EOY 0	0	(50,000)	0	(35,000)
EOY 1	15,000	(35,000)	10,000	(25,000)
EOY 2	20,000	(15,000)	10,000	(15,000)
EOY 3	20,000	5,000	10,000	(5,000)
EOY 4			10,000	5,000

Table 25.3 Example of payback

Using the information in Table 25.3:

- the payback for investment A is 2 years and 9 months
- the payback for investment B is 3 years and 6 months.

Therefore, investment A appears the better option because the payback period is shorter.

However, there are other factors to consider:

1. How easy will it be to borrow £35,000 or £50,000? There is no information on the business's ability to borrow money, so all that can be said is that, normally, £35,000 would be easier to borrow than £50,000.

2. There is no indication of how many years each of the investments could last, beyond the payback period. A vehicle bought for the business may not last as long as an extension to the factory.

3. The table does not show how accurate are the two sets of figures for the net cash inflows.

4. It is not clear whether the two options would face competition that may affect the net cash inflows.

5. The nature of the two investments is not clear; one may pay back earlier but in the long run lead to a far greater level of sales and subsequent profit.

It is for the last reason that another investment appraisal technique is used. Table 25.4 offers a summary of the advantages and disadvantages of the payback method of investment appraisal.

Advantages of payback	Disadvantages of payback
It is easy to calculate and understand, and is therefore a cost-effective way of assessing an investment.	It ignores the value of money over a period of time; the purchasing power of money falls as prices rise. Inflation erodes the spending power of money.
It is a quick and useful guide to the level of risk involved in an investment. The longer the payback, the greater the risk.	It does not take into consideration any cash inflows after the payback period.
Because payback puts an emphasis on how quickly an investment is paid back, it is an effective method for companies in markets which are constantly changing.	There is no indication of when within any given year the cash inflows will occur.
	It does not measure the level of profits from the investment.

Table 25.4 Advantages and disadvantages of payback

The last disadvantage in this table explains why it is wise to use an additional method of investment appraisal.

Accounting rate of return (ARR)

This method of investment appraisal measures the profitability of any investment. The profit is expressed as a percentage of the cost of the investment. By taking the annual average return, this method also takes into consideration the life of the investment, unlike payback.

The higher the rate of return, the better the investment. Alternatively, another way to judge the success of the investment is by comparing the rate of return with the interest rates within the economy. If the percentage rate of return covers the percentage interest rates, then the investment may be seen as worthwhile. Similarly, if the percentage rate of return is more than the percentage interest rates that could be obtained from putting (investing the money into a bank savings account), then the investment is worthwhile.

The rate of return may need to be higher than the rate set out in the objectives of the business.

Examiner's voice

This method of investment appraisal is often known as average rate of return or annual average rate of return. It is vital that you are familiar with any of these three terms, even though they mean the same thing.

Example 1

An investment in a new digital printing machine which lasts for five years costs £15,000. The cash inflows (revenue – direct costs) from this printer are shown in Table 25.5.

To formulate:

- Calculate the total cash inflows (add each year for life of investment) = £60,000
- Subtract the cost of the investment (15,000) to gain the profit = £45,000
- Divide the total profit by the life of the investment (5 years).
- Divide the answer by the initial cost of the investment (£15,000) to gain the percentage ARR.

Year	Cash inflows
EOY 0	(15,000)
EOY 1	10,000
EOY 2	11,000
EOY 3	13,000
EOY 4	15,000
EOY 5	11,000

Step 1 Total cash inflows = 60,000

Step 2 Total cash inflows – cost of investment = profit
60,000 – 15,000 = 45,000

Step 3 $\text{Average annual profit} = \dfrac{\text{profit}}{\text{life of printer (five years)}}$

$\dfrac{45,000}{5} = £9,000$

Step 4 $\text{Return on investment} = \dfrac{\text{annual average profit}}{\text{cost of investment}}$

$= \dfrac{9,000}{15,000}$

$= 60\%$

Table 25.5 Cash inflows

Advantages of ARR	Disadvantages of ARR
It takes into account all of the cashflows throughout the life of the investment.	There is no indication of when the cash inflows occur within any given year.
It measures the profitability of the investment.	It ignores the value of money over time. The purchasing power of money falls as prices rise.
It is relatively easy to calculate and understand.	The life of the investment needs to be known and may alter over time.
It allows for a simple comparison between two or more investment opportunities or the opportunity cost of the investment.	It is harder to calculate than the payback and therefore will cost more in time and money to appraise potential investments.

Table 25.6 Advantages and disadvantages of ARR

Net present value (NPV)

Both methods (payback and ARR) have the disadvantage of not taking into consideration the value of money over time. In order to gain a realistic measure of any investment, the net present value method needs to be used. This method of investment appraisal considers the value of money over time. It converts all monetary values into today's values to allow for a realistic assessment of the returns in the years ahead.

Such a technique overcomes the problems of looking at cash inflows for three, four or even ten years' time, and being able to realise that £100 in ten years' time will not buy £100 worth of goods at today's prices. One only has to look at the changes in the price of oil in 2008/09 to realise the significance of such changes, and how they may affect the actual decision on whether to undertake an investment.

This method works on the assumption that any inflows will be worth less than the same amount today. The technique discounts the value of money over time by a given percentage rate. This discounted value allows the calculation of the **discounted cash flow (DCF)**.

For example: if you invested £1,000 in your bank and interest was paid at about 5% a year, after one year there would be £1,050; after two years, £1,102.50. Consequently, £1,000 in two years' time is worth £1,102.50; or £1,102.50 in two years' time is only worth £1,000 in today's money.

Examiner's voice

There is no need to worry about the particular percentage discounts or the actual figures as these will be given to you in a chart or table. There are examples for you to consider below.

The actual percentage discount rate will depend mainly on the likely level of inflation within an economy. Although this rate is not easy to forecast, it is better than not allowing for changes in the value of money at all! Other factors affect which discount rate is used, some of which are determined by the business itself. It may have undertaken similar investments in the past and therefore have a set figure in mind.

The length of the investment may also be a consideration. The longer the life of the investment, the higher the discount factor in order to take account of the fall in the value of money over time.

Example 1

Year	Discount rate 5%	Discount rate 7%	Discount rate 10%
0	1.0	1.0	1.0
1	0.952	0.935	0.909
2	0.907	0.873	0.826
3	0.864	0.816	0.751
4	0.823	0.763	0.683

Table 25.7 Example of net present value

Table 25.7 shows the discounted figures for various rates: 5%, 7% and 10%.

It is interesting to note how the value of £1 falls over four years. If discounted by 10%, £1 in four years will be worth 68p.

Using the information in Table 25.7, a business can now calculate the net present value of an investment.

If a business wanted to buy a new machine which costs £10,000, and applied a discount factor of 5%, the net present value is shown in Table 25.8.

Year	Net return	Discount factor at 5%	Present value (Net return × discount factor)
0	(10,000)	1.0	10,000
1	4,300	0.952	4,093.6
2	3,100	0.907	2811.7
3	2,650	0.864	2289.6
4	1,850	0.823	1522.5
Total (returns − cost)	1,900		
			10717.4 − 10,000 £717.4

Table 25.8 Example of net present value

The original figure of £1,900 after the discounted factor of 5% is now only £717.40. However, the net present value is still positive and is therefore considered worthwhile.

Examiner's voice

Again, although there is no need to put the figures in a table, ensuring that the information is clear both to you and the examiner is important.

Example 2
For the same investment, but with a discount factor of 10%, the figures are shown in Table 25.9.

Year	Net return	Discount factor 10%	Present value (net return × discount factor)
0	(10,000)	1.0	(10,000)
1	4,300	0.909	3908.7
2	3,100	0.826	2560.6
3	2,650	0.751	1990.1
4	1,850	0.683	1263.5
Total	1,900	0.621	(277.1)

Table 25.9 Example of net present value

With a negative answer, the investment is not worthwhile. This means that although the cost of the investment takes place immediately, the returns from the investment (the inflows) come in over four years, and during this period of time, the value of money is being eroded; so much so that in today's values, the investment will not cover its costs.

The examples in Tables 25.8 and 25.9 clearly show how significant the discount factor is in the decision process. The higher the discount factor, the greater the returns need to be to cover the falling value of money.

Advantages of net present value	Disadvantages of net present value
It takes account of the value of money over time.	It is more complicated to work out than payback and ARR.
All cash inflows are accounted for (not so for payback).	Because it is more complicated, it takes longer to make a decision and is therefore more expensive.
	Its value as a decision-making tool is limited by the selection of the discount factor, which is at best only an educated guess as to the value of money over time.

Table 25.10 Advantages and disadvantages of net present value

Although all of the three investment appraisal methods have their limitations, collectively they are a valuable method of deciding if a particular investment ought to go ahead. All of the methods considered are based only on financial data and as a consequence, do not take into consideration any other factors that may be important in the decision-making process.

Non-financial factors affecting investment decisions (qualitative)

The objectives of the business
There are occasions when a business will know what sort of return it requires on any investment and, equally important, whether such returns satisfy the objectives set.

Resources available, productive capacity, labour, finance
Although a particular investment may be financially attractive, the business may not have the required

labour to operate the new machine. A significant amount of training may be required that would be too costly added to the cost of buying the new machine.

Although the potential investment is worthwhile, the finance to purchase the new machine may not be available, either because there is no funding available or that the business cannot afford to borrow sufficient funds.

The economy

- The state of the economy can have a dramatic effect on investment decisions.
- The level of inflation may affect the discount factor used, which in turn may lead to an investment no longer being worthwhile.
- If the economy is moving towards a recession, there may be insufficient demand in the future to justify the investment. The lack of demand would affect the likely cash inflows and therefore affect the likely return or payback period.
- If a UK business sells goods or services abroad, the value of the pound could greatly affect sales and consequently affect the cash inflows of the business. Furthermore, the value of different currencies can fluctuate daily, making any forecast for inflows almost impossible.

The data sources

The ability of the business to forecast accurately the demand for its products or services may depend upon the validity of its market research and other available data.

Who is making the decision?

Although the investment appraisal techniques are a useful method of deciding if an investment should go ahead, the person who is responsible for making the decisions may have his or her own agenda! There may be some status or kudos in going ahead with a project (look at the Millennium Dome debacle in 2000), even if the figures do not support such a decision. Self-interest for a particular department of the business or government service may mean that the financial evidence is ignored.

Hospitals have only a certain budget at their disposal, but may spend money on a renal unit rather than a physiotherapy unit, even though the latter is a better option financially.

Internal rate of return

The net present value does not yield any specific information on the actual return on the investment. The internal rate of return is a method of investment appraisal that does allow the return to be calculated. However, the net present values are used in determining the internal rate of return.

Method of calculation

Two discount factors are used; the first where a positive net present value is produced, and the second where a negative net present value is produced. Using two discount factors and therefore having two net present values, one positive and one negative, means that a discount factor that produces a net present value of nought (zero, 0) is found.

The net present value of zero means that this is in fact the rate of return on the project in question.

Examiner's voice

If the NPV is positive, the rate of return is higher than the discount rate. When the NPV is negative, the rate of return is lower than the discount rate.

Finding the discount factor at which the NPV is equal to nought will provide the rate of return (see Table 25.11).

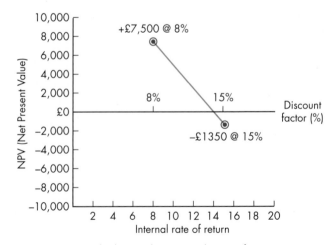

Figure 25.2 Calculating the internal rate of return

	Cashflow	Discount factor 8%	DCF	Discount factor 15%	DCF
EOY 0	–75,000	1	–75,000	1	–75,000
EOY 1	40,000	0.93*	37,200	0.87	34,800
EOY 2	30,000	0.86	25,800	0.76	22,800
EOY 3	20,000	0.79	15,800	0.66	13,200
EOY 4	5,000	0.74	3,700	0.57	2850
		NPV**	7,500	NPV	–1350

* To calculate the DCF: 40,000 x 0.93 = 37,200

** To calculate the NPV, add the DCF for each of the four years and then subtract the initial investment of 75,000.

Therefore: 37,200 + 25,800 + 15,800 + 3,700 = 82,500

82,500 – 75,000 = 7,500

Table 25.11 Calculating the internal rate of return

The internal rate of return can be found by plotting the NPVs on to a graph (see Figure 25.2). The positive NPV is plotted above the line of the discount factor, and the negative NPV is plotted below the discount factor line. The point where the line cuts the discount factor line (where the NPV is zero) represents the approximate return on the investment. In this example the return on a project is approximately 14.2%.

Key Terms

Internal rate of return: the discount rate at which the NPV is equal to zero.

Question Time allowed 25 minutes

1. Calculate the payback period from the following information: (4 marks)

Year	Net cash inflow
0	(20,000)
1	6,000
2	9,000
3	10,000
4	12,000
5	10,000

2. Calculate the ARR and net present value (5% discount factor) from the following information: (6 marks)

Year	Project 1 Net cash flows	5% discount rates
EOY 0	(50,000)	1.0
EOY 1	12,000	0.952
EOY 2	15,000	0.907
EOY 3	20,000	0.864
EOY 4	13,000	0.823

3. Explain why using the internal rate of return is useful when attempting to appraise a potential investment project. (4 marks)

(14 marks)

Your Turn

Case Study Time allowed 40 minutes

F&H's Sports Schools

Felix and Holly have run their business for over 10 years, providing the local area with summer and Easter sports schools. Each school offers training by qualified coaches and chances to participate in competitions of a high standard. They have a good reputation in and around their home town and the courses or schools are usually booked up before the holidays start.

The major schools have been rugby and hockey, which have been highly successful with a high degree of repeat customers each holiday. However, Felix is keen to expand the business and has suggested that the two of them give careful consideration to opening another school in order to satisfy the demand for soccer. The local team has recently gained promotion to the football league and Felix is keen to capitalise on this success.

Although also keen to see their business expand, Holly doubts if there are enough boys in the area to run rugby and soccer schools, and therefore thinks that offering a netball school will be more successful. She argues that the hockey school, aimed at the girls, is always fully booked before the rugby school, and with few facilities at the local schools, this would be a successful investment.

The soccer training school will cost about £45,000 for the site and equipment. The netball training school will cost less because the amount of land is so much less, even though the area for the actual netball court would need tarmac. Holly estimates that the total cost will be about £25,000.

They have both estimated the likely cash inflows (see Table 25.12) using demographic predictions and the likely prices that could be charged. Their knowledge of coaching wages means that both are happy with the figures put forward for their own schemes. They are keen to ensure that their particular idea is undertaken, but it is clear that they cannot afford to invest in both ideas.

Having asked an accountant which idea is the best financially, they were told that some investment appraisal would need to be undertaken.

The lifespan for the soccer school and the netball school are both five years.

1. State two advantages of payback as a method of investment appraisal. (2 marks)

2. Explain two factors that may affect the discount factor that would be used to ascertain the NPV for an investment. (4 marks)

3. Using quantitative and qualitative information, suggest which school Felix and Holly should invest in. (16 marks)

(22 marks)

Year	Soccer school	Net cash inflow (£000)	Netball School	Net cash inflow (£000)
EOY 0		(45)		(25)
EOY 1		10		7
EOY 2		15		10
EOY 3		15		12
EOY 4		15		10
EOY 5		10		8

Table 25.12 Case study

26 Unit

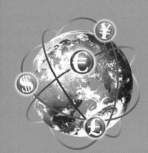

COMMUNICATION OF BUSINESS OBJECTIVES

Introduction

People within organisations cannot act in isolation. Employers and employees work in groups, have varying objectives, either as individuals or as groups and affect the business's operations and performance.

Human resource management does not take place in isolation. As with all of the functions within a business, it is dependent upon the other functions of the business. The objectives of the business will determine the level of labour required to work within the business and how the structure of the business is organised. The pay of employees will be governed by the budget constraints as laid down by the finance department. The employees will affect the level of production and the productivity rates and therefore costs. The quality of the products will also be affected by the morale and motivation of the workforce. In turn, the marketing will be made easier if the quality of the products is of a high standard.

Effective communication is vital for a business to operate in an efficient manner. Regardless of what needs to be communicated, it is essential that the information to be imparted is clearly understood. Imagine being an employee on the production line at a car plant where the level of noise may be significant, and needing to hear what the supervisor is trying to explain about a particular task. If the employee fails to hear the message correctly, serious errors may occur. Similarly, if a pilot aboard a jumbo jet fails to understand an instruction clearly as to which course to fly, this inability to understand the instruction may have fatal consequences.

Communication is important for business for a number of reasons:

1. Effective communication will ensure that the number of mistakes made within the business is reduced. If such mistakes can be reduced then this will have an effect upon the costs of the business, in time and consequently money.

2. If the level of communication within the business is clear and effective, then the employees within the business will feel a sense of belonging (Maslow's theory) and involvement (Mayo's theory).

3. If communication can take place quickly and effectively, this will enhance the decision-making process of the business. As a consequence, the business will be able to progress and be more competitive.

4. Effective communication can be a marketing tool for the business; if communication reaches its target market successfully, via higher sales, the business should be able to generate additional income.

Examiner's voice

When answering examination questions, it is a good idea to try to justify your points by relating any specific theory. The comments about the importance of effective communication have been justified by mentioning motivational theorists.

Communication involves the transmission of information from one person to another. The information or the message can be in many forms and can be transmitted in many ways. Communication involves:

1. the information to be imparted (the message)

2. the transmitter (who ever sends the information)

3. A form of transmission (a form of signal using sound or vision)

4. a receiver.

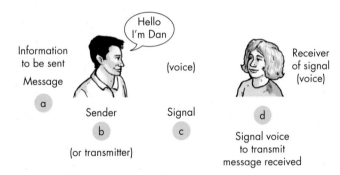

Figure 26.1 The communication process

Types of communication

There are several different types of communication:

- one-way and two-way
- formal and informal
- open and closed
- vertical and horizontal.

Figure 26.2 One-way communication

One-way communication

One-way communication is the simplest form of communication.

Advantages	Disadvantages
Easy to use.	Less reliable as there is no way to check message. (no feedback)
Cheaper than two-way.	May cause frustration for the receiver.
No pressure on the sender to justify what is being communicated.	

Table 26.1 Advantages and disadvantages of one-way communication

Two-way communication

Two-way communication involves both a sender and a receiver of information.

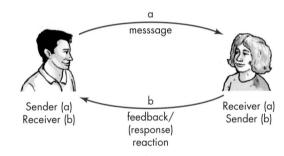

Figure 26.3 Two-way communication

Advantages	Disadvantages
More effective/reliable, because the receiver is able to gain clarification (feedback).	Takes more time and is therefore more expensive.
Receiver feels more involved because he/she is able to seek clarification.	Puts the sender of the information under pressure to justify/explain the information being sent.

Table 26.2 Advantages and disadvantages of two-way communication

Formal communication

Examiner's voice

One of the easiest ways to distinguish between formal and informal communication is the location or environment in which the communication takes place.

This type of communication is often associated with how information is communicated, often using agreed rules or procedures. The 'house' style of communication is usually something that is made clear in an induction process, when a new employee joins a business.

This type of communication has been officially sanctioned by the business.

The formality may refer to the type of language that is used, to whom one speaks or the media that is used to communicate.

Many businesses insist on an established procedure for answering the phone or laying out letters or emails. Most businesses will also establish a procedure for communicating with staff higher up the hierarchy. Similarly, there will be 'pro forma', (a document with a specific purpose and layout) that is to be used for various activities such as requests for holidays, appraisal or training, and salary information.

Many of the legalities that a business has to deal with use formal language. Documents such as the Memorandum of Association and the Articles of Association, which are necessary for the incorporated process, use formal terms and in many cases, a formalised layout. Contracts between businesses will also use formal language.

Information stored by a business, regarding for example sales figures or employees details, are examples of formal communication.

Informal communication

As the word implies, the type of communication in this instance has little or no established rules for how communication takes place. This applies to the type of language used, the procedures for communication and how such information is communicated. The setting for informal communication usually takes place outside of a work environment. There is usually no strict programme for communication and no particular rules on how such communication can take place. The language and type of information passed on is unique to the people involved in the communicating process. If a group of friends are talking in a school dining room, what and how they communicate about is entirely their decision.

In the majority of cases, informal communication is not written down but passed on verbally. There are exceptions to this, when people are communicating by email or by text message, where a 'form' of the written word is used.

Open communication

This involves the use of language that will be understood by the vast majority of the population. Such communication tends to be free of technical language and jargon.

Open communication is very important if the business intends to reach a large audience. Using language that is not easily understood will reduce the number of people who can understand what the business is trying to state. This is particularly true within marketing. Often a clear, simple message will yield better results, than a detailed, complicated and technical message.

If effective communication is to take place between the various stakeholders of the business, then an appropriate type of communication needs to be used. In most cases, open communication is required for any communication with the stakeholders outside of the business. If the stakeholders of the business are internal (within the business), then it is more likely that closed communication will be used.

Closed communication

A business may have its own language for activities, procedures and components within the business. Such communication, once learnt, will be be understood by those within the business, but not by anyone outside of the business.

Students and teachers understand the significance of a 'U' grade at AS and A2, but there will be many people within the population who have no idea at all!

Such language may well be a form of slang or a convenient abbreviation in order to save time. Many of the terms used within government and the civil service are a series of initials, which are quicker to use than having to state in full the exact title of a particular body. The examination board, OCR, is in itself, a form of closed communication, as most people do not know what the initials stand for.

Closed communication may also include formal language relating to the business.

Vertical communication

This is normally associated with communication from the management being passed down to the employees on the shop floor. However, any communication between the different layers of the business is referred to as vertical communication. Such communication can take place in an upwards direction. Employees at the lower end of the business hierarchy may pass on vital information to the management about difficulties with production or useful information about consumer attitudes to a specific product or service. This type of communication may just involve the day-to-day discussions between management and those that have to implement the business's strategies.

Being able to communicate with different levels of the organisational structure within a business may be highly beneficial to all concerned. It provides an opportunity for employees to feel involved (Mayo's theory) and helps alleviate any frustrations within the working environment (Herzberg, hygiene factors).

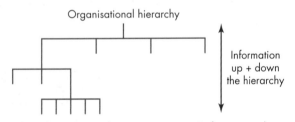

Figure 26.4 Vertical communication (information between different layers of hierarchy)

Horizontal communication

This type of communication involves communication between people on the same level of the organisational

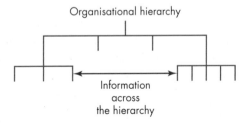

Figure 26.5 Horizontal communication (information between the same layers of hierarchy)

structure. Communication between two employees involved with the research and development of a product, or employees discussing a marketing plan for a new advert, or two people within the finance department looking at a cashflow forecast, will all be undertaking horizontal communication.

Examiner's voice

The difference between vertical and horizontal communication is not what is being said, but the route or channel of communication that is used.

Channels of communication/ communication networks

Different businesses may operate different communi-cational networks of channels. The channel or network will vary for different reasons:

- the type of leader
- the size of the business
- the experience of the employees
- the type of organisational structure.

All of these may be important, but there is no set rule as to which network or channel that is used. There is a link with the type of organisational structure, however; the more centralised the structure, the more likely is the business to use either a 'wheel' or 'chain' network.

The chain

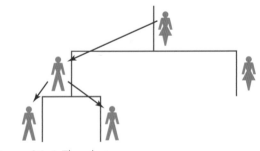

Figure 26.6 The chain

This type of network is normally associated with a formal and vertical hierarchy. Information can be communicated up and down the hierarchy, although it is more likely that much of the communication will be down the hierarchical structure. A typical organisation that would use this type of communicational network is a large one such as the civil service or a local authority. There is likely to be a lack of opportunity for those employees at the lower end of the hierarchy to feel involved or be able to communicate with higher levels of the hierarchy directly. There is also the possibility of information becoming distorted as it travels through several layers of the hierarchy.

If communication is to be two-way, there is likely to be a problem in terms of time; any message that has to travel through every level of the hierarchy will take time, which is costly for the business.

The wheel

Figure 26.7 The wheel

The 'wheel' has the leader, chief executive, or board of directors at the centre. All communication goes through the leader (centralised structure), and this type of network enables the leader to keep in touch with everything that is taking place within the business. However, this network may discourage employee initiative and responsibility as the leader is involved with all communication. This type of network is not associated with delegation.

The Circle

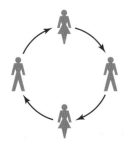

Figure 26.8 The Circle

This is a restricted network in terms of communication. Communication can take place between employees, usually within a department or on the same level of a hierarchy. As communication takes place between two people, it will be time-consuming and therefore expensive.

All networks

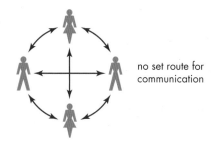

Figure 26.9 All networks

This network, as Figure 26.9 shows, has no set route and allows communication between anyone within the business. This informal network means that communication may be quicker, as those who need to communicate with each other, can do so without going through a formalised network. Such a network is more likely to be appropriate for a smaller business, which does not need a highly structured process of communication.

Communication media

The communication media refers to how the message is imparted to the receiver or receivers. Television, radio, text message, telephone, noticeboard, fax, memo, email and video-conferencing are some of the most frequently used media.

All of the above have their advantages and disadvantages, in terms of accuracy, speed, cost and formality.

The use of information communication technology (ICT) has speeded up the process of communication considerably; however, there may be problems with regards to the clarity and therefore the reliability of the information being imparted. Nevertheless, business has invested in ICT in a big way, as the cost of communication, coupled with its speed, has led to significant savings, even allowing for considerable set-up costs (particularly for the hardware).

The usage of ICT is not always successful; the National Health Service has spent billions of pounds on computer systems that have not managed to provide the required benefits. Whether this is due to inappropriate software or technical issues with the hardware is difficult to ascertain, in spite of the Freedom of Information Act!

Video-conferencing has had a significant effect upon costs for businesses. Sales teams no longer need to meet, but instead, can 'link up' and hold a meeting with each person, even in different countries.

Examiner's voice

It is important to be consistent in your usage of terminology. Communication media (or medium if just one) is what is used to impart the message. The channel of communication or network is concerned with the route of the message. The types of communication are concerned with the manner in which the message is imparted.

Barriers to effective communication

Effective communication can be hampered by 'barriers'. Shannon and Weaver's theory of communication highlighted three main barriers to effective communication:

1. **Technical:** this barrier is concerned with the ability of the receiver to receive the information being communicated. If there is too much noise, the information will not be heard. You have only to think about the difficulty of hearing some of the announcements made at a railway station as a train approaches! Similarly, if a written message is sent but cannot be read by the receiver, this too would be a 'technical' barrier.

Examiner's voice

Any interference that prevents the receiver from being able to receive a message is described as a technical barrier.

2. **Semantic:** This barrier relates not to the ability to receive the message, but the receiver's ability to understand what is being sent.

   A text message may well be received by a parent from a son, but may not be understood, especially if predicted text has been used! The message may use closed communication that will not be understood by someone outside the family.

3. **Effectiveness:** If there are no technical or semantic barriers, the final barrier is whether the information being communicated has been acted upon in an appropriate manner.

   If the message asked for an employee to contact their manager, the employee contacting their manager suggests effective communication. The employee has received the message, understood the message and acted upon the request within the message.

Examiner's voice

Technical and semantic barriers are both relatively easy to identify, although ensuring that semantic barriers are removed may be harder to achieve. Dealing with the 'effectiveness' barrier is significantly harder because there may be several reasons why the message has not been acted upon. In other words, there may exist additional barriers to effective communication, not covered by Shannon and Weaver's theory.

Additional barriers to effective communication

The skill of the sender of the message

The ability of the sender may affect the effectiveness of the communication process. If the sender is inexperienced and has not given sufficient thought to the media for the communication or the nature of the message, these factors will act as a barrier to effective communication.

Similarly, the sender's ability to choose the right words or the right timing could also affect the reliability of the communication.

The ability of the receiver

Irrespective of the ability of the sender, communication can be ineffective due to the lack of ability of the receiver. If there is an inability to read or understand the significance of the message, problems may occur.

Body language

Regardless of the content of the message, body language may affect the effectiveness of communication; a serious message will not be received in the right way if the body language is contradictory. It is little wonder that undertakers are not known for their constant smiling and laughter, given the nature of their work and the information that needs to be imparted.

Body language can be used to put a greater emphasis on a message. Similarly, the tone of the voice can be used to help express a message. A phone call may enable the receiver to gauge feelings by the message and the tone of the voice, something that is not possible if emails or text messages are used.

Inappropriate medium used

Communication may be ineffective if the wrong medium is used. Informing an employee that he or she has been made redundant by a sing-a-gram would be totally inappropriate!

Similarly, there would be no need to formalise an invitation to a meal after work from one employee to another. Using text messages to your parents even for a simple message of 'c u latr', may not be received clearly.

Cultural differences

Communication between different cultures may run into difficulties because the words used or the tone of the message is not perceived by the receiver in the same way as the sender intended. This is true regardless of whether any actual communication between the two parties was intended. In 2007, an English teacher working in Sudan allowed one of her pupils to choose the name Mohammad for a class teddy bear. This act caused offence to the Muslim population, which resulted in the teacher being prosecuted and sentenced to prison; such was the perceived level of offence caused by the 'innocent' act.

The size of the business and the number of layers in the business hierarchy

Communication becomes harder as a business grows. There will be more layers within the organisation, more messages issued and more employees to receive such messages. There may be more links in the chain of command and a higher number of employees within the span of control.

For the very large multi-national companies, communication will become even harder due both to language differences, with meaning being lost in translation, and cultural differences (see above).

The greater the numbers of layers within an organisation, the more opportunities for the communication to break down. A message may become distorted as it passes through the various layers within the business. You may be able to think of instances when your friends have passed on a message and managed to confuse it; or where a friend has not heard the information correctly and passed on information that is no longer accurate.

As the size of a business increases, there may be a greater degree of decentralisation, which will reduce the communication chains and therefore improve the effectiveness of any communication.

The amount of information

If there is a lot of information to pass on and particularly if the media use is verbal, there is a much greater risk of errors occurring, making the communication ineffective. How easy it is to absorb a large amount of information will also be affected by the skill of both the sender and receiver.

Once a particular media becomes popular, there is a tendency to present too much information, which is sometimes known as 'information or communication overload'. Users of email are often guilty of this, sending a mass of information which could be better presented by alternative media.

Examiner's voice

It is important to note that no single factor can be considered in isolation. It is essential that you think about the context of the case and a range of factors when considering how effective any communication will be.

Type of Communication	One-way	Two-way
	Formal	Informal
	Open	Closed
	Vertical	Horizontal
	Internal	External
Communication channels/networks	Chain	Wheel
	Circle	All networks
Communication Media	Text/Email	Telephone/Fax
	Letter/printed word/Conversation	

Table 26.3 Summary of communication aspects

Your Turn

Questions Time allowed 20 minutes

1. State four different types of communication
(4 marks)

2. Suggest an appropriate type of communication for the following, and justify your answer. (4 marks)

   A. An instruction from the manager to a shop floor worker.

   B. Communication between two friends planning a night out.

   C. Communication in the form of an advert aimed at its consumers.

   D. Communication between two technical experts discussing a new machine.

3. For the following circumstances, suggest an appropriate communicational media:

   A. Communication to employees informing them that Fred is having a retirement party.
   (2 marks)

   B. Communication to employees informing them that a new prospective customer is to visit the factory next week. (2 marks)

4. Explain how effective communication may improve employee motivation. (4 marks)

5. Explain the difference between open and closed communication. (4 marks)

(20 marks)

Case study Time allowed 40 minutes

The Fruits of the Farm Ltd (FFL)

Tim Thomas started his fruit farm back in the 1980s, along with his sister Emma. They slowly built the fruit farm up from a family firm to a highly successful business, supplying a major supermarket as well as the local shops within the county of Somerset.

Emma was responsible for the recruitment, training and retention of the staff, and as the business grew, found her task more difficult. Finding the right staff at the right wage took up more of her time. It was not just the nature of the work (harvesting the fruits was still undertaken by hand), but the fact that of course, many of the employment opportunities were seasonal. Students were available when the majority of the fruits were ready for picking, and also willing to work long hours and for just above the minimum wage in order to fund either holidays or reduce their overdrafts, but there were few other obvious sources of labour willing to undertake such tasks.

Emma had spoken to other fruit farmers in the area who had managed to overcome their labour problems by using recently arrived workers from eastern Europe. Under EU law, there is free movement of labour between member states, and many people had made their way to the UK, hoping to make their fortunes.

Tim was less sure about such an approach; he could see the benefit to the business that they would be willing to work for only the minimum wage, and was conscious that as the supermarket operated on very competitive prices, FFL had to work within tight margins. However, he was concerned about foreign workers being unable to understand what was required, and how he would be able to explain that they should only pick the ripe ones or the fruit that was nearly ripe but without insect damage. The supermarkets were very particular about the appearance of the fruit and had very strict guidelines for what was acceptable.

Tim knew that FFL could not afford to lose the supermarket contract. He was particularly concerned because he and Emma had discussed buying some more land in order to take up additional orders for their fruit. The country was increasingly keen to eat their 'five portions a day' in order to improve their health.

After much debate, Emma agreed to advertise for more workers, and as expected, she was quickly faced with her first communicational problem: how to interview the eight people who had arrived at the farm gates within a couple of hours of contacting the local job centre near Taunton. She thought that they were from Romania and Slovakia but it was difficult to communicate with them; one person's spoken English was sufficient for him to be appointed the unofficial interpreter for her.

1. Discuss the most appropriate methods of communication that Emma could use when trying to explain how to harvest the fruit.   (15 marks)

2. Analyse the main barriers to effective communication for FFL that may exist when employing foreign workers.   (15 marks)

(30 marks)

THE NATURE OF MANAGEMENT

What do managers do?

What is the purpose of managers? Certain broadly defined functions can be identified, whichever section of a business they work in. These include:

- communicating
- controlling
- coordinating
- decision-making
- evaluating progress
- leading
- motivating
- planning.

There is no particular significance in the order of these activities. It can be argued that all are equally important aspects of a manager's role. What is important is that the resources of the business (finance, employees and time) need to be managed with the aim of using them as efficiently as possible in order to reach the business's objectives.

Many of these functions apply not only to a manager's specific department in isolation, but to others also. Planning one department's activities cannot be undertaken in a vacuum. For example, production managers need to know what to manufacture; marketing managers cannot try to sell products that the business cannot make, and so need to know and understand production capabilities; new technology in any department cannot be installed without finance managers sanctioning and allocating the funds. Furthermore, communication and coordination between departments, once the business's strategic plan is underway, is crucial if the business's strategic objectives are to be reached.

Examiner's voice

A useful definition of management appeared in *The Observer* in 2007. Simon Caulkin wrote: 'Management is supposed to amplify effort by providing a creative framework for individual expression that benefits the team.' It is worth bearing this in mind when evaluating whether the actions of a manager are 'good' or 'bad'.

Management style

There are essentially four styles of management. The style that is chosen can have a dramatic impact upon employees and their motivation.

Autocratic

Typical characteristics of an autocratic manager:

- sets the work and expects it to be performed precisely as directed
- does not involve employees in decision-making
- very strict
- does not believe in employee autonomy
- believes in 'top down' communication and does not encourage employees to contribute
- believes in close supervision
- thinks that employees are solely motivated by money.

Figure 27.1 Different management styles

Democratic

A typical democratic manager:

- encourages employee input into decision-making
- believes in employee autonomy
- encourages two-way communication
- allows employees to use their initiative
- believes that the motivation of employees is not simply financial.

Laissez-faire

Typical characteristics of a laissez-faire manager:

- the manager is remote from employees
- the manager provides very little direction for employees
- a 'let them get on with it' approach is adopted
- employees often have to set their own tasks and objectives.

Paternalistic

Typical characteristics of a paternalistic manager include:

- wanting the workforce to feel involved in decision-making
- consulting employees
- persuading employees to accept his/her view, regardless of their own views.

This style of management has traditionally been associated with Japanese companies.

Differences between management styles

Managers adopting these styles also tend to adopt a particular tone of voice and body language. Autocrats tend to be stern and abrupt, with an 'I'm the boss' manner. Democrats can be friendlier, willing to listen and often adopt a 'my door is always open' approach. Those who are laissez-faire may appear distant, with either a 'just get on with it' semi-autocratic manner or a dismissive 'I'm sure you can handle it on your own' type of comment, neither of which is very helpful. Paternalistic leaders often adopt a 'you see, the trouble with your approach is ...' manner, in order to persuade employees to think negatively about their views. This 'mock consultation' will not be successful in the long run.

Autocratic managers are often found in businesses that are highly centralised, i.e. all of the important decisions are taken by those at the top of the hierarchy, and strict company procedures are laid down for everyday operation. Democratic managers are more likely to be found in a decentralised business, where those at the top encourage creativity and autonomy at all levels.

There is a tendency to regard the democratic style as the 'right' one, but this is not necessarily the case. A good manager will vary style according to circumstance and will not remain permanently in one particular mode. For example, there may be an important deadline approaching which means that some aspects of an autocratic approach need to be adopted, for a time at least.

The democratic approach is certainly inclusive and should lead to better decisions being taken. However it means that the process will take more time and this is not always available. Sometimes discussion continues without agreement being reached, and it will have to be cut short.

Finally, once a particular project is underway, a laissez-faire style may deliberately be chosen for a while, because a manager does not want to be seen to be constantly 'checking up' on subordinates (this could be perceived as a lack of trust which could demotivate them). This style can work well if employees are well-motivated and enjoy responsibility, but will be much less effective if this is not the case.

Key Term

Centralisation: the amount of control exercised by senior executives over decision-making. The business is highly centralised when middle managers and employees have little autonomy.

Examiner's voice

It is important to be able to identify the different sorts of situation where a particular management style will be appropriate. A good manager will vary style according to circumstance.

Theory X and Theory Y

Douglas McGregor's work is often misunderstood. It is sometimes presented as a theory of motivation, but strictly speaking this is not true. It is a theory of how managers view employees. The view adopted will affect how the manager believes employees should be treated and motivated. The theory states that there are two broad sets of assumptions about employees; these are known as Theory X and Theory Y.

Figure 27.2 Douglas McGregor developed a key theory explaining how managers view employees

Theory X

A theory X manager views employees as:

- inherently lazy, disliking work and responsibility
- lacking the will and ability to work unsupervised
- lacking initiative
- largely motivated by money.

A manager adopting such a view is likely to manage in an autocratic manner, offering little if any scope for employee input. Communication will be limited. The way in which work is carried out will take little account of job satisfaction, because it is assumed that the employee's driving force is money. Piecework will probably be the favoured method of payment and remuneration. This is the kind of leadership fostered by Frederick Taylor.

Theory Y

A theory Y manager regards employees as:

- enjoying their work if the right conditions are created
- willing to accept responsibility and challenges
- creative and willing to contribute
- able to exercise self-discipline
- not just motivated by money.

A manager adopting a theory Y view will view employees as valuable assets rather than as a cost to be minimised. The style will be democratic, with employees encouraged to set their own goals and exercise self-control. Motivation comes from factors such as variety, challenge and self-development. Training needs will therefore be identified and employees encouraged to develop their skills. Such a style is more in keeping with Maslow and Herzberg.

The tendency is to think that theory Y must be right since it is a much less pessimistic view of employees than theory X. Indeed, McGregor thought that such an approach was likely to be more effective. Nevertheless, there may be situations (particularly in low skilled jobs with little opportunity for self development and where labour turnover is high) that a theory X approach may be adopted, with all that it implies for management and motivation. However this view might become a self-fulfilling prophesy; autocratic treatment and poor motivation may bring the very response from employees that managers thought existed in the first place.

Many of these issues are considered further in the next chapter.

Task and people needs

Another way of considering how managers manage is to consider task and people needs. A narrow view of management is that its function is to 'get the job done'. Such a view ignores the fact that achieving this effectively depends on people doing their jobs effectively. There is therefore something of a dilemma between 'task needs' and 'people needs'. A manager who has an overriding desire to 'get the job done' will be task-orientated. A manager whose principle aim is to make employees contented and keep them in high spirits, will be people-orientated. Most managers are a mixture of the two to varying degrees. Neither choice is 'right' or 'wrong', but it is possible for a manager to identify his/her leadership style and advise skills to be developed in order to improve performance.

One of the best known ways to approach this was developed by Robert Blake and Jane Mouton in 1964. The grid (usually referred to as the Leadership Grid or 'Blake's grid') is very easy to understand and to apply. Along the horizontal axis are 'task needs'. 'People needs' are plotted on the vertical axis. By considering a manager's responses to a research questionnaire, their style of leadership can be established by where they are placed on the grid. Figure 27.3 indicates the five possibilities that can arise from the manager's actions and priorities.

> ### Key Terms
>
> **People needs:** the needs of employees. A manager who concentrates on people needs will try to make employees contented and keep them in high spirits. This may be at the expense of getting the work done.
>
> **Task needs:** the opposite of people needs. A manager who has an overriding desire to 'get the job done' will be orientated towards the task rather than employees' needs.

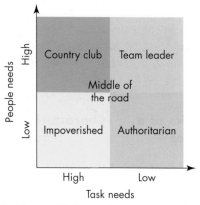

Figure 27.3 The Blake and Mouton leadership grid

Country club leadership

This manager is concerned about the well-being and feelings of their team of people rather than completing the required tasks. While morale may be high, some employees may take advantage, and if deadlines are missed there may be repercussions on other areas of the business which depend on the completion of a task by a certain date.

Authoritarian leadership

An authoritarian manager will be concerned with the task rather than the employees. This manager believes that the needs of the employee must always take second place to completing the task. Leadership will be authoritarian and motivation very much a secondary consideration. A lack of attention to employees' needs can lead to resentment, a lack of commitment and other human resource problems.

Impoverished leadership

This manager will have a lack of concern for either task or people needs. He or she will be unable to devise procedures to ensure that work is completed to the required standard or on time, or to stimulate and motivate employees. This sort of leader is very ineffective at everything. Morale and productivity are both low and this leader's actions are therefore likely to affect other areas of the business negatively.

Team leadership

This manager will have a strong and equal regard for both employee and task needs. This is what a manager should aim for. These leaders believe that if employees are treated as genuine stakeholders, then their needs and the business's task needs will be in harmony. High levels of motivation will be accompanied by high productivity.

Middle-of-the-road leadership

By definition, a middle-of-the-road leader compromises between the two sets of needs. This implies that neither set of needs is truly met, and less than optimal outcomes for each are achieved. Such leaders may be indecisive and timid.

Once a person has identified their place on the grid, areas for leadership development can be identified, although the grid has to be used in context. Leadership styles have to be varied as the occasion demands. If a crucial contract needs to be fulfilled on time then a greater emphasis on task needs will be appropriate; whereas a country club approach may be adopted as the Christmas holiday period approaches. The grid can nevertheless be a timely reminder to a leader of what they should be aspiring to, and to avoid being stuck in one particular style.

> ### Key Term
>
> **Blake's grid:** a method of identifying the actions, priorities and therefore leadership style of a manager. This is undertaken through an analysis of task and people needs.

Types of manager

There are different types of manager, both in terms of hierarchy and function.

Senior managers

These are at the top of an organisation, and are usually led by a Chief Executive Officer (CEO) who will work closely with the board of directors. Some businesses refer to their directors as senior managers. These managers are more concerned with long-term planning and strategy than day-to-day implementation of policy. Nevertheless, a particularly important function of senior managers is to ensure that their departments communicate with each another, so that the business runs smoothly from day to day. The different functional areas of a business have to work together: they cannot exist in isolation.

'Middle managers'

These managers will have more operational (i.e. day-to-day) control than senior executives, and are responsible to them for implementing their strategy. It is not considered good practice for a senior manager to interfere with the way in which middle managers choose to organise their departments.

Junior managers

This term can refer either to management trainees (destined for higher positions) and those in supervisory positions who have a degree of authority. Their work will involve some of the functions of a manager outlined above.

Line and staff managers

In terms of function, two types of managers exist: line managers and staff managers.

Line managers

Line managers have direct input into and responsibility for policy on the business's products. A line manager has 'line authority', i.e. the authority and power to order subordinates in their department to perform appropriate tasks.

Staff managers

Staff managers exist to provide advice and support to the line managers; e.g. the management information services department (which is essentially the numerical database of the firm) can provide all sorts of data for decision-making and also design software support to the line managers. Staff support also includes personnel management, secretarial work and maintenance. Although there will still be a hierarchy within

departments offering staff support, staff managers have no line authority over those whom they support. A high-ranking personnel manager has authority over his subordinates but cannot tell employees in the marketing department what to do.

Key Terms

Line managers: managers who have a direct input into and responsibility for policy on the business's products.
Staff managers: managers whose function is to provide advice and support to the line managers.

Differences between a 'manager' and a 'leader'

'Leadership' is not the same as 'management', although they are linked. A really effective manager will almost certainly be a successful leader. Managers 'manage' via their organisational skills, whereas a leader is more inspirational. Some differences between the two are highlighted in Table 27.1.

Characteristics of a manager	Characteristics of a leader
Obeyed by subordinates	Followed by subordinates
Minimises risk	Risk-taker
Prefers the status quo	Embraces change
'Steady state'	Creative
Sets an example	Inspires others to behave in a certain way
Tells employees to follow procedure	Encourages new ways of thinking
Not very outgoing	Charismatic

Table 27.1 Differences between a manager and a leader

Leaders still require managerial skills (e.g. maximising the use of people's talents and using time effectively) and have to be proficient in their job, but will be 'followed' rather than 'obeyed'. This is not because of their position in the hierarchy but because employees respect and trust them. Leaders are passionate about what they want to achieve and how they want to achieve it. A leader is usually more courageous than a manager, and will take greater risks. A leader will set an example and stimulate others to work towards his/her goals.

It is important to avoid stereotyping. None of the above means that managers are dull remote individuals, rarely moving from their office, pushing routine paperwork up and down the chain of command and generally stifling employees' creativity, while the dynamic leader speeds around motivating everyone by their charisma and enthusiasm!

Where management skills and leadership qualities are harmonised, the business will benefit hugely. However a manager cannot just become a leader. It has been said that great leaders are born, not made, and there may be some truth in this. Leadership skills can certainly be learned, but unless a person is comfortable with the idea of adopting a leadership role, it will not be easy to put those skills into practice. It also has to be acknowledged that a dynamic, creative and charismatic leader can also become a loose cannon if they do not work within the framework of the business's deadlines and objectives.

Management of specialist departments within a business

A large business will have a number of different departments that perform specialist functions. It should not be assumed however that these are rigidly compartmentalised; all managers manage at least a few people, and so every manager has a degree of personnel responsibility even if they are not a personnel manager. Similarly, they have to set and adhere to budgets even if they are not finance managers. The departments are production, marketing, personnel and finance.

Production management

Production management involves more than just making the products. It is concerned with a variety of issues including production scheduling, purchasing, stock control, quality control and maintenance.

Marketing management

This position involves issues such as market research, the development of pricing policies, promotional campaigns and ensuring that the distribution of the product reaches the customer when they want it.

Personnel management

Personnel management is concerned with organising people. This encompasses issues such as recruitment, training, performance appraisal, offering advice on motivation, dismissal etc to the line managers, ensuring that employee records are correct, wages and industrial relations.

Financial management

Finally, financial management is concerned with the housekeeping of the business accounts. All receipts and payments, however small, need to be recorded in order to ensure that the business is solvent and able to meet its overall financial objectives. It is also concerned with the raising of finance and the analysis of costs.

Other areas of management

These are the four main functional areas within a business but this does not mean that there are always only four departments. A business may for example have a research and development department ('R and D') where new products are developed and tested. It may have a management information services department for ICT support.

However many departments actually exist, the need for coordination and cooperation between the functions should be obvious. Production must produce what marketing tells them to make, since this is how the customer is satisfied and repeat purchases are generated. However this coordination cannot be done in isolation. The financial objectives of the business will have come partly from a consideration of the capabilities of the production department and the ability of marketing to sell the products. The finance department must ensure that even if products are being successfully produced and sold, the business is not overtrading; i.e. ensuring that the cash flow is sufficient to support the growth. Personnel will have to ensure that the business has a manpower plan to make certain that all departments have the right people to achieve this.

In a small business such as a sole trader, these functions still exist but will have to be performed by a single person, who may not be enthusiastic or effective at all of them. This sort of managerial specialisation results in managerial economies of scale.

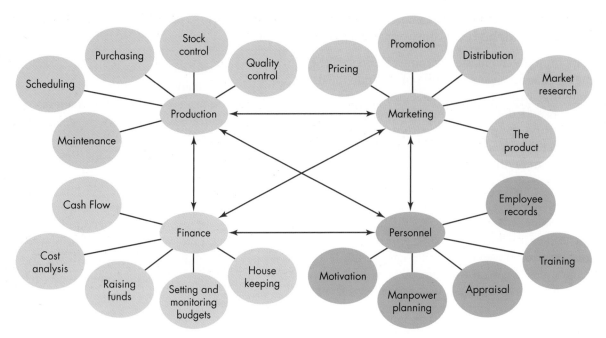

Figure 27.4 *The four main departments in business and their most important functions*

Examiner's voice

When answering a question involving the four functional areas of a business, bear in mind that integration and cooperation between them is essential if the business is to operate successfully and meet its strategic objectives.

Figure 27.5 *Input into the product*

The organisation of a business

Broadly speaking, there are two ways for a business to be organised: by system or by product.

Organisation by system

Here, the business is split into specialist areas which operate together to make the business function efficiently, rather like the parts in an old-fashioned clock. This means that each part of 'the system' has some input into the output of the business' product(s).

The achievements (or failures) of the business arise from the outcome of the interaction of a number of different departments. This seems very sensible; each part of the system (i.e. department) contains specialists who can concentrate on what they do best. Specialist functions (departments) are not duplicated but there are several points to bear in mind:

- There can be a tendency for each department to operate as a separate entity or/and to treat itself as the most important part of the business. If this occurs, managers in such a department fail to operate with the strategic objectives of the whole business uppermost in their mind.
- Without a high level of integration, coordination and some degree of compromise (e.g. over timescales and deadlines), the business will become fragmented with each department working largely to its own agenda. Such fragmentation will damage the overall productivity of the business.
- It can be difficult to evaluate performance and identify whether or not a particular product is particularly successful, since there are several departmental inputs affecting performance. Some departments may try to take most of the credit for success and/or may blame others for failure.

- It is not always easy for managers in one department to see a direct result between their contribution and results.

Organisation by product

Alternatively, the company could be organised by product, i.e. the business is organised around recognisable individual products. These are known as **profit centres**.

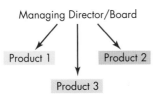

Figure 27.6 Organisation by product

Each product is 'a company in miniature' with its own finance, marketing etc department. This too seems a sensible way to organise for the following reasons.

- It is easier to see which products are performing well. Each profit centre can be easily evaluated.
- Managers of each product can concentrate their energies on one product rather than several.
- Each centre has considerable autonomy which can increase motivation.

- Managers can see the direct result of their decisions and so may be more motivated.

Needless to say, there are also drawbacks with this form of organisation:

- Different products compete for resources (such as finance); this can create winners and losers and so can lead to conflict.
- Are resources wasted? Would it be better to have one finance department, one marketing department etc. (thus achieving managerial economies of scale) rather than several?

It is for the board to decide on the most appropriate method of organisation, given the business's situation and its objectives. Once a choice is made to change from one method of organisation to another, it will not be easy to change back.

Further resources

www.kevindecker.com/page.asp – a website containing practical details on how to become a successful manager, and especially how to build a successful team.

www.nwlink.com/~donclark/leader/bm_model.html – the Blake's grid questionnaire. Where would you be on the grid?

Your Turn

Questions Time allowed 15 minutes

1. Define the term 'organisation by system'. (2 marks)
2. Define the term 'organisation by product'. (2 marks)
3. State and give one characteristic of the four styles of leadership. (8 marks)
4. Outline two differences between a manager and a leader. (4 marks)

(16 marks)

Case Study Time allowed 25 minutes

Harvey plc

Harvey plc is a medium-sized, growing company making household products. It achieved success with the brand 'Sparkle', an all-purpose non-scratch cleaning fluid. It has always sold well, and indications are that it will be possible to export it abroad in the near future.

The company also makes 'Jewellgleam' (a gold and silver cleaner), 'Pineoshine' (a scented household cleaner) and 'Duropad' (a plastic scourer for washing up). These have sold satisfactorily but not spectacularly well.

A year ago, a new product for window cleaning was launched, 'Windowgleam'. This has not been a success at all; the whole project has been dogged with disasters.

Ray Crimp, the managing director, feels rather guilty about this, as 18 months ago he instigated a complete change in the company's organisation. It was previously organised by product (each with its own team), but is now based on a systems basis with specialist functions. The change was made on the grounds of cost-effectiveness. He argued that the duplication of each function (finance, marketing etc.) was costly and unnecessary. The Board agreed, the change was made (several people being made redundant in the process which was also costly), and each function is now headed by a director.

Ray and the directors are gathered at the quarterly board meeting, and one of the items on the agenda is to discuss recent events, in particular the shambles surrounding 'Windowgleam'.

Attending the meeting with Ray are:

- Bob Lemar, the marketing director; rather short-tempered.

- Ahmed Singh, the production director. He too has a short temper.

- Cath Tolland, the firm's senior accountant. A rather self-important woman who takes her job very seriously. She is nevertheless an excellent accountant.

- Mary Julius, the personnel director. Highly competent but dislikes arguing and likes to work independently.

Ray began the board meeting.

Ray: As you know, there have been a few minor problems with 'Windowgleam ' and I'd like to iron them out today. Now then Bob, how are things in marketing?

Bob: A few minor problems? Let me tell you how it is. We research the product and we find the customer wants it. We find out how they would like it packaged; we design the package. We send out our sales teams to sell and what happens? Production doesn't make enough of them! We can sell well but we can't deliver. Our distributors must think we're totally incompetent.

Ahmed: Don't try and blame it on us Bob. Let me tell you how it is in production. I've been concentrating my resources on 'Sparkle', which pays our wages after all. I haven't had the time or money to concentrate on your precious 'Windowgleam'.

Bob: Not enough time? We planned this launch about two years ago. How long do you need?

Ahmed: Are you deaf? I said time and money. I've not had the finance to install the proper technology onto my production lines. If I had, I would have exceeded my budget.

Bob: I know that. Do you think I know nothing about finance? Sorting out your line would have only meant exceeding your budget by about £90,000; that's a measly, pathetic 3%.

Ray: Now, could we …

Cath: Excuse me. Did you say 'only 3%'? Only 3%? £90,000 is a lot of money. We don't set budgets for fun you know. The financial position of the company is rather important.

Bob: You accountants never see the real world do you? It's all just columns of figures, balance sheets and, and …

Owen: And what, Bob? And, all the other thousand and one things we're supposed to do: like make sure we don't have a cashflow problem, like ensure we pay the VAT on time, like analyse our performance. Considering I'm actually two members of staff short in my department, I think I'm doing rather better than you.

Ray: Ah yes, I was coming to that. Mary, what's going on in your department?

Mary: Now then, you can't blame it all on personnel you know.

Ray: I'm not blaming anyone, I just wanted to…

Mary: The new procedures don't make life very easy. Whereas previously every manager did the advertising and interviewing themselves, now my department does it all. I get a bit of paper with something like 'The applicant will need to know about cost and control procedures' written on it. That doesn't mean much to me. Managers often complain they are to busy to attend interviews or that they can't attend the interviews I've set up. Why can't we go back to the old system, when the people who knew what they needed conducted the interviews?

Cath: It's your job, Mary. I've enough on my plate already without doing your department's work.

Bob: I see what she means though, Cath, even if you don't. With the old system, I had a sum of money and I set my own budgets. Now someone from the accounts department who knows nothing about marketing starts acting like a dictator.

Cath: Look Bob, you simply cannot blame me for your own over-zealous behaviour. You shouldn't have sent your sales teams out until we were completely ready.

Ray: OK. OK. Let's cool down a bit, shall we? Now I have a proposal from Bill Longman, in the R and D department.

Ahmed: Where is Bill anyway? Why isn't he here?

Bob: Frightened to show his face, I shouldn't wonder.

Ray: He's actually in another meeting but he's sent along a proposal for a new product.

Bob: Another one? We haven't properly launched the last one yet. Those idiots in R and D live with their heads in the clouds.

Ahmed: That's the first sensible thing you've said all day, Bob. They come up with these weird and wonderful ideas without bothering to think if we can actually produce it.

Bob: Or if the customer wants it.

Cath: Or if we've the money to do it!

Mary: Or if we've the right staff to deal with it.

Ahmed: Well, at last we all agree on something! Let's forget this new thing, whatever it is.

Ray: Now hold on, I think we should at least discuss it.

Bob: We've no time, Ray. Let's end now, go away and solve our own departmental problems. Until they are sorted we'll never make any progress. We'll have a formal meeting in about two months' time.

Mary: Fine.

Ahmed: Suits me.

Cath: Good idea.

Ray: No, wait a second, let's all …

[But he was talking to an empty room.]

1. Analyse two problems that have occurred at Harvey plc as a result of the reorganisation.

(6 marks)

2. Recommend and justify a strategy to solve the organisational problems at Harvey plc.

(18 marks)

(24 marks)

MANAGEMENT AND MOTIVATION

If someone is asked what they understand by 'motivation at work', they might reply by using phrases such as 'people working hard', 'employees believing that what they do makes a difference', or 'people wanting to do their best'. Certainly these sentiments form part of what makes a motivated employee.

There are sometimes misconceptions about what constitutes motivation. Motivation at work is caused by positive factors; when an employee is motivated, it is because the right conditions have been created and the employee *wants* to behave in a certain way. On the other hand, if an employee is told that unless his conduct improves he will receive a formal warning, his behaviour may change but he will not feel *motivated* to do so.

A motivated person has a strong desire to act in a particular way and to achieve a certain result. A motivated employee is therefore one who wants to work hard, takes a pride in his/her work and is committed to achieving the business's goals.

'Motivation' is not the same as 'morale'. The two are linked but there is a difference: morale can be defined as 'spirit', in the sense that if morale in a team (or indeed an individual) is high, then team members are supportive of each other and there exists a spirit of confidence and purpose. This is likely to lead to increased motivation.

Key Terms

Motivation: a strong desire to act in a particular way and to achieve a certain result.

Morale: 'spirit'; if morale in an individual, group or team is high then there exists a spirit of confidence and purpose.

Why is motivation important?

The business's purpose in motivating its employees is not only an ethical decision to make their working lives as stimulating as possible; in the final analysis, a business wants its employees to be motivated so that they can be fully effective in helping the business to meet its objectives. The benefits of a motivated workforce are readily apparent.

- Employees who are motivated will be less prone to absenteeism and have lower rates of labour turnover, which will help lower costs.
- Motivated employees will regard themselves as true stakeholders rather than 'workers' and will be more productive, committed and willing to 'go the extra mile' for the business.
- High levels of motivation make change easier to implement.

In short, motivated employees help to give a business a competitive advantage.

Motivational theorists

Minimum standards of pay and safety at work are laid down by the law, but a business that wants motivated employees will have to exceed those standards. A large number of people have undertaken research into what causes employees to be motivated. A summary of the best known follows here.

Examiner's voice

Candidates are mistaken if they think that presenting the findings of the motivational theorists in a few words such as 'Taylor said people only work for money' or 'Mayo said people have social needs' will be sufficient to score high marks. At A2 level, examiners are looking for more depth and a clear understanding of how the work of the theorist can be applied to the specific business in the case study.

Frederick Taylor (1856 – 1917), scientific management

Frederick Taylor was an American theorist, writing in the early years of the twentieth century. His famous 'Principles of Scientific Management' was published in 1911. Taylor thought that a scientific approach could be used to motivate employees, whatever tasks they were performing. The approach meant that the principles he believed in could be replicated and applied in most industrial settings.

Essentially, the approach meant that jobs would be carefully observed to see exactly what tasks were being performed. They would then be broken down into simple tasks to ensure a high division of labour. Those who were best suited to each job would be recruited and then trained to perform the specialised task. They would be paid on a piece rate, the basic premise being that money was the key motivator. By using these principles, a way could be found to use workers efficiently to increase productivity and link reward to their effort. This, Taylor claimed, would mean that the objectives of both managers and employees would be harmonised.

The theory is in many ways a product of its creator and its time. Taylor was an engineer (not a psychologist, like Mayo; see below) specifically interested in productive efficiency and not the psychological understanding of employee behaviour. Furthermore, at the time it was quite rare for the concept of job satisfaction to be uppermost in managers' minds. Employees might have wanted more than simply 'a day's work', but were often grateful that they had any work at all. If they complained about a lack of satisfaction at work they could be dismissed. Society was more hierarchical, and employees were being seen as little more than machines;

although Taylor was not against employee welfare and good industrial relations. However, he believed that these would naturally arise from the scientific principles that linked the output desired by the managers to the rewards available for the employees.

Taylor's work was adopted by many businesses in the 1920s (notably at Henry Ford's car plants) but the approach, at least in the way that Taylor originally envisaged it, went out of favour as society changed and new theories of motivation began to emerge. Nevertheless the concept of money as the principal motivator for employees is still referred to as 'a Tayloristic approach'. Furthermore, many of the principles of modern work study (see Unit 48) owe much to his work.

Key Term

Scientific management: the concept (originated by Frederick Taylor in the 1920s) that a set of principles could be developed and applied by managers to motivate employees in most types of business. A central part of the theory is that employees are largely motivated by money.

Elton Mayo (1880–1949), human relations management

Elton Mayo was an American psychologist whose most significant work was conducted in the 1920s and 1930s. Like Taylor, he was interested in improving employee productivity, but he approached the issue from a

Figure 28.1 Elton Mayo

different perspective; he felt that scientific management alone could not explain the behaviour, attitude and productivity of employees.

Mayo is associated with the term 'Hawthorne effect'. This is because his most famous research was undertaken at the Hawthorne plant of the Western Electric Company in Chicago. The experiments were of different types and lasted over a period of several years.

The initial research at the plant was concerned with altering the brightness of the lighting in a particular area of the firm. It was discovered that the productivity of employees nearly always rose when it was changed – although it later returned to normal. It was thought that the presence of the researchers had an effect on productivity. The employees liked the fact that someone was taking an interest in them.

The second set of experiments involved a particular group of women assembling telephone components. These were the so-called 'relay assembly experiments'. Various changes were made to rest breaks and the length of the working day. Furthermore the employees were allowed to choose who they wished to work with. They also had a supervisor who adopted a consultative attitude to the changes and who implemented some of the changes they suggested. The result was that the increase in breaks and the shortening of the day, coupled with being able to work in a group and being managed by a democratic supervisor, led to an increase in productivity. The first of these points was quite significant as it was against the prevailing wisdom of the time, that breaks should be minimised in order to increase output. To some extent the debate over 'are long hours good or bad?' continues today.

Further research was conducted into groupwork and payment by results in the 'wiring room experiments'. A group of male employees was observed soldering telephone equipment. It was discovered that being paid according to results on an individual basis did not always raise productivity. This was because the men were worried that if output rose by a large amount, the business would reduce the rate they were being paid, and that would mean having to work harder for the same pay. Mayo also observed that despite the individual piecework system in place, the men chose to work in specific groups, and that there was a social hierarchy that was not necessarily reflected in the differences in jobs; the person who was doing the most important job did not necessarily have the highest status in the group. These group members bonded closely together and formed a united front when dealing with managers; each member gave the same sort of response to any question asked.

A further series of experiments involving alterations to the working environment and employee teams indicated once again that cooperation and teamwork raised productivity – as did meeting group norms, i.e. performing to the expectations of the group rather than to those of the business.

Broadly speaking, Mayo reached the following conclusions:

- Employees respond to changes in the working environment.
- A sense of recognition and consultation is important to employees.
- The workplace is a social system. Employees like to work in groups.
- Communication with management and group norms affect productivity.

With several different experiments being conducted over a period of years it can be difficult to generalise as to exactly what is 'the Hawthorne effect'; people use the term to mean different things. Sometimes it is used to mean one of the above factors, and sometimes several. Some researchers use the term to mean the effect on employees' behaviour and productivity as a result of being observed.

Examiner's voice

Make sure that you know the conclusions which Mayo drew from the Hawthorne experiments, but be careful when using the term 'Hawthorne effect'; it can be used to mean different things.

Nevertheless, Mayo's conclusions pointed to the fact that there was more to increasing productivity and motivation than Taylorism suggested. Psychological factors were also important. He felt that a more humane approach to breaks, coupled with teamwork, communication and an interest from management could bring quite significant results. As a result, businesses started to change in order to reflect this, introducing greater use of consultation, better communication, improved welfare facilities, and groupworking.

Mayo's work was conducted among employees at one plant in the first part of the twentieth century, and therefore cannot be regarded as applicable to all employees in the twenty-first century. His work has also been criticised on the grounds that several variables were often changed at once, and so identifying the exact cause of a change in productivity is difficult. Furthermore as the experiments went on for years and not days or even months, it could be expected that employees' abilities would improve, and that this was the cause of the increase in productivity.

Whatever one's view, when looked at from the perspective of a modern business, his conclusions seem rather obvious although at the time they were quite radical. They marked a distinct break from Taylor's theories, and Mayo is regarded as the founder of the human relations school of management, in which psychological factors are seen to have a large influence on productivity.

Abraham Maslow (1908–70), the hierarchy of needs

Abraham Maslow is famous for his work on human needs. Like Mayo he was a psychologist, and in 1954 published a theory of the hierarchy of needs. Maslow had originally worked with animals and observed that some needs were fulfilled before others: e.g. the need to satisfy thirst was met before the need to feed. Building on this observation with further research created his famous hierarchy of needs.

Some of the work relating to the hierarchy is couched in quite complicated psychological jargon, but in terms of application to business it is essentially this: employees have a variety of needs at work that have to be satisfied, and until the lower order needs are met, the higher ones cannot be. Once a person's needs are met at a particular level, they cease to be motivated by them and will need to 'move up' to a higher level (unsatisfied needs are a motivating factor). On the other hand, if lower order needs are not satisfied, then an employee will no longer be concerned about achieving higher order (esteem and self-actualisation) needs.

- **Self-actualisation needs.** 'Self-actualisation' is hard to define precisely, but Maslow suggested that it was concerned with personal growth and the achievement of one's full potential as a human.
- **The esteem needs.** Humans look for self-esteem. They seek the respect of others, some recognition and recognition for effort as well as a degree of status.

- **The love and belonging needs (usually called social needs).** Humans as social animals do not like loneliness and isolation. They have a need for friendship and positive relationships with others.

Figure 28.2 Maslow's hierarchy of needs

- **Safety and security needs.** Once physiological needs are taken care of, humans seek security, stability and protection.
- **Physiological needs.** These include the need for shelter, water, and food.

Although the theory was not designed specifically for business use, its significance in the business world is that if employees are to be motivated, managers must provide the conditions for needs to be met and employees to progress up the hierarchy.

Therefore:

- **To meet physiological needs,** a business would have to pay a fair wage for a fair number of hours worked, and allow appropriate breaks.
- **To meet the security needs,** a business would have to ensure a high standard of health and safety, as well as making sure that appropriate policies on issues such as bullying, discrimination, and discipline are in place.
- **To meet the social needs,** there should be an opportunity for social interaction with others; both employees via (e.g.) teamwork and managers via a consultative, democratic approach.
- **To meet esteem needs,** there should be the opportunity for leadership and promotion.
- **To meet self-actualisation needs** of employees, managers should try to identify what these needs are (using methods such as appraisal), and help to guide employees towards appropriate goals and challenges. Training should be provided to help meet them.

The theory has its criticisms. Two of the most important are:

1. The theory was not specifically designed for use in the business world. It will be difficult if not impossible for a manager to identify each and every employee's needs to help them progress.

2. It is something of a generalisation. Do employees necessarily seek self-actualisation through work? It could be argued that once their lower order needs are met by an employer, an employee may seek self-actualisation through non-work activities such as sport, playing the guitar or painting.

Nevertheless, there are some interesting issues here with lessons to be learned for motivation: the need for managers to be democratic and to help employees identify goals to be met at work; the fact that employees require a satisfactory social situation at work for motivation to occur; and the fact that if lower order needs are not met (i.e. without an adequate wage earned in an environment free from health risks and victimisation), the higher ones are likely to be meaningless.

Peter Drucker (1909–2005), the 'father of modern management'

It is not possible to mention 'management' or 'motivation' without reference to Peter Drucker. Drucker was born in Austria in 1909 and was a writer, lecturer and consultant for over 60 years. He published a large number of books on management; the two best-known are probably *The Practice of Management* and *The Effective Executive*, in which he identified the sort of skills necessary for managers to succeed in their role, such as time management, knowing how or where to apply talents, prioritising and planning, and making effective decisions. Drucker also spoke on the subject of motivation, and so wide and pervasive has been his influence that he has sometimes been called the 'father of management'. As far back as the 1950s, his key beliefs were stated:

1. The most important asset of any organisation is its employees, who should be recognised as such and not treated as costs to be minimised. Drucker claimed that a manager's primary purpose is to enable people to perform. He wrote of the business as a community built on trust and respect for its employees.

2. He coined the phrase 'knowledge worker' long before others appreciated how significant a commodity knowledge would be in a post-industrial society. Unlike traditional skills, knowledge changes rapidly and so employees need both formal education and ongoing training. The development of this idea was to be very persuasive in later years.

To try to do justice to Drucker's work in a few sentences is impossible, but some of the most important factors for managers if they want an effective and motivated workforce are to:

- decentralise and delayer the business as much as possible, to allow organisational freedom for managers and employees to respond quickly to consumer demands.
- take an interest in their employees and value their contribution to the organisation.
- offer ongoing training to create and nurture 'knowledge workers'.
- try to create a 'plant community' where individuals' social needs can be met.
- keep a sense of perspective when it comes to reward. He was very critical that senior managers could reap huge rewards as a result of closing down plants and making thousands of employees redundant. He called this 'morally and socially unforgivable'.

These straightforward ideas brought major benefits to American corporations in the post-war period, and they continue to hold their significance today. Many researchers and theorists developed these ideas.

In the 1980s he began to have grave doubts about the behaviour of many large US businesses and the executives who ran them. He claimed that the way in which businesses were being run was fundamentally wrong. Employees were expendable, at board level self-interest ruled – high levels of executive pay particularly irked him – and there was little sense of the community that he believed should exist. Thirty years after making his name as the person who laid down the groundrules for creating a successful business, he emerged as one of corporate America's most outspoken critics.

Frederick Herzberg (1923–2000) The two-factor theory

Unlike Maslow's theory, Frederick Herzberg's was constructed specifically for the workplace. He was particularly interested in the factors that cause job satisfaction and job dissatisfaction. Perhaps unsurprisingly, he found that factors such as interesting work, responsibility and the opportunity for self-development proved to be motivating. However his

Figure 28.3 Frederick Herzberg

research also demonstrated that factors such as pay, pensions, working conditions and the relationship with the line manager did not result in job satisfaction. Herzberg called these 'hygiene' factors. They are also known as 'maintenance factors'.

This gave rise to the 'two-factor theory'.

The hygiene factors

These are similar to the lower levels of Maslow's hierarchy. They do not motivate employees, no matter how 'good' they are. This however does not mean that they are of no significance; Herzberg discovered that the absence of them causes job *dissatisfaction*. Improving these factors will improve the working environment generally and can lead to reduced discontentment and a reduction of the 'management doesn't care about us' attitude.

The motivating factors

Hygiene factors are therefore important, but Herzberg discovered that the reduction of job dissatisfaction is not enough to ensure motivation. If employees are to be motivated then certain other factors must be in place. These motivators (which are similar to the higher levels of Maslow's hierarchy) relate to the job itself and not the working environment. They are factors such as responsibility, recognition, meaningful and rewarding work, and the opportunity for promotion.

In conclusion, a business will need hygiene factors in place to prevent job dissatisfaction, *and* motivators in place to motivate.

Examiner's voice

The presence of motivators will motivate but the presence of hygiene factors will not; they just prevent dissatisfaction. The two are not the same.

Herzberg's original research was conducted amongst white collar employees (accountants and engineers), and has been criticised on the grounds that the conclusions may therefore not be applicable to all employees especially 'frontline' blue collar workers. Subsequent research by other people has not been conclusive, but if Herzberg's findings are accepted then there are a number of practical issues for management.

- There should be scope for **job enlargement**. This does *not* simply mean 'giving people more work' but redesigning and broadening the nature of a job. Employees should be encouraged and supported (e.g. via training) to take on new and more challenging tasks if they want to.
- Employees need greater autonomy at work and the chance to accept responsibility. Therefore, there is a need for **job enrichment**; the job itself needs to be interesting and enriching to the employee. This means that jobs need to be analysed and redesigned to allow personal growth. This enrichment could take the form of employees taking more responsibility for work being undertaken (i.e. getting rid of unnecessary supervision) and greater involvement in decision-making. Where possible, employees should be able to complete a whole task, not just a part of it.
- There should also be **job rotation** which allows greater variety in the tasks to be undertaken and should help prevent boredom. It will also enable employees to gain experience for promotion. This is not the same as job enrichment, because it does not involve an increase in responsibility.
- People like to be praised for their efforts. Herzberg emphasised the importance of positive feedback to provide recognition and a sense of achievement.

In practice, job enlargement, enrichment, and rotation will be very time-consuming to plan and implement. This is not to say that managers should not bother with them, but it must be recognised that if these are to be undertaken properly, a large amount of resources will have to be channelled into the process. Any proposed changes will need to be negotiated with employees, who otherwise may see the process purely as an attempt to give them more work.

Furthermore it is not always easy to enrich unskilled, repetitive jobs, but it could be argued that managers are paid, in part at least, to try to do so.

Key Terms

Job enlargement: redesigning and broadening the nature of a job so that employees can take on new and more challenging tasks if they want to. It does *not* simply mean 'giving people more work'!

Job enrichment: making sure that a job is interesting and enriching to an employee, e.g. through a greater variety of tasks, more responsibility, greater involvement etc.

Tom Peters (1942–), 'In search of excellence'

Tom Peters is a management 'guru' rather than 'a motivational theorist'. He is a charismatic speaker and also has a very individual style of writing. Peters was born in Baltimore USA and came to prominence in the early 1980s with the publication of '*In search of excellence*', a book looking at how to improve corporate performance, which became a best-seller. This was followed by a string of other successful publications, including '*Thriving on chaos*' and '*Crazy Times Call for Crazy Organizations*'.

'*In search of excellence*' caused something of a revolution at the time because Peters was very critical of the way that most large corporations in the USA were being run. His research found cautious executives who disliked change and who were obsessed with three things: numbers, bureaucracy, and control. This obsession he claimed was a mistake, because these issues did not focus on the things that really mattered to business success – people, customers and action. On the twentieth anniversary of the publication of this book, he stated:

'I was scratching the Douglas McGregor itch. Doug was the guy who invented Theory X and Theory Y, which basically said that people are a really important

Name	Theory	Key points	
Taylor	Scientific management	• Organise employees like machines • Tight control and direction of workforces • Pay on the basis of piece rates	
Mayo	Human relations management	• Hawthorne effect (Western Electric, Chicago) • Working conditions changed to improve productivity but motivated by: – recognition – sense of involvement	
Herzberg	Two-factor theory	Motivators: • sense of achievement • recognition • responsibility • promotion • meaningful work/tasks	Hygiene/maintenance factors: • working conditions • pay • company bureaucracy • status • job security
McGregor	Theory X and Theory Y	Theory X: • money motivators • supervision of workers required • workers have little initiative • workers do not make decisions	Theory Y: • job satisfaction motivates • workers are able to work on their own • workers have initiative and can make decisions • workers are motivated by rewards and recognition
Maslow	Hierarchy of needs	• Physiological needs • Security needs • Social needs	• Status needs • Self-actualisation needs

Table 28.1 Theories of motivation, a summary

part of business and that you can't motivate them by controlling and tyrannizing them. Everybody knew that what he said was true, and everybody continued to treat their workers like s*** and then kept asking why companies didn't perform better.'

(*Fast Company*, Issue 53, November 2001)

Many of Peters' basic premises are not in themselves new (and also not solely concerned with motivation), but the early 1980s were a good time for a restatement of some simple but important ideas. For example, Peters pointed out that problems are not likely to be solved quickly or effectively when a business is governed by bureaucratic policies, rigid organisation and multiple layers of hierarchy. Second, a business must focus on its customers and be run with the customers rather than itself in mind. Third, if employees are to be motivated, they need to be valued and empowered at all levels of the business. Taylorism as a motivational tool, which was back in fashion in many corporations, was often a mistake.

'Taylor showed how he could increase productivity, reduce mistakes and make even the dumbest ox of a man a dependable employee. Hardly an uplifting view of work or your employees.'

(*Fast Company*, Issue 53, November 2001)

Many of Peters' suggestions mirror previous ideas. They include:

- acknowledging employee achievement and effort, and also giving praise (giving employees a sense of recognition)
- Involving and empowering employees (which gives employees a sense of involvement and belonging)
- encouraging participation (giving employees a sense of involvement and responsibility)
- trying to offer continuous employment (giving employees a sense of security).

Peters remains an influential figure in business literature, and in 2007 was voted the second most influential leadership professional by Gurus International in an independent internet study.

Key Term

Empowerment: allowing employees to make decisions about when and how a task is performed

Who is right?

There cannot be a definitive answer to this question; what motivates some employees will not do so for others. The factors that motivate professionals may not be the same as those that motivate workers in unskilled jobs. Some people may not want to seek fulfilment at work and may do a perfectly good job, but not be the slightest bit interested in any responsibility or self-development in a work-based context. However it cannot be claimed that this is true across the whole workforce. Such a 'theory X' attitude (see Unit 27) is very outdated.

It should however be apparent that certain factors arise repeatedly as motivators, whatever the nature of the employment; fair pay, managers taking a genuine interest in employees' work and development, allowing the business to meet employees' social needs, and some variety, autonomy and challenge, to list just a few. There can be no single right way to motivate employees, although clearly certain broad principles need to be followed.

Figure 28.4 Motivation can arise from a variety of different factors.

However, such principles cannot be treated as a 'tick list' that will guarantee a motivated workforce. In general, the factors affecting the chosen method(s) of motivation depend on:

- The culture of the business. A new manager arriving at a business run on autocratic lines will find it difficult to introduce employee involvement, job enrichment and empowerment. As with almost all successful initiatives, the support for this motivational route must come from the top of the organisation.
- The nature of the workforce and (referring back to Douglas McGregor) the manager's expectations of it.
- A manager's 'people skills' and leadership style. A person who is naturally at ease in delegating and discussing different points of view will find it easier to empower employees than a confirmed autocrat.
- The resources available. If the money for initiatives such as increasing pay, building a new canteen to facilitate social interaction, or sending people on training courses is not actually forthcoming, all of the proclamations about 'valuing employees and their contribution' will sound rather hollow.

Examiner's voice

While it is important to know and understand the different motivation theories, simply quoting them will not access the highest levels of the mark scheme. You need to evaluate which one (or ones) will be most appropriate for the business in the case study. You can do this by considering the practical implications of implementing the theory. For example, who will initiate the strategic changes necessary? What timescale will be appropriate? What are the resource costs? This will be a more fruitful approach than just quoting the nature of the original research or (as some candidates do) saying 'they should use Maslow'.

Further Sources

http://www.accel-team.com/motivation – a useful site that looks at motivation in theory and in practice. It deals with all of the major theorists.

www.leadershipgurus.net – a brief outline of the 30 most important business gurus.

www.tompeterscompany.com – the website of Tom Peters offers information on what his management consultancy and training firm can offer to the modern business.

Your Turn

Case Study Time allowed 40 minutes

Stanton Solutions Software Ltd (SSSL)

Greg Stanton runs a software development company, Stanton Solutions Software Ltd (SSSL). Greg founded the business four years ago and has gained a reputation as a business that 'delivers', i.e. projects are on time and the software performs well. The business deals mainly with software for chemical engineering projects. This requires employees with specialist knowledge, who can be hard to find. Greg has recently been thinking of diversifying into other engineering software as well.

Greg however has a problem with labour turnover. Apart from himself, there are six employees at SSSL, all of them graduates with a considerable number of years of experience and expertise. Two of these (Nick Gerret and Anna Navarro) have handed in their notice and will be leaving in a month's time. In one way Greg will not be sorry to see them leave, as they had been arriving for work late and taking time off work sick with minor ailments on an increasingly regular basis. Both of them have been with SSSL for less than a year.

Luckily, the projects they are working on will be completed by the time that they leave, but there are several new ones that are waiting to be started. These two are only the latest to leave; there is not one employee who was with Greg when he started the firm and, looking back, he thinks that SSSL has had 17 different employees since it began. This did not seem to matter when employees could easily be found, but the rate at which people are leaving means that Greg has to take on more work himself, and he is becoming rather stressed. He has been forced to offer higher salaries to recruit employees, but this has not solved the problem.

He has always acknowledged to himself that he is not a 'people person'. While he is technically very competent, he tends to work on his own; he rarely delegates important jobs, preferring to keep the important projects under his direct control. There is limited involvement over what work will be undertaken by employees; Greg simply allocates projects to staff according to his perception of their strengths and interests. Being a rather private person, he has never attempted to organise any social events for his staff.

He has asked the two employees why they are leaving and they were quite honest with him.

'It's a bit dull here, Greg,' said Nick. 'Nothing personal but you don't exactly go out of your way to make things interesting and you keep all the major projects to yourself. It's like you never trust us properly. Also, the business I'm joining offers a bit more of a chance to progress'.

Anna had said something similar, that she wanted more scope for her own input. Greg protested that he had been trying to help by keeping most of the complicated work to himself. 'Yes, but you know what I mean,' she replied. Greg was not sure he did.

He has recently been studying some motivational literature but is unclear just how the concepts he has read about such as 'Taylorism', 'the Hawthorne effect', and 'the hierarchy of needs' might actually be applied to his business. He does however recognise that something will have to be done soon to address the problem, otherwise he simply will not have the staff to fulfil his contracts.

1. Outline what is meant by the following terms:

   A. Taylorism

   B. Hawthorne effect

   C. hierarchy of needs

   D. knowledge worker

   E. hygiene factors.   (5 x 4 marks)

2. Analyse **two** reasons why a motivated workforce is important to Stanton Ltd.   (6 marks)

3. Recommend and justify a strategy that Greg could use in order to improve motivation at Stanton Ltd.
                                           (18 marks)

                                      (44 marks)

EMPLOYMENT LAW

Relations between employers and employees are governed by the law. Until the 1960s, British industrial relations largely followed the tradition of voluntarism. This meant that, although various pieces of legislation existed, neither employers nor employees looked to the law to achieve their objectives. Unions were sometimes suspicious that the judiciary would be biased against them, while managers were concerned that any increase in legal constraints would limit their ability to manage in the way that they wanted. The attitudes of both were to be profoundly affected by the behaviour of trade unions in the 1970s and the employment legislation that followed.

Going to court to settle a dispute between an employee and an employer creates a winner and a loser. This does not make for harmonious industrial relations once the case is concluded. For this reason, the government funds an independent organisation dedicated to improving industrial relations. This organisation is Acas, which stands for Advisory, Conciliation Arbitration Service. This is exactly what it offers. It gives advice on industrial relations to employees and managers, and it offers them a conciliation (i.e. mediation) service. It aims to reconcile different positions and resolve disputes of employment law before they come to court.

Key Term

Acas: the Advisory, Conciliation and Arbitration Service. It gives impartial advice and support to employees and managers on industrial relations issues.

There are a very large number of laws governing the treatment of employees. It is no defence in law for employers to claim ignorance of a particular piece of legislation, or that they thought the Act did not apply to them. It is essential for a business to keep up to date with any new legislation, and indeed changes to existing laws if they want good industrial relations and to avoid prosecution.

The rest of this unit is divided into three sections, exploring the law relating to:

1. the recruitment process

2. employees

3. the termination of employment.

The law relating to recruitment

Prevention of discrimination

Discrimination occurs when an employer treats a person less favourably than another employee without any justification. It is important to note that discrimination can occur not only when employing someone, but also when promoting someone, or allowing them access to training courses.

The Disability Discrimination Act 1995

This Act aimed to end the discrimination which many disabled people had to face at work and also as consumers when accessing the services of a business. A business is breaking the law if it refuses to employ (or promote) a person on the grounds of disability. The disabilities may be mental, physical or sensory, i.e. people who are partially sighted or deaf. The Act affects any business with 15 or more employees, and makes it illegal for a business to treat its disabled employees, or potential employees, any differently from others.

The Act also applies in terms of access to facilities and services. A business has to make 'reasonable adjustments' to the way in which products and services are delivered so that disabled people can use them. The adjustments can be physical, e.g. changes to the actual building such as ramps and handrails, or procedural, e.g. always having a member of staff available to help a disabled person.

The implications for a business are as follows:

- There needs to be a clear policy on how services are to be provided to disabled people.
- This policy needs to be clearly communicated to all staff.
- The policy needs to be reviewed and monitored. The Act makes it clear that it is not a 'one-off' but a continuing duty on a business.
- The policy includes training issues in terms of a disabled person's rights and the way that disabled people are to be treated.

Examiner's voice

You will produce an analytical answer and achieve a good grade in the case study if you can detail the implications for the business in complying with the law.

The Sex Discrimination Act (1975) and the Race Relations Act (1976)

The laws are similar to the provisions governing disability. A business is breaking the law if it refuses to employ (or promote) a person on the grounds of race or sex. Similarly, it would be illegal to draw up an advertisement for a job that specifies that the business will only employ a person from a particular racial group, or only a man, or only a woman. There are limited exceptions to this; e.g. if a swimming pool has separate changing rooms for men and women, it would be legal to advertise for a female changing room attendant.

Since 2003 there has been similar legislation applying to a person's sexual orientation and also religion. There may be cost implications for the business in implementing religious rights, e.g. permitting extended leave for religious holidays, and ensuring that any canteen facilities meet religious dietary requirements.

Finally, the law now provides protection against discrimination on the grounds of age when recruiting, promoting, training and also when considering redundancy.

The law relating to employees at work

A **contract of employment** is an agreement between a business and an employee, under which each of them has certain obligations. As soon as someone begins work, a contract comes into existence. It does not need to be in writing; it could be oral or implied. The implied terms of a contract are those that are so obvious they do not need to be explicitly agreed; e.g. duties on employers to pay wages and take reasonable care of employees. In return, employees must 'render service' (work properly) and obey lawful and reasonable instructions.

If a business employs someone for a month or more, within two months of starting work the employee must be given 'a written statement of employment particulars'. This is a document setting out the main aspects of a person's employment. The sort of information in a statement would be: the hours of work (including overtime or shift work), pay, sickness entitlement, pension scheme details and the period of notice required. It is not in itself a contract, although it will cover most of the particulars in the contract.

The existence of a contract and the written statement of employment particulars mean that both the business and the employee are clear about their rights and responsibilities.

The Health and Safety at Work Act 1974 (HASWA)

As well as duties at work, there is a vast amount of law relating to employee rights. One of the most important is the right to a healthy and safe working environment. An employee's health, safety and welfare at work are protected by law. The 1974 Act was a very important piece of legislation which has since been amended and extended to take account of new issues and hazards such as repetitive strain injury or possible damage to the eyes from working at computer screens. Furthermore, since 1993 all employers have been required to make estimates of workplace health and safety risks and to take the steps to manage and minimise them.

Not only do businesses have 'a duty to take reasonable care' of employees, but the criminal law lays down minimum safety requirements. There is a positive obligation to create a safe and healthy working environment; breaches of the law can lead to criminal prosecution as well as civil proceedings for compensation.

The provisions of the Act relate to:

- the place of work
- the system of work
- the working environment
- any machinery used
- the use and storage of substances
- employees.

The implications are that a business must:

- ensure that the building is safe. Entry to it and exit from it must be safe.
- coordinate the whole system of work so that it is safe.
- ensure that the temperature in the working environment is within certain limits; the atmosphere must be safe to breathe, the floors must be safe to walk along etc.
- fit guards onto machinery to prevent accidents. Employees must be provided with the correct safety equipment (and clothing), and trained to use it.
- provide training in any hazards associated with the work, e.g. the lifting of loads and the handling of substances. A business that failed to provide any training 'because it was common sense for an employee not to lift a heavy load' would not have a legal defence if the employee became injured.
- have a written safety policy which states who is responsible for safety issues. This policy must be clearly communicated to employees.

Examiner's voice

Stating the implications of an Act such as the HASWA (e.g. training and other cost implications) rather than simply quoting the basic requirements of it, will lead to marks being awarded at Level 3 for analysis.

The Act also places a duty on employees to comply with the Act. All employees must:

- take reasonable care of their own health and safety and of others who could be affected by their actions.
- comply with lawful instructions relating to safety matters; an employee who was trained and told to use

lifting equipment could not try to sue the business for an injury to his back if he ignored the instructions.
- not interfere or misuse anything provided for heath and safety purposes; e.g. letting off a fire extinguisher for malicious purposes or 'in fun' is a serious matter, for which an employee can be summarily dismissed.

The Act says that a business must comply 'so far as reasonably practicable'. A business may dispute that it can afford to comply with every single part of the Act, saying that the expense is not reasonably practicable. If an accident occurred and the business was prosecuted then the court would decide whether it was reasonably practicable or not.

Figure 29.1 The law requires employees to comply with safety rules

Health and Safety Commission (HSC)

The organisation responsible for health and safety in the UK is the Health and Safety Commission. This is a government-funded, independent body accountable to Parliament via the Under Secretary for the Department of Work and Pensions. The HSC's role is to protect people's health and safety by ensuring that risk in the workplace is properly controlled, to conduct research, promote training and provide an information service on health and safety issues.

Health and Safety Executive (HSE)

The Health and Safety Executive and local government are the enforcing authorities who work in support of the Commission. The HSE is responsible to the HSC for the regulation of risks to health and safety in organisations such as nuclear installations, mines, factories, farms, hospitals and schools, gas and oil installations, and the movement of dangerous goods and substances. Local authorities are responsible to HSC for enforcement in offices, shops and other parts of the services sector.

If an employee feels that there is a health and safety issue, s/he should first discuss it with their manager – possibly involving their trade union or safety representative if one exists. If the issue is not resolved, the HSE can be contacted for advice on the law. The HSE has the power to ensure that the law is complied with, and if a breach of the Act is serious enough or there is repeated disregard for it, the HSE can close a business down. Needless to say, this is very much a last resort.

Smoking in the workplace: the Health Act 2007

On 1 July 2007, workplaces in England became smoke-free environments (Scotland, Wales and Northern Ireland had already implemented this law). This includes offices, factories, shops, bars, restaurants, and work vehicles that are used by more than one person. Indoor smoking rooms are no longer allowed; anyone wishing to smoke must go outside the premises.

The 'anti-smoking law' should be taken seriously by a business. A business ignoring it or failing to prevent smoking inside the premises will be liable for prosecution and a fine. An agreed policy (including disciplinary procedures for employees breaking this law) should be in place, which should be carefully monitored to ensure compliance. If a business recruits a person who smokes, that person should be informed of the implication of the Act so that any breaches of the law are unlikely.

The Equal Pay Act 1970

This Act aims to prevent discrimination in terms of pay and other benefits. It states that if the work being done by someone 'is the same or broadly similar' to work being done by another person, then the rate of pay and other terms of employment should be the same. Nevertheless, repeated studies have shown that this Act has not closed the pay gap between men and women. However, in 2008 the Office for National Statistics reported that the gender pay gap was the narrowest since records began. The difference in prize money for men and women winning the Wimbledon tennis championship was a glaring example of inequality, until equal prize money was introduced in 2007.

The reasons why an employer might get away with breaking the law are complicated, but contributory factors are that women tend to be less unionised than men, more women work part-time than men and, on average, part-time employees receive lower hourly earnings than those working full-time. In other cases it can be a matter of intimidation by an employer who threatens to dismiss an employee. Needless to say, such an attitude is not conducive to harmonious industrial relations in the long term.

The Minimum Wage Act 1999

This Act lays down the minimum level of pay to which employees aged 16 years and over in the UK are entitled. It does not matter if an employee is in part-time or full-time employment.

If employees are paid on a piece rate (a certain amount for each item produced), the business has to ensure that the system of work enables enough items to be made for the employee to earn at least the minimum wage. The idea is not only to guarantee a certain level of wages but to ensure a 'level playing field'; i.e. that all businesses compete on the basis of quality of products, efficiency and customer service. Employers who treat and pay their employees well cannot now be undercut by others whose low prices are based on low rates of pay.

The minimum wage paid depends on age. Table 29.1 shows the wage rates in October 2008.

Age	Hourly rate (£)
22 years and over	5.73
18–21	4.77
16–17	3.53

Table 29.1 Minimum wage rates in 2008

Age discrimination: the Employment Equality (Age) Regulations 2006

Although age discrimination could occur in any age group, the new law is particularly significant for older workers. As the working population becomes older, there will be fewer younger workers in the labour force. Also, with increased life expectancy, many employees are retiring later than previously.

It was noted above that the law now gives employees protection against discrimination on the grounds of age when recruiting, promoting, training and also when considering redundancy. Furthermore, employees now have the right to request to work beyond retirement age; they cannot be presumed (or forced) to retire at 65 years of age. The Act does not however mean that a business should discriminate in favour of an older worker!

Equality policies

Acas strongly suggest that all businesses have an equality policy to ensure fair and consistent treatment of all employees. Managers should ensure that all employees are aware of this policy and its implications; i.e. that it is unlawful for someone to be discriminated, bullied or harassed on the grounds of sex, race, sexual orientation etc., and that disciplinary action will follow if they engage in any such behaviour. Employees should know about the business's procedures and whom to approach if they think they are not being treated in accordance with the policy. Acas stresses that the policy needs to be reviewed and monitored. The Act makes it clear that this is a continuing duty on a business.

> **Key Term**
>
> **Equality policy:** a policy to ensure fair and consistent treatment of all employees so that they are not discriminated, bullied or harassed on the grounds of sex, race, sexual orientation etc. Managers should ensure that all employees are aware of this policy and its implications.

Maternity/paternity provision: the Work and Families Act 2006

There has been an entitlement to maternity leave and maternity pay for many years. The main provisions of this Act came into force in April 2007, and the right to paternity leave and pay has also now become clearly enshrined in law. The rights to paternity leave give eligible employees the right to take paid leave to care for the child or support the mother. If a female employee has worked continuously for six months, then she will be entitled to a year's maternity leave of which half will be unpaid. If a male employee has worked continuously for six months, he is entitled to two weeks' leave on full pay and up to six months' leave unpaid.

The Act also introduced rights to paid leave for parents adopting children, and the right for parents of young children to apply to work flexibly. These rights aim to give parents greater opportunities to balance work and family life.

There are clearly implications particularly for a smaller business. There have been complaints that although large businesses might be able to cope with the cost and managing the absences, smaller businesses may not be able to so easily. To assist with the cost, the government allows a proportion of the pay for both maternity and paternity leave to be claimed back from HM Revenue and Customs. It is illegal to dismiss someone because they are pregnant and are intending to take maternity leave. Absences might be managed by employing staff on short-term contracts.

The Data Protection Act 1984 (updated 1988)

Even if a business is complying with the law in all of the above matters, it may still fall foul of the law if it fails to keep its employee records properly.

Any business will need to keep all sorts of employment-related records on its employees, but it is not allowed to disclose this information to other individuals within the business or another organisation. The Act is designed to prevent harm resulting from the misuse of any data that is held. Information about an employee's sickness or disciplinary record for example could easily be misused – particularly if the information had become outdated. The Act tries to balance the need for a business to process essential information with the individual's right to privacy.

The Act was updated in 1988. The law was broadened to cover 'paper-based' data recording systems, and it also now applies to any data on the business's customers.

All users of personal data must register with the Data Protection Registrar. A business making this registration must detail the nature of the data and the purposes for which it is held, as well as a list of the parties to whom the data may be made available. It is a criminal offence to hold unregistered data, and breaches of the following principles can also lead to prosecution.

- Data must only be kept for the specified purposes.
- Individuals are entitled to reasonable access to the data.
- Data can only be passed to a third party with the consent of the individual concerned.

There are several implications of this Act for a business. First, there is a legal obligation to protect the security of any data on an employee. In the past, much of the data held by a business used to be kept in filing cabinets and was only accessible by senior members of staff. With storing information on computers, data can be collected, viewed, altered and passed on easily (often without leaving a clearly identifiable trace), and so it is important that safeguards are in place. This obviously has training and other cost implications.

European Union (EU) laws

Finally, it needs to be recognised that some laws affecting UK businesses have come from the EU. The EU's Social Charter is a charter of rights for employees concerning areas such as working conditions, wages and consultation of the workforce. UK businesses have to adhere to these EU laws just as if they had originated from the UK parliament. There are two types of EU law:

1. **Regulations:** must be adopted and applied in a certain way.

2. **Directives:** must also be applied as law, but it is up to the individual member country to decide how to implement it.

The Working Time Directive

This EU Directive is an example of law coming from the EU. It became part of UK law in 1998 and states: a business must not allow an employee to work more than 48 hours per week on average. The Directive is partly aimed at reducing the UK's culture of long working hours. There are also provisions relating to an employee's entitlement to rest breaks and the pattern of shifts that can be worked. An employee can sign away their legal rights to these if they wish, but if a business dismissed a person for a refusal to do so, this would constitute unfair dismissal. Some employees (such as the police) are exempt from the Directive.

Key Terms

EU Regulations and Directives: legislation emanating from the European Parliament. Regulations have to be adopted and applied in a certain way, whereas it is up to the individual member country to decide how to implement a Directive.

The business, trade unions and the law

A business must comply with a considerable body of law relating to an employee's trade union membership. This includes the right for:

- an employee to belong to a trade union (and the right not to belong to one if the employee so chooses).
- an employee not to be discriminated against because of trade union membership.
- a union to be 'recognised' (i.e. an employer will meet with union representatives and negotiate members' pay and conditions) if there are at least 20 employees and the majority of the workforce belong to a union.

Unions also have certain responsibilities under the different Acts, such as having to inform managers in advance of the intention to strike, and having to hold a secret ballot of members before taking strike action.

This legislation and its implications are covered in more detail in Unit 70.

The termination of employment

This is potentially a very difficult area of employment law, and businesses have to be very careful to avoid legal complications when terminating employment. Termination could occur through redundancy or dismissal. It is important to be clear about the difference.

Redundancy

An employee is not made redundant because they have done anything wrong. Redundancy arises from a situation where the job that used to be performed no longer exists and so the employee is surplus to requirements. This might arise because a particular job is mechanised or where a section or all of a factory or office is closed down. Employees made redundant are entitled by law to a redundancy payment, which varies according to how long they have worked for the business. It is of course open to a business to pay them more than this.

The Acas guidelines for selecting employees for redundancy state that a business:

'should be using objective criteria wherever possible, precisely defined and capable of being applied in an independent way. This is to ensure that employees are not selected unfairly. The chosen criteria (e.g. skills, experience, standard of work) should be consistently applied. There should also be an appeals procedure.' (source: ACAS website)

Dismissal

There are different types of dismissal but the one most commonly before an employment tribunal is unfair dismissal. A dismissal has to be justified and must be fair if it is to be legal. Employees who have been employed for a minimum of one year have the right not to be unfairly dismissed. Summary (i.e. 'on the spot') dismissal is only 'fair' in two instances; gross misconduct, e.g. an employee physically assaulting a customer, or gross negligence (a reckless or wilful disregard for the safety of others), e.g. a manager at a theme park allows a ride to remain open when he knows that a safety fault exists.

Other types of dismissal that can be justified as fair are:

- repeated poor conduct such as lateness or failing to comply with reasonable requests (to perform tasks) from a manager.
- incapacity, e.g. being too ill to work at all or taking time off work when genuinely ill on a regular basis.
- capability: repeated inability to do the work required, or a major incident such as losing the business a very valuable customer.
- redundancy: if the employee's job no longer exists and there is no work to do.
- 'some other substantial reason': a tribunal would look at each case on an individual basis.

If one of these is the reason for the dismissal, then it will normally be fair as long as the employer has acted 'reasonably'. This means that the employer has not summarily dismissed the employee but has followed appropriate disciplinary procedures.

For any disciplinary-related dismissal, the employer should follow the Acas guidelines. Summary dismissal is not appropriate in the overwhelming majority of cases. The guidelines state that there are certain stages to be followed if the dismissal is to be fair and legal:

1. The manager should give at least one verbal warning to the employee.

2. This should be followed by at least one written warning.

3. There should then be a final written warning. By law an employee has to receive all allegations in writing, and attend a formal meeting to discuss the issues. It would be normal practice to allow a trade union representative or a friend to accompany an employee in such a meeting.

4. There also has to be an appeals process. It must be made clear to the employee how to appeal and to whom.

There are two other types of dismissal: wrongful dismissal and constructive dismissal. Either of these can proceed to a tribunal, although constructive dismissal can sometimes be hard to prove.

Wrongful dismissal

This occurs where there has been a breach of the employment contract. What is 'wrongful' will therefore vary according to the terms of the individual contract. For example, an employee who is entitled to eight weeks' notice of termination of employment but is only given four weeks' notice would be wrongfully dismissed.

Constructive dismissal

This happens when the behaviour of a manager or managers forces an employee to leave the job. This could result for example from bullying, or changing the conditions of employment without consent; e.g. forcing the employee to work at weekends when their contract states 'Monday to Friday'.

Employment tribunals

Alleged breaches of employment law are heard in an employment tribunal. This is a special sort of court which deals with employees' claims for matters such as unfair dismissal, discrimination or victimisation by their employer. Employment tribunal hearings usually take place before a legally qualified chairman and two 'ordinary' members, one nominated by the employer and one by the employee.

A tribunal is less formal than a criminal court, and almost all hearings are open to the public. A very large number of cases are settled before they ever reach the tribunal. This is partly because by law an Acas conciliator has to be assigned to the case, and this person will work impartially with both sides to settle out of court.

If the tribunal rules in favour of the employee, it will order the business to make a payment to the employee to compensate for what has occurred. There are 'caps' (i.e. limits) on what can be awarded, except in cases of discrimination when it is unlimited.

Key Term

Employment tribunal: a special sort of court dealing only with employment law; e.g. an employee's claim for unfair dismissal, discrimination or victimisation by their employer.

The rights of part-time employees

Part-time employees now have the same statutory employment rights as other employees. Until 1999, part-time employees had to work for three years continuously for the same business before they were entitled to any employment protection. This meant that part-time staff were easier to discriminate against in matters such as pay, holiday entitlement and redundancy rights. The adoption of the EU Directive on part-time rights at work now means that part-time employees who have been employed for a year are entitled to exactly the same legal rights as those in full-time employment.

Further Sources

www.acas.org.uk – the Acas website. Very informative and extremely easy to navigate. It includes some 'movie' clips that can be watched to illustrate the issues.

www.berr.gov.uk – Department for Business, Enterprise and Regulatory Reform, the government department working to create the conditions for business success. Useful not only for employment-related issues but also for matters relating to business competitiveness.

www.disability.gov.uk – disabled rights. Information for businesses on how to meet their legal obligations.

www.employmenttribunals.gov.uk – the nature of tribunals, procedures, how to claim etc.

www.hse.gov.uk – the Health & Safety Executive. Advice on improving workplace health and safety and the benefits to businesses that can occur as a result of a healthy and safe working environment.

www.statistics.gov.uk – all sorts of data about economic and social issues and trends. Useful for data on the differences in pay between men and women.

Your Turn

Case Study Time allowed 35 minutes

Mears plc (MP)

Marcus O'Hanlon is the Human Resource Director of Mears plc, a printing business based in Birmingham and Solihull. He is reviewing the progress reports on various human resource issues sent to him by Adam Boyd, his young deputy, who was appointed two months ago. Marcus is beginning to think that the appointment was a mistake. Right from the start Adam has wanted to make an impression, and he has certainly done that. Adam graduated from university three years ago and has a very authoritarian manner. Although well-qualified, it seems to Marcus that he has not yet developed any real skill in managing people in awkward situations.

Marcus does acknowledge that Adam has made some progress on the tasks given to him since joining the business. The board of directors wants MP to be clearly recognised as an equal opportunity employer, and Marcus is pleased that Adam has made a good start on MP's new equality policy; what he has written follows from a useful consultation exercise and it

looks as though the policy will eventually command a good deal of support. Marcus reflected that it would have to be launched properly so that all employees are fully aware of it.

The preliminary work that Adam has undertaken over the redundancies scheduled for MP's Solihull factory is less promising. Marcus now regrets delegating the task to Adam. Marcus has usually had a useful working relationship with the union representatives at the firm (from the Transport and General workers' union, recognised by Mears), but Adam has antagonised them by trying to impose a strict 'last in, first out' redundancy policy with no exceptions. This is causing much difficulty, and the union representatives are now telephoning and emailing Marcus to say that they want to deal with him and not Adam.

Even more difficulty has arisen with a dismissal. Adam has written in his report on the incident that he had found an employee, Ray Balden, smoking in the loading bay with some lorry drivers from another business who had just unloaded a delivery of paper and ink. Ray was standing a couple of metres away from a large drum of chemicals marked 'flammable'. Adam had told Ray to report to him in his office immediately. On checking his employment record, he discovered that Ray has one previous verbal warning for smoking in the building, and both a verbal and a written warning for lateness. He therefore dismissed him summarily without informing either Marcus or Ray's line manager, Helen Abbey. The senior union representative wants to speak to Marcus about this as well.

In addition, there is also the issue of a wrongful dismissal claim made by Valerie Engle. She is claiming that her line manager, Nic Warboys, gave her a succession of jobs that she was not trained to do and then repeatedly criticised her when she did not perform them properly. Valerie is not a member of the union but in a letter to Nic said that she was going to contact Acas and then 'sue the business for everything it has'. Marcus does not feel that he wants to trust Adam with this human resource problem.

1. Outline the difference between 'dismissal and 'redundancy'. (4 marks)

2. Outline what is meant by 'unfair dismissal', 'wrongful dismissal' and 'constructive dismissal'. (6 marks)

3. 'Adam has made a good start on Mears' new equality policy'. State two purposes of an equality policy. (1 mark)

4. State two ways by which a business could make its employees aware of its equality policy. (2 marks)

5. Analyse the contribution that Acas might make to the current industrial relations situation at Mears. (6 marks)

6. Discuss the implications of Adam's decision to summarily dismiss Ray Balden. (18 marks)

(37 marks)

EMPLOYEE PARTICIPATION

Modern management theory emphasises the beneficial effects of employees being consulted and participating in decisions that affect them at work. This participation is also known as 'industrial democracy' and has long been an objective of the trade unions. However, not everyone agrees that employee participation is beneficial to a business, and even those who believe in its benefits cannot agree on a single model or framework that can be applied. Although it may be acceptable to have a law insisting that multinational companies in the EU with large numbers of employees must have a formal consultative works council with elected employee representatives (see page 175), such an approach would not be appropriate for a small cornershop employing six people, four of whom are part-time workers. If successful participation is to occur in a business, then an appropriate method has to be found which is broadly acceptable to both employer and employees.

Issues for consultation

A business is legally required to consult with its employees via their representatives or trade union, on issues such as:

- redundancies (if the number planned is 20 or more)
- health and safety
- changes to contracts of employment or pension schemes
- a takeover.

Some managers may not wish to see their 'right to manage' affected, and may refuse to do anything other than comply with the letter of the law. While this means that they are not in breach of the legislation, there will be a problem if they employ over 250 people. The Companies Act 1985 states that a company with an average of 250 or more employees must include in its annual report:

'a statement describing the action that has been taken during the financial year to introduce, maintain or develop arrangements aimed at providing employees systematically with information on matters of concern to them as employees and consulting employees on a regular basis so that the views of employees can be taken into account in making decisions'.

An absence of this statement might affect the corporate image of the business and deter potential investors and customers.

Consultation could also prove useful on other matters, many of which will in practice be interlinked. These could include a change in working practices, a change to methods of remuneration, or the introduction of new technology. In fact, it is hard to imagine managers being able to manage effectively without some form of consultation with employees.

Reasons for employee participation

Participation measures such as appraisals (see Unit 33) and similar human resource initiatives should not be introduced for their own sake. Participation should be used to help the business achieve its strategic objectives. There are several ways it can help to do this:

Increased levels of motivation

If employees feel that their view counts, they may become more motivated. Industrial relations (the relations between employees and their employer) can improve. This may cause productivity to rise. It can also lead to a greater acceptance of decisions, since employees have been part of the decision-making process and understand what the business is trying to achieve.

Better communication

Participation should mean better communication between managers and employees. Even if the business has a clear set of objectives and a strategy to achieve them, this cannot guarantee success. The commitment of employees will play a major part in whether the strategy succeeds or fails. Participation can improve trust, lead to agreed goals and improve that commitment.

Improved quality of decision-making

Managers do not and cannot 'know it all'. Employees often complain that senior managers have little idea of what goes on at 'the sharp end'. Employees know the processes and methods that work (i.e. actually help to complete the job), and those that do not. They know from direct experience where the real problems lie and whether these are technical, financial or procedural. Such information would be very useful to managers, especially when planning for change. Therefore management decision-making is improved.

Employees' expectations

The modern approach to learning at GCSE and AS/A2 level places more emphasis on analysing all sorts of data and making decisions based upon it. Employers need to realise that education now deliberately encourages a questioning approach for pupils, with the emphasis on selecting information and justifying their decisions. If this has occurred for 11 or more years at school, young people may expect some level of involvement and participation once they are at work, rather than blindly accepting someone else's view. If this is not forthcoming, morale and motivation are unlikely to be high.

Compliance with the law

Consultation is now a legal requirement for many issues (e.g. redundancy) and for certain types of business. Non-compliance would be a breach of the law and would be likely to attract bad publicity. This may affect recruitment.

All of these appear to be very positive reasons for introducing some form of participation, but it would be naïve to assume that all participation and consultation will be successful immediately or in the long term.

Problems with employee participation

There are several ways that consultation could be introduced (see below), but it is important to bear the following in mind, whichever method is chosen.

Slower decision-making

Decision-making is certainly slower with participation. There will be a trade-off between the need to reach a consensus and the speed with which some business decisions are made. This has important implications for the employees involved in the consultation process and leads to the next issue.

Format of consultation

When will any consultation take place, and with whom? How many employees will be involved? From which sections of the factory/office will they be drawn? How will they be chosen? When will the meetings be held? Any employees involved in consultation have the legal right to paid time from work during the working day, but they may not want to attend a meeting before or after work unless they are paid for this as well. Who will 'cover' for the employees while they are being consulted? Also, if the business operates a bonus scheme, how will employees' bonuses be affected by 'absence' due to the consultation process?

The business' culture

Participation should be genuine and needs to be part of the culture of the business. A business which has approachable managers who adopt a democratic style will find it relatively easy to introduce some form of participation. A business which has been managed in an authoritarian, autocratic manner cannot just introduce participation and expect it to succeed; the whole culture of the firm will be against it. Furthermore, if the process is just for show and employees are not listened to (i.e. no action is taken as a result of the participation), they will become cynical and disinterested. The culture of such a business will have to change if the participation is to be successful. This is not easy and will need a clear change of direction from senior managers. The alteration of a business's culture is complex; people are used to behaving in a certain way, and it takes time to change this.

Lack of expertise for decision-making

Employees may lack the expertise to make decisions. An employee may find it hard to analyse data effectively as part of the consultation without training. This is particularly true of statistical or accounting information, which could be open to different interpretations. However, this problem may not occur if the employee is a member of a trade union that has paid for him/her to attend some sort of business course. If this is not the case, some thought must be given to how to address this problem. Will the employee(s) be given (paid?) time off work to attend a course? Will the business offer to pay for evening class education? This would demonstrate a commitment to the process but will involve a cost.

Lack of trust

There may be a problem of trust. Some managers might feel that disclosing potential sensitive information, e.g. about launching a new product or opening a new plant, might be leaked to competitors, either accidentally or out of spite.

Disinterested employees

Employees may not be interested in the process of consultation. Perhaps there have been personality clashes, or poor treatment of the workforce in the past, which can be very hard to overcome.

Successful consultation

The problems listed above are not insurmountable. Success depends on the following factors:

1. **Genuine consultation,** i.e. whether employees' views are actually listened to and acted upon. The Acas website states: 'Making a pretence of consulting on issues that have already been decided is unproductive and engenders suspicion and mistrust about the process amongst staff'.

2. **Investing time and money in the process.** Like many business initiatives, the process must be driven from 'the top'. If junior managers see that senior managers are not really interested or concerned with participation, they will not devote much time and effort to it either.

3. **Managers accepting that positive results are unlikely to be immediate.**

4. **Managing employees' expectation of consultation.** Employees will have to accept that their views may not always be accepted or acted upon. There may be sound financial or organisational reasons for managers not accepting their ideas. Employees also have to accept that they are involved in decisions that had previously been 'management territory'. Some of these decisions will be difficult, especially in areas such as redundancy.

5. **Avoiding confrontation.** A 'workers versus managers' style of confrontation is not conducive to successful participation.

6. **Structure the consultation procedure.** The way in which the participation is structured and the degree of consultation will affect its success.

Achieving effective participation

An extension of collective bargaining

One way for the consultation to occur would be with the union representatives, if there is a recognised union in the business. A trade union is an organisation of employees that seeks to protect and improve the interests of its members. If a union is recognised by an employer, its existence is accepted and the managers agree to negotiate with it over terms and conditions of employment. It shows a willingness to treat employees as stakeholders. This negotiation is called 'collective bargaining'.

If the collective bargaining process is already established, the arrangements for the timing of the meetings, pay issues and the personnel involved are already established. The scope of the meetings would be extended beyond simply 'bargaining', and would be a logical way to proceed.

If there is no union, managers may want to consider recognising one. Indeed, as so much rests on how genuine the participation process is, it would be difficult for managers to claim to be truly interested in achieving industrial democracy and then refuse to accept a union's existence!

Recognising a union can mean:

- better communication between managers and staff. Communication can improve trust, lead to agreed goals and improve that commitment.

- assisting managers in identifying employees' training needs.
- assisting managers in ensuring that health and safety procedures are complied with.
- early identification and resolution of problems, as union representatives often have considerable experience and training in employment law.
- a formal structure for bargaining that can be extended to cover participation and consultation.

The strategic benefits of union recognition could therefore include:

- reduced labour turnover and therefore recruitment costs
- increased staff motivation and morale
- fewer days lost through work-related injuries and illnesses
- improved productivity
- the establishment of a formal channel of communication that could assist with achieving change.

However there will be costs: union representatives will press for better wages and conditions for their members which, if granted, will reduce the business's profits, at least in the short term. Only if there is greater productivity and profitability in the long term will recognition and participation be beneficial in financial terms.

Further information about the nature of trade unions, their role in the management of change, and their legal position for industrial action can be found in Unit 70.

> ### Key Terms
>
> **Collective bargaining:** managers and employee representatives (usually their union) negotiate over terms and conditions of employment.
>
> **Union recognition:** an employer accepts the existence of a union and agrees to negotiate with it over terms and conditions of employment.

Quality circles

These are one of the components of lean production, and are regular short meetings of a group of employees during working hours. The objective is to discuss and resolve work-related problems. Through quality circles, managers can gain a much greater awareness of employees' problems and concerns.

As the name suggests, historically they have been established to improve the quality of output. Some businesses operate quality circles in each different section of the firm. However, as the quality of the final product is dependent on many factors from suppliers to stock control, some businesses operate a quality circle with employees drawn from various different departments of the business. In some ways, this is a miniature version of the Works Council (see below). Whichever model is chosen, at these meetings employees have the opportunity to comment on processes and procedures that affect the product. It is usual for employees to select at least some of the issues they wish to discuss, rather than the managers setting the agenda. The UK company Wedgwood introduced quality circles to senior management, middle management and unions over 25 years ago, and others have followed their example.

Many of the advantages of quality circles relate to participation. Elton Mayo (see Unit 28) noted back in the 1920s that involvement improved employee productivity. Furthermore there is a clear focus on quality, which is very important in a competitive world. However, there remains the issue of which employees will be involved. Participation is usually voluntary, but what happens if employees do not want to participate, or too many people want to? When will quality circles meet? These issues will have to be resolved, as will the problem of persuading employees to make suggestions if they fear that they may be made redundant as a result. In the past, car manufacturers Rover has guaranteed that employees will not lose their jobs as a result of any cost-saving suggestions put forward. This is not an easy commitment to make.

Furthermore, although quality circles mean that employees are participating, this is a rather limited and narrow version of industrial democracy. In recent years businesses have often widened the scope of the quality circle. Quality is certainly not the only aspect of the business that affects employees, and there are likely to be other issues (e.g. pay and training) that they also want to raise. If this opportunity is not available because of the narrow focus on quality, the participation is not really serving its proper purpose.

It is also open to debate as to whether quality circles can successfully be used to consult on big issues such as redundancy or relocation.

> ### Key Term
>
> **Quality circle:** a regular short meeting of a group of employees during working hours. The objective is to discuss and resolve work-related problems. Managers can gain a much greater awareness of employees' problems and concerns.

Works Councils

A works council is a formal meeting of managers and employees in a particular factory (or the business as a whole) to discuss pay and working conditions or grievances, and negotiate on issues such as changes in working practices

The works council model (also known as a consultative committee) for participation and consultation has existed among some firms in the UK for many years, and in 1994 it became a legal requirement from an EU Directive. Only certain types of business are required by law to have a works council, but any business not covered by the criteria could still adopt the model.

The 1994 Directive created the European Works Council (EWC). It applies to any company with 1,000 or more employees, including at least 150 in two or more EU member states. EWCs give employees the right to information and consultation on their company's decisions. Consultation was defined as 'the exchange of views and establishment of dialogue between employees' representatives and management'.

It was hoped that EWCs would deal with a large range of issues (such as the business's impact on the community within which it operates and the wider environment). It was envisaged that the majority of EWCs would meet once a year, with the possibility of additional meetings of a small steering committee (of EWCs' members) to meet at short notice if required. Senior managers would then work towards implementing agreed decisions.

Apart from the usual problems with participation, matters are made more difficult by the fact that some representatives have to travel abroad, translators may be necessary and payment must be made for travel and accommodation. These problems are not impossible to solve, but are additional complications; as are the issues of how many representatives will come from each country and how long they will serve on the council.

The Directive has not been an unqualified success. On the whole, while the larger multinationals have complied, other smaller companies have not always done so. It has been possible to argue that the number of employees fell below 1,000 for a period of time, or that some people in the business were in fact agency workers and therefore not part of the real workforce. If these facts are true, the establishment of the works council is not necessary. These sorts of arguments have to be tested in court, and a union might not feel that a costly and lengthy legal battle is worthwhile.

Also, it is legal for managers to withhold 'sensitive information which might seriously harm the functioning of the business'. It has been claimed by some trade unions that this has been used as an excuse to limit the data presented to the council, thereby preventing the employee representatives from making a fully informed contribution. Some companies have sought to limit the scope of the EWC to debate wider issues.

In 2007 the European Trade Union Confederation (ETUC) met in Brussels to push for an urgent revision of the Directive, specifically to demand a legal clarification of 'sensitive information' and also what consultation and participation rights actually exist. This is yet to be forthcoming.

Key Term

Works Council: a formal meeting of managers and employee representatives to discuss pay and working conditions and to negotiate on issues such as changes in working practices. There is a legal requirement on certain types of company operating in the EU to set up a European Works Council.

Employees as shareholders

The owners of a company's ordinary shares are entitled to vote at the Annual General Meeting on the basis of one vote per share. If employees are encouraged to buy shares in their company, or are given them as a bonus or a reward for long service, it could be argued that this ability to vote is a form of participation.

However the meeting is by definition annual, and so the opportunity to participate is restricted. Furthermore, if employees own a modest number of shares (such as 500) and there are millions of other shares, they may feel that their 'voice' (even if joined by several hundred other employees) will not be heard since they can easily be outvoted.

This is not to say that employees owning shares in their company is not valuable. It may assist with motivation but as a method of participation in decision-making, its value is rather limited.

Examiner's voice

If in the examination you decide that some form of employee participation would be beneficial to the business, you need to think carefully about the nature of the business before reaching any judgement on the form it should take. What is the culture of the business like? What about size? Is the business small with no formal employee representation? Or is it a large multinational with recognised unions? What resources are available for the consultation process? These sorts of issues will be crucial to your analysis and suggestions.

Further sources

www.berr.gov.uk – the Department for Business, Enterprise and Regulatory Reform. Useful section on EWCs and many other employment related matters.

www.etuc.org – the European Trade Union Confederation. This organisation's aim is 'to promote the interests of working people at European level and to represent them in the EU institutions'. Very useful for straightforward explanations of EU directives relating to industrial relations.

www.hutchins.co.uk – a useful outline of the use of quality circles in UK businesses. Contains other helpful links to the topic.

Your Turn

Case study Time allowed 40 minutes

Cameron and Andrews Landscaping Ltd (CALL)

Cameron and Andrews Landscaping Ltd is a private company operating in a town in the Midlands. It was founded by Mick Cameron and Dean Andrews in 2003 and has grown successfully, building on a reputation for competitive prices and quality. CALL undertakes a variety of gardening and landscaping jobs both for private individuals and increasingly for the local council. Due to the seasonal nature of the work, the business is at its busiest in the summer. There are nevertheless 14 skilled full-time employees who work all the year round, and in the summer, a number of semi-skilled employees are hired as required.

CALL's financial year has just ended, and although profits have risen once again, the increase has been rather smaller (1.4%) than in previous years, when they have averaged 5%. Mick (who prepares the accounts) feels that this is because the organisation and allocation of jobs has been rather haphazard over the past 12 months. The business has been something of a victim of its own success. The vast growth in work has meant that Mick and Dean have barely been able to keep on top of the paperwork and general organisation. There have been several problems with incorrectly ordered materials which have delayed the start of jobs, and lately there has been some difficulty with CALL's VAT paperwork. Mick's secretary has been off sick for nearly three months and the temporary staff that have been sent along by the employment agency have not been very competent or enthusiastic.

There has also been some slight disagreement between Mick and Dean. Three weeks ago, two of the full-time employees who are team leaders approached Mick to say that they were unhappy with being sent to the wrong place at the wrong time and often with the wrong materials. They suggested that they could organise their own schedules and order their own materials, if they were given some instruction on the nature of the jobs to be done in advance.

The team leaders also told Mick that they had heard of a new supplier about eight miles away, that they had subsequently visited and found to be excellent in terms of product range, quality, and price. They had several ideas on how CALL might save money, with some slight changes to the current purchasing policy. Mick was pleased by this initiative but Dean was not very sympathetic. Dean likes to feel in control of the business and dislikes participation from the workforce.

Mick argued that greater autonomy and participation in decision-making would motivate the employees, but Dean was doubtful. 'They would only want more money,' he replied, and then added 'and we can barley afford that, from the state of the accounts'. Mick pointed out that the company was still profitable even if the rate of growth of profit had slowed. Dean looked unconvinced.

Yesterday the team leaders went to Mick and raised the same matters again. Mick had another meeting with Dean, who was as sceptical as before. 'I know the permanent workforce are all skilled but in the summer there will be many of them who are not. They can't all participate, and anyway what is there to participate in? I can't see any point. And another question, when are they going to do all this talking?'

Mick tried again. 'Come on, Dean,' he said. 'Let's show them a bit of trust. This sort of thing could make life easier all round for everyone. Our team leaders want a response from us.'

Dean promised that he would think about it.

1. Define the term 'employee participation'. (2 marks)

2. State three issues on which a business might consult its employees. (3 marks)

3. Analyse two benefits to CALL that might arise from employee participation. (6 marks)

4. Analyse two problems that might arise at CALL from employee participation. (6 marks)

5. Recommend and justify a strategy by which CALL could introduce effective participation. (18 marks)

(35 marks)

METHODS OF REMUNERATION

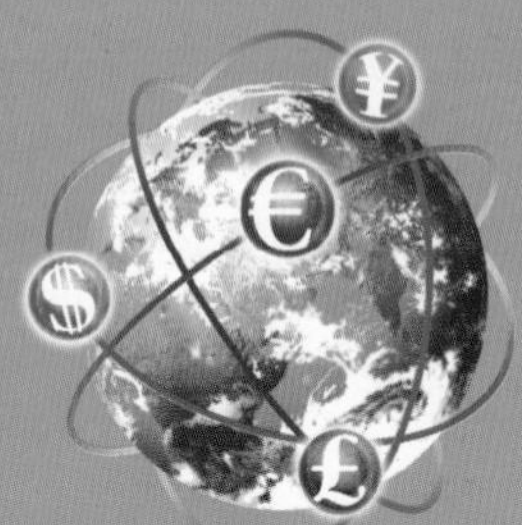

Money may not be the main motivating factor for all employees in every type of business, but it is still a very significant one. It is therefore important to consider the different methods of remuneration that are available to a business, and the advantages and disadvantages of using those methods. If employees feel that they are not receiving a reward that reflects their ability and contribution to the business, this may lead to a number of negative implications such as low morale, low motivation and a lack of commitment.

Pay and payment systems have a huge effect on industrial relations and indeed the whole operation of a business. It is essential to choose methods of remuneration which makes employees feel adequately rewarded. The methods can be divided into two basic types:

1. time-based systems
2. performance-related systems.

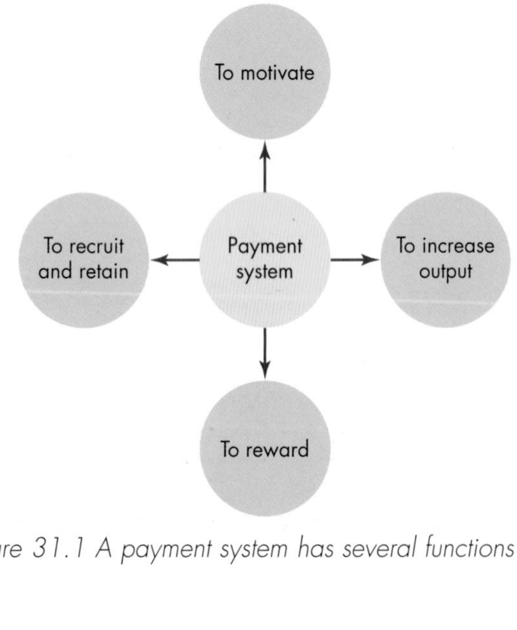

The method(s) of remuneration must be chosen very carefully so that the desired results are achieved. Payment systems may be designed to increase output, motivate, reward, recruit (and retain), or a combination of these outcomes. If the wrong system is chosen, or a change is made without adequate consultation, these outcomes are unlikely to be forthcoming.

Examiner's voice

In textbooks or newspaper articles you may come across the phrase 'methods of payment'. This usually refers to the basis on which the money is earned (e.g. a time rate, a piece rate etc.), and not to how the money is paid (e.g. in cash or by bank transfer). The examination question will ask about the basis on which the money is earned.

Time rates

In this method of payment, the wage is based on the number of hours worked, multiplied by the hourly pay rate. This does not mean that there is only one wage rate in a business. Many organisations have a scale through which employees can progress as they gain new skills and experience. This is the case for occupations such as teaching and police work.

If an employee agrees to work longer hours than those on his contract, then it would be usual for these 'overtime' hours to be paid at a premium rate (at more than the normal hourly rate), e.g. 'time and a half' or 'double time'.

Figure 31.1 A payment system has several functions

A time rate has a number of advantages as a method of remuneration for the employee and for the business. For the employee, there is certainty about the wage to be received. For the business, the employment costs are easily calculated, and time-based systems of pay are usually relatively inexpensive and easy to administer. Also, as employees are not rushing to finish a task, the work is likely to be completed properly, creating fewer items of poor quality.

On the other hand, there are disadvantages, the most obvious being the lack of any link between effort and reward. Whatever the level of output, pay will remain the same, which may lead to resentment. If there is no difference in the reward for effort, employees may perceive this to be an unfair system. Motivation levels may be negatively affected.

Time rates are the most useful when:

- employees perform similar work
- it would be difficult to try to identify individual effort (e.g. people working in a group)
- the amount of work performed is not under the employee's control (e.g. a shop assistant)
- quality is more important than quantity (e.g. a doctor dealing with patients).

Wages and salaries

A salary is a fixed amount of money earned per year which is paid monthly into a bank account, rather than in cash. Twelve payments of an equal amount are made; it does not matter how many days there are in the month. This is distinct from a wage, which is calculated at an hourly rate and usually paid weekly. Salaries have traditionally been paid to professionals and managers rather than other employees, but these differences are not as rigid as they once were, and it is increasingly common for white-collar employees of all types to be paid a salary.

In both cases, the amount received by the employee might be supplemented by additional pay, e.g. in the form of a bonus or some sort of performance-related pay (see below).

Piece rates

A piece rate is where an employee is not paid by the number of hours worked, but by the amount of output produced. Employees thus have an incentive to produce more items. There is a clear link between effort and reward under this system. This will be beneficial if employees are wholly or mainly motivated by money. However, there are a number of implications.

First, a successful piece rate system must ensure that output is clearly attributable to a particular employee. This might mean the employment of extra supervisors to check and authorise payment for what has been produced. This will mean extra expense. If output is not attributable to a particular employee, this may lead to conflict over who should be paid what, which may lower motivation levels.

Second, a 'pure' piece rate system (see Figure 31.2) where employees are paid strictly on what they produce, is in reality unlikely. It is usual for there to be a basic (i.e. minimum) level of pay, with an amount for piecework paid on top of that. This means that a careful calculation must be made to ensure that, whatever the level of output, employees can earn at least the minimum wage (see Figure 31.3). Some system of work study (see Unit 48) must be carried out to determine how long a particular task takes to complete so that it can be linked to a payment per item produced. The calculation can be costly to undertake as it must be done very precisely. Furthermore, once employees realise that they are being studied, they may choose to work more slowly to distort the data. They can then 'speed up' once the system is in place, and earn more money based on the inaccurately gathered data. The business does not want to set a piece rate that allows wage costs to spiral out of control.

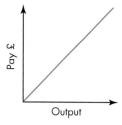

Figure 31.2 A 'pure' piece rate system with no minimum level of pay

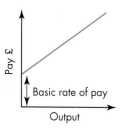

Figure 31.3 A piece rate system incorporating a minimum level of pay

Third, there are also issues with quality and health and safety. There is no point in developing a pay scheme that encourages quantity at the expense of quality. This is literally a waste of money, even if some items can be recycled. It is also important that employees do not rush work and become involved in an accident or develop a long-term health problem such as repetitive strain injury.

Finally, the output produced must be sold. This is a clear example of why a method of remuneration has to be linked to a key function of the firm; marketing. There is no point in producing huge amounts of goods if these are not linked to customer demand. In some cases the piece rate changes after a particular level of output to deter huge amounts of output that may not be saleable. In Figure 31.4, the relationship between output and pay changes after point x. Increases in output still achieve a higher rate of pay, but the rise in the rate of pay is less generous than before. This will deter employees from producing output that cannot be sold.

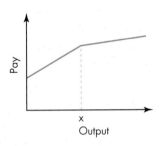

Figure 31.4 The piece rate can vary with the level of output

Performance-related pay

This links pay to performance and results. It can take a variety of forms:

Payment by results: piecework, commission or bonuses

Piecework
This is the most basic form of performance-related pay and has been examined above.

Commission
This is a method of payment often used for employees who are involved in selling. Their pay would be similar in structure to Figure 31.3 where a basic amount is paid and then pay increases made in line with the amount (or value) of sales. This means that employees who are attuned to meet customer needs (e.g. agreeing to meet when it suits them, carefully explaining the nature of the product etc.) can earn a lot of money.

There is of course the danger that sales staff may try to sell products that will benefit themselves rather than the customer – especially if the customer does not have full and detailed knowledge of the product. Some of the criticism over the misselling of personal pensions in the 1980s has been on this very issue.

Bonuses
A bonus is a sum of money, usually paid annually. It can take different forms: a fixed proportion of the employee's salary or wage, dependent on the business' profits, or arising from an appraisal of the employee's individual performance (see below).

If the business is a company then an additional method of paying a bonus would be through giving shares to employees. They will receive an extra payment when the company pays out its dividend to shareholders. Theoretically this will increase commitment to the business and encourage employees to work hard so that company profits increase, the value of its shares rise, and a large dividend is paid.

In practice, matters may be different. There is no direct link between individual effort and reward; an employee working in a branch of a large supermarket may reason that his effort, however great, will only make a tiny difference to the overall performance of the business. There is therefore absolutely no reason to overexert himself. If all employees, or the majority of them, feel like this, the incentive will have the opposite effect to the one desired.

There are similar problems with profit-sharing where employees are not given shares but receive a bonus based on the business's profits. This raises further issues: on what basis will it be paid? Will it be linked to current salary/earnings? If this is the case then those earning the most will receive the greatest bonus. If senior managers receive vastly more than employees further down the hierarchy, this will be regarded as unfair, and may worsen industrial relations.

Also, if the amount available for sharing is small, receiving a tiny amount can demotivate and appear insulting (especially if employees feel that they have worked hard and expectations are high).

Bonuses are intended to motivate and reinforce the employee's sense of worth to the business, and used in the right way, they can do this. However, a bonus may come to be regarded as 'a right' to be enjoyed every year. If this happens then any motivational effect will disappear, as the employee simply expects to be given the bonus as a matter of course.

Measured day work (MDW)

MDW incorporates elements of both a time rate and a piece rate, and in so doing gains the advantages of each method. Employees receive a regular and guaranteed rate of pay in an agreed time period, in return for achieving agreed output targets incorporating both quantity and quality.

It operates like a sort of stepped piece rate. Looking at Figure 31.5: if agreed output is in range B, then payment is made at level 2. If output falls into range A, then payment is made at level 1. If output targets are exceeded (e.g. in range C) then pay increases to level 3.

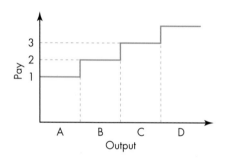

Figure 31.5 Measured Day Work

As with any piece rate system, there can be disagreement on the amount paid (in this case per level) and the amount to be produced to qualify for higher payments (in this case the width of the band).

MDW as a method of remuneration is not as popular as it once was. For the employees there is constant pressure to maintain output, backed up by the penalty of lower pay if it falls. For managers there is the possibility that, unless output levels are calculated very carefully and coordinated with the sales department, the business could end up with a vast amount of output produced at inflated wage rates that cannot be sold.

Appraisal

This sort of performance-related pay is common in managerial and professional jobs. Normally an employee will set several personal targets at an annual appraisal meeting with his/her line manager. These targets should result in outcomes that should be beneficial to both the employee and the business – e.g. achieve a basic level of proficiency in a foreign language. The following year at the appraisal meeting, the employee fills out a question and answer sheet relating to the previously agreed targets. The employee comments on the extent to which s/he feels that they have been met. The progress towards the targets and the comments will then be reviewed by the employee's line manager. An employee may then be rated against the targets with statements such as 'fully met', 'partially met', or 'no progress towards target'. If targets have been met satisfactorily then an extra payment is made. The advantage of this method is that employees have an incentive to reach their targets, and this achievement will benefit the business also.

However, this sort of performance-related pay can backfire. Inappropriate targets might be set; an employee may have unrealistic expectations of what s/he can actually achieve. Also, sometimes a line manager may 'push' an employee to accept a target that they do not really want. None of these situations will be helpful to the process. A manager should ensure that the employee's targets, like the business's objectives, are 'SMART' (specific, measurable, agreed, realistic, and time limited). There is no point in setting an employee up to fail, especially if there is a degree of performance-related pay at stake.

Furthermore, there is always an element of subjectivity in judging targets. What one manager regards as 'good progress' might not be perceived in the same way by another manager. Inconsistency in appraisals across a business will be very divisive.

Finally, in any form of performance-related pay, the employee could feel insulted if the sums of money involved are small. A bonus of £1,000 might seem acceptable at first sight, but if the employee is a higher rate taxpayer then the deduction of tax at 40% and then National Insurance will considerably reduce what is actually taken home. Appraisal is examined in detail in Unit 33.

Key Terms

Appraisal: an annual assessment of an employee's performance (also known as 'performance management'). It can be linked to a performance related bonus.

In summary, performance-related pay:

- can help with the recruitment and retention of employees
- can motivate via higher rewards
- rewards loyalty and commitment.

However it can also:

- encourage a focus on what will be rewarded rather than on 'the wider picture'
- be divisive and demotivate employees
- discourage teamwork.

Performance-related pay cannot just be imposed upon an existing pay structure without careful thought as to the way in which it will operate, the potential costs (both monetary and to morale, motivation and teamwork) and benefits. Any change to a pay system requires consultation with the workforce well in advance if it is to be successful; employees at all levels of an organisation are acutely sensitive to any change (actual or perceived) in their worth.

Key Term

Performance-related pay: some, or all, of an employee's pay depends on individual (or group) performance.

Non-monetary method of remuneration

Not all methods of remuneration are monetary. Non-monetary rewards, which are sometimes referred to as 'fringe benefits', or 'perks', can also be used by a business. These include private health care, gym membership, subsidised nursery provision for employees' children, a company car, subsidised season tickets for travel to work, etc. The business may also benefit from the provision of these. For instance, if an employee is provided with a private health policy, s/he will probably receive medical treatment on falling ill sooner than on the National Health Service, and will therefore be able to return to work sooner.

Key Term

Fringe benefits (also known as 'perks'): non-monetary methods of remuneration, e.g. private health care, a company car etc.

Method	Advantages	Disadvantages
Time rate	• Easy for the business to calculate payroll costs and to operate. • Fewer problems with poor quality output. • Employee can easily calculate earnings.	• No link between effort and reward. • Demotivation due to some employees feeling that they are working harder than others and yet gaining the same reward.
Piece rate	• Effort linked to reward. • If employees are motivated solely by money, this will be an effective method of remuneration. • Increased output.	• Disagreement between employees and managers on a 'fair' rate. • A system of verifying individual output will be necessary. • Will only work effectively if employees are motivated by money. • Quality and safety issues.
Performance-related pay	• Some link between effort and reward. Those who work hard are rewarded for it. • Can be linked to targets that are mutually beneficial to both the employee and the business. • Increased commitment to the business.	• The nature of the extra payment might mean that the link between effort and reward is very indirect. • Different payments can cause jealousy and resentment. • May vary from year to year. Small payment will be seen as derisory. • May come to be taken for granted and cease to motivate.

Table 31.1 Summary of the advantages and disadvantages of the main methods of employee remuneration

Deductions from pay

Considerable deductions are made from an employee's pay, whatever form it takes. Income tax has to be deducted by the business at the appropriate rate (and then paid to HM Customs and Revenue), as does the employee's national insurance contribution. These are statutory deductions from pay, and the employee has no choice over whether or not to pay them.

If the business operates a contributory pension scheme and the employee wishes to join, this will also mean a further deduction. Such a deduction would, however, be voluntary.

For every employee on the payroll, the business must also pay an employer's national insurance contribution to the government. This is different from the employee's contribution that it deducts from the employee's pay and then passes on. This statutory payment is effectively 'a tax on employment', and the more people which a business employs, the more contributions it has to pay. A rise in the amount of employer's contribution is always met with disapproval by those running a business, since it makes people more expensive to employ.

When considering the cost of taking on a new employee, a business must take into account not only the wage (and any performance-related pay), but also the national insurance contribution it must make. If the business offers its own contributions to the employee's pension scheme, this is a further expense. These extra payments are often referred to as 'on costs' – i.e. 'on top of' the basic employment costs.

Key Term

Statutory deductions from pay: the legal deductions that have to be made by a business from an employee's pay: income tax and the employee's national insurance contribution.

Changing the method of remuneration

As has been seen, payment systems are broadly of two types; time rates, and those based on performance. Acas guidelines should be followed, whichever method is used. Acas stands for Advisory, Conciliation and Arbitration Service, and offers unbiased guidance on matters of industrial relations. Acas is funded by the government which ensures that it is independent.

The Acas website makes it clear that for a payment system to be successful it should:

- be carefully selected to take account of the needs of the organisation and its employees
- have the commitment of all employees and all levels of management
- be developed and maintained with the participation of employees and their representatives.

If a payment system is to be changed, these points are very important. It does not matter what the change is; whether it is a change from a basic rate payment per hour to a piece rate, a change in the nature of a bonus, or the introduction of appraisal. Change of any kind always makes employees nervous and so their involvement in matters affecting pay is crucial.

Any strategy for achieving a successful change to a pay system will need to follow these points.

- Identify why the old system is unsatisfactory. Are there any parts of it that command agreement from all involved (e.g. a Christmas bonus)? If so, a good starting point is to keep and build on these.
- Identify precisely what the new system is supposed to do, e.g. encourage recruitment and retention, increase individual effort etc.
- Involve employees or their representatives at the earliest possible stage. Managers must explain the reasons for the change and be prepared to modify their initial proposals.
- Ensure that the proposals mean that as few employees as possible (and preferably none at all) will be financially worse off than previously; also, that wage differentials (the pay difference between one grade of employee and another due to skill, experience etc.) are not reduced. Any proposals failing to take account of these issues are extremely unlikely to secure much support from the workforce.
- Ensure that any change fits in with the business's culture; e.g. a culture involving teamworking may be upset by a new appraisal system designed to reward individual effort.
- Ensure that the proposed system fits in with the business's objectives. A strategy designed to achieve an increase in market share from repeat business via customer satisfaction is unlikely to succeed if employees dealing with customers feel cheated and undervalued by the new system.
- Try to ensure that any of the changes are agreed rather than imposed.

- Monitor and evaluate the change. What has been the reaction from employees? Have the changes succeeded in the way they were supposed to? If not, what sort of adjustments might be appropriate?

Examiner's voice

Payment systems affect motivation and output, as well as the recruitment and retention of employees. If you are asked to consider changes to a payment system, you will need to analyse and evaluate the implications of any change on these issues if you want to access the higher levels of the mark scheme.

'New' and 'old' pay

In the 1990s the phrase 'new pay' started to be used. 'New pay' reflects changes in the business environment. With 'old pay', the payment system reflected the structure of the business, usually organised in a tall hierarchy. The level of pay was based around rigidly defined jobs arranged in hierarchical levels. Increases in pay were based on progression up a fixed scale, in line with the number of years of service or alternatively with a promotion. The payments on the scale would usually be increased in line with inflation. Once at the top of a payscale, the employee 'hit a pay ceiling' which meant a limit on the amount that could be earned.

'New pay' is different, and reflects the changing nature of the modern business world. Many businesses now favour flatter organisation structures (to improve communication and facilitate employee empowerment), and the old style hierarchy of jobs has disappeared in many organisations. New pay is accordingly much less hierarchical and means that the remuneration employees receive is based not on the number of years of employment at the business or their job title, but on their contribution to the business's success and their willingness to acquire useful skills.

Under an old pay system, employees who plodded along loyally for years doing the same job could expect to move up a grade over a period of time as the person in the job above them retired, and in so doing gain a pay rise. New pay is very different and emphasises that pay should reflect self-development (supported by the

Characteristics of 'old pay'	Characteristics of 'new pay'
Related to a hierarchical pay structure.	Related to a flatter organisational structure.
Inflexibility over the work performed.	Flexible approach to the work performed.
Increases in pay based on length of service, promotion, and the rate of inflation.	Increases in pay based on the individual's worth to the business.
Payment system is rooted in past practice.	Payment system is closely allied with the business' strategic objectives.

Table 31.2 'New' and 'old' payment systems

Key Terms

New pay: the remuneration which employees receive is based not on the amount of time spent in employment at the business, or their job title, but on their contribution to the business's success and their willingness to acquire useful skills.

business e.g. through training), flexibility and the actual worth of the employee to the business. It is rooted in the market worth of the employee.

It is certainly true that many businesses are moving away from a rigid pay hierarchy that values the job, towards a pay system that values individuals and the contribution they make. It is not difficult to see why; the most talented and skilled employees expect to be rewarded accordingly and will simply leave if they do not receive a reward in line with their market worth. The argument that 'I'd like to pay you more, but I can't because of the payment system' is now impossible to sustain if a business wants to retain the very best employees.

Further Sources

www.acas.org.uk – the Acas website. Practical guidance for businesses on how to successfully introduce, operate, and change a payment system.
www.peoplemanagement.co.uk – the online magazine for the Chartered Institute of Personnel and Development. Useful not only for pay-related matters; lots of up-to-date articles about all kinds of human resource issues.

Questions Time allowed 20 minutes

1. State two characteristics of a time rate. (2 marks)

2. State two characteristics of a piece rate. (2 marks)

3. State two instances when a time rate would be an appropriate method of payment. (2 marks)

4. State two instances when a piece rate would be an appropriate method of payment. (2 marks)

5. Explain two advantages and two disadvantages of a bonus system. (8 marks)

6. Outline two differences between 'old pay' and 'new pay'. (4 marks)

(20 marks)

Case study Time allowed 20 minutes

Trouble with TLRs

Teachers in the UK are paid on a time rate. Piece rates are not considered appropriate given the nature of their work, although bonuses can be paid for achieving good examination results in some instances. In state schools there is a pay scale up which teachers can progress, according to length of service and qualifications. A similar scale exists in independent schools. However, in state schools there is very little flexibility over pay. There is usually little opportunity for the sort of 'new pay' systems that exist in the business world.

A major change in teachers' pay in all schools in the state sector came into effect in January 2009. Up until this time, any teacher undertaking an additional role in the school would often receive a payment of some kind. This remuneration took the form of a 'management allowance' and was paid whatever the nature of the responsibility. These varied according to the amount of responsibility involved, and were paid whether the teacher was a Head of Department or was in charge of the school magazine.

However from January 2009, by law any allowances paid have to be *specifically* related to teaching and learning. This means that all teachers with posts of responsibility such as Heads of Faculty, Heads of Department, Heads of Year etc. are to receive payments which will be called Teaching and Learning Responsibility payments (TLRs) instead of 'management allowances'. Like the previous system of allowances, TLRs will vary according to the level of responsibility.

The situation is less clear for those who had until 2009 had a non-teaching responsibility, such as helping with school examinations, being responsible for audio visual equipment, or being in charge of the school fair. These responsibilities do not qualify for a TLR payment because they are not directly related to teaching and learning. The Department for Children, Schools, and Families stated that the reason for the change was that teachers should teach and not be involved in other jobs in school which could be performed by non-teachers. This sounds sensible but it worried those receiving allowances for these non-teaching responsibilities because of the potential loss of earnings and the reduction in pension rights that would also occur because of the possible cut in salary. They argue that they were happy doing these jobs and should be allowed to continue performing them.

There are a number of trade unions that teachers can belong to, but all of them (except one, the National Union of Teachers) agreed to accept the TLR proposals. This caused a large number of teachers to accuse the unions of 'selling out'. In 2008 a union spokesman stated that 'unless the TLR issue is carefully managed by head teachers, there is massive potential for discontent and a reduction in morale'.

Assume that it is January 2008. The proposals are to be implemented in one year's time. Recommend and justify a strategy by which a head teacher could successfully introduce the TLR proposals.

(18 marks)

Recruitment

The recruitment process is vitally important to any business. Finding the right person for a particular job can be expensive in terms of time and money. Appointing someone and then discovering that he or she is the wrong person for the job, or that they leave quickly, makes the process even more costly. The catering trade has higher than average labour turnover, partly because workers fail to realise that the work is demanding and that the hours are unsocial.

JOB DESCRIPTION

POST: After School Care Assistant

REPORTS TO: Head of Preparatory Department

DUTIES AND RESPONSIBILITIES:

a. General: To operate an after school care service for pupils of the Preparatory Department as directed by the Head of the Department.

b. Detail: To keep a register of pupils remaining after school and to record the times they are collected;

To supervise, control and ensure the safety of pupils remaining after school;

To implement a planned programme of activities;

To collect, and serve a light snack and to clean up after service;

To prepare classrooms for activities and to ensure that they are left in a tidy condition;

To maintain a safe environment for the pupils.

Figure 32.1 A typical job description

Job description

The first part of the process is to prepare a job description. This is usually prepared by the human relations department or its equivalent, and sets out the job requirements.

Person profile

Once there is a job description, the business can start to look at the ideal characteristics of the person to undertake the job. This may include some or all of the following:

- qualifications
- previous experience
- ability to work with a team
- willingness to travel
- work under supervision or independently
- ability to use initiative
- flexibility.

Internal or external appointment

The recruiter needs to decide whether to recruit internally or externally. This decision will depend on the nature of the job and whether or not there are suitable candidates within the business. Very often, internal candidates will be considered alongside external applicants.

The benefits of appointing an internal candidate

- Recruitment will take less time because the prospective candidate is already known to someone with responsibility in the business.
- There is no need to undertake costly advertisements.
- There will be less need for induction training.
- The ways in which the business works will already be known to the candidate.

- There is less risk of being impressed by someone at interview who then turns out to be a poor appointment.
- The opportunity of promotion may motivate internal candidates to achieve similar success for themselves in the future, and encourage good workers to stay rather than look for promotion elsewhere.

However, there is a risk that internal candidates who are not successful may react badly and sour the working relationship. It is also possible that a worker who worked well in a previous role, e.g. as part of a team, fails to work well in the new position, e.g. in a managerial role.

Advertising

When a business decides to advertise a job externally, there are a number of important factors to be taken into account.

- The job advert must contain enough information to attract suitable applicants and deter unsuitable ones.
- Certain vital information must be included, such as the title of the job and any required qualifications. Other information about the job can be put on a website or sent in the post.
- The advert must be put in the right place to attract suitable applicants. For example, Chester Zoo would put an advert for a new director in the broadsheet daily papers like *The Times* and *The Independent*; it would advertise for animal keepers in the periodicals aimed at employees who keep or look after exotic species; if it needed shop workers and ice-cream sellers for the summer months, the adverts would be placed in local newspapers.

Applications

Many businesses use application forms so that the process of comparison between applicants and choosing who to interview is made easier. In the initial stages, these forms might ask for basic information on experience and qualifications. There might then be a more complex form which asks for information about past experience in a number of areas. This might include extended questions about whether the candidate has worked well as part of a team or has had to make decisions under difficult circumstances. Most of these forms are now filled in online.

Figure 32.2 Procedure for online applications at Sainsbury's

Interviews

As the next stage of the process, many large businesses perform a telephone interview to reduce costs. The candidates to be interviewed face-to-face will be selected after the telephone interview.

An interview is regarded as the most successful method of finding the right person for a job. However, some people feel that the process is flawed and that decisions are made on first impressions rather than on facts. An interviewer will decide whether a person is able to do the job on offer in the first 60 seconds of an interview. The judgment will be based on punctuality, confidence, handshake, appearance and ability to make conversation in the initial stages of meeting.

The following factors are important for the business in the interview process:

- Having the right number of people on the interview panel.
- Deciding beforehand what information is to be gathered.
- Making sure that the interviewee is put at ease and is not interrogated.
- Allowing adequate time for the interview to take place.
- Giving the interviewee the opportunity to ask questions.

Alongside interviews, businesses may also conduct other tasks to help them in the recruitment process. These may include:

- team tasks and activities
- presentations on a requested topic to the selection team

- personality tests
- teaching a lesson.

At the end of the process, the business will hope to have a new employee who matches the initial job description, will adapt well to the workplace, and contribute positively to the success of the business.

Training

The need for training an employee begins as soon as they start to work for a business, and should then continue for the length of their employment. In recent years the need for ongoing training has become increasingly important for UK businesses. This is partly as a result of government incentives, initiatives and legislation, but also because businesses have experienced benefits from investing in the training of their employees. These benefits may include better motivation and performance (see discussion of Abraham Maslow, Unit 28) and also give the business access to new markets; e.g. meeting the government's ISO targets for quality and assurance is now a requirement for businesses if they wish to become suppliers to large UK businesses (see Unit 2).

Induction training

Starting a new job is a difficult time for any individual. Many employers find that this is the time at which labour turnover is at its highest. Perhaps there is something wrong with the recruitment process, or the induction process is so unsatisfactory that the employee feels uncomfortable in the job role or the work environment. Getting induction right is therefore crucial if the business wants its new recruits to stay. The cost of recruitment is high for any business, so money spent in ensuring that successful candidates stay in the job is well spent.

The factors that should be included in induction training are included in Figure 32.3.

Figure 32.3 The induction process

It is possible for induction programmes to discourage new workers rather than making them enthusiastic about the job. This may happen if the induction bombards the employee with huge amounts of information about the business and its operation (see Figure 32.1). New workers are often most concerned about finding their way around the building, following correct procedure and avoiding silly mistakes. They are not particularly interested in the disciplinary procedure and the history of the business. Some of the things they need to know will be learned over the first few weeks; others are better explained on the job by a line manager rather than as part of a series of endless presentations in the first few days.

Management needs to think carefully about what needs to be in the programme to allay fears, explain systems and keep the introductory programme short. It is then possible to ensure that other information is acquired as the employee fits into the business.

Training methods

There is a variety of training methods that businesses can use to improve the performance of their employees. In choosing the method, employers need to think about the nature of the training to be given and the employees to be trained. What suits one situation and group of workers will not necessarily suit all.

On-the-job and off-the-job training

Training can either be at the place of employment or at a different location. In either case, the training can be delivered either by employees of the business or by outside specialist training organisation personnel.

On-the-job training

There are advantages to this type of training, including the following points:

- It may be easier to do a series of shorter training sessions where the worker is released for part of the day.
- It is likely to be much cheaper, especially if it is provided by the business's staff.
- It can be tailored to the specific requirements of the business.

However, there are disadvantages:

- It may be regarded as less valuable, especially if it is delivered by people who work within the business.
- It can be regarded as tedious, unimportant and a waste of time.

Off-the-job training

This type of training will probably cost more, but has the following advantages:

- For many workers this may be regarded as a perk, involving time away from work in pleasant surroundings.
- Being away from the workplace may encourage employees to think more seriously about training issues.
- It is an opportunity to spend time with colleagues in a different environment, which may change perceptions and break down barriers between managers and other workers.

Other training methods

There are many different ways in which training can be delivered to workers (see Unit 32). Some of these will be through the involvement of the employer, but in other cases the individual may decide to invest time and money in his own training and development.

These are just a few of the methods of training:

- Learning by watching and doing. This is sometimes called 'sitting next to Nellie'. You may have seen this type of training in operation at a supermarket checkout or in a bank. This type of training depends on the business having spare capacity so that an experienced member of staff can deliver the training.
- Apprenticeships. These involve training that is both on-the-job and in college on a day-release system. It is a method that is used in skilled trades such as plumbing and car mechanics.
- Distance and e-learning. Individuals take responsibility for their own work under the supervision of a mentor or tutor, who will give feedback and assistance as required, in addition to marking assignments.
- Courses. Businesses can use this method in a variety of ways. For example, the introduction of a new computer system will require training for all staff who use the system. Other courses may be used if it is felt that a particular group of workers is not working efficiently, or if the business feels that there are efficiency savings to be made through new work practices.

In addition to these methods, the government is now involved in a number of training initiatives, both for individuals and businesses. These include:

1. Investors in people. This involves developing skills in the workforce to meet government criteria in areas such as customer service. When a company achieves the target, it is given a display plaque to confirm the achievement.

2. Learning and Skills Council. This organisation works in a number of areas with employees over 16. It aims to give people with few conventional qualifications the training and skills to become integrated and successful in the workforce.

Training Needs Analysis (TNA)

Training needs analysis is the way in which a business ensures that its workers are given the skills that they need to do their job effectively. In doing such an analysis, the business will collect information from workers, customers, managers and suppliers, as well as observing the way in which jobs are performed in different areas. It is important that the whole workforce, including managers, is included in this exercise. There may be skill shortages in a particular area that have been overlooked in the past because no one has noticed the lack of training or there has been a failure in communication. TNA should help to resolve the problem by highlighting such problems in particular areas of the business.

This feedback will be collated and analysed, to make sure that training is appropriate and not a waste of money or time. The end result should be a better trained workforce, able to do its job more effectively.

The following factors ought to be considered as part of a TNA:

- The firm must first decide what it wants to achieve for the future, maybe in terms of sales, output, productivity or market share.
- From the results gained in the initial survey, decisions must be made about who is to be trained and how.
- It is vitally important at this stage to involve people who are to be trained in the process, so that they can have an input into the type of training they need. This will be particularly important when a new product or process is being introduced.
- Decisions must be made about how the training is to be delivered. Can some of it be done within the firm? How much should be done by external providers?
- External training providers need to be chosen carefully, to match the style of the business and the budget.
- The cost of a particular training solution needs to be considered before it is undertaken. Will the results be worth the expense?
- The number of people who need training is also an important factor. If it is only one or two people, it would probably be most cost-effective to send them on a course. If it is a large group, it may be better to deliver the course inhouse.

Evaluation of training

Once the training process has been completed, managers need to assess the work that has been done. Businesses often undertake costly training programmes without considering whether the exercise has delivered value for money, and without looking at what, if anything, has been achieved by way of improvement.

In some areas it will be easy to see the benefits of training. For example, the training for the introduction of a new computer system will have measurable results. It will be possible to measure the ease with which employees adapt to the new system, to look at problems that arise and address them. In a similar way, if a supermarket trains its staff in customer service, a survey among customers will demonstrate if the training has been successful.

In other areas it is more difficult to assess the results of training. This may be so for courses involving management training. If feedback is sought from the participants of the course, they will often not be able to see how they are putting its content into practice; they are more likely to comment on the delivery of the course than its success in helping them to do their job better.

Businesses also need to do a cost-benefit analysis on any training provided, to enable better decision-making in this area in the future and avoid wasting money. Training at any level is expensive, and it is important that businesses ensure that money spent on training achieves positive benefits for the future.

Further Sources

www.businesslink.gov.uk
www.trainingzone.co.uk

Task

Find someone who has undertaken training at their workplace in recent months. This could be a parent, relative, friend or one of your teachers. Discuss the training with them, and find out about some of the following things:

1. When did the course take place? How long was it? Who delivered it?

2. What was the main purpose of the course?

3. What sort of training techniques did the course use?

4. What was learned from the course?

5. If the interviewee had been running the course, how would s/he have done it differently?

6. How has s/he used what was learned from the course at work?

Case study   Time allowed 1 hour

Coup Sauvage

Grace Williams runs a ladies' hairdressing salon in a busy market town. She has built the business up over a period of 10 years, and now it is very successful with a regular and loyal customer base. Grace regards her business as 'up-market', and the prices she charges reflect this. Her customers are prepared to pay her high prices because they are happy with the quality of the service she provides.

Grace employs a variety of workers at different levels of experience. She takes some young people from the local college who are completing hairdressing courses. They work with her on some days of the week and attend college on other days to complete their qualifications. Grace works with the college to deliver on-the-job training and to provide experience of working in a busy salon.

Grace also has two experienced members of staff who have been with her from the beginning of her business. She knows that she can trust them and their work, and she is happy to leave them in charge of the salon. In addition to this, Grace employs six hairdressers who have been qualified for between three and five years. They come to Grace to increase their experience of hairdressing and to work in a large, prestigious salon.

In recent months however, Grace has begun to experience staff turnover problems among this last group of workers. They are often very enthusiastic about joining the business, and usually have excellent qualifications. Grace is sure that she is choosing the right people; she is not sure what she needs to do to persuade them to stay longer.

Grace tends to leave this group of workers to do their jobs. She knows that they are fully qualified, so apart from the occasional bit of advice, she does not see the need to do more.

This staff turnover situation is beginning to cause problems for Grace. Apart from the time taken interviewing replacement workers, Grace's customers are beginning to complain. Customers become used to a particular stylist and they like to return to the stylist whom they like. Reluctantly, Grace is beginning to think that she needs to treat newly qualified employees in a similar way to those who are still at college, by giving them training in further aspects of the job and running a large salon.

1. Explain two ways that on-the-job experience can help with the training of the college students.

(6 marks)

2. Analyse the costs and benefits for Grace of taking college students to work in the salon as part of their training. (14 marks)

3. How should Grace tackle the problem of high staff turnover among newly qualified workers? Justify your answer. 20 marks)

(40 marks)

APPRAISAL

An appraisal is an assessment of an employee's performance, and for this reason it is also known as 'performance management'. While it is clearly part of a manager's job to monitor employee performance in a general sense throughout the year, this is not usually regarded as 'appraisal'. An appraisal is usually a formal meeting between an employee and their line manager once a year, during which the employee is encouraged to reflect upon achievements, workload and development needs, and to agree targets to be achieved in the next year. The process should be a positive one, with any criticism being constructive rather than disparaging.

Until fairly recently, appraisals tended to be restricted to people in management posts, but it is now increasingly popular for them to be introduced in one form or another for employees at all levels in a business. Responding to employee needs can help give a competitive edge over rivals through increased motivation, productivity and commitment to the job.

Although there is no legal requirement for a business to have a system of appraisal, there are many potential benefits for a business in appraising its workforce. However, appraisals are often regarded with deep suspicion by employees who may view the process as 'spying' and showing a lack of trust in their ability to complete the job. It is therefore very important that any appraisal system is introduced and operated with as much cooperation from employees as is possible. Without this, it may be regarded by the workforce as irrelevant and a waste of time.

Key Term

Appraisal: an assessment of an employee's performance.

The objectives and benefits of appraisal

Careful thought needs to be given to exactly what the process is designed to achieve before it is introduced, because this will affect how the process is designed, how it will operate and how it is perceived by employees. Will it be for reviewing performance? Will it be to identify training and development needs? Will it be linked to some sort of bonus or other reward? In practice, it may be all three.

Key Term

Development needs: the requirements that an employee has in order to perform their job more effectively or/and gain the skills and abilities necessary for promotion.

The main purpose and benefit of appraisal is to identify an employee's strengths and weaknesses; although a better term to use would be 'development needs', as the word 'weakness' has negative overtones. A judgement can be formed as to whether the employee is effective in their current post. If not, then the reason for this can be determined. Thus an appraisal can be used to gather information for human resource planning, and employee development needs can be linked to a programme of training in order to make the employee more effective.

An employee's potential for promotion can be considered. The appraisal presents an opportunity for an employee to discuss their expectations of the future. If these are linked to training and initiatives such as work shadowing, the employee will feel valued by the business. Such investment in career development is likely to be motivating as it is helping to meet self-esteem and achievement needs (see Unit 28).

The employee's workload can also be considered. This is important because of the obvious link to morale and motivation. Appraisals can be used to see if the workload has changed over the past year. Is there too much work? Too little? Also, with employees now able to sue for non-physical injuries such as stress, a discussion of workload with a formal record kept of the meeting could prove crucial if this ever occurs.

There will also be a discussion of how work is actually performed, and it can therefore highlight any procedural issues, communication problems or other difficulties that are hindering efficiency.

Introducing appraisal

Appraisal should never be introduced for its own sake. It is not a stand-alone process; it should be clearly linked to human resource issues such as training and pay.

Managers need training. Perhaps a production manager is perfectly competent with the technology his department has to use, but his interpersonal skills are not good. Such a person will need training in listening skills, making criticism constructive and giving praise when it is due. Unless line managers feel comfortable with the process and see that senior managers are committed, they may regard the process as a waste of time.

Figure 33.1 Appraisals are an opportunity to discuss past performance and future goals

Appraisal is sometimes linked to an increase in pay or a bonus of some kind, based on the assessment of performance. If this is the case, the process must be transparent and judged objectively. If employees feel that there is a degree of favouritism when bonuses are awarded, they will become distrustful of the whole process. Apparent bias towards some people will not be conducive to high morale and teamwork.

Employees must be clearly briefed on how the process will operate. There may be conflicts here as to whether the person conducting the appraisal is a 'judge' or a 'helper'.

Key Term

Performance management: another term for the process of appraisal.

Examiner's voice

Many candidates make statements such as 'appraisal will motivate people'. Appraisal in itself is very unlikely to motivate employees! Employees need to be able to perceive clear and direct benefits from the process for this to occur.

Creating effective appraisal systems

What will make appraisal ineffective?

- A lack of commitment by senior staff. A proper system of appraisal can be expensive. Treating it as a cost to be minimised will not bring the desired results.
- An inconsistent approach by line mangers. If some managers are too negative in their assessments, employees appraised by them will rightly claim that they have been treated differently to others. This can lead to discontent, especially if the appraisal is linked to a reward.
- Inadequate time allowed for the appraisal process. If managers give the impression that they are keen to be doing something else, this will be recognised by employees who will then regard the process as a waste of time.

- A failure to respond to employee concerns and aspirations. If an employee acknowledges that s/he needs training in for example some aspect of IT, then if the opportunity to attend a course which was promised at the appraisal never materialises, this will lead to a lack of confidence in the process, and also in the line manager.
- Unrealistic targets being set. Employees may have unrealistic expectations of what can actually be achieved. Also, sometimes a line manager may persuade employees to accept targets that they do not really want. Neither of these is helpful to the process. A manager should ensure that the employee's targets, like the business's objectives, are 'SMART' (specific, measurable, agreed, realistic, and time-limited). There is no point in setting an employee up to fail.
- The use of ambiguous language such as 'you have not done too badly; at least you've achieved some of your targets'. This sort of statement can leave an employee unsure of whether they are being praised for success or criticised for failure.

What will make appraisal effective?

- Senior managers must ensure that all managers are committed to the process, and that sufficient resources are available.
- Consultation with employees (via their trade union if one exists) at the earliest opportunity on the objectives and procedure.
- Ensuring that employees understand the system and how it will affect and benefit them.
- Ensuring that line managers are adequately trained in the skills necessary to perform an effective appraisal, e.g. listening skills and 'SMART' target setting.
- A willingness to modify the process if it is seen to be failing in reaching its stated objectives.
- Allowing employees to comment on the outcome of their appraisal.

Key Term

'SMART' target setting: a framework within which to set an employee's targets for the coming year. Targets should be Specific, Measurable, Agreed, Realistic and Time-limited.

Examiner's voice

Careful thought must be given to the business's culture when answering a question about appraisal. When answering a question about introducing (or changing) an appraisal system, it will be beneficial to develop a strategy building on the business's existing 'people' strengths.

The appraisal process

There is no single process that will suit all organisations; different businesses must develop different appropriate models, although reference to Acas guidelines would be a sensible idea. There are however some common characteristics for most processes.

First, it is usual for the employee to fill out a question and answer sheet relating to the targets that were agreed the previous year. The employee can comment on the extent to which s/he feels that they have been met. These targets and the employee's comments will then be reviewed by the line manager. An employee may be rated against the targets with statements such as 'fully met', 'partially met', or 'no progress towards target'. In the case of the latter, an employee should naturally be given the opportunity to offer an explanation; perhaps a key member of their staff who was crucial to the meeting of the target has been on long-term sick leave. In any event, the inability to meet a target should be approached by offering support to achieve it (if it is still appropriate) the following year, rather than a barrage of negative criticism.

That is not to say that a manager conducting the appraisal can only be 'nice', and an employee may have to be told that their performance has, in one or more areas, fallen short of the required standard. Even so, a constructive approach focusing on improvement and development is likely to prove more beneficial in terms of employee morale than condemnation.

Second, there is also likely to be a section for 'other achievements', and a section for the employee to comment on development needs for the future. The idea is for employees to have 'ownership' of their targets and career. Those who set unchallenging targets for themselves and show little interest in development can hardly complain that the business is ignoring them in terms of their career.

Finally, all sections are then discussed with the line manager and an overall judgement on the employee will then be made. A formal written record of the appraisal meeting and any forms completed will be kept. It is sensible, common practice for an employee to be given a copy.

In some businesses, certain types of employees have 'assessment sheets' that are completed monthly. A sales assistant for example might be assessed on factors such as appearance, ability to work without supervision, the level of customer service provided etc. These sheets can be filled in fairly quickly and the employee graded by ticking a box which corresponds to a certain level of achievement. However, great care must be taken to avoid labelling the boxes to be ticked with words such as 'satisfactory', 'adequate' or even 'good', since such terms are ambiguous. A clear descriptor is necessary. If customer service is 'good', what does this actually mean? Words such as 'always pleasant and helpful' would be more useful.

These sheets are not really 'appraisals' in the true sense of the term, although the grades recorded on them may be used at the appraisal interview as part of the overall appraisal process.

Further Sources

www.acas.org.uk – the Acas website. Practical guidance for businesses on how to introduce and operate a successful appraisal system.

www.peoplemanagement.co.uk – the online magazine for the Chartered Institute of Personnel and Development. Useful for information on appraisal. It also contains up-to-date articles about human resource issues of all kinds.

Your Turn

Case study Time allowed 30 minutes

KBJ Hotels plc

The KBJ Hotel group owns four hotels in London, and Janet O'Donovan is its new Chief Executive Officer. One of the problems facing her is the appraisal system left in place by her predecessor, Max Phillips. Max retired early following the introduction of several failed human resource initiatives. Appraisal was one of these, and Janet felt that the whole system had been introduced far too quickly, in a very haphazard manner and with virtually no consultation.

The objective which the board has set for Janet is 'to significantly increase shareholder value' over the next three years. Janet feels that this is a rather vague objective, but did not want to refuse the job offer as it was her first opportunity to take up a senior managerial position.

The system left in place by Max means that staff appraisals are conducted twice a year in a meeting between an employee and their line manager. Each hotel is run by a senior manager, all of whom have complained that a twice-yearly appraisal is too often and a waste of time because it distracts both them and the staff from other duties.

The same complaint has been echoed by nearly all of the line managers in charge of the different sections of the hotels. They have also pointed out that as labour turnover among frontline staff (such as chambermaids and restaurant/bar staff) is so high (on average it is 30% per year across the four hotels), the process is worthless since many of the staff have left by the time of the next appraisal session.

Janet is wondering how to improve the appraisal process, or whether to abolish it and concentrate on improving recruitment and selection. She thought that if the right calibre of employee were employed in the first place, there would be less need to appraise them.

1. State three objectives of an appraisal process.

   (3 marks)

2. Analyse the benefits of appraisal to a business such as KBJ.   (6 marks)

3. Recommend and justify a strategy that Janet could use to improve the appraisal process at KBJ.

   (18 marks)

   (27 marks)

EVALUATING WORKFORCE PERFORMANCE

A motivated and productive workforce will give a business an advantage in reaching its strategic objectives. However, there needs to be a way of evaluating just how satisfactory motivation and morale strategies actually are. A variety of simple techniques exist that enable a business to do this.

Data relating to workforce performance (e.g. employee absence and labour turnover) is useful for identifying problem areas in the business and also for planning purposes. For example, if the average annual labour turnover in a particular department of 50 employees is 10%, the human resource department can plan ahead on the basis that five employees a year will have to be recruited if the department is to be fully staffed.

Examiner's voice

Students often take one look at a table of numbers and say 'I can't do that,' without even considering what it is that they are being asked to do! In most cases, all that is required is GCSE level mathematics, such as the calculation of a percentage. Putting a simple calculation into an A2 context is an easy way to create an analytical answer and score marks.

Quantitative data on any business issue is subject to a number of limitations, and this is particularly true when applied to human resource issues. Some of these limitations are discussed at the end of this chapter. Nevertheless, the use of figures is an important and essential aspect of measuring employee performance.

Labour turnover

Labour turnover is concerned with measuring the number of employees who have left the business, and is usually calculated as an annual percentage by the following formula:

$$\frac{\text{Number of employees leaving during the year}}{\text{Average number employed during the year}} \times 100$$

If the average number of employees in a business was 150, and over the course of a year, 25 people left, the rate of labour turnover would be calculated as follows:

$$\frac{25 \times 100}{150} = \frac{2500}{150} \text{ or } \left(\frac{25}{150}\right) \times 100$$

The rate of labour turnover = 16.7%.

The higher the figure obtained, the more likely it is that motivation is low, otherwise why would so many employees be leaving? However the figure does not explain *why* employees are leaving. It might be due to retirement or personal reasons rather than dissatisfaction and disillusionment with work. The figure is useful as a guide to motivation, but if managers want to evaluate the situation correctly, they will need to look behind the data to obtain an accurate picture of what is occurring. Acas (see Unit 70) provides a specimen 'analysis of labour turnover' form that a business can download and use – or modify – for this very purpose.

The Acas form also contains the formula for calculating labour force stability – the **labour stability index**. This shows the extent to which the experienced employees are being retained.

acas

Analysis of labour turnover

Length of service	Sex	Left voluntarily	Dismissed	Redundant	Total
Less than 1 month	M				
	F				
1-3 months	M				
	F				
4-12 months	M				
	F				
1-5 years	M				
	F				
Over 5 years	M				
	F				
Total	M				
	F				

	M	F	Total
(a) Total employed at beginning of period			
(b) Total number of leavers during period			
(c) Total starters during period			
(d) Total employed at end of period			
(e) Average number employed during period = (a) + (d) ÷ 2			

Labour turnover (%)

$$\frac{\text{No. of leavers during period}}{\text{Average employed during period}} \quad \frac{\text{(b)} \times 100}{\text{(e)}}$$

Labour Stability Index (%)

$$\frac{\text{No. currently employed with 1 year's service or more} \times 100}{\text{Total number of employees 1 year ago}}$$

Figure 34.1 Acas labour turnover analysis form © Acas

So, for example, if the number of employees with one or more year's service is currently 89, and the number of employees one year ago was 120, the calculation would be:

$$= \frac{8900}{120}$$

The labour stability index = 74.2%

A high figure on this index indicates that experienced employees are remaining within the business, whereas a low figure indicates that there are a lot of new employees. These employees have been recruited because others have left, and so a low figure for the business (or an individual department) should prompt the question, 'Why is this happening'?

Finally with labour turnover, it should be remembered that while high rates are undesirable (because of the cost implications of recruitment and selection, disruption to work, the fact that new recruits are more likely to make mistakes, etc.) a workforce that has a zero rate of labour turnover is likely to become stale and resistant to change. This is especially true at management level; a certain level of labour turnover can therefore actually be desirable.

> **Key Term**
>
> **Labour turnover:** a measure of the number of employees who have left the business (usually over the past year), relative to the number employed in that period. A high percentage is an indicator of poor morale and motivation.

Absenteeism

Absence from work imposes an extra cost on the business in the form of a replacement employee, or puts pressure and stress on existing staff who have to do extra work to cover for their absent colleague. However a distinction must be made between different sorts of absence, and when analysing data on absence this must be acknowledged.

Long-term absence

This is where an employee is off work for a lengthy period, and is usually due to illness. A high number of absences due to illness or injury could be symptomatic of an unsafe and unhealthy working environment.

Short-term absence

This is a different situation, where an employee is absent from work for a day (or a few days) because of a minor ailment such as an upset stomach or a headache. It is this sort of absence that is referred to as 'absenteeism', and can be used as an indicator of the level of morale and motivation.

This is the most common type of absence. A certain amount of short-term sickness can be expected in any business, but where there is an upward trend overall or in a specific department, it is indicative of a problem.

A record of all absences and reasons for these should be kept by the business. This will be crucial if disciplinary action for recurring absence is ever taken against an employee. If a pattern of absenteeism starts to emerge with a particular individual or individuals (e.g. repeated absences on the same day of the week), this might be an indicator of a problem that should be tackled.

The formula to be used is similar to the one used for labour turnover. The following is based on one day's absence in a month for an individual employee. It could also be used with hours instead of days, and over any appropriate time period. Whichever is chosen, the calculation gives what is known as the **lost time rate**.

The calculation is useful for an overall picture of lost time in the business as a whole. It should also be undertaken for all areas of the business, because it can show up those departments with a particular absence problem.

The lost time rate generates an answer in the form of a percentage and is calculated as follows:

$$\frac{\text{Total days absent in the month}}{\text{Total available working days in the month}} \times 100$$

Consider the following:

- There are nine employees in a particular department.
- There are 23 available working days in the month.
- Eleven days are taken off work with the reason given as 'sickness'.

The lost time calculation is therefore:

$$\frac{1100}{207} \ (9 \times 23)$$

The lost time rate = 5.3%

Key Term

Absenteeism: employees are absent from work with minor medical ailments such as an upset stomach or a headache. Absenteeism can be a key indicator of low morale and motivation levels.

High absence rates need to identified, analysed (is it one or two employees who are causing the high figures, or is it across the department?) and dealt with.

There is a distinction between 'authorised' and 'unauthorised' absence. The latter refers to the sort of short-term absences mentioned above; the former is where an employee asks for time off for a particular reason such as a medical appointment, to visit a relative who is ill, or to attend an important meeting at a child's school. This sort of absence can be hard to deal with because an employee cannot always have a medical appointment out of normal working hours. A business needs a clear and consistent policy on allowable absence (and whether employees will be paid for it). It cannot grant permission to one employee to be absent for a doctor's appointment during working hours and then refuse permission to another, without stirring up resentment. Once again, a record of these absences should be kept to see if a pattern emerges.

Lateness

Exactly the same principle can be applied to lateness. If there is a perception among managers that many employees are arriving late to work, this needs to be investigated and monitored properly. As in all matters relating to employee attendance, an individual record should be kept and the number of instances of lateness in a week or month can be recorded quite easily. Acas provides a sample form to record this.

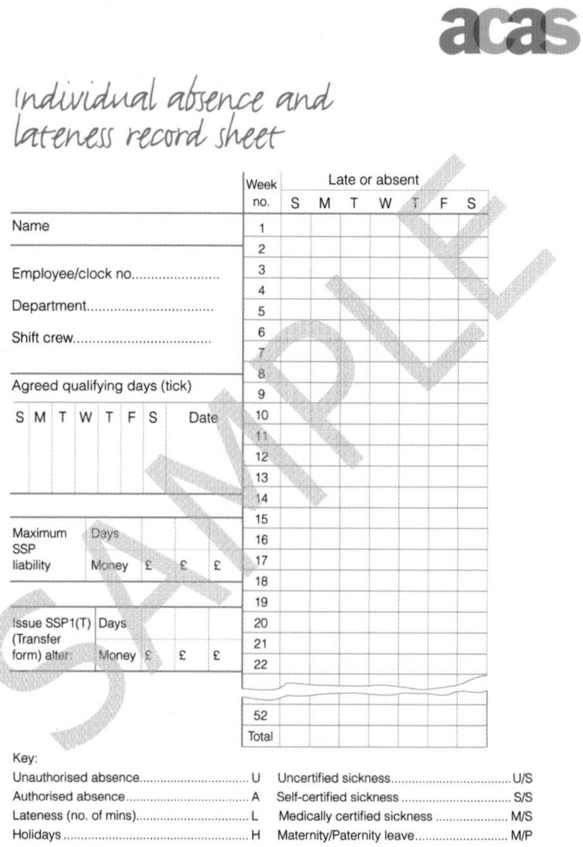

Figure 34.2 Acas individual absence and lateness sheet © Acas

In addition, a calculation could be done by a department or section to see if the lateness is a general or a localised problem.

In a particular section of a factory there are 20 employees. Suppose that last April there were 23 working days, and the total number of late arrivals in April was 58. The calculation would therefore be:

$$\frac{\text{Total number of late arrivals}}{\text{Total number of scheduled attendances}} \times 100$$

$$\frac{5800}{460}$$

The departmental lateness rate = 12.6%.

A high percentage is usually a good indicator of low motivation levels; a person who is motivated and who enjoys work is rarely late. The manager responsible for that area would need to examine the data to see whether the problem was being caused by a specific individual or individuals. Employees may be occasionally late for valid reasons, from childcare problems to traffic difficulties on the way to work. However, persistent lateness shows a disregard for taking the appropriate actions to arrive at work on time, i.e. a lack of motivation.

Workforce productivity

An important indicator of workforce performance is how productive employees are. This is not just a measure of how much is produced; it is a measure of output relative to input. At its simplest, it is a measure of output per employee.

Consider this example: 100 employees typically produce 1,000 units of output in one month. The business introduces some new technology that leads to 50 redundancies. The remaining 50 employees continue to produce 1,000 units per month. This is an improvement in productivity because output per employee has increased.

The formula is:

$$\frac{\text{Output (per week/month/year)}}{\text{Average number of employees}}$$

Using the example above, labour productivity (average output per employee) was initially:

$$\frac{1000}{100} = 10$$

After the change it has become:

$$\frac{1000}{50} = 20$$

Productivity has therefore increased.

Productivity is harder to measure in the tertiary sector where there is no physical product being produced.

Key Term

Productivity: a measure of output per employee. Productivity is a key indicator of performance.

Wastage rates

A measure of employee performance that could be used alongside labour productivity is the level of waste and/or rejects produced. A business will seek to minimise these because a high percentage is very inefficient – costs are higher than they could be.

Whether measured on an individual or departmental basis, the calculation is straightforward:

$$\frac{\text{Number of rejects produced (by employee or department)}}{\text{Total number of products produced}} \times 100$$

Therefore, if the number of rejects produced by employees on a particular factory shift was 543 and the total output was 7,500, the wastage calculation is:

$$\frac{543}{7500} \times 100$$

The reject rate = 7.2%

Waste and reject rates need to be minimised in order to maximise business efficiency. High rates can be due to poor quality inputs from suppliers or from outdated capital equipment, but they can also be indicative of an indifferent attitude by employees. If high rates are identified, the cause needs to be investigated.

Other methods of assessing employee performance

Appraisal

In Unit 33, the process of appraisal was considered. An appraisal is usually a formal meeting between an employee and their line manager once a year during which the employee is encouraged to reflect upon achievements, workload and development needs, and to agree targets to be achieved in the next year. The main benefit of appraisal is to identify an employee's strengths and weaknesses, although a better term to use would be 'development needs' as the word 'weakness' has negative overtones. A judgment can be formed as to whether the employee is effective in his/her current post. If not, then the reason can be determined. An appraisal can be used to gather information for human resource planning, and employee development needs can then be linked to a programme of training in order to make the employee more effective.

Employee assessment forms

Whereas appraisal tends to be for white-collar jobs on an annual basis, it is becoming increasingly common for businesses to assess employee performance on a more regular basis using a simple 'tick sheet'. This sheet grades employees on certain aspects of their job.

Both of these methods emphasise the need to look beyond mere numbers when evaluating performance.

Assessing employee performance

Examples of key areas in job*	Outstanding	Very good	Good	Fair	Unsatisfactory
Judgement					
Oral ability					
Written ability					
Numerical ability					
Technical ability					
Relations with colleagues					
Relations with public					
Management of staff					
Management of resources					
Acceptance of responsibility					
Drive and determination					
Reaction to pressure					
Overall performance					

*not all these aspects will be contained in every job

Figure 34.3 Acas sample employee assessment form © Acas

Additional measures of morale and motivation

- The number of customer complaints.
- The frequency of industrial action at the business, e.g. work to rules, strikes etc.
- The number of times in which the business's grievance procedure has been used.

Limitations to the use of quantitative data

There are a number of issues to bear in mind when using figures to assess employee performance, and it is important to highlight them.

Consider the following basic data relating to labour turnover in the four main departments of a business. The figures for the last 12 months are shown in Table 34.1. What do they indicate? On the face of it, an overall figure of 15% for the business is not very impressive, and the accounts department in particular is a disaster in terms of motivation.

Department	Labour turnover
Accounts	33%
Marketing	5%
Personnel	2%
Production	20%
Average for all departments	15%

Table 34.1 Labour turnover for different departments

However, there are several points that can be made on the validity and use of these figures in forming a judgment on performance.

Averages can be misleading

The 15% figure for the business as a whole is not representative of any of the figures for the individual departments. To use a single figure for the whole business would disguise the differences in the data and be misleading.

Not all departments employ the same number of people

The figure for the accounts department has contributed significantly to the final 15%. Assume that only six people work in that department. If one of them leaves, this will have a large impact on the departmental (and the overall business) figure. Two people must have left, because the figure is 33%. This makes a key indicator of motivation in the business as a whole appear worse than it actually is. On the other hand, the production department has a lower percentage figure, but if that area of the business employs 100 people, then 20 of them have left; this is a significantly larger number of employees than the two from accounts.

A single figure in isolation is of limited use

The figure for production looks poor. However, if the figures for the previous three years were 27%, 25% and 22%, the current 20% looks rather different. It is still too high but there is a continued improvement. 'Headline' figures can certainly highlight a sudden change (for better or worse), but trends in the data are significant and need to be monitored.

Numbers do not explain the situation

Figures for employee performance cannot explain what is happening in the workplace. Labour turnover is 20% in production, and the board of directors may rightly consider this unsatisfactory. However, having gathered the figures, their next job is to find out exactly why so many people are leaving. The employees might have been complaining that they are poorly paid. However, a knee-jerk reaction to pay them more to solve the problem might be an expensive mistake. The true reason might be an unsafe working environment or poor management. Many businesses conduct 'exit interviews', or ask employees to fill out a questionnaire to discover the reason for leaving.

Examiner's voice

Questions involving calculations do not stand alone. The results are there to be used, usually in the next question. Once you have performed a calculation, think how you could use it to support your argument. This will help you gain marks for analysis. The questions that follow will help you to do this.

Case study Time allowed 45 minutes

Terry's Toys Ltd (TTL)

TTL makes a variety of large children's cuddly toys such as bears, lions and penguins. It has discovered that there is a growing demand worldwide for high quality toys of this nature, and so it does not attempt to compete with businesses from the Far East on price. The toys are made very carefully with a considerable amount of hand stitching, and are not mass-produced on a production line. As a result, TTL's products command a premium price.

Two years ago, TTL introduced an extra shift to its factory which works at night to meet the growing demand. The night-shift employees have a shift premium and are paid a basic wage of £1,750 per month, whereas the day-shift workers are paid a basic wage of £1,600 per month. There are 25 employees on each shift.

When the change was made, nearly the entire existing workforce chose to remain as day-shift workers. Night-shift workers therefore tend to be employed via local agencies. They have a higher rate of absenteeism than those on the day shift (shift A), and also tend to have a much higher rate of labour turnover. If night-shift workers call in sick, it can be difficult to persuade day-shift workers to cover for them – even if several hours overtime are offered.

Throughout last year it proved very difficult for TTL to meet its contractual obligations to customers; despite the introduction of some new capital equipment, employees sometimes did not produce enough output.

Average output of toys	Monthly bonus to each employee
301–350	£20
351–375	£25
375–400	£30
400–425	£35

Table 34.2 Calculating the monthly bonus for employees

As a result, at the start of the year (January), a new performance-related pay scheme was introduced. This meant that if the average employee output exceeded 300 toys per employee a month, a bonus is paid to each employee on a sliding scale as follows:

Output has risen, but so have the number of rejects (toys that cannot be sold because of their poor quality). These rejected products are not easy to recycle. The Managing Director of TTL, Alex Terry, is not keen to sell the rejects as 'seconds' in retailers at the discount end of the market, as this would conflict with the brand image that he has worked hard to establish.

The data for the past four months is shown in Table 34.3.

Alex is currently considering the implications of this data.

1. Calculate the percentage increase in the number of rejects in each section between December and March. (4 marks)

2. Taking into account the number of rejects, calculate the labour productivity (average output per employee) in each section during March. (4 marks)

3. Using your answer to question 2, calculate the gross payment made in March to an employee in both sections. (4 marks)

4. Analyse two consequences to TTL of its reliance on agency workers. (6 marks)

5. Discuss whether the introduction of the bonus scheme at TTL has been a success. (18 marks)

(36 marks)

	Shift A (Day) 25 staff		Shift B (Night) 25 staff	
	Output	Number of rejects	Output	Number of rejects
December	9500	52	9890	60
January	9601	73	10300	65
February	9624	83	10789	90
March	9629	101	10456	118

Table 34.3 Data for the last four months

PRODUCTION

Unit 35

LOCATION OF INDUSTRY

Introduction

As with all of the functions within a business, production cannot stand alone. Without marketing to stimulate sales, there would be no reason to produce the product. The objectives of the business will have a significant effect on the productive capacity of the business and its actual level of output.

Once the objectives of the business are known, production facilities for producing the required products will be discussed and planned. However, planning within the production function of the business cannot take place without an awareness of the budgetary constraints as laid out by the finance department.

The planning within production will need to take note of the human resource requirements as well as the outlay on machines. Workforce planning cannot operate in isolation.

The chapters within this section cover the requirements as stated within the specification. To avoid unnecessary duplication, certain topics that also appear within other options may be located elsewhere.

Deciding where to locate a business will depend on a variety of factors to be discussed in this chapter: see Figure 35.1 for an illustration.

Figure 35.1 Factors influencing the location of industry

Examiner's voice

It is important to realise that although there are a wide range of factors that affect the location of a specific business, it will be important in the examination to select the relevant factors for the question, rather than write out a list.

Type of business and its product/service

If the business is involved in the primary sector of the economy, it may have little or no choice as to where to locate, as the raw material will govern its location. A coal industry will be located wherever the coalmines are! Similarly, any industry involved with the extraction of a raw material is to some extent governed by the source of that raw material.

While there has been a fall in the level of activity within the primary and secondary sector, the tertiary sector has expanded rapidly. Providing a service to consumers usually means that the location of such services is vital to achieve success. Ensuring that consumers are served in a convenient way is crucial. Consumers want services on their doorstep, and with the rising cost of fuel for transport, a convenient location is even more important.

The nature of the product is important if bulky raw materials are required. Reducing the cost of transporting the raw materials, especially if the product is in a competitive market or is a low value product, will be a key objective. For both, minimising costs will be a factor affecting location. Crisps are good example of a low value product which is also bulky to transport.

Type of market and significance of costs

The greater the degree of competition within a market, the more likely it is that any locational decisions will be cost-orientated. A monopolist may not be as concerned about costs due to the lack of competition, and therefore will not view locational decisions in the same manner.

Costs of the factors of production

The cost of production, land, labour, capital and enterprise will affect the location of any given site. The cost of land will be significant, depending upon the nature and size of the business.

The significance of the cost of labour will again depend upon the nature of the business, and the level of labour required. If the business is labour-intensive, then locating to a cheap and plentiful supply of labour will be paramount. Selecting an area where unemployment is high may mean that there is a high supply of labour, which will make the cost of labour cheaper. However, if particular skills are required, an area where such skills exist will be a significant factor in the choice of location.

Cost of site (demand and supply of such a site)

The cost of any site is determined by the level of demand and supply. Any increase in the level of demand for a particular site will increase the price of such a site (see Figure 35.2).

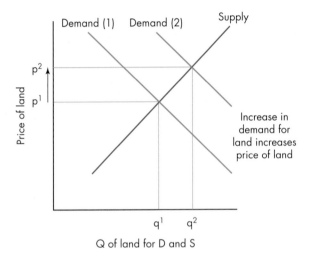

Figure 35.2 Cost of site affected by demand

Similarly, any change in the level of supply of appropriate sites will tend to reduce the cost of the sites (see Figure 35.3).

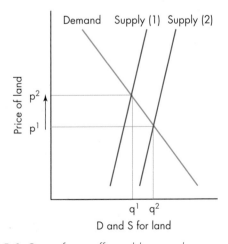

Figure 35.3 Cost of site affected by supply

Before the 'credit crunch' of 2008, the number of industrial sites was increasing rapidly. However, with a fall in the demand for these sites, the price level has fallen dramatically. This meant that potential buyers of offices and factory sites could negotiate a better deal.

Infrastructure

Businesses will look carefully at the infrastructure within the area. The infrastructure includes the facilities within the area such as transport links, schools, health services and other industrial facilities. If a business is to relocate to a new area, it may want to take some or all of its employees with it. The employees will want to be sure that there is a good range of housing in the area and good educational and health facilities within the area before contemplating any move.

The business needs to ensure that it can move its finished goods quickly and easily to its particular market; good transport links are therefore essential. It is no coincidence that the majority of new industrial buildings are located near a motorway junction.

The degree of competition within the area

Most businesses will want to locate away from their competitors. However, there are occasions when it will deliberately select to locate alongside its competitors. In Birmingham, jewellery shops are all located together in what is actually called the jewellery quarter. This may seem strange, but consumers will make a conscious decision to go the jewellery quarter, knowing that there will be a massive amount of choice within a small area of Birmingham.

Location of consumers

Depending on the nature of the product or service, being close to the consumers can be significant. For those involved in retailing, being close to the consumer is often the most significant factor. Local shops provide a range of products and services for locals. Consequently there is a real need to be located in a convenient location for the consumers. Local cornershops such as the Spar chain survive because they meet a consumer need in a convenient manner.

Similarly, a supplier to the car industry may want to be near to its consumer (the car plant) in order to deliver the components when required. With the heavy reliance on just-in-time (JIT), suppliers tend to locate as near to the 'consumer' as possible. Tesco Metro stores are usually located in areas of high density population, often in a business district, in order to meet its customers' needs.

Some international businesses choose a new location because of the access which that location gives to new customers. Nissan and Toyota wanted to locate within the UK at Sunderland and Derby in order to access consumers in the EU. Such locational decisions also allow the business to beat import duties and therefore offer effective cost incentives. In these two cases, both locations had the added incentive of financial inducements to provide a substantial improvement in regional unemployment difficulties.

Any of the above benefits will need to be assessed against the problems related to the currency changes that may occur and therefore create uncertainty regarding prices.

Government incentives

The government has always attempted to alleviate unemployment by offering incentives to industry to locate in areas where the level of unemployment is high. Ever since the 1960s when Development Areas where introduced, and in the 1980s when Enterprise Zones were established, governments have offered financial help to industry.

Today, the government operates assistance to areas of high unemployment through its Assisted Areas scheme. In addition, through the EU grants available under its regional policy (see Figure 35.4), the Assisted Areas are allowed to claim aid; this began on 13 February 2007.

The two main grant schemes available are the SFIE and the RSA:

- Selective Finance for Investment in England (SFIE) helps to fund new investment projects that will lead to long-term improvements in productivity, skills and employment.
- Regional Selective Assistance (RSA) operates in Scotland and aims to encourage new investment

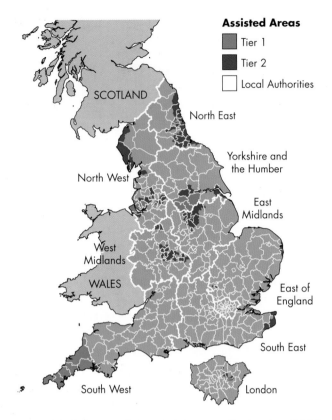

Assisted Areas
- Tier 1
- Tier 2
- Local Authorities

Figure 35.4 State aid Assisted Areas in England in 2008

projects that aid employment in the area. Regional Selective Assistance Wales (RSA) operates in the same way in Wales.

EU regional policy

In addition to UK government incentives, the EU offers a range of grants and 'contributions' to the economy. The European Council agreed a new Financial Perspective in 2005, which covers funds for 2007–13. The funds include money for structural and cohesion fund expenditure. Any funds used to improve the infrastructure of a region will usually make that area more attractive to industry. New objectives were issued alongside the funding, aimed at enhancing employment within certain areas. Yorkshire and Humberside will receive over 583 million euros.

Planning regulations

A planning bill was put forward in November 2007 which proposed an eight-point plan to speed up planning applications for major developments.

On 16 July 2008, the House of Lords completed its second reading of a controversial bill to speed up the process for the approval of infrastructure projects, which would include the building of motorways and power stations. Delays for such projects can be very costly to the economy and individual businesses, and therefore anything to speed up the process may be considered as a move in the right direction. The new bill was aimed at changing who is responsible for the granting of permission to proceed with such projects. Prior to the bill, local authorities were responsible for planning permission in the main. If there were any major disputes about a particular project, a public inquiry could be undertaken. Unfortunately, such inquiries take a very long time and therefore may damage the economy. The proposed bill would allow permission to be taken by an independent 'Infrastructure Planning Commission' (IPC). Concern was raised in the House of Commons as to whether such a body would be suitable, especially if an additional runway at an airport was being decided by this proposed new body. However, supporters of the bill highlighted the huge delays that had taken place under the old system, when deciding whether to give permission to build the fifth terminal at London's Heathrow airport. Permission was finally granted after seven years!

On 14 July 2008, the deputy director of the CBI suggested that any delays would threaten Britain's ability to 'keep the lights on' if a new energy infrastructure was not built quickly!

Globalisation

Globalisation has meant that the level of competition has increased as businesses face a much larger (world) market. The main consequence of globalisation is the need to be highly competitive. This in turn has encouraged businesses to locate where costs are at their cheapest. Many call centres are now located in India because of the low labour costs, as communications technology means that there is no need to be located within the market country. Car manufacturers have benefited from locating in eastern European countries to take advantage of cheap land and labour, coupled with EU grants. Even the UK film industry has located to countries such as Hungary, where the cost of land is minimal when compared to the UK and labour is significantly cheaper.

One obvious downside to locating abroad may be the language barrier. If a clear understanding of the language is required, this may incur additional costs to cover interpretational fees. There may also be cultural differences that affect production.

On 10 August 2008, it was reported in the *Sunday Times* that Ford's plant at Southampton where the Ford Transit vans are made, was under threat. The Southampton plant faces competition from other Ford plants in Turkey and Romania, both of which are able to offer cheaper production facilities.

Special requirements

There are some businesses that require special conditions or requirements for its operations to take place. A port obviously needs to be located by the sea! However, airports will not only require a large amount of land to provide all the facilities expected, but also have to avoid populated areas because of noise pollution. At the same time, airports need to be near to good transport links and sufficient population to warrant its usage. This therefore presents a dilemma. On the one hand, being near to the population is important but on the other, being too near will create pollution problems for those people who live nearby.

Further Sources

BERR (Department for Business Enterprise & Regulatory Reform)

www.berr.gov.uk/regional/assisted-areas

www.nomisweb.co.uk

www.investmerseyside.com

assistedareas@dti.gsi.gov.uk

Your Turn

Questions Time allowed 25 minutes

1. State two ways in which the UK government may affect the location decisions of a business.
(2 marks)

2. With the aid of a diagram, explain how an increase in the amount of industrial units built will affect the price of such sites. (4 marks)

3. Analyse the main factors that will affect the location for a new supermarket. (10 marks)
(16 marks)

Case study Time allowed 20 minutes

Pipers crisps

In 2004, Alex Albone and three co-owners started a business in Lincolnshire, manufacturing and distributing crisps. The crisps are sold under the brand name of Pipers.

The majority of the crisps are sold to a group of small retailers, the National Trust and public houses. In addition, some are sold to Kew Gardens, the department store, Harvey Nichols, and also abroad in Norway and Ireland.

The business uses a large quantity of potatoes and flavourings based on regional products such as Somerset cider.

(adapted from the *Daily Telegraph*, 22 July 2008)

Evaluate the major factors that Alex and his co-owners would have considered when deciding where to locate their business. **(13 marks)**

TYPES OF PRODUCTION

36 Unit

There are three main methods of production, job, batch and flow. Cell production is a variant of flow production.

Job

Job production often involves producing a single item or product. Various terms are attributed to job production, such as bespoke, unique, tailor-made, one-off.

Job production usually involves satisfying a consumer's specific needs, and can also refer to the production being undertaken by one employee who completes the whole task. This type of production is often undertaken by small, local businesses. For example, a customer requests flowers for a wedding, which will be ordered and arranged in the chosen colours and requested arrangements. Similarly, a football team may order a logo for its shirts in a distinct design with specific colours. A person may want a garden makeover to meet certain requirements and with a particular layout. Each of these jobs is unique, specifically requested and produced to satisfy that individual customer.

The size of job production can however vary, depending on what is being produced. A business producing crisps may order a machine that packages the crisps. This machine will be made to meet the specific demands of the crisp manufacturer and be unique, made to order.

Job production tends to be labour-intensive, as the number of goods produced would not make it worthwhile investing in an automotive process.

The costs of setting up a job production process are significantly less than batch or flow. The process is more expensive in terms of labour costs and the cost of materials as there are few opportunities to gain from bulk-buying economies of scale.

Costs are however lower in terms of stock held. For job production, there will be little work-in-progress, and materials need only to be bought for a particular job.

Figure 36.1 Some job production projects can be very large but still a single product!

An example of job production of a large product is the construction of the magnet railway system being built in Dubai, United Arab Emirates. This is a massive project but is a one-off job, meeting the specific requirements of the Dubai government.

Benefits of job production

- It can meet customer needs exactly.
- The quality of work is usually high as only one item is being produced.
- It is easier to motivate workers involved in the production process, as they will build the product from start to finish in many instances.

- There is complete or considerable flexibility to produce whatever is required.
- It is easier to add value due to the highly specialist work that is undertaken.
- Little stock is tied up.

Drawbacks/limitations of job production

- There are usually no opportunities for benefiting from economies of scale.
- There are higher costs of production.
- Labour is more likely to be skilled, therefore harder to find and more expensive to employ and train.
- In most instances, it will be a slower process.
- It is difficult to gauge the costs for the job, as in many instances it will not have been done before! Jobs tend to be costed on an hourly rate for labour with additional costs for the materials used and the hire or purchase of any specialist equipment.

Batch

Batch production is used when there is a set procedure and stages that the production process needs to go through in order to create a product. One process has to be completed before the next stage of the production process can be started.

Every batch of goods goes through every stage of the process together. The process is then repeated, when the next batch goes through exactly the same processes. As each stage of the production process is the same, different products can be produced using the same process. A batch quantity will vary according to the nature of the product and how it is made. There can be some variations within each batch process to suit specific orders, as long as the actual process remains the same.

For example, to make bread, the raw materials need to be mixed, then put into an oven and finally wrapped (packaged) or left unwrapped. However, at each stage, every batch of bread being produced can be different because different ingredients can be used in the first process; e.g. to make white bread, brown bread, wholemeal bread, and so on.

Pottery manufacture is another good example of batch production. A batch of the raw materials are mixed in the first stage of the production process; then the batch will be moulded into the required shape (mugs); the moulded shapes will then be heated and once cooled finally painted to a specified design. The next batch of raw material will be moulded into different shapes (cups) and will then follow exactly the same process.

Benefits of batch production

- The system is able to produce in larger quantities than job production.
- There may be some economies of scale, depending upon batch sizes.
- Batch production is generally faster than job production due to the larger number of products produced.
- As a greater quantity of goods is produced, the unit costs should be lower, benefiting from some economies of scale.
- There is more flexibility than flow production to meet the needs of the consumer.

Limitations/drawbacks of batch production

- There may be a time delay between batches which means that nothing is being produced (downtime).
- When batches of parts are produced with presses (dies), the change over to a different press can take several hours, during which time nothing happens for that process in the batch production process.
- The increased downtime between batches reduces the level of output when compared to flow production.
- As the level of production is higher, a higher level of stock needs to be held, adding to the cash outflows of the business.
- Storage space for products waiting to go into the next batch process may be needed. This space could have been used for productive purposes.
- The amount of variation will not be as great as it is for job production.
- There is less variety of work and a lower level of skill required, therefore the tasks may not be as motivating as with job production. This in turn may affect the morale and subsequently the productivity of the workforce.

Flow

Flow production provides a continuous process, utilising a conveyor belt approach whereby the product is assembled on a production line with employees undertaking specific repetitive tasks for each stage of the individual processes.

The manufacture of cars is a good example, although there are lots of products that are assembled in this manner. Most 'white' goods are assembled using a flow system.

Flow production is used in order to produce vast quantities of a standardised product. The division of labour means that the employees concentrate on one particular task in the production process and therefore are able to increase the level of productivity (see Unit 37).

Due to the large numbers that are produced, the level of capital equipment used in the production process is very high. Flow production is often automated. This is an example of a capital-intensive factory (a greater reliance on machines rather than labour).

Figure 36.2 Automated production

Benefits of flow production

- The business is able to gain the benefits from economies of scale and therefore reduce the unit cost of production.
- Due to the large-scale production, the business can benefit from the division of labour and therefore reduce costs still further.
- The business can produce a standardised product in very large numbers much more quickly than the other methods of production.
- Unlike batch production, because the process of flow production is continuous, there is little downtime and therefore production levels are optimised.

- It enables a business to remain competitive due to low unit costs and large scale production, to enable demand to be met.

Limitations/drawbacks of flow production

- The initial set-up costs are very high because of the cost of the robots and automated systems.
- It takes a considerable amount of planning to organise the flow system and timings to ensure that all components and sub-assembly is completed in the right order at the right time to keep the line moving at all times.
- It lacks the flexibility to produce a wide range of products.
- If the line stops for any reason, the whole production process is stopped, unlike batch production where another stage of the production process could continue.
- Any significant fall in demand will make the process uneconomical. (This happened during the recession that started in 2008, causing several car plants to reduce its production levels or even close down.)
- Given the repetitive nature of the production tasks, the employees are less likely to be motivated, which may affect productivity, absenteeism and labour turnover levels. All of these have a negative effect on costs.
- There will be large amounts of stock in terms of work-in-progress.

Changing the method of production

One of the main dilemmas facing a business when thinking about changing the method of production is whether it is right to do so, and deciding when is the best time to change.

Changing from batch to flow may increase efficiency, but the initial outlay is very expensive. Buying all the machines in order to operate flow production may be too expensive for some businesses. Furthermore, while the changeover is taking place, there will inevitably be a loss of production.

A very small business that operates in a niche market, satisfying its customers' specific needs, may not want to switch to batch production and risk being unable to satisfy its customers so easily.

Characteristics of the production process	Job	Batch	Flow
Quantity produced	Often one	More than one and increasing in number	Increasing in number – very large quantities
Variety of product	Each one is unique	Some variation for each batch produced	Standardised product but with some variation often in colour
Examples			
Capital required	Can be high because a one-off product	More capital outlay due to size of production	Large capital outlay for convey system and automated processes
Skill of labour	Often highly skilled because each product is unique, therefore skill needs to be adaptable	A particular part of the batch process might require a level of skill	Less skilled as jobs are more likely to be repetitive
Organisation type	Organic		Mechanistic as size increases

Table 36.1 Methods of production

It is possible to switch from batch and flow to cell production, though much will depend upon the skill of the workforce and their ability to change the manner in which they work. It will also depend upon the quantity of products that are produced. Although cell production may be better in terms of job satisfaction for the employees, the ability to produce products as quickly is in doubt.

The decision to change will depend on the:

- nature of the products involved
- financial situation of the business
- significance/importance of its customers in terms of meeting their specific needs
- degree of competition in the market in which the business operates.

Examiner's voice

Questions that relate to the different types of production and possible changes need to be answered in the context of the case material. This will avoid a generic answer that will not gain many marks. Think about the finances and other resources of the business, its objectives and the likely demand for the products.

Cell production

The definition of cell production varies considerably. Some people define it as a production system that has employees working in teams who are responsible for the whole of the production process for a given product. Within the factory, there will be a number of such teams operating in the same manner. This complete cell production process is expensive to set up, as the tooling for the process has to be duplicated depending upon the number of teams involved. The Volvo Kalmar plant in Sweden operated a cell production process with considerable success, especially as this method gave the employees the satisfaction of producing a whole car or a significant part of it, from start to finish. The alternative flow production for manufacturing cars means that employees are normally only involved in one small part of the production process, and it is therefore considered harder to achieve any sense of pride in the finished product, unlike the members of the cell teams.

The layout of a cell production plant is often U-shaped to enable the process to be contained within a given area in which a team operates. Canon, the camera manufacturer, has used this approach with some considerable success.

A reduced version of cell production operates when a team is responsible for a section of the production process or collection of workstations within the productive process. This is a diluted form of cell production, with the intention of trying to empower the workforce and encourage them to take more responsibility for the work they do and consequently gain more pride and a sense of achievement (see Mayo's theories of motivation, Unit 28).

Benefits of cell production

- There are improved working conditions because the employees operate in a team and are therefore responsible for their particular cell. This provides a greater degree of motivation and reduces boredom and absenteeism.
- As the employees are responsible for the work within their own cell, there is an incentive to ensure that the quality of the work is high. This reduces the amount of waste and therefore reduces costs.
- Encourages a sense of responsibility and pride in the work (see Herzberg's theories, Unit 28).
- There are opportunities for job rotation (Herzberg) within the team.

- It allows the employees to set their own pace of work. As long as the tasks are completed within a specified time, the team can organise and decide the pace of work at any stage of the day to suit themselves. Products can be stockpiled following a period of a high work rate, and used when they decide to have a period of a slower work rate.

Businesses are constantly looking for ways to increase the standard of their products and improve the productivity, in order to gain even the smallest competitive advantage. In 2007, Volvo spent millions on a new automated multi-task cell at its aero plant in Trollhattan, Sweden. The cell, one of the world's most advanced, undertakes several tasks within a confined space in a fully automated manner. This is an unusual example of a production method that is both cell and flow production!

Further Sources

www.themanufacturer.com/uk/magazines/the manufacturer
www.businessweek.com
www.sweetart.co.uk

Your Turn

Questions   Time allowed 30 minutes

1. State three characteristics of job production.
   (3 marks)

2. Explain the likely costs of setting up a flow production process.   (4 marks)

3. Analyse the impact on the employees of operating cell production.   (6 marks)

4. Explain how a wide range of products could be produced, using batch production.   (4 marks)

5. State three products that are likely to be produced using:
   A. job production
   B. batch production.   (3 x 2 marks)

   (23 marks)

Case Study   Time allowed 40 minutes

Sweetart cakes for all occasions

Heather Higgins has operated her bespoke cake business for several years. It is based in Staffordshire, but is known well beyond this county. She has specialised in the designing and making of cakes for all occasions. Her cakes are bought for weddings, birthdays and other special occasions. Not only does she produce cakes; sugar sculptures are also available and can be produced to match customer requests or selected from a vast range of designs available in albums.

Weddings customers are able to have tasting sessions to choose the type of cake and the filling. Fruitcakes, sponge cakes and cakes containing champagne are all available and produced to exacting standards.

Figure 36.3 Sweetart cakes

Her website states that she can design humorous sculptures, which are influenced by puppets, gothic art and doll artists in America. She explains, 'I have no desire to illustrate from life, I much prefer to use my imagination so there are no rules!'

Such is the standard and uniqueness of her work that she has won national and international awards. Heather designs and crafts each sculpture by hand to each client's unique specification, no matter how outlandish the idea.

1. Explain why Heather's business is most likely to use job production. (4 marks)

2. Analyse the benefits of job production for a stakeholder of Sweetart. (6 marks)

3. Should the business change the production process from job to batch in order to meet increased demand for Heather's cakes and sculptures? (18 marks)

(28 marks)

SIZE OF PRODUCTION

Economies of scale

Businesses attempt to grow in size in order to gain certain benefits. Growth is achieved in two distinct ways:

- Internal growth (organic)
- This is growth that tales place over time, as the business gradually increases its ability to produce more goods.
- External growth
- This is a much quicker method of growing, achieved by takeovers, mergers and acquisitions.

Whichever method of growth is used, economies of scale are the key benefit. Economies of scale refer to the savings (economies) that can be achieved due to the level (size) of production. Economies are gained when the unit costs (cost per unit of production) falls as the level of production increases. Being able to take advantage of such economies (savings) is crucial to businesses, because the economies help to keep prices competitive.

The economies also help the business as it grows to charge lower prices; assuming the reduction in costs is passed on to the consumer, it therefore can undercut smaller businesses that are not able to gain from economies of scale because of their small size. Therefore, as the larger businesses grow, more benefits from economies of scale will ultimately force the smaller businesses out as they can no longer compete.

There are several types of economies that can be gained.

Internal economies

Internal economies are benefits which a business gains by growing in size. There are several types of internal economies.

Buying-in-bulk economies

As the level of production increases, more supplies and components are required. The business will be able to negotiate a better price for such large quantities, and therefore is able to reduce its costs per unit. Supermarkets are able to extract huge bulk-buying discounts from its suppliers, who want to ensure that they are able to keep supplying the supermarkets.

Nestle, the world's largest food group, stated that the sales in Britain of its Kit-Kat brand had increased by 18% in 2008. As the business sells more bars of Kit-Kats, it will also be able to buy more ingredients and wrappers, purchased at a lower unit cost.

Reducing the unit costs of production also means that the contribution per unit (cpu) will increase. This means that the total contribution (cpu x sales or level of production) will increase and therefore there will be more funds available to cover the overheads of the business.

Pearson group Holdings owns a large variety of names in publishing, including Penguin, Dorling Kindersley, Ladybird, Puffin, Viking, Putman, Addison Wesley Longman, Adobe Press, Cisco Press and Macmillan USA. In addition it owns *The Financial Times*, *Investors Chronicle* and *The Economist*! All of these businesses use paper and printing presses, and therefore the group may be able to command huge discounts in purchasing.

Financial economies

As a business increases in size, it has more assets to use as security to obtain a loan. However, as the amounts involved will be larger, the business is often able to negotiate a better rate in terms of the interest to be paid.

Technical economies

The simple illustration in Figure 37.1 shows the savings to be made from technical economies. The capacity of lorry B is 80% greater, although the size of the lorry is only 50% larger. Being able to carry a much greater percentage increase in boxes will mean that the cost of transporting each box will be less.

Lorry A, Capacity 40 Boxes

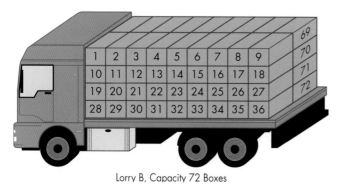

Lorry B, Capacity 72 Boxes

Figure 37.1 Technical economies of scale

Although the lorry is much larger, there is still only one driver required, and although extra fuel will be needed for the larger lorry, the additional amount will not be as high an increase as the increase in the capacity of the lorry. Similarly, the extra excise duty is not increased on the same scale as the additional capacity. As a consequence, the technical economies lead to huge savings and a subsequent fall in the unit costs of transporting the loads.

Marketing economies

As the business increases in size, marketing economies can be gained. This is because the larger business can afford to hire specialist marketing staff who will improve the marketing of the business. In addition and probably a larger cost saving, the business can 'buy' cheaper advertising slots due to buying in bulk, and therefore gain a discount on the advertising rates.

The business will also be able to spread the cost of its marketing over more goods, causing the unit cost to fall.

Spreading the costs over more goods is one of the most obvious benefits of economies of scale. See Table 37.1 as an example: such a reduction in the unit cost provides such a competitive advantage to the business.

Number of goods produced	Total cost of Marketing (£s)	Unit cost of marketing Cost of staff Number of goods produced
10,000	100,000	£10
25,000	100,000	£4

Table 37.1 Marketing economies

Managerial economies or specialist employees

Table 37.1 highlights the benefits of spreading the cost of specialist staff over more units of production. It can however increase its expenditure on such specialist staff, and although the total costs will increase, the unit costs will not necessarily increase by the same rate.

Number of goods produced	Total cost of specialist staff (£s)	Unit cost of specialist staff
10,000	100,000	£10
25,000	150,000	£6

Table 37.2 Unit costs of specialist staff

In Table 37.2, the additional cost of hiring specialist staff (an extra £50,000) is spread over more goods produced, and therefore the unit costs still falls to £6.

Risk-bearing economies

As the business grows and the availability of finance improves either by increased profits or financial economies, the business can diversify into different markets unrelated to each other. The benefit of doing this is that the business has spread the risk by having an interest in differing markets. If one market suffers, the business has another in which to operate.

Tobacco businesses invested in markets that have no links with the core business of tobacco. BAT (British American Tobacco) has at one time owned Saks retailers, Argos and financial services.

Examiner's voice

Any fixed cost will be spread over more units of sales or production, and therefore the average fixed cost will be reduced.

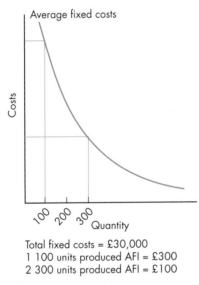

Total fixed costs = £30,000
1 100 units produced AFI = £300
2 300 units produced AFI = £100

Figure 37.2 Falling average fixed costs

External economies

External economies are benefits which the business and the community gain as the industry grows. In other words, benefits are gained outside of the business when it grows.

For example, when a business expands, ancillary businesses benefit and the local area benefits from the high level of employment and the expenditure that takes place in the area of the business. Local newsagents will benefit, as trade will increase when more employees are taken on at the major business.

In addition, benefits are gained by the business when the industry grows. If the industry in the area expands, additional infrastructure may be added which benefits the businesses in that area. The Toyota factory near

Derby led to an improvement in the road links around the area; roads were upgraded, helping Toyota to transport their cars more easily and quickly.

Another way of viewing the external economies of scale is when a business benefits as a consequence of an industry being concentrated within a particular area.

The actual benefits could include:

- improved transport infrastructure
- suppliers locating near to the business
- a good supply of skilled labour within the area due to the concentration of the industry. The Staffordshire area (known as the Potteries) is a good example.

The key benefit to be gained from economies of scale is the reduction in the unit costs of production (see Figure 37.3). This in turn allows the business either to reduce its prices to improve its competitiveness, or increase its profits.

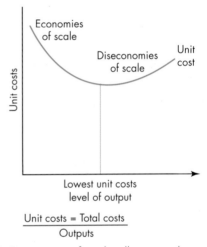

Unit costs = Total costs / Outputs

Figure 37.3 Economies of scale allow a reduction in the unit costs of production

Diseconomies of scale

Just as there are advantages of growing in size or operating production on a large scale, there are also disadvantages. These are summarised under the heading of diseconomies of scale.

- As the level of production increases, the complexity of running the plant will increase. More expenditure may be needed to organise communications within the plant. A greater amount of time will be needed to coordinate the whole process that is now on a much larger scale. Both of these factors add to the costs and therefore explain why the unit costs start to rise (see Figure 37.3).

- As a business grows in size, effective communication becomes harder. More layers are formed within the organisation and the span of control may increase, reducing effective communication still further. Additional costs may be incurred in an attempt to improve communication within the now larger business.
- The decision-making process may also suffer as more people are involved in the process, making consensus less likely, and compromise solutions being put forward or delaying the decision-making process. Such delays will add to the costs of the business.
- As the size of the business grows, the sense of belonging (remember Maslow's theories, Unit 28) may be reduced or even lost. Employees may feel that they are only numbers rather than part of a family business. This may lead to an increase in labour turnover that in turn adds to the costs of the business.

task quickly becomes repetitive and therefore boring. Although the task is easy to fulfil, the boredom may override the ability to complete the task quickly, resulting in a poor standard of workmanship.

Similarly, if the task is too repetitive, a repetitive strain injury may occur. This in turn may lead to an increase in absence.

Breaking down a task into smaller specialist tasks may allow a particular task to be automated, saving further on costs in the long run.

Concentrating on one or two small tasks rather than on a multitude, an employee will save a considerable amount of time because s/he will not be changing tools to perform differing tasks. The amount of non-productive time will therefore be reduced.

Examiner's voice

This is an opportunity to use a diagram to illustrate the implications for the business of having a reduction in costs. A simple demand and supply diagram with a new supply curve to the left could be drawn.

Specialisation

As a business expands, it can start to afford to hire specialist staff. They will be experts in their field and are therefore likely to generate more income for the business, either directly or indirectly.

The business may change its production process in order to take advantage of specialisation and the division of labour (see below). Specialisation is often used to justify international trade.

Division of labour

This occurs when a job is broken down (divided) into separate tasks. The job will be easier to perform, it will be cheaper to train an operative, and the skill level will not need to be so high. Once the task is learnt, the operative (worker) will be able to complete the task more quickly, increasing the productivity rate and therefore increasing output.

However, the key problem of dividing labour so that each person specialises in a particular task, is that the

Productivity

Productivity considers the relationship between inputs and outputs. The greater the output in relation to the input, the higher the level of productivity. In its most simplistic form,

$$\text{productivity} = \frac{\text{Output}}{\text{Input}}$$

This ratio measures the efficiency of a business in its ability to convert inputs (resources) into output (manufactured products).

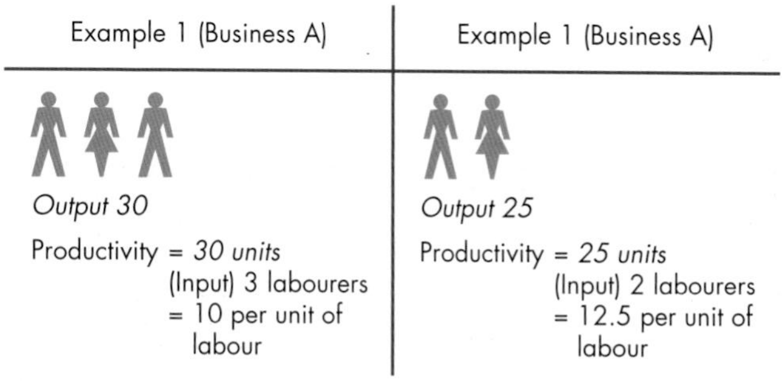

Example 1 (Business A)	Example 1 (Business A)
Output 30	Output 25
Productivity = 30 units (Input) 3 labourers = 10 per unit of labour	Productivity = 25 units (Input) 2 labourers = 12.5 per unit of labour

Figure 37.4 Productivity

In Figure 37.4, the number of employees in business B is fewer, but although they do not produce as many goods as business A, their productivity is higher. Each unit of labour in business B produces 12.5 goods, compared with business A where each unit of labour produces 10 goods.

Alternatively, by introducing the specialisation of labour (division of labour), their output should in theory be higher although it may mean an increase in the number of workers required. A higher level of output per worker suggests a higher rate of productivity (see Figure 37.5).

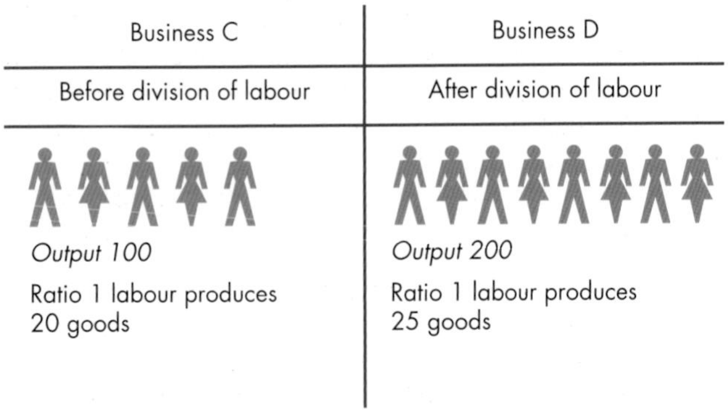

Business C	Business D
Before division of labour	After division of labour

Output 100

Ratio 1 labour produces 20 goods

Output 200

Ratio 1 labour produces 25 goods

Figure 37.5 Division of labour and productivity

In Figure 37.5, business C has five units of labour producing 100 goods. After division of labour is introduced, the number of units of labour actually increases but the output increases to 200 goods. The input to output ratio for business C is 20 goods per unit of labour, whereas the input to output ratio for business D is 25 goods per unit of labour. The productivity rate is therefore higher in business D where division of labour operates.

How an increase in productivity can be achieved varies, but the two main ways are:

- fewer inputs for the same level of output
- increased output from the same input.

Savings as a result of productivity can be significant. Table 37.3 shows the wage rate, the productivity rate per employee and the subsequent cost of labour per car produced.

Average wage rate per employee (per month)	Productivity rate per employee	Labour cost per car
£2,500	10	£25
£2,850	15	£19

Table 37.3 Productivity rates and labour costs

The consequence of an increase in productivity is a significant fall in the labour costs for each car produced. Regardless of the cost reduction, the increase in productivity will enable the business to produce the goods more quickly and in a more efficient manner.

It may be thought that a high level of productivity is directly linked to the size of the business and its ability to take advantage of economies of scale. That would not necessarily be the case. Although size may affect the ability of a business to benefit from economies of scale, productivity gains are more concerned with how goods are produced and not just the cost of producing them (though cost benefits often arise).

Productivity can be measured in a variety of ways:

- $\dfrac{\text{Number of goods produced}}{\text{Average number of employees}}$

- $\dfrac{\text{Output}}{\text{Number of employees and machines}}$

- $\dfrac{\text{Sales revenue}}{\text{Number or value of machines (fixed assets)}}$

- $\dfrac{\text{Sales revenue}}{\text{Wage bill or number of employees}}$

Productivity rates are likely affected by:

- The level of technology
  Increased technology will allow a greater quantity of products to be produced for a smaller amount of machinery, as it is more advanced and efficient.
- The level of training given to the employees
  Training will allow employees to be more 'productive', thereby increasing their output.
- The ergonomic design factors
  Taking careful consideration to arrange the workstation in such a manner as to improve the ergonomic layout, will increase output. Even ensuring that all the tools required are within easy reach of the employee can quickly improve the level of productivity.
- The level of motivation in the employees
  It is assumed that a motivated workforce is contented and therefore more productive. The BSI scale for observed ratings used to calculate the basic time for a task works on this principle.
- The level of effective management (to reduce waste and supervise employees)
  According to Mr Cahill, the Chief Executive of Trinity Horne Consultants, '... more time spent on active supervision correlates with an increase in worker productivity' (*The Times*, 12 November 2008).

Further Sources

The Global Productivity Report (12 November 2008)
Getting More From the Same (November 2008), The Management Consultancies Association
www.growthbusiness.co.uk
www.moneyterms.co.uk/economies-of-scale

Questions Time Allowed 20 minutes

1. Draw a diagram to show the consequences on average fixed costs if production levels increase.
   (3 marks)

2. Explain how an increase in productivity will reduce the unit costs of the business. (4 marks)

3. Explain how productivity levels could be increased if training was undertaken. (4 marks)

4. From the lists below, match the best type of economy of scale to explain the benefit stated.
   (4 marks)

Benefit gained	The economies of scale
A Being able to gain a cheaper loan due to higher value of assets	1 Marketing economies
B Employing a specialist employee	2 Financial economies
C Gaining a reduction in the cost of purchasing raw materials	3 Risk-bearing economies
D A business which manufactures suntan lotion starts to produce paint	4 Technical economies
	5 Bulk-buying economies

(15 marks)

Case Study Time Allowed 45 minutes

Bottles for All Ltd (BFAL)

Bottles for All manufactures and distributes bottles for medicine and medicinal tablets, which are sold to chemists throughout the country. It has been manufacturing the bottles for over 40 years and has seen several expansions in that time. It has only recently started to manufacture bottles for tablets, even though many tablets are sold in packets.

The business has always tried to expand in order to benefit from being a large manufacturer. As production levels have increased, its lorries have experienced difficulties in keeping up with deliveries, and have started deliveries at night to some of the larger chemist chain stores and supermarkets.

In 2008, although the UK economy was suffering from the effects from a recession, BFAL was keen to guarantee its survival. The demand for its bottles was inelastic, nevertheless the managing director, Tom Schubob and the finance director, Danni Wat had considered buying a lucrative printing business located next to the bottling factory, just in case their market faced difficulties.

Megan, the production director had been concerned about the productivity levels and other problems that had arisen after the last major expansion, when BFAL increased its production capacity by over 25%.

Tom was delighted, as he thought that BFAL was now probably the market leader in the manufacturing of bottles for medicines, but also concerned about the rising level of costs within the factory.

1. State the formula for productivity in its simplest form. (1 mark)

2. With the use of a diagram, explain how a consumer may benefit from BFAL growing in size.
   (4 marks)

3. Explain two likely internal economies of scale which the business is likely to gain. (4 marks)

4. Analyse how the consumer may not benefit from BFAL growing in size. (6 marks)

5. Evaluate the extent to which the stakeholders of BFAL will benefit from its expansions. (16 marks)

(31 marks)

Critical path analysis (CPA) is the process that allows for the overall time of a project to be calculated, and to allow a diagrammatic network to be drawn which shows when activities should start and finish.

It also allows planners to see which activities can be undertaken simultaneously. Once the network is drawn, it allows the business to monitor the progress of the project.

The building of Terminal 5 at Heathrow took years to complete. Nevertheless, much of the work went into the planning stage, before a brick was laid or single amount of concrete was poured. Each activity that was necessary to be undertaken in order for the terminal to be finished, would have been allocated a period of time in which to be completed. Certain activities would have been examined to determine the order in which they were to be tackled, and if certain activities could be undertaken at the same time.

Examiner's voice

Critical path analysis is sometimes known as network analysis.

A node and an activity

Figure 38.1 A node

A node represents:

- the start of an activity
- the end of an activity
- both the start and end of an activity.

Figure 38.2

An activity represents a task that is actually undertaken; e.g. laying foundations, building walls, assembly of roof trusses (supports), tiling roof, installing electrics. For simplicity and convenience, each activity is given a letter; see Figure 38.2.

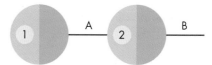

Figure 38.3

In Figure 38.3, A starts and is followed by activity B. This means that B cannot start until activity A has been completed. Consequently, the path diagram helps the user see which activities are dependent upon which other activities.

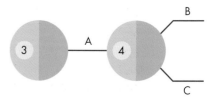

Figure 38.4

The network is also able to show which activities can take place simultaneously.

In Figure 38.4, activities B and C cannot start until A is finished, but can take place simultaneously. To show this, B and C are drawn in parallel.

Where two activities have to be completed before another activity can start, as in Figure 38.5, the node will have two activities joining before the start of another activity. For example, G cannot start until both E and F have been completed.

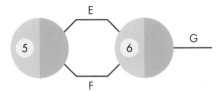

Figure 38.5

In Figure 38.5, node 5 represents the end of an activity and the start of activities E and F. Node 6 represents the end of activities E and F AND the start of activity G. It may also be the case that two activities cannot start until other activities are completed. The approach is exactly the same. Activities are drawn parallel and both have to be completed before the others can start. In Figure 38.6, activities S and T have to be completed before both V and W can start.

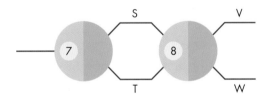

Figure 38.6

In Figure 38.6, node 7 represents the end of a previous activity and the start of both S and T. Node 8 represents the end of activities S and T AND the start of activities V and W.

At this stage, the nodes and activities have been drawn to represent the order of events (activities). In addition, it is now clear as to which activities have to be completed before other activities may start.

However, what has not been included is the actual amount of time that each activity takes. Introducing a time element is essential if the activities are to be in the right order, and for a time for the overall project to be calculated.

To help keep the diagrams (networks) simple, the nodes and the activities are used to show the length of time involved and other essential information, such as earliest starting times and latest finishing times (see below).

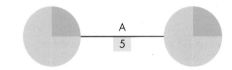

Figure 38.7

In Figure 38.7 the length of the activity is usually posted under the activity line.

Earliest starting time

To calculate the earliest starting time (EST), add the length of the previous activity and put the answer in the next node (see Figure 38.8).

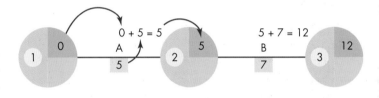

KEY:

Figure 38.8

In Figure 38.8, the activity takes five days. To calculate the EST for activity B, simply add the EST for the previous activity to the length of the activity. There is nothing before A, therefore 0 and A takes 5 days:

$$0 + 5 = 5$$

The answer is then placed in the node at the start of B.

Examiner's voice

Where the EST is placed within the node may vary. It is therefore important to ensure that whenever you draw a network, you always include a key (see Figure 38.8). There is no right way, though most favour the first example.

Calculating the EST for the next activity, C:

EST of previous activity (5) + length of activity (7) = 12

Therefore, 12 is placed in the node at the start of the next activity.

If there is more than one activity going into another activity as in Figure 38.9, then it is important to realise that the highest number of days needs to be taken, as the next activity cannot start until BOTH activities are complete.

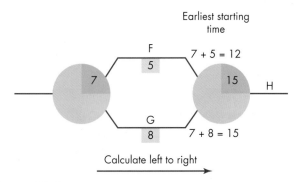

Figure 38.9

In Figure 38.9 both F and G needs to be finished before H can start. The earliest starting time for H needs to be the HIGHEST figure.

EST of previous activity (F = 7) + length of activity (G = 5) = 12

Or EST of previous activity (7) + length of activity (G = 8) = 15

Therefore the EST for H = 15. This is because H cannot start until both F and G are complete, and G will take longer to complete.

At the end of the activities, the last EST is also the overall duration of the project as a whole (see Figure 38.10).

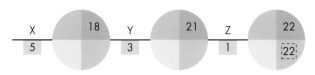

Figure 38.10

In Figure 38.10 the last activity is Z and its EST is 22 days. As there are no more activities in the project, 22 days is the total length of the project

Latest Finishing Time (LFT)

The latest finishing time refers to the latest time in which an activity can be completed without causing a delay to the next activity.

To calculate the latest finishing time (LFT) you need to work from right to left. Calculations are started from the end of the project. The starting point is at the end of the project, so that in Figure 38.10, if the EST in the last node is 22 days, the LFT will also be 22 days.

To calculate the LFT:

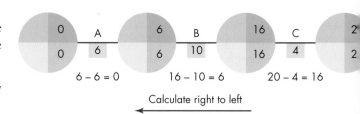

Figure 38.11

LFT at the end of an activity minus the duration of the activity.

In Figure 38.11, to calculate the LFT for activity B:

LFT at the end of the activity (20) – length of activity B (4) = 16

Therefore 16 is placed in the node at the end of activity B.

Similarly, to calculate the LFT for activity A:

LFT at end of B (16) – length of activity (10) = 6, which is placed in the node at the end of activity A.

Examiner's voice

It is always the case that the very first node at the start of the project should have a LFT and EST of 0. If you do not have this then you have made a mistake.

Whenever there is more than one activity going into a node from right to left, the LOWER number is taken.

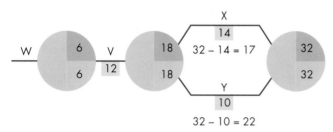

Figure 38.12

In Figure 38.12 activities X and Y 'feed' into activity V. To calculate the LFT for V:

LFT of X = LFT at end of X – length of activity X = 32 – 14 = 18

LFT of Y = LFT at end of Y – length of activity Y = 32 – 10 = 22

Taking the lower figure means that the LFT for V = 18 and the LFT for W:

LFT of V = 18 – 12 = 6.

Finally, a whole network may look like Figure 38.13.

Critical paths

The critical path is where in a given node, the EST and the LFT are the same. Looking at Figure 38.13, the critical path is A, C and F. For these activities the EST and the LFT are equal.

This means that for these activities, any delay will affect the length of the whole project and is therefore a serious issue.

The route of the critical path is marked with parallel lines on the activity.

Examiner's voice

It is also worth remembering that adding the duration of each activity on the critical path ought to be the length of the overall project. This is another check which you can use to ensure that you have worked out the ESTs and LFTs correctly.

Writing out the critical path as well as marking it on the diagram is to be encouraged. When a critical path is identified further resources can be deployed for these activities.

Dummy activities

A dummy activity is an activity that has no significant time but is an essential link between other activities. Because it has no real time factor, it is marked with a dotted line (see Figure 38.14).

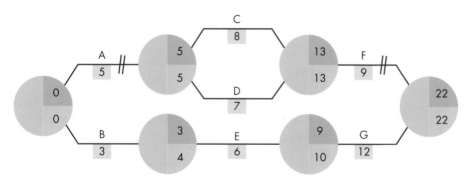

Project takes 22 days

Critical path = ACF ‖

Figure 38.13

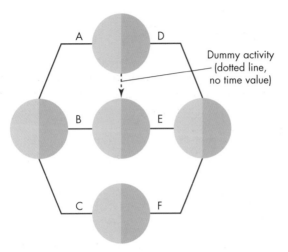

E requires A + B but only D follows A
If E joined A + B ??? ??? D ???? use a dummy to
simplify the diagram

Figure 38.14 Dummy activity

Activity	Duration of activity	Previous activity
A	5	–
B	8	–
C	10	–
D	10	A
E	9	B
F	6	B
G	12	B
H	2	D and E
J	9	H and K
K	5	F and G
L	3	J

Table 38.1 Construct a network

Examiner's voice

Questions may ask students to draw up a network from the information provided (see the sample question below). Although this is probably too long to be set as an examination question, it is nevertheless a good test of your ability to draw networks! It is more likely that the network diagram will be given to you and that you will be asked to calculate the ESTs and LFTs in order to calculate the total length of the project. In addition, calculating the floats is a common question.

This example is set in the Your Turn section at the end of the chapter.

Sample question: Buzzboards are thinking about producing their own surfboards, and have attempted to work out the activities that have to be undertaken in order to produce the boards. Construct a network and calculate the length of the project given the information in Table 38.1.

Floats

A float shows how much time an activity may overrun (be delayed) before it has an effect on either the next activity or the project as a whole. There are two types of float: a total float and a free float.

Total float

A total float represents the longest time by which any activity's start may be delayed without affecting the length of the project as a whole. This is the most serious type of delay, as a delay in the overall finishing time of the project may mean that additional costs are incurred, or a penalty fee may need to be paid to the customer. Penalty clauses are common in the construction industry. Total float is concerned with the total path of the project, and is calculated:

LFT of the activity – duration of activity – EST of the activity.

For example: using Figure 38.13, calculate the total float for activity D:

LFT of D = (13) – duration of D (7) – EST of D (5) = 1

This means that the start of activity D can be delayed by one day without affecting the overall length of the project of 22 days.

If the float was more than one in this example, the overall length of the project would be affected.

The total float for activity C:

LFT (13) – duration (8) – EST (5) = 0

This means that there is no room for any delay: any delay in the start of C would delay the whole project.

Free float

The free float refers to the effect upon the next activity and not the project as a whole; consequently, any such delays are not as serious.

The free float is calculated as shown:

EST of the next activity – duration of the activity – EST at the start of the activity.

Using Figure 38.13, the free float for G =

EST at end (22) – duration (12) – EST at start (9) = 1

This means that the start of G can be delayed by one day before it will affect the start of the next activity, assuming there is one.

Examiner's voice

It is worth remembering that the total float is always larger or equal to the free float, otherwise you have made a mistake with your calculations.

Using the network

By calculating the floats and having a knowledge of the ESTs and LFTs, critical path analysis can help to resolve problems related to delays. Where the total float for an activity is one or more, any delay at the start of the activity will not delay the overall length of the project. However, if the total float is zero, this means that any delay **will** lead to a delay in the project as a whole.

If the figure is one or more for free floats, this means that any delay in the start of the activity will not affect the start of the next activity, unless the delay is greater than the value of the free float. If the free float is zero, a delay at the start of the activity will cause a delay at the start of the next activity but NOT the overall project.

Knowing the float times may allow management to switch resources away from activities with a positive float to the critical activities, in order to resolve any delays.

Examiner's voice

Apart from the values of the floats, it is still important to consider the context of the question. Knowing not only the length of the delay but the cause of the delay, may be of significance.

Gantt charts

The precursor to Gantt charts was created by Karol Adamiecks in 1896, although Henry Gantt designed his version at the time of the First World War. A Gantt chart is a graphical representation of the order and duration of given tasks within a project. It is a simple and useful tool for planning and monitoring progress of a project. It can be used to calculate how long a project will take, and which activities are dependent upon other activities. It also shows which activities should be completed at any given time within the duration of the project.

In other words, it is similar to a critical path or network diagram!

However, it can also be used to show simply how particular resources such as labour can be assigned to a given activity.

Because it is a simplistic version, it is less valuable for more complicated and lengthier projects.

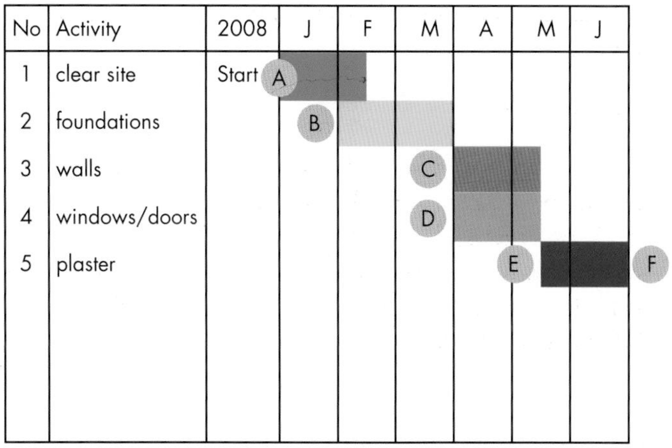

Figure 38.15 Gantt chart

The nature of the activity within the project is written on the left, and the duration of the activities is usually presented along the horizontal axis. The timescale should be included to allow for progress to be monitored and for a visual version of which activities are dependent upon which.

A. represents the start of the project, at the beginning of January.

B. represents the foundations which start at the beginning of February. Note that the foundations can start before the end of the first activity.

C. and **D.** (the walls and windows) start when the foundations are complete at the end of March and the beginning of April.

E. plastering starts when the windows, doors and walls (C and D) are complete.

F. is the end of the project which is due to finish at the end of June.

By displaying the activities in this simplistic manner, it is easy to compare what is actually happening with what ought to be happening. It is of course not able to show so easily which activities are critical, and is therefore limited in its usage.

However, it is useful in solving some resource problems related to specific activities. See Figure 38.16 for a simple network diagram.

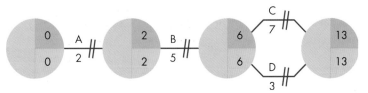

Figure 38.16

This network can be shown in a Gantt chart (see Figure 38.17).

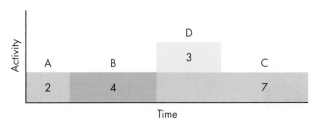

Figure 38.17 A Gantt chart

Activity	Number of employees required
A	10
B	8
C	18
D	8

Table 38.2 Figures for use in a Gantt chart

However, if the units of labour are now added to the chart it is clear as to who is doing what: see Figure 38.18.

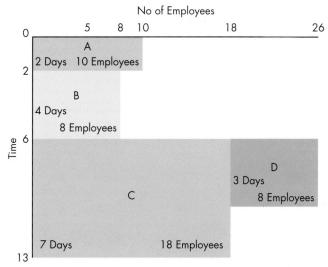

Figure 38.18

Activities C and D take place at the same time, so there could be a shortage of labour to complete these activities. In other words, the number of workers required could be greater than the number of workers available. By drawing a Gantt chart, this could be displayed and resolved.

Examiner's voice

To draw the Gantt chart with an allocation of the resource labour, the time axis can be changed to the vertical axis, and the horizontal axis used to display the time.

Benefits and limitations of critical path analysis

Benefits

- CPA is a simplistic visual form of communication to show the order and timing of activities.
- It offers a simple method to calculate the shortest time in which to complete the project.
- It gives a method to identify the activities which are critical.
- Knowing the EST allows for supplies to be delivered just-in-time (JIT).
- It helps a business to see when finance (cash) will be needed to ensure that supplies are ready for any given activity.
- CPA allows management to see the consequences of potential delays.

Limitations

- The value of CPA depends upon the accuracy of the activity times.
- Knowing that some activities are critical may encourage a reduction in quality in order to complete the activity on time.

- CPA only considers the timings of activities, but does not consider any of the cost implications.
- CPA does not consider changing external factors.

Benefits and limitations of Gantt charts

Benefits

- It is a simplistic visual representation of a project.
- It is easy to use for monitoring progress of a project
- You can see at a glance what activity should be taking place at any given moment in time.
- It shows both time and a resource allocation such as labour.

Limitations

- It cannot allow the user to see which activities are critical.
- It does not allow the user to see at a glance the ESTs and LFTs.
- The calculation of floats, although possible, is not straightforward.

Your Turn

Questions Time allowed 40 minutes

1. State two reasons for using critical path analysis.
   (2 marks)

2. Explain the difference between total float and free float.
   (4 marks)

3. a. Using the information below in Table 38.3 and Figure 38.19, calculate the ESTs, LFTs and the length of the project. (5 marks)

   b. Calculate the total and free floats for each activity B,C and E. (3 marks)

4. If there was a delay of two days for each of the activities B, D and E, analyse the likely consequences. (6 marks)

   (20 marks)

Activity	Duration of activity	Previous activity
A	5	–
B	8	–
C	10	–
D	10	A
E	9	B
F	6	B
G	12	B
H	2	D and E
J	9	H and K
K	5	F and G
L	3	J

Table 38.3 Data for questions

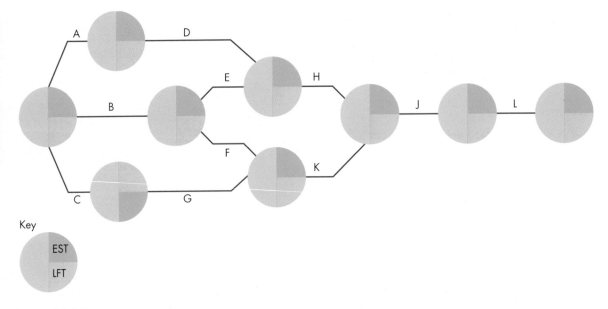

Key

Figure 38.19

Case Study   Time allowed 40 minutes

Niki Smythe is about to open a travel business specialising in adventure holidays for the over 50s. She had the idea several months ago and has organised and planned the opening of her online business.

Figure 38.20 represents her plan for the marketing and opening of the website and subsequent launch of the business.

However, she has been told that there is likely to be a delay of four days on activity F, which is receiving

the video of the various holiday hotels and adventure activities she has commissioned from a film company who specialise in marketing videos. Once the video is received it will need to be put on to the website to allow potential consumers to see the various locations and activity holidays (K).

She has already had some difficulties with completing brochures on time (activity J), ready to be distributed to consumers, to save them having to download the material from the web.

1. Evaluate how serious such a delay on activity F will be for Niki.   (16 marks)

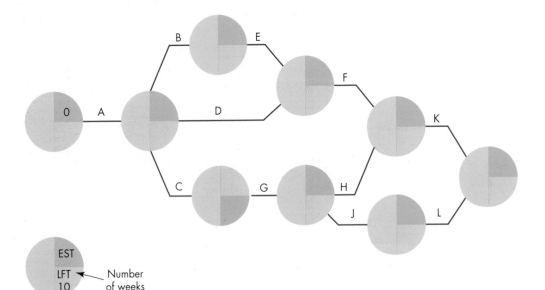

Activity	Weeks	
A	10	–
B	8	A
C	10	A
D	6	A
E	4	B
F	14	D + E
G	8	C
H	12	G
J	16	G
K	4	F + H
L	6	J

Figure 38.20 Marketing and launching the website

CONSTRAINTS ON PRODUCTION

Many of the constraints on production are caused by factors outside of the business. External factors are usually beyond the control of the business, and are often difficult to predict or deal with.

The main external constraints upon a business are:

- the economic climate
- government economic policy
- the market
- competitors
- legislation (laws)
- environmental and ethical issues
- suppliers.

The economic climate

This is one of the major constraints on a business, over which it has little or no control. Changes in the economic climate can occur for a multiplicity of reasons.

The 'credit crunch' of 2008 has been blamed on American bankers. However, regardless of who or what was to blame, the consequences for business and the production of goods have been significant. Within weeks of banks being closed or taken over, the downturn in the UK economy escalated, leaving demand for many products (especially houses) at its lowest for decades. Consequently, building companies reported record falls in profits and even recorded losses. In addition, all the businesses that supplied the builders suffered a similar fate due to the economic concept of **derived demand in reverse**. Just as there is a natural increase in demand for bricks when there is an increase in the number of houses

demanded and being built, the opposite is the case; as the demand for houses fell dramatically, the demand for bricks and similar house-building components fell dramatically also.

The economic cycle (see Unit 58) often acts as a constraint on production. A downturn in the economy in 2007–08 and into 2009 led to recession conditions and a subsequent fall in the level of demand within the economy. Many businesses were forced to reduce their production levels, and in turn reduce the number of shifts that operated or number of hours worked by employees. Some businesses even operated a four-day week in response to the very low level of demand within the economy.

For some businesses, the recession led to their closure or partial government takeover. The airline Zoom, the travel company XL and the building society Bradford and Bingley were significant casualties in September 2008.

Figure 39.1 Zoom was one of the many businesses hit hard by the recession

A fall in the level of demand within the economy inevitably leads to a fall in the demand for labour, and as a consequence the level of unemployment rises. Industry will take note of such changes and alter its production levels accordingly, if affected.

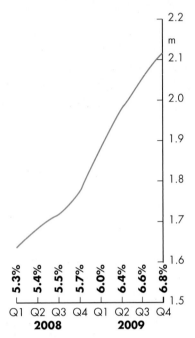

Figure 39.2 Unemployment forecasts released by the CBI in September 2008

As the 'credit crunch' effect deepens, businesses are affected by consumers turning to cheaper alternatives for their usual brands of goods. Not only are the products that are bought affected, but also the shops that consumers visit. Prior to the economic downturn, supermarkets Lidl and Aldi were perceived as retailers for the lower income groups. However, as consumers changed their shopping habits in an attempt to find bargains, these two retail outlets saw a large increase in business.

Government economic policy

The government will respond to economic conditions in a variety of ways. Monetary policy and fiscal policy changes can affect the production levels of a business.

Monetary policy may lead the Bank of England to alter interest rates that will affect businesses in three ways:

1. A change in interest rates may change the cost involved with any planned loans a business may want to take out. Depending on whether rates increase or decrease, such changes can increase or decrease the costs. An increase in interest rates will add costs for a business, and it may try to pass on such increased costs to the consumer.

2. However, as consumers are probably faced with increased costs to finance mortgages, consumers will have less money to spend and therefore sales will become harder for business.

4. An increase in interest rates will affect the value of the pound and therefore affect exporters and importers in different ways. Usually, an increase in interest rates increases the value of the pound and therefore makes exporting conditions harder, as the cost of buying UK goods increases. However, if interest rates fall, this is welcomed by UK exporters.

5. The opposite is the case for importers. The extent to which such changes affect production levels will be affected by the elasticity of the products.

Fiscal policy is an important part of government economic policy. Budgets are announced annually, when the government states its intentions as to the level of government expenditure and the revenue to be collected through taxation.

Naturally, changes in the level of income tax and income tax allowances greatly influence the amount of disposable income available to the consumer. If taxes are increased, consumers' disposable income falls, which in turn affects the sales of goods and services offered by business.

Similarly, changes in taxes that are on goods and services (indirect taxes) affect the price of the products sold by manufacturers. Any increases in such taxes may encourage businesses to find ways of either passing on the increases to the consumers, or absorbing the increases and therefore not passing the rises to the consumers.

The consequences on production will be varied. The size of what is produced could be reduced, thereby not passing on the additional cost of the tax to the consumer. However, such a strategy may affect the image of the business.

If businesses are faced with continually rising taxation, one consequence is that consideration may be given to setting up the production process abroad, where costs can be significantly cheaper. Sir James Dyson moved some of his manufacturing production from Malmesbury in Wiltshire to Malaysia and Singapore in 2002, to reap the benefits of cheaper production costs.

The market, competitors and competition law

The action of competitors is an obvious constraint on any business. The type of market in which a firm operates may influence its behaviour within that market. There are occasions when businesses abuse their power. The Office of Fair Trading exists to monitor the behaviour of businesses to ensure that they act in the public interest. It has the power to refer firms to the Competition Commission, whose task is to investigate the alleged behaviour of firms, and to decide what the facts are and the remedies to be put in place to prevent unfair practices.

The type of market may affect what is produced and in what quantities. There are several categories of market:

Monopoly

Operating as a monopolist allows the firm to charge higher prices and produce quantities to suit itself. With no competitors and therefore no substitutes, the monopolist has few incentives to increase production or improve its products.

However, there are few real monopolist firms today due to the globalisation of markets. In addition, the Competition Commission exists to ensure that monopolists do not act against the public interest.

Oligopoly

In an oligopolistic market, there are few businesses that tend to compete on a non-price basis. Prices tend to be very similar and therefore the businesses compete for consumers by offering a better product or service. It is in oligopolistic markets that collusion is more likely to occur (when rival businesses agree prices). To prevent this, the Competition Commission has the role of monitoring the behaviour of such activities.

- It was reported in 2008 that British Airways and Virgin Atlantic agreed to pay nearly £100 million in compensation to passengers who had been affected by price-fixing on fuel surcharges.
- In March 2007, the Office of Fair Trading referred BAA to the Competition Commission under the Enterprise Act 2002, to investigate the ownership and operation of BAA's airports. The findings of the CC suggested that BAA should not own both Glasgow and Edinburgh airports if competition was to exist.

- Similarly, Gatwick, Heathrow and Southampton should not all be owned by BAA if there was to be effective competition between the airports. It was therefore suggested that BAA should sell one of these airports.

Monopolistic

In a monopolistic market where there is much more competition because there are more businesses in the market, there is less opportunity for businesses to act against the public interest. Businesses will compete both on prices and the quality of the goods and service they offer.

Mass market

Another way to classify markets is related to the size of the market in terms of the number of potential consumers. In a mass market, businesses concentrate on satisfying large numbers of consumers. As a consequence, the businesses will be keen to try and take advantage of large-scale production in order to gain the benefits of economies of scale.

The method of production is more likely to be flow, in order to efficiently produce the large numbers of goods required within the market. Often the production process will produce standardised products.

Niche

For a niche market, the number of potential consumers is lower, which will lower the level of production. It follows that in many instances, the method of production will also reflect the smaller numbers of goods being produced. Batch or job production will probably be the chosen method.

Legislation

The government (UK or EU) can pass laws that affect how a business operates and how it produces its goods and services. The legislation can sometimes become a burden to businesses, who may feel weighed down by the amount of red tape (bureaucracy) involved.

The legislation concentrates on:

I. health and safety issues

II. the manufacturing of products and waste management

III. food safety

IV. vicarious liability

V. environmental issues.

Health and safety

The building trade has been transformed in the last decade with regards to health and safety. In order to protect the health and safety of employees on building sites, they are now required to wear appropriate safety equipment, which may include hard hats, appropriate boots with steel toe-caps, protective goggles when undertaking certain tasks and possibly masks.

All of this equipment has to be provided by the employer and so adds to the costs of the business, not only in terms of purchase but also in supervising its usage.

Additional costs are incurred when risk assessments have to be undertaken, with appropriate forms being filled in, checked and stored in case of problems. Within the car industry, anyone entering an area where spot-welding is taking place must now wear a protective screen, to prevent sparks hitting their face.

The manufacturing process

Much of the legislation concentrates upon the packaging of products, especially for food (see labelling regulations below). There are several regulations that have to be considered before someone can manufacture products.

Designs

There is a form of protection for designs or specific branding. Registering designs at the UK Intellectual Property Office or the UK Designs Registry can protect them. Shapes or particular appearances can be protected.

Trade marks

This is another form of protection, where a brand name or a brand slogan can be protected to prevent others using it or trying to imitate it.

Copyright

Ideas, text, graphics music and film can be protected to avoid copying. For example, it is not permitted for anyone to copy the contents of this book, as the authors own the intellectual rights to the words (see the inside cover of the book).

Patents

A patent gives the inventor the right to stop other people from manufacturing or selling the invention for a limited period of time. However, once the patent expires, anyone is free to copy the invention and make his or her own version.

The patent was introduced to encourage people to be innovative and to benefit from their invention for a given period of time. In the UK, the most important rule regarding what can be patented is that the invention must be new.

Environmental considerations

There is pressure on manufacturers to produce in an environmentally friendly manner. More attention is now given to the use of renewable and recyclable products. Similarly, manufacturing processes need to conform to environmental regulations within the country where the product is manufactured or the raw materials sourced.

Bureaucracy (red tape)

The amount of rules and regulations can seriously affect the ability to produce goods. At the end of 2008, Sir James Dyson wanted to establish an engineering school in Bath. However, he was faced with a plethora of planning rules and procedures that hampered his ideas. Sir James commented, 'It's not the third runway at Heathrow. It's an engineering school that everyone says they want, but we have this planning system that's clogging it up.'

The government often receives criticism for the amount of red tape affecting business. The Better Regulation Executive has suggested that it has helped British industry to save over £800 by identifying and reducing unnecessary legislation. However, according to an HSBC survey in the *Sunday Times* on 24 August 2008, 81% of British firms claim that government red tape and bureaucracy is on the increase.

Waste management

By reducing or eliminating waste, it is possible for all businesses to reduce their costs and remain competitive in the global markets. The essence of lean production (see Unit 46) is to increase the efficiency of the production process from design to the product leaving the factory. Virtual design processes have eliminated the need to make 'mock-up' cars of clay in order to test the aero-dynamics of the car. Eliminating the need to build prototypes has saved a large amount of time and resources.

The Japanese have an expression, 'Muda', which refers to the reduction and elimination of all waste within the production process.

The careful control of waste can actually help reduce the production costs and therefore help to maintain a competitive edge in the market. Having spent significant amounts of money on purchasing materials needed for the production process, businesses are spending more time thinking about how to bring out the best from these materials.

Toyota has been concerned about the elimination of waste for a long time. All employees are involved with the process of questioning the way in which they perform their jobs, looking for a more efficient manner in which to complete each task.

There are several elements to waste:

- Defects due to poor quality: waste via defects means that either a finished product or part of a finished product has to be scrapped.
- Overproduction: producing excess products in relation to the level of demand means that the excess products will have to be stored. This may be a waste of valuable space.
- Conveyance: every time a component or a finished product has to be moved it represents another activity, which will cost time and money.
- Waiting: if employees are waiting for resources, they are not actually producing anything. This could be classed as idle or downtime.
- Inventory: holding any stock, whether it is raw materials, work-in-progress or finished goods, is expensive as it ties up space and capital.
- Motion/poor factory layout: if an employee or a machine is moving unnecessarily it is a waste. Ergonomics tries to reduce the amount of unnecessary movement in order to reduce wasted time.
- Over-processing: making a product too complicated or elaborate and beyond the needs of the consumer is a form of waste.

The cost of disposing of waste has escalated significantly, and with the government increasing the taxes on landfill waste, businesses have to try to eliminate waste as much as possible while also being mindful of the environmental impact of waste. Packaging that protects the delivery of components is being reduced in order to reduce waste. Jaguar at Castle Bromwich has the majority of its components delivered in returnable cases. If components are delivered from a country where the cost of returning the packaging would be too high, then cardboard protective packaging is allowed. However, this cardboard is carefully collected ready for collection and subsequent recycling. The excess metal from the sheets of aluminium that are used for the majority of Jaguar cars is automatically collected and moved via a conveyor belt below the actual presses to large skips, ready to be collected for recycling.

Lean production (see Unit 46) contributes to a reduction in waste, either in materials or time, which can have significant consequences for costs. Lean production describes the following processes:

- Just-in-time (JIT) delivery in order to reduce stock levels.
- Coordinating the work and delivery of suppliers' products to prevent excess stock-holding and idle time for the employees.
- Improved layout of the factory to improve the efficiency of employees' movement within their working area.
- Improved communication between the production and marketing departments to produce only what is required by the consumer. The majority of cars produced today have already been sold and are subsequently made to order. This eliminates stock levels and over-production.
- Improved quality control processes such as Kaizen and Jidoka.

Food safety

The amount of legislation related to producing food which is 'fit for human consumption' has increased. Complying with the legislation has a cost implication, but choosing not to comply would have a greater effect upon costs as a result of possible fines and the loss of trade due to inevitable bad publicity. One can debate whether Cadbury were guilty of any breach of regulations by not informing the food agency of a problem with a batch of its chocolate bars. However, withdrawing the chocolate from shops led to a significant loss of sales and costs in wasted production. Legislation related to food has not just been about the actual food. The labelling of food is covered by law, with the purpose of protecting the consumer. Under the Food Labelling Regulations 1996, companies have to comply with several sections for all prepared food:

Name of the food

If the purchaser could be misled without such information, the name should give an indication of whether the food is powdered, smoked, pasteurised, or homogenised. Otherwise the actual name or brand name will be sufficient.

If this information cannot be visible to the consumer, e.g. when food is sold in a vending machine, there should be a notice on the front of the machine.

List and quantity of ingredients

There should be an obvious label as to what the product is, such as 'egg and cress sandwich'. This should be followed by a list of ingredients in descending weight order. Any additives or flavourings must also be listed.

Shelf-life or date-marking

For products that have a very short shelf-life such as perishable products, there has to be a 'use by' date on the label. For other foods, a 'best before' date needs to be shown.

Specialist storage instructions

If products require specialist storage, this should be stated with suggestions.

Name and address of manufacturer or packer

This is essential information as it enables consumers to write if a complaint needs to be made.

Alcoholic content

For alcoholic drinks over 1.2% in alcoholic strength, the label must state the strength by percentage volume.

The country of origin

This information should be given where necessary.

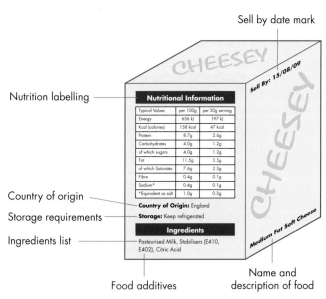

Figure 39.3 Much packaging information is now compulsory

All of these points concentrate on the consumers' right to have clear information on food. Such regulations may add to the costs of businesses, but allow the consumer to make a more informed choice as to what to buy. However, the regulations are a constraint for businesses that have to be taken seriously and complied with in order to avoid fines and the loss of goodwill or reputation for the business.

EU regulations

Quotas imposed by the EU affect the level of production for a range of products. In 2008, minimum prices were imposed for poultry imported from outside of the EU, along with a quota on the actual amount that can be imported. The aim was to protect EU farmers from cheaper imports. Such moves affected the production levels of EU farmers who are now protected from cheaper alternatives.

Vicarious liability

This term refers to the responsibility of the employer for the actions of its employees, when one person is liable for the negligent actions of another person, even though the first person was not directly responsible for the damage or injury. An employer can sometimes be vicariously liable for the acts of an employee. Employers are vicariously liable, for negligent acts (torts) or omissions by their employees in the course of their employment. For an act to be considered vicarious, two main conditions must be satisfied:

- The employee must be acting on behalf of the employer as part of his or her employment contract.
- The 'act' that caused damage, must have been committed during the normal course of employment.

In other words, the person concerned must be acting with the authority of the employer and be employed by the employer. If the employee commits a 'tort' (wrong-doing), but is acting against the rules and requests of the employer, the employer may not be liable for the behaviour of the employee.

Similarly, if a person uses a contractor, that person is not vicariously liable. To help decide whether a person is employed or is a contractor who has been hired to complete a specific task, the law has certain tests that can be applied:

Control test

A person is employed if s/he can be told not only what tasks have to be performed, but how to perform those tasks. A contractor may be told what tasks to perform, but the manager will not tell the contractor how to undertake such tasks.

Someone employed in the car industry and who works on the final trim assembly where the dashboards, carpets seats and CDs are fitted, will be told what tasks to perform and how they are to be performed; furthermore such employees may be told when to perform each task as well. Under these circumstances, the employer is in control.

Multiple test

Being able to ascertain who is responsible for the provision of work clothes and specialist equipment, and ensuring that tax and national insurance is deducted, will help decide if a person is employed or contracted. If a person is responsible for providing their own equipment and paying their own tax and national insurance, that person is contracted and not employed.

Integration test

Trying to find out the extent to which a person is involved in a particular business, e.g. by belonging to the office soccer team or being eligible to attend the business's Christmas party, may help to decide if a person is employed by the business.

Examiner's voice

As well as looking at the two main factors to decide if an employer is vicariously liable, it is important to consider all the evidence and not just the tests, to help decide if the person involved is actually employed by the business.

Example

Jack owns a window-fitting business which employs three staff on a full-time basis. The business fits windows into new office blocks and shops. When working at a new shop, Tom spills his beer over the newly fitted carpet. Jack has a company rule that employees are not allowed to consume alcohol while at work.

To decide if Jack is vicariously liable for the damage to the carpet, it is important to apply the two main conditions. First, Tom is an employee of Jack (stated) and the damage occurred during the normal course of his employment. However, Tom was not acting with the authority of Jack.

Although there is some doubt as to whether disobedience would be a sufficient defence, it may depend upon the level of supervision by Jack.

Examiner's voice

Applying the two main 'tests' is crucial, although it is quite likely that the examiner will be looking for some signs of evaluation, using the context of the question.

The principle of vicarious liability can also be bypassed by applying 'Employers' Indemnity'. When an employer is successfully sued, they have the option to sue the 'tortfeasor' (the person who caused the damage) for an indemnity to recover the damages back.

Environmental and ethical issues

The amount of legislation in this sphere has increased significantly in recent years. The growing concern for the environment and consequential effect upon our climate has led to governments around the world passing legislation.

Pollution

Pollution and waste have now become key issues that businesses have to consider as part of any production process. Manufacturers must seriously investigate how they produce goods, to take account of pollutants that may be caused both by what is produced and how it is produced.

Careful consideration of carbon emission laws has had a significant effect on car manufacturers around the world. A higher priority is now given to the level of carbon dioxide emissions of the cars to be produced, to ensure that they comply with a range of regulations. When cars are being designed, the aerodynamics (shape) of the car, its fuel efficiency and its emissions rate are factors that have to be considered as a high priority.

Sustainability

Sustainability has also become much more significant when considering the raw materials that are used in a production process. Book publishers who use paper that has come from sustainable trees, or even recycled paper, are keen to state within the book cover the source of the paper used. This is a marketing and ethical statement of the publisher's care for the environment.

Ethics of production

There are ethical considerations of the product to be made.

A. The sale of contraceptives is viewed by some people as an essential product to counter unwanted pregnancies, but regarded as ethically unacceptable to others, especially certain religious groups.

B. Tobacco, a proven killer, is sold legally. Steps have been taken to curb its consumption however. The advertising of cigarettes has been banned for many years, and more recently health warnings on the packets of cigarettes have increased in size. In 2008, it was decided to introduce vivid pictures on cigarette packets of the likely health damage as a result of smoking.

Similarly, since the introduction of the law banning smoking in public places, the sale of alcohol in public houses has fallen. Production of beer has changed to take account of the fact that although less beer is sold in pubs, more is being sold in cans to be consumed at home. An awareness of this trend meant that manufacturers had to respond by altering the packaging of the beer.

C. The Labour government extended the drinking hours for public houses, at the same time as spending millions of pounds on advertising campaigns which highlighted the dangers of excess drinking.

D. The sale of replica guns may be viewed as an ethical issue, given the rise in gun crimes within the UK.

E. GM crops have regularly created a debate on the ethics of such production.

F. Manufacturers of chocolate have been faced with the challenge of countering obesity, in an attempt to be seen as ethical and moral producers. The Food Standards Agency issued a report in 2008, highlighting their concerns about the sizes of portions offered to consumers; Cadbury reduced the size of its Dairy Milk bars.

G. Ethical issues not only affect the actual production of goods but also the advertising to encourage purchases. Businesses are affected by pressures from lobby groups, who suggest that advertising of products that contribute to obesity or so-called binge-drinking should be drastically reduced. Such pressures may affect the demand for the products and therefore affect production levels.

Figure 39.4a An old-fashioned plastic bag
Figure 39.4b A new environmentally friendly bag

H. Concern over the production of single-use carrier bags issued by supermarkets led to a fall in production levels of such bags. Supermarkets responded by introducing bags that were made from 100% recycled plastic and designed by Cath Kidston.

Further Sources

www.google.co.uk for more photos of health warnings on cigarette packets
www.leauk.org
www.competition-commission.org.uk

Questions Time allowed 20 minutes

1. State three ethical issues affecting production.
(3 marks)

2. Explain why reducing waste is important in the production process. (4 marks)

3. State two economic factors that would lead to a fall in production. (2 marks)

4. List two ways in which firms in an oligopolistic market may compete. (2 marks)

5. Explain the difference between being employed and being contracted to perform a task.(4 marks)

6. State five items which a manufacturer would need to include on food labels under the Food Labelling Regulations of 1996. (5 marks)

(20 marks)

Case study Time allowed 45 minutes

Packed and Boxed (P&B)

Parminder and Becky are setting up a new business that will offer a packing service for presents and food hampers. The food on offer is to be homemade and will only be available at the busy Christmas period. They have decided to offer a range of specialist jams, biscuits and chocolate cakes for the festive period, knowing that many people treat themselves over Christmas.

The packaging materials vary greatly, ranging from highly decorative cardboard, plastic bags and glass containers to polished wooden boxes. Their idea is that many people do not have time to spend wrapping up their presents, and are convinced of a market for their service.

However, Parminder and Becky have already argued over the type of materials to be used for the packages. Parminder is concerned about the sustainability of the materials that Becky wants to use. Becky is more concerned with making the packaging look good, rather than worrying about any environmental issues. She is also more concerned about the legal issues when labelling their range of food.

Recent reports about obesity have caused both of them to think about other issues.

1. Explain two legal requirements for the labelling of food that P&B should consider. (4 marks)

2. Analyse the likely ethical issues for P&B if the business is to sell the range of food suggested. (10 marks)

3. Should R&B use the range of packaging stated for their packaging service? (18 marks)

(32 marks)

Costing is the act of measuring the effects of any business activity in financial terms. In costing an activity, a business can work out whether it is likely to be worthwhile and profitable, or not worth pursuing. It can also help the business to plan for the future and find ways to reduce costs and maximise efficiency.

Standard costing

Standard costing is the cost that the business would normally expect for the production of a particular product, or to complete a particular activity. The setting of a standard cost is a target for the business to achieve.

Example

A hairbrush manufacturer may say that the standard cost for a hairbrush is £3. This is what the business expects the final cost of production to be, and is the standard cost. This can be compared with the actual cost to see whether it has been achieved. The difference between the standard cost and the actual cost is called the **variance** (see Unit 15).

The use of standard costing helps a business to monitor its performance. If the hairbrush manufacturer finds that it has actually cost £3.50 to make a hairbrush, it will be able to investigate why the target is not being achieved, identify the area that is causing the negative variance and put processes into place to resolve the situation. It may find that the raw materials for the bristles were more expensive than anticipated and that this increased the actual cost. The manufacturer could either try to find a cheaper supplier or negotiate a better price with its existing supplier. If no solution is

	Standard cost	**Actual cost**
Raw materials	80p	130p
Labour	90p	90p
Indirect costs	130p	130p

Table 40.1 The standard and actual costs of producing a hairbrush

possible, the manufacturer may need to reassess the standard price for the future.

In Table 40.1, the manufacturer needs to find out why the cost of raw materials is so much higher than was anticipated. This could be as a result of a change in the value of the currency affecting import prices, or because an increase in oil prices has increased the price of the materials used.

The advantages of standard costs

Standard costs can:

- give a business a good idea of the target cost they should be aiming for. They can use their own estimates combined with information from outside the firm.
- give employees a target to aim for and can alert them to problems as and when they arise.
- be used within the reward and motivation policy of the business so that bonuses could be offered when positive variances are achieved.
- encourage workers to look for better and more efficient ways of completing a job so as to achieve positive variances.

The disadvantages of standard costs

- Collecting information to arrive at a standard cost may be time-consuming. The process will need to be repeated at regular intervals, especially in periods of rapid inflation and in changing business environments.
- The use of standard costing, especially when tied to bonuses for workers, may result in a situation where quality is sacrificed to keep costs of production down. This will not be helpful to the business in the long term.
- If the business is not careful in reassessing the figures used periodically, it may find that standard cost has become an inaccurate measure of the actual cost because so many factors have changed.

Cost centres

A cost centre is a specific part of a business where costs can be identified and allocated with reasonable ease.

Example

The Curtain People is a business which provides an interior design and manufacture and fitting service for domestic customers. Their business is divided into three cost centres: interior design; the making of soft furnishings; and the fitting of soft furnishings and carpets. The costs of the business are allocated between these three divisions in relation to the number of employees in each division.

The total costs for 2008 for The Curtain People was £4,500,000. The number of employees for each department are as follows:

- design department: 3
- making: 12
- fitting: 5
- total: 20.

The allocation of costs for each centre is calculated using the proportion of the 20 workers in each department. For example, the design department employs 3/20 of the workforce, so it will be allocated this proportion of £4,500,000 as its costs. The other allocated costs are as follows:

- design £675,000
- making £2,700,000
- fitting £1,125,000.

There are a number of ways in which a business can choose to allocate costs to cost centres. These include:

- the product being produced: The Curtain People could split the costs instead between curtains, carpets and other soft furnishings.
- the individual department: this might be appropriate for a larger business with departments for marketing, human resources, finance etc.
- the location: a business based on different sites is likely to use each of its sites as an individual cost centre.
- the capital equipment used in each department: this may be used in businesses like electricity generation where one department may have most of the costs and capital equipment employed.
- the physical size of the department in terms of space.

Benefits of using cost centres

The use of cost centres can benefit a business and makes its performance more efficient in a number of ways.

- The information will help to highlight those departments that are performing well and those that are not, making it possible for management to make the necessary changes. If the only information available was for the business as a whole, it would be difficult to pick out the problem areas.
- The information gained can be used to help motivate the workforce. For example, achieving a stipulated reduction in costs in a department could be tied to a bonus payment for the workers in that department.
- The availability of the information may encourage management to look for new suppliers or more efficient production techniques to bring costs down. Without this information, managers may be unaware of rising costs and their implications on the performance of their departments.

Disadvantages of using cost centres

The use of cost centres may result in conflict and a lack of motivation.

- As previously, the act of collecting and separating out the information into different cost centres is likely to be expensive in terms of time and money.
- In some businesses it is difficult, if not impossible, to separate out the costs into different departments. There may be an overlap in the production process; some costs may apply to the business as a whole.

Suppose that a large business like a building society decides to sponsor a local premiership football team. How should the cost of this be split amongst its different cost centres? Should branches close to the team ground have more of the costs allocated because they are likely to benefit most, or should the costs be allocated according to the size of the branch?

- The way in which costs are allocated can have a significant effect on the performance of a particular cost centre. In the previous example of the building society, some branches may not benefit at all in terms of business, and therefore an allocation of the cost would make their performance worse.
- Some of the costs for a business may be outside its control. The large rises in oil prices during 2008 pushed up the costs of all businesses to a greater or lesser extent.
- If the allocation of costs is felt to be unfair or unreasonable by some departments, this may lead to conflict between departments. Instead of motivating employees, it can have exactly the opposite effect.

Profit centres

A profit centre is similar to a cost centre, except that in this case the profits coming in are ascribed to different parts of the business. From this, management can judge which products, outlets or divisions are the most profitable parts of the firm's operations. The firm may use the same criteria for dividing the business into cost and profit centres. Sometimes however a department (such as marketing) may generate costs for the business but will not receive profit directly, so this will not be possible.

Absorption costing

In this costing method, all the indirect costs or overheads of a business are absorbed by different cost centres. The methods used for allocating overheads to different cost centres will vary. The easiest method is to use the output of each unit or its proportion of direct costs, to allocate the overheads.

Example

A business produces two types of kettles, electric and hob kettles; see Table 40.2. The overheads are £250,000.

	Electric	Hob
Output per annum	60,000	20,000
Direct costs	£200,000	£100,000

Table 40.2 Output and direct costs for electric and hob kettles.

To use output to allocate overheads, work out the percentage of total production for each product.

For electric kettles: $\dfrac{60,000}{80,000} \times 100 = 75\%$

For hob kettles: $\dfrac{20,000}{80,000} \times 1000 = 25\%$

The overheads will be allocated:

- 75% of £250,000 to electric kettles = £187,500
- 25% of £250,000 to hob kettles = £62,500

If instead the business decided to allocate overheads in relation to direct costs, then the division would be different.

To use direct costs to allocate overheads:

For electric kettles: $\dfrac{200000}{300000} \times 100 = 66.7\%$

For hob kettles: $\dfrac{100000}{300000} \times 100 = 33.3\%$

The overheads of £250,000 will now be divided as follows:

66.7% of £250000 = £166,750 to electric kettles
33.3% of £250,000 = £82,500 to hob kettles.

This costing method will be time-consuming and expensive to complete. There is also a risk that the information is old and does not represent the current situation. The alternative is to use full costing, which takes all the overheads of the business and divides them using one simple criterion.

Example

A business has overheads of £50,000 a month made up of rent, salaries, clerical costs and depreciation. The firm produces four different products. These overheads can either be split:

- equally, so that each production centre is charged £12,500.
- by revenue: one product brings in revenue, so it is allocated twice the overheads of the other three.

One product will be allocated £20,000 and the others will be allocated £10,000 each.

The main benefit of using absorption costing is that it ensures that all the overheads are covered somewhere in the business. This therefore means that if price exceeds the cost for each unit of the good or service, a profit will be achieved. In addition, the overheads will not have been allocated in an arbitrary or haphazard manner.

Contribution or marginal costing

Contribution or marginal costing is a method whereby fixed costs or overheads are ignored and the business considers only the variable costs of production (see Unit 41). Contribution is the selling price of a product minus the variable cost of producing it. This can be calculated as a total across all production or the contribution made by each extra unit produced. Once the variable cost has been covered, anything left over can be used as a contribution towards fixed costs.

Contribution per unit (cpu) = price – variable cost per unit

Total contribution = sales × cpu

It is important that contribution is not confused with profit. Output making a positive contribution may increase profits, but this is not necessarily the case. Businesses are most likely to consider contribution costing when they are considering accepting an order that will not increase their overheads (see Unit 41). For example, an airline like British Airways may consider filling the last few seats on a plane by costing them to cover the extra variable cost or marginal cost of carrying that passenger. These marginal costs will be the cost of food, the extra fuel to carry an extra passenger and the costs of the ticket itself. All the other costs like the crew, the fuel and services and parking slots at the airports will already have been paid. Any extra income can then be used to contribute towards the overheads of the business. Therefore, BA will be happy if the price it achieves for the last few seats gives a positive contribution.

The business will not cost so that revenue fails to cover variable cost because in this situation the business will make a loss on each unit sold.

Example

Middleport Mugs has been approached by a large supermarket and a department store with a request to produce a special edition mug as a limited addition. The business has some spare capacity over the summer and could therefore satisfy one of these orders. The figures are shown in Table 40.3.

	Supermarket	Department store
Size of order	20,000	10,000
Price per mug	£1.00	£2
Variable costs:		
Raw materials	40p	50p
Labour	40p	40p
Other variable costs	30p	30p

Table 40.3 Potential order figures for Middleport Mugs

The supermarket is only prepared to pay £1 for a mug that will cost £1.10 in variable costs to produce; therefore it is not worth accepting this order. The department store will pay £2 for a mug with variable cost of £1.20, so each mug sold will contribute 80p towards the firm's variable costs. and the business's profits will be increased or its losses reduced. If the business has the capacity to meet this order it will be worth accepting. The business does not have to take its fixed costs into account, because they will not be affected by the acceptance of this order.

Further Sources

www.labspace.open.ac
www.is4profit.com
www.accountingcoach.com

Your Turn

Questions Time allowed 10 minutes

A business with overheads of £60,000 a year decides to allocate them between the two products it makes, in proportion to the output of each product. The business produces 2,000 units of product X at a direct cost of £3 each and 5,000 units of product Y at a direct cost of £5 each.

Calculate:

1. The amount of overheads allocated to product X and product Y.

2. The total cost of producing the output of product X and product Y.

Case study Time allowed 1 hour

Andersen's Hotel

Naomi Lesley runs a small family hotel in Whitstable in Kent. The hotel is situated on the sea front, has 20 en-suite rooms and a very successful small restaurant. Naomi employs 30 people, some of them full-time and some part-time.

Naomi bought the hotel ten years ago, and she has worked hard to build it into a successful and profitable business. One of the problems she still has, however, is the seasonal aspect of the business. Naomi generally closes the hotel completely for the month of January so that she can have a holiday, but apart from that she is open all year. The hotel is full over Easter and Christmas and also throughout June, July and August, but at other times of year there are always rooms available and the restaurant often has spare capacity, particularly during the week.

Naomi has decided to start looking at the way in which she costs her different services, and to think about the opportunity to use contribution costing at quiet times of the week and year. She feels that she may attract more customers both for the hotel and the restaurant at off-peak times.

The indirect costs of keeping the hotel open each week are £4,000. This includes heating, lighting, interest charges on a loan from the bank and the cost of the permanent staff like the chef, receptionist, house manager and restaurant manager. The direct costs are mainly the other staff and the cost of food and other consumables.

The restaurant relies on local custom through the year as well as from residents, so it is difficult to vary the price for meals. The usual charge for a double room is £150 a night in high season (from Easter to the end of October) and £100 at other times of the year.

Naomi has been approached by a coach holiday company from the Midlands. They want to bring groups of about 25 pensioners to Whitstable for five-day holidays (Monday to Friday) during May and September. They are willing to pay £240 per room for the four-night stay. Naomi is considering the implications of accepting this offer.

1. Explain one other costing method that Naomi could use for her business. (5 marks)

2. Analyse other methods, apart from contribution costing, that Naomi could use to tackle the seasonality of her business. (15 marks)

3. Evaluate the factors that Naomi should take into account when deciding whether to accept the offer from the coach company. (20 marks)

(40 marks)

CONTRIBUTION

A business needs to cover its costs in order to make a profit. A profit is not made as soon as goods start to be sold, and contribution analysis can help the business to decide whether a product is making a profit, i.e. contributing towards a profit.

Contribution is the revenue received from selling a product minus the direct costs (OR variable or unit costs) of producing that good. Assuming that the revenue is greater than the direct costs of making the good or providing the service, there is a contribution to the overheads (fixed costs). In some cases, if the overheads have already been paid for, any contribution will be making a profit.

Contribution costing is also sometimes called marginal costing.

Examiner's voice

Examiners will accept whatever figures the candidate has used, in the event that a mistake has been made. The 'own figure rule' can only be used to your advantage if you have clearly shown your working!

Contribution or marginal costing

The contribution per unit (cpu) is the contribution of each unit of production overheads. To calculate it:

Cpu = price – direct or variable costs

Example

Ahn and Shivan decided to run a disco for their GCSE business enterprise. They had fixed the price of the tickets at £7. This price included entrance to the disco and some food. The cost of the food to be provided for each person was £3, whereas the hire of the hall and the fee for the DJ came to £175. To calculate the contribution for each ticket sold:

Cpu = price – direct costs
    = £7 – £3
    = £4.

To calculate the total contribution (how much in total is contributing to the overheads), multiply the cpu by the sales. Therefore if 70 tickets were sold:

Total contribution = cpu × sales
          = £4 × 70
          = £280.

The profit of the disco is the revenue left over after paying the overheads:

Profit = total contribution – overheads or fixed costs
    = £280 – £175
    = £105.

Examiner's voice

Remember to show your working clearly so that the examiner can follow what you have done. If this is done, marks can be awarded even if your answers are incorrect. It is also important to write out any formula/equation you use, as this will show the examiner you know what to use, even if the figures you have used are wrong.

The principle involved in the contribution method is illustrated in Figure 41.1.

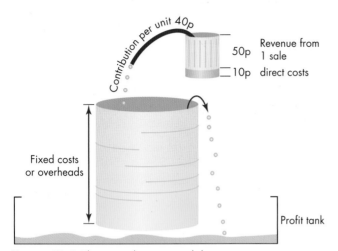

Figure 41.1 The contribution model

The contribution method can be used to calculate how much an individual product contributes to the overheads or profits (Table 41.1), and to compare how more than one product within a business contributes to the overheads of that business (Table 41.2).

Contribution allows a business to assess the level of profit for each product it makes:

- Model 1, £30,000
- Model 2, £18,500
- Model 3 £11,750.

The method also allows the business to see which products or models are contributing the most to cover its overheads. In Table 41.2, Model 1 contributes the most, £40,000. All three models are contributing in a positive manner because the revenue is greater than the direct costs.

In Table 41.2, the overheads of the business have been shared equally between the three models. There is no reason why the business cannot allocate as a percentage of sales or any other means it chooses.

The advantage of contribution costing is that the overheads do not have to be allocated at all.

In most cases, a business will not worry about the individual model in terms of how much of the overheads it should pay. Instead, the contribution from all three models can be added together;

Product: Sunshield glasses	Value in £s
Price	100
Direct costs	30
Contribution per unit	
(price – direct costs)	70
Sales = 520	
Total contribution (Sales x Cpu)	36,400
Overheads	35,000
Profit (total contribution – overheads)	1,400

Table 41.1 Calculating the profit for a given product

Products: Sunshield glasses	Model 1 Sunshield shades	Model 2 Sunstops	Model 3 Sunseekers
Price	100	120	180
Direct costs	20	25	35
Contribution per unit (price – direct costs)	80	95	145
Sales	500	300	150
Total contribution (sales x cpu)	40,000	28,500	21,750
Overheads £30,000	10,000	10,000	10,000
Profit for each model: (total contribution – overheads)	30,000	18,500	11,750
Total profit (Model 1 + 2 + 3)			

Table 41.2 Calculating the profit for three products

Products Sunshields	Model 1	Model 2	Model 3	
Price	100	120	180	
Direct costs	20	25	35	
Contribution per unit (price – direct costs)	80	95	145	
Sales	500	300	150	
Total contribution per model (sales x cpu)	40,000	28,500	21,750	
Total contribution (model 1 + 2 + 3)				90,250
Minus overheads				–30,000
Total profit				60,250

Table 41.3

£40,000 + £28,500 + £21,750 = £90,250

Then the overheads can be deducted to calculate the profit:

Profit = total contribution for all three models –
      overheads
    = £ 90,250 – £30,000
    = £60,250.

The table would normally look like Table 41.3.

Table 41.3 shows how contribution is usually used by business. As long as the overheads are covered, it is not important as to which of the products pays for them. What is important is that products are making a contribution to the overheads. For many businesses, it is almost impossible to work out which product should pay what percentage of the overheads as sales and direct costs vary, and therefore the best method of ensuring that the overheads are paid is for all products to contribute.

Examiner's voice

Most of the exam questions will concentrate on calculating the total contribution of products and then subtracting the value of the overheads (Table 41.3), to ascertain the level of profit or loss. In some questions, there may be reference to labour costs and the cost of materials. Both are classed as direct costs unless otherwise stated.

Special orders

If the business were to be offered an additional or special order, the calculation of contribution is very helpful.

Examiner's voice

This is a popular question in the option papers and is a concept that needs to be clearly understood.

The concept of contribution can be used to decide whether it is worthwhile for a business to take on an additional or special order.

Example

Energise Drinks is a business which produces energy drinks that are sold to a range of fitness centres. It has overheads of £105,000. The drinks are sold in small cartons for ease of usage and transportation for the manufacturer and the end user. The business has not been trading for long but has already managed sales of 200,000.

The manufacturer already sells a range of drinks (five different types in total, but with almost identical costs), but is keen to attract an order from a supermarket chain. The price of the drinks to the retailer is normally 90p, with direct costs of 30p. Table 41.4 shows the sales and costs of the drinks.

Energise Drinks	2008 figures
Price of drink	90p
Sales	200,000
Overheads	£ 105,000
Contribution per unit (price – direct cost) (price 90p – dc 30p)	60p
Total contribution (sales x cpu) 200,000 x 60p	£ 120,000
Profit (total contribution – overheads) £120,000 – £105,000	£ 15,000

Table 41.4

Examiner's voice

Take care when calculating the total contribution as the sum may involve the multiplication of pounds and pence, which may cause confusion.

The supermarket wants to place an order for an initial amount of 25,000 drinks for one region, but is only prepared to pay 40p per drink. What should the owners do? For this type of business decision, contribution is particularly helpful. Calculating the contribution is done in exactly the same way as before.

Energise Drinks	Special Order	
Price of drinks for supermarket	40p	
Sales for special order	25,000	
Direct costs	30p	
Contribution per unit (price – direct cost) (40p – 30p)		10p per drink
Total contribution (cpu x sales) (10p x 25,000)		£2,500

Table 41.5

It is necessary to ascertain whether the total contribution from its existing sales cover its overheads. Table 41.4 shows that the total contribution of £120,000 covers the overheads of £105,000 and therefore the business makes a profit of £15,000. By taking on the additional order, although the business is only making a contribution of £2,500, it is an additional contribution and will therefore add to the profit of the business because the overheads have already been covered.

This example assumes that the business does not incur any additional overheads to meet this extra order and has enough capacity spare to produce the 25,000 extra drinks. If this is only an initial order, there are other factors to consider:

1. How many drinks will the supermarket want in the future?

2. Will Energise Drinks be able to produce the number of drinks that may be ordered in the future?

3. How will its existing customers be affected?

4. Will additional overheads be incurred?

5. Will the business have enough staff to take on the potential increases in production?

6. How keen is Energise Drinks to gain the supermarket order as a long-term source of business?

A business is often willing to take on a special order even if it appears to be unprofitable or produces only a small level of profit. This is because of an expectation of profits in the future. In the example above, Energise would be able to undertake the special order because it may lead to substantial increases in orders in the future. Increasing the number of drinks sold may enable the business to benefit from economies of scale and consequently reduce its direct costs per unit. Although the supermarket is only prepared to offer a lower price than its other customers, the potential reduction in unit costs will compensate to some extent.

Careful consideration will need to be given to the potential increase in overheads. Additional machines and extra labour may be necessary which would increase overheads overall, in turn affecting the profit levels.

However, even an initial 'loss' may be worthwhile in the long term if additional orders are a possibility. Table 41.6 shows the figures for Energise and an alternative special order. For this additional order, another supermarket wants Energise to packet the drink slightly differently, which will mean Energise buying an additional machine to package the cartons. The cost of the additional machine is £1,500.

Energise Drinks	Special Order	
Price of drinks for supermarket	35p	
Sales for special order	25,000	
Direct costs	30p	
Contribution per unit (price – direct cost) (35p – 30p)		5p per drink
Total contribution (cpu x sales) (5p x 25,000)		£1250
Additional overheads	£1,500	
Profit (total contribution – overheads) £1,250 – £1,500		Loss of £250

Table 41.6

It would appear from the information in Table 41.6 that the additional order is not worthwhile as a loss of £250 is incurred. However, whether the order is taken will still depend upon the list of factors raised above.

Examiner's voice

Sometimes examination questions require you to work out the contribution per unit and other figures, but are slightly hidden. For example, questions have stated that the direct costs are 20% of the price. In other words, there is an additional stage to be undertaken before you have the figures in the format that you require. Remember to always show your working so that what you have done is clear.

Key Terms

Contribution: revenue – direct costs
Contribution per unit (cpu): price – direct costs
Profit: total contribution – overheads
The emphasis for contribution is on the difference between revenue and direct costs, rather than the fixed costs.

Your Turn

Questions Time allowed 25 minutes

1. State the formula for calculating contribution per unit (2 marks)

2. Total contribution – overheads = ? (1 mark)

3. Explain why contribution is an important decision-making tool for business. (4 marks)

4. If a business sells 100,000 magazines at £2.50 each and the direct costs are 80p and fixed costs are £125,000, discuss whether the business should stop selling magazines. (14 marks)

(21 marks)

Case study

Spiders Time allowed 40 minutes

Stuart and Harveer have run their website business, 'Spiders', for just over four years with considerable success. It is operated from within Harveer's home in order to reduce the overheads of the business. Most of the expense is due to the amount of equipment required to create the websites for its customers. There is some expenditure on marketing for their business, but not a significant amount as much of their business has relied on word of mouth and the careful placement of 'pop up' adverts on the internet.

The overheads for the business are £65,000.

Stuart and Harveer have been approached to produce a new website for a client, who has asked for a special price because if the website is good, there will be the possibility of many more to follow. However, the requirements are quite unusual and neither Stuart nor Harveer have tackled this kind of work before. Stuart is keen to try something new, and thinks that the business should accept the order.

Harveer is much more cautious and does not think it is worth it. He says, 'This new order will mean we will not be making any money from it. I have worked out the costs, which are as follows. The price wanted is £1,300 and our labour costs and raw materials will come to £1,250'.

1. Calculate the contribution per unit for each of the original three websites, A, B and C. (6 marks)

2. Calculate the level of profit from the original websites in Table 41.7. (4 marks)

3. Calculate the contribution of the proposed new website. (3 marks)

4. Discuss the additional factors which might influence 'Spiders' to take on this special order. (14 marks)

(27 marks)

Websites	Website A	Website B	Website C
Price £	1,800	2,200	2,600
Labour costs	900	1200	1,300
Sales	50	10	5

Table 41.7 Figures for Spiders

BREAK-EVEN ANALYSIS

Break-even analysis is another tool which businesses can use in order to aid the decision-making process. The break-even point or level can be found by:

- using a chart
- calculating (using a formula)
- using a graph.

It is used to find the level of output necessary to cover all costs. Break-even is the point where total revenue covers (is equal to) the total costs.

Finding the break-even level by chart

In its simplest form, the break-even may be found using a chart, where the total revenue (TR), is equal to the total costs (TC). A table of figures may be shown to enable you to find the break-even level of output in this manner.

The break-even level of output (TR=TC) is at 500.

Examiner's voice

When looking at such a chart, be careful to read the correct amounts, whether they are in millions or thousands of pounds. Getting the right formula and calculation but writing out the wrong answer because you have not noted carefully the denominations, may cost valuable marks.

Having to produce a chart in order to find the break-even level could be time-consuming. There is a quicker method available which uses a formula for calculation.

Units of Output	sales revenue £	fixed costs	variable costs	total costs	profit/loss
0	0	50000	0	50000	−50000
100	12000	50000	2000	52000	−40000
200	24000	50000	4000	54000	−30000
300	36000	50000	6000	56000	−20000
400	48000	50000	8000	58000	−10000
500	**60000**	**50000**	**10000**	**60000**	**0**
600	72000	50000	12000	62000	10000
700	84000	50000	14000	64000	20000

Table 42.1

Units of Output	Sales revenue	Fixed costs	Variable costs	Total costs	Profit/loss
200	40,000	45,000	5,000	50,000	−10,000
400	80,000	45,000	10,000	55,000	25,000

Table 42.2

It may also be the case that within the chart, there is no obvious break-even level as it falls between two numbers within the chart (see Table 42.2).

It is clear from Table 42.2 that the break-even level of output is somewhere between 200 and 400 units. In this situation, the chart is of little value and using a formula is more beneficial.

Finding the break-even level by formula

To calculate the break-even point, contribution can be used (see Unit 41).

$$\text{Contribution} = \frac{\text{Fixed costs}}{\text{Contribution per unit}}$$

(Remember: contribution per unit equals price – direct/variable costs.)

Examiner's voice

When using the formula for break-even, it is important to remember that **total** fixed costs are divided by **unit** contribution. It is a common error to put the formula the wrong way round, or put total contribution.

Example
A business making wooden puzzles has fixed costs of £20,000 and the direct costs are £1.50p for each puzzle made. The intended selling price is £2. The number of wooden puzzles that need to be sold to break-even is:

$$= \frac{£20,000}{£0.50 \ (£2 - £1.50)}$$

= 40,000 wooden puzzles

This break-even figure can now be used to assess whether it is possible to achieve this number of sales.

Examiner's voice

It is always worth commenting upon an answer for break-even. Is it very high or low? Is it possible to make this many?

This formula can also be used to show the likely consequences for total revenue and the break-even if there is a change in price. Increasing the price will mean that the contribution per unit increases and as a consequence, the number of goods that need to be sold to break-even will be less.

If the selling price for the wooden puzzle increases to £2.50:

$$\frac{£20,000}{£1.00 \ (£2.50 - £1.50)}$$

= 20,000 wooden puzzles

The small increase in price led to a large fall in the number of puzzles that need to be made in order to break even. Pricing strategies can be measured as to how they will affect the break-even level and the margin of safety (see below).

Similarly, if there is an increase in the variable (direct costs), the formula quickly enables the new break-even level to be calculated.

Examiner's voice

It is quite possible that on the option papers, you may have to 'find' the figures you require before applying the formula.

Example
Calculate the break-even when the fixed costs are £10,000 and the direct costs are 20% of the price, which is £2.

$$\text{Break-even} = \frac{fc}{cpu\ (p-dc)}$$

$$= \frac{£10,000}{20\%\ of\ £2}\ (40p\ therefore\ cpu = £2 - 40p$$

$$= 6250\qquad = £1.60p)$$

Finding the break-even level by graph

Break-even can also be shown graphically. It is important to understand how the various lines are calculated.

Cost lines

Fixed costs

Fixed costs (overheads or indirect) do not alter with the level of output, and are therefore represented with a horizontal straight line.

Fixed costs will exist even if no output is taking place, and therefore are drawn starting at 'x'.

If a business uses a machine (a fixed cost) which costs £10,000, the fixed cost when output is zero is £10,000 (see Figure 42.1).

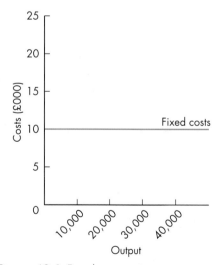

Figure 42.1 Fixed costs

Variable costs

Variable or direct costs vary directly in proportion to the level of output. As output increases, the level of variable costs increases (see Figure 42.2). It is possible to use the graph to read off the particular total variable costs at any given level of output.

Examiner's voice

If an examination question asks you to work out a given variable cost for a certain level of output, the graph would be clearly marked to allow you to do this, rather than guess/estimate the level.

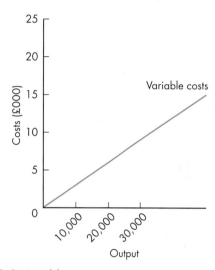

Figure 42.2 Variable costs

Total costs are the addition of fixed and variable costs. Note that the total cost line does not start at zero. Even when a business is not producing any goods, it still has costs (fixed costs). The business will have bought the factory premises and the machines necessary to produce the goods. The total cost line therefore starts at £10,000; see Figure 42.3.

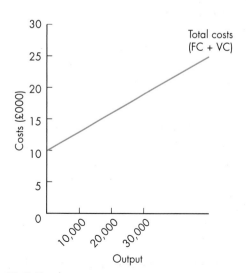

Figure 42.3 Total costs

Revenue line

Total revenue = price × level of output

The total revenue line will be a line with the same gradient, as it is assumed that there is only one price which does not change (see Figure 42.4).

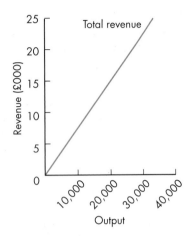

Figure 42.4 Total revenue

The level of the price will determine the gradient of the total revenue line; the higher the price, the steeper the total revenue line will be (see Figure 42.5). Similarly, if the price falls, the gradient of the total revenue line will fall.

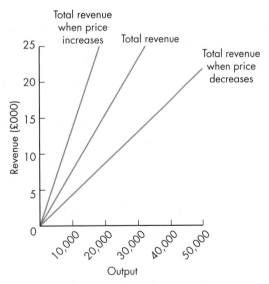

Figure 42.5 Total revenue line changes when price changes

Once the individual lines are known, the break-even point and level can be established. This is where the total revenue line cuts the total cost line; see Figure 42.6.

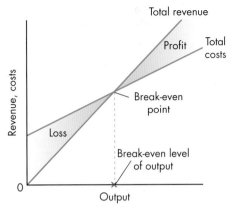

Figure 42.6 Break-even, profit and loss

Knowing the break-even level of output will enable a business to assess profit if output is above the break-even. Looking at the diagram below (Figure 5) any output level to the right of the break-even level will be profitable, whereas any level of output to the left of the break-even level will mean that a loss is incurred.

The break-even level of output is shown as 'x'. Once the break-even level of output is known, a business can easily assess its level of profit or loss by looking at its particular level of output (see Figure 42.7).

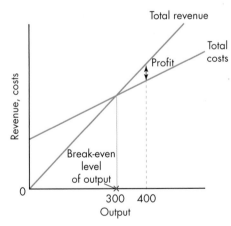

Figure 42.7 Comparing output for break-even

Using Figure 42.7, if the break-even level of output is 300 units and the actual level of output is 400, it is clear from the graph that the business is making a profit. If the scale is clear it will be possible to show the actual level of profit when 400 units are produced (xx).

It is also possible on a break-even graph to show the consequences of a change in price. It has already been shown how the total revenue line changes when the price is changed (see Figure 42.5); but it is also possible to show what happens to the break-even level of output when the price is changed (see Figure 42.8).

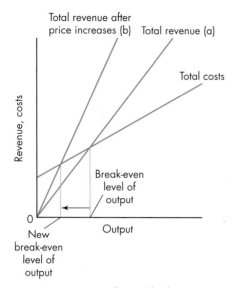

Figure 42.8 Consequences for profit if price is increased

In Figure 42.8 following a price increase, the total revenue line becomes steeper (TR b), and as a consequence, the break-even level of output falls.
It is worth noting that, although the break-even level of output falls, which means a profit will be earned at an earlier/lower level of output, there is no guarantee that the output will be sold at the higher price.

Examiner's voice

It is important to realise that any of the costs may change and therefore need to be shown on a diagram.

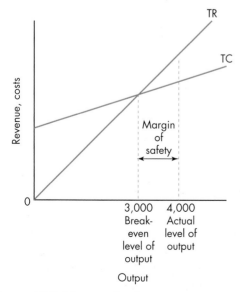

Figure 42.9 Margin of safety

Margin of safety

The graph also allows a business to see its margin of safety. This is calculated by subtracting the actual level of output from the break-even level of output; i.e. the difference between the actual and break-even level of output (see Figure 42.9).

The margin of safety allows a business to assess the consequences of any change in its circumstances that may affect its output, its prices or its costs (see Figure 42.10).

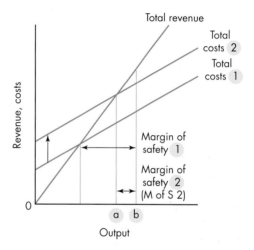

Figure 42.10 Changing margin of safety

In Figure 42.10, an increase in costs moves the total cost line upwards and as a consequence the break-even level of output increases from a to b. This in turn means that the margin of safety falls in size from margin of safety (M of S) 1 to M of S 2.

A business will find this useful because it can assess the impact of any changes in either the actual level of output or the break-even level. As a consequence, the business will know the significance of any change in output. The smaller the margin of safety, the less flexibility the business has to deal with any change in circumstances. The margin of safety allows a business to know the likely effects on the profit of the business; the lower the margin of safety, the lower its profits.

Example

Table 42.3 shows the figures for a business producing ice cream.

At a), the difference between the actual and break-even level of output is 300 units of ice cream (1200 – 900).

Actual level of output	Break-even level of output	Margin of safety
a) 1200	900	300
b) 1000	900	100
c) 900	900	0

Table 42.3 Figures for an ice-cream producing business

At b), there has been a fall in the level of output due to a shortage of labour, and therefore, assuming all other variables are constant, the margin of safety will fall.

At c), a further fall in actual output due to one of the machines requiring a service, now means there is no margin of safety, and therefore any other disruption to output will mean a loss being incurred. With no margin of safety, there is no difference between the actual level of output and the break-even level of output; hence no profit is being made.

Examiner's voice

Always state the formula in any question that requires a calculation. Any mistakes you may make subsequently will be marked using your own answer. There are usually some marks for stating the formula!

Benefits and limitations of break-even analysis

Benefits

1. Tables and diagrams are easy to view and comprehend and easy to interpret. This makes it a valuable tool, as it does not take a long time to calculate or use.

2. Break-even analysis is a beneficial management tool to aid the decision-making process. This is especially true for new businesses, which can use break-even analysis as part of their business plan. It will offer an opportunity to consider the level at which break-even occurs, and decide how realistic the chances are of such a level of output or sales being achieved.

3. It can be used to show the level of profit at a given level of output, and to set targets for achieving profits.

4. The margin of safety can be established.

5. It is possible to assess the consequences of changes in circumstances by looking at the margin of safety.

6. Similarly, a business can use break-even to consider the impact of changes for a particular product.

Limitations

The overall problem with break-even as a decision-making tool, is that it is based on the utilisations of predicted figures. There is no certainty that the actual fixed costs, variable costs and prices will be accurate or constant. The cost of raw materials such as fuel can quickly render any break-even calculations almost worthless. The huge increases in the cost of oil and subsequently, gas and electricity, had a dramatic effect on the costs of industry in 2008.

1. The direct or variable costs may change, depending upon the quantities involved. A manufacturer is likely to be able to negotiate a discount for buying in large quantities. This will alter the VC line and therefore the total costs, which in turn will affect the break-even position. A new diagram or table would have to be drawn, which is time-consuming.

   As the level of production increases, the opportunities to gain the benefits of economies of scale will have an effect on the unit costs.

2. If batch production is being used, which may involve the production of fixed quantities for each batch, the break-even level of production may not be obtainable. Producing batches of 50 units with a break-even level of 840 will mean that the business must decide whether to produce 800 (which will mean a loss) or 850 (which is beyond the break-even but may be more than the demand for the product).

3. If there is more than one product or service involved, it may be difficult to allocate the fixed costs (see absorption, Unit 40). Calculating the break-even may be very difficult.

4. Calculating the total revenue relies on just one price. In business, this is unlikely as discounts may be offered for large purchases or promotional offers may be used, especially in the early stages of the product life cycle.

For many businesses, trade discounts and prompt payment schemes make calculating the price and therefore the break-even difficult.

5. There is an assumption that if the price increases, total revenue will also increase. This is often not the case as an increase in price can lead to a fall in sales and therefore a fall in revenue. This in turn will affect the actual ability to break-even and the margin of safety.

6. There is sometimes some uncertainty as to whether costs are fixed or variable (labour is an obvious example).

7. There is no certainty that all goods will be sold. Circumstances change within the business environment and therefore may affect sales.

8. Assuming all output is sold.

Key Terms

Break-even: the point where total revenue is equal to total costs. (TR = TC). At that point all costs have been covered.

Fixed costs: Costs that do not alter with output.

Variable costs/direct costs: Costs that do vary with output.

Total costs: The addition of fixed and variable costs.

Total revenue: Price × sales or output.

Margin of Safety: the difference between the actual level of output and the break-even level.

Questions Time allowed 25 minutes

1. State the formula for calculating the break-even level of output. (2 marks)

2. Faye sells handbags at £40. Her direct costs per item are £10, with fixed costs of £7,500. Calculate the break-even level of sales. (4 marks)

3. **A.** If Faye was able to sell 320 handbags, calculate the level of profit made (remember to show your working). (3 marks)

   B. What is her margin of safety? (2 marks)

4. If Faye were to increase her prices, use a diagram to explain what would happen to her break-even level of sales. (5 marks)

5. From Figure 42.11:

   A. Calculate the selling price. (2 marks)

   B. Calculate the total variable costs at the break-even level of output. (2 marks)

6. Fill in the missing figures for each line in Table 42.4. (5 marks)

   25 marks

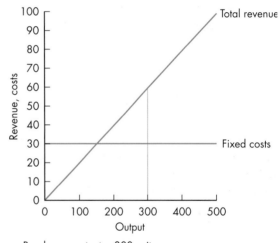

Break-even output = 300 units

Figure 42.11

Examiner's voice

Whenever you include a diagram in your answer, ensure that you explain what has happened. Do not just draw it and assume it is obvious. Ensure that all parts of your diagram have clear labels.

Actual output	Price £s	FC £s	VC £s	Profit Loss £s	Breakeven level	Margin of safety
A. 15,000	4	6,000	3	9,000		
B. 5,000	10	2,000	6			

Table 42.4

Case Study Time allowed 40 minutes

Danni Watt is keen to set up her own business, providing revision courses for AS and A level Business Studies students in her local area. She has bought a laptop and PowerPoint projector for £2,500. After she had conducted some market research, she found that the cost of hiring a suitable hotel conference room was £500, which included a sound system and a screen for the Powerpoint projection. The room would hold up to 200 students. Danni had already spent £100 on a mailshot to schools in her region.

She calculated that the cost of providing revision material in a folder was £5 per student. This would cover the cost of a folder and all the photocopied revision sheets. In addition, the hotel would charge £6 for water and cola drinks per student.

Not having undertaken such courses before, Danni wanted to make sure that she had some support, and decided it would be a good idea to employ an assistant for the day of any revision course. In an attempt to keep her costs down, she chose to employ a student from her own school and agreed to pay Kelly £50 for the day.

She was uncertain as to what price to charge, even after further research into similar courses that had been advertised in a Business Studies magazine. After much thought, Danni decided to charge £24 for the day course.

1. Calculate the total fixed costs for Danni's revision course. (2 marks)

2. Calculate the break-even number of students for her revision course. (4 marks)

3. If a total of 145 students attended her first revision course:

   A. Calculate the level of profit she made. (4 marks)

   B. Calculate the margin of safety for the revision course. (3 marks)

4. If Danni decided to increase her prices to £27 for the day's course, calculate by how much the break-even level of output has changed. (3 marks)

5. Using the break-even information, analyse which price may be best for Danni's revision course. (9 marks)

(25 marks)

CAPACITY UTILISATION

Using the resources of the business in an effective and efficient manner is essential to a successful business. Most resources used are scarce and therefore costly; any method in which such resources can be used to the maximum will be beneficial.

Knowing the level of capacity utilisation is important to a business, because it affects the covering of its fixed costs. If fixed costs are £10,000 and the business is operating at 50% of its capacity (its maximum is 1,000 units of production), it only has the 50% of its productive capacity to cover all its fixed costs. (There is a smaller level of production to cover all the costs.) However, if the business operates at 100% capacity (its maximum), there is twice the output to cover the same level of fixed costs; consequently the average fixed cost would be considerably lower, allowing the business to either lower its prices or increase its profits.

$$\frac{\text{Fixed costs of £10,000}}{(50\% \text{ of } 1,000 = 500)} = £20$$

whereas with the same fixed costs but increased capacity:

$$\frac{£10,000}{(100\% \text{ of } 1,000 = 1,000)} = £10.$$

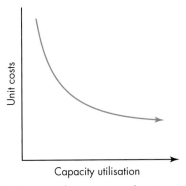

Figure 43.1 Increased capacity utilisation: unit costs fall.

By operating at a higher utilisation of capacity, the business is able to reduce its costs and become more competitive.

Calculating the capacity utilisation

The calculation for capacity utilisation is as follows:

$$\frac{\text{Actual or current level of output}}{\text{Maximum possible output}} \times 100\%$$

Example
If a business produces 1,200 units and has the productive capacity to produce 2,000 units, the capacity utilisation is as follows:

$$\text{Capacity utilisation} = \frac{\text{current production level}}{\text{maximum output}} \times 100$$

$$= \frac{1,200}{2,000} \times 100\%$$

$$= 60\%$$

Examiner's voice

Remember as always to state the formula and show your working.

With reference to Table 43.1, the capacity utilisation of Liverpool Football Club on match days is:

$$\frac{44,500}{45,276} \times 100\% = 98.2\%$$

Football club	Maximum capacity	Typical Attendance 2008	Capacity utilisation %
Arsenal	60,000		
Aston Villa	43,300		
Bolton Wanderers	28,723	21,095	
Chelsea	42,000	41,693	
Fulham	24,525		
Hull City	25,504		
Liverpool	45,276	44,500	
Manchester United	76,180	75,398	
Middlesborough	34,500	25,164	
Newcastle United	52,387		
Portsmouth	20,338	18,416	
Stoke City	28,383	26,704	
Sunderland	49,000		
Tottenham Hotspur	38,000	36,183	
Wigan Athletic	25,000		

Table 43.1 Capacity utilisation at Premier League football grounds

whereas the capacity utilisation for Bolton Wanderers is:

$$\frac{21,095}{28,723} \times 100\% = 73.4\%.$$

Reaching full capacity

There are several ways in which full capacity can be obtained:

1. Increase the demand for the products produced.

   The marketing department may undertake a variety of campaigns aimed at increasing demand, and consequently more goods will need to be produced thereby reaching full capacity. There is a danger of increasing demand beyond full capacity, which would require further investment that may not be possible or viable. In addition, the response to marketing may not be immediate, and therefore reaching full capacity may take a long time.

2. Producing different additional products with the same resources.

   If the resources are sufficiently flexible, it may be possible to produce other goods or variations to increase output and therefore reach full capacity.

3. Reducing capacity

   Although this may appear rather drastic, in certain economic circumstances it is a viable option. It is sometimes achieved by 'mothballing', when some of the capacity is kept but taken out of usage. It may be literally wrapped up and stored, ready for any upturn in the economy or demand for the given products.

   On other occasions, the productive capacity is actually reduced. This is often the case when the economic climate or demand for the given product falls significantly. Corus, the Anglo-Dutch steel manufacturer, announced a reduction in its capacity at the end of 2008.

Corus and BT cut jobs and production capacity as crunch spreads through industry

Two of Britains biggest business will cut production and move jobs off the payroll in further evidence of the economic downturn's impact on the real economy.

Corus, the Anglo-Dutch steelmaker is to halt more production just weeks after it imposed initial cuts across its operations. The Tata-owned group will cut output by 30 per cent and temporarily shut down three blast furnaces. The cuts will run until the end of March.

Last month Corus said that it was cutting production by 20 per cent, or the equivalent of one million tonnes of crude steel, to run to the end of the year. The group, which was formed from the merger of British Steel and Hoogovens, will close blast furnaces at its plants in Scunthorpe in Humberside, Port Talbot in South Wales and in the Netherlands. In Britain, Corus has four blast furnaces at Scunthorpe, although one was already idle two at Port Talbot and one Teesside, which will not be affected at the moment.

Philippe Varin, chief executive, said: " The current slowdown requires us to adapt our operations to the changing environment with maximum speed."

Source: *The Times*, 8 November 2008, Christine Buckley and Lilly Peel)

Constraints on reaching full capacity

- The level of competition within the market in relation to the size of the market. If there are many competitors competing for a limited number of consumers, there is less likelihood that full capacity will be obtained.
- The stage of the product life cycle; if demand for the product is declining, operating at full capacity is unlikely.
- If the product is seasonal, there will be occasions when demand is lower and therefore production levels will be below full capacity.
- New, superior alternatives have entered the market, therefore reducing demand and the level of production.
- Increased capacity will reduce the ability to reach full capacity, especially if too much investment has taken place.
- Outsourcing will reduce the utilisation of capacity.

Benefits and costs of operating at full capacity

Benefits

- As capacity utilisation increased, the average unit cost will fall (see Figure 43.1, Spreading the cost between more sales). The fixed costs are spread over more goods and the variable costs may benefit from economies of scale (bulk-buying).
- Less wastage of resources.
- Profits increase, as a result of falling unit costs.
- Employees are busy therefore probably more motivated, as a full order book indicates prolonged employment.
- Opportunities for employee bonus payments through overtime or profit-sharing.
- More competitive due to reduced costs, enhancing survival and market domination opportunities.
- Bankers, shareholders, suppliers and consumers will all see full capacity in a positive manner.

Costs/disadvantages

- There is little or no opportunity for maintenance and therefore breakdowns will mean 'downtime' (when the production stops so that no goods are being produced).
- Any additional orders will either be impossible to meet (especially in the short term) or will require significant additional costs in overtime. The profit on any additional orders will probably be lower.
- Working at full capacity may put pressure on the employees who may therefore become stressed, leading to an increase in the level of absence. This will put even more pressure on the rest of the employees.
- As the emphasis is on producing the goods with all resources being fully employed, there is little or no time for inhouse training.
- The level of quality may be affected. There may be occasions when, in an attempt to satisfy as many orders as possible, certain processes are hurried which lead to mistakes being made, affecting the quality of the finished product. This may lead to a fall in sales as the reputation of the product is damaged.

Over-utilisation of capacity

This can only be a short-term factor, when resources are pushed beyond their normal levels. Workers may be asked to work additional shifts or hours, or some work may be subcontracted to satisfy a surge in demand. However, employees can only work additional hours occasionally before any detrimental effect on output occurs.

Examiner's voice

It is important for students to consider carefully the nature of the product and its market, in an attempt to assess the likely consequences of full capacity or its abilities to achieve this. The context of the question is, as always, crucial.

Further Sources

www.growthbusiness.co.uk

Your Turn

Questions Time allowed 20 minutes

1. Explain what is meant by capacity utilisation.
   (4 marks)

2. Calculate the capacity utilisation if a factory is capable of producing 6,500 units but is presently producing 5,000 units. (3 marks)

3. If production is 200 units and the capacity utilisation is 80%, calculate the maximum level of production. (3 marks)

4. Analyse **one** likely benefit for a business of operating at full capacity. (6 marks)

   (16 marks)

Figure 43.2 An Emirates aircraft

Case Study Time allowed 35 minutes

Emirates, the UAE airline

Emirates Airline flies to over 100 destinations, using its fleet of 114 wide-bodied passenger planes. Zawya Dow Jones reported that the seat occupancy on Emirates flights fell in the latter months of 2008 by 1.8%. However, the President of Emirates, Tim Clark, stated that the average seat factor (seat occupancy) was between 70% and 77%. He said that he was surprised that the airline was able to carry so many passengers despite the world financial crisis, and that the fall in the value of the pound had not stopped the flow of British tourists flying with Emirates.

The overall seating capacity for Emirates planes has increased by 15.6% recently, and seat occupancy was increased by 3.6% before the financial crisis of 2008.

One of the problems facing Emirates is to decide the most appropriate seating configuration (the number

of seats and the type of seats within the plane). One decision that has to be made is which combination of classes to have within its planes (first class, business class and economy class).

On its Airbus A330-200 planes, the passenger capacity/seating configuration can either be 237 passengers if all three classes are provided, or 278 passengers if just two classes are used (see Figure 43.2).

(Adapted from an article by Ivan Gale, *The National*, 30 October 2008)

1. With the use of a diagram, explain how a decrease in capacity utilisation will affect unit costs. (4 marks)

2. Evaluate the likely consequences for the operation of an increased capacity utilisation (seating occupancy). (16 marks)

   (20 marks)

STOCK CONTROL

The quantity of stock held by a business is vitally important. Insufficient stock may mean that the business runs out of stock and cannot satisfy orders for its products. Too much stock will mean that the business is not being efficient, as too much cash will be tied up in stock. It is therefore essential that the right amount of stock is held; enough to meet orders from customers, but not too much to avoid unnecessary costs. How much stock needs to be held depends upon the type of business. Supermarkets will need large quantities of stock as they sell FMCGs (fast-moving consumer goods), while a garage selling cars would not need to hold much stock.

What is stock?

Stock is usually one of the following:

1. Raw materials
2. Work-in-progress
3. Finished goods.

Raw materials

This is stock that includes all the raw materials or components that are needed to produce a finished good. Many businesses will only buy in stock once an order has been gained.

Work-in-progress

This includes the raw materials and components that are partly assembled or used to produce the finished good. At any one time much of the stock may have already been used in the production process, but it is not as yet a finished product that consumers would be willing to buy.

Finished goods

This is the completed product that has yet to be delivered to the consumer. Some products are stored and then delivered. How much stock will be in this form will depend upon the nature of the product and the size of a given order. The business may be storing the finished goods until the number required by the consumer has been completed, which are then delivered in one despatch. This is often the case when products are to be exported.

For many products, the amount of finished goods stock is minimal, because the finished goods have already been sold and are therefore transported out of the factory immediately. This is particularly true for a business with a high rate of stock turnover (see financial efficiency ratios, Unit 22).

The major issue is trying to decide on the right level of stock, balancing the benefits and the costs of holding stock.

Benefits of holding stock

Satisfying demand

It is important to be able to satisfy a demand for the products that are produced by a particular business. Creating a demand that cannot be satisfied often leads to a loss of goodwill, with potential customers turning elsewhere for their goods. This leads to a loss of revenue.

Coping with fluctuations in demand

This is similar to the previous benefit; however, being able to take advantage of a surge in demand, for whatever reason, may lead to further sales and a potential increase in orders and revenue. Furthermore, if orders increase due to the business's ability to meet the sudden increase in demand, the business may be able to reduce costs, as the additional production costs may benefit from the savings due to economies of scale.

Buffer stock to meet late deliveries

Not only does buffer stock ensure that there is sufficient stock available before a delivery is due, it ensures that there is no disruption to the production line. Stopping a production line because there is insufficient stock could cost thousands of pounds in 'downtime' (when production is not taking place).

Cost savings due to economies of scale purchases

By purchasing a large quantity of stock may allow for cost savings due to buying in bulk. Providing that the cost of holding the stock is not greater than the savings made by buying in bulk, it may be worthwhile. It also assumes that there is adequate space to store such quantities.

Costs of holding stock or inventory

Storage costs

Using warehouse space is expensive. The actual costs of purchasing the warehouse to hold stock or the cost of rent has to be covered either immediately, or if rented, on a regular basis regardless of any sales patterns and subsequent revenue.

It is not only the actual warehouse that needs to be provided, but also some sort of storage facilities even if it is just shelves. In many factories the stock storage is computerised and uses automotive equipment for stocking and distributing; all of which is an additional cost to the business. Depending upon the nature of the products or raw materials to be stored, there may be heating or freezing costs.

Opportunity costs

By paying for stock, it has prevented the business from undertaking alternative expenditure.

Depreciation/obsolescent costs

Stock may depreciate over time, especially if it is perishable and reaches its sell-by date. It may also be damaged and will therefore lose value.

Stock can also suffer from becoming obsolete. While in storage, stock can become redundant as tastes change, or a new product arrives on the market that supersedes the stored item. Although the stock has been paid for, it is unlikely that a return in the form of sales revenue could be gained.

Security costs

Most goods will require some form of security. CCTV cameras or security guards are both expensive. The level of security will depend upon the nature of the products and raw materials involved.

Administrative costs

These costs are related to the costs of obtaining the stock. Raising orders, agreeing transport delivery times and checking the stock on arrival all incur costs.

Insurance costs

As the risks of holding stock increase, the cost of insurance will increase. Insuring the stock is an unavoidable cost.

Out-of-stock costs or stock-out costs

Although the above points highlight the often significant costs of holding stock, there are additional costs of not having sufficient stock which are usually referred to as out-of-stock costs.

If a business runs out of stock and is therefore unable to continue to produce goods, the inevitable loss will be the inability to complete and satisfy the order. Although this cost can be calculated by taking the value of the order, what is harder to gauge is the value of any future

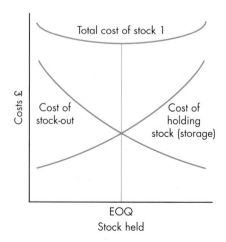

Figure 44.1 Optimum stock level (economic order quantity)

orders that may have been lost as a result of not meeting the existing order.

Traditionally, businesses would hold sufficient stock on the basis of 'just-in-case'; however this can also be costly as often too much stock is held. Finding the optimum stock level can be achieved by considering the cost of holding stock and the cost of a stock-out. Figure 44.1 weighs up the cost of holding stock against the cost of not having stock!

Stock control charts

Once a level of stock has been decided upon, the management of that stock needs consideration. Stock control charts are usually used to monitor the levels of stock. They show the total cost of the stock on an annual basis, once both costs have been taken into consideration.

Figure 44.2 shows some of the key aspects and terms found in stock control charts.

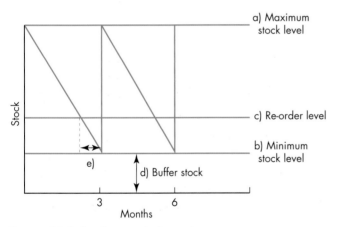

Figure 44.2 Stock control chart

Maximum stock level

This is represented by a) on Figure 44.2. This amount will be determined by several factors:

The storage capacity of the factory or warehouse
The larger the storage capacity, the more likely the business will be able and willing to hold more stock. Additional storage space may be available for expansion in the future.

The product
The characteristics of the product in terms of its rate of turnover (stock turnover levels), its size and value are all factors that will affect the level of maximum stock.

The level of sales
A high level of sales will often mean that the maximum stock level will be higher.

The cost of storage
Storage space will probably incur costs.

The degree of competition
If the market is competitive and there is an opportunity to gain more sales, the business will probably have a higher maximum stock level to be able to cope with any unexpected surge in sales. However, the cost of holding such stock levels will still need to be considered, if costs are to be kept under control.

The timing of marketing campaigns
If a business has launched a marketing campaign to introduce a new product or improve sales of an existing product, it may decide to hold a higher level of stock in the hope of increased demand.

The time of the year (seasonal sales)
Businesses involved with selling seasonal products may have to stock-pile products, so a higher maximum level of stock will be required to satisfy the surge in demand whenever it occurs.

Minimum stock level

This is represented by b) on Figure 44.2. This will be determined by the following factors:

The level of sales
If stock is sold quickly, the minimum stock level is likely to be higher.

The amount of time taken to deliver new stock
If the lead time is substantial, then a higher minimum stock level will probably be used.

The history of unforeseen circumstances
If stock has run out previously, the business is more likely to have a higher minimum stock level.

Re-order level

Represented by c) on Figure 44.2, this is determined by the following factors:

- The amount of time that is taken from re-order to the actual delivery, which is known as the **lead time**.
- How near the supplier is to the factory.
- The sales records to date. If the trend of sales has been increasing, the business is more likely to have an earlier re-order level.

Buffer stock

Buffer stock is represented by d) on Figure 44.2, and is the difference between the minimum stock level and holding no stock. It should be viewed as emergency stock. The level of the buffer stock will be determined by:

- the likelihood of delays with deliveries
- the speed of the production process
- reliability and location of suppliers
- the level and pattern of demand.

Lead time

This is shown as e) on Figure 44.2 and represents the length of time between re-ordering the stock and its arrival (see Figure 44.3).

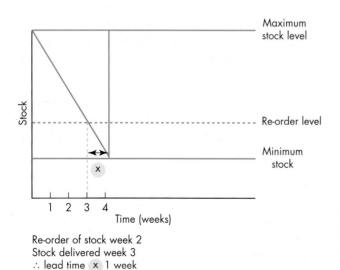

Re-order of stock week 2
Stock delivered week 3
∴ lead time ⊗ 1 week

Figure 44.3 Lead time

The gradient of the line indicates the rate of sales. The steeper the gradient, the faster the rate of sales. Figure 44.4a shows a steep gradient that is typical for a FMCG; Figure 44.4b shows a less steep gradient, typical for a slow-selling product such as furniture.

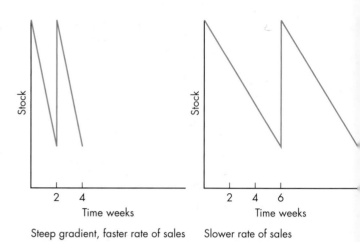

Steep gradient, faster rate of sales   Slower rate of sales

Figure 44.4a and b The rate of sales

However, there is an assumption that the rate of sales is constant (hence the straight line). In reality, the rate of sales will vary according to the time of year and because of other business environment factors that affect sales.

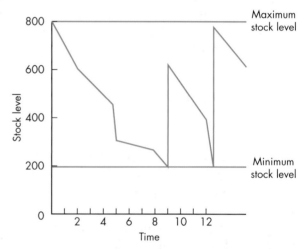

Figure 44.5 Variable sales pattern

Figure 44.5 shows that sales are more likely to vary over time. The amount of stock ordered varies. Even though the maximum stock level is 800 units, if a business knows its sales trends, it may not re-order quantities to ensure that maximum stock is held.

As lean production has been adopted within the UK (see Unit 46), the level of stock has been one obvious area of concern. The utilisation of just-in-time (JIT) has led to significant falls in the overall levels of stock held. Consequently, a typical stock control chart has also changed. (For more details on JIT, see Unit 44).

In Figure 44.6 it is clear to see that the maximum stock, the minimum stock and the re-order level of stock

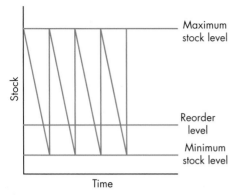

Figure 44.6 Just-in-time (JIT)

have all changed. This is because JIT is an attempt to reduce costs in order to be 'leaner' and therefore more competitive.

Examiner's voice

It is unlikely that you would have to draw a stock control chart in full. However, understanding how the stock control chart would change when circumstances change would be helpful.

Examples

- If a business is growing in size, it will no doubt need more stock. It will therefore need to consider the consequences for its re-order and buffer stock levels, as well as the maximum stock levels. Ensuring that supply is maintained is vital to the business and therefore a higher buffer stock may be needed to avoid any stock-out situations.
- Seasonal products may require more frequent deliveries and in larger quantities at certain times of the year, to coincide with the peak selling periods. A firework manufacturer is likely to hold much greater levels of stock in the run up to 5 November, bonfire night, and New Year celebrations, than in the summer months.
- The weather, the dates of public holidays and special events can trigger a change in stock levels. A business selling soft drinks will watch the long-range weather forecast with interest. Knowing that a heatwave is on the way will mean an increase in the level of stock held, in order to meet the potential surge in demand.

Calculating the average level of stock

To calculate the average level of stock:

$$\frac{\text{Maximum stock level} + \text{minimum stock level}}{2} = \text{average stock}$$

For example, if the maximum stock level is 15,000 items and the minimum stock level is 4,000 items, the average stock is:

$$\frac{15,000 + 4,000}{2} = 9,500$$

Examiner's voice

If actual stock levels are given average stock levels can be calculated by:

$$\text{opening stock} + \text{closing stock} \div 2$$

The control of stock levels

Concern over the levels of stock held has encouraged businesses to persuade suppliers to hold the stock until required (roughly how JIT operates); or alternatively, to persuade the customer to take the stock and store it! In this case, the supplier usually will not charge the customer until the stock is used or sold.

Apart from JIT, there are other ways in which the level of stock can be both monitored and controlled. The obvious method of controlling stock levels is by careful stock rotation.

LIFO and FIFO

These acronyms stand for last in, first out (LIFO) and first in, first out (FIFO). LIFO and FIFO are stock control terms that are also used for accounting valuations. The terms are related to the order in which stock is sold and how restocking takes place.

If new stock is simply placed on the shelves in front of the old stock, it will be sold first; hence, first in first out! Such a system is acceptable if the products in question have a long shelf-life such as paint or canned foods.

However, it would not be an appropriate way of controlling stock if the products were perishable and therefore have a short shelf-life. If this is the case, a more stringent system needs to be used. LIFO is a better system for the control of stock if waste is to be avoided or reduced. Selling the older stock before any new stock will help to ensure that stock does not go beyond the sell-by date. This system does however assume that shelves are stacked correctly. If staff do not bring all the old stock to the front of the shelves and then stack the new stock at the back, the system breaks down. Some stores are able to fill some cabinets from the back to ensure that the old stock is sold first; however, this is not possible on supermarket shelves, and therefore the success of FIFO relies on the efficiency of the employees.

Using EPOS

Just as the Kanban system is necessary to effectively operate JIT, EPOS (electronic point of sale) is invaluable in ensuring stock levels and the re-ordering of stock is done efficiently. The EPOS information is scanned by bar codes. Each product has a unique bar code number which is read electronically at the checkout desk, and the information passed via electronic data interchange (EDI) to a computer that will automatically re-order stock at the required level.

Further Sources

www.thebarcodewarehouse.co.uk

Questions Time allowed 25 minutes

1. State three factors that would affect the maximum stock level held by a business. (3 marks)

2. Explain how a stock control chart would change if the rate of sales changed. (4 marks)

3. Explain the difference between LIFO and FIFO. (4 marks)

4. If the maximum stock level was 25,000 units and the minimum stock level was 4,000 units, calculate the average stock level. (3 marks)

5. Explain what is meant by out-of-stock costs. (4 marks)

6. Draw a diagram to show the economic order quantity. (4 marks)

(22 marks)

Case study Time allowed 30 minutes

Logo Designs Ltd (LDL)

Logo Designs is a business specialising in the designs and printing on T-shirts that are used for merchandising. It sells to other businesses who want their corporate logos put on to T-shirts for promotional activities and as gifts to clients. LD has recently gained the contract to design and print the T-shirts ready for the premier of a new blockbuster James Bond film. Although it has regular orders from existing clients, this particular contract is much larger than any of its previous orders. One of the problems it faces is judging how many T-shirts will be provided. The film distributor is anxious that the merchandising is a success and has indicated to LDL that additional orders may follow. Although LDL has the ability to print the T-shirts, its storage capacity is not large. The production manager, Ron, is concerned about storing the blank and completed T-shirts before they leave the premises to be delivered to the various cinemas and promotion venues.

1. Evaluate the stock control factors that LDL will need to consider having gained the new contract.

(18 marks)

Consider this simple quality control test.

Statistical Quality Control 100% Inspection Exercise

Consider the letter "f" – capital or small – as a defect. How many defects in the following text?

"Effective quality control in manufacturing enterprises, in office operations, in service functions, and in job shops has undergone many innovations of late. From early times it has been presumed that if you had few inspectors and they were on the ball, your quality of product would be okay. If your firm still adheres to this outmoded concept, you may be missing an immense potential for quality improvement and defect elimination for your operation. If this test demonstrates anything, it should show the difficulty of finding all defects, even if you have 100 percent inspection. Far better to never build defects into the product in the first place. How can this be done? Many firms have found the total approach to quality control is the only systematic way to achieve perfection in quality, but it does mean that from first to last you'll have covered most of the possible loopholes in purchasing, receiving, material control, process design, and shipping and packing, at which key points in final product quality are checked out. Above all, quality control is a team effort, which should energise the entire organisation toward a common goal."

Your count: _____   Actual Number: _____

Conclusion:

This is a very simple test of quality, and you attempted it just once, without pressure or distractions; yet you may have missed some of the 'faults' and failed to think carefully about what was written. It may now be easier for you to understand how mistakes are made and why they are not always spotted and subsequently rectified. It is important to try and ensure the any checks are not just left for people to make.

What is quality?

Quality is concerned with:

- the design of the product
- the reliability of the product
- ensuring that the product is properly checked while in production and not only when completed.

Being fit for purpose

Quality includes ensuring that the product is fit for purpose and is safe to use, will be reliable and last an appropriate time (durable).

Quality is also important for services. A survey in 1993 by Mintel suggested that consumers looked for an efficient service, with helpful and knowledgeable staff.

Satisfying legislation

Legislation is passed which sets the standard for certain products. Toys have to be manufactured within several legal guidelines as to the material used, the type of paint used and the way in which parts are assembled together. Food has to be fit for human consumption; cars have to pass several crash safety tests.

Why is quality important?

Quality has become more important in today's markets because consumers now expect it as standard and not an additional extra. Any good that is purchased and then has to be returned because it is faulty, brings bad publicity for the business and may lead to a loss of goodwill. When a business has to recall products because a major fault has been discovered, not only are sales lost but the reputation of the business is damaged. Recovering a good reputation requires time and money, and if it is lost irretrievably, sales will be lost for ever.

Consumers are now more likely to complain and publicise their complaints on consumer television programmes. They will often select a product because of its perceived quality and its reputation for reliability.

Quality assurance

Quality assurance is concerned with the way in which a business sets out its procedures to assure its consumers that the products produced are of the right quality. Systems should be in place to ensure that quality is appropriate.

Inspection v cost of rejects/returns

For the business, the cost of inspecting products for quality must be balanced against the cost of the consequences of poor quality products.

Costs of inspection	Cost of poor quality products
Installing procedures to improve quality.	Wasted materials.
Time taken to check and inspect.	Cost of repairing.
Employing people to inspect, or requiring employees to use part of their time to inspect instead of producing.	Production losses to rectify faults.
	Damage to reputation of the business and loss of sales.

Table 45.1 Costs of inspection and returns

This creates a dilemma for most businesses. It may not be possible or economically worthwhile to check that every pencil is exactly the same length and colour; the value of the end product has to be considered. However, ensuring that a particular part of a car engine is exactly the right size may be crucial if all the other components are to fit correctly. In other words, the decision on whether or not to inspect products for faults will depend upon the product and its function. The degree of tolerance depends upon the nature of the product.

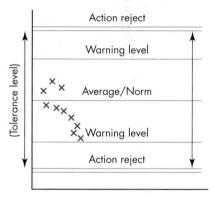

Figure 45.1 Control chart tolerance levels

Figure 45.1 shows the tolerance levels for a given product. Every time a product or part of a product is tested, it must fall within the tolerance levels (between the arrowed lines). If a test discovers a product outside of the permitted tolerance level, it should be rejected as a defect (action level).

Every time a test is undertaken, the actual reading is usually plotted, and it is possible to plot a trend that may indicate that something is going wrong and can be rectified before it is too late. Each 'x' represents a test result, and the trend of the tests in Figure 45.1, although within the tolerance levels, suggests that it is getting close to the warning level. If the warning level is reached, it should trigger questions as to why the test results are moving towards and beyond the warning level.

How much tolerance is allowed will depend upon the sophistication of the product and its function. Many of today's factories prefer prevention rather than cure (see Dr Deming and P Crosby's views below).

Figure 45.2 shows sensors that prevent a fault occurring while building a car. Before the press comes down to cut and shape the various panels of a car, the sensors detect whether the steel or aluminium is aligned correctly. If it is not, the press will not come down, therefore preventing serious damage to the steel, aluminium or even the press itself.

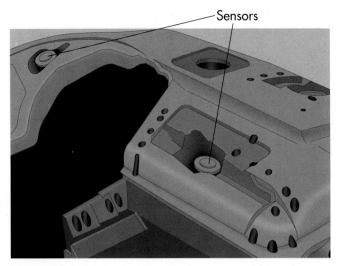
Sensors

Figure 45.2 Sensors to prevent damage and loss of materials

Statistical quality control

Dr Deming, a quality guru, suggested 14 factors to improve quality performance; see Table 45.2.

Another guru, Philip Crosby, has only four items on his list to aid quality management.

As you can see by looking at Tables 45.2 and 45.3, what constitutes quality and how to achieve it, varies! However, there is one constant theme that arises: prevention of faults is preferable to detecting faults. As a consequence, sampling completed products is now not the main approach or method of achieving a good quality product. Sampling is still used, but as part of a range of procedures.

Total quality management (TQM)

This approach became extremely popular in the 1980s. Total quality management considers the efficient usage of all the resources used within the production process, directly or indirectly related to the actual production process. The word 'total' is the significant factor, as it is an essential part of this practice that all employees are responsible for the well-being of a business and not just those that produce the product. Employees are empowered to take the responsibility for the work they do.

1	The message about quality should be consistent throughout the business.
2	There should be a commitment to improve continuously.
3	Improvements are not just about the product itself.
4	Encourage employees not to fear improvements; they are not negative.
5	Remove any barriers within the organisation that may prevent the improvement of quality.
6	Ensure that the organisational structure of the business supports all of the other 13 points.
7	Ensure that all suppliers are concerned about quality, and award business to them on this basis.
8	Encourage everyone to be involved in quality, and train employees to think in this way.
9	Training is vital.
10	The role of supervising employees needs to change to a training and helping role.
11	Switch from the detection to the prevention of faults.
12	Remove barriers that prevent employees from having a pride in their work.
13	Dispose of slogans and unrealistic targets.
14	Dispose of work quotas.

Table 45.2 Dr Deming's plan for improving quality performance

1	Meeting conformance requirements: standards either meet the requirement or fail to do so.
2	Prevention not detection: build quality into the product.
3	The standard for performance is zero defects.
4	Improved quality is free (no costs of repairing or correcting), therefore the cost of good quality pays for itself!

Table 45.3 Philip Crosby's four points

It is a different approach to the control of quality within a business. The emphasis is on finding ways to prevent mistakes rather than inspect for mistakes. This approach fits with the philosophy of both Dr Deming and P Crosby.

Toyota, the car manufacturer, adopted a TQM approach within its car plants. The components of TQM are listed within its 'house', shown in Figure 45.3.

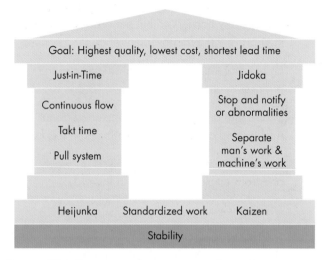

Figure 45.3 Toyota production system 'house'

TQM helps a business to:

- focus on the needs of the consumer
- improve quality in all its departments
- encourage a team approach by its employees
- encourage employees to be involved
- find ways to improve performance and quality
- seek out waste and any inefficiencies.

However, TQM may take time to implement, as employees may have to learn a new way of thinking and operating. It will require financing to pay for the training and installation of new procedures and approaches to organising the business.

Benchmarking

In its simplest form, benchmarking is achieved by comparing a business with that of a competitor that is usually the market leader, in order to improve its own practices. It involves setting standards for the performance of the business.

Benchmarking is concerned with the identification of the 'best practice'. This is done by comparing the products produced and how they are produced, with other businesses in the same industry. By improving its practices within the business, costs may be reduced, quality should be improved and a business should aim to improve standards on a constant basis.

There are several stages to effective benchmarking.

- Decide which products or activities/processes are to be benchmarked.
- Be aware of the existing processes in the business (to enable a comparison to be made).
- Analysis of those operating 'best practice' (if accessible).
- Make a comparison and identify gaps or areas for improvement.
- Take action to improve where necessary, to ensure that the practice of the business is close to being 'best practice'.
- Ensure process is ongoing (as for Kaizen, see below).

Types of benchmarking

There are a number of different types of benchmarking:

External benchmarking
External benchmarking is the most common type, where comparisons of performance are made between one business and another.

Internal benchmarking
Internal benchmarking is when comparisons are made within a business, usually between one department and another.

Competitive benchmarking
A comparison is made with the best competitor. Although gaining information from a competitor may not be easy, some exchange of information may be available through the trade association for that type of industry.

Functional benchmarking
Comparisons are made between businesses with similar processes, though not necessarily for similar products. It could involve comparing how businesses collect their research data, or how they undertake the design processes.

Strategic benchmarking
This is not related to a specific process but is concerned with the overall strategies that businesses use. If a business needs to improve its overall performance, considering the various strategies used by successful businesses is a good way forward.

Limitations of benchmarking

- Limited access to sensitive material (trade secrets!).
- Difficult to find which business offers 'best practice'.
- Difficult for a business to implement improvements to reduce gaps between itself and 'best practice' business; this may be due to insufficient employees of the right calibre, a lack of finance or an inflexible workforce.

Kaizen

Kaizen is the philosophy of attempting to gain 'continuous improvement'. The days of occasionally managing to find a way to improve the process of producing a product have gone. No business can afford to stand still if it is to remain competitive. 'Continuous improvement' refers to the production of the product and how to improve the quality of the product.

This approach is achieved more easily if all the employees are encouraged to take part in the process, and not just management. Often, the people best placed to make suggestions for improvements are the production workers, who know what the job actually entails.

Quality circles

Quality circles are a voluntary scheme where employees meet within the working day to consider problems affecting their work. Quality circles were established in Japan in 1962, and their main functions are to identify, analyse and attempt to solve problems within the workstation. Quality circle groups tend to be concentrated within manufacturing companies.

Management are consulted but rarely involved within the actual quality circle. This is because operating a quality circle for workers provides a sense of responsibility (Herzberg) and a sense of involvement (Mayo), and therefore provides an obvious source of motivation for the employees. The consequence for the business when quality circles operate is an increase in productivity, less absenteeism and an increase in the morale of the workforce.

There may however be disadvantages. If suggestions to improve workstations involve a reduction of the jobs that are performed and even a possible reduction in the number of employees required, such ideas will conflict with the employees' basic need for a job!

Evidence shows however that such fears are unfounded, and that quality circles have been adopted by many businesses.

Example

The concept of quality circles was introduced at Wedgwood, the pottery business, as early as 1980. This was an ideal type of business to adopt this process for improving quality and dealing with specific problems that arose on the shopfloor/workplace. A variety of problems were tackled, including:

- the elimination of clay waste
- a reduction in the level of dust
- a re-design of several workstations
- a better method of maintaining specialist equipment used to paint pots and plates
- a re-design of the paintbrush holder and paint bowl used for gold paint.

BS 5750 Kitemark and Quality standards ISO 9000

The British Standards Institution (BSI) rewards businesses that have adopted certain quality procedures. Originally, BS 5750 was the most common standard, awarded for operating a procedure to ensure the quality of products. The reward for 'passing' BS 5750 was that the business could show the BS symbol, demonstrating to potential buyers that the products from this particular business were likely to be of a high standard because the procedure for ensuring quality was practised. There were many businesses that insisted that their suppliers were registered as 'BS 5750' standard.

The international version of BS 5750 is ISO 9000.

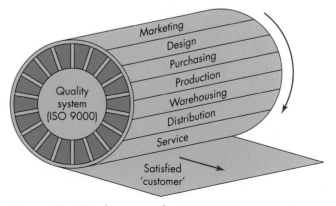

Figure 45.4 Quality system for ISO 9000
Source: Total Quality Management (1989) J S Oakland

These relate to a series of quality management systems. There are various different standards that can be awarded.

1. ISO 9000: this introduces the user to the concepts behind the management systems, and specifies the terminology used.

2. ISO 9001: concentrates on the design and development of products

3. ISO 9002: production

4. ISO 9003: final inspection tests

5. ISO 9004: quality management and systems.

Who is it relevant for?

ISO 9001 is suitable for any organisation looking to improve the way in which it operates and is managed, regardless of size or sector. However, the best returns on investment come from those companies prepared to implement it throughout their organisation rather than at particular sites, departments or divisions.

Figure 45.5 Kitemark symbol

Being able to display these various labels is an important marketing tool. A potential consumer (another business or an end-user) knows that the business displaying the marks has achieved a particular standard or undertaken certain quality procedures. The products should be of a high standard in terms of their quality.

Zero defects

By applying the concept of zero defects, a business should be able to benefit from an improvement in quality and therefore a reduction in costs, as less defects equals less waste. If a policy of zero defects is to be successful, the business needs to ensure that the right conditions are in place.

The needs of the consumer are paramount and the product is then built with these needs in mind. If the needs of the consumer are met, this should increase consumer satisfaction and lead to further orders or consumption. This in turn may lead to brand loyalty, and allow the business to establish its market share and even benefit from economies of scale as orders increase. If the expectations of the consumer are not met, this could have a damaging effect upon the image of the business.

However, the cost of achieving zero defects needs to be considered carefully against the likely benefits (refer back to Table 45.1).

Further Sources

John S Oakland (1992) *Total Quality Management*, Butterworth-Heinemann Ltd
Francis Mayle (1999) *Identifying Best Practice in Benchmarking*, Holloway, Hinton, CIMA
www.hutchins.co.uk/Cs_Wedg (for details of quality circles at Wedgwood)

Questions Time allowed 40 minutes

1. State three types of benchmarking. (3 marks)

2. Explain what is meant by tolerance levels. (4 marks)

3. Analyse one benefit of a business being able to display an ISO or BSI standards logo. (6 marks)

4. Apart from achieving improved quality, explain an additional benefit to the operation of the business if it introduces quality circles. (4 marks)

5. State the term for continuous improvement. (1 mark)

6. Should a business introduce the concept of zero defects? (10 marks)

(28 marks)

Task

From the list of products listed below, decide upon the most appropriate quality control tests that you would want to undertake. You should consider what to test out on the product, the timing and frequency of the test, and at what stage of the production process of the product. Think carefully about the cost versus control issues.

- biro
- lawnmower
- tin of soup or a can of Coca-Cola
- a chair
- a toy teddy bear.

LEAN PRODUCTION

Globalisation has increased the level of competition for many manufacturers. Ensuring that the best possible product is produced at the lowest possible price is now of paramount importance if a business is to survive in the international marketplace.

In order to remain competitive, it is essential that businesses find ways to reduce costs and to improve their productive efficiency.

What is lean production?

Lean production originated from Japan, and is an approach in which all employees are involved in putting into operation a series of working practices that will help the business to meet the demands of the consumer in an efficient and effective manner.

Apart from the price of a good, the consumer now expects a reliable product that has quality built in as standard and can be delivered on time. By operating lean production, the above requirements of the consumer are more likely to be met.

Lean production is a whole-business approach to achieving and maintaining a competitive product in the highly competitive markets of the world. It concentrates on the elimination of waste in its broadest sense. It not only looks at how a business can reduce its waste in terms of materials used, but waste in terms of time. Anything that helps to reduce the time it takes to introduce a new product, produce a new product and deliver a product, is related to the lean approach. By reducing waste in its broadest sense, the business should be able to reduce its costs and therefore become more competitive.

Car manufacturers Toyota followed the original ideas that had been used by Ford, and improved on them to

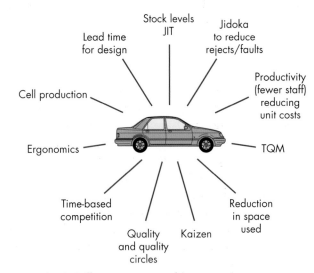

Figure 46.1 Different aspects of lean production

increase productivity further and gain the maximum output from the minimum inputs. The Toyota Production System is seen today as the benchmark for the industry.

Main elements of lean production

Time-based competition

This is an attempt to reduce the time taken between the generation of the idea for a product and it going into production (lead time).

This can be speeded up by the usage of computer-aided design (CAD) and virtual design techniques that can eliminate the need to build prototypes. Instead, any new designs can be tested virtually before the actual product is put into production. This saves valuable time and the cost of building prototypes.

Total quality management

Total quality management considers the efficient usage of all the resources used within the production process, whether directly or indirectly related to the actual production process. The word total is the significant factor, as it is considered vital that all employees are responsible for the well-being of a business, and not just those that produce the product. Employees are empowered to take the responsibility for the work they do. It is a different approach to the control of quality within a business. The emphasis is on finding ways to prevent mistakes rather than inspect for mistakes.

Jidoka

This is a process for building into the production process an ability to detect and reject faulty goods and components at the earliest possible moment in the production of the good. It is essential to try to keep the production line operating. If it stops, this is known as downtime, and means that no production on this line is taking place. The cost of downtime can be very expensive and is therefore to be avoided if at all possible. Jidoka is an aid to prevent defects occurring which may eventually mean that the production process has to be stopped.

Figure 46.2 Jidoka in process

The Andon Lamps signs which are usually displayed alongside every line enable management and supervisors to check the progress of each section of the assembly line. Each number refers to a particular workstation, and the status of the problem can be shown with amber and red lights. This enables a quick response to the right part of the line, in an attempt to keep the line moving and thereby avoid any downtime.

Figure 46.3 Andon lamps. Amber light: warning if a problem on the line is being dealt with; red light: line stopped, downtime

Kaizen

Kaizen is a philosophy which regards improvements in quality as an ongoing phenomenon, and not just something that takes place occasionally.

Striving for 'continuous improvement' is the key factor for the Kaizen approach. It is also achieved more easily if all employees are encouraged to take part in the process, and not just the management. Often, the people best-placed to make suggestions for improvements are the production workers who know what the job actually entails.

Improving one part of the production process often encourages improvements in other parts of the process. If flow production is taking place, the saving of several seconds in an early process in the production line will mean that other processes will have to find time-savings, otherwise bottlenecks on the line will occur. This acts as an incentive to find improvements further down the production line in order to facilitate the smooth flow of the whole process.

However, if continuous improvements are being made, eventually jobs may be affected; consequently, employees may be reluctant to make too many suggestions on how to improve the production process, for fear of losing their own jobs. There is also a view that continual improvement programmes put great pressure upon the employees, who then tend to suffer either from accidents or stress. It has been suggested that job rotation helps reduce such concerns.

The alternative viewpoint is that without improvements, the business will become uncompetitive and jobs will be lost due to a falling demand for the products.

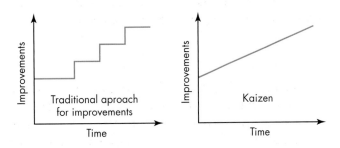

Figure 46.4 Kaizen

Quality and quality circles

As quality is now considered as something that needs to be built into the product that is produced, the business needs to focus on how quality can be improved and maintained (see also Unit 45, Quality).

To complement the Kaizen approach, some manufacturers have adopted quality circles. This is a voluntary scheme where employees, often between four and ten in number, are allowed to meet in working hours to discuss problems related to their working environment and workstations. They will also aim to create solutions to problems, and pass on these suggestions to management. By involving the employees, there are motivational benefits that may contribute to an improvement in the level of productivity for the business.

Just-in-time (JIT)

This is a method whereby levels of stock are low in order to reduce the amount of space required for storing stock. By ordering stock in smaller quantities but with more frequent deliveries, the business is able to hold less stock with all the related advantages. (see Unit 44, Stock Control).

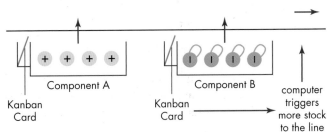

Figure 46.5 Kanban system to operate JIT

Kanban

In order to operate JIT successfully, a Kanban system needs to operate.

A Kanban system helps to organise the flow of components onto the production line at the right place at the right time. In Figure 46.5, the production assembly line is fed with components A and B. As the components are used, the level of stock by the line falls, and at a predetermined quantity, the kanban card is removed and 'posted'; the details of the kanban are within the bar code, so a computer will recognise the type of component, the quantities required and where the component is required on the production line.

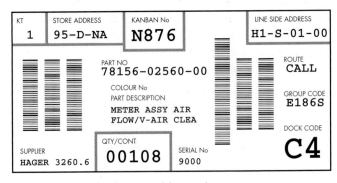

Figure 46.6 A kanban card barcode

The computer will automatically trigger a withdrawal of additional stock to be fed on to the line at the correct point in the process. It will also help organise the production and timing for any sub-assembly that takes place within the factory, so that these parts are ready in time to be used at another stage of the production process. The new stock will have a kanban so that the process can start all over again. Automatically additional stock from the suppliers will arrive on time, just-in-time to be used on the line.

For the kanban system to work effectively:

1. all components must have a kanban attached to the parts or the container of the parts

2. no parts should be moved without a kanban.

Naturally, there is a significant initial set-up cost if JIT and the associated kanban system are implemented. However, the long-term benefits far outweigh these capital costs.

Example

Car manufacturer Jaguar holds only two hours' stock of many of its components! At their plant in Castle Bromwich, Birmingham, the kanban cards have, for some components, been replaced with an electronic push-button kanban. This sends the message for additional stock automatically, therefore saving more time as the kanban does not have to be collected and delivered to a computer.

The push-button kanban is located at the workstation related to a particular part or raw material.

Cell production

Cell production is a form of teamwork. Employees are placed in different teams, with each team responsible for a particular part of the production process. Their responsibility includes the control of quality for their particular part of the production process, and ensuring that the parts that are delivered to their area or part of the process are of an acceptable standard.

The team is also responsible for the health and safety of their area, and for deciding who performs the tasks and when they are to be completed. As long as the particular process is completed in time to be passed to the next stage of the production process, and the tasks have been completed to the right standard, the employees within the cell can rotate their jobs to enhance job satisfaction.

Allowing employees some responsibility and involvement (Herzberg and Mayo's theories) contributes to a more contented workforce and consequently a higher level of productivity.

Ergonomics

Ergonomics looks at the relationship between the employee and the capital equipment (machine or tool) being used. An effective ergonomic design is one where the minimum amount of time is wasted in using the machine or equipment. In many car plants, drills and such tools are deliberately hung on spring coils so that workers can literally let go when the task involving that particular tool is complete, saving valuable seconds in not having to walk to place the tool back on a bench. Although such savings appear minute, when multiplied by the number of times a repetitive process is undertaken, they become significant in terms of both time and costs.

Further Sources

www.leanuk.org/pages/lean
The Toyota Production System 1996

Your Turn

Questions Time allowed 20 minutes

1. Explain what is meant by TQM. (4 marks)

2. Explain why Jidoka may save the business money in reduced costs. (4 marks)

3. State how Kaizen is a benefit to a business. (2 marks)

4. State two ways in which time-based competition can be improved. (2 marks)

5. Explain how the use of cell production may increase the motivation of the employees. (4 marks)

(16 marks)

Case Study Time allowed 35 minutes

The Crusty Cob Bakery (CCB)

A bakery is attempting to become more competitive. At present it produces a wide range of loaves and cakes for a well-known supermarket chain. The supermarket is constantly asking for the price of the bread produced by CCB to be cut. The supermarket is the largest customer for CCB's bread, and consequently the business is keen to keep its orders from the supermarket.

In order to increase CCB's competitiveness, its owners have decided it needs to become 'leaner'. Although it already operates a JIT system for its stock, it has yet to implement any other ways of being 'lean'.

It has a very loyal workforce, many of whom have been working at the bakery for many years. In addition, many employees often stay for only a short period of time and then leave, claiming that they find the work boring, with little or no opportunity for responsibility or real involvement in their tasks.

The production manager is keen to introduce a range of cost-cutting and efficiency-improving measures. However, many of the likely changes are not welcomed by some employees.

1. State four possible 'lean' changes that CCB could implement. (4 marks)

2. Analyse ONE problem of implementing Jidoka at the bakery. (6 marks)

3. Should CCB introduce cell production? (10 marks)

(20 marks)

TECHNOLOGY

Technology is extremely important for businesses. The pace of technology is such that no business can afford to ignore it. Failure to keep up with technological development may mean a loss of competitiveness.

Technological progress has raised the standard of living for most people. It has brought a wide range of innovative advances that enable a business to produce goods of a higher quality and in a more efficient manner. If a business can improve the efficiency of the production process, it may be able to reduce its unit costs and thereby become more competitive. This resulting efficiency provides the business with the opportunity to increase profits or pass on any savings in the cost of production to the consumer.

Many electrical and electronic consumer goods have fallen in price, partly as a result of technology. Products such as the PC, digital camera, mobile phone, plasma television, DVD and mp3 player, satellite television and computer consoles have been introduced during the last 20 years, and are now commonly found in the home.

Examiner's voice

Technology will be welcomed by some people and feared by others. The stakeholders of a business undertaking technological change will have different views. Depending upon the exact wording of the exam question, higher order marks will be awarded if you refer to how technology affects or helps each stakeholder.

Technological progress can be applied in all three stages of production.

The primary sector

Extractive technology has transformed the way in which our raw materials are collected, from the relatively older technology of a combine harvester, to the newest techniques for finding and extracting oil in remote areas previously out of reach.

Advances in genetically-modified (GM) technology have seen the advancement of GM crops, although this is a controversial issue.

The secondary sector

The usage of computer-aided design (CAD) and computer-aided manufacture (CAM) are well-established and help to reduce the lead time for the manufacturing of products:

- The usage of virtual sites within the design process has allowed designers to view their creations prior to producing prototypes, and in some cases have done away with the need to have such prototypes.
- Technology within cars continues, although lately there has been a greater emphasis on safety, such as parking sensors and external sensors that provide a warning that the car in front is too close or warn a driver when the car drifts out of lane. Technology to 'combat' speed cameras is selling well, as are GPS satellite navigation ('sat-nav') systems, which direct the driver to a given location by voice instructions and or visual display units.
- Information technology transformed the production process, enabling control of the production process, the stocking for the production and quality to be monitored and implemented.

- JIT relies heavily on IT to activate notification of stock levels and subsequent re-ordering of the required components.
- The newspaper industry uses robots to collect the rolls of paper that will be used on the printing presses. These robots are able to use their 'intelligence' to collect the right rolls of paper and deliver them to the correct printing press.

The ability of a business to reduce its unit costs may be vital if it is to remain competitive.

Example

Airline manufacturers have responded in different ways to the demand for flights. Boeing has developed a plane with a longer non-stop capability, whereas Airbus has developed the A380, which was unveiled in 2005 and ought to be in service before the end of the 2006. The A380 will probably be configured to carry about 550 passengers, but has the capability to carry 850. The technology to enable such a vast plane to take off and fly has resulted in the design of a new range of Rolls Royce engines, which are capable of lifting such a plane into the sky. Technology has also been used within the plane: intelligent lighting helps lessen the effects of jet lag by assimilating the right time of day throughout the length of the journey.

Such technological development will however bring additional problems as well as benefits. The existing infrastructure (airport terminals and some runways) may need to be altered in order to facilitate such a large plane.

The tertiary sector

Technology is having a massive impact on this sector of business.

Newspapers

Such is the speed of technological progress within the tertiary sector, that traditional media such as newspapers and magazines are being threatened.

Orange is trailing its e-newspaper, 'Read&Go'. This service uses an integrated e-paper technology, which does not use the traditional back lighting of LDC screens and is therefore easier to see in direct sunlight. 'Read &Go' is also the first of its type to offer Wi-fi in addition to a connection to the 3G network. The news service will be updated every hour.

Technology has allowed the service to have a storage capacity of 1Gb, sufficient to hold more than 200 newspapers. It was reported in June 2008 that if the service was successful while on trial in France, it would be launched internationally.

Television

'Freesat' began broadcasting in May 2008, and provides a satellite alternative to Freeview. Freesat has over 80 free digital channels and is accessible by over 98% of the UK households.

The significance of the technological advancement is not only for the businesses directly involved in the satellite industry, but it has also provided companies with another media in which to market their goods. Such channels allow businesses to target specific consumers more easily.

Retail sector

The retail industry has been transformed due to technological change. EPOS systems have improved efficiency changes in the distribution and delivery of produce.

Estate agents

The usage of virtual sites has transformed the estate agency sector. Potential house-buyers can 'visit' houses for sale on the estate agent's website, and view each room, thus saving the need to visit these houses. Similarly, designs for a new kitchen or bathroom can now be viewed in 'virtual reality' to enhance the decision-making process. This technology has saved retailers valuable time and therefore costs.

Electronic transfer of data

The ability to transfer data electronically has allowed industry to be more mobile, especially for its workforce. Staff can work remotely, which can make enormous savings for the business. The concept of 'hot-desking' has evolved, which is the practice of sharing desks or workstations between workers (who also work remotely and therefore do not need a permanent office space), as a means of saving space and resources.

Training

Training can now take place within house via e-learning, which negates the need for expensive travel and off-the-job training. This provides the business with further cost savings.

Personal entertainment

Personal entertainment has changed dramatically as a result of technological advances.

Example

Nintendo's Wii has transformed home entertainment. The motion-sensing Wii allows users to play tennis, golf, ten-pin bowling, baseball and other sports in a proactive manner and see the results of their efforts on the screen, making virtual play one of the fastest growing areas within the service sector.

Wii has rapidly expanded its product portfolio to include WiiFit. This particular 'game' has been so successful, that during the first two days of sales when the product was introduced in 2008, 240,000 units were sold, yielding over £17 million.

Mr Iwata, President of the Japanese computers games group, has indicated that Nintendo is working on the next generation of games. There is speculation that a television screen would no longer be needed to display the games; instead, a display screen inside a mask may be worn by the participant. Perhaps a mind-controlled console that fitted like a helmet could one day become a reality.

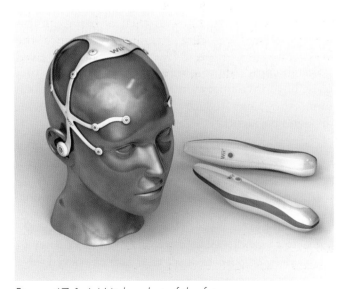

Figure 47.1 A Wii headset of the future

Opportunities (potential benefits)

In a competitive market, ensuring that costs are kept to a minimum is important. Using technology to reduce costs may allow the business either to spend more on marketing and offer a higher specification, or reduce the price of the product.

Technology allows for a faster lead time (the time taken from the idea for a new product to its completion). Having a faster lead time allows a business to be more competitive:

- It will enable the business to be first on to the market and therefore be seen as an innovator.
- IT allows a producer to 'see' a design in three dimensions, therefore sometimes reducing the need to build prototypes. This not only saves time but can reduce the possibility of expensive errors.
- Technology may help reduce the lead time for a business, and therefore be able to satisfy demand quicker and have a competitive edge.
- Technology can improve the quality of the product; robots can be used to ensure a consistently higher standard of work, reducing the number of rejects or returns to the business. Improving quality helps to eliminate waste and reduces costs to enhance competitiveness further.
- Computers allow for the production process to be streamlined (e.g. CAD, CAM), saving on costs and offering a more reliable production process.

Threats

Costs

Technological progress relies heavily on research, which can be very expensive, and there is no guarantee of success! The dilemma for any business is whether to wait and see what its competitors do and then try and imitate, or initiate progress by attempting to be a market leader.

Each approach may bring its own problems. If a business does not undertake technological innovation, it will be left behind. Being innovative may be good for the business in the short term, as a competitive advantage may be gained. However, businesses that copy a new development have not incurred the same research and development costs, and can therefore produce a similar product much more cheaply.

Example

The costs involved can be huge. Abu Dhabi's Masdar company, disclosed plans to invest £1.02 billion in a solar power project. The money is to be spent on producing a very thin photovoltaic film, which is then applied to the surfaces of buildings in order to generate power. The technology means that the cost is much lower than using conventional panels that harness the sun in order to generate electricity. The Middle East is an obvious place to utilise solar energy.

The potential savings to industry, given the rising cost of conventional sources of power, are enormous. However the risk is also great, with no guarantee of a cost-effective return on the investment.

Figure 47.2 Traditional solar panels

Unemployment

New technology may lead to a loss of employment. If there is a possibility of job losses as a result of technological change, the employees or their union representatives may resist such changes. A redundancy package may be negotiated which will be an additional cost to the employer. Employees may fear redundancies and changing work practices, leading to low morale and motivation levels.

Although the usage of a machine such as a robot may mean there is less need for labour and therefore redundancies will take place, there may also be more job opportunities involved with the production of the new technology.

An important point to note is that a failure to keep up with technology may lead to a loss of competitiveness, and result in job losses as a consequence of falling demand for the products of a given business.

Costs of training

New technology may require employees to retrain, and therefore the business will face additional costs in implementing the new technology. In some cases, the new technology may involve fewer skills and therefore the employee may suffer in terms of motivation, as they become machine-minders.

When to invest?

A major difficulty for many businesses is whether or not to invest in the latest technology. The pace of change is now rapid, with improved versions and new developments appearing frequently. The dilemma facing a business is not only when to buy but also, which to buy. Waiting for the next improved version may lead to a loss of competitiveness, but buying too early may mean that the competitors buy at a later date a much improved version of the required equipment.

Examiner's voice

Technology does not always mean that employees will be made redundant. There are often employment opportunities that arise as a result of technological progress. Losses in one sector of the economy may be replaced by more jobs in another sector. The banking sector has fewer employees at branches around the country, but because of technological advances, many more are now employed in call centres in order to meet the demand for tele-banking. It is therefore important to consider the positive as well as the possible short-term negatives that may arise. It is important to show how technology affects a business, and how that business may react to changing technology.

Shareholders' 'short-termism' may mean that they resist huge investments in technology as, in the short term, they may reduce profits, therefore reducing dividend payments.

> ### Key Term
>
> **Technology:** a means of improving the efficiency of resources used. It enables a business either to increase its productivity or to reduce its unit costs, both providing a way of remaining competitive.

Questions Time allowed 45 minutes

1. State two ways in which technology can help a business. (2 marks)

2. Explain how technology may reduce costs. (6 marks)

3. Analyse one consequence of technology for either a supermarket or a holiday company. (6 marks)

4. Evaluate the likely implications of technological change for the stakeholders of a business. (16 marks)

(30 marks)

Case Study Time allowed 45 minutes

BMW goes Electric!

BMW, the German car manufacturer, has spent heavily in applying technology to solving the problem of carbon dioxide emissions. It is developing an electric car with zero emissions.

It is hoped that the car will be available in 2012. Research suggests that private transport in cities needs to be carbon-friendly and efficient. Circumstances have meant that there is now room for an electric car in the marketplace. Stricter carbon-dioxide emission regulations, coupled with increases in taxation for cars with high emissions and the likely increases in the London congestion charge, have all meant that a battery-operated car is now viable.

Norbert Reithhofer, BMW chief executive announced that BMW is evaluating its battery-powered model.

Mercedes revealed that it is working on an electric Smart ForTwo.

The car industry is notorious for 'me-too' products and components. Rivals are quick to try and eliminate any new initiative that has provided a technological advantage in the marketplace. With very small margins in the car industry, ensuring the technological investment will be profitable has yet to be seen.

(Adapted from *The Sunday Times*, 23 March 2008.)

1. Explain the problems for BMW of being innovative. (6 marks)

2. Discuss how technology may affect BMW's stakeholders. (16 marks)

(22 marks)

WORK STUDY

Work study is a term created by Russell Currie, an employee of chemical manufacturer ICI, to cover the various techniques associated with performance improvement.

The aim of work study is to increase the productivity of the given resources of a business. It is an attempt to gain the optimum usage of the available resources.

Work study consists of two elements, shown in Figure 48.1.

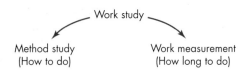

Figure 48.1 Work study

Method study

Method study considers how a job or task should be done, and the order of tasks required to complete the job. It is also used to improve how a job is performed. In the nineteenth century, Gilbreth looked at the methods used in the production process. Analysis and observation of the actions and movements of employees led to the creation of symbols to represent basic movements that the employees made as they worked. Gilbreth worked on the objectives of lightening the workload wherever possible, and spreading the work out in a more even period of time.

These observations helped bring about the study of ergonomics (see also Unit 46), the relationship between people and machines. It concentrates on how productivity can be increased by ensuring that the machines and tasks to be performed by the employees are undertaken in the most effective and time-efficient manner. Machines should be easy for employees to operate and located in the most appropriate position for the employee.

Method study can be divided into certain key tasks or steps.

- **Select the job or task for study.** The main reasons for selecting a particular job to be studied are:
  A. high costs
  B. creating bottlenecks
  C. low productivity
  D. poor quality.
- **The existing method is observed and noted.** The key elements of the job will be noted and include:
  A. the amount of movements involved in undertaking the task
  B. the length of any delays
  C. checking the quality.
  In order to streamline this observation, symbols are used (see Table 48.1).

Flow chart of job	
Symbol	**Explanation**
●	Operation/task
➡	Movement (of equipment/documents)
▽	Storage (of documents etc.)
◗	Delay
■	Inspection

Table 48.1 Symbols for job observation

- **Examine the observations.** It is important to try and find why a job is done in a particular way.
- **Consider better alternative methods.** Finding a cheaper, faster, more time-efficient and ergonomic method of completing the task.
- **Introduce new methods.**

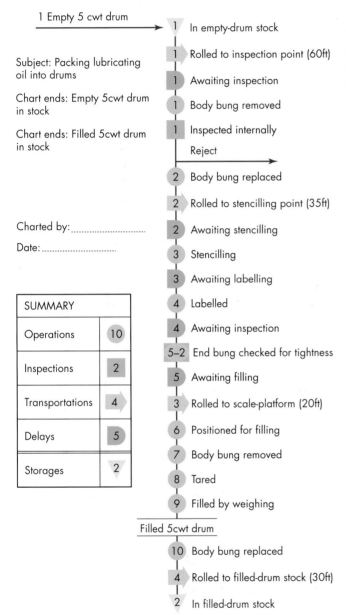

Figure 48.2 Flow process chart

Figure 48.2 illustrates a job that has been observed, charted and considered as to what actually happens. This is then examined and better alternatives considered.

Work measurement

Work measurement considers how long a job or task should take to complete. The process involves attempting to establish basic and standard times for a given job or task.

In order to achieve an appropriate time for a job, the cooperation of employees is required. It is important to establish an accurate time for any given job, and the study must therefore reflect how long it takes an average employee, working with some degree of enthusiasm.

The process will involve:
- selecting the task to be examined and observed
- measuring the time for each stage of the job
- rating the performance of the employee
- deciding what criteria is to be used to rate the performance
- applying the formula to calculate the basic and standard times.

Basic time

The basic time is calculated to see how long a particular job takes, in order to work out labour costs. It may be one small task related to the assembly of a product. The basic time for all tasks is recorded, to calculate the total time needed to complete the whole job. This information can also be used to help construct a network diagram (see Unit 38).

This is calculated by applying the formula:

$$\text{Basic time} = \text{observed time} \times \frac{\text{observed rating}}{\text{normal/standard rating} \ (100)}$$

Example 1
Observed time $\qquad$ = 180 minutes
Observed rating $\qquad$ = 125
Normal standard rating = 100

$$\text{Basic time} = 180 \times \frac{125}{100} = 225 \text{ minutes}$$

You will notice that the basic time for the job is longer than the actual observed time. This is because of the observed rating that has been applied. An observed rating of 125 suggests that the employee observed was working very quickly and therefore above the average. To gain a realistic time for the job, it is important to take into consideration the experience and ability of an employee.

Examiner's voice

Selecting the 'right' observed rating is essential. A high rating will lengthen the basic time when compared to the observed time, and a low observed rating will shorten the observed time. This is essential if an appropriate time is to be set for a job.

Example 2

Observed rating   = 310 minutes
Observed rating   = 50
Normal/standard rating = 100

Basic time = $310 \times \dfrac{50}{100}$ = 160 minutes

In this example, the observed employee was very slow and therefore received a low rating of 50. As a consequence, the basic time is shorter than the observed time, to compensate for the very slow performance. It would be wrong and expensive to set the time for the job based on the speed of the employee in this example.

To help fix a rating for the observed performance, the British Standards Institute (BSI) has produced a series of guidelines, describing and rating the different types of performances (see Table 48.2).

The results of the two observations are added together and an average is then taken:

Basic time from example 1   225 minutes
                                    plus
Basic time from example 2   160 minutes

$$= \frac{385 \text{ minutes}}{2}$$
$$= 192.5 \text{ minutes}$$

This final figure is used as the basic time for the job. It is faster than the novice employee and slower than the experienced employee, and is therefore a fairer time in which the job has to be completed.

In order to gain the 'right' time for a task, it is important to collect accurate information. The following factors need to be considered:

BSI rating score	Description of rating
125	Very fast, above-average worker performance.
100	Standard performance, good pace attained by a skilled and motivated average worker. Quality of work is maintained.
75	Normal performance, steady pace of unmotivated supervised worker.
50	Very slow, showing no interest in task performed.

Table 48.2

- the number of times in which a job is observed
- when the job is observed
- the person observed undertaking the job
- what is observed.

Examiner's voice

There is no 'right' number of observations that have to be undertaken or a 'right' number of employees that need to be observed. It is important that the numbers reflect the employees involved and for the basic time calculated to be reliable. Care needs to be taken to ensure that the observer is not 'duped' by an experienced worker.

Standard time

Once the basic time has been calculated, additions to this time need to be made if an accurate time is to be used. People need breaks, and do not perform at the same pace throughout the day. Consequently, allowances are made for rests, visits to the toilet and other contingencies. Once these additions to the basic time have been made, a standard time is achieved.

Therefore, to calculate standard time:

Standard time = basic time + additions for 'breaks'

Your Turn

Questions Time allowed 35 minutes

1. State the two major elements of work study.
   (2 marks)

2. Explain the term 'ergonomics'. (4 marks)

3. Calculate the basic time form the following information. Show your working! (5 marks)

Employee	Observed time (minutes)	Observed rating	Normal rating (100)	Basic time
Richard	140	75	100	
Holly	95	100	100	
Sanjeev	80	125	100	
Nicki	130	50	100	

4. Analyse the factors to be considered when undertaking observations in order to calculate a basic time. (9 marks)

5. Using the table above, calculate the standard time for Sanjeev if allowances of 15 minutes are made. (3 marks)

(23 marks)

Task

Take an everyday task such as making a cup of tea. Using the symbols in Table 48.1, plot the task, its movements, storage and delays and inspections.

Once you have done this, attempt to apply a work measurement approach to improving how the task is done.

As an alternative to making a cup of tea, try packing a box with ring binders, sealing it with sellotape and writing an address label.

You can also try to decide what observed rating you would give to the different students in your group who attempt the task.

RESEARCH AND DEVELOPMENT

What is research and development?

Research and development is essential for many businesses, particularly those in a highly competitive or technological market. Keeping up with or being ahead of the competition is vital if a business is to survive. Any business involved with mobile phones, cameras, airplanes or medical drugs will spend significant sums of money on research and development, in an attempt to beat the competition within the market.

However, there are problems with spending such sums of money. There are no guarantees of success; the money spent may not yield any profits and is therefore an addition to costs without any returns.

Furthermore, a business may spend a significant amount of money on research that yields a breakthrough in technological progress and gives the business an edge on its competitors; a competing business may copy the idea without having spent the same amount of money on research and therefore gain success without huge costs. (These are sometimes referred to as 'me too' products.) Patents provide an opportunity to protect the latest innovation that the business has developed.

The importance of research and development has grown for many businesses as a consequence of increasing globalisation. Many markets are truly international and therefore open to other competitors, many with a significant advantage in terms of labour costs (this is true of some of the Eastern bloc economies and China). Consequently, one obvious way to remain competitive is to ensure that sufficient amounts of money are spent on research and development to gain in terms of technological advancement.

In simplistic terms, research and development is a process that enables the creation of new or improved products to meet the needs of its consumers. Research and development:

- is necessary to launch new products successfully, to ensure that they meet customers' needs.
- examines how to improve the production process and its efficiency.
- explores alternative materials to produce the goods.
- aims to reduce the amount of waste generated in the production process.

These actions will help a business to maintain or gain a competitive advantage. Innovation can allow the business to charge a premium price as a reward for its high costs.

Problems related to research and development

The cost

Research and development can be very expensive. The cost depends upon the nature of the product. Pharmaceutical companies may spend millions of pounds on research, and gain nothing.

Risk

There is no guarantee of success, as research does not necessarily yield effective results. Consequently, the money spent will be a cost without any revenue to cover such costs. This often explains the high prices of certain products.

Copying from other businesses

Even if the research and development is successful, there is a danger of other companies copying any new initiatives. Although such research can be protected, patents do not last forever. Furthermore, companies that copy will not have incurred the same research and development costs, and could therefore charge less for their product.

Limited protection of new ideas

Patents do not cover all aspects of new products. Also, nothing can prevent a copy being made if no patents have been applied for. There are additional problems of ensuring that companies do not copy, as it can be time-consuming and expensive to prove that a copy has been made.

Coping with such rapid changes in technology

For certain industries, the rate of change is significant. The mobile phone industry is a good example. The technological rate of progress is so fast that without research and development, a business could fall out of the market very quickly if it failed to keep pace with the level of changes being made.

Constant changes may annoy consumers

Again, the mobile phone provides a good example. Although some consumers crave for the latest model, others are happy with the type and model they have, and become annoyed if their next phone operates in a totally different way. This is particularly true for older consumers.

It may also be annoying to the consumer if replacement parts for old models are no longer available because of new models. In this case, consumers may feel they are being forced to update their mobile phones unnecessarily.

Unemployment

Constant improvements because of research and development have meant in many cases a shift from labour-intensive processes to capital-intensive processes. This can have a significant effect on the level of employment, to which trade unions object.

Technological changes

Technological advancement in communications as a result of research and development has led to many changes in the working practices of employees. The workplace has been altered by hot-desking, and video and telephone conferencing, and more people are now able to work from home. Although this may have several advantages for both the employer (costs) and the employee (convenience and costs), there are disadvantages in terms of isolation and in the lack of team-building.

The process for research and development

Some businesses spend a huge amount of money on research and development. Car manufacturer Ford announced in July 2006 that it would be spending over £1 billion on UK research in an attempt to cut carbon emissions. On average, Ford spends £330 in the UK on research and development.

Before a product is produced, great care is given to several key aspects.

Market research

The business needs to ensure that the product will be something which the consumer will want to buy. It is essential to undertake market research to ensure that a market-orientated approach is adopted. There are very few types of product which are product-orientated, where market research is not undertaken.

Research into market trends is important. Fashions and consumer lifestyles change, and it is essential for a business to be aware of such trends. If the business is a pioneer, it may wish to try to influence or even set such trends! How easy this is to achieve will depends on many factors, including the size of the business, its financial status and the skill of the research and development department.

Research may also take place within the business to assess its capability to produce any new product. This will involve a consideration of the resources required to make the new product, both in terms of capital equipment and the materials to be used.

Brainstorming

Whether this takes place before or after any initial research will vary, according to the type of business and the products involved. However, morphological studies can generate ideas very quickly.

> ## Key Term
>
> **Morphological study**: a method generates a lot of ideas very quickly and therefore more cheaply.

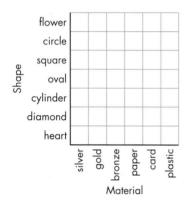

Figure 49.1 Morphological study for decorations, using two axes/grids

Figure 49.1 shows simply how morphological studies can be used so that an idea can quickly be developed with a wide range of alternatives. In this example the matrix shown has only two axes or grids. One represents the shape of the decoration, and the other the material to be used. By having the two grids, the number of ideas or options is quickly multiplied.

If additional axes or grids are added, the number of ideas or options generated is even greater. In Figure 49.2, the number of ideas generated is 125.

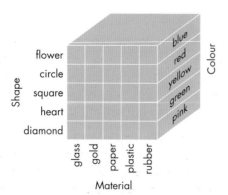

Figure 49.2 Morphological study for decorations, with additional grid

When designers are developing a new product, consideration will be given to three key aspects. This involves the process of value analysis.

Value analysis

There are three aspects to value analysis:

- function
- cost
- aesthetics.

Function

The nature of the product will determine its task. It is essential that a lawnmower is capable of cutting the grass, as this is its main function. A kettle needs to boil water, a mobile phone needs to be capable of making and receiving calls and texts, and a car needs to be able to move and carry people! For many products the functional aspect is taken for granted by the consumer, but at the research and development stage, this is of paramount importance, simply because if it does not fulfil its function, the item will be useless.

Cost

The significance of the cost will vary depending on the nature of the product and the market in which it is to be sold. Nevertheless, keeping down costs for any product allows the business to be competitive and/or more profitable. It can also improve how the product is perceived; being good value for money may be attractive to the customer.

It is often a challenge to guarantee the functional element of the product without incurring high costs. Different materials can be considered, ensuring that they do not reduce the functional ability of the product.

Aesthetics

This is where the looks of the product become important. For some goods, the look is of little or no consequence. The water bottle for spraying a car windscreen is hidden under the bonnet of the car, therefore its appearance is not important. However, the shape and style of the car as a whole is important, as this influences many potential consumers.

Clothes are a strong example of when the aesthetics of the product are probably the most important aspect. Ensuring that the product (and its packaging) appears attractive is vital for many goods.

The difficulty for the research and design department is how to balance the three aspects of the value analysis.

All three aspects should be covered, but the nature of the product will determine which aspect is prioritised.

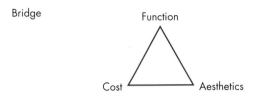

Figure 49.3 Function is the most important aspect

Figure 49.3 shows that in it simplest form, the triangle can be used to prioritise the three aspects.

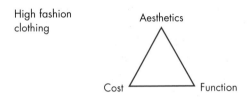

Figure 49.4 Aesthetics is the main aspect

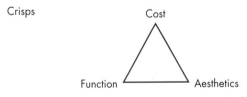

Figure 49.5 Costs are important for this product

For the products shown in Figures 49.3, 49.4 and 49.5, a different aspect of value analysis takes priority. In Figure 49.3, the product is a bridge, which must be able to support the weight of the vehicles that are using it to cross the river (function). Regardless of its costs and aesthetics, if it does not withstand the loads upon it, it will cease to function.

However, in Figure 49.4 the main priority switches to the aesthetics, as the look of the product is highly significant. Figure 49.5 is also different. Because the product is in a highly competitive mass-market and is also a low value product, the main priority is to produce the product at its lowest costs. The functional qualities are not completely ignored, but cost is a high priority.

There are some products where it is hard to suggest which aspect of the value analysis triangle takes priority. Using a car as an example, the price and therefore its costs are very important, especially as most cars are sold in a highly competitive market. However, the various components of the car will have different priorities attached to them regarding costs, function and

aesthetics. The engine has to function, with costs being a consideration, but aesthetics as a low priority. The overall shape of the car must consider aesthetics, be conscious of costs and also emphasise function, particularly with aerodynamics affecting its performance and petrol consumption. Finally, hub caps covering the wheels are an aesthetic touch, with some cost consideration but little functional qualities.

The above example shows that the research and development process is not straightforward, and the complexity will vary according to the product. Cutting costs may affect the quality and the reliability of its functional qualities. Spending too much on either functional aspects or the aesthetics may affect the ability of the marketing department to sell the product.

Factors affecting the level of research and development

The level of competition in the market

If the product in question is in a highly competitive market, it is more likely that research and development expenditure will be higher. A competitive advantage may be gained, but any additional research and development expenditure may affect the costs of the business. Increases in costs may affect the level of pricing (and therefore the product's competitiveness) and also the profit margins, which may already be tight in a competitive market.

International markets can be highly competitive, in which case additional research and development could be essential to attract the customer faced with so much choice.

The product

The more sophisticated the product in terms of technology, the more likely that research and development will be needed to keep up with technological developments.

The pace of technological development within the telecommunications industry is very fast. Research and development expenditure within the pharmaceutical industry, particularly for cancer drugs, has grown immensely.

The external environment

Following the vast increase in the cost of oil in 2008 (nearly $150 per barrel), the car industry responded with further research and development into better fuel consumption. There was also additional research and development expenditure to lower carbon emissions, following the government's decision to introduce a progressive road fund licence tax based on emissions.

The state of the economy

When the economy is in recession, it is more likely that businesses will undertake cutbacks. One such cutback is research and development expenditure.

Responding to a particular problem

Coca-Cola bottle suppliers were faced with the problem of distributing large bottles to be filled at different plants. They quickly worked on the problem to reduce costs, as distributing empty one- and two-litre bottles was expensive.

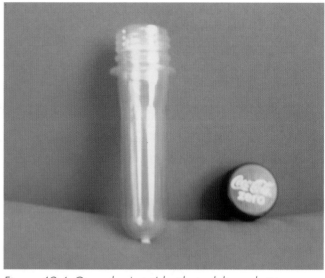

Figure 49.6 Once the 'mini' bottle is delivered, it is 'blown-up' to its full size, ready to be filled.

Further Sources

www.daiichi-Sankyo(pharmaceuticals)

Your Turn

Questions Time allowed 15 minutes

1. Drawing a value analysis triangle, suggest the order of priority for the following products.

   A. textbooks   **B.** cosmetics   **C.** laptop

   Justify your answers.   (9 marks)

2. List the major problems facing a research and development department.   (4 marks)

   Why is a morphological study a cost-effective way to generate many ideas?   (4 marks)

   (17 marks)

Case Study Time allowed 45 minutes

The Plastic Bag Company (PBC)

The environmental lobby has made huge progress in bringing to the public's attention the damaging effects of plastic bags. The main culprits in terms of environmental damage are those distributed by supermarkets. Until 2008, little concern had been expressed by the supermarkets as to the consequences of millions of bags being used everyday.

However, in 2008, Marks & Spencer announced that it would be charging 5p for its plastic bags in all of its food stores. During a trial in the southwest of England, there was a 70% fall in the demand for plastic bags.

This approach was followed by the Chancellor of the Exchequer, Alastair Darling MP, who suggested that the government may introduce charges for plastic bags in 2009.

In spite of the estimated 13 billion plastic bags that are used by customers every year in UK supermarkets, no real alternative has been proposed. Different attempts have been made by supermarkets to encourage its customers to use fewer of these bags, such as reusing sturdier canvas bags.

The managing director of PBC was concerned about the steps being taken by the supermarkets. One of the major supermarkets was PBC's major customer, so any initiative that reduced the demand for the plastic bag would have serious consequences.

At the recent board meeting, it was agreed that additional money should be spent on research and development. An attempt would be made to come up with an alternative bag that would fit the purpose, and at the same time satisfy the environmental issues.

It was decided to concentrate on finding an alternative to the plastic bag, rather than finding alternative uses for its product. This was because it was the plastic bag that was seen as the environmental issue; no change of use could alter this.

1. Explain why research and development may involve a high degree of risk. (4 marks)

2. Analyse the implications for PBC if it lost significant sales as a result of falling demand from the supermarket. (9 marks)

3. Evaluate the benefits of using value analysis as a process to help PCB find an alternative to its existing plastic bags. (19 marks)

(32 marks)

STRATEGIC MANAGEMENT

50 Unit

OBJECTIVES

Introduction

This compulsory module is mainly a synoptic paper. Although there are new topics and concepts to be explored, it is assumed that your work from the AS modules will be revisited.

The key word is strategy. This is an overview; it is a management perspective and considers both the long-term and short-term consequences for any decisions.

Deciding the most appropriate strategy, implementing the chosen strategy and being aware of the likely consequences when implementing such strategies, are all crucial factors to be considered in your answers to the questions in this module.

To gain a high mark, you will need to develop an integrated approach (knowing how the different functions of the business affect each other). When forming your answers, you should consider the long-term objectives of the business, the stakeholders, the environment in which the business operates and the resources available to the business.

Most business organisations create objectives for the business to meet. These may be for the short or long term, and may be easy or difficult to achieve. The larger

the organisation, the more complex the setting and achieving of objectives will be. The communication of ideas and targets to large numbers of people by several managers makes the whole process of setting objectives and formulating strategy much more difficult. As the number of people who are involved increases, so does the likelihood of conflict between those involved, because of differences in ideas and expectations. In addition, different stakeholder objectives make it more difficult to ensure that all parties are satisfied by a particular course of action.

Mission statements

The mission statement sets out the purpose of the business to all its employers, shareholders and any other interested stakeholders. The mission statement usually includes information about the values and ethos of the business, as well as the aims and objectives. The increased importance of environmental awareness, fair trading and non-discriminatory practices in employment has also encouraged firms to include mention of these issues in their mission statements.

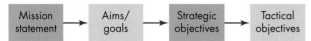

Figure 50.1 *A company's mission statements, goals and objectives*

> The following statements have been taken from UK company mission statements:
>
> 'Continually increasing value for customers to earn their lifetime loyalty.'
>
> Tesco
>
> 'To creatively balance the financial and human needs of our stakeholders. To passionately campaign for the protection of the environment and human and civil rights and against animal testing within the cosmetics and toiletries industry.'
>
> The Body Shop
>
> 'Cadbury's means quality'
>
> Cadbury's

Using the mission statement

The purpose of the mission statement is to make everyone associated with the business aware of its aims and objectives, and the purpose of its existence. The mission statement usually makes reference to those stakeholders that the business feels to be important in its operations. Increasingly, businesses refer to their employees, the community and the environment, as well as shareholders or owners of the business.

However, a mission statement is not an end in itself. Having formulated the statement, the business must then ensure that it has an impact on all aspects of its operations, from day-to-day management to employment practices; from the identity and logos used to the advertising policies.

Aims and objectives

Once the business has established its mission statement, it needs to determine how it will achieve the aims and objectives. Many businesses now use objectives as a way of managing the business at all levels, so that policy can be directed towards a particular goal.

The objectives of any business will depend on a number of different factors, including the following:

- the age of the business
- the size of the business
- the market in which the business is trading
- whether the business is a public or private company with shareholders, or a sole trader or partnership
- the wishes and priorities of the owner or board of directors.

Strategic objectives

Any business is likely to have one or more of the following objectives:

- survival
- profitability
- growth
- market share.

> ### Aims/goals
>
> Aims or goals are more specific than a mission statement, but they are sometimes confusingly used as alternative terms for the main objectives of a business. The principal aims of most businesses includes:
>
> - **survival.** For a new business, the most important aim is survival, especially if the business is trying to compete with well-established companies.
>
> - **breaking even.** It is not likely that a business will be profitable straight away. There are many costs to cover, especially those of the premises and all the fixtures (fixed costs or overheads). Therefore, it is more realistic to set a target of breaking even within a given time period.
>
> - **share of the market/growth.** Much depends on the type of business and the market in which it operates. Capturing a larger share of the market not only increases sales with all the benefits that follow, but also puts the business in a position from which it can try to dominate the market.
>
> - **profit.** This is a longer-term goal than survival. The ability to make a profit depends on the type of products or services offered by the business and the amount of competition in the marketplace.

The achievement of these strategic objectives will require a number of tactical objectives to be put in place.

> ### Key Term
>
> **Strategic objective:** an objective for the whole business for the long term, determined by senior management directors.

Key Term

Tactical objective: an objective set for a department or group of people. It is implemented at departmental level by middle management and is a short-term objective. Tactical objectives are employed in achieving strategic objectives.

Survival

In its early years, a new business will need time to establish itself in the market and to start to become profitable. Very few businesses are successful from the outset, and most will need to recoup the outlays like shop-fitting, advertising or purchasing stock they made before and during the setting-up period.

Many businesses will fail at this stage of the development, despite having a good idea or product and a ready market for entry. The reasons for failure at this stage are numerous but the most common one is because of inadequate cashflow to meet commitments. Setting realistic aims at the outset and adhering to them are important strategic objectives for the new business (see Chapter 74 in AS Business Studies, second edition, Mottershead, Challoner and Grant (2008)). If the business does survive, it can then move on to the next stage of profitability.

Profit

The amount of profit which the business aims to achieve will depend very much on the wishes of senior management and the shareholders. Some sole traders will make a combination of profit, workload and quality of life their strategic objective, particularly as the business becomes established. For larger businesses, the choice of financial targets may have to be made with reference to shareholder objectives and financial institution requirements (see Unit 23).

Growth and market share

Having become profitable, the business will then wish to establish a competitive advantage over its rivals. This will usually involve a strategy of growth into areas of the market where this advantage can be achieved. This could mean expanding into existing markets, moving into new product ranges, finding new markets or diversifying. All this is explained in Ansoff's Matrix which lays out the options available to a business that wishes to grow (see Unit 7).

Other strategic objectives

As part of the main objectives, the business may also have other aims to satisfy particular stakeholders in the firm. These could be any or all of the following:

- shareholder returns, either in terms of earnings per share or return on capital employed
- market leadership and status, either within the business or among shareholders
- diversification to spread risk and access new areas of the market
- concentration on a core activity rather than trying to achieve in a number of different markets
- green or ethical considerations such as reducing carbon emissions.

Stakeholder objectives

Traditionally, objectives for businesses were often directed at achieving the maximum return for shareholders, as the owners the organisation. Shareholders could make demands and the managers would have had to respond to them. For example, businesses like Royal Doulton had to meet profitability targets to satisfy corporate shareholders in the business, at a time when their objectives should have been focused on their product range and their competitors in the emerging economies of the Far East.

It is now increasingly the case that managers are responding to the needs of a range of stakeholders, such as customers, employees, suppliers, the community and the environment, in the belief that this will give a long-term advantage to the business. For example, environmental pressures are forcing businesses to respond to stakeholder groups for information about their sustainable business practices. Customers are particularly important because they may be represented in all of the major stakeholder groups as employees, shareholders or members of the local community. According to Geoff Lane:

'Companies will always have their problems, but they're more likely to get the benefit of the doubt if they're seen to be transparent.'

(*The Times*, 12 October 2007)

If the business treats its employees well, responding to their needs and improving their experience of work, the result is likely to be a better motivated workforce and a more successful business. For example, if a business such as Reuters is willing to operate family-friendly policies for employees with young children, it may experience lower staff turnover, and higher morale and commitment, and the retention of expertise.

A business which treats its suppliers well may be rewarded with greater cooperation and reliability, together with a willingness to help if there is a problem (such as an immediate demand for delivery from a valued customer). Many large businesses are very slow to make payments to their suppliers; this action may result in a poor relationship between the customer and supplier.

The local community may be vital in either ensuring the success of a business or hindering its progress. Supermarket giant Tesco has had a very aggressive policy towards local competition when setting up stores in new areas. As a consequence, many communities now lobby councils to try to prevent planning permission being granted to new Tesco stores.

Care for the environment and an understanding of our impact on the world and its resources is becoming an increasingly important issue for consumers in the developed world. Businesses cannot afford to ignore this; to do so is to run the risk of bad publicity. Demands made by consumers and the press for a reduction in the issue of plastic bags in supermarkets forced a change of policy throughout the retail industry in 2008.

(See Unit 67 for information on all these issues.)

Using stakeholder objectives

Businesses might find it difficult to meet the needs of both its shareholders and its other main stakeholders. The shareholder is likely to feel that they are part-owners of the business, and that they are risking their money by investing in it. They will expect to see a return for the investment. On the other hand, neglecting the other stakeholders may result in the company being less successful in the long term.

Our expectations of business change with society. In the past it was possible for firms to concentrate on returning profit for their shareholders, almost to the exclusion of everything else. Businesses could still do this, but they run the risk of alienating their workers, customers, suppliers and the wider community. In the days of rapid communication and media interest, this is likely to result in bad publicity and falling sales. The demands made of managers in balancing these different expectations are increasingly complex and difficult.

Areas of stakeholder conflict include the following:

- The need to balance a demand for profit from the shareholders with ethical practices in trading. An example here would be the lending policies of some financial institutions in the period before the 'credit crunch' of 2008.
- The requirement to treat workers well in terms of payment needs to be balanced with the demands of customers for low prices. Companies such as Gap

and Primark have received bad publicity because of their employment policies in developing countries.
- The need to consider the health and safety of customers alongside low costs of production.

Risk and reward

The attitude, ethics and culture of a business will all have an influence on the contents of its mission statement and its behaviour in the market. The willingness of the managers or owners to take risks will also be affected by these factors, together with the nature of the market in which the firm operates. It is generally the case that the higher the risk that a business takes, the higher the reward will be if the business is successful. This situation can be seen in the research and development undertaken by the major drug companies: it will be very costly in terms of time and money, and very little of it is likely to yield positive results in terms of new treatments. The consequence of this risk is that, when a new drug is found to be effective in treating a particular condition or illness, its initial price is very high. This situation often causes an outcry in the media, especially if the drug is too expensive to be prescribed by the NHS. Patients and their families will understandably feel upset in these circumstances, particularly if a life-threatening condition is involved. Although it may seem that the drug companies are making huge profits at the expense of ill people, the reality is likely to be that they are taking rewards for the huge risks they have taken.

In industries like micro-electronics, where the product and the demand change constantly, the business has to be prepared to take risks in order to survive. Managers know that there will be occasions when new products fail, so occasional failure has to be associated with a 'no blame' culture for employees. Failure in this type of business will be seen as a necessary risk of success.

In other businesses, the culture will be one of safety and risk-aversion, in which the result of failure will be to attach blame. Employees will be reluctant to take risks. A business that is risk-averse is unlikely to undertake new and untested projects, and their ability to earn profit will be limited.

Further Sources

www.missionstatements.co.uk
www.bized.co.uk
www.ey.com: the top ten business risks
www.thetimes100.co.uk

Questions Time allowed one hour

1. Use the internet to find the websites of two well-known companies. Find their mission statement and compare the differences in their objectives.
(5 marks)

2. Describe two factors that the mission statement tells you about the operations of this business.
(6 marks)

3. From the information on the company's website, analyse the culture of this business in terms of its willingness to take risks and its approach to stakeholders.
(9 marks)

4. Explain the differences between strategic and tactical objectives.
(4 marks)

(24 marks)

Case study Time allowed 1 hour

Petals and Pastries

Sophie James launched 'Petals and Pastries' in 2005 in a small market town in Shropshire when her youngest child started school. As a single parent she knew she was taking a risk, particularly as she had always worked for others previously rather than being a sole trader. Sophie is a trained florist, but she had always been a good cook, and her artistic training meant that she was also a very talented cake decorator.

Sophie's initial idea for the business was for it to operate mainly in the wedding market, providing a service for flowers and wedding cakes. However, the nature of the business has gradually changed over time. Sophie now sells cut flowers from the unit she rents on a trading estate, as well as delivering bouquets and arrangements within a ten-mile radius. Most of the business comes from recommendation and from a small advert in a glossy monthly magazine.

When Sophie was planning the business, she wrote a mission statement for herself, the bank and the relatives who were lending her money. She knew what she wanted the culture of the business to be,

both for herself and for various other stakeholders. Her mission statement was as follows:

Petals and Pastries will:

- provide an outstanding service to our customers regardless of the size of the order.
- use ethically produced and organic flowers wherever possible.
- produce cakes that contain no additives and the best possible ingredients.
- provide a family friendly working environment for our employees.

Although Sophie started out working by herself, she very quickly found that she needed to employ other staff. She realised that the best alternative would be to offer part-time work to mothers with young children, like herself. The demand for her flowers and cakes was rarely urgent, so she could be fairly flexible with employees as far as hours were concerned.

The decision to sell cut flowers to the public was a risk for Sophie. It meant that she had to have flowers in stock at all times to meet demand (unlike previously), and that there was a much greater risk of waste from this part of the operation. Nevertheless she now realises that the gamble has paid off. Many of the customers who come to her to buy flowers have returned for 'special event' flowers or cakes, or have recommended her to friends.

Sophie is confident that she will soon have repaid all her start-up loans and that the business will be yielding a substantial profit. She now needs to decide whether to be satisfied with this or to risk expansion into a different area.

1. What does the extract of Sophie's mission statement tell you about the nature of her business?
(6 marks)

2. Evaluate the benefits that have resulted from Sophie's 'stakeholder objectives' approach to running the business.
(15 marks)

3. Analyse the conflict of objectives that might occur if Sophie decides to expand.
(15 marks)

(36 marks)

STRATEGIC PLANNING

Planning is an important tool in ensuring the future success of a business. Most of the tools available to the business to enable it to plan effectively will have been covered in the AS courses or as part of the A2 optional module. You need to be able to use tools like decision trees, critical path analysis and investment appraisal in any discussion about strategic planning.

Successful businesses need to plan for the future in all sorts of ways, and they need to ensure that the objectives that have been set for the future of the business fit with planning. They need to consider new products, changes in their markets, cashflow and investment decisions in order to remain competitive. Managers may need to take risks in order to maintain or increase profits; effective planning will help to minimise these risks and ensure that the business knows clearly what its future course of action will be. Businesses that refuse to plan ahead are likely to find that they are overtaken by competitors and that profits are affected.

Developing a strategy

In order to formulate a strategic plan, it is necessary to collect information on many aspects of the business. This will involve an internal and external audit of the business, which should be executed on a regular basis. The internal audit looks at the strengths and weaknesses of the business, and the external audit looks at the opportunities and threats in the trading environment of the business.

Internal audit

An internal audit allows a business to assess its strengths and weaknesses in relation to its competitors across the whole of the business. Many businesses employ external

Figure 51.1 An internal audit

organisations to complete these surveys, although it is possible for management to do them in for their own departments. The purpose of the audit is to provide accurate information about each particular department, and it is therefore best to use accounting or statistical data wherever this is possible. For example, the human resources department could provide figures for absenteeism and turnover, while the marketing department looked at market share and advertising elasticity of demand. In each case, the business should be comparing itself with its major competitors to see where it has strengths and weaknesses.

External audit

The external audit looks at the opportunities open to the business and the threats which it faces in its external environment. All businesses operate in a constantly changing environment. The business needs to be aware of these changes, and must then assess the extent and implications of them on future success. Figure 51.2 shows the range of external factors which might affect a business. Factors included in the external audit are referred to by a variety of different acronyms, but the main ones are included in a PEST analysis, standing for political,

Figure 51.2 An external audit

economic, social and technological factors. PEST analysis now also covers a variety of other issues.

Volkswagen and the car industry

Volkswagen has built up an image of quality and reliability for its cars, which is reflected across the whole range. This has been done in response to competition and customer demands. In recent years, VW has managed to transfer this image to its Eastern bloc brand, Skoda. The business acquired this make of car, and changed it from a car renowned for unreliability into one which is now still inexpensive, but produced with a commitment to quality in the factory in the Czech Republic.

A car manufacturer might have to respond to any of the factors shown in Figure 51.2 at any particular time. In recent years, safety and carbon emissions have become increasingly important issues for the consumer when purchasing a new car, and manufacturers have had to address these consumer concerns in their specifications for new models. The environmental effects of transport are now at the centre of concerns about climate change across the globe; no car manufacturer can afford to ignore these issues if they are to succeed. In 2008, the UK government showed a new determination to tackle the problem of car emissions with legislation to make greater variations in road fund tax, dependent on the emission level of car engines.

Political

The actions of government can have a major impact on the way in which a business operates (see Unit 64). Legislation on employment, health and safety, competition and taxation are all examples of government policies that have an impact on employers and businesses. In addition, the government's influence is now moving into new areas of the business environment such as environmental and ethical issues.

Economic

The economy and government economic policy are key areas of concern for all businesses, because of the impact which they have on consumer demand (see Unit 60). Inflation, interest rates, the value of the currency, unemployment and the economic cycle will play their part in influencing the success of the business and in determining its actions. For example, car dealers may need to offer low-cost finance terms or lengthened periods of repayment in order to attract new customers at times when interest rates are high.

Social

The characteristics of the population are important factors for business demand. Changes in the distribution or spending habits of consumers are constantly taking place, making it vital that businesses are aware of these changes and act accordingly (see Unit 65). For example, an increase in the number of retired people, many of whom have higher disposable incomes and are physically active, has produced a large and growing demand for specialist holidays. This relatively new sector of the market is referred to as the 'grey economy'. Similarly, growth in the number of students in the UK has led to increased demand for rented accommodation in university cities.

Technological

Changes in technology offer businesses new opportunities, but also create new risks (see Unit 65). A successful business must be ready to implement new procedures and train staff in their use. They also need to recognise situations where existing processes and machinery have become obsolete. The music recording industry has moved from tapes, through compact discs and on to internet downloads with increasing rapidity.

Successful and innovative businesses will already be preparing for the next product in such a cycle. For example, the Apple business is continually updating the specification of the ipod and the Apple phone, in order to generate new demand from customers to have the latest 'must-have' equipment.

Competition

The extent of the competition and the threat which it poses will have a considerable impact on the success of the business. It might be necessary to change the price or product range in response to competition; e.g. the arrival of a 'Sainsbury's local' store will have an impact on local shops and newsagents.

Culture

Businesses need to take account of the characteristics of the local population and their shopping habits. Food stores in Indian, Chinese or Pakistani neighbourhoods often do not sell dairy products because they do not form part of their customers' diet.

Ethics

Businesses must be aware of the demand for ethical trading and its effect on customer demand (see Unit 67). Television coverage of chicken farming in the UK by well-known presenters, like Jamie Oliver, has led to an increase in demand for free-range chicken in supermarkets.

Pressure groups

Pressure groups can exert pressure on businesses. Animal welfare organisations have put pressure on shops to sell meat products that are produced in humane conditions.

Environment

Environmental factors are becoming increasingly important. The high price of domestic fuel and an increase in awareness of global warming have led to a rapid rise in the demand for low-energy light bulbs and a consequent fall in their price.

In terms of formulating strategy, SWOT is only one of the tools that the business can use, and it is important not to use a SWOT analysis in isolation from all the other information which a business might gather. A SWOT analysis only gives part of the picture, and it should be viewed alongside information such as market research, ratio analysis and other financial data, sales figures and government economic statistics. For a business considering growth, Ansoff's Matrix could also be another useful tool to use with a SWOT analysis, because it would help the business to consider the best direction for changes to achieve growth (see Unit 7).

It is also important to remember that a SWOT analysis is not an end in itself. It is something for the business to use in determining objectives and strategy. For example, the knowledge that new competition is entering the market might lead a business to look at different opportunities in its environment that might help it to survive and grow. It is also vital to remember that the usefulness of all of this planning will depend on the information being gathered in a way that is unbiased and objective. To achieve this, it might sometimes be necessary for the business to use an outside agency.

Using the information

Once the audits are complete, the business needs to put the information into a summarised format. The usual way of presenting this sort of information is in a SWOT analysis to show the strengths, weaknesses, opportunities and threats for the business (see Unit 7).

Further Sources

www.iia.org.uk
www.dfid.gov.uk
www.businessballs.com
www.businesslink.gov.uk
www.trainingzone.co.uk

Your Turn

Case Study

co₂balance

co$_2$balance is one of the major carbon offsetting companies in the UK. The business recognises that people's actions have an impact on the local, regional, national and global environment. They offer businesses and individuals the opportunity to reduce the climate impact of their activities through a range of projects to reduce the world's carbon emissions. Some of these projects are in the UK, but others are overseas.

An example of one of these projects is the company's work with groups in East Africa to replace open fires for cooking with solar ovens. The ovens do require some fuel but are 75% more efficient than open fires. The result of their use is that less greenhouse gas is produced, fewer trees are chopped down and the environment for the population is healthier and safer.

(Source co$_2$balance website)

Group activity

Working in groups, use the co2balance website to prepare an external audit to be presented to its shareholders. If you make assumptions about the business, you should clearly state what these are. Write up your audit as a formal report.

Questions Time allowed 40 minutes

1. Give two uses and two limitations of SWOT analysis.

(4 marks)

2. Evaluate the ways in which a business like Waterstone's, the booksellers, might make use of a PEST analysis to help in its strategic planning.

(16 marks)

(20 marks)

STAKEHOLDER OBJECTIVES AND STRATEGIC MANAGEMENT

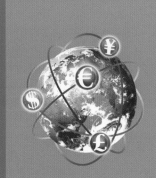

A stakeholder is a person or party that has an interest (i.e. a 'stake') in the success of a business. Stakeholders want to see a business succeed because they will benefit from its success. It was shown at AS level that the objectives of stakeholders can be used to create a useful framework to help analyse the operation of a business. The same framework can be developed at A2 level to analyse the setting of a business's objectives and also the strategy it develops to reach them.

The business/stakeholder relationship is extremely important and cuts both ways; the business affects the stakeholders, and the stakeholders affect the business.

The sorts of issues for consideration are the extent to which the stakeholders regard the business as a success, how the different stakeholder groups might view change, which stakeholders are the most important, and how the objectives of the different stakeholder groups might affect the strategic decisions of the business.

Examiner's voice

It is important that you understand the relationship and the interaction between a business and its stakeholders. You need to be able to identify what each stakeholder wants from the business, and also evaluate the influence which each stakeholder can bring to bear on the business's strategic decision-making.

Key Term

Stakeholder: a person or party with an interest in the success of a business.

Stakeholder objectives

In theory, all stakeholders will benefit from a business's success, but in reality they may not. Furthermore even if all stakeholders *do* benefit, they may not do so equally. It is very important to recognise the potential conflicts between the objectives of the different stakeholder groups. In order to analyse why, it is necessary to recall the objectives of each stakeholder in the business.

To these stakeholders should be added 'the government'. The government is not a direct stakeholder in the same way as the others, but nevertheless it has an interest in any business's success. This is because if more people are employed as a result of a business's activities, the government will pay out less social security benefits and receive increased tax revenue from the business and its employees.

Examiner's voice

There is some debate as to whether a competitor is actually a stakeholder or not. It is true that a competitor has 'an interest' in a rival business, but it is unlikely that they have an interest in (i.e. want to see) it succeeding. It would presumably rather see it fail and succeed themselves! You will not be penalised for adopting either point of view, as long as you make clear how you view 'a stakeholder'.

These stakeholder objectives have to be addressed by a business, for these reasons:

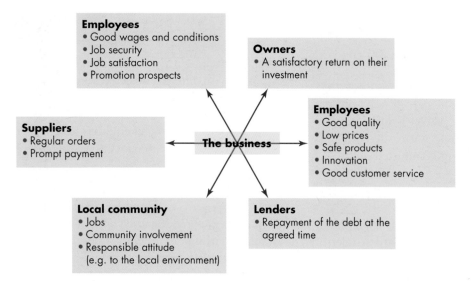

Figure 52.1 A summary of a business's stakeholders and their objectives

- **Employees** who feel valued will be more productive, be less resistant to change and less likely to leave. It should be noted that there are different types of employee. Directors and managers are certainly 'employees' but may have different objectives to 'front-line' workers. They may be expecting a greater element of career progression.
- **Customers** who do not feel exploited and like the standard of products and service will generate repeat custom.
- **Suppliers** who are treated as true stakeholders rather than 'suppliers' are more likely to be loyal and committed because they have 'a stake' in the business. This has important implications for the short term (i.e. needing a quick delivery) and also for the successful implementation of strategy.
- **Owners** will want a return that they feel is satisfactory. If the business is a company, shareholders will expect (at least) the sort of dividend that investors in a similar business have received. They will also be expecting a rise in the share price over time. If these are not forthcoming, they will sell their shares. This will drive the share price down and could leave the business open to a takeover.
- **The local community**, while not a single coherent entity, could generate negative publicity for a business if it creates social costs such as pollution or congestion. There are also examples of how a community can turn against a firm. A good example of this concerns *The Sun* newspaper. In its coverage of the 1989 Hillsborough football stadium disaster in Sheffield, where 96 people died and over 700 were injured, *The Sun* ran the headline 'THE TRUTH',

claiming that some Liverpool fans stole from victims and others urinated on members of the emergency services when they arrived to help. This caused outrage among thousands of people in Liverpool, and even now the newspaper sells poorly in the city as many newsagents refuse to stock it.

Stakeholder conflicts

A business must take into account stakeholder objectives when making strategic decisions. However this can lead to a variety of conflicts and, in the short term at least, there will probably have to be trade-offs between the various groups.

A business might set the strategic objective of increasing profits by £15 million over the next three years. This may seem to be valid, and meets some of the 'SMART' criteria. However, this objective is to be achieved through price increases and making employees redundant. The fact that 'in the future there is the possibility that all stakeholder groups will benefit from the greater profits' will be of no consolation to employees who are going to lose their jobs, or a consumer facing a large price rise. It is therefore quite possible to see how conflict between these two groups and the shareholders is likely to arise as a result of this particular strategic objective being chosen.

Stakeholder influence

The influence that the particular stakeholder groups can exert on the business is not likely to be equal; in any given business some stakeholders will have a greater influence than others. Some issues for consideration are detailed below.

Employees

How many are there? Is there a union that the business recognises (see Unit 70)? If so, how many members belong to it? Are there a large number of 'career' employees (who could not easily be replaced), or is the workforce largely uncommitted with a high rate of labour turnover?

Shareholders

If the business is a company, is it private or public? In a private business, it can be hard to identify the actual price of the shares as they are not traded on the open market. However, in a public company shareholders will be very sensitive to changes in price, and indeed the dividend which they receive. They have the power to vote directors off the board, whereas employees and suppliers cannot. Therefore in a public company, directors may feel that shareholders are key stakeholders whose views must form a very important part of strategic decision-making.

Suppliers

Is the supplier in a monopoly position, or could similar products be bought from elsewhere? If the latter is the case, then potentially it has considerably less power than if it supplies a unique, essential product.

Local community

To what extent might any bad publicity affect the business in the long term? Might bad publicity 'blow over' quite quickly?

Creditors

If a business is finding it difficult to keep up with its mortgage (or other loan) repayments, it may have to delay payments to suppliers to improve its liquidity position, so as not to default and run the risk of the loan being recalled.

Key Term

Key stakeholder(s): One(s) with a large amount of influence on the business. A key stakeholder's views will play an important part in strategic decision-making.

The legal situation

Faced with potential conflicts arising from stakeholders with differing objectives and influence, can those running a business look to the law for guidance? In the case of a company, it has until recently been the case that the objectives of shareholders (as the owners) were expected to be the main concern for directors and managers.

The Companies Act 2006 has altered this. It is an important piece of legislation that consolidates and updates existing law relating to the running of a company. It caused a lot of debate when passing through parliament. Section 172 is particularly important, putting into law for the first time a statutory statement of directors' duties and responsibilities. It states that each director must act in a way that they consider in good faith (i.e. honestly) would be most likely to promote the success of the company (although the term 'success' is not actually defined in the Act).

Directors must now 'have regard' for a number of factors that include:

- the likely consequences of any decision in the long term
- the interests of the company's employees and the company's business relationships with suppliers and customers
- the impact of the company's operations on the community and the environment.

In some ways the new legal position still leaves the issues regarding conflict unchanged. While 'having regard' for different stakeholders is now enshrined in law, this does not remove the likelihood of stakeholder conflict. It still will not be possible to satisfy all groups all of the time. If a plant has to close 'for the long-term success of the company' this will be obviously be against the interests of the employees that are made redundant and the company's suppliers. The concept of 'having regard' for stakeholders in a particular instance may need to be tested in court for the issue to be clarified.

Nevertheless, under Section 172 directors who make very unsuccessful decisions could be in breach of their legal duty. Any serious (e.g. fatal) health and safety failures, or a failure to protect the environment from significant damage, could result in prosecution. Directors will have to be more attentive to a wider variety of stakeholder interests than was previously the case.

Examiner's voice

When approaching a question involving stakeholder needs, try to adopt a balanced view and then reach a conclusion as to which group(s)' needs are most important or significant at that particular time for that business.

Key Terms

Companies Act 2006: this has put into law for the first time a statutory statement of directors' duties and responsibilities. This includes 'having regard' for employees, suppliers, and the environment.

Further Sources

http://www.companieshouse.gov.uk/ – information about and the legal situation regarding companies in the UK.

Your Turn

Case Study Time allowed 30 minutes

Cabin crew ballot to ground Virgin

Virgin Atlantic cabin crew are to ballot for strike action next week, threatening to pile misery on air passengers in the New Year. The union, Unite, has 3,100 cabin crew members at Virgin, and a prolonged dispute could lead to chaos at some of the UK's already overstretched airports.

The seven-month-long Virgin dispute is over pay. Staff complain that they have been undervalued for too long and that the airline pays less than some rivals. Virgin Atlantic cabin crew flying on business routes say they earn £10,000 less than their counterparts at British Airways. Those working on holiday routes say they also earn considerably less than other airlines's cabin crews.

Virgin Atlantic is 51% owned by Richard Branson's Virgin group and 49% by Singapore airlines. The Asian operator has been trying to offload its holding for some time.

(Adapted from *The Observer*, 2 December 2007)

1. List **five** likely stakeholders in Virgin Atlantic.
   (5 marks)

2. State **two** likely objectives of each stakeholder in Virgin Atlantic. (10 marks)

3. Analyse **two** possible stakeholder conflicts that could arise within Virgin Atlantic. (6 marks)

4. Evaluate how the stakeholders in Virgin Atlantic might be affected if a prolonged strike occurs.
   (18 marks)

(39 marks)

MARKET ANALYSIS

Knowledge of the market and consumer needs is vital information for any business, old or new. Without this information, a business can lose market share, finding that valued customers are turning to competitors. Many well-known and successful businesses have failed when launching new products without analysing the market carefully beforehand, whereas others have successfully launched themselves into new markets without difficulty.

The Virgin Group has experienced both success and failure in its attempts to diversify. Virgin Atlantic has been successful and built up a good reputation in the air travel market, whereas the Virgin Brides and soft drinks sectors have been failures for the group.

Figure 53.1 The Virgin brand has diversified into many markets

Consumer information

One of the most important ways of acquiring information about an existing or potential market is to carry out market research among consumers. This might be qualitative research completed by market research companies directly with consumers, but today there are many other ways of collecting information about the consumer and their perceptions.

Collecting consumer information

- The business can use its own sales staff to collect feedback from retailers. For example, if a chilled dessert manufacturer such as Muller introduces a new range, the sales staff can talk to purchasing managers at the major supermarkets about the launch and ask about consumer comments in store. They will also receive feedback of the flavours that consumers prefer from sales figures.
- Large businesses such as like Levi Strauss are likely to run their own customer focus groups to obtain their opinions on adverts, new products and the perception of competitors among their target market.
- Internet market research sites such as 'YouGov' carry out ongoing research for their clients about consumer perceptions, asking questions about good and bad publicity in recent months. They will also carry out specialist surveys, although this type of survey will be very expensive.
- Organisations such as banks use online customer panels to give feedback on performance and customer care.

- Some hotels and restaurants ask customers to fill in a short questionnaire before leaving to get immediate feedback.
- Many government bodies and utility companies may now ask customers when contacting them by phone to complete a short survey at the end of the call.
- Specialist magazines such as *Marketing* (see Table 53.1).

	Last week	Brand	Agency/TV buyer	%
1	(–)	Asda	Fallon London/ Carat	58
2	(–)	Loyd Grossman Sauces	MCBD/Mediavest	49
3	(–)	Abbey	WCRS/Carat	46
4	(–)	Pizza Hut	Wieden & Kennedy/ Mediavest	45
5	(–)	British Army	Publicis/Carat	44

Table 53.1 The top five commercials remembered by consumers in the week of publication

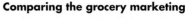

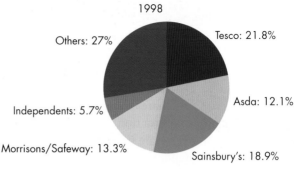

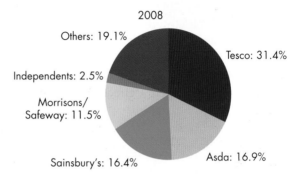

Figure 53.2 Comparing the grocery market
Source: TNS Worldpanel

Market share

Market share is the proportion of a market under the control of a particular business. For many large businesses, market share is vitally important and an indication of the success of the firm; this is particularly the case in situations of oligopoly.

Key Term

Oligopoly: competition among a few large businesses. It is typically found in sectors such as banking and supermarkets.

This concern about market share can be seen in the UK in the competition between supermarkets. When the annual accounts of companies like Tesco and Sainsbury's are quoted, there will always be mention of the market share of each business. For Tesco, their place as market leader is the best indication possible of their success and shows them that Tesco is 'getting it right' as far as the customer is concerned. Whenever there is criticism of Tesco in the press, the business can refer to the fact that their customers are happy with what they are doing.

Being market leader gives the business a number of advantages in terms of publicity and future sales. Tesco is able to negotiate competitive contracts with its suppliers because of the large volume of orders placed; launching new lines or diversifying into new markets will mean that there is already a large market in existence with a good impression of the business's activities; one short, high-profile advertising campaign may be sufficient to create consumer awareness; if the product is newsworthy, for example, an ethical clothing range, it will also receive a large amount of free publicity in the media when the product is launched.

However, the incidence of bird flu at a Bernard Matthew's turkey farm in 2007 shows that even market leaders can find themselves in serious trouble with their customers if they make a mistake. The result is likely to be a falling market share and a falling share price on the stock exchange.

Examiner's voice

There is an overlap between market share and market growth for any business. A situation where the market is growing, but the business's market share is stable or falling, would suggest that there are problems to be addressed.

Market size and growth

Market size can be measured in terms of volume or value of sales. Businesses need to have this information so that they can monitor any changes in the size of the total market, and can assess their share of the market. A business with a shrinking share of a growing market will need to investigate the situation and take remedial action. The fall in market share may be a result of a lack of competitiveness or failure to keep pace with change and innovation. Such a situation could indicate either a lack of awareness of customer needs, or competing against an aggressive competitor who is more in tune with the market. For example, after the success of its 'Razr' phone, Motorola have found it difficult to find a new handset to compete effectively with the competition.

Market growth is an increase in the size of the total market, providing an opportunity for a business to increase its sales. The growth may arise as a result of a number of factors.

- An improvement in living standards and disposable income might lead to an increase in car ownership.
- Increased opportunities in export markets.
- An increase in the size of the population or number of consumers.
- Changes in tastes, styles and society are particularly important for businesses in the fashion sector.
- A change in expectations amongst consumers. The expectation of lower unemployment might mean that consumers start to increase their spending.

The individual business cannot do a great deal to change the growth of the market, but it can undertake measures to ensure that it maintains or increases its share of a growing market.

One course of action that a business might take to overcome problems in a growing or shrinking market is to buy out or merge with a competitor.

> In 2008, when airlines were struggling to cope with rapidly rising fuel prices and aggressive competition from budget airlines BA and Iberia, the Spanish airline started to discuss a merger. Both companies knew that they could gain through economies of scale, particularly through shedding labour and combining routes.

The international perspective

Most businesses now need to monitor and assess overseas markets as well as their domestic market (see Unit 6). A large number of UK businesses exports goods and services, and even businesses that do not trade internationally may be affected by a change in an overseas trading situation.

All world markets are particularly vulnerable to changes in the situation in the USA. The collapse of the sub-prime mortgage market in the USA in 2007 has rippled through developed economies throughout the world, affecting demand for goods and services and the financial services sector. A clear effect of this for UK consumers has been the difficulty faced by buyers in obtaining mortgages from increasingly cautious banks and building societies.

The environment

As well as monitoring their sales and changes in their markets, businesses now need to assess the environmental impact of their operations (see Unit 67). This is important for a number of reasons:

- The rapidly rising price of fuel and power has an impact on the costs of all businesses. It makes sense for firms to ensure that these costs are kept to a minimum.
- A business taking action to reduce its carbon footprint can use this as a selling point to attract customers who place environmental awareness high on a list of priorities.
- Increasingly, governments both in the UK and elsewhere in the world are legislating in areas that will reduce global warming and climate change. It makes sense for business to be at the forefront, with changes implemented after careful thought and planning, rather than racing to put in the changes once the legislation is announced. As a consequence, some businesses have put in energy-reducing policies and measures to reduce carbon emissions, ahead of government legislation in these areas. These actions benefit the business, but they are also a useful marketing tool with consumers who are increasingly environmentally aware.

Reviewing the market climate

Analysis of the market is an essential part of any business strategy for a successful firm. If an organisation has up-to-date knowledge of its market and is in tune with the needs of its consumers, it will be able to satisfy those needs effectively. This market analysis must be reviewed at regular intervals, because of the rapid pace of change in developed economies. A good or service desired by a consumer may be replaced by a new good or service within the year, month, or even week.

Further Sources

www.businesstimesonline.co.uk
www.yougov.com
Marketing published by Haymarket Publications

Your Turn

Case Study   Time allowed 1 hour

Stonyfield Farm

Stonyfield Farm is the world's largest organic yoghurt producer and is a majority-owned subsidiary of Danone, the French multinational business. In America, Stonyfield is the market leader, with over 80% of the market for organic yoghurt products, and sales that exceed $200 million.

In 2006 Stonyfield set out to achieve similar success in Europe by investing in a relatively small Irish dairy, Glenisk. Glenisk was small by UK standards, using a tiny fraction of the total organic milk produced by British dairies and having no market outside Ireland.

There were two main reasons for Stonyfield investing in Glenisk. The first was a shortage of supply of organic milk from UK producers, making it difficult to guarantee yoghurt supplies to retailers. The second was that Stonyfield had little knowledge of the European market, while Glenisk would be able to provide expertise and information about the tastes and requirements of European consumers. Stonyfield realised that it could not assume that European consumers would want the same products as American consumers. In addition, although Danone had wide knowledge of the European yoghurt market, it only had limited experience of marketing organic products.

In the UK, two producers, Yeo Valley Organics and Rachel's Organics were already established brands, so the market was not going to be an easy one to break into. The shelf space for chilled desserts and yoghurts in supermarkets was already crowded, with a bewildering range of products.

Another cautionary note was sounded by the fact that Muller, the leading yoghurt producer in the UK, had withdrawn from the organic yoghurt market within a year of entering, because of difficult trading conditions. 'Like many other companies, Muller learned that multi-million euro launches are no guarantee of success in the organic food industry.'

(Adapted from www.organicmonitor.com)

1. Explain two methods that Stonyfield could use to assess the market for organic yoghurts in the UK.
   (4 marks)

2. Analyse possible reasons for Muller experiencing difficulties in entering the organic yoghurt market.
   (10 marks)

3. Evaluate methods that Stonyfield could use to ensure that their entry into the market is a success.
   (18 marks)

4. Analyse the reasons why Danone might want to move into the organic yoghurt market. (10 marks)

   (42 marks)

FORECASTING (TIME SERIES ANALYSIS)

Forecasting is the use of existing data to predict future trends. Businesses need to use forecasting so that they can make plans for the future. For example, a bathroom supplier might forecast the growth in housebuilding so as to assess the future demand for its products. A business can use forecasting for costs, market size, but the most important use for forecasting is sales. From this, the business will be able to look at its market share and the likely demand for labour, marketing and training. For example, if a business finds from forecasts that it is likely to experience growing sales in the next two years, it will need to recruit and train new workers and to ensure supplies of raw materials.

There are a number of quantitative methods that the business can use for forecasting, but this chapter will consider the use of time series analysis, which is a moving average. A moving average looks at data over a period of time and combines it over different periods to give averages. Time series analysis is the use of a moving average using past data, calculated over a period of time which is then projected to give forecast figures for the future. It is particularly useful for a business that faces cyclical or seasonal changes in demand, because the analysis will iron out the variations and give a long-term trend for the data. The analysis makes the assumption that past performance can be used as an indicator for the future, which may not always be the case.

The business will want to find four components from the information given by time series analysis:

- **The trend:** the raw data or actual figures that make up the data may fluctuate over a period of time. For example, an ice-cream seller will find that sales vary with the weather. These fluctuations may make it difficult to see whether the overall movement of sales is upward or downward. The trend figure will smooth out these fluctuations to give an overall picture.
- **Cyclical fluctuations:** these are the variations that occur as a result of the business cycle, and recessions and booms in the economy (see Unit 58). For example, a house-builder may find that demand for properties change with the rate of interest and the availability of credit.
- **Seasonal fluctuations:** these are changes that occur over the year; they will affect some businesses more than others. For example, a toy manufacturer would expect sales to increase in the run-up to the Christmas period and holidays.
- **Random fluctuations:** these are changes in sales that might be difficult to predict. For example, the ice-cream seller might find that sales increase at unexpected times if the weather is warmer than normal.

Finding the trend

Identifying the trend in sales figures will show a business whether the overall movement in its sales is upward or downward. In order to do this, the raw data must be used to calculate a moving average. This average can be calculated over any period of time, but the choice will depend on the cycle of sales which the business faces. For example, if a business has seasonal sales that fluctuate over quarters of the year, it would use a three-month average. If it faces variations over a three-year period, the average would be a three-point calculation.

Examiner's voice

It is very unlikely that you will be asked to calculate a moving average under examination conditions because the process is time-consuming. However, you may need to calculate one for a pre-issued case study. It is also important to understand the process and what the figures mean.

Calculating the three-period totals

Year	Sales (£000)
1995	120
1996	110
1997	115
1998	130
1999	112
2000	121
2001	133
2002	121
2003	127
2004	145
2005	133
2006	138
2007	154
2008	144
2009	151

Table 54.1 Calculating the three-year periods

Year	Sales (£000)	Three-period total
1995	120	
1996	110 (a)	(a) 345
1997	115 (b)	(b) 355
1998	130	357
1999	112	363
2000	121	366
2001	133	375
2002	121	381
2003	127	393
2004	145	405
2005	133	416
2006	138	425
2007	154	436
2008	144	449
2009	151	

Table 54.2

Table 54.1 shows the figures for a business where sales peak at three-year intervals. In this case, a three-period moving average should be used. To calculate the three-period average, add together the first three numbers and put the total alongside the middle of the three years; in this case, 1996.

120 + 110 + 115 = 345

This number should be put in the total column as shown in Table 54.2. The first sales number then drops out and the following three numbers are added for 1996, 1997 and 1998. The total of these numbers is placed alongside 1997. This process is continued down the table, with the top number dropping out at each stage and the next three being added until the final three numbers are reached. The final total will be placed alongside 2008.

Calculating the three-period averages

This will be the fourth column in the table, and the figure is found by dividing the totals in the third column by three to find the average figure.

Year	Sales (£000)	Three-period total	Three-period moving average
1995	120 ⎫		
1996	110 ⎬ (a)	(a) 345 / 3	(a) 115
1997	115 ⎭	355	118.3
1998	130	357	119
1999	112	363	121
2000	121	366	122
2001	133	375	125
2002	121	381	127
2003	127	393	131
2004	145	405	135
2005	133	416	138.7
2006	138	425	141.7
2007	154	436	145.3
2008	144	449	149.7
2009	151		
2010			

Table 54.3

To calculate the value of (a):

$$\frac{345}{3} = 115$$

Plotting the information on a graph

If the sales figures are plotted on a graph, they will fluctuate as shown in Figure 54.1. This graph is not appropriate for forecasting because it is impossible to see any long-term trend in it.

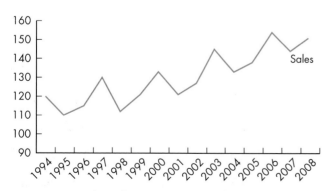

Figure 54.1 Sales information in a graph

When the moving average figures are plotted, they should not be joined together. Instead a straight line should be drawn through them, which is called the **line of best fit**. This line will show a long-term trend and can be used to forecast future sales; this is shown in Figure 54.2. This is now an appropriate graph for forecasting purposes because it can be used to predict a long-term trend. The data is extrapolated in this process; the line of best fit will be extended to show what might be expected to happen in the future.

> **Key Term**
>
> **Line of best fit:** a line drawn through the points on a graph so that the points are distributed as evenly as possible above and below the line.

Once this line has been drawn in, it is possible to extend or project it so that forecast figures for future sales can be read if the long-term trend remains the same; see Figure 54.3.

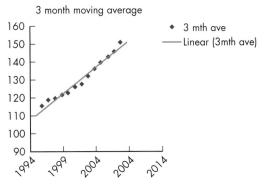

Figure 54.2

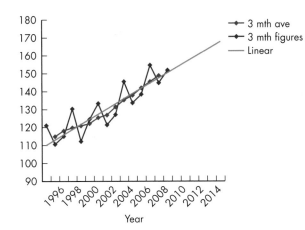

Figure 54.3

In Figure 54.3 the line of best fit through the moving average figures has been extended up to 2014. If the current trend in sales figures remains the same, it will be possible to read off the sales figures from this line for the next five years.

Calculating the cyclical variation

Although it is possible to read off the trend in sales from the moving average line on the graph, accurate figures for annual sales are not given. As Figure 54.1 showed, sales figures for each year will fluctuate. By calculating the average variation of sales in each of the periods (three, in this example) and applying this to the figures, it is possible to obtain a more accurate forecast of annual sales.

The cyclical variation is the amount by which the actual sales in a period vary from the moving average figures. In Table 54.4, the actual sales for 1996 are £110,000, whereas the moving average sales are £115,000. This means that the cyclical variation is:
actual sales – moving average sales = 110 – 115 = –5
It is important to show the sign in the calculation.

Each of the periods has been given a period number in the final column. This is a three-period average, so starting at the first year, 1995, with year 1, go through

Year	Sales (£000)	Three-period total	Three-period moving average	Cyclical variation
1995	120			
1996	110	345	115	−5 period 1
1997	115	355	118.3	−3.3 period 2
1998	130	357	119	+11 period 3
1999	112	363	121	−9 period 1
2000	121	366	122	−1 period 2
2001	133	375	125	+8 period 3
2002	121	381	127	−6 period 1
2003	127	393	131	−4 period 2
2004	145	405	135	+10 period 3
2005	133	416	138.7	−5.7 period 1
2006	138	425	141.7	−3.7 period 2
2007	154	436	145.3	+8.7 period 3
2008	144	449	149.7	−5.7 period 1
2009	151			

Table 54.4

and allocate the period to each of the following years. It is then possible to calculate the average of the cyclical variations for each period.

For **Period 1**, the average is:
$$\frac{-5 + (-9) + (-6) + (-5.7)}{4} = -6.425$$

For **Period 2**, the average is:
$$\frac{-3.3 + (-1) + (-4) + (-3.7)}{4} = -3$$

For **Period 3**, the average is:
$$\frac{11 + 8 + 10 + 8.7}{4} = 9.425$$

Using these average cyclical variations with their signs to adjust the values taken from the projected line on the graph, will help to make the figures a more accurate forecast of annual sales.

For example, in Figure 54.3, the projected sales figure for 2012 is £160,000. The year 2012 is period 3 in the cycle and the average cyclical variation in period 3 from the calculation above is £9,425. This means that sales for that year are forecast to be:

£160,000 + £9,425 = £169,425

Similarly for 2011, which is period 2, the reading from the graph is £158,000. From this £3,000 must be subtracted because the cyclical variation for period 2 is a negative value of £3000:

158,000 – £3,000 = £155,000

Examiner's voice

Questions about moving averages on papers without pre-issued case studies are likely to ask you to calculate or apply cyclical variations to a set of figures or a graph of moving averages that has been given to you. There is an example of one of these questions at the end of the chapter.

Centring

This process has to be used if an even number of periods is used. If a four-period moving average is used, there is no middle point to put the figure alongside. In this process a four-point total is found first and placed between the two periods at the centre; i.e. between the second and third periods for the first total, and so on. These totals are then added together in groups of two to give an eight-period average. This total can then be divided by eight and centred as shown below (see Table 54.5).

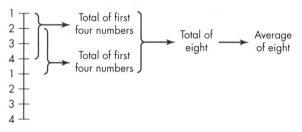

Figure 54.4

A four-period average using quarterly figures, like the one above, would be particularly useful for businesses such as garden centres or theme parks, where the sales are

Period	Sales	Four-period total	Eight-period total	Moving average
Quarter 1	100			
Quarter 2	150			
Quarter 3	170 (a)	510 (a)	1030 / 8	128.75
Quarter 4	90	520		
Quarter 1	110	550		
Quarter 2	180	605		
Quarter 3	205	590		
Quarter 4	95			

Table 54.5

seasonal and are likely to fluctuate considerably. The use of the moving average will smooth out the fluctuations and give a better overall picture of the direction of sales.

Summary

1. Find the trend period; e.g. 3, 4 or 5.

2. Calculate the moving total.

3. Calculate the moving average.

4. Calculate the cyclical variation.

5. Calculate the average cyclical variation.

6. Plot the trend line on a graph and extrapolate the forecast from the projected line of best fit.

7. Add or subtract the average cyclical variation to the forecast figures on the graph.

The use and limitations of forecasts

Forecasts are likely to be useful to businesses in showing the trend in figures like sales, but they need to be used with caution.

- Any forecast will only be as reliable as the data that is used to formulate it. It is vital in preparing forecasts to use accurate and reliable information.
- Businesses need to be careful about making assumptions about the future based on the experience of the past. While past performance may be a reasonable indicator of the future most of the time, events in political and economic spheres can occasionally make forecasts less useful.
- The most recent information is often the most useful and relevant. The use of moving averages does not distinguish between recent and distant information in formulating the forecast.
- The forecast does not take account of any change in the objectives of the business. For example, the business may want to increase its sales by a larger percentage in the next few years or, if the economic outlook is not good, it may be happy simply to maintain sales at their current level.
- It is important nevertheless for businesses to try to estimate future revenue and costs so that they can take action to improve their overall performance. The use of a moving average will help to show the business how well it is likely to perform in the future, other things remaining equal.

Your Turn

Questions   Time allowed 1 hour

1. Using the figures below, calculate a three-period moving average and the cyclical variations for each of the periods. (20 marks)

Year	Sales £000
1	50
2	60
3	48
4	55
5	70
6	50
7	60
8	75
9	50
10	70

2a. On a sheet of graph paper, plot the points given below for sales and join them point-to-point.
(4 marks)

Year	Sales £000	Moving average
1	40	
2	30	47
3	70	48
4	45	50
5	35	52
6	75	57
7	60	58
8	40	62
9	85	65
10	70	68
11	50	70
12	90	

2b. Plot the figures for the moving average. Draw in the line of best fit through the plotted points.

(4 marks)

2c. Project this line to show the trend for the next year. (1 mark)

2d. From the graph, find the forecast sales for each of the three periods of next year. (3 marks)

2e. The cyclical variations for each of these periods are as follows:

Period 1 = −3

Period 2 = −19

Period 3 = +20

2f. Calculate the likely value of sales, having taken account of these cyclical variations. Show your working.

(6 marks)

(18 marks)

DECISION TREES

A decision tree is a technique that is used to aid the decision-making process. Whenever a business is considering two or more options, decision trees can be used to show the likely financial return for undertaking each of the options. Decision trees combine the risk (costs) and the likely return (revenues) from a given undertaking. The 'decision' is based on two aspects:

1. the probability of a particular outcome (the risk)

2. the estimated monetary reward of a given option (the reward).

Decision trees consider the risk in relation to the possible level of reward. Each of the above factors is estimated and calculated in order to reach an amount. One of the advantages of using decision trees is that the technique is usually drawn, allowing for a visual presentation of the choices and their likely returns. The visual approach allows the business to see the options available, along with the likely outcomes and their possible monetary values.

Figure 55.1 A decision tree

The diagrams

As for many techniques, particular symbols are used.

The symbols used in Figure 55.1 are:

A. The square represents a decision; to do something or not to do something, or to do one thing or another. The number of lines drawn from the square represents the number of options, from which one will eventually be chosen.

In this example, the decision is between selling and not selling.

B. The circle represents the possible outcomes once an option is selected. The outcomes may be simple, such as success and failure. However the outcomes could be for different products or even days on which particular goods are sold. Whatever the possible outcomes once a decision is made, a line represents each such outcome from the circle.

In this example, if the decision were to sell, then the possible outcomes would be to sell online or sell at the market.

C. If a decision is made to sell, it is necessary to end the alternative choice. This is done by drawing parallel lines on the option that is not selected.

To build a decision tree, the information available has to be 'converted' into a diagram.

Converting information into a diagram

For example: a building company has some land and it needs to decide whether to build some houses on the land or do nothing.

1. The first step is to draw the initial decision: to build or not to build! Action: draw a square to represent the decision (see (i) on Figure 55.2).

2. Now consider how many outcomes there are of building the houses. In this example there are two possible outcomes:

   • the houses are built and successfully sold OR
   • the houses are not sold.

   Action: draw a circle to represent the outcomes and label each option (see (ii) on Figure 55.2).

3. It is also important to state (usually below the outcome line), the probability of that outcome occurring: (iii) on Figure 55.2.

4. The final piece of information to be put on the diagram is the likely monetary value of a particular outcome. This is called the estimated monetary value or the likely revenue. This information is placed to the right of the outcome line: see (iv) on Figure 55.2.

Calculating the expected values

Figure 55.2 now has the complete picture of the decision to be made. The tree is now used to calculate the 'expected values'.

The expected value = EMV × probability.

For example:

Success in selling the houses
= £1.2 million × 0.4 = £0.48 million
Failure in selling the houses
= £0.3 million × 0.6 = £0.18 million

The two outcomes are added together to gain an expected of £0.66 million; see (v) in Figure 55.2.

This expected value is then placed into the outcome circle (Figure 55.2, (vi)). If one of the outcomes is negative then this figure is subtracted from the positive outcome.

Finally, the cost of the particular decision selected is subtracted form the expected value, to give an amount that is the likely result of taking the decision to build the houses:

£0.66 million – £0.5 million = £0.16 million or £160,000

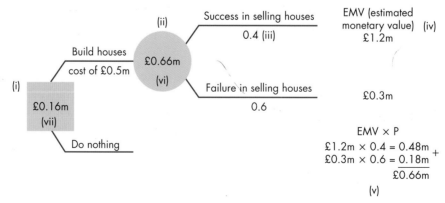

Figure 55.2 A decision tree

This figure is then placed into the decision box (assuming it is a higher positive figure than any alternative), Figure 55.2 (vii).

This figure can be compared with any of the other possible decisions. In this example there was no alternative apart from doing nothing. However, this could still be important. If to do nothing costs nothing and consequently yields nothing, this may be a better choice if the choice to build the houses had meant making a loss.

It is quite possible that there will be several options to decide upon.

In Figure 55.3 there are three possible options to be considered.

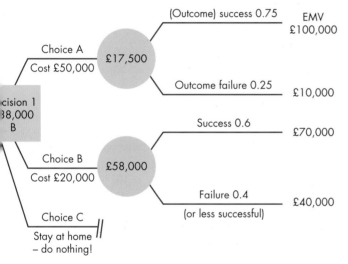

Figure 55.3 A decision tree

To choose the best option, the following calculations should be undertaken.

Choice A EMV × p = £100,000 × 0.75 = 75,000
          EMV × p = £10,000 × 0.25 = 2,500
                                        77,500
Choice B EMV × p = £70,000 × 0.6 = 42,000
          EMV × p = £40,000 × 0.4 = 16,000
                                        58,000
Choice C no value or cost involved   0

Each figure would be placed in the circles and then the cost of each of the choices is subtracted.

Choice A   £77,500 – £50,000 = £27,500
Choice B   £58,000 – £20,000 = £38,000

Therefore the 'best' choice would be B.

There are instances where there are a series of decisions to be made. It is important to remember that the process for calculating the expected values remains the same.

In Figure 55.4, the initial decision is to decide whether to launch a product on a regional basis, or not launch at all. If it is decided to launch on a regional basis, there are three possible outcomes:

- high success with a probability of .5
- medium success rate with a probability of .3
- a poor response with a probability of .2.

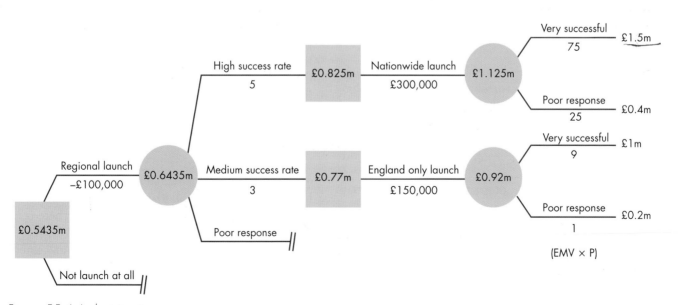

Figure 55.4 A decision tree

The expected values for the nationwide launch and the England-only launch are:

Nationwide launch	$£1.5m \times 0.75 =$	$£1.125m$
	$£0.4m \times 0.25 =$	$£0.1m$
	Expected value =	$£1.125m$
	Cost of launch =	$-£.3$ million
		£0.825 million
England-only launch	$£1$ milllion $\times 0.9 =$	$£0.9$ million
	$£0.2$ million $\times 0.1 =$	$£0.02$ million
	Expected value =	$£0.92$ million
	Cost of launch =	$-£0.15$ million
		£0.77 million

Each of these final figures is written in the decision boxes and now become the EMVs for the outcomes of the initial regional launch.

The calculation process is now repeated with the new figures.

Regional launch	
High success	$£0.825 \times 0.5 = £0.4125$ million
Medium success	$£0.77m \times 0.3 = £0.231$ million
Poor response (no EMV)	$£0$
	$£0.6435$ million
Cost of launch	$-£0.1$ million
	£0.5435

Based on the decision tree calculations, the answer is:

A. Undertake the regional launch and the nationwide launch if the regional one is a high success.

B. The overall expected value allowing for all costs will be £0.5435 million.

There may be other factors to consider that may be offered in a case study, which can be used as context. Such factors may include:

- The amount of finance available in the first instance
- If the launches fit with the objectives of the business
- The reliability of both the EMVs and the probabilities
- The business environment, such as the state of the economy
- If the £0.5435 million is a sufficiently high return on the investment
- What, if any, are the alternative investments that could be undertaken?

Examiner's voice

1. It is important to note that this process of using a decision tree, considers only the value of a choice and nothing else. A consideration of the affordability of the initial cost and whether the choice fits in with the objectives of the business is equally important. In other words, the context of the case is once again vitally important.

2. It does not matter how complicated the decision tree appears to be, the process for working out the best choice remains the same. It is quite possible that the decision tree diagram will be given to you, for you to calculate the best choice.

3. Be prepared to offer evaluative comments as to the reliability of the figures involved.

The benefits and limitations of using decision trees

Benefits

- It is a simplistic, visual method to aid the decision-making process when faced with several alternatives.
- It is a relatively quick and therefore cost effective method of aiding the decision-making process.
- By applying the probabilities, the technique does attempt to account for the level of risk involved, which other decision making techniques do not.
- May be accurate if a similar selection of choices has been considered before, making the figures more reliable.

Limitations

- Much depends upon the accuracy/ reliability of the figures used. The probabilities are crucial to calculating the expected values on which a decision is based. Consequently, if these probabilities are only guesses, then the reliability of the technique is limited. This is especially true if the decision to be made relies on making 'guesses' for the probability of a certain outcome, when such an outcome has not occurred before. This prevents basing the probabilities on experience and the figures are therefore even more of a liability. (This is particularly true if such decisions are being made for the first time and therefore there is no experience to aid reliability of data.)
- When 'selecting' the probabilities, the management may be in favour of one particular choice and therefore be tempted to load the probabilities in the favour of that choice.
- Similarly, the ability to gauge the EMV (estimated monetary value) of an outcome may be difficult as

there are so many variables that could affect the financial outcome.

- There is often no mention of a time period over which the decision is based. The longer the 'life' of the outcome, the less reliable the figures are likely to be.

- Decision trees concentrate on the quantitative and consequently, qualitative evidence is not considered, which may be crucial.

- There is no reference to the 'human element'. Even though a decision does not have a financial implication, it may affect how the business operates and therefore have an implication for employees.

Questions Time allowed 30 minutes

1. State three benefits of using a decision tree in the decision-making process. (3 marks)

2. Calculate the expected value given the following information:

   - EMV of £50,000 and a probability of .8
   - EMV of –£10,000 and a probability of .2
   (4 marks)

3. Mario's, a local restaurant is trying to decide if it should open on Sundays or remain closed. From research it has estimated that the chances of success by opening on Sundays are about 80% (0.8) with EMV of £600 and failure 20% (0.2) with an EMV of £200. The cost of opening on Sunday would be £200.

   Draw and complete a decision tree using the following information to decide if it is worthwhile opening the restaurant on Sundays. (6 marks)

   (13 marks)

Case Study Time allowed 45 minutes

Tamhar's Corner Shop

Tamhar Pickup and her associate, Harpinder Singh run a local corner shop selling a wide range of groceries, newspapers and other convenience products. It is located in the middle of a large residential estate in a town in the Midlands. Many of the residents worked at the car plant, which was only a mile away from the shop.

Tamhar is an adventurous entrepreneur who is always looking how to increase the profit made by the business to allow her to spend more time at home and less time working.

Harpinder is more cautious and always wants to be certain that any new product that Tamhar wants to sell will be successful, as room in the shop is limited.

Tamhar has also been offered the opportunity to sell and rent DVDs. To do this the shop would have to buy the display stands and the initial stock for both selling and renting for £2,000. The salesman has advised her that the likely revenue from the DVDs is around £8,000 a year.

She was told that it would be an 80% certainty that this level of revenue would be gained and if the business was unlucky (only a 20% chance), the business would still make about £4,000.

Tamhar had also thought of installing and operating a digital photo machine. The machine would enable customers to insert their memory card into the machine and print out photos of various sizes in an instant. The machine would cost a small installation charge and a yearly rental of only £1,000. The profits on this type of photo machine are normally high and if the machine is a success, the estimated revenues are about £5,000; or £3,500 if a limited success.

Harpinder was still concerned and suggested that Tamhar could only pursue one of her ideas

1. Using Figure 55.5, decide which option Tamhar and Harpinder should take. (6 marks)

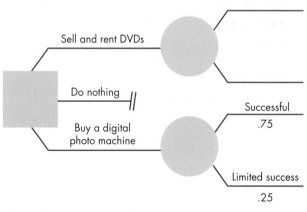

Figure 55.5 Tamhar's Corner Shop

2. Evaluate the best option for Tamhar and Harpinder. (14 marks)

   (20 marks)

MEASURES OF PERFORMANCE: PEOPLE

Any business needs to be able to measure the performance of its workforce in a variety of areas. Some factors such as job satisfaction and motivation will be difficult to assess in an accurate or objective manner, but it is possible for the business to calculate other indicators and to show them in a numerical form. The main measures that can be calculated are productivity, absenteeism and labour. From these and other measures, it may be possible for the business to draw some conclusions about the motivation and job satisfaction of its workforce, and to make comparisons with competitors and other areas of the business world.

Labour productivity

Labour productivity is one of the most important factors in assessing a business's performance and success. It is a measure of the efficiency of the workforce.

Examiner's voice

Be careful not to confuse productivity with production. Production is the total output of the business, sector or country whereas productivity is the output per worker.

Productivity per worker is calculated in the following way:

$$\text{Productivity} = \frac{\text{total output}}{\text{number of employees}}$$

For example: in a small bakery employing six workers, the total output of decorated cupcakes per week is 5,400 cakes. This means that the productivity per worker is 5,400/6, which is 900 cakes per week.

The higher the productivity, the greater the efficiency of the workforce and the lower the wages costs per unit of output. Most businesses will want to increase productivity and consequently cut its costs, if possible.

Productivity has become increasingly important in all areas of the economy in recent years, from the output of manufacturing industry to the efficiency of postal workers. Sectors of the UK economy (such as the car industry) where productivity used to be low have been turned around by new production techniques, many of which were introduced by Japanese managers. Quality circles and Kaizen production techniques have helped to motivate the workforce, reduce waste and improve performance (see Unit 46).

With the impact of globalisation (see Unit 68) and the emergence of developing economies such as China and India, it is increasingly important for businesses to make their production as efficient as possible if they are to compete effectively. Labour is usually cheaper in emerging economies than in the developed world. The more advanced economies need therefore to take advantage of their ability to invest in the newest technology and to ensure that their workers have the skills and resources to maximise productivity.

Absenteeism

Absenteeism is another measure of performance that the business can examine. It may give an indication of the morale of the workforce and the level of job satisfaction.

Absenteeism is measured by looking at the total number of working days lost across the whole business, as a percentage of the total number of working days for all employees.

If a business employs 20 workers who each work a five-day week for 46 weeks of the year, the total number of working days is:

$20 \times 5 \times 46 = 4{,}600$ days

Over the period of a year there are 120 working days lost through absence. The rate of absenteeism is:

$\dfrac{120}{4600} \times 100 = 2.6\%$

Absence is inevitable in any employment situation, but management should be concerned about a high level of absenteeism, because it usually indicates that employees are not happy about some aspect of their job.

The factors that contribute to absenteeism will be specific to the individual and to the business. In some cases, all workers may be unhappy with a particular situation, but in others the problem may arise from the relationships between particular workers. The main factors are as follows:

- Lack of job satisfaction, boring repetitive work and lack of challenge.
- Work that is too challenging in a situation where the worker has insufficient training for the job.
- Poor management which is either too controlling or too easy-going.
- Stress created form a range of factors in the work environment – heavy workloads, unrealistic expectations by management, little opportunity to work independently.
- Workplace relationships. This may be a problem either between groups of workers or between managers and workers.
- Lack of recognition either in terms of poor pay for the job or from management.
- Poor working conditions.

In any situation, absenteeism imposes costs on the business. These arise mainly from lost production and the need to pay for others to cover necessary work, but there may also be other more long-term costs for a business. Customers may find that they are not receiving good service and take their business elsewhere; other employees may begin to feel resentful if their workload increases as a result of persistent absence by one particular worker; morale and attendance in general may suffer throughout the business.

Some absenteeism is inevitable, but its levels for the workforce as a whole and for individuals need to be carefully monitored, and action taken if levels become high. There are several options for a business to tackle absenteeism problems.

Possible actions for reducing absenteeism

Many businesses are now proactive in the management of absence at every stage. Even a short absence will result in an interview either with a superior or a member of the human resource team. This will make it possible to find out the cause of the absence and may discourage a culture among workers, where an occasional day for 'sick leave' is seen as a right. Where the absence is longer term, the worker's return may include a visit to Occupational Health and a phased return to work.

Managers need to ensure that workers have the necessary training to do their job well, but also that they are given sufficient and appropriate work to do. Recent studies have identified a problem that they have called 'rusting' (2 January 2008, *The Guardian*). For many workers, the main problem is boredom and a lack of challenging work. It is as important to make workers feel valued and useful as it is to ensure that their training is adequate and ongoing.

Where the work is necessarily boring and repetitive (e.g. on a production line), it may be helpful to change this system so that the work is more varied and demanding. This could mean changing to job rotation or to cell or team working (see Unit 28).

Some businesses like Royal Mail have tried to offer incentives to improve attendance. This could come in the form of a bonus for attendance or recognised extra leave. In the case of Royal Mail, the inducement was entry to a raffle for an expensive foreign holiday.

Labour turnover

Labour turnover is another quantifiable measure of performance, but once again it is a measure that should not be used in isolation. It is calculated in the following way:

$$\text{Labour turnover} = \dfrac{\text{number of people leaving within the period}}{\text{average number of workers on the payroll}}$$

If a business has a workforce of 200, and 10 people leave over the course of a year, its labour turnover for that year is:

$\dfrac{10}{200} \times 100 = 5\%$

Businesses can use labour turnover statistics most effectively to compare different departments or to look at changes over a period of time. This may highlight employment problems in different parts of the business or show the effects of introducing new work initiatives on labour. However, the figures need to be used with caution and with regard to the nature of the business or department; for example, a supermarket is likely to have higher labour turnover in departments where it employs students and school pupils than elsewhere in its business. These employees are likely to be working part-time and may be forced to leave as their educational circumstances change.

Costs and causes of high labour turnover

The recruitment of labour will always impose high costs on any business if it is done properly. The process of recruiting new workers is time-consuming for managers and human resource departments, involving advertising, interviewing and selection. Once the new employees are recruited, further costs are incurred by their induction and training for the work. While some labour turnover is good and can have a positive impact on the business, it is also necessary to ensure that labour turnover is kept within acceptable limits.

If the rate of labour turnover is high or begins to increase, the business needs to investigate the causes and should then address the problem. The most common causes for high labour turnover areas follow:

- The recruitment process itself may be at fault for one of several reasons (such as the wording of the advertisement or the interview methods). If the 'wrong' workers are being attracted and appointed, they are likely to become disillusioned and to leave.

A recent survey has shown that a larger number of UK businesses continue to spend money on recruitment when it fails to produce the right people, rather than trying to assess the reasons for the failure (Emma Parry, *Personnel Today*, March 2007).

- Lack of appropriate induction and training for a job may make the new employee feel uneasy and inadequate. Many workers leave within a short time of being appointed for this reason.
- Workers who do not feel challenged or valued by management will often start to look for new work very quickly.
- If pay rates are below those paid elsewhere in the region or sector, this will result in dissatisfaction with the job and an increased likelihood that employees will begin to look elsewhere.
- A shortage of particular skilled workers in an area may contribute to higher than normal labour turnover.

In conclusion, businesses need to use labour turnover statistics with care. If a business is to change and progress, it is important to have some staff turnover. New workers may bring different ideas and vibrancy to an organisation which can motivate and inspire existing employees. It is also important to use the statistics in relation to past experience and competing businesses.

Further Sources

www.le.ac.uk
www.eef.org.uk
www.bbc.co.uk
www.employersforwork-lifebalance.org.uk
www.acas.org.uk

Case study Time allowed 30 minutes

Absenteeism in the Civil Service

Government ministers have been considering introducing an incentive scheme offering cars and holidays in an attempt to cut absenteeism, similar to that used by Royal Mail. As a result of their scheme, Royal Mail cut the average absence per employee from 6.1% to 4.8% in a three-year period. By the end of the scheme, 37 employees had won a Ford Focus car and 74 had won a £2,000 holiday voucher. All of the 90,000 employees who met the specified target

for unbroken attendance were given a bonus of £150. A Royal Mail spokesman said that the cost of the scheme was more than outweighed by its benefits.

Ministers have been considering a similar scheme for government departments because research statistics show that absenteeism in the public sector is consistently running ahead of that in the private sector. In 2007, the figures for average days off per worker were 6.3 for the private sector and 9 for the public sector. In 2005, a record-breaking 5.1 million working days were lost by government departments, costing the UK taxpayer £450 million.

(Adapted from *The Telegraph*, 8 January 2007)

1. Discuss the ways in which the Royal Mail scheme will have yielded benefits that outweigh its costs.

   (10 marks)

2. Why might the problem of absenteeism be worse in the public sector than in the private sector?

   (6 marks)

3. The public sector figures show that the worst figures for attendance are in HM Customs and Excise and the Prison Service. Why might this be the case? (6 marks)

4. Evaluate other methods that government departments might use to reduce absenteeism.

   (18 marks)

   (40 marks)

Case Study   Time allowed 1 hour

Nando's

Nando's is a chain of chicken restaurants that first started operating in the UK in 1991. The UK business now has 122 restaurants employing 3,000 people. In each of the restaurants, the human resource and training issues are dealt with by two 'buddies'. Nando's places a very strong emphasis on motivation and provides a budget to each area manager to give days out to staff. The group believes that motivated and happy employees will result in better customer service and higher returns.

Having established the business in the UK, Nando's began to grow rapidly. In this situation, senior management became concerned that the result of this rapid growth might be the loss of enthusiasm, motivation and passion among the workforce.

The solution to the problem they were facing was a series of training programmes aimed at leadership within the business. This was first delivered to directors and then to lower levels of management within the company. It was not always easy to deliver

the programme because, although the enthusiasm was there, there was little time to carry out the training. However, having completed the programme, the results have been excellent. Turnover of managers has fallen from 35% to 20%, which compares very well with the averages for the industry as a whole. In a survey of staff, 91% said they had fun at work, 96% said they were proud to work for the company and 87% were confident in their manager's training to do the job.

One of the main areas covered in the training programme was the issue of diversity in employment. The programme encouraged the use of different pathways and pipelines in recruitment and identifying recruitment criteria, which were fair and objective in identifying the right talents for the job. In particular, line managers were encouraged to be aware of their own biases and stereotypes and then to ensure that these were not reflected in the way in which they recruited staff.

With hindsight, the development manager felt that the only mistake they made was to introduce the training too quickly. A more gradual approach would have made it easier to support the changes. From the employee perspective, it has been an overwhelming success. One employee commented, 'I was blown away by the approach. It makes more sense to encourage team members to take responsibility. People enjoy their jobs more now. They know what they're doing and are ultimately more effective.'

(Adapted from *Personnel Today*, October 2006)

1. Evaluate reasons why labour turnover might be higher than the UK average at Nando's.

   (20 marks)

2. How might the strategic direction of Nando's be affected by its new employment training and recruitment?

   (20 marks)

   (40 marks)

THE NATURE OF ECONOMIC ACTIVITY

The economy is a major influence on all types of business; indeed, it could be argued that it is the most important influence. This chapter explores the concept of **macroeconomics**, the study of the whole economy.

Key Term

Macroeconomics: the study and analysis of the behaviour of the whole economy

Anyone who says that economics is irrelevant to their life is definitely wrong! The main groups involved in the operation of the economy are highly interconnected and a business can find its situation considerably changed by economic events, such as a fall in consumer spending or a change in the exchange rate. These economic events may force the business to change how it operates, in ways that might not be positive for some of the business's stakeholders.

Consider a UK firm that has been exporting sports equipment to a large retailer in Germany. The German retailer subsequently finds that it can buy equipment of the same sort of design and quality from a new supplier in Poland at a much more competitive price. The German retailer therefore does not renew its contract with the UK business.

The emergence of this new low-cost supplier will make the UK business's life very difficult, and it may have to make some of its employees redundant. Thus, an employee who thought he had a reasonably secure job in a business selling to a growing area of the leisure market suddenly finds his life turned upside down by economic events entirely outside his own control. How is it, he may ask, that the Polish firm can produce these products so much more cheaply than his firm can? Furthermore, what action could his business take in order to avoid the job losses?

What is meant by 'the economy'?

The **economy** is not a single entity. It refers to the collective behaviour of a number of different groups. These are:

- all the different businesses in the UK, ranging from sole traders to multinational companies
- people acting as both employees of businesses and consumers of their products
- the government, which sets the economic framework within which businesses have to operate, and is also a major provider of many goods and services which it finances through taxation and borrowing.

Key Term

Economy: collective behaviour of a number of different groups such as businesses, people as employees and consumers, and the government.

In addition to these, any study of the economy must also take into account the UK's trading relationship with other countries, especially the European Union (EU).

Examiner's voice

Although a clear understanding of macroeconomic issues is essential, examiners are not looking for highly detailed and technical explanations of how the economy works. What is much more important is for you to be able to analyse how the economic environment affects the behaviour of businesses.

The economy is dynamic; it changes all the time. People become unemployed, then find jobs; some people retrain to gain new skills and others retire. Some businesses close down or get bigger; others start up. The government also changes its role in the economy. Until the 1980s, the government owned whole industries such as coal, steel, water and electricity. The economy is very different now from how it was 50 or even 20 years ago. Businesses have to adapt to the changing nature of the economic environment in which they operate.

The nature of economics

Economics is not a science in the same way as chemistry and physics. Whereas scientists can conduct laboratory experiments using the same conditions time and time again, the economist's 'laboratory' never stays the same. The economy, as already noted, is dynamic. This means that the effects of a particular policy at any one time may be different from the effects that occurred previously from the same policy.

Consider a cut in the rate of income tax. Lowering the rate of tax to increase spending on the grounds that it was successful in a similar situation 10 years ago, may not be a sensible policy today. The economy will have changed since then: many of the businesses within it will be different, consumer spending patterns will be different, and the UK's trading position with other countries will also have changed. Comparing the economy today with the economy 10 years ago is not comparing like with like.

In addition, although economists would agree that a cut in the rate of income tax will increase consumer spending, the *extent* of the increase in spending might be the subject of considerable disagreement. Will it be a lot or a little? When will it happen, within six months, a year or longer?

It is important to approach macroeconomics in a structured way. The analysis of how the economy influences businesses can be divided into the following five clear steps:

1. Explaining what is meant by the term 'economic activity'.

2. Identifying the economic variables (i.e. factors) that affect economic activity.
(These two steps are dealt with in this chapter.)

3. Analysing what can cause the variables to change. This involves an understanding of an important concept known as the economic cycle. This is dealt with in Unit 58.

4. Explaining what the government's macroeconomic objectives are likely to be, since what objectives it is trying to achieve and how it is trying to achieve them will have a major effect on businesses. This is dealt with in Unit 59.

5. Explaining what the government and/or the Bank of England might do as a result of any change in the variables. Economic policy is explored in Unit 60.

What is 'economic activity'?

'Economic activity' refers to the production of goods and services. Production can be primary, secondary or tertiary, and the level of economic activity refers to output in all of these sectors (see Figure 57.2).

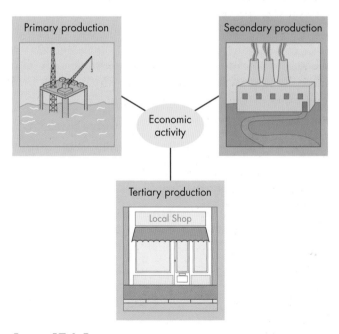

Figure 57.1 Economic activity

A term often used when discussing economic activity is **gross domestic product**. This is usually shortened to GDP. It means the total output of all goods and services produced, usually in a year. 'Gross' in this case means total, and 'domestic' means within that particular country, in this case the UK.

This is distinct from *gross national product* (GNP), which is GDP plus the output of any UK businesses operating abroad. Another term that is used to discuss economic activity is 'national income'. Any of these terms can be used to describe economic activity, but GDP is the most commonly used measure.

Usually, a high level of economic activity (i.e. rising GDP) is beneficial for everyone. It means that there is likely to be a high level of employment, since if the demand for products is rising, businesses will need to employ more people in order to produce them. Jobs are also more likely to be secure when GDP is rising and this, coupled with increasing incomes, means that people's spending power will increase.

Businesses too will benefit: if spending is rising, there will be more demand for products and (assuming that their costs are not rising too much) profits will also rise. This is good for the business's stakeholders. It also means that more money is available, which can be used for further expansion and development.

The government should also benefit from rising GDP, since high levels of spending and output caused by the rise in economic activity mean more tax revenue from people and businesses. This can then be used for spending in socially desirable areas such as the health service and education. Alternatively, the government could use this extra tax revenue for tax cuts. Both these measures will be popular and may help to get the government re-elected.

Conversely, a fall in GDP is not normally welcomed by wage-earners, consumers, businesses or the government.

Factors that affect economic activity

The simplest way to analyse how the whole economy operates is to divide it into two groups: households and businesses. In the households group, people go to work and earn income. There is therefore a flow of income from businesses to households as payment for the work done.

Most of this income will promptly be spent and therefore there is a flow of income in the opposite direction from households to businesses. Economists call

this **consumption**. Of course, economists are not saying that people spend their income at the same business at which they work, although this could be true in some cases (e.g. if someone worked in a supermarket). They are saying that businesses in the economy pay their employees and then receive income back when people, acting as consumers rather than employees, spend it. Figure 57.3 shows this diagrammatically.

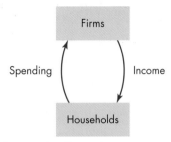

Figure 57.2 The circular flow of income

The **circular flow of income** begins with the flow of income that households have earned being spent on goods and services. This spending then enables firms to acquire the money they need to finance the next round of production.

Consider a starting position where the level of economic activity is quite high and GDP has been rising. If consumption spending by households is sufficient to buy the whole output produced by businesses, businesses will be very pleased because they will have made a profit and will not have unsold stocks of goods. Businesses will continue to employ the same number of people and may even think of expanding output.

However, this situation may not occur automatically because some of the income earned by households is not going to be spent. This means that businesses run the risk of not having all their output purchased by consumers. If this happens, they will have unsold goods that will not earn them any profit.

There are three reasons why all the income earned by households in the UK will not go directly to UK firms:

1. **Taxes.** The government takes a proportion of income through taxes.

2. **Savings.** Whatever remains after tax from an employee's wages is known as disposable income and people may decide to save some of this. Any income saved is obviously not spent.

3. **Imports.** Some income left after taxation and saving does not get spent on products made in the UK, even

though they might have been bought from UK retailers. Products that are made abroad and purchased by UK households are known as **imports**. When income is spent on products that are imported, there is a flow of income to foreign, rather than UK, firms.

These three reasons mean that there are **leakages** from the circular flow of income, which is why UK businesses do not receive back all the income that they have paid out to their employees. The diagram of the circular flow of income in the economy, including leakages, looks like Figure 57.4.

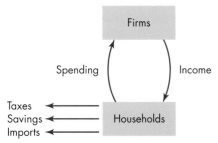

Figure 57.3 The circular flow of income, including leakages

Key Terms

Circular flow of income: the (continuous) flow of income from businesses to households as payment for work, and from households to businesses as payment for products.
Imports: purchase of goods from abroad.
Leakages: income that 'leaks away' from the economy and so does not get passed back to UK firms from households; this comprises taxes, savings and imports.

There are, however, a number of **injections** of income into the economy, which help to offset the leakages. These injections do not arise from UK consumers; they come from elsewhere. They are:

• **Government spending.** The government is a big spender in the UK on services such as schools, hospitals and defence. Many billions of pounds that businesses receive from the sale of their goods and services come not from household consumers, but from central and local government.
• **Exports.** Consumers abroad will buy goods from the UK. The sales of products made by UK businesses to other countries are known as **exports**. The products go abroad, but income flows into UK businesses in payment.
• **Investment.** Investment (also known as capital spending) by businesses is very important. It involves businesses buying products such as new buildings,

machinery and improved technology, in order to make themselves more competitive and productive in the future. Notice that when economists talk about investment, they are not talking about the business depositing money in a bank. That action would represent saving, which has the opposite effect on the economy to investing. Saving reduces total spending, while investment increases it.

Key Terms

Injections: income coming into the UK economy that does not come from UK households; this comprises investment, government spending and exports.
Exports: sale of goods to other countries by UK businesses.
Investment: purchase of capital equipment and/or buildings by businesses.

We can now amend the circular flow of income to show both leakages and injections, as in Figure 57.5.

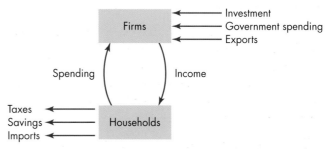

Figure 57.4 The circular flow of income, including leakages and injections

In summary, the circular flow of income is a continuous process. People are earning and being taxed, saving and spending (sometimes on imports) all the time. Businesses are continuously employing and therefore paying people income. They are also exporting products abroad and investing in capital equipment. The government takes in tax revenue and spends it.

What happens to economic activity when the variables change?

Even though the circular flow of income never stops flowing, this does not mean that the level of economic activity stays the same. When one of the variables changes, the level of economic activity is likely to change. In reality, several variables are likely to be changing at the same time, and what actually happens to the economy depends on whether a change in one variable is offset by another.

Assume that a newspaper report states that 'imports rose by £10 billion last month'. Imports are a leakage from the circular flow and so economic activity could be expected to fall. However, it may be the case that, over the same period of time, businesses have invested £10 billion. In this case (since investment is an injection), the net effect on income, and therefore the level of activity, in the economy will be nil.

Take the statement 'investment has risen by £5 billion'. Investment is beneficial (the economy needs modern factories) and it should increase the level of activity. Suppose, however, that at the same time households had decided to save £5 billion more than before. This leakage from the circular flow would offset the injection of income from investment. Furthermore, if the rise in saving was in fact greater than £5 billion, then, despite the rise in investment, the level of economic activity would fall.

This shows that when considering any news about the state of the economy, those running businesses need to consider what is happening to all the relevant variables. When reading headline statements in the press, they must ask themselves 'Yes, but what else has happened?' before passing a judgement on the likely effects of a change.

- **If total leakages are greater than total injections, the level of economic activity will fall.** This means that some businesses will experience a drop in the demand for their products, may make employees redundant, will invest less (as they are not very optimistic about the future) or may even close down.
- **If total injections are greater than total leakages, the level of economic activity will rise.** This means that demand will rise and businesses will take on more employees and invest more. However, rising injections of income may mean that spending is increasing too fast, and that businesses cannot meet the rising demand for their products. The result will be that prices will start to rise rapidly and this can be very damaging for the economy (see Unit 59).

In reality, small differences between leakages and injections do not matter much. Economic policy is not concerned with trying to balance them to the last pound, or even the last billion pounds. Economic policy is about creating a stable macroeconomic environment within which businesses can succeed. The government and the Bank of England are trying to prevent the potentially damaging effects of either a huge rise or a huge fall in GDP. Their policies to achieve this can have significant effects on businesses, as you will see in Unit 60.

Further Sources

www.hm-treasury.gov.uk – macroeconomic data and information about current government economic policy; the site includes a powerful search facility for all sorts of economic/business issues.

www.whystudyeconomics.ac.uk – information about the nature of economics and advice on how to study it.

What happens to economic activity if leakages do not equal injections?

The total amount of leakages from the economy in any given period of time is highly unlikely to be exactly the same as the total amount of injections.

Your Turn

Questions Time allowed 20 minutes

1. State the difference between GDP and GNP.
(2 marks)

2. State what is meant by 'the level of economic activity'.
(2 marks)

3. Outline the difference between imports and exports.
(4 marks)

4. Outline the difference between saving and investment.
(4 marks)

5. Analyse the importance of the circular flow of income to a business.
(9 marks)

(21 marks)

An understanding of the concept of the economic cycle is important because it makes possible an analysis of the macroeconomic variables that affect a particular business. Unit 57 showed how these variables are represented in the circular flow of income, which is reproduced in Figure 58.1. The economic cycle is likely to affect all these variables, both the injections and the leakages.

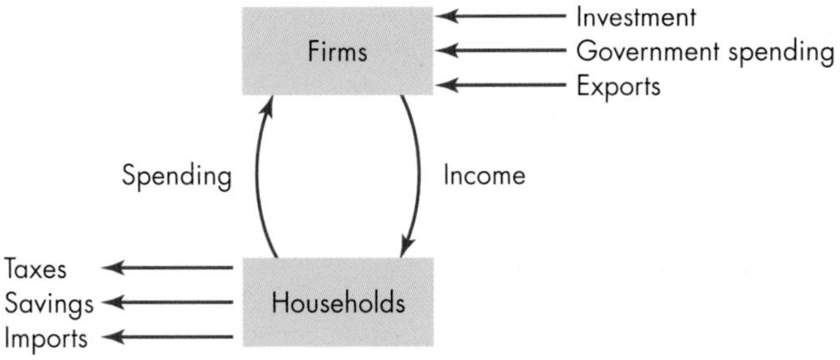

Figure 58.1 The circular flow of income

What is the economic cycle?

The **economic cycle** refers to the changes that occur in the level of economic activity over a period of time. It is also known as the business cycle or the trade cycle.

> ### Key Term
>
> **Economic cycle:** rises and falls in economic activity; these follow a pattern that can be identified as boom, recession, slump and recovery.

Economic activity in industrialised countries tends to proceed in cycles. Sometimes gross domestic product (GDP) is rising and sometimes it is falling. A period of economic prosperity is followed by a period of slower or economic prosperity is followed by a period of slower or

falling economic activity. Then, after a time, this gives way to a rise in GDP and the cycle starts again.

The economic cycle is usually represented by the graph in Figure 58.2. The trend (i.e. the general direction) in GDP is upwards, but the actual level of economic activity does not follow the smooth path of the trend.

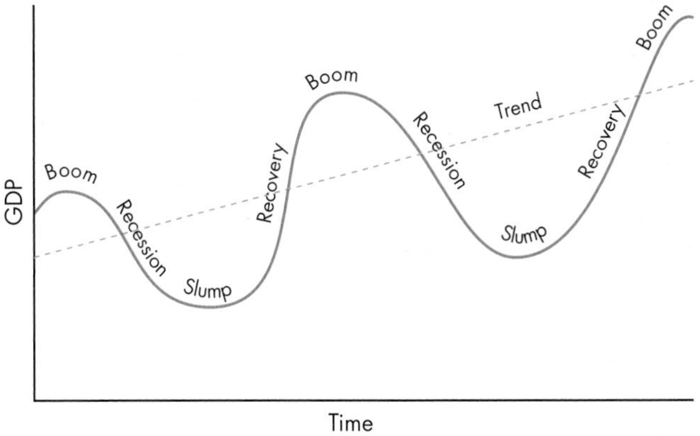

Figure 58.2 The economic cycle is divided into four stages

What happens at each stage of the cycle?

Boom

In this stage of the cycle, there is a high level of employment and consumption, and therefore a high demand for products. Businesses are profitable and feeling confident about future sales. This may encourage them to invest in new plant and machinery, which in turn leads to further rises in GDP. The boom eventually reaches a peak and GDP will not rise any further in that particular cycle.

Recession

A recession is defined as *two successive quarterly falls in GDP*: in other words, output falls for two consecutive three-month periods. In a recession, sales are falling and so business confidence about future consumer demand in some sectors is low. Initially, this may only happen in markets for luxury products, such as new cars and foreign holidays. This causes a fall in investment in those industries, since no business wants to invest in equipment and buildings that are going to be underused.

Figure 58.3 In a recession sales are falling and business confidence about future consumer demand may be low

The affected businesses make employees redundant, and this increased unemployment reduces consumer spending. This lowers demand and profits in other sectors of the economy, which is likely to depress investment even further. The government and the Bank of England need to act before a recession becomes too serious, otherwise business confidence will collapse, which could lead to a slump.

Slump

The symptoms of a slump (also known as a **trough** or a depression) are similar to those of a recession, except that they are more serious and widespread. In a depression, almost all the economy is affected, not just a few sectors. This leads to high levels of unemployment in many different industries, low business confidence, low levels of consumer spending, low levels of investment and low profits for businesses.

Recovery

In the recovery phase of the cycle, economic activity rises. Consumers start spending again and demand increases. Business confidence starts to increase as profits rise. Businesses take on more employees, and higher employment in turn increases consumer spending. This is how the upturn in economic activity gets under way. This eventually leads on to the next boom.

The time taken to complete a cycle can vary, as can the length of each particular phase. Obviously, it would be better for businesses if recessions were as brief, and booms as long, as possible.

How might a business evaluate where the economy is in the economic cycle?

A business needs to know where the economy is in the cycle in order to plan ahead and make decisions about output, employment and marketing. Much of this can be done through desk research (see Unit 3). Several sources of data should be used; a business should not rely on just one. Possible sources of data include:

- output/sales trends from the business's own plant(s)/shop(s)
- national/regional/local output and sales levels in the business's own sector
- national/regional/local employment levels
- national/regional/local spending levels
- national/regional/local sales levels
- professional journals/reviews of the economy, such as the Bank of England's Inflation Report
- news coming from managers' or directors' contacts with other (local/ regional/national) firms about the state of their business.

Why does the economic cycle exist?

There are many different views as to why the economic cycle exists. Figure 58.4 shows the economic cycle

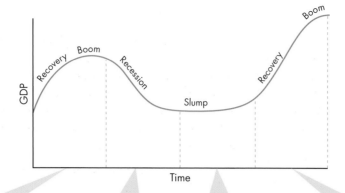

The high level of spending means that total demand in the economy exceeds supply. This starts to cause demand-pull inflation.

The boom in spending may suck in a large volume of imports. This will worsen the UK's trading position.

The counter these effects, the Bank of England puts up interest rates which slows down spending.

The government may also cut back on its level of spending.

As spending falls, some sectors of the economy start to experience a fall in the demand for their products.

These businesses then begin to lay off employees.

Spending falls further

Businesses are highly interdependent, so these falls in spending multiply across the economy, causing even larger falls in consumption.

As a result, many businesses postpone investment in new plant and equipment

---

The Bank of England will probably cut interest rates, as inflation is not likely to be a threat at this stage of the cycle.

The government may also stimulate demand by its own spending.

Businesses eventually have to undertake investment in the upkeep of buildings and machinery if they are to keep trading at all.

These three actions cause spending to rise.

Output and employment also start to grow – and the cycle begins again

Figure 58.4 Reasons for the economic cycle

again, but this time includes an explanation for the various changes in GDP at each stage of the cycle.

There are other explanations for the cycle. Some theories look at technological change and how it can increase GDP but also make employees redundant. Other theories look at changes in stock levels and the effect of businesses becoming either more pessimistic or optimistic about the future; their views on how much stock they need to hold will obviously affect their suppliers' output and employment decisions. Another possible cause is a 'shock' from an event such as the terrorist attacks on the World Trade Centre on 11 September 2001, or Hurricane Katrina, which devastated much of the Gulf of Mexico and its oil production in 2005.

Whatever the cause, the cycle exists and is a major influence on a business.

Effect of the economic cycle on the macroeconomic variables

In order to examine the effects of the economic cycle on businesses, it is first necessary to consider briefly how the macroeconomic variables themselves are affected as the economy moves through the cycle.

Consumption

Consumption depends mainly on *income*. The higher the level of employment (and therefore income) in the economy, the higher will be the level of consumption. The position of the economy in the cycle is therefore the major determinant of consumer demand for a business's products. Of course, in a recession or slump, consumers can still borrow money to spend.

Figure 58.5 An important additional determinant of consumption is the availability of credit

Investment

Businesses will always undertake a certain amount of **investment**, whatever the level of economic activity. There will always be a need to replace equipment that has worn out, and to keep up with competitors. However, a large amount of investment is related to GDP. If GDP is falling and a recession is predicted, businesses are unlikely to build new factories or install the latest technology. The reverse is also true: if GDP is rising, businesses will feel more confident about future sales and will invest in order to meet demand.

> ### Key Term
>
> **Investment:** purchase of capital equipment and/or buildings by businesses.

Government spending

Government spending is also known as *public spending*. It is important not to confuse 'public spending' with 'spending by the public', which is consumption spending.

> ### Key Term
>
> **Public spending:** spending by central and local government for the public's benefit, either on essential services or to change the level of economic activity.

Government spending can be used as a tool to stimulate or reduce the level of economic activity. As government spending is an injection into the circular flow of income, any rise in it will increase the level of economic activity, while any reduction will slow it down. This is known as *fiscal policy* (see Unit 60) and is of considerable relevance to the economic cycle.

Exports

The demand for exports is partly affected by their price. However, as they are goods that are sold abroad, they are not affected by the level of GDP in the UK; they depend on the level of economic activity in other countries. It is therefore possible for most of the UK economy to be doing quite well, but for particular businesses dependent on exports to be struggling because of a recession in continental Europe or the USA.

Taxation

Assuming that the government makes no change to the percentage rates of tax that people and businesses have to pay, as GDP rises, the tax revenue collected by the government will also rise. In a recession, the reverse will be true. Tax revenue is therefore determined to a large extent by the economic cycle.

Saving

Higher levels of *income* are generally associated with higher levels of saving in the economy. Two other factors also affect saving:

1. **The rate of interest.** For many people, this is unlikely to be the major factor affecting saving. If a person is earning the minimum wage and interest rates rise, this is unlikely to generate much more saving because of their relatively low income. On the other hand, if a person's income doubles as a result of finding a new job, this might increase the amount saved.

2. **Expectations of the future.** If people feel that they are about to lose their jobs, they may try to save more money. However, if people are confident about the security of their jobs, they may see little point in saving.

Imports

A rise in the level of economic activity is associated with an increase in the amount of imports. This is for two reasons:

1. As spending rises, some of it will be spent on goods that have been produced in other countries.

2. As businesses increase output to meet rises in demand, they will need more raw materials and capital equipment. Some of these will have to be imported.

How does the economic cycle affect businesses?

Not all businesses in the economy are affected in the same way by changes in economic activity caused by the economic cycle. Consider the following examples.

A business selling PCs

How might this business be affected in a recession? To what extent are PCs essential for everyday life? If they are considered necessary, there may be little effect at all on demand. Presumably though, some people who are worried about losing their job will now cancel their planned purchase of a PC. Others will keep using their old model rather than upgrade. Demand is therefore likely to fall.

However, even if the market for PCs to be used at home suffers a fall in demand, PCs are often provided for people at work. To what extent will businesses cancel purchases or delay upgrading? If businesses continue to buy PCs in large quantities, the effect of the recession on the firm selling them will not be so severe.

A business selling mobile phones

Mobile phones have quickly changed from being a luxury item to a necessity for some people. If there is a recession in the UK, to what extent will sales be affected? This could be an even more difficult question to answer than the one concerning PCs. This is because the groups who buy mobile phones are different.

The business may find that demand from young people, who use mobile phones partly as a fashion statement, will be largely unaffected. This is because these consumers see them as essential for their lifestyle. They will almost certainly continue to buy the latest models. A business selling mobile phones would need to consider demographics very carefully. If the proportion of younger people in the population is relatively small, the fact that they continue to buy mobile phones may not offset the decline in purchases (and upgrades) among other age groups.

A supermarket chain

If the economy moves into recession, will there be any change in demand for a supermarket's products? On the face of it, the answer is no, since people must eat in order to live. They also require other household goods, such as washing powder. However, if incomes are falling, there is likely to be an increased demand for 'budget' or 'value' products, so the supermarket will need to start stocking more of these if it is to meet consumer requirements. New suppliers may have to be found for some of these products. At the same time, the business may alter its advertising and promotional policies to reflect the change. Both these factors will involve additional expense.

Examiner's voice

Questions in the examination will centre around one specific business, not all the businesses in the economy. Therefore, you will need to apply your knowledge of the economic cycle and its effects to a particular business.

Summary

Businesses are, to a large extent, at the mercy of the state of the economy, but that does not mean that they can and should do nothing when the level of economic activity changes. The likely effect of a recession on a business depends on how it chooses to respond.

Further Sources

www.statistics.gov.uk – data on the macroeconomic variables, the overall state of the UK economy and the different regions and sectors.

Case Study Time allowed 35 minutes

A. A. Alarm Systems

Alan Armstrong runs a small private company that installs alarm systems to households and businesses. He decided to start his own business, having worked for 10 years as an engineer for one of the major installation companies in the region.

He founded A. A. Alarms in 2003 and business has grown steadily. He won a major contract with a large housebuilding business early on, and his good workmanship here earned him a reputation that has since generated a steady stream of customers. He now employs three other people.

Alan, however, was slightly puzzled by the economic reports in his morning newspaper that seemed to be contradictory. One article discussed the government's intention to press on with more housing developments in several parts of the country, which included Alan's. Reading this pleased him and made him feel optimistic about the future. But another article stated that although there had been a rise in GDP over the past six months, it was less than had been predicted by the government. This, the article said, meant that the increase in consumers' income and spending had also not been as large as expected. Alan was not so pleased with this.

He was also not pleased when one of his employees, Nick, told him that morning that he was handing in his notice in order to work for a new alarm installer that had just started up in the area. Nick told Alan that the new company was offering installations at up to 20% less than A. A. Alarms, so he felt that his job would be more secure and that the prospects were better.

Alan decided to do some careful planning. He had been thinking about investing in some new technology that would be a major help to him and his engineers when diagnosing faults in a system. Now he was not so sure. He thought it would be best to start planning by establishing just where the UK was on the economic cycle.

1. Outline **one** effect of an increase in consumers' income on A. A. Alarms. (4 marks)

2. State **two** ways in which Alan could assess the state of the economy. (2 marks)

3. State **two** ways in which the government might benefit from a rise in GDP. (2 marks)

4. Outline **two** factors that could influence Alan's decision to invest in some new technology. (4 marks)

5. Evaluate the extent to which a downturn in economic growth might affect AA Alarms. (18 marks)

(30 marks)

THE MACROECONOMIC OBJECTIVES OF GOVERNMENT

Most economists would agree that a government has four **macroeconomic** objectives:

1. **A low and stable rate of inflation.** The current government has set a target of 2% a year for the rate at which prices in the economy should increase.

2. **A high level of employment.** As many people as possible should be in work.

3. **Economic growth.** There should be an increase in the amount of goods and services produced in the economy each year.

4. **A balance of payments equilibrium.** The value of the payments that the UK makes for imports should be similar to the value of the income it earns from exports.

Key Term

Macroeconomics: study and analysis of the behaviour of the whole economy.

A textbook from 30 years ago might have said 'another possible objective is a fairer distribution of income and wealth'. Since then the gap between those at the top of the income distribution and those at the bottom has become wider, so what has happened to this objective?

The government *is* still interested in the distribution of income and wealth, but policies to tackle inequality are now different from those of the past. Previously, money was taken in tax from the relatively wealthy and distributed in the form of various benefits to the less well off. This was sometimes called the 'Robin Hood' approach. Although, of course, the relatively poor still receive benefits, the emphasis now is on the government providing opportunities for people to improve their employment prospects. Unemployment

benefit has been replaced by a Jobseeker's Allowance to reflect this. The government tries to improve people's ability to find jobs (and therefore earn more income via their own efforts) through policies on education and skills training, and by creating the right conditions in the economy for people to set up their own businesses and run them successfully.

These right conditions involve achieving as many of the four objectives as possible. When these objectives are not being met, it creates problems for the economy and therefore for businesses. This chapter considers these problems and why the achievement of the macroeconomic objectives is so important if businesses are to succeed.

A low and stable rate of inflation

People often say that inflation means rising prices, but this is only partly correct. At any one time, some prices in the economy will be rising but some will be falling. It would therefore be more accurate to say that **inflation** is a persistent general tendency for prices to rise. A high rate of inflation is bad for the economy and therefore bad for businesses.

Inflation makes UK exports uncompetitive. As a result of **globalisation**, identical products (e.g. the same model of car, brand of clothes, can of soft drink) can be made almost anywhere in the world. If the UK has a rate of inflation that is higher than those in other countries, the price of UK exports will rise, making them less attractive to consumers abroad. A fall in the level of exports will mean less income for businesses, which could affect employment.

Inflation can also affect investment. Multinational companies look to produce in the cheapest possible location. This means that when they invest in a new plant, they choose the country with the lowest rate of inflation. They do not want to locate in a country where the price of labour and raw material inputs is rising sharply, because this would make their products uncompetitive.

Inflation creates uncertainty. Managers dislike uncertainty about what the return on an investment will be. It is one thing to estimate that the profits from an investment will be £100,000 a year for the next 10 years, but if inflation is running out of control, how much will this be worth **in real terms**: in other words, what quantity of products will this sum of money actually buy? Low inflation allows businesses to plan their investments with some degree of certainty about their return and so encourages investment.

Key Terms

Inflation: persistent general tendency of prices in the economy to rise

Deflation: the opposite of inflation, it occurs when there is a persistent tendency for prices in the economy to fall.

Globalisation: ability of multinational companies to purchase inputs, make products and sell them, all over the world

In real terms: adjusted for the effects of price rises.

Examiner's voice

When inflation falls, this does not mean that prices have gone down; it just means that the rate of increase in prices has fallen.

In summary, inflation is bad for businesses because it:

- makes UK businesses uncompetitive internationally
- can lead to unemployment
- creates uncertainty, which can deter investment.

Deflation

Deflation is the opposite of inflation, and occurs when there is a persistent tendency for prices in the economy to fall. It is important to note that when inflation falls,

this is not deflation because it does not mean that prices have fallen; it simply means that the rate of price increases has slowed down.

A simple example can illustrate this principle. Assume that a product originally costs £100 and after 12 months it costs £110. This represents a rate of price rise (i.e. inflation) of 10%. If inflation continued to rise at 10%, then the following year the product would cost £121. If however inflation falls to 5% then the price of the product will now be £115.50. Inflation has fallen but the price of the product is still rising, but not at such a fast rate. For *deflation* to occur, the price of the product would have to actually fall. In reality, economists are interested in the prices of all products, but the principle is exactly the same.

At first sight deflation would appear to be beneficial; if prices are falling then consumers and businesses receive more for their money. However therein lies the problem. If consumers expect prices of products such as clothes, cars and houses to continue to fall, they tend to postpone consumption on the grounds that if they wait a month or two then the price will be even lower. It was noted in Unit 57 that falls in consumption lead to lower output and sales from businesses.

Furthermore, businesses will then react to this. If demand is falling as consumers wait for even better deals, employees will be made redundant. This will lower national income, and therefore demand in the economy, even further. Businesses will also postpone investment in new factories, offices, and technology. After all, why build a new factory if the demand for products is falling? Also, the business might well reason that instead of the value of a new office block rising over a period of time, with deflation it might fall. Why make an investment which is going to lose value? As investment is an injection into the circular flow of income, any fall in investment will worsen the fall in national income. Deflation could bring about a slump, which is not beneficial to businesses.

Japan suffered badly from deflation at the turn of the century, but it is not something that has historically troubled the UK economy, although some economists in 2009 were predicting that the sheer depth of the recession could mean that deflation might occur.

A high level of employment

The government wants a low level of unemployment for three reasons:

1. **Unemployment is a waste of human resources.** If unemployed people were at work producing goods and services, society as a whole would have more goods and services to enjoy. People would have a higher standard of living.

2. **Unemployment is bad for the individual.** Unemployment is often associated with social problems such as vandalism and drug abuse. The lack of a job can also be damaging to a person's self-esteem.

3. **Unemployment is bad for society as a whole.** The problems associated with drugs and vandalism have to be paid for. In addition, benefits have to be paid to people who have no job. 'Society' has to pay, in the sense that this money could be spent in other, more productive areas, such as education and health.

In summary, unemployment is bad for businesses because:

- it means lower levels of spending and therefore lower demand for businesses' products
- it can lead to social problems, which have to be paid for.

Economic growth

The benefit of **economic growth** is that, if more goods and services are produced, people have a higher standard of living. Over the past 30 years or so this objective has changed slightly. It is not just a continuous growth of goods and services that is desired; the growth should be sustainable. In other words, where possible, growth should come from the use of renewable resources, and damage to the environment resulting from growth should be minimised. Moreover, the needs of future generations should be considered. Issues such as the ozone layer and global warming have put this sharply into focus.

Key Term

Economic growth: an increase in the volume of goods and services produced each year.

In summary, a lack of growth is bad for businesses because it:

- causes unemployment and so reduces the demand for businesses' products
- means that people's standard of living (and therefore spending) is not increasing as fast as it could be.

Figure 59.1 Sustainable growth has become much more important in recent years.

A balance of payments equilibrium

'Balance of payments' is the term used to describe the financial records of the UK's trade with the rest of the world. For example, someone who stays in a hotel abroad makes a payment to the hotel, which is recorded as an *outflow* of income from the UK. If a UK company operating abroad sends its profits back to the UK, these are recorded as an *inflow* of money.

The balance of payments is about the measurement of all these types of inflows and outflows, but the most important component of the balance of payments is known as the **balance of trade**. This is the record of all the UK's **imports** and **exports**. It is this figure that is usually used in the news.

Key Terms

Balance of trade: difference between the value of exports and imports. If exports exceed imports, there is a balance of trade surplus; if imports exceed exports, there is a balance of trade deficit.

Imports: purchase by UK businesses and consumers of products made abroad.

Exports: sale of products from UK businesses abroad.

An excess of imports over exports is known as a *trade deficit*; an example is shown in part (a) of Figure 59.2. An excess of exports over imports is known as a trade surplus; an example is shown in part (b).

Why is the balance of trade important? If people spend more than they receive in income, at first their savings will be run down and then, if the pattern of earning and spending continues, they will have to borrow. It is the

(a) Trade deficit   (b) Trade surplus

Figure 59.2 Balance of trade

same principle for a country if it continuously imports more than it exports. All countries have balance of trade deficits from time to time, but a prolonged deficit causes problems because the imported goods have to be paid for somehow. It is important that the UK exports sufficient products to 'pay its way' internationally.

In summary, a trade deficit is bad for businesses because:

- UK businesses are losing out on sales to foreign businesses because of imports, and this will cause unemployment.
- UK businesses are not earning sufficient revenue from exports to pay for the country's volume of imports.

Why do these problems occur?

The problems of inflation, unemployment, balance of trade deficits and low economic growth have to be tackled if businesses and the society they operate within are to prosper. In order to do this, it is necessary to establish their causes.

What causes inflation?

Why do prices rise? The answer is deceptively simple: because businesses put them up. There are two main reasons for this:

A rise in costs

The price of a product is made up of the total cost of all the inputs that go into it, such as labour, raw materials and interest rate charges, plus an amount for profit put on top: the mark-up. If any of the input costs rise, the business will probably put up prices in order to maintain the same mark up. In the example shown in Figure 59.3, if the cost of raw materials rises from £5 to £8 per unit, the business is likely to try to increase the selling price

from £25 to £28 in order to make the same amount of profit. When rising costs force UK businesses to increase their prices, this is known as cost-push inflation.

The level of demand in the economy

If total demand in the economy exceeds supply, this will cause prices to rise. If a business's telephones are ringing constantly with customers asking for more products, managers will feel confident about putting up prices without there being any adverse effects on demand. Where there is too much demand and not enough supply, there is said to be demand-pull inflation.

Figure 59.3 Effect of a rise in costs on selling price

> **Key Term**
>
> **Market failure:** where a market does not produce the desired outcome. In the case of the labour market, it means that there is unemployment.

What causes unemployment?

Unemployment means that the labour market in the economy has failed; i.e. not everyone who could work is actually working. The total supply of workers is less than the total demand for them. There are several reasons why this might occur.

Some people choose not to work and try to exist on benefits; these people are said to be *voluntarily unemployed*. There is also seasonal unemployment, which means that some employees (e.g. in the hotel or agricultural sectors) tend to be unemployed at certain times of the year. Finally, there are always people moving from job to job; when people are between jobs, this is known as frictional unemployment. Economists tend not to worry too much about these types of unemployment because they are usually short term. Other causes of unemployment can be much more serious because the problems are longer term:

A slowdown in the level of economic activity

This causes the demand for products and thus the demand for workers who produce those goods to fall.

This type of unemployment is known as demand deficient (or cyclical) unemployment (see Unit 58).

Wages are too high

High wages create more spending and so help prevent demand-deficient unemployment. However, if they rise too high, this will cause businesses to lay off workers and/or try to replace them with machines. This type of unemployment is known as 'real wage unemployment'. Of course 'too high' is a matter of opinion; workers will view wage rates rather differently from the businesses that pay them.

A decline in certain types of industry

When industries decline, workers have to try to find jobs in the expanding sectors of the economy. This is not always easy because they may not have the right skills. If someone has been a coal miner for 30 years, he cannot easily find work in one of the new, fast-growing labour markets of the economy, such as designing software games for children. If unemployment results from a change in the whole structure of output in the economy, this is known as 'structural unemployment'. The traditional industries that made Britain 'great' during the Industrial Revolution, such as coal, steel, shipbuilding and textiles, declined rapidly after the Second World War.

The problem in the labour market can be reversed. If the demand for workers is greater than their supply, then there are shortages of labour and wages will tend to rise as businesses offer higher pay to attract employees. Either a surplus or shortage of workers could occur right across the economy or at local level. There could be an excess supply of workers in one area and excess demand in another; unemployed semi-skilled assembly workers in the Midlands (causing the rate of wage growth to slow in that region), and a shortage of engineers in the South East of England (causing the growth of their wages to rise).

People do not 'flow' easily from one job to another due to skill limitations (known as 'occupational immobility') and family ties (known as 'social or geographical immobility'). This means that even when government assistance for retraining and relocation is available, these problems in the labour market can take years to correct.

What causes a poor rate of growth?

Several causes of a low growth rate may be suggested:

A lack of investment

If businesses do not invest, they will lack modern factories with the most up-to-date capital equipment with which to compete with businesses in other countries. This could mean that UK goods are priced uncompetitively and/or are of lower quality than those made abroad, so consumers will not buy them.

Laws may hinder business activity

If the UK's legal framework (sometimes called 'red tape') is tougher on businesses than other countries, this will deter entrepreneurs and may also put off inward investment into the UK from foreign firms.

The workforce may lack skills and qualifications

If so, the UK will not have a highly productive workforce capable of producing high-quality products.

What causes a balance of trade deficit?

A trade deficit for the UK means that it is importing more than it is exporting. The causes are twofold:

- **Imported products are cheaper or of better quality than those produced in the UK.** If this is the case, it is not surprising that UK consumers buy them.
- **UK businesses are not selling sufficient quantities of goods that consumers in other countries want.** This could be because the design or quality is poor and/or their prices are high. Sometimes the exchange rate makes UK exports expensive abroad. There is often little that UK businesses can do about this problem, which is considered further in Unit 61.

Further Sources

http://eh.net/hmit – to find out the purchasing power of money in different years (e.g. to buy the equivalent of £1,000 worth of goods bought during the Second World War, you would need around £29,000 today).

Case study Time allowed 30 minutes

Greenland Electrical

Greenland Electrical Ltd (GEL) was established in 2002. It is a small company producing motors, pumps and other components for washing machines. The design of the components means that the washing machines that they are used in are very efficient in terms of water and power use. The company employs 30 people, most of whom belong to a trade union.

The chief executive, Rory Palmer, is the person who originally created the ideas and established the business. This proved very difficult to do because he had little previous experience of running a business. He had a lot of trouble raising sufficient finance to get started and even now cashflow is often a problem. The company does not make the whole washing machine; it sells its products to two established manufacturers.

The use of Greenland's technology means that the final selling price of the machines is higher than ordinary models, but as they are targeted at the middle and higher income groups this has, so far, not been a problem. GEL's two customers have been very effective in their advertising and sales have been growing. Rory has been approached by a distributor in Germany who wants to open negotiations for sales to be made in Europe. He has therefore been thinking recently of expanding the business and moving to a larger factory unit. He was, however, concerned when he heard a news bulletin warning about a possible rise in the rate of inflation. He was also alarmed that some economists were talking about the possibility of a rise in unemployment as well.

1. State the four macroeconomic objectives of a government. (4 marks)

2. State what is meant by the term 'standard of living'. (2 marks)

3. Analyse how rising inflation might affect GEL. (9 marks)

4. Evaluate how a rise in the level of unemployment might affect the strategic decisions of GEL. (18 marks)

(33 marks)

ECONOMIC POLICY AND ITS EFFECT ON BUSINESSES

Economic policy is conducted in three ways: through monetary policy, fiscal policy and the exchange rate. All of these can be used to influence the economy. To speak of the government controlling the economy would be wrong; a better phrase might be 'steering it in the right direction'.

The government cannot alter the behaviour of people and businesses simply by telling them what to do, so it has to use economic policy to try to alter their behaviour. The economic policy or policies that are used depend on what economic objective(s) the government or the Bank of England is trying to achieve (see Unit 59).

Monetary policy

Monetary policy is concerned with manipulating the level of demand in the economy through the rate of interest. 'Rate of interest' has two different meanings:

1. To borrowers it is the cost of borrowing; what has to be paid back to the lender.

2. To savers it is the reward for saving; the return on their money.

When interest rates change, they all move in the same direction: when rates rise for savers, they also rise for borrowers.

Until 1997, monetary policy was decided by the Chancellor of the Exchequer and then put into effect by the Bank of England. One of the first actions taken by the then Chancellor of the Exchequer, Gordon Brown, when Labour came to power in 1997, was to make the Bank of England independent and hand control of monetary policy to the bank's **Monetary Policy Committee (MPC)**. The MPC is a panel of experts from the financial and business world, which meets once a month to decide whether to change the rate of interest. Although the government owns the Bank of England, the MPC is entirely independent.

Key Terms

Bank of England: the central bank in the UK; as banker to the government and other banks, it conducts monetary policy and is not involved in personal banking.

Monetary policy: manipulation of the level of demand in the economy using the rate of interest.

Monetary Policy Committee (MPC): committee of the Bank of England that meets once a month to decide whether to change the rate of interest.

When monetary policy was in the government's hands, there was always the temptation to use the rate of interest for political purposes. For example, a government might lower the rate of interest before a general election in order to induce a feel-good factor, even if the economy was at the wrong place on the economic cycle for this to be the appropriate policy. If the level of demand was already rising too fast, a *rise* in interest rates would have been the correct policy.

As a result of this, when interest rates were eventually raised, they would have had to go higher than would have been necessary, had the government acted economically rather than politically in the first place. High rates can be damaging to businesses.

Virtually all economists now agree that giving the Bank of England control of interest rates was a good decision; governments can no longer meddle with the economy for political reasons.

What is the Bank of England trying to achieve?

The Bank of England is responsible for meeting the government's target for the rate of inflation in the UK economy. This is currently 2%. A low and stable rate of inflation is beneficial to businesses (see Unit 59).

The bank does look at factors such as the level of unemployment and output when assessing the level of demand (and therefore the possibility of inflation exceeding the target), but low inflation is its priority.

How does monetary policy work?

The rate of interest is essentially the *price of money*. The price of something affects its demand, and therefore the demand for money responds to changes in the rate of interest.

If the Bank of England wants consumers and businesses to spend less, it raises the rate of interest. Figure 60.2 shows that if the rate is increased from r_1 to r_2, this will discourage borrowing and spending. The demand for money will fall from Q_1 to Q_2. It may also encourage some people who have surplus cash to save. The opposite would apply if the bank cut the rate to r_1.

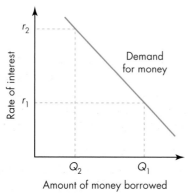

Figure 60.1 The demand for money

To quote from the Bank of England's website:

> Monetary policy operates by influencing the cost of money. The Bank sets an interest rate that affects the whole pattern of rates set by the commercial banks for their savers and borrowers. This, in turn, affects spending and output in the economy, and eventually costs and prices.

Therefore, if the Bank of England wants to slow down the economy and control inflation by lowering consumer spending and business investment, it puts up the rate of interest. If it wants to encourage people to spend and businesses to expand, it lowers the rate of interest.

Effects of a rise in the rate of interest on businesses

A rise in the rate of interest is likely to have the following effects.

Investment will fall

Businesses are more likely to make do with older, less efficient machinery and hardware because the cost of borrowing money to replace them has risen. This will have a knock-on effect on their suppliers. In addition, businesses know that a rise in interest rates will slow down consumer spending: this will make it even less attractive to invest.

A fall in investment will slow down the level of economic activity, and if the fall in investment is severe enough, it may cause a recession (see Unit 58).

Consumer spending will fall

As the interest payable on mortgages, loans and credit cards increases, spending on other products will fall. The demand for luxury items, which are often bought on credit, will fall.

It is often said that when rates rise, people save more. This, however, ignores the reality of the effect of a rate rise on a typical household with for example £2,000 in savings and a mortgage of £100,000.

Using these figures, let us consider this point in more detail. First, we make some assumptions to simplify the analysis, as shown in Table 60.1.

Table 60.2 shows what happens to the Smiths' finances when the rate rises.

Some people (probably those with no mortgages or other loans) can save more when the interest rate rises, but for the 20 million or so people like the Smiths with

The Smiths have a disposable income of £1,500 per month.	+£1,500
The household has £2,000 saved in the bank, earning 3% interest. This means that the interest paid to them is £60 per year, or £5 per month.	+£5
The rate of interest on the family's £100,000 mortgage is 6%. This makes the monthly interest charge £500 (£6,000/12). The household also has to make a capital repayment of £400 each month towards the money it owes. The total monthly repayment is therefore £900.	−£900
The household's total monthly income available for spending is: £1,500 + £5 − £900 = £605	**£605**

Table 60.1 The Smiths' family budget with a 3% interest rate

Assume that disposable income is still £1,500. Employees do ask for higher wages when interest rates rise, but even if granted this will not happen at once.	+£1,500
At the bank the £2,000 savings now receives interest at 4%. This means a yearly return of £80. The monthly interest paid increases from £5 to £6.67 (£80/12).	+£6.67
As the rate of interest is now 7% repayments on the mortgage go up to £7,000 a year. This means a monthly interest repayment of £583 (£7,000/12). Add on the £400 capital repayment and that is a total of £983.	−£983
This means that income left for consumption is now £523.67. The Smith household is worse off by over £80. £1,500 + £6.67 − £983 = £523.67	£523.67

Table 60.2 The Smiths' family budget with a 4% interest rate

various loan debts, this is unlikely to be possible. The main reason for the fall in consumer demand when interest rates rise is the *rise in borrowing costs*, not an increase in saving.

Conversely, a cut in the interest rate will raise consumer spending, not so much because it is no longer worth saving, but because of the effect on consumers like the Smiths of having to pay less on their loans.

A rise in the interest rate will also slow down the rate of growth of house prices. When this happens, there is a *wealth effect*. As people see that the value of their property is no longer rising (and it may even be falling), they feel less confident about spending and this reduces demand.

The exchange rate is likely to rise

When UK interest rates rise, the pound becomes a more attractive currency to invest in and the increased demand for sterling causes the exchange rate to rise. This means that any business selling abroad will find that its exports become more expensive to foreign customers. It also means that imports become cheaper. This will be good if a business uses imported raw materials, but not so good if it is competing with foreign imports of a finished product (see Unit 61).

Effects of a fall in the rate of interest on businesses

A fall in the rate of interest is likely to have the following effects.

Investment will increase

A lot of investment is made with borrowed money. Any fall in the rate of interest means that it is now cheaper for businesses to borrow money to finance expansion and capital spending. They will therefore increase their purchases of new buildings, machinery and technology.

Any investment will raise the level of economic activity and this means more spending by consumers and a further boost to GDP. The installation of modern plant and equipment will also help UK businesses to be more competitive internationally.

Consumer spending will increase

Anyone with a mortgage (or any other type of loan) will now pay less interest and so their purchases of other goods and services are likely to rise, although not all businesses will be affected in the same way. For example, a travel agent is more likely to expect an increase in demand as a result of a fall in interest rates than a baker. When it comes to spending on credit, consumers will now be prepared to borrow to buy consumer durables such as cars, DVDs and washing machines.

The exchange rate is likely to fall

How this occurs and the precise effects on businesses are explained in Unit 61. For the moment, it is sufficient to say that a fall in the exchange rate makes UK exports cheaper abroad, so any business that sells abroad will find that its exports become more attractive. It also means that imports become more expensive. This causes an unwelcome rise in costs if a business has to buy raw materials from abroad. On the other hand, a fall in exchange rates will benefit any UK firms that are competing with foreign imports.

Figure 60.2 If interest rates are cut, consumer spending is likely to rise

The 'credit crunch'

Monetary policy was used in trying to counteract 'the credit crunch' of 2008/9. This term referred to the problems in the financial sector of the economy. By the end of 2007 it became clear that in America many banks had made billions of dollars worth of loans to customers with poor credit ratings and that these borrowers were starting to default on their repayments. In 2008 it was obvious that many UK financial institutions had lent money in a similar manner and were experiencing the same difficulties. A bank, like any business, needs a stream of income (from its loan repayments) to pay bills and to keep the business growing through loans to new customers. Without this income a bank is going to be in severe difficulty.

A crisis in the financial sector of the economy is very serious. Once customers think that a bank or building society is financially insecure they try to withdraw their savings. This is exactly what happened with Northern

Rock, and this further loss of finance can only worsen the bank's situation. Following the crisis at Northern Rock many banks in the UK became worried that a sizeable number of customers (and even some UK banks themselves) were so financially weak that they began to reverse their policy of 'easy loans for all' and increasingly started to lend only to those with very secure credit ratings. Mortgages and other loans began to cost more and were harder to obtain. This became known as 'the credit crunch'.

There are serious implications to this sort of situation; once lending slows down then so does economic activity, with the danger of a recession and a steep rise in unemployment. If this happens, business confidence can collapse, causing further falls in investment and spending. One of the measures the Bank of England took to avoid this was to lower the rate of interest to make it easier (i.e. cheaper) for personal and business customers to repay loans. This meant that the banks could start to feel more confident about lending again.

How quickly do changes in interest rates take effect?

The Bank of England works on a timescale of around 18 months: this is how long it takes for changes in interest rates to have their full effect on investment and consumption. Suppose that the bank increases the interest rate. Although some investment planned for the future will be cancelled or postponed, many projects will already be under way. Once the construction of a factory has been started, it has to be completed.

Consumers also take time to react. Spending patterns do not change overnight and for millions of people it could be many months before their behaviour adjusts to the fact that they have less to spend. This is partly because there is a strong element of 'keeping up with the neighbours' when buying goods such as cars and mobile phones. For quite a long time, people may run down their savings to maintain levels of spending.

This time-lag is not necessarily a disadvantage to the Bank of England. When it puts up interest rates, what it is hoping for is that the slowdown in economic activity is gradual rather than sudden; it wants a 'soft landing' rather than a recession. The bank hopes that as demand slows down, businesses will try to lower their costs and hence the prices they charge to their customers. If price rises slow down, that is precisely what the bank is trying to achieve in terms of its inflation target.

Similarly, when interest rates are cut, the Bank of England is hoping for a steady, sustained increase in output, which will encourage long-term prosperity in the economy, rather than a burst of inflationary growth that has to be swiftly curbed by rate rises.

Fiscal policy

Fiscal policy is conducted through taxation and government spending. It is controlled by the government through the Chancellor of the Exchequer, the member of the cabinet responsible for the government's finances. The Chancellor works closely with the Treasury, which is the ministry responsible for helping to determine and implement the government's economic policy.

Key Terms

Fiscal policy: economic policy conducted by the government through taxation and public spending.

The Budget: an annual statement of how much the government intends to spend in the next year and how this spending will be financed.

Fiscal policy affects the level of demand in the economy and so has a significant impact on businesses. In order to evaluate what is likely to happen to the demand for its products, a business needs to analyse **the Budget**. The Budget is the occasion (usually in April) when the Chancellor states how much the government intends to spend in the next year and how this spending will be financed.

Examiner's voice

To discuss the likely effects of fiscal policy on a particular business, it is important to understand the nature of the various types of tax, the purposes of government spending and the effects of these.

Taxation

There are two types of tax: direct and indirect.

Direct taxes

Direct taxes are taken directly from:

- a person's income when they work. This is called income tax.

- a business when it makes a profit. The type of tax paid by a business depends on its legal status: sole traders and those in a partnership pay income tax, whereas a company (private or public) pays corporation tax.

There is another direct deduction from a person's income called *national insurance*. This is taken as a contribution towards the state pension and treatment under the National Health Service. It may not be called national insurance tax, but it is deducted by law directly from a person's income and so can be treated as a direct tax. A business also has to pay a certain amount of national insurance for every employee. The more employees a business has on its payroll, the more it has to pay. For this reason, national insurance paid by a business is sometimes called a payroll tax.

There is also direct taxation at local level. Households pay *council tax* to the local authority for services such as refuse collection, street cleaning and the fire service. Businesses have to pay the business rate to help fund the same services. This local authority taxation on a business is in addition to any national insurance payments and taxes that are paid to central government.

Indirect taxes

These taxes are not paid when a person or business earns money, but when they *spend* it; that is why they are 'indirect'. Most products have value added tax (VAT) put on them. This means that a percentage of the selling price is paid to the government as a tax. VAT is currently 15%.

On many goods there is another indirect tax as well as VAT. The government puts *excise duty* on certain products. This duty is a fixed amount of tax on each item rather than a percentage rate, but the effect is the same: it makes the product more expensive and raises revenue for the government. Examples include car tax (the proper name of which is vehicle excise duty), tobacco, alcohol and petrol.

The government taxes businesses and people (see Figure 60.3) in order to:

- raise revenue
- affect the level of economic activity
- influence the pattern of expenditure.

Raising revenue

The government plays a major role in the economy, and the amount it spends amounts to around 40% of GDP. Much of this spending comes from tax revenue.

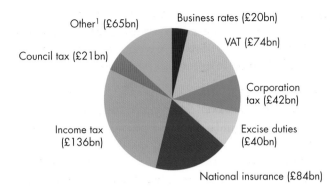

¹ Other sources include capital taxes, stamp duties, vehicle excise duties and some other tax and non-tax receipts (e.g. interest and dividends).

Source: HM Treasury

Figure 60.3 Sources of UK tax revenue, 2005/06

Affecting the level of economic activity

In the years following the Second World War, the government often tried to manipulate the economy to achieve full employment and low inflation through tax and expenditure changes. However, the idea that this can be done with any precision is no longer popular; experience shows that the policy may have the wrong effect. This is because there are *time-lags* before the effects occur. This means that when the effects eventually come through, the economy may have moved on to a situation in which the policy is no longer appropriate. For example, if taxes are cut to avoid a recession, by the time the extra spending starts to happen the economy may already be recovering strongly, which is likely to have the unintended consequence of a rise in inflation.

Nevertheless, the principle of using tax and expenditure changes to 'nudge the economy in the right direction' is still accepted. Lower taxation should encourage spending by consumers and businesses, which will boost the level of economic activity. Likewise, an increase in government spending can have the same effect. The increases in spending on public services at the start of the millennium are said by many economists to have helped prevent a recession in the UK. Similarly in 2008, even with the budget deficit larger than expected, many economists were urging the chancellor not to cut public spending because the outlook for the economy was very uncertain. Cuts in government spending would have reduced the deficit but would have slowed the economy down further. On the other hand, if too much demand is causing inflation and/or too many imports, the government could increase tax rates, which will reduce spending.

Influencing the pattern of expenditure

The government tries to encourage certain kinds of behaviour and discourage others. Lower rates of tax are placed on products that the government is trying to encourage people to buy; for example, unleaded petrol has a lower rate of tax than leaded. Taxes are put on products that can be harmful, such as cigarettes and alcohol, in order to discourage their use.

Public spending

The government intervenes in the economy through **public spending** (see Figure 60.4). It does so for three main purposes.

> ### Key Term
>
> **Public spending:** government spending on goods and services for the public (e.g. health, education and defence).

To provide essential services that the private sector is unlikely to offer

This is another example of how a market can fail because 'the market', i.e. private businesses, will not usually want to supply services such as a police force, a fire service or street lighting, as these are unlikely to make a profit. This means that central or local government has to provide them. Other examples are healthcare and pensions. It is likely that many people will fail to realise how important these are (and therefore will not save any money to pay for them) until it is too late, i.e. when they become ill or old. This means that the government has to do it for them by taxing people and providing the services when they need them. These goods are known as **merit goods**.

> ### Key Term
>
> **Merit goods:** goods and services provided by the government that the private sector would not supply in sufficient quantities because they are not profitable.

Merit goods are important for UK businesses. Some of these services are, of course, provided by the private sector. However if, for example, education were left completely up to people to buy privately, they might not buy 'enough' education for their children. This would not be good for an economy whose businesses need an educated workforce. The same argument applies to healthcare. The economy needs a healthy workforce because healthier workers are more productive. If the government thinks that people are not getting enough of these sorts of products for businesses to function effectively, it will increase its spending on them.

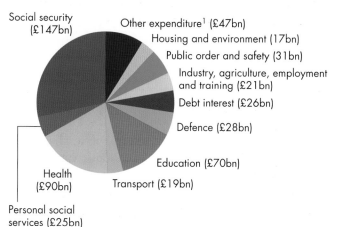

Social security
(£147bn)
Other expenditure[1] (£47bn)
Housing and environment (17bn)
Public order and safety (31bn)
Industry, agriculture, employment and training (£21bn)
Debt interest (£26bn)
Defence (£28bn)
Education (£70bn)
Transport (£19bn)
Health (£90bn)
Personal social services (£25bn)

[1] Other expenditure includes spending on: general public services; recreation, culture, media and sport; international cooperation and development; public service pensions; spending yet to be allocated and accounting adjustments.

Source: HM Treasury

Figure 60.4 Where taxpayers' money is spent, 2005/06

To influence the level of demand in the economy

The government can influence the level of demand by its own spending as well as through taxation. If the amount of government spending rises, this will increase the level of economic activity. The reverse is also true. As has been noted, spending in the economy might be too high or too low. The economy as a whole can 'fail' in terms of inflation from the high level of demand or unemployment from the lack of it.

To assist certain regions in the UK

The government targets some of its spending (Regional Development Assistance) at specific regions of the country where industry has been in decline for a number of years. This is known as **regional policy**, and some of the funds for this assistance come from the European Union.

Key Term

Regional policy: government economic measures to try to encourage businesses into regions of the country where economic activity is low.

Some areas of the UK suffer from much higher levels of unemployment than others, while the more prosperous

regions get overcrowded, creating congestion and pollution as well as pressure on facilities such as schools and hospitals. As well as preventing this, the aims of Regional Development Assistance are to:

- safeguard jobs in order to support communities
- encourage new businesses into the area and create jobs
- improve people's skills to make them more employable and productive
- minimise the loss of tax revenue to the Treasury; unemployment causes government spending on benefits to increase
- encourage investment and so boost the local economy
- help firms survive and/or grow, so they can compete more effectively abroad and also domestically against imported products
- help tackle social exclusion: this is where people (particularly young people) feel that they have little chance of participating in society and so turn to crime, vandalism and drugs; creating job opportunities will help prevent this.

The amount of assistance given to a business depends on the extent to which it will help meet these aims. A project that creates a lot of jobs that are likely to be permanent will receive more assistance than one that creates a few jobs that may only be short term. As well as finance for businesses, funds are available to local authorities for urban renewal and infrastructure improvement, so that an area can be made more attractive to businesses.

The multiplier

Put simply, the **multiplier** means that if businesses experience a change in the demand for their products, this will have a knock-on (multiplier) effect on the businesses that supply them. The multiplier is a very useful concept not only for analysing the effects of fiscal policy, but also for considering other changes in economic activity.

Key Term

Multiplier: the effect of changes in economic activity in one sector on other sectors; if one business experiences a rise or fall in demand for its products, this has a knock-on effect on businesses supplying it.

A cut in income tax will increase the demand for cars made in the UK and this increase in demand will cause a multiplier effect (see Figure 60.5). Car manufacturers will order more of all sorts of components from their suppliers — everything from brake shoes to bumpers, seats to CD players, and windscreens to wheels.

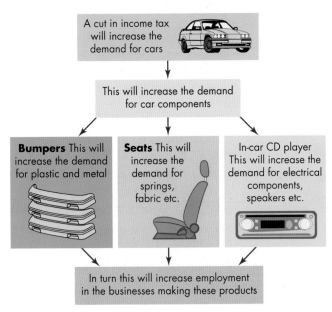

Figure 60.5 Multiplier effect of a cut in income tax

Income is being created at each stage of the process. This causes a rise in spending, and therefore employment is multiplied across the economy. The same would apply if there were an increase in UK exports of aircraft engines, for example. This would have a multiplier effect on the businesses that supply the exporter. Quite a small rise in spending in one or two industries can quickly generate increased demand for products elsewhere.

The multiplier also operates in reverse. A fall in demand will cause spending to fall, which in turn has a multiplier effect across the economy. Any government putting up taxes to raise more revenue or cutting public spending must consider the multiplier effects of such a policy.

The multiplier also helps to explain why the closure of a large business such as a steelworks, car plant or shipyard can be so devastating. Not only does the area lose a major source of employment, but in addition, all the smaller firms that depend on the large business suddenly find themselves with vastly reduced order books. This is why there was so much concern about the closure of the Rover car plant in 2005.

As unemployment rises, there is less spending in the local shops on consumer items such as televisions, clothes and carpets. When the multiplier 'goes into

reverse' nationally, for whatever reason, unless action is taken by the government or the Bank of England, a full-scale depression might occur.

Evaluating the effects of a change in economic policy

Examiner's voice

When evaluating the likely effects of a change in economic policy (or indeed, any economic variable) on a business's strategy, it is important to weigh up the issues carefully.

A good starting point for evaluating the effects of a change in economic policy is to consider the nature of the demand for the product. The demand for essential food items will be affected differently to that of the demand for new cars if spending changes, but this is only part of the evaluation.

The remainder of the evaluation can be done by considering three things. These can be remembered by the mnemonic 'TED':

- **T**: the **trend** in the variable
- **E**: the **extent** of the change
- **D**: the likely **duration** of the change.

Consider a question concerning the effects of rise in the rate of interest on a business. It is tempting to say 'this will mean a drop in sales as consumers will spend less. Also the business will invest less as well because loan repayments are more expensive'. This is correct so far as it goes, but is hardly a strategic approach. A better answer will consider 'TED'.

- **T**. If interest rates have been rising steadily for the past 12 months because the Bank of England has made it clear that it is concerned about inflation, the latest rise will not be unexpected. A business may already have anticipated it. This may mean that it has a marketing campaign ready to be launched to persuade consumers to buy, even if they have less to spend as a result of their mortgage repayments rising.

  On the other hand, if the rise comes unexpectedly and is against the trend (e.g. there has been no change in the rate for the last six months), this may come as more of a shock.

- **E**. Interest rates usually change by a quarter of 1% at a time. Thus although there has been 'a rise in the interest rate', this may not have a very large effect in the short run. Consumers may run down their savings rather than cut down on consumption. It may be that several increases occur before there is a significant impact on spending. The effect on a business's ability to repay a loan will also be affected by an increase in interest rates. The result of this depends (again) partly on the extent of the increase and partly on how much finance has been raised by the business in the form of loans.

- **D**. Businesses and consumers are likely to consider how long the rate rise will last. If it is expected to be short term, it will have little effect as everyone expects economic life to return to normal quite soon. A business is unlikely to cancel the building of a strategically important factory just because the rate of interest has risen by a quarter of a per cent in one isolated change! If however it is expected that the rise will not be reversed for a year or more (with possibly more rises on the way), a business's reaction could be very different.

Therefore a small rate rise in line with the trend, which is expected to be reversed shortly, will have much less effect on strategic decisions than an 'out of the blue' rise, against the trend, accompanied by the Bank of England making it clear that rates will have to stay high for a long period of time.

The same 'TED' reasoning can be applied to changes in tax rates, government spending and exchange rates. Remember, to evaluate any change in an economic variable on business strategy, use 'TED': Trend, Extent, Duration!

Further Sources

www.dti.gov.uk/regional – part of the Department of Trade and Industry website that gives information and data on regional policy and other government assistance for businesses.

www.thebankofengland.co.uk – what the Bank of England does, and how monetary and exchange rate policies operate.

www.hm-treasury.gov.uk – a good source of economic data and other useful information about current economic policy.

Your Turn

Case Study   Time allowed 40 minutes

Big Pit (BP) and Aberpergwm Colliery (AC)

The South Wales valleys are not always well served in terms of infrastructure and this is a deterrent to the attraction of new businesses. As part of its regional policy, the government has designated much of South Wales as a Development Area. This regional financial assistance is channelled via the Welsh Assembly.

In the nineteenth century, coal-mining was the main industry in South Wales. However, the twentieth century saw a steady decline in its fortunes, and new competitors in the world market had a cost advantage that the Welsh mines just could not match.

Today there is one important reminder of the past glories of the Welsh coal industry. It is the oldest mine in South Wales, the 'Big Pit' in Blaenafon which finally closed 1980. The coal had run out and it seemed as if Blaenafon and the surrounding area were destined to suffer the same high level of unemployment as the rest of South Wales.

However, Big Pit was reinvented as a tourist attraction and it now houses the National Mining Museum of Wales. The main attraction at the museum is a 90 metre deep journey into the underground workings, using the same cages that once transported the miners. A former miner accompanies the tourists on a guided trip below ground where they can see at first hand what life was like for the men who worked at the coal face.

Like all national museums in Wales, admission is free. The museum has a number of interactive displays and a large collection of mining tools and equipment. There is a gift-shop selling souvenirs and books, meals are available, and there are facilities for disabled people. The museum has done much to regenerate the area which has recently been designated a World Heritage Site.

Another poignant reminder of the past is Tower Colliery, which finally closed in January 2008. It had been owned and run by its own workforce and its closure was a sad event. The pit had run into financial difficulty in the 1980s and was scheduled to close. The miners kept it open by putting much of their redundancy money into it and taking out a loan. Some regional assistance was also available. It used to employ 300 people. In late 2006 the mine was however once again struggling against international competition and finally had to close. However some of the men and equipment will go to the newly-opened Aberpergwm Colliery in the Neath Valley.

1. State what is meant by the terms 'fiscal policy' and 'monetary policy'. (2 marks)

2. State who is responsible for the control of fiscal policy. (1 mark)

3. State who is responsible for the control of monetary policy. (1 mark)

4. **A.** State **two** taxes that Aberpergwm Colliery will have to pay. (2 marks)

   B. Analyse one likely effect of a rise in VAT on Aberpergwm Colliery. (6 marks)

5. Big Pit museum could be described as a merit good. Explain what this means. (2 marks)

6. As part of its regional policy, the government has designated much of South Wales as a Development Area. Outline **two** likely reasons for the government offering support for businesses in this area of Wales. (4 marks)

7. Assume that the rate of interest rises. Evaluate which of the two businesses (Big Pit and Aberpergwm Colliery) is likely to be affected the most. (18 marks)

(39 marks)

THE EXCHANGE RATE

The UK trades with many different countries and these countries use different currencies. It is therefore important to understand the nature and effects of the exchange rate.

The **exchange rate** is the value of the pound in terms of another currency. When people travel abroad, they usually take an interest in how much foreign currency each pound will buy, and how many pounds they are likely to get for any currency brought back. It is exactly the same for UK businesses.

The exchange rate can have a number of different effects on a business, which can significantly affect its operation. Before these are examined it is necessary to consider how the exchange rate is determined. It is not 'fixed' by the government, although the government can try to influence it. Currencies are traded in a market, in this case, the **foreign exchange market**. This market is global: wherever banks and other financial institutions trade currencies, they are part of the foreign exchange market.

Key Terms

Exchange rate: the value of the pound in terms of another currency.

Foreign exchange market: the market for currency, which is not in a single location but exists globally whenever buyers and sellers deal.

How is the exchange rate determined?

As in any market, the price (in this case the 'price' of the pound, i.e. the rate of exchange) is determined by the interaction of demand and supply.

What determines the demand for pounds?

The demand for pounds on the foreign exchange market is determined by several factors, as shown in Figure 61.1.

Foreign investment in the UK
Any foreign business wishing to build a factor or office in the UK will have to use its currency to demand pounds in order to pay the UK construction companies.

Desire of foreign customers to buy UK exports
If a UK firm sells clothes to a business in Germany, it would want to be paid in pounds, not euros.
This is because it does not want to go to the trouble and expense of exchanging euros into pounds. The German retailer must therefore use euros to demand pounds in order to pay the UK exporter. Similarly, German tourists coming to the UK would go to their bank and use euros to demand pounds.

Demand for pounds

'Hot money' flows into the UK
Hot money is money that flows from country to country in search of the highest possible rate of interest. If UK interest rates are higher than those in other countries, foreign banks will use their surplus foreign currency to demand pounds, which they will then deposit in UK banks. Hot money is dealt with in more detail later in this chapter.

Figure 61.1 Determinants of the demand for pounds

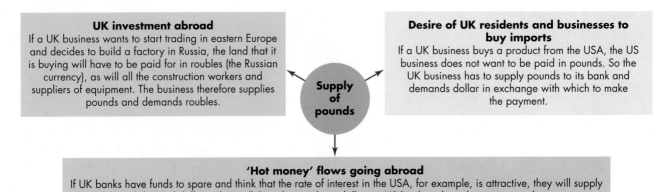

Figure 61.2 Determinants of the supply of pounds

What determines the supply of pounds?

The supply of pounds on to the foreign exchange market is determined by the factors shown in Figure 61.2.

The interaction of the demand for and supply of pounds establishes the exchange rate, as shown in Figure 61.3.

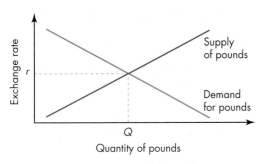

Figure 61.3 Determination of the exchange rate

What are the effects on a business if the rate of exchange changes?

Assume that there are 1.5 euros to the pound. This means that:

- for every £1 supplied, a business will receive €1.5
- for every €1.5 supplied, a business will receive £1.

Consider an Italian pizza producer that sells a box of 20 'Mama Mia' pizzas' for €100. A restaurant in London imports them from Italy. This transaction is shown in Figure 61.4.

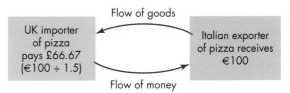

Figure 61.4 Cost to the UK importer of pizza

Just down the road from the London restaurant is a business that sells fountain pens. It sells a box of five for £100. A lot of its business is in the EU. A stationery shop in Italy buys these for its more exclusive customers. This transaction is shown in Figure 61.5.

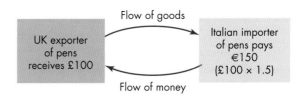

Figure 61.5 Cost to the Italian importer of fountain pens

What happens if the exchange rate rises?

Assume the rate is now £1 = €2. This means that the pound is now stronger and therefore buys more foreign currency than before. Both of the two businesses will be affected, as shown in Figures 61.6 and 61.7.

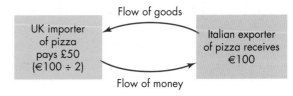

Figure 61.6 Effect of a higher exchange rate on the UK importer of pizza

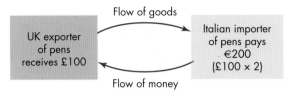

Figure 61.7 Effect of a higher exchange rate on the Italian importer of pens

The effect of a rise in the exchange rate is to make imports cheaper, but exports more expensive.

What happens if the exchange rate falls?

Assume that the rate is now £1 = €1. The pound is now weaker: that is, it buys less foreign currency than before. Once again, both businesses will be affected, as shown in Figures 61.8 and 61.9.

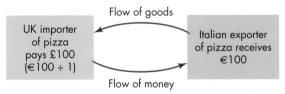

Figure 61.8 Effect of a lower exchange rate on the UK importer of pizza

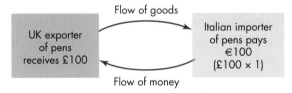

Figure 61.9 Effect of a lower exchange rate on the Italian importer of pens

The effect of a fall in the exchange rate is to make imports more expensive, but exports cheaper.

The interaction of the supply and demand for pounds causes the rate of exchange to change on a daily basis. Unless there is some factor that is out of the ordinary, such as terrorist attacks, a war or an unexpected change of government, these daily changes are minor. This is just as well because the changes in costs and prices caused by sudden large changes in the rate of exchange can be very destabilising and damaging to a business.

The Bank of England and the exchange rate

The Bank of England undertakes what are sometimes called 'smoothing operations'. It buys and sells currency whenever it is thought necessary in order to stop ('smooth out') potentially damaging changes in the exchange rate. However, it certainly does not seek to bring about large changes on a regular basis. For example, if the bank thought the rate was slightly too high, it would sell (supply) pounds and buy foreign currency or gold. This is shown in Figure 61.10; the sale of pounds lowers the exchange rate from r_1 to r_2.

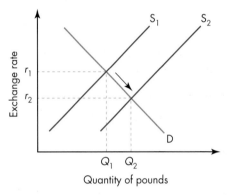

Figure 61.10 Effect of the Bank of England selling pounds

Alternatively, if it thinks the rate is too low, the bank will buy (demand) pounds using reserves of foreign currency or gold to do so.

Hot money

The Bank of England can also use flows of **hot money** to alter the rate of exchange.

Rises in the rate of interest affect the exchange rate via flows of hot money. It is important to understand this relationship because hot money is a major determinant of the exchange rate. Consider the following: someone receives £100 as a birthday present and decides to save it rather than spend it. Naturally, s/he will look for the bank or building society that offers the best rate of interest.

Exactly the same principle applies to international finance: international banks are looking for the best rate of interest for their money. Suppose there is a Japanese

Key Term

Hot money: flow of money from country to country, which is chasing the highest rate of interest it can possibly get.

investment bank in Tokyo and that interest rates are 2% in Japan while UK banks are offering 5%. If the Japanese bank has some surplus funds, it will transfer them to the UK because the return is better. However, it will have to change its yen into pounds first. This increased demand for pounds will raise the price of pounds, i.e. the exchange rate.

So, if the Bank of England wants the exchange rate to rise, instead of buying pounds itself (using foreign currency or gold), it can put up the rate of interest. This will encourage inflow of hot money into the UK to take advantage of the higher returns. This will shift the demand curve in Figure 61.11 from D_1 to D_2 and raise the exchange rate to r_2.

Alternatively, if the bank wants the rate of exchange to fall, it can lower the rate of interest. This makes deposits of money in the UK less attractive and the rate of exchange will fall.

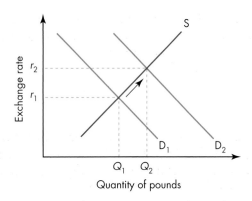

Figure 61.11 Using hot money to raise the exchange rate

The exchange rate as a tool of economic policy

What is the Bank of England trying to achieve when it intervenes? Apart from smoothing out temporary fluctuations, the bank may intervene for other reasons.

Inflation

Raising the rate of exchange can be a useful part of an anti-inflationary policy. Imports become cheaper, which lowers the cost of raw materials bought from abroad. This means that UK businesses can keep costs, and therefore prices, down.

In addition, an increase in the value of the pound means that the price of UK exports rises. The prices charged by any UK businesses exporting now appear uncompetitive, and they must try to cut their prices if they want to continue to export. This means they will have to keep control of wages and other costs. This will help to lower the rate of inflation.

Economic growth

Lowering the rate of exchange can help to increase economic activity. A lower rate makes UK exports cheaper, which is useful if the UK is not exporting enough. A fall in the rate helps boost exports and in doing so creates employment and economic growth.

Unfortunately, a lower rate may cause *imported inflation*, as any raw materials purchased from other countries will become more expensive.

Are all businesses affected in the same way by changes in the exchange rate?

The answer is 'no'. Consider the following three examples.

A UK business that exports but does not import

If the rate rises

Consider the business mentioned earlier that exports pens to Italy. It sells boxes of pens at £100. The original rate of exchange is £1 = €1.5, so the euro price of the pens is €150. Assume the exchange rate rises to £1 = €2. This means that the selling price has gone up in terms of what foreign countries must now pay: the price is now €200. This may make the product uncompetitive compared with pens produced in other countries. So why does the UK business not lower its selling price to £75, which would put the euro price back down to where it was before at €150?

A price reduction of £25 per box of pens is quite substantial. If it wanted to keep profits per box of pens at the same level, the company would have to lower costs by £25 per box. However, it may not be able to find a cheaper supplier of the components that go into the pens, and its employees are unlikely to take a pay cut.

If the costs of production are £70 and the pens now sell at £75, this means a profit of only £5 per box. Worse still, if the total cost of making the pack in the first place was £80, the business will now make a loss if it sells them abroad.

The business is now faced with the issues of:

- selling fewer pens abroad because the foreign exchange price has risen
- trying to sell more pens in the UK to make up for reduced sales abroad
- trying to offset the rise in the exchange rate by lowering costs and therefore the selling price
- selling at a loss abroad because it is taking a long-term view of its relationship with its Italian customers (but how long can it keep this up for?).

If the rate falls

A fall in the exchange rate means that the foreign currency price falls, although the price in pounds is still £100 per box. The business is now faced with the issues of:

- increasing the profit per box (i.e. deciding whether it could raise the selling price in pounds); if the rate fell to £1 = €1, the selling price could be raised to £150; this would be equivalent to €150 (the same euro price as before).
- leaving the price unchanged at £100 (which is now equivalent to €100) and hoping the Italian importer will buy more because they are now cheaper.

A UK business that imports but does not export

If the rate rises

UK businesses that do not export products will not be affected by the higher foreign currency price of exports. An example of this would be a hairdresser.

However, even if they do not export, many businesses will import raw materials or components. For example, a hairdresser might import shampoo and conditioner from Spain. If the pound rises, these imported products will become cheaper. What will the owner of the salon do? If her costs have fallen by 5%, she is now faced with the issues of:

- passing this saving on to her customers in the form of a price cut, if she feels that this will generate a lot of extra business
- taking a larger profit margin, if she decides that she has enough customers already and wants to take advantage of the cost reduction.

If the rate falls

A fall in the exchange rate means that the cost of the imported shampoo and conditioner rises. The business's owner is now faced with the issues of:

- passing the cost increase on to her customers: will this be possible or will they go elsewhere?
- absorbing the increase in costs, accepting lower profits: this may be likely if the situation is not expected to last very long.

In both of these instances, if the shampoo and conditioner costs were only a small percentage of total costs of the business, the impact of the rate change would not be very significant. If they were a large part of total costs, the impact would be greater.

A UK business that both imports and exports

Consider a business that imports various components in order to make tractors. It assembles them into finished tractors, which it then exports. If the exchange rate changes, whether it is 'good' or not depends on the relative magnitude of the two effects.

If the rate rises

Imported components are now cheaper, but this good news may be offset by bad news in the form of the higher foreign currency selling price of the product. Fewer finished tractors may be sold abroad.

If the rate falls

Exports are now cheaper and so, theoretically, more tractors should be sold abroad. However, the fall in the rate will mean that the imported parts that the business uses have become more expensive. This could mean a rise in the final selling price, and this bad news may offset the good news.

Summary

In conclusion, there will not be an exchange rate that is satisfactory for all UK businesses; it depends on their circumstances. The various effects of changes in the exchange rate are summarised in Table 61.1.

Rise in exchange rate	Fall in exchange rate
The pound will buy more foreign currency than before	The pound will buy less foreign currency than before
UK exports become more expensive	UK exports become cheaper
Imports into the UK become cheaper	Imports into the UK become more expensive

Table 61.1 Summary of the effects of a change in the exchange rate

Can a business avoid the effects of a change in the exchange rate?

There is a way for a business to shield itself from exchange rate fluctuations. Just as a business can opt for a fixed rate loan from a bank, it is possible to sign a contract to buy foreign currency in advance of when it is actually required. The rate will be fixed at the agreed figure. The business will then be certain of what it has to pay or what it will receive. However, the bank will charge a fee for this *future trading*, and this will be a further cost to a business. Managers must assess the risk of any rate changes and their impact, and in the light of this decide whether it is worth signing up to the fixed rate.

Examiner's voice

You will not be asked to perform any explicit calculations involving a change in the exchange rate, although if the figures are stated and you are able to do so, it may assist with your analysis. However you will certainly need to be able to form a judgement on the extent to which a business's strategy may be affected by a change in the exchange rate, if you want to gain marks for evaluation.

You will need to consider issues such as the amount of goods exported. With the tractor business above, if exports were only 5% of the business's total sales, it might not be too concerned about a rise in the rate. However, if 50% of its sales were abroad, this would be much more significant. Should the business now make the strategic decision to try to switch sales to UK customers? On the other hand, if the business needs to import then it must consider the value of the components imported. If these are only a small proportion of its total costs then it will not be badly affected by a fall in the rate. Furthermore, can any cost increases (caused by a fall in the rate) be easily 'passed on' to customers?

The 'TED' framework can also be applied again here: trend, extent, duration.

- **Trend.** Was the rate change part of a trend? If the rate fell and this fall had been expected then it may have little effect on a business's strategy. Its managers may have bought currency in advance as explained above. Alternatively, an unexpected change against the trend (especially if it is a relatively large change) may be more problematic.
- **Extent.** Was the rate change large or small? In reality, large changes in the value of a currency are quite rare. The value of the pound against the Euro for example tends to change by tenths of a cent at a time. This means that while a change from 1.434 to 1.432 euros to the pound is indeed 'a fall in the exchange rate', it will not produce the same reaction amongst businesses as a fall from 1.434 to 1.234.
- **Duration.** Is the rate change expected to be temporary or more permanent? Rates of exchange change every day and therefore 'a change in the exchange rate' in itself is not an unexpected event and, in itself, hardly likely to be the cause of any major strategic changes! However, even with a small rate change it is important for a business to try to take into account how long it might last for. Consider the change above. Suppose a business plans to invest 100 million euros in France in one year's time. At the rate of 1.434 euros to the pound, this will cost £69,735,007. If the rate falls to 1.432 and the business expects it to remain there then, if it is correct, the cost of the investment will now be £69,832,402 – almost £100,000 more. This might have an effect on the business's strategic plans.

'TED' is important!

Further Sources

www.thebankofengland.co.uk – what the bank does and how exchange rate policy operates

www.x-rates.com – one of many websites that offer foreign exchange services; it is useful for explaining why currency values change, and offers a conversion table and the ability to plot rate changes over time in virtually any currency

Your Turn

Case Study   Time allowed 35 minutes

TTL

Tyler's Tracking Ltd (TTL) is a manufacturer of 'high tech' vehicle-tracking equipment. It is particularly useful for consignments which need security. It has performed well since it was established in 2004, and the Chief Executive and majority shareholder Doug Tyler was delighted to win a contact with a German company in 2005, that led to further European orders very quickly. The business now exports a significant amount of its output (see Table 61.2). Doug found it hard to conduct negotiations directly with businesses abroad and so has established a network of agents abroad who TTL supplies. These agents relieve Doug of all the trouble of negotiating in a foreign language, but take a commission of 15% on all sales. This is more than the percentage charged by TTL's UK agents, which is only 10%.

Doug is rather concerned about the recent rise in the exchange rate, and he is not certain exactly how TTL will be affected. A news bulletin stated that exporters were suffering because of it and it was hoped by many that the Monetary Policy Committee might reduce the rate of interest at its next meeting in order to weaken the value of the pound.

TTL currently sources all of its components from within the UK. Doug has, however, been investigating the possibility of importing components from a business in California that is offering what TTL requires at around 10% less than the cost from his current suppliers. The reason he has not signed a contract with the firm yet is that he still feels a certain loyalty to his original suppliers, whom he regards as stakeholders and who helped him considerably when he was becoming established.

The sale of tracking equipment is something of a niche market but Doug is well aware that there are nevertheless competitors abroad and in the UK who are determined to reduce his market share. TTL prides itself on its after-care service for customers which Doug is convinced helps maintain consumer loyalty.

	2007	2008	2009
Direct sales in UK	30	22	20
UK sales via agents	30	30	30
Direct sales abroad	20	33	35
Sales abroad via agents	20	15	15

Table 61.2 TTL Percentage sales revenue by distribution channel

1. Outline **one** difference between 'the rate of interest' and 'the rate of exchange'.   (4 marks)

2. State what is meant by the term 'hot money'.   (2 marks)

3. Analyse the factors that affect the rate of exchange.   (9 marks)

4. Discuss the extent to which the strategic behaviour of TTL would be affected by a rise in the rate of exchange.   (18 marks)

(33 marks)

62 Unit

THE EUROPEAN UNION

The European Union (EU) is a group of 25 countries that aim collectively to improve the standard of living of their citizens. This is achieved by:

- creating a large market where businesses can compete, prosper and, in doing so, benefit their stakeholders
- generating economic and political stability
- achieving balanced economic growth across all of Europe
- protecting all EU citizens' rights via a common framework of law.

Membership of the EU has a significant effect on UK businesses.

Free trade and the single market

A thriving business community improves standards of living and promotes growth. One of the major goals of the EU is to create a large market where member states can trade freely. That is what 'single market' means: countries can trade freely with a common (i.e. single) set of regulations and rules on the movement of goods, people and finance, rather than having different regulations for each country.

This single market can help to make trade easier, and so businesses can sell more. This creates more wealth and jobs. The problem is that trade is not always free.

Trade barriers

Countries sometimes import more than they export (see Unit 59). Many people think that the solution to this is straightforward: a country in this position should restrict

Figure 62.1 Member countries of the European Union

Key Terms

Free trade: trade without tariffs or quotas being imposed when products are traded.

Single market: a market in which there is a single (i.e. common) set of laws and regulations relating to the movement of products, people and money; all businesses in the single market have to abide by these.

the number of imports allowed in. This is known as imposing a *quota*. Another way to solve the problem would be to put a tax on goods entering the country from abroad. This would make imports more expensive and home-produced goods relatively cheap. This tax is known as a tariff.

The problem with these actions is that other countries will retaliate. This can result in a quota and tariff trade war that is damaging to businesses in all the countries concerned. Quotas and tariffs are *trade barriers*, and using them could mean that businesses in all countries that trade abroad end up selling less.

The removal of trade barriers

One aim of the single market is to remove these trade barriers between member states. However, goods entering the EU from outside (e.g. from the USA or Japan) face a barrier called the *common external tariff* (CET), but it is thought that the negative effects of any retaliation are outweighed by the benefits for members of trading within the single market. Furthermore, many businesses outside the EU are encouraged to build their own factories in EU countries in order to avoid the CET. This inward investment creates employment in the EU.

Another example of the removal of trade barriers is the *harmonisation* (i.e. adopting a similar set) of specifications, safety standards and testing requirements for products. Before the single market came into being (on 1 January 1993), these were different in each EU country. This meant that a UK business that sold electrical components and was thinking of starting to export them faced considerable duplication of work. Moreover, different standards in different counties meant that it was expensive (perhaps impossible) for some businesses to comply with all of them, and in some cases they did not even bother to try to trade. Now, a single set of rules makes trade easier and has opened up a larger market.

Labour market barriers are also being removed through, e.g. the harmonisation of qualifications needed to do a certain job. Previously, a professional person might have needed a qualification gained in a specific country to be allowed to work there. Now, individuals with the appropriate qualification (e.g. doctors, teachers and social workers) have the right to work in any EU country, not just the one in which they were trained. In this way, people can improve their own lives and the lives of others in the country to which they move.

Finally, restrictions on moving money around within the EU have been abolished. This is helping to encourage investment in profitable opportunities, and promoting competition in the financial world. It should give both borrowers and savers a better deal.

All of these measures encourage free trade, and free trade brings competition. Competition is good because it brings down prices, drives up quality and improves customer service. Any business that does not strive to improve in these areas will find its customers taken by those who do.

The single market is intended to create the sort of virtuous circle shown in Figure 62.3. The hope is that the circle will continually repeat itself, with competition in the single market ensuring that the best businesses and their stakeholders prosper.

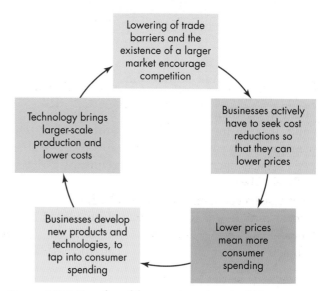

Figure 62.2 Benefits of free trade within the EU

Critics point out that a huge burden of EU laws and regulations distract businesses by taking up a huge amount of management time to ensure compliance.

What are the implications of trading in the EU for a UK business?

A business does not just start selling in Europe. There is an almost endless list of implications. Some of the most important are as follows:

- Someone in a senior position in the business must be put in charge of analysing the strengths, weaknesses, opportunities and threats in the proposed EU markets. They need to conduct and update market research, which takes up a lot of time and other resources.
- Employees in the business have to be fluent in different languages and have an understanding of the culture of other countries. This requirement

applies not just to senior executives but also to staff at all levels.

- It is not only competition for customers that has to be considered. With the free movement of workers, businesses offering the best employment package attract the best staff. This is particularly true for young graduates, who are very mobile. Recruitment policies have to be reviewed.
- Businesses have to comply with the common requirements on specifications, standards and labelling if they want to trade. This can be costly.
- Marketing policies need to be adapted, and links established with a reliable distributor, bank and, probably, lawyer abroad.
- Competition is not all one way. EU firms can take UK businesses' customers away. UK businesses must fight to be efficient, concentrating on their strengths and maximising opportunities arising from their competitors' weaknesses.
- A business operating in other countries can gain economies of scale. These are the advantages in terms of lower unit costs that come from large-scale production. Lower costs per item mean a larger profit margin.
- Selling in other EU countries can increase a UK business's stability. It no longer has all its eggs in one basket.
- Customers in Europe may insist on paying UK businesses in euros, since that is the currency they use with all other European firms. If this is the case, the UK business has to bear the cost of exchanging the money into pounds.

The euro

The **euro** came into existence because it made no sense to have a single market with over ten different currencies operating in it. So, in 1999, most of the member countries gave up their individual currencies and adopted the euro as a common currency. The UK did not join the euro, but it is clearly still an important economic issue both for the UK as a whole and for its businesses.

Key Term

Euro: the single currency that came into being in most EU countries on 1 January 1999.

Advantages to UK businesses of joining the euro

Adoption of the euro would offer UK firms a number of advantages.

It would encourage trade

UK businesses would no longer have to pay commission for buying or selling euros. Anyone who has been on holiday abroad recently will have had to pay commission to buy currency and travellers' cheques. Although this will probably have amounted to only a few pounds, they might still have felt quite annoyed. For a UK business buying from, and selling to, EU countries, the commission may be quite considerable. This extra cost might discourage some businesses from exporting, and so reduce trade.

Prices would be more transparent

Different currencies make it difficult for firms to compare prices. The euro enables businesses to compare prices of raw materials and components from other EU countries quickly. Finding the best deal is a lot easier.

Less uncertainty over costs and profits

With a single currency there is less uncertainty over costs and profits. The possibility of a changing exchange rate can mean a great deal of uncertainty for a UK business. At present when there is the possibility of a fall in the exchange rate this will make imported raw materials more expensive. This causes lower profit margins for businesses that have to buy them. At present, while the UK is not a member of the eurozone, if the exchange rate changes then this could disadvantage a UK company. Suppose this company agreed to buy 1 million components at €3 each and the exchange rate was €1.5 to the pound: the cost is €3 million. In pounds this would be £2 million. If the rate falls to €1 to the pound, the cost in pounds rises to £3 million. This could easily wipe out any profit that has been budgeted for.

Alternatively the rate of exchange may rise, making the euro price of exports rise (which will deter some foreign customers from buying). A UK business could be selling a product at £10,000. If the rate was €1.5 to the pound, the cost to a customer in the eurozone would be €15, 000. If the rate rose to €2 to the pound, the euro cost would now be €20,000. This increased price is likely to make the product produced by the UK business unattractive.

Such large changes in the rate are unlikely (in the short run at least), but they do illustrate how an exchange rate can 'move against' a UK business. If the UK joined the eurozone, neither of these events could happen. Thus, it is often argued, membership of the euro should help to create greater business confidence in the likelihood of success when trading with other EU countries.

> ## Key Terms
>
> **Eurozone:** the collective name for countries that have adopted the euro as their single currency.
> **European Central Bank (ECB):** the central bank that sets interest rates for the whole of the eurozone.

Disadvantages to UK businesses of joining the euro

Membership of the euro presents some problems too.

Loss of control over monetary policy

Decisions on interest rates are made by the **European Central Bank** (ECB). This could cause problems if not all economies in the EU are at the same stage of the economic cycle. Suppose that the UK joined the euro at a time when the UK economy was in a mild recession, while the rest of the EU was booming. The correct policy for the ECB to adopt would be to increase the rate of interest. This, however, would mean that economic activity in the UK would slow down further, perhaps even provoking a slump. This situation would clearly not be beneficial to UK businesses. Joining the euro could mean UK businesses suffering for the good of the others.

'Outer' countries may get left behind

Economic activity in a country is often concentrated around its capital and a few of its other important cities. Sometimes the regions 'get left behind', which is why governments have a regional policy. Exactly the same argument applies to the EU as a whole. Some people think that economic power, prosperity and decision-making will become centred on the leading member countries, especially France and Germany. Businesses in other countries could suffer unless they received considerable financial assistance. Where, it is often asked, will the funds for this assistance come from? One source could be increased taxation on UK businesses. This would be an unwelcome burden.

At what exchange rate should the pound join the euro?

This is potentially the most significant problem. If the UK joins the single currency, on an agreed day, all pounds will be converted to euros. Suppose that, for a long time, the rate of exchange has been €1.5 to the pound. Now, as the day for joining approaches, the pound rises so that it is worth €3. Is this the correct rate?

At first sight, it would be a good idea to have as many euros to the pound as possible on the day of joining. If there were €3 to the pound, then a pound would have a lot of purchasing power in the rest of the EU; imports would be very cheap. This would be good for UK consumers, but bad for UK businesses because they might not be able to compete with the flood of cheap imports. However, the reverse of this would mean that businesses in other EU countries would have to supply €3 instead of €1.5 for every product that previously cost a pound. This would make UK products very expensive, and so all exporting firms would suffer. This could lead to unemployment.

Alternatively, if the pound fell in value to €1 just before the date for joining, this would make exports cheaper but would make imports from the rest of the EU, including raw materials, a lot more expensive, since £1 would only buy €1. This could also lead to inflation and unemployment.

Joining the euro would be a one-off: it would not be a reversible decision. It is therefore extremely important that the correct rate is agreed before the UK joins. It is essential that the pound is not locked into a rate that is permanently damaging to businesses. However, there is little agreement on what the 'correct' rate actually is.

Examiner's voice

There is no clear answer to the question of whether joining the euro is appropriate for UK businesses or not. It depends on an individual business's circumstances.

Further Sources

www.cbi.nl – the website of the 'employers' organisation', the Confederation of British Industry (CBI); it has a useful 'export readiness checker', featuring an excellent list of issues for a UK business considering exporting for the first time.

www.ecb.int – for the European Central Bank and the euro; it contains useful EU economic statistics.

www.eurofound.eu.int – trends in EU consumer spending and living standards.

Case Study Time allowed 35 minutes

Tony's Plastics

Tony Walker is the majority shareholder and chairman of a business producing goods made out of recycled plastic. The business was established six years ago and has proved very successful.

The products that Tony's factory makes are not of high quality but are low cost and easy to produce. They are also cheap for consumers to buy, but despite this, there is quite a large profit margin on them.

The main items that the business sells are plastic cutlery, coat hangers and clothes pegs. The fact that the colours of these products can vary is not a disadvantage to Tony, and can actually be turned into an advantage when selling products such as 'children's party packs' of cutlery and cups.

Two years ago, Tony led the business through a successful diversification into making plastic carrier bags for shops. It is quite straightforward to change the logo on these and this has proved to be a growing market. Tony's business is reliable and competitive with a very good reputation. He now thinks that with his business expertise and experience he should start to export some of these products to countries in the eurozone. He has called a board meeting today because there are a number of issues that he wants to discuss and clarify.

1. State **two** aims of the EU. (2 marks)

2. Outline, using examples, what is meant by the term 'trade barriers'. (4 marks)

3. Outline **two** advantages and **two** disadvantages to UK businesses of joining the euro.
(2 × 4 marks)

4. Discuss the strategic implications of Tony's decision to start exporting to countries in the EU.
(18 marks)

(35 marks)

BUSINESSES AND THE LAW

The law is a key aspect of the business environment and a very important constraint on strategic decision-making. It can be quite difficult for a business to keep up with legal changes (particularly a small business such as a sole trader). Nevertheless it has to be done; in the event of a business doing something illegal it is no defence for a director or manager to say that they were not aware of the law. Time must be devoted to keeping up with legal changes. Also, where necessary, employees have to be informed and trained.

Types of law

There are two different types of law in the UK:

1. civil law

2. criminal law.

Civil law

This law is concerned with the rules that govern the relations between businesses and/or people, e.g. employment rights, and consumer rights. A breach of civil law does not make a business or person a criminal. If the civil court's decision goes against a business or person, they are not fined or imprisoned but have to pay 'damages'. This is a payment to compensate the 'injured' party (business or person) for any loss or injury, to restore them to the position that they would have been in, had the law not been broken.

Criminal law

This law defines the actions that the state has decided are 'wrong', and the punishment that will result from these actions. In a criminal court, if a business or person is found guilty the result can be a fine or imprisonment. Because of this, the 'burden' (standard) of proof is higher in a criminal court. The court has to be convinced 'beyond reasonable doubt' (i.e. certain) that the defendant is guilty, whereas in a civil court it is on 'the balance of probabilities'; i.e. 'it is more likely than not' that one party is correct.

> ### Key Terms
>
> **Civil law:** law concerned with the rules that govern the relations between businesses and/or people, for example employment and consumer rights.
>
> **Criminal law:** this law defines the actions that the state has decided are 'wrong' and the punishment that will result from these actions.

EU Law

Some laws affecting UK businesses have come from the European Union. Many of these have originated from the EU's Social Charter which is a charter of rights for employees concerning areas such as working conditions, wages, and consultation of the workforce (e.g. the Working Time Directive, under which a business must not allow an employee to work more than 48 hours per week on average). UK businesses have to adhere to these EU laws just as if they had originated from the UK parliament. There are two types:

- 'Regulations' which have to be adopted and applied in a certain way.
- 'Directives' must also be applied as law, but it is up to the individual member country to decide how to implement it.

Why have laws?

The law aims to make individuals and businesses behave in a responsible way. Laws define the kind of behaviour that is unacceptable. Without laws a business could:

- dismiss employees at a moment's notice for any reason with no explanation
- provide dangerous and unhealthy working conditions that may lead to the injury or death of employees
- change the amount of money it had agreed to pay to a supplier for a particular delivery
- pollute and destroy the environment;

while employees could:

- turn up for work whenever they liked, completely disregarding the hours they had agreed to work
- remove products from their place of work and use facilities such as telephones or photocopiers for their own purposes
- ignore instructions about work from their managers.

A civilised society simply could not operate in this manner; there needs to be a framework for the protection of rights. Laws mean that there are legal minimum standards that must be adhered to by all businesses. If laws are to be effective, they have to be enforced, which is why the state provides the judicial system.

At A2 level it is important to know about three areas of legislation and their implications for business, governing:

- the relationship between one business and another
- the way in which a business treats its consumers
- the treatment of employees.

Examiner's voice

You need to be able to identify the main pieces of legislation that affect a business's behaviour, particularly its strategic outlook. Be aware of the implications of a business complying (or not complying) with the law.

Laws governing the relationship between businesses

Contract law

A contract is a legally binding agreement between two or more parties. Most business relationships are of a contractual nature and so contract law sets out the basic framework of rights and obligations. A contract may be an offer to supply something at a particular time and/or of a particular quality.

A contract is binding on both parties; it is against the law for one party to change the terms of the contract without the other's agreement.

The breach (breaking) of a contract is a breach of the civil law and means that the aggrieved party (i.e. the person or business who has been wronged) can recover damages. Suppose a business selling frozen desserts has signed a contract to deliver £10,000 worth of ice cream to a supermarket in one month's time. Its ability to do this depends on the ingredients being delivered one week before by its own supplier. Suppose that the supplier failed to deliver the ingredients. This means that the dessert business is unable to make the product or deliver to the supermarket. Naturally the supermarket does not pay because the goods did not arrive. The dessert business would be able to sue its supplier for damages, i.e. for the revenue lost as a result.

> ### Key Term
>
> **Contract:** a legally binding agreement between two or more parties. Most business relationships are of a contractual nature and so contract law gives the basic framework of rights and obligations.

Competition law

Consumers benefit in terms of price and quality when businesses compete against each other for customers. In the UK (and the EU) it is illegal for businesses to restrict competition. This could occur in various ways:

- a relationship between businesses aiming to restrict supply
- businesses conspiring together to keep up prices (known as a cartel)

- a business charging an artificially low price in order to destroy a competitor, or to deter any new entrants into the market
- a business forcing its distributors to stock all of its products under the threat that if they do not do so, they will not be supplied at all.

The two organisations that aim to ensure that UK businesses comply with the law are the Office of Fair Trading (OFT) and the Competition Commission. They will also consider whether a merger between two businesses is likely to result in any sort of anti-competitive behavior. The OFT has a special 'cartel-busting squad' with wide-ranging powers of entry into business premises to look for evidence. It is now a criminal offence to obstruct their investigation, and actions such as shredding important documents can result in a prison sentence. For breaches of the Act, a business can be fined up to 10% of its turnover.

Laws governing consumer protection

The Sale of Goods Act 1979
This has always been an important Act, and like the Health and Safety Act of 1974 it has since been extended, particularly by the Consumer Protection Act 1987. All goods:

- must be of 'satisfactory quality' (i.e. the product must not be damaged or defective)
- must be 'as described'. This applies not only to advertisements but also to any explanations given by a shop assistant
- 'must be fit for the purpose for which they were intended'.

If any of these conditions are not met, a business must provide the consumer with a replacement or their money back. A business cannot avoid the law by saying that it has a policy not to accept returned goods! The Act also imposes a duty on a business to ensure that its products are safe to use.

In addition to these civil laws there are the following criminal laws:

The Trade Descriptions Act 1968
A consumer cannot be expected to understand everything about a product. This law is to prevent consumers from being intentionally misled when they buy. The law states that any description of the goods on sale must not be false or misleading. The law refers to all types of description; sign, advertisement or verbal.

The Weights and Measures Act 1985
It is an offence to give 'short measures' or an incorrect indication of the amount of a product on sale. If a product is labelled as containing one litre or weighing one kg, that is what it should contain or weigh.

The Unsolicited Goods Act 1971
It is illegal to demand payment for services that have not been ordered. If a publishing business delivers a quantity of books that had not been ordered to someone's house, and then demands payment for them, the business is breaking the law.

The Trading Standards Authority is a public body that investigates breaches of consumer laws. They will also assist consumers with taking a business to court if it refuses to comply with its legal obligation.

Laws governing the treatment of employees

Prevention of discrimination
Discrimination occurs when an employer treats a person less favourably than another employee without any justification. This discrimination can occur in various ways; employing someone, promoting someone, or allowing them access to training courses.

Acts such as the Sex Discrimination Act (1975), the Race Relations Act (1976), and the Employment Equality (Age) Regulations 2006 and the Disability Discrimination Act 1995 mean that a business is breaking the law if it refuses to employ or promote a person on the grounds of race, sex, age or disability. For disabled people, a business has to make 'reasonable adjustments' to the way in which products and services are delivered so that disabled people can use them. Since 2003 there has been similar legislation applying to a person's sexual orientation and religion. There may be cost implications for complying with these rights, such as permitting extended leave for religious holidays or ensuring that any canteen facilities meet religious dietary requirements.

The implications for a business are:

- There needs to be a clear equality policy to ensure fair and consistent treatment of all employees.
- This policy needs to be clearly communicated to all staff. Managers should ensure that all employees are aware of this policy and its implications (i.e. that it is unlawful for someone to be discriminated, bullied or harassed on the grounds of sex, race, sexual orientation etc.) and that disciplinary action will follow if they engage in any such behaviour.
- Employees should know about the business's procedures and who to speak to if they think that they are not being treated in accordance with the policy.
- The policy needs to be reviewed and monitored. The Acts make it clear that it is not a 'one-off' but a continuing duty on a business.

Examiner's voice

It is necessary to have a working knowledge of employment law, but it is also very important to be able to recognise the implications to the business in the case study. This approach will score higher marks.

The Minimum wage

This Act which came into effect in 1999 lays down the minimum level of pay to which all employees in the UK (except those under 18) are entitled. It does not matter if the employee works part time or full time. If employees are paid on a piece rate (a certain amount for each item produced), the business has to ensure that the system of work is sufficient for enough items to be made for the employee to earn at least the minimum wage.

Health and safety

The Health and Safety Act 1974 was a very important piece of legislation. It has been extended to take account of new issues and hazards, such as repetitive strain injury or possible damage to the eyes from working at computer screens that people were not fully aware of or did not exist when the original Act was passed.

Not only do businesses have 'a duty to take reasonable care' of employees, but the criminal law lays down minimum safety requirements. There is *a positive obligation*

to create a safe and healthy working environment; breaches of the law can lead to criminal prosecution as well as civil proceedings for compensation.

The provisions of the Act relate to the:

- place of work
- system of work
- working environment
- machinery used
- use and storage of substances
- employees.

The business must comply with the following regulations:

- Ensure that the building itself must be safe. Entry to it and exit from it must be safe.
- Coordinate the whole system of work so that it is safe.
- Ensure that the temperature in the working environment is within certain limits; the atmosphere must be safe to breathe, the floors must be safe to walk along, etc.
- Fit guards onto machinery to prevent accidents. Employees must be provided with the correct safety equipment (and clothing), and trained to use it.
- Provide training to guard against any hazards associated with the work; e.g. lifting loads and handling substances. A business that failed to provide any training 'because it was common sense for an employee not to lift a heavy load' would not have a legal defence if the employee injured themselves.
- Draw up a written safety policy, making clear who is responsible for safety issues. This policy must be clearly communicated to employees.

Employees must also comply with the Act. They must:

- take reasonable care of their own health and safety and of others who could be affected by their actions.
- comply with lawful instructions relating to safety matters; an employee who was trained and told to use lifting equipment could not try to sue the business for an injury to his back if he ignored the instructions.
- not interfere or misuse anything provided for health and safety purposes; e.g. letting off a fire extinguisher for malicious purposes or 'in fun' is a serious matter, for which an employee can be summarily dismissed.

The Act says that a business must comply 'so far as reasonably practicable'. A business may dispute that it can afford to comply with every single part of the Act, claiming that the expense is not 'reasonably practicable'. If an accident occurred and the business was prosecuted, the court would decide whether it was 'reasonably practicable' or not.

Smoking in the workplace

On 1 July 2007, workplaces in England became smoke-free environments; legislation was already in place in Scotland, Wales and Northern Ireland. This includes offices, factories, shops, bars, restaurants, and work vehicles that are used by more than one person. Indoor smoking rooms are no longer allowed; anyone wishing to smoke must go outside the premises.

The 'anti-smoking law' will need to be taken seriously by a business. A business ignoring this law or failing to prevent smoking inside the premises will be liable for prosecution and a fine. An agreed policy (including disciplinary procedures for employees breaking this law) should be in place, and this needs to be carefully monitored to ensure compliance. If a business recruits a smoker then that person should be informed of the implication of the Act so that any breaches of the law are unlikely.

The Health and Safety Executive (HSE)

This is the organisation responsible for the regulation of risks to health and safety at work. If a breach of the Act is serious enough or there is repeated disregard for the law, the HSE can close down a business.

The termination of employment

This could occur through redundancy or dismissal. It is important to be clear about the difference.

Redundancy

An employee is not made redundant because they have done something wrong. Redundancy arises from a situation where the job that used to be performed no longer exists and so the employee is surplus to requirements.

Dismissal

Dismissal usually occurs for reasons of discipline or capability. Any dismissal has to be justified and must be 'fair' if it is to be legal. If an employee has accrued one year of continuous service with an employer then summary ('on the spot') dismissal is only 'fair' in two instances:

- gross misconduct (e.g. an employee physically assaulting a customer)
- gross negligence: a reckless or wilful disregard for the safety of others (e.g. a manager at a theme park allowing a ride to remain open when he knows that a safety fault with it exists).

It is more usual for dismissal to result from actions such as:

- repeated poor conduct, such as lateness or failing to comply with reasonable requests from a manager

- incapacity: e.g. being too ill to work at all or taking time off work when genuinely ill on a regular basis
- capability: e.g. repeated inability to do the work required, or a major incident such as losing a very valuable customer from the business.

If one of these is the reason for the dismissal, it will normally be fair as long as the employer has acted 'reasonably'. In essence this means that the employer has not summarily dismissed the employee but has followed appropriate disciplinary procedures. For any disciplinary-related dismissal, the employer should have given at least one verbal warning, followed by at least one written warning, and then a final written warning to the employee. By law an employee has to receive all allegations in writing, and attend a formal meeting to discuss the issues. It would be normal practice to allow a trade union representative or a friend to accompany an employee in such a meeting.

There also has to be an appeals process. If the business has not complied with these three stages, the dismissal will not be fair and will therefore be illegal.

What happens if a business breaks the law?

Breaches of **employment law** are heard in an employment tribunal, a special sort of court that deals with employee's claims for matters such as unfair dismissal, discrimination, breach of contract and victimisation by their employer. If the tribunal rules in favour of the employee, it will order the business to make a payment to the employee to compensate for what has occurred.

Key Terms

Employment tribunal: a special sort of court that only deals with employment-related issues such as victimisation by an employer, unfair dismissal, and discrimination.

For breaches of **criminal law**, the business will be prosecuted in the criminal courts; either a magistrate's court for the more minor offences or the Crown Court where the penalties are more severe for the more serious matters. If found guilty, a business can be fined and/or those responsible for the breach could be imprisoned. Any breach of the **civil law** will be heard in the County Court where the business can be sued for damages.

If a business fails or refuses to pay damages or compensation, the business or person that is owed the money can apply to the County Court for payment to be enforced. The Court will not be impressed with a business that has failed to pay someone what is due to them. County Court judgments against a business can generate a lot of bad publicity and the hearing will be expensive. Furthermore, an adverse County Court judgment can affect a business's ability to obtain loans and other forms of credit in the future.

A strategic approach to complying with the law

It is usual for the government to announce changes in the law well in advance so that compliance with the change can be built into a business's strategic planning process. Discussion of the government's stated proposals should start at a senior level as soon as possible. Changes in the law are likely to affect one of more stakeholder groups, especially employees, and their views should be sought. Management of any change in the law must start from 'the top'; employees cannot be expected to know how they are to behave without guidance.

The actual detail of the legislation may be complicated, and it may be necessary to contact a lawyer for advice in the first instance (many websites including Acas offer advice and publications), and/or when the business has a plan in order to ensure that it actually does comply.

With legislation affecting employees (such as the prevention of smoking in the workplace), it is advisable to involve them at the earliest stage and to build their views into any plans. However, the consultation needs to be meaningful if the law is to be effectively complied with. Where possible it is useful for employees to have some 'ownership' of the changes. The manager that 'consulted' by asking the employees where they wanted the outside smoking shelter is not likely to have been as successful as the one who not only asked this question, but negotiated exactly how 'cigarette breaks' were to be taken: deducted from existing breaks or introduce extended breaks for non-smokers to ensure fairness? In addition, some managers brought in health professionals to offer guidance and support on how to give up smoking to minimise problems resulting from the change.

When there are changes to employment law (such as the Equality in Age Regulations) it is necessary to revise the business's existing employment policy and to ensure that employees (especially those in authority) are clear about the change. Someone at senior level needs to have responsibility for this; matters cannot be allowed to 'drift'. There are therefore resource implications such as, who will do this? and when? will the communication with employees and any necessary training be in work time, or will some employees have to be paid to attend a training session?

Compliance must be carefully integrated into the business's strategic plan.

The strategic benefits of complying with the law

- The avoidance of fines (these can be large especially in matters of health and safety) which will lower profits.
- The avoidance of claims for compensation, which will lower profits.
- The avoidance of bad publicity (e.g. from discrimination, illegal safety measures or breaches of consumer law) that may deter potential employees and so leave important posts in the business unfilled.
- The avoidance of bad publicity that may deter customers and so lower sales and ultimately profits. There are for example over eight million people in the UK with disabilities, and compliance with the law may attract disabled customers to the business.
- The poor treatment of employees means that they will not achieve their full potential. Where a business adopts practices to avoid discrimination, it should benefit all employees.
- Compliance with health and safety legislation means fewer accidents and days off through injury or sickness. This may also result in a better relationship between managers and employees, which could make objectives easier to achieve, such as implementing change.

Further Sources

www.hse.gov.uk – the Health & Safety Executive. Advice on improving workplace health and safety and the benefits to businesses that can occur as a result of a healthy and safe working environment.

www.businesslink.gov.uk/regulationupdates – information on new and changing regulations affecting UK businesses.

www.disability.gov.uk – disabled rights. Information for businesses on how to meet their legal obligations.

www.employmenttribunal.gov.uk – the employment tribunal system in the UK.

www.legislation.hmso.gov.uk/acts.htm – Acts of Parliament at a glance.

www.oft.gov.uk and www.competition-commission.org.uk – information about consumer protection and the regulation of anti-competitive behaviour.

Case Study   Time allowed 1 hour

Discountec

Mrs Richardson bought a new washing machine from her local branch of Discountec plc, a well-known national chain of shops selling electrical consumer goods. When she used it for the first time, there was a strong smell of burning. As soon as she became aware of this she switched it off, but it then flooded water all over her new carpet that had cost £2,000. The flooding meant that she had to phone a plumber who charged £75 for an emergency call out.

When she went back to the store she was not in a very good mood. This was worsened by the fact that at the entrance she tripped over some bricks that some workmen had left scattered around, and cut her ankle. It looked to her as if they were building some sort of ramp for disabled people to access the store but neither any workmen nor any 'work in progress' signs were anywhere to be seen.

When she eventually saw the manager, he demanded to know who had installed the machine. She replied that it was her son 'who was not an expert but knew how to connect two taps'. On hearing this, the manager refused to accept any responsibility, saying that her son must have had plumbed it in wrongly and broken it. Then he suggested that Mrs Richardson contact the manufacturer and take the matter up with them. She refused to do this and as their discussion was becoming noisy he agreed to replace it 'as a goodwill gesture from an ethical company', but said that he was prepared to do no more. Mrs Richardson said that if this was the case then she would take the business to court and sue it under the Sale of Goods Act. The manager replied that 'she could do what she liked', and in an aggressive tone asked if she knew how much it was going to cost her 'when she lost the case'.

Mrs Richardson decided to seek some advice from her local Trading Standards office. On explaining her problem the person she spoke to said 'Discountec again! Have you seen our local paper this week?' He showed a copy to Mrs Richardson and on the front page was an article about two female employees from the same store who were going to an employment tribunal on the grounds that they had been discriminated against with regard to access to training. The manager of the local branch was reported as saying 'They can do what they like. This business is an equal opportunity employer and we have a clear equality policy. They should be aware of that before they take the matter any further.'

1. Outline two differences between civil law and criminal law. (4 marks)

2. The branch manager of Discountec says the business is an equal opportunity employer with 'a clear equality policy'. State the purpose of an equality policy. (1 mark)

3. State two ways by which a business could make its employees aware of an equality policy. (2 marks)

4. State the purpose of an employment tribunal and give one example of the sort of cases that are heard at a tribunal. (2 marks)

5. Analyse two strategic benefits to Disountec of complying with the law. (6 marks)

6. Discuss whether Mrs Richardson would be wise to sue Discountec plc under the Sale of Goods Act. (13 marks)

7. Other than the Sale of Goods Act, evaluate the legal influences that are likely to affect the strategic operation of a branch of Discountec plc. (13 marks)

(41 marks)

The political environment in which a business exists will have an impact on its actions, performance and success. In the UK, the tiers of government include the European Union, national government and local authorities. The political ethos of these bodies will have an effect on the way the business can operate. It is also important to remember that the UK operates within the world's economic and political scene and therefore, events in other countries may have an impact on the UK. For example, the lending crisis in the USA in 2007 had an impact on British banks and mortgage lenders, like Northern Rock, affecting their ability to lend and maintain liquidity.

Key Term

Liquidity: the ability to turn assets into cash and the speed with which it can be done in order to meet savers' demand for cash liquidity.

The European Union

As a member of the EU, the UK is bound by all its rules. These include:

- regulations which are legally binding immediately and imposed directly by the EU.
- directives that require legislation in the member country.
- recommendations and opinions that express the view of the particular body.

For example, rules controlling driving hours and the use of tachometers on heavy goods vehicles are applied and enforced by the EU throughout all member countries. The introduction of the Single European Market in 1999 brought a number of changes that had an impact on business and the way it operates. The intention had always been that the EU should operate as a single market, but until 1999 that was far from the case. There is some way to go in this process, but nevertheless, UK businesses are now able to supply to a market of more than 459 million people (the third largest in the world after China and India), with all the opportunities and risks from competition that this market creates.

The main changes introduced by the Single European Market legislation were:

- freedom of movement for all EU citizens within member countries
- free movement of capital within the EU
- harmonisation of rules and regulations applied to products and services making it possible for businesses to sell in all member countries; e.g. the requirement to sell all electrical appliances with a moulded plug already attached
- removal of some of the checks on crossing frontiers between member countries
- harmonisation of tax rules for individuals and businesses
- removal of internal tariffs and a common external tariff.

The result of all these changes has been an increase in the competition faced by all businesses, regardless of the extent to which they trade in the EU. Managers have realised that efficiency is vital for success in such a huge market and this has resulted in specialisation, growth within and outside national boundaries and a drive to achieve economies of scale in areas like marketing and production. Huge companies like Nestle own production units and supply markets throughout the EU, taking advantage of the economies of scale that this brings to all sectors of the business. They can manufacture for a much greater market, achieving huge cost savings through long production runs.

European Monetary Union

The EU introduced the single currency in January 1999, and in January 2002 all money transactions for those countries in the system moved into euros. For a number of reasons, the UK chose then and continues to choose, not to be part of the single currency. This has implications for the UK economy and businesses in the following ways:

Figure 64.1 The City of London remains outside the eurozone

- All transactions between UK business and firms in the eurozone create costs, because businesses need to change currencies into and out of sterling.

Examiner's voice

In case studies and questions, you may find that the UK currency is sometimes referred to as sterling and at other times as the pound.

- The exchange rates between the euro and pound with countries outside the EU may vary, leading to different trading conditions; e.g. since the single currency was introduced, the pound has performed better than the euro against the dollar. This means that UK firms exporting to the USA find that their goods are relatively less competitive against those from EU countries using the euro (see Unit 61).
- Some multinational companies may have located elsewhere in Europe or considered moving their businesses into the eurozone. This is to gain the benefits from removing currency transaction costs from trade across frontiers. Japanese businesses such as Sony, Nissan and Toshiba have all discussed the possibility of moving their production out of the UK if it continues to remain outside the single currency. These businesses have so far remained in the UK, but would prefer a situation where the UK was a member of the single currency.
- Financial sector businesses, with their large movements of money, are likely to be seriously disadvantaged by the existence of transaction costs. Although it was felt that this might have implications for London's future as a major financial market, the City of London has confounded predictions and become increasingly important in European and World markets as a major money and banking centre.

Key Term

Eurozone: those countries in the EU that are now using the euro as their currency.

The growth of the European Union

As the EU continues to expand its boundaries, it creates many new opportunities for business, while introducing new problems and risks. The new member countries of the EU have a population base that is much more diverse than the one that existed previously, and businesses need to be aware of these differences before they move into those markets. Many of the eastern European economies have much lower standards of living than those in Western Europe, and their economic systems have only recently moved to becoming market economies after being centrally planned for many years. Care needs to be exercised in trading or moving production to these areas because the business framework is still very fragile and the risks for business are therefore large.

Most of these countries are anxious to move their economies forward as rapidly as possible. They want to increase the range of consumer goods, to provide better jobs for their populations and to import from other EU countries. This means that there are opportunities for UK businesses to move into the areas in many ways:

- A number of UK firms have moved some or all of their production to the newer member countries to take advantage of their lower cost labour, but also to give them easier access to these new markets. For example, many of the big 'blockbuster' films requiring large numbers of extras are now filmed in Hungary and the Czech Republic to take advantage of lower production costs.

- There is a demand for new infrastructure and technological development in these countries that UK businesses are well placed to meet. A number of UK businesses have taken the opportunity to set up joint ventures with firms in these countries. Europolis is working on a joint venture with Polish businesses to build the largest logistics centre in Central and Eastern Europe. This is attracting attention from large businesses in Western Europe such as IKEA and Unilever.

- UK business has taken advantage of workers coming into the UK from the new member countries. These workers often move into areas where there are skill or labour shortages and therefore help the UK economy operate more efficiently. For example, fruit farmers in East Anglia rely heavily on overseas workers from Eastern Europe to pick their crops, and many areas of the tourism and catering industry are increasingly reliant on foreign labour from EU countries. Polish workers have moved into many areas of the UK workforce, from dentistry to building and construction. In October 2007, there were 400 Polish bus drivers working in the West Midlands region.

Management and the European Union

The decision to move into Europe is an important strategic one for management, and it needs careful consideration before any such move is undertaken. Although the EU is now a single market, this does not mean that it is uniform throughout; in fact, the opposite is the case. Within the EU there is a huge diversity in terms of consumers, competition, demand and production; these factors must be taken into account. If a business is trading in a market that is fragmented and geographically separated, it is going to experience difficulties in supplying to that market unless there has been a thorough investigation of the market, and the business is aware of the sectors in which it wishes to trade. For example, a business producing an item at the premium end of the market will not want to move into a low income economy to sell its product, but it may be interested in producing in such an economy. Burberry has moved some its production to eastern European countries in recent years in an attempt to cut costs and increase profit margins.

Above all, the managers of a business entering Europe need to have clear objectives for the future, both in terms of the existing domestic market and the new overseas market. There are both opportunities for managers to take in terms of higher sales; for example, Melton Mowbray Pork Pies will benefit from 'Protected Geographical Status' (see below). However, there are also risks involved in moving into the unknown. Managers need to minimise these risks through careful planning, an understanding of the new market and a willingness to be adaptable to the new situations they face.

Protection for Melton Mowbray's pies

Melton Mowbray The Melton Mowbray pork pie has finally joined Cornish clotted cream, Whitstable oysters and Welsh Lamb on Europe's list of protected food.

After a ten-year battle, the world-famous pie has been given protected geographic status by the European Commission.

This means only producers making these pork pies to the traditional recipe and in the vicinity of the Leicestershire town of Melton Mowbray will have the right to use its name. The Melton Mowbray Pork Pie Association has fought hard for the status, which will come into effect on October 4 providing no other European states object. Matthew O'Callaghan, chairman and local councillor, said: "The award of [protection] for Melton Mowbray pork pies safeguards our regional food heritage, protects our local jobs and gives the consumer value."

Central government intervention

The extent to which the government intervenes in the economy will vary, and depends on one or more of the following factors:

- The political persuasion of the party in power will be significant. In general, Labour governments are more likely to intervene in the working of the economy than Conservative governments. *The Independent* newspaper gives a figure of 3,000 new pieces of legislation introduced under the Blair government, one for every day it was in office. Many of these laws had effects on the day-to-day running of businesses.

- The state of the economy may be an important factor. Governments are likely to feel the need to respond more when the economy is in difficult circumstances, such as a situation of rising unemployment. A government coming up to a general election, with an economy experiencing low growth, may try to stimulate demand through the use of fiscal policy.

> ### Key Term
>
> **Fiscal policy:** the use of government spending and taxation, through the government's annual budget, to influence the level of demand in the economy.

- The views of the electorate may also play a significant role in influencing government opinion. In 2008, the Brown government had to bow to public pressure and introduce measures to reduce the effects on the low paid of the removal of the 10p rate of income tax.
- Sometimes local governments intervene and affect the operation of businesses. The decisions by Ken Livingstone, the former mayor of London, to introduce the congestion charge and later the pollution charge in parts of the capital have had a big impact on businesses in the area. Businesses need to take a change in policy like this into account when making decisions on location or relocation and in the provision of vehicles for their employees or for distribution.

Competition policy

The UK's policy on monopoly is to allow it to exist, but to prevent the use of restrictive practices that operate against the public interest. The Office of Fair Trading considers any business with more than 25% of the market to be a monopoly. If a proposed takeover bid or merger would result in a monopoly situation, it will be the subject of investigation by the Competition Commission, requiring permission from the Commission to go ahead.

> ### Key Term
>
> **The Office of Fair Trading (OFT):** the government organisation that makes markets work well for consumers. This is achieved by promoting and protecting consumer interests and making sure that business is fair and competitive. Anti-competitive policies by businesses will be investigated to prevent abuse of the consumer.

The main areas of restrictive practices operated by businesses are connected with price-fixing or restriction of selling outlets. In recent years, the mobile phone industry has been the subject of a number of different inquiries by the Competition Commission. These have included investigations into roaming costs within Europe, the cost and ease of switching between contract providers, and the grocery and supermarket sector.

> ### Key Term
>
> **Monopoly:** in terms of UK and EU competition policy, this is any business that controls more than 25% of the market share.

Examiner's voice

The UK and EU definition of a monopoly is that it is a business controlling more than 25% of market share, but the term 'monopoly' is also used in some cases to refer to a single supplier who controls a market. Microsoft could be used as an example of a monopoly in this situation.

In some cases, a group of businesses may operate restrictive practices together, through a joint and secret agreement. This practice is called 'collusion'. It is easiest to collude where a few large firms dominate an industry. This is because the fewer people who know of the agreement, the more likely it is to be undetected. The operation of collusion between businesses is illegal in the UK and elsewhere in the EU. As a result of OFT investigation into collusion, British Airways was fined in 2007 for price-fixing fuel surcharges with Virgin Atlantic; Virgin was not fined because they reported the offence to the American Aviation Authority.

Privatisation and deregulation

The main period of privatisation of public sector businesses took place in the 1980s and 1990s under Conservative governments, particularly those of Margaret Thatcher. Privatisation is the act of passing ownership of a business from the public to private sector by selling shares in the business. In general, the businesses being privatised were monopolies within the UK, although some, like British Airways, faced considerable foreign competition even before their privatisation.

The arguments in favour of privatisation are as follows:

- Private sector businesses are subject to market forces and therefore need to operate efficiently, being aware of supply and demand conditions.

- A business that is privately owned needs to be profitable and to satisfy its shareholders in order to be able to survive.

The arguments against are:

- Many nationalised industries, like that of electricity supply, were natural monopolies. If privatisation results in new suppliers this may lead to the duplication of expensive investment which is inefficient and not in the interests of the general public.
- In some cases, it was felt that the businesses were sold off too cheaply and that valuable long-term assets were turned into short-term cash which was not used prudently by the government of the day. Harold MacMillan, a former Prime Minister referred to privatisation as 'selling the family silver'.
- Private sector businesses will not trade in unprofitable areas, leading to a variation in provision across the country.

To avoid problems of overpricing after privatisation, the privatised utilities were put under the control of regulators such as OFWAT for the water industry and OFFER for the electricity suppliers. Regulators have the power to cap price increases and demand efficiency savings through investment. Their intervention has been particularly evident in the telecommunications market, where OFTEL has been responsible for a number of pricing interventions to the benefit of the consumer.

The UK regulators are:

- OFREG: Office for the Regulation of gas and Electricity
- Ofcom: Office of Communications
- OFGEM: Office of Gas and Electricity Markets
- OFWAT: Office of Water Services
- DWI: Drinking Water Quality

At the moment, the Post Office remains the only major public sector industry not to be privatised, although they now face private sector competition from numerous courier firms in areas such as parcel delivery and fast and guaranteed letter delivery.

The process of privatisation was also accompanied by that of deregulation in a number of sectors of the economy during the 1980s. It was felt that outdated rules and regulations were stifling competition and that the result for the consumer was high prices and poor levels of efficiency. For example, bus provision in most areas of the UK was subject to a number of local authority laws, most commonly ones that limited the number of providers, often creating monopoly situations.

The removal of these laws led to a rapid increase in providers, sometimes to unsustainable numbers in the short run. The effect of deregulation is shown on the supply and demand diagram in Figure 64.2 with a shift to the right of the supply curve. This will result in lowering the price to the customer.

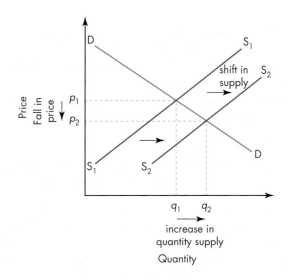

Figure 64.2

In the longer term, there has been mixed results. Some areas of the market have better services, with more choice and greater efficiency; others face inadequate provision or a complete lack of services.

Labour markets

In recent years governments have shifted their intervention in labour markets from the demand to the supply side. They have used measures to try to encourage an increase in the number of people entering the labour market, but also to try to improve the skills and quality of that labour. These supply-side measures may take a long time to have an impact on the economy, but they are less likely to have the adverse economic effects that may come with demand management (see Unit 60). At the same time, the government has removed some of the legislation and red-tape that affected the employment of workers. For example, although many UK employers now honour the working hours agreement, it is still possible to ask employees to work longer hours, as long as agreement is sought from the worker

Labour market supply-side policies

Training and education are vitally important in any labour market, but this is more likely to be the case in a developed economy where there is likely to be less demand for unskilled workers. The government has tried to improve the skill level of the UK population through measures like the National Curriculum, access to university, training schemes for the long-term unemployed and the New Deal for young unemployed workers.

Government bodies for training initiatives

- **Training for work:** retraining and re-skilling for those experiencing difficulty in finding employment.
- **The New Deal:** aimed at moving 18–24-year-olds from unemployment into work.
- **Skillseekers:** funding for training to help young people improve their employment prospects when they leave school at 16, 17 or 18.
- **Modern Apprenticeships:** help for young people wanting to gain a vocational qualification in areas like car mechanics, plumbing and electrical work.

Employment regulations have been reduced to make it easier for employers to take on extra workers. Rules governing part-time work and the employment of women have changed, as have the rules about short-term contracts. At times these changes may create problems for the individual worker by giving them fewer rights than full-time workers, but they have benefited the UK economy in attracting overseas businesses whose managers want to relocate to a country where employment practices are less restrictive for employers.

The overhaul of Trade Union legislation since 1980 has also helped to make the UK labour market much less restrictive. This legislation has covered issues like postal ballots and secondary picketing (see Unit 63). The fall in working days lost through industrial action as a result of this legislation, together with the fact that UK employment laws are less restrictive than elsewhere in the EU, has also helped attract inward investment to the UK.

Minimum wage

The use of a policy to guarantee a minimum wage for low paid workers has a number of advantages and disadvantages.

For the individual worker it means that they receive a reasonable rate of pay for their work and that the possibility of exploitation should be removed; this should mean that all employees are guaranteed at least a basic standard of living. In 2008 the rates were £5.73 for workers over 22, £4.77 for those between the ages of 18 and 21 and £3.53 for under-18s who had left compulsory education.

For the employer, the effect of the minimum wage is to increase the costs of employing labour. This may mean that the employer reduces the number of workers employed to reduce the wage bill, which is not in the interests of the employees. Since the introduction of the minimum wage in the UK there is little evidence that this is the case. However, there are still employers who are working outside the law, paying their employees below minimum wages; this is most likely to happen with home workers in industries such as textiles, where wages are paid in cash to workers who are isolated, unaware of the law and perhaps too reliant on the job to risk losing it.

Examiner's voice

The legislation on employment and the rates of minimum wage are frequently changed. You can check for up-to-date information on www.direct.gov.uk/employment.

Further Sources

www.europe.gov.uk
www.europa.eu
www.competition-commission.org.uk
www.dt.gov.uk

Your Turn

Questions Time allowed 35 minutes

1. Outline two ways in which UK businesses are affected by its membership of the EU. (4 marks)

2. Discuss the effects of an increase in the minimum wage rates for the owner of a small Chinese takeaway business. (10 marks)

3. Imagine that Nissan was considering moving its European production unit from the UK to Greece to take advantage of their lower cost labour and to be in the eurozone. Evaluate the effects of this on:

   A. the UK economy. (10 marks)

   2. the Nissan company. (10 marks)

   (34 marks)

SOCIAL CHANGE

Any successful business will need to be aware of changes in the society in which it operates, so that the organisation of the business and the goods or services it produces will meet the demands of all stakeholders.

Demographic changes

The distribution and size of the UK population have undergone many changes since the Industrial Revolution in the nineteenth century. Similar changes will have occurred in major trading partners in Europe and North America. These changes have an impact on the nature of demand faced by business, as well as the size and characteristics of the workforce.

The following demographic factors have an impact on the markets in which businesses operate.

Changes in the age of the population

From the late twentieth century onwards, there has been a growth in the proportion of old people in the UK and a fall in the proportion of young people. In addition, many of these elderly people now have access to large incomes through pensions and savings, together with better health and a longer life expectancy than was previously the case. All this has resulted in increases in demand for products like specialist holidays and mobility aids.

Many businesses have had to revise their recruitment policies. A lack of young people entering the job market has encouraged some businesses to employ older workers with the necessary skills. Hardware store B&Q now has a policy of actively recruiting retired workers, whom

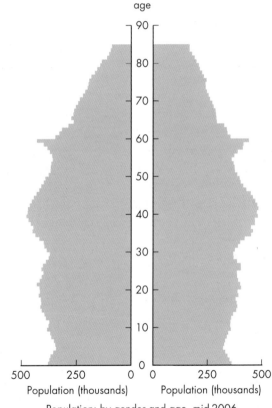

Population: by gender and age, mid-2006

In mid-2006 the resident population of the UK was 60,587,000, of which 50,763,000 lived in England. The average age was 39.0 years, an increase on 1971 when it was 34.1 years. In mid-2006 approximately one in five people in the UK were aged under 16 and one in six people were aged 65 or over.

The UK has a growing population. It grew by 349,000 people in the year to mid-2006 (0.6 per cent). The UK population has increased by 8 per cent since 1971, from 55,928,000. Growth has been faster in more recent years. Between mid-1991 and mid-2006 the population grew by an average annual rate of 0.4 per cent and the average growth per year since mid-2001 has been 0.5 per cent.

Figure 65.1 Population estimates

they have found to be more reliable and knowledgeable in dealing with customer enquiries.

Ethnic diversity

The UK has a more diverse ethnic mix now than was previously the case. Part of this is a result of the free movement of labour in the EU and the increase in its size as countries from eastern Europe have joined in recent years. In many cases these different nationalities create demand for different ranges of goods and also bring aspects of their culture to existing UK residents. For example, most small towns and all cities have Indian and Chinese restaurants and takeaways, and all the major supermarkets now carry ranges of the foods from these countries. Indian and Chinese food is now part of the British way of life.

Immigrants bring with them demand for different products and services, together with new ideas and customs. The influx of Polish workers has led to a demand for different foodstuffs, such as carp, in local supermarkets. Polish workers are now an important part of the bus network in the West Midlands. As a result of this the bus companies have had to introduce classes in English and local information to ensure that their Polish drivers can cope with requests for help from passengers.

Changing patterns of employment

The employment of women

The role of women in society has changed considerably in recent generations. Before the Second World War, most married women would not have been in the workforce. Today, the opposite is the case; the vast majority of women of working age, even those with young children, are in paid employment, at least part of the time. This has increased demand for more flexible working patterns so that both women and men can fit employment around childcare. Businesses now have to offer maternity and paternity leave to their employees by law, but other businesses offer extended leave and flexible alternatives like job-sharing and home-working to ensure that they keep or attract the best possible female workers.

Education

A larger proportion of young people now stay on to pursue some sort of further education after the official school leaving age of sixteen. In 2007 the UK government stated its intention to extend the school leaving age to 18 in the near future, although this will be combined with an increase in the provision of practical and vocational courses. This means that most young people now enter the workforce at a later age than previously and often with more qualifications. However, many of these young people will be involved in part-time working while pursuing their studies. The catering and retail sectors employ many of these students in temporary and part-time jobs, particularly in the evening and at weekends.

Flexibility

Businesses in the retail sector now need more flexibility in employment because of extended opening hours. Seven-day trading and twenty-four-hour opening require full- and part-time workers to cover the longer time period if they are to operate successfully. These jobs are often attractive alternatives for students or women with children.

Technology

The growth of the internet, emails and improvements in other forms of electronic communication have made it possible for workers in some sectors to work either exclusively or partly from home. Meetings can be held using video-conferencing, and work can be circulated quickly around the globe. This type of working is more likely in jobs which rely on communication technology, like journalism, but it is an increasing feature of the business world. For the individual it removes the need for costly and time-consuming travel, and for the business it reduces the costs associated with providing office space.

Agency work

The use of agency workers has also increased in recent years. The businesses using these workers pay the agency for their use, and the employees will be paid by the agency where they are registered. This gives the business the flexibility to vary their employment level from week to week to meet demand levels. It therefore also releases the business from responsibility for payroll, PAYE and National Insurance payments. Alternatively businesses can outsource parts of their work to other organisations. This might be done because the other business has greater economies of scale or because the business needs to free up labour to meet orders and commitments. For example, a clothing firm might outsource the design of its fabrics to businesses with expertise in this area.

Examiner's voice

Outsourcing means passing on all or part of a specific job to another firm. Outsourcing is used for the following reasons: greater efficiency in the outsource business, lack of capacity in the main business, ability to complete an order quickly.

All of these social changes have implications for the demand faced by businesses. An increase in demand, as a result of a change like immigration, will shift the demand curve to the right, while a fall in demand, as a result of fewer babies being born, will shift demand to the right (see Figure 65.2).

Examiner's voice

It is important to remember that the final paper is synoptic and includes the whole syllabus. It is useful therefore to try to include theory that you learned earlier in your course. The use of a demand and supply diagram in this section would show that you know how to apply your AS Business Studies knowledge in a strategic situation.

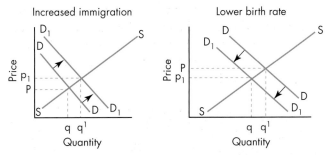

Figure 65.2 Demand and supply diagram

Corporate responsibility

An important and relatively new area of awareness for the business world is that of corporate responsibility. Most businesses include profitability as one of their main objectives in order to satisfy stakeholders such as shareholders. Corporate responsibility goes further than this and includes the wider responsibility of the business to other stakeholders and society in general.

This is an extract from Barclays' statement on its corporate responsibility:

'At Barclays we set ourselves goals for the way we conduct our business across a wide range of issues and we take our commitment seriously. These commitments include defining our responsibility to customers and employees and addressing the critical issues of financial exclusion and environmental impact.'

This approach is now typical of many industries in the UK. It stems from a recognition of the fact that business is no longer judged solely on its ability to deliver the good or service, but that the manner of the delivery is increasingly important. Businesses need to be aware of the wider concerns of the general public and of their impact on society and the environment.

Bad publicity in any area can bring a business to its knees. In 1994, Starbucks coffee shops were made the target of widespread protest, both in the UK and USA because they were paying Guatemalan coffee-pickers less than a living wage. The reason that Starbucks was chosen as the main target for the campaign was not because it was the worst offender or because it alone could make changes, but because of its high profile. Many of those protesting had had no direct stakeholder connection with the company. As a result of the bad publicity and boycotts of its business, Starbucks introduced a new code of conduct and a number of 'ethical' products. Clever use of marketing may have turned all the bad publicity into increased sales and awareness.

Figure 65.3 Starbucks was targeted by protestors for fair trade

Businesses have to consider their corporate responsibility in a number of different areas:

Environment

As the publicity about global warming, pollution and other environmental issues increases, businesses have had to respond to the demands of society and government to play their part in these areas. Most supermarkets now operate schemes to encourage customers to use fewer plastic bags, and producers are looking for ways either to reduce packaging or to make it biodegradable. Businesses can use their actions in these areas in promotion and publicity.

Charity and fundraising

Most large businesses are now involved in charitable and community work to raise their profile. EDF Energy gives all of its employees one day off a year to work on projects in local schools and in addition, employees are encouraged to take part in the Young Enterprise Scheme with student businesses. Others businesses such as Tesco gain huge amounts of publicity and goodwill from schemes that pay for sports and computer equipment for schools and sports clubs.

Diversity

Many businesses feel that their operations should better represent and include the wide range of diversity of the population in the UK. In October 2007, the fashion designer, Vivienne Westwood was openly critical of the fashion industry and women's magazine publishers for their failure to use black models. Good publicity for her and bad publicity for others might have an effect on future sales.

Financial responsibility

In recent years UK banks and building societies have been criticised for their failure to lend money responsibly to customers. As a result of this, the financial sector has had to become increasingly aware of the need to exercise control of access to credit cards and loans, particularly to people who are more financially vulnerable.

It is therefore important for a business to use its corporate responsibility policy to show employees and the wider community that it cares about more than profit. The costs of doing this may be relatively small in monetary terms, in relation to the returns in the form of profit. It also helps to motivate workers and improve the image of the business projected to society in general.

> ### Further sources
>
> Look at the section on corporate responsibility on the website of any major UK firm such as Marks & Spencer (www.marksandspencer.com), Nat West (www.natwest.com) www.statistics.gov.uk – the Labour Force Survey has information on areas like ethnicity, identity and lone parents in employment.
> www.city-and-guilds.co.uk – the ageing workforce.

Case Study   Time allowed 1 hour

Older Staff still facing bias at work

There are wide discrepancies in the way that businesses in the UK have responded to the legislation introduced in 2006 to meet EU regulations on age discrimination.

Employment tribunals have been swamped with complaints about age discrimination in recent months. There are reports of practices by well-known UK companies that are regarded as 'abhorrent' by organisations representing workers. The public sector is shown to be particularly poor in its treatment of workers approaching retirement.

Age Concern has pointed to Abbey, Nationwide and B&Q as companies who actively recruit older workers and who have good policies in place for the employment of older workers. It also mentions a number of US firms operating in the UK who force workers to retire at 65, something that would break the law in the US.

More encouragingly, the report says that the situation is showing signs of improvement, particularly with regard to flexible working for older workers who want to stay on after retirement.

(Adapted from *The Financial Times*, 4 October 2007)

1. Give **two** examples, other than age, of ways in which businesses can discriminate.   (2 marks)

2. Evaluate the strategic effects on recruitment at Nationwide created by the ageing population.   (15 marks)

3. Analyse other ways in which the changing age distribution of the UK population is likely to affect UK businesses in future.   (10 marks)

(27 marks)

TECHNOLOGICAL CHANGE

People have come to expect an ever-increasing rate of change in technology, both at home and in the workplace. Keeping pace with what is available can be time-consuming and difficult for the individual, but is even more daunting for the manager of a business. New technology can be introduced and then become obsolete before there is time to take the required change on board (see Unit 66).

The effects of technology on business

Perceived disadvantages

Technological change at work is often felt to be threatening because of its possible effects on the individual worker. There are a number of reasons for this.

- Technological change is often associated with unemployment in employees' eyes. The introduction of computers in banks and of robotic processes in car plants led to a reduction in the number of workers employed in those areas. Workers in sectors where new technology is being introduced may feel that their job is threatened.

- New technology makes it necessary for workers to acquire new skills; those involved in this process may feel that they do not have the qualities required to learn the skills, or that they are too old to take on the task.

- The changes caused by new technology may require employees to move to different departments or to work with new colleagues and managers. Many people will find such changes difficult, particularly if they have worked with one group of people for a long

time, or there is someone in the new group whom they have found to be difficult. These types of changes often require a change of culture or way of thinking; many, particularly older employees find it difficult to adapt in this way. It removes their sense of belonging, built up over their years of service.

Examiner's voice

Look at the work done by Mayo in this area. Using theory to justify your answers is to be encouraged.

- In countries such as Japan and the USA, the 'new' is regarded as exciting and desirable. In the UK we have a tendency to cling to the 'old' ways and to regard new products and ideas with suspicion. This is particularly the case in established manufacturing industries such as the production of china and glass tableware.

Benefits of technological change

On the other hand new technology may bring numerous opportunities and advantages with it.

- Rather than creating unemployment, the introduction of new technology may bring a net increase in employment by increasing demand for the product or service. The introduction of computers in banking may have reduced the demand for counter cashiers, but it has made the huge growth in the financial services sector possible and created thousands of new, but different jobs as a consequence.
- New technology creates new demand among consumers. Japanese industry built its success in the late twentieth century by identifying the next

product or trend and then making sure that they were first to bring it to market. This helped make their businesses successful and created employment for Japanese workers.

- Learning new skills and implementing the changes involved in introducing new technology can have positive benefits for the morale of the workforce and the self-esteem of individual workers. The result may be better motivation and an increased willingness to accept change in future. However, it is also important to remember that these situations may result in redundancy for some workers (see Unit 28).

Managers and employees need to understand that continuing to do the same thing is the highest risk of all. This might not be the message that employees and unions want to hear, but they need to be convinced. There are numerous examples of businesses where the need for range was either not recognised or was ignored.

Swatch

The Swiss watch industry was confident that cheap quartz watches coming on to the market from Japan posed no threat to their very specialist product; they thought that the demand for hand-made watches was guaranteed. They eventually responded and took on the Japanese threat. The Swiss company, Swatch, began to produce a competing, mass-produced quartz watch, and managed not only to become market leader, but also to secure the future niche markets of companies like Omega and Tissot, by showing them the benefits of greater efficiency and better promotion in their markets.

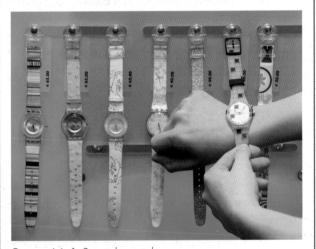

Figure 66.1 Swatch watches

Implementing technological change

One of the major difficulties in implementing technological change is the timing. If a business holds back too long before introducing new technology, it may begin to lose markets and market share, and run the risk of being out of date. This may happen if a business wants to wait until new technology becomes cheaper or until the equipment has proved its worth. On the other hand, moving too soon may mean that a business has to pay higher prices and that it becomes involved in the inevitable teething troubles of new equipment. The situation is exactly like that of buying the newest games console. Do you buy it now when it is more expensive and there are not many games to play on but you are ahead of the game, or do you wait until it is cheaper but everyone has already bought it and there are lots of games? There is no right answer.

Businesses considering the introduction of new technology must also look at the way it will fit into their overall situation. Too many businesses buy new equipment in a piecemeal fashion, a little at a time, having failed to make a strategic assessment of the complete situation. In order to make a reasoned decision, it is important to look at the investment in terms of its ability to reduce costs and its potential to improve the business's capability to respond to changes in the marketplace.

The costs and benefits of installing new technology in a business may not be immediately obvious, particularly in the area of human resources. Installing new technology in isolation, without training or organisational change, is unlikely to bring the benefits that the business might expect or want. The more complex the organisation, the more comprehensive the cost-benefit analysis needs to be in its scope before any decision is taken.

In some cases, it may make more sense for a business, particularly a small or new one, to choose not to invest in the newest technology and to use resources outside the business instead. For example, small businesses considering putting in new e-business systems may find that the benefits at this stage of their existence do not justify the expense that would be required. In these circumstances it would be sensible to look at external suppliers of such systems to see if they offer a better and cheaper alternative in the short term. Going down this route may also mean that the risk of rapid obsolescence is minimised because the supplier has to upgrade to the new technology.

Key Term

Obsolescence: existing capital equipment is replaced by new developments in technology; e.g. the replacement of the typewriter by the word processor.

Rapid technological change is a key factor in the business world. Its existence creates a situation of uncertainty as well as the possibilities of dealing with an increasingly complex market. Any decision in this area needs strategic planning and investigation. Managers should not assume that new technology will always be better or more useful in their business, but neither can they afford to ignore possibilities that might improve the performance of their businesses and there competitiveness in the market.

Further Sources

www.businesslink.gov.uk
www.itweek.co.uk
www.manufacturingtalk.com

Your Turn

Case Study Time allowed 1 hour

Getting the best from new phone technology

Stamco Timber is a timber and builders merchants which supplies building firms across the south east of England. The business has four offices which are 40 miles apart.

When the business opened a new branch in 2000, a decision was taken to install a new phone system, and the contract was put out to tender. One of the suggestions received was from a Voice over Internet Protocol (VoIP) telephone system. This system was at the forefront of technology at the time, using either a leased line or broadband to route calls between the internal sites of a business. Internal calls are free and can be transferred between extensions quickly and easily. External calls are charged at the standard provider's charge. Stamco decided that the VoIP system would be the best option for them.

The new phone system required specialist handsets and computer network cards. It cost £20,000 to install. As Stamco already leased a line between two of its sites and could use broadband between the others, no extra costs were incurred there.

Although this may sound like a great deal of money for a phone system, Nicholas Wilde, the financial director, says that the system paid for itself in a very short period of time. From the start, the company saved £300 to £400 a month in phone calls. In addition, VoIP has added to the professional image of the business in a number of ways. When customers ring a local branch, they are now routed through a call centre. If all the lines there are engaged, the call is routed back to a local office. This means that the customer never gets the engaged tone and is therefore less likely to put the phone down and ring a competitor.

Nicholas says that there are one or two important factors to remember when installing a phone system like this. The leased line was always more efficient than the broadband because there was no risk of it going down and losing them business. Stamco have now installed leased lines throughout the business. It is also important for the business to do thorough research on alternative quotes and to ensure that the chosen provider delivers what has been ordered and paid for. The most important part of the installation, however, is to ensure good staff training for the new system and to make sure that everyone is expert in its use. This removes the need for expensive call-outs and makes it possible to tweak the system to suit the needs of the business and its workers at the training stage.

(Adapted from *Business Link*, April 2008)

1. Explain the importance of the phone system to a business like Stamco. (4 marks)

2. Analyse the problems that businesses are likely to encounter if they choose to use cutting-edge technology. (10 marks)

3. Evaluate the costs and benefits that Stamco should have taken into account when making the choice of a new phone system. (16 marks)

(30 marks)

THE ENVIRONMENT

Consideration of the environment is another external factor that affects the working of a business. Damage to the environment (a **social cost**, **external cost** or **negative externality**) is moving higher up the agenda for politicians and the general public. Consequently, businesses cannot afford to ignore the problem.

It is not just an issue for the UK economy; throughout the world the demand for energy resources has serious environmental repercussions. China consumes 12.1% of the world's energy resources, second only to the USA. With only modest oil reserves, China relies on coal, which causes huge environmental damage.

The type of cars we drive have been targeted by an alliance of environmental groups, who staged protests in January 2005 in an attempt to shame drivers of 4×4 vehicles into buying smaller cars which consume far less fuel and emit less pollution. Some versions of the Range Rover produce 389 grammes of carbon dioxide per kilometre, double the rate of the Ford Mondeo (Ben Webster, *The Times*, 8 January 2005).

Sales of 4×4 vehicles had increased in 2004 by 12.8%, more than double the number sold a decade ago. By 2008, with a change in the tax regime making cars with high emissions a lot more expensive to tax, manufacturers were rapidly attempting to reduce emissions!

Car and plane usage has added considerably to the air pollution from emissions. Even those of us who are trying to stay fit by cycling to work, face the risk of heart disease according to the British Heart Foundation. Dr D Newby of the British Heart Foundation stated:

'Cycling through congested traffic exposes the cyclist to high levels of air pollution especially as the exercise of cycling increases breathing and the individual's exposure'.

(*The Sunday Times*, 21 January 2005)

Examiner's voice

This topic is highly controversial and you should guard against 'banging a drum' with emotive language and political dogma. It is better to put forward a balanced view highlighting both the positives and the negatives of a business that may or may not be responsible for a particular form of pollution. Marks are awarded for the way in which you write your points and NOT for any particular viewpoint.

Environmental issues and their consequences

Air pollution

Much publicity was given to the level of air pollution in Beijing, the host city for the 2008 Olympics. 'Smog' descends upon the city at regular intervals, forcing some athletes to withdraw for fear of damage to their health. In an attempt to reduce the smog, the Chinese government stopped industrial production in the area and took over one million cars off the road.

The massive rate of economic growth, both in China and India, has a serious effect upon the air quality in and around these countries.

Our air continues to be polluted by a wide range of industrial processes. The power stations that generate our electricity, and incinerators which burn some of our rubbish, are a major cause of air pollution according to experts.

It is not only industry that creates the pollution. Cars and planes used by consumers are another major source of air pollution. The Environment Agency is responsible for monitoring the amount of air pollution caused by industry.

> The biggest consequence of pollution seems to be on our climate. Weather conditions do appear to becoming more extreme, with more frequent winds of greater intensity, rainfall in greater quantities that causes flooding are now something that is even affecting the UK. The consequences of global warming and the rising sea levels are that London will need to build another barrier to supplement the Thames barrier if regular flooding is to be avoided.
>
> Researchers found that without a sharp reduction in green house emissions, sea levels could rise far more than the 2ft to 3ft already expected by 2100.
>
> (Adapted from *The Sunday Times*, 9 January 2005)

However, in 2007 intense rainfall caused serious damage to buildings and houses in Hull, Gloucester and Tewksbury. The amount of rainfall was so severe and over such a short period of time that floods were inevitable. Many people were forced out of their homes for several months and in some instances, over a year. Sadly 2007 was not a 'freak' year; August 2008 was one of the wettest on record.

Figure 67.1 Flooding caused extensive damage in 2007

Noise pollution

Living close to a motorway or an airport will mean a considerable amount of noise pollution. House values are usually reduced as a consequence of their proximity to the source of noise pollution. Expensive anti-noise measures have been fitted to houses close to the runways of some airports (double or triple glazing), while large fences are erected on motorways to deaden the constant noise. Such measures add to the expense of the transport system, but are essential if the social costs are to be tolerable.

The fear of further noise pollution led to serious opposition to another runway at Heathrow.

River or sea pollution

Water can be easily contaminated by industry when discharging its waste. Chemical plants have in the past been guilty of causing environmental damage as a result of careless disposal of waste or insufficient treatment prior to disposal. Oil is spilt into the seas around the world on a regular basis. Some of the spills have been due to accidents as ships have run aground. The consequences of these accidents are significant. Oil spills are expensive to clear up and the damage to wildlife and the land is enormous. Money spent clearing up such spills could be better spent providing more hospitals or new schools.

Land pollution

Deforestation and land scarred by quarrying or mining is a form of pollution. Brazil has continued to fell millions of its hardwood trees, leaving the land bare as there are no trees to hold the soil in place. Once the land is reduced to a barren state, nothing can be grown on it and therefore another resource has been lost.

Congestion

Traffic congestion is an environmental issue because cars in traffic jams are still using petrol and polluting the atmosphere. In addition, such traffic often leads to a call for more roads to be built, which erodes the amount of land for other uses.

Government measures

Sustainable Development Strategy

The government introduced its 'Sustainable Development Strategy', which aims to deliver a better quality of life for everyone. It proposed the following:

- a reduction on vehicle excise duties for cars with low emissions
- an increase in the standard rate for the landfill tax (a charge for disposing of waste related to the amount disposed)
- tax allowances for industry, which invests in environmentally-friendly technology
- recycling schemes operated by local governments; many households now have additional bins and containers for plastic waste and papers.

Moving freight off the road

The EU Transport Committee is contemplating a project aimed at moving freight off the roads of Europe and on to rail. Numerous EU studies have shown that switching from road to rail provides a plethora (many) of social and environmental benefits.

Environmental stewardship

Launched in August 2005, 'Environmental Stewardship' is a new agri-environmental scheme which provides finance to farmers in England who deliver 'effective environmental management on their land'.

Waste Management Programme

Defra (Department for Environment, Food and rural affairs) introduced the Waste Management Programme following a report ('Waste not, Want not') which set targets for the disposal of waste.

By 2010, the amount of biodegradable waste that is placed in landfill is to be 75% of the amount in 1995; by 2013, the rate is to be down to 50% of the 1995 amount.

The climate change levy

This is a tax on the use of energy in industry and commerce.

Carbon Trust Standard

Launched on 24 June 2008 by Environment Secretary, Hilary Benn and businesswoman and 'dragon' on the BBC's television programme, 'Dragon's Den', Deborah Meaden, this is a kitemark for being environmentally friendly. The kitemark proves that the company has reduced its carbon footprint. B&Q and Morrisons have already gained their kitemark.

Department for Transport

The DFT announced that it was widening its definition of 'promotional literature'. This will mean that the advertising of cars will have to include information on carbon emissions and fuel on outdoor adverts (billboards) as well as other media. The information must be displayed with equal prominence to the rest of the wording within the advert.

The Carbon Trust

This government-funded body offers advice to firms on carbon-emission reduction.

Congestion charges

The government has also allowed local governments to introduce road congestion charges. The London Congestion charge started at £5 each time a vehicle entered the congestion zone. Although traffic fell by up to 15%, the charge was increased in 2005 to £8 per vehicle. Professor Begg, a government adviser on road issues, stated that the London congestion charge would have to be increased to £15 per vehicle before it would have a significant effect on the levels of traffic. This is due to the fact that car usage is highly inelastic and therefore the charge needs to be significant if it is to have any real effect.

Alternative sources of energy

The government has invested money into alternative sources of energy. The number of wind farms has escalated in the last few years, but face problems from local residents who object to them because they are unsightly. At present, wind farms only generate a single figure percentage of our total energy generation.

Harnessing the power of the tides (tidal energy) has not been prolific, which is perhaps surprising considering that the UK is an island.

Kyoto Treaty 1997

The Kyoto Treaty commits the industrialised nations to reducing emissions of greenhouse gases such as carbon dioxide by about 5% below the 1990 levels within 10 years.

Unfortunately, the United States would not sign the treaty. It is hoped a revised version of the treaty will be in place by 2008.

Under the Kyoto Protocol, by 2008–12 the UK must reduce its baseline emissions of six major greenhouse gases by 12.5 per cent from a baseline target set in 1990. Furthermore, the draft Climate Change Bill commits the UK to reductions in carbon emissions of at least 26% by 2020 and a long-term goal of 60% by 2050.

Pressure groups

Environmental damage is not only expensive for businesses to reduce, but may bring unwanted publicity. Pressure groups such as Greenpeace and Friends of the Earth exist in order to highlight environmental issues. Negative publicity may affect sales or damage the image of the business.

Business has had to respond to demands for environmental issues to be addressed. Car manufacturers have responded by meeting the changing demand for cars. Consumers have been switching to smaller, more fuel-efficient vehicles, as a result of environmental concerns and the rising costs of petrol and diesel (the price increased by over 30% in 2007–08).

According to the Chief Executive of the Society of Motor Manufacturers and Traders, the percentage of small cars such as the Ford Fiesta and the Vauxhall Corsa sold 10 years ago was 27%; today that percentage has increased to nearly 33%. At the other end of the market, sales for the 'gas-guzzler' car, Hummer, have fallen significantly from a peak in 2006 (70,000) to a projected figure of about 35,000.

Key Term

Social costs/negative externalities: the cost to society of an activity.

Further Sources

www.unilever.com
www.shell.com
www.greenpeace.org.uk
www.defra.gov.uk
www.realbusiness.co.uk
www.climatechangecorp.com
www.carbontrust.co.uk
www.energysavingtrust.org.uk

Your Turn

Questions Time allowed 25 minutes

1. Give two alternative terms for a social cost.
(2 marks)

2. State two social costs of building another runway at an airport. (2 marks)

3. Explain who pays for the social costs incurred after an additional runway is built. (4 marks)

4. State one way in which the government is trying to reduce environmental damage. (1 mark)

5. What are the likely costs of trying to improve the environment? (4 marks)

6. Explain why it is difficult for a government to increase taxes on cars and petrol in order to reduce pollution from car emissions. (5 marks)

(18 marks)

Task

Using any of the listed websites above (or any others you may find), offer an updated list of what:

A. the government and

B. business

are doing to try to reduce the 'carbon footprint'.

THE MANAGEMENT OF CHANGE

Change is an inevitable fact of life for everyone, including the business environment. Over recent years, the pace of change has become increasingly rapid, as scientific and technological development makes it possible to do things in new ways and to introduce new products and techniques into the industrial process and the market. Each of these changes makes it necessary for us to learn new skills in our home and work environments. Some of us will make the changes and learn the skills more easily and quickly than others.

Whatever the case, change creates uncertainty in the workplace. A failure to manage change without careful strategic planning and an appreciation of the problems that may arise will mean that the business is likely to suffer.

Communication and change

In his book, 'Making it happen', Sir John Harvey Jones says the following:

'I have never understood why some managers are so terrified of telling their people the full economic facts. In a situation where there are inevitably going to be some job losses it is surely better to try to reassure as many people as possible, even if you cannot reassure everyone, than to end up with everyone in the outfit being anxious.'

In his opinion and that of many other successful and enlightened managers, it is always better to give everyone as much information as soon as possible. At ICI, managers always ensured that employees were the first people to hear of possible redundancies, and gave help to those involved from the beginning to the end of the process – and sometimes beyond them leaving the business. In general, people can cope better with a situation where they know the facts, however bad they

may be, than one where there is secrecy and rumour. Inevitably, in the latter case, people begin to work in a climate of fear and suspicion, which does not create an atmosphere where change will be accepted. In addition, if the rumours are incorrect, a great deal of time and effort will be wasted in putting things right.

Communication of information in a clear way from the top to the bottom of the hierarchy is essential; it must be done in an appropriate way, with the opportunity for workers to talk further with those who can allay their concerns, particularly if they involve job losses. It is equally important in the process of change to communicate good news to people; all too often this aspect of change is overlooked. Workers need to be told that they have done a good job, they have succeeded in a particular task, the profits have improved and the business is doing well. If these things are said and all good news is communicated, the atmosphere in the workplace will be more positive, workers will see the benefits of the changes they have implemented and be more likely to embrace change in the future.

The causes of change

Changes in a business can arise from internal or external sources, and the business's ability to control them may vary accordingly. Some strategy should be in place to identify likely problems and deal with them before they start to create difficulties for the business.

Internal change

Objectives

As businesses grow, it is likely that their objectives will change. In its early years a business will focus its efforts on surviving and ensuring an adequate cashflow, but gradually, if the business is viable, this focus will begin to change to profitability and possible growth in the long term. At each stage, the new objective will result in a change of emphasis for the running of the business that is likely to impact on everyone associated with it. A new business will need to keep tight control over costs in order to survive, whereas a business looking to grow may need to spend large amounts of money to achieve this objective.

Personnel

Changes in personnel are always likely to have an effect on the running of the business, and the more senior the personnel, the greater the possibility of major changes. The appointment of Stuart Rose as Managing Director of Marks & Spencer in 2001 was a key feature in the change in their fortunes. New people bring their own ideas and methods of working, so that even though it may take time and the scale of the effects may vary, their priorities and methods of working will eventually permeate through the business to colleagues.

Skill levels

The skill level of staff will also change over time as society's attitude to education and learning changes. This is likely to have an effect on the business, depending on the number of personnel it employs and the skills they require to do their job. Companies like Microsoft have experienced difficulties in recruiting high level software workers in recent years because of the low number of graduates coming out of IT courses at UK universities at present.

Finances

The financial status of the business may also force it to make changes. New procedures, products or legislation may force a business to undertake large-scale investment. Trading losses or a drop in profit levels may make it necessary to reorganise the workplace with the possible need for redundancy.

Waterford Wedgwood has faced very difficult trading conditions for a number of years, both in home and export markets; this has resulted in newer and more efficient production, the movement of some production overseas and redundancies at a number of its sites.

Conversely, improved trading conditions may make it necessary to take on new staff and to alter the responsibilities of existing employees. Changes like this are likely to result in uncertainty, disappointment and friction.

Innovation

If the business is innovative in its market, it may develop new products that result in changes in the processes it uses or the markets it supplies. This is particularly evident in sectors such as pharmaceuticals, electronics and communications, where the pace of change is very rapid. Companies such as Sony and Dyson continually innovate and change their product base in order to stimulate new demand. For Dyson this may involve a relatively small electronic adaptation or a new colour used for the vacuum cleaner, to signal a new model; for Sony it is likely to involve ground-breaking new technology in products such as its Play Stations.

External change

Globalisation

One of the most significant contributors to the change faced by all businesses in recent years is that of globalisation. The growth of China and India as major industrial nations has had huge implications for the business world. These countries are now significant both in terms of their production and consumption, and their low-cost labour also makes them attractive to businesses in the developed countries for outsourcing or relocation. The improvements in communication and the growth of cheap air travel bring these countries increasingly closer to the rest of the business world. Businesses in the developed world need to find markets where they can maintain an advantage over lower cost producers. As these newly industrialised countries develop and increase their capabilities, this is becoming increasingly difficult.

> ## Key Term
>
> **Globalisation:** the growth of the world so that it can be viewed as a whole place rather than a number of separate countries. The result for business is increased interdependence and the ability to trade in the world as if it were one market.

The environment

Environmental issues are becoming an increasingly important factor in the market, forcing changes on business either because of dwindling and expensive fossil fuel supplies or because of the threat of global warming and carbon emissions. Consumers now expect businesses to make major changes in their products and production because of the perceived threats to the planet; these changes may be to do with packaging, energy efficiency, recycling or production methods.

Failure to respond may have dramatic consequences for future demand levels for some businesses. Electricity providers such as EDF Energy have started to provide 'green' tariffs, where the electricity is generated by renewable sources to meet a demand for environmentally-friendly products from customers who want to reduce their carbon footprint.

Figure 68.1 The desire for renewable energy will bring great change to the energy industry

Technology

The speed of technological change has become increasingly rapid in recent years. New products, production methods and changes in information technology are increasingly significant factors in changing the business environment. Any business failing to take account of such changes is likely to find difficulty in maintaining success and profitability, particularly in the long term. An example of this can be found in the market for mobile phones, where consumers want to change their handset at regular intervals to take advantage of new features and styles.

The customer base

The customer base itself may change (see Unit 65). There may be a change in its composition; for example, the age and ethnic distribution of the UK population has changed greatly throughout its history and is continuing to change as eastern European countries enter the EU and their workers enter the UK workforce. Supermarkets in Coventry and elsewhere in the West Midlands now sell a range of products for the Polish customers who have recently settled in the area.

At the same time, the demands of the population may also change, forcing business to react, as is the case with the growth in demand for organic food production. This has forced the major supermarkets such as Sainsbury's and Tesco to stock a wide range of organic fruit and vegetables, where demand is growing rapidly and profit margins are high.

The economy

The economic situation and the stage of the economic cycle (see Unit 58) in the UK and world economy may also inflict change on a business. A downturn in economic activity will force a business to look at its markets and finances, and to take steps to minimise any adverse effects. Globalisation also has an impact here because businesses are increasingly dependent on international markets, both for supplies and for customers.

Competition

Businesses may also have to change in response to competition and once again globalisation makes this a more serious threat; any business now faces competition on a worldwide basis. Businesses need to be aware of the actions of their competitors, and must introduce measures to secure their market share. Marks & Spencer's failure to take account of the growth of competition from retailers like Next, Top Shop and Zara and to change its product range accordingly, had a serious impact on it profits in the late 1990s. Businesses that have been market leaders can sometimes feel that they do not need to change. This may make a fall in their market share more disastrous and difficult to cope with. More recently, smaller supermarkets such as Kwiksave and Somerfield have had to respond to the rapid growth of Tesco and its expansion into many different areas of retail trade. While Somerfield survives in small rural towns with a niche market, Kwiksave has found it impossible to respond to the intense competition and has ceased to trade.

The government

The government and its policies can also impose change on businesses. This is most likely to come in the form of new legislation, either at a national or local level. For example, the government has recently increased maternity leave to one year. Changes in the rights to paternity and maternity leave may force a business to reorganise its deployment of staff. The government's policy on taxation may have a significant impact on the financial situation of the business, and could create a need for financial stringency and redundancy.

The management of change

The management of change is likely to be one of the most difficult roles facing managers or owners of a business. Human nature generally prefers stability and is suspicious of change. However, change in any environment is inevitable and continuous, and with forethought, planning and consideration for the feelings of others, change can be introduced effectively. Unfortunately, there are numerous examples of the opposite scenario; for instance, when workers read in the media rather than hearing from management about the closure of their factory and forthcoming redundancies, it is obvious that the management of change has gone badly wrong.

Anticipated change

Experienced managers may be able to anticipate changes in some areas of the business and respond in ways that minimise the adverse effects. For example, if a business has an efficient market research and forecasting department, it may be possible to anticipate a fall in demand and develop a new product or find a new market. Similarly if labour shortages are expected, the business can begin to train new workers or offer training schemes to existing staff. This sort of change is referred to as anticipated change. A business should always be in a state of incremental change where managers are responding to the day-to-day changes in their trading environment. The benefits of incremental change are that its effects are less dramatic and staff can contribute to its introduction; employees are therefore less likely to be unsettled by it, and its implementation is likely to be smoother.

Unfortunately not all change can be anticipated. Events such as the terrorist attacks in New York, 2001 and London, 2005 can create major problems for a business. In these cases tourism and travel businesses such as major transatlantic airlines, were particularly badly affected in the aftermath to both events. Similarly, the outbreak of foot and mouth disease in 2001 affected small businesses such as farmers and the UK tourist industry as a whole.

Unanticipated/catastrophic change

Although the business has no control over **unanticipated** or **catastrophic change**, they still need to have contingency plans for worst-case scenarios. Contingency plans to deal with catastrophic change are likely to be the responsibility of a small department. For

example, the debate on childhood obesity in the UK has had a huge impact on the catering industry, with huge falls in demand for products like burgers and pizzas. McCain Chips used their contingency planning to fight back when there was bad publicity about the quantity of chips that children in the UK were eating. McCain encouraged discussion and debate to gain press coverage and give them the opportunity to emphasise the low-fat aspects of many of their products. McDonald's has also had to look closely at the range of products it offers, both in the USA and the UK in response to consumer interest in healthy eating.

In doing this, both businesses managed to gain valuable publicity from numerous articles and features where their name was mentioned. Specialist companies working in contingency management encourage businesses to be ready to respond to criticism in an immediate and positive manner, exactly like the McCain approach.

Factors for successfully managing change

The effective management of change in any business situation will depend on the extent to which the managers have been successful in managing the following.

- Managers need to have created an environment of mutual trust between themselves and their employees. If either group feels that their credibility or efforts are being undermined by the other, the introduction of change is unlikely to go smoothly. Suspicion is counter-productive in any working relationship and will almost certainly create a climate where change results in difficulties in managing the business.
- Communication is vital to any process of change. If the communication is timely, clear and truthful, appropriately delivered and gives a complete picture, it stands a much better chance of receiving a positive hearing. It is never going to be possible to counter all resistance to change, but if employees feel that management is being honest with them, a source of friction is removed, giving change a better chance of success.
- In a fast-moving business which has experienced change many times, employees will become used to change, realise its necessity and view it as less threatening. It will always be more difficult to introduce change to a business that has remained static over a long period of time. For many years, companies such as Royal Doulton and other pottery businesses resisted change because they thought the

consumer wanted a traditional product. This resulted in inefficiency and a lack of investment. When the need for change became imperative, it was difficult to introduce the changes needed because of the resistance of the workforce.

- The inclusion of employees in the process of change is always more likely to give a successful outcome. They will feel that they have 'ownership' of the changes and they may suggest helpful ideas. Participation often allows the changes to go further than management would have dared to consider if they were acting by themselves.

Examiner's voice

This is an example of the work of Mayo (see Unit 28). If you can refer to different areas of business theory in your answers, it will show that you are aware of different aspects of a topic.

- Whenever employees become involved in the process of change, management need to be prepared to listen to them and they must also be willing to compromise if the requests are appropriate and sensible. Making small changes to a plan to satisfy the concern of employees will often make it possible to introduce the much bigger changes.
- Above all, management needs to have a clear strategic plan of the process for change which they must be able to explain and justify to those involved in its implementation.

Changing location

The strategic decision to move all or part of a business to a new location is difficult to manage and can cause concern and uncertainty for all involved. There will be a variety of reasons for a business choosing to relocate (see Unit 35):

- the opportunity to move to a lower cost site
- the availability of cheaper labour
- the availability of suitably qualified or trained labour
- limits placed on expansion at the current site
- the personal wishes of the owner
- a large consumer base/market.

Relocation is a major strategic change for a business and it will almost always be long term in its implementation, requiring an analysis of possible costs and benefits arising from the move. Increasingly, the decision to relocate may involve a move to an overseas location for all or part of the business, often to take advantage of cheaper labour costs.

Employees at all levels may view relocation as abandonment of their work, and may make workers feel undervalued. Even relatively new businesses manage to build up a corporate ethos and history that will be symbolised in many of the ways it operates. Moving to a new site will suggest the abandonment of this ethos, and there may be a tendency for people to cling to the 'old ways' even when they know that change needs to happen.

The decision to relocate is not one to be taken lightly. All aspects of the move need to be considered and discussed in detail, because any mistake could be costly. In 2006, Powergen made the decision to move its Indian call centre back to the UK in an effort to retain customers and win back market share. Presumably the initial decision to move to India was thought worthwhile in terms of labour costs, but it will have caused redundancies in the UK at the time, with all the associated problems for those concerned. Powergen's initial decision to move to India ought to have involved research into the likely effect on its customers and its market. The end result has been costly both in monetary terms and distress for two groups of workers – those in the UK who lost their jobs initially, and those in India who now find themselves without an income.

Figure 68.2 Small businesses suffered when the congestion charge was introduced to London

The location of the operating facility is critically important for some businesses, but not as vital for others. Many small retail businesses rely on personal customers for all of their business. A good location, possibly with parking facilities close by, will be vitally important to the level of demand they might expect. The introduction of the congestion charge in central London hit many small businesses very hard.

In small rural towns, a business such as a dry cleaner is likely to be affected if parking is prohibited outside the shop or car parking charges are introduced in the town centre. For businesses operating call centres, the location is less likely to be as vital in terms of the market which is why, in the era of cheap and easy telephone communications, many businesses have moved their call centres overseas. For a call centre, the location will be determined by the availability and supply of labour. For other businesses, good road communication is the most important factor. The junction of the M1 and M6 in Northamptonshire is surrounded by large warehouses operated by companies such as Tesco and Amazon, to give them easy access to the major road network.

Each business needs to consider the market it serves and the constraints placed on it in getting the good or service to that market. The decision to relocate needs to be considered from all these points of view. In addition the costs of moving should be considered, not just in terms of redundancy and physical movement, but also in terms of the effect of the move on the morale of those who remain with the business. If 'the survivors' are unhappy or unsettled by the move, the business will be affected whether they have relocated or not.

The process of change needs to be viewed as long term and continuous and should not be imposed by management. It is important to know what is valued and needs to be kept, as well as what needs changing in an organisation. Each change needs to be justified and should be operating effectively before the management moves on to the next change. Above all, managers should be aware of the effects of change on their employees, and they need to show concern about the needs and concerns of their employees in order to create an atmosphere of trust and an adaptable workforce.

Further Sources

www.businessstudiesonline.co.uk
BBC online lectures The Reith Lecture 1999 (Globalisation)

Your Turn

Questions Time allowed 35 minutes

1. Suggest two reasons for change in the business environment and give an example of each.
(4 marks)

2. Define globalisation and give an example of its effects on a business. (4 marks)

3. Explain why communication is so vital in managing change. (6 marks)

4. Analyse the problems for Tesco in recruiting workers with the right skills and qualifications.
(10 marks)

5. Analyse the ways in which Marks & Spencer has had to change its product base to deal with globalisation and competition. (10 marks)

(34 marks)

Case Study Time allowed 1 hour

Kingfisher chief executive warns of tough times ahead

In September 2007 the chief executive of Kingfisher DIY, Gerry Murphy gave a warning about falling consumer confidence and tough trading times ahead for the business. He mentioned rising interest rates as one of the main causes of the problems facing the business. The rate of interest has an impact on the company by increasing the cost of its overdrafts and loans, but its impact on customers is even more worrying. Rising mortgage repayments and higher interest charges on credit cards have an impact on high street sales for the businesses in the group.

Kingfisher is the biggest DIY chain in Europe, owning B&Q in the UK and other DIY groups in Europe. B&Q profits for the first half of 2007 were hit by the worst summer in living memory. The situation in the UK looks likely to worsen, with a slow down in the housing market and the effects of earlier interest rate rises beginning to be felt by home owners. However, fortunately for Kingfisher, there are other markets where the situation is not so gloomy. Profits in France and Poland had climbed over the period to help offset some of the problems. The group has businesses across the globe from Ireland to China, and its international business now accounts for more than half its sales.

In the home market, in an attempt to attract a different sector of the population, B&Q is trying to make its stores more attractive to female customers. Research has shown that they are interested in ideas for improving their homes, but can often be put off stores if there is too much space given to DIY and building items. B&Q are planning more room settings to show off their ranges of homeware and furnishing products. They want to move away from the typical DIY image of row upon row of paints, nails and electrical components.

(Adapted from *The Guardian*, 21 September 2007)

1. Evaluate the benefits for Kingfisher of having interests all over the world. (10 marks)

2. To what extent is it possible for a business like Kingfisher to deal with the effects of changes in interest rates in the UK? (10 marks)

3. Explain some of the difficulties that Kingfisher might face as a result of trading in so many diverse markets. (6 marks)

4. Recommend whether B&Q should try to feminise its stores.

(20 marks)

(46 marks)

CHANGE WITHIN THE BUSINESS

As we saw in the previous chapter, change is necessary to ensure that a business is in touch with its consumers and its market. For change to work, management and employees need to work together and cooperate at every stage of the process. There are many ways in which this atmosphere can be created and encouraged in the workplace by both groups. Some situations will involve just managers and employees, but others will involve outside agencies such as unions and government bodies.

The effects of motivation and leadership on change within a business

Most of these measures will have been covered elsewhere in this book or the accompanying AS textbook, so you can read about them in more detail in the relevant chapters.

Teamwork

The use of teamwork in the workplace has expanded greatly since the 1980s, particularly with the introduction of Japanese work practices into UK industry. Making groups of workers responsible for particular tasks, allowing job sharing and encouraging worker participation in development with Kaizen methods (see Unit 46) all make workers more involved in and more responsible for the final output of the business.

Cooperation

Enlightened management should understand that a well-motivated workforce will be more likely to work effectively in a climate of cooperation. There are many ways of motivating workers (see Unit 28). It is important to ensure that the motivation used is appropriate for the circumstances and the group of people involved; this is where management skills are vital. To use motivation effectively, managers need to know and understand employees, to engender a spirit of trust at work and to create good two-way communication channels.

Organisational culture

An organisational culture where issues like these are considered to be important is likely to be one where it is easier to introduce change; the atmosphere is likely to be one of cooperation and a common understanding of the needs of the business. This does not mean that the introduction of change will be easy; problems will inevitably be raised. What it does mean however, is that there will be an ethos and culture that makes it possible to discuss problems and deal with them to mitigate their adverse effects wherever possible.

The role of employer/ employee relations

Every business will have a different way of managing the relationship between employer and employee. Whatever the system, the processes should be clearly understood and trusted by all parties.

Individual relations

On a day-to-day basis, communication between management and workers on an individual level is vitally important. The more distant individual workers are from their managers, the more likely it is that problems will arise. Management need to know about the situations that their employees face in their jobs, and workers need to realise that managers have many different constraints that affect their actions. If there is mutual understanding and a climate in which people can discuss their roles and the situations they face, the need for change will be better understood and accepted, albeit reluctantly.

Collective relations: trade unions

At a collective level, many businesses have workers who are members of trade unions. The role of trade unions and the legislation which governs them is covered in Unit 70. This situation has changed considerably since the 1980s when the then Prime Minister Margaret Thatcher introduced a wide range of legislation to reduce the power of the unions. At the time this caused increased tensions in a number of industries, notably with the National Union of Mineworkers, but after the initial conflicts of opinion the situation has improved greatly. The UK now has a much better record on industrial relations than was previously the case. Nevertheless, any introduction of change where the workforce is unionised should include union representatives in their discussions from the outset.

The role of the trade union is ultimately to protect the rights of their members. This will often put them in conflict with management, particularly if planned changes will result in redundancy or the reduction of workers' rights. This sort of conflict has been experienced at British Airways. They have suffered a number of crippling strikes as a result of changes in workers' rights and working practices.

Sometimes a more sympathetic approach to the management of change might help avert a strike, but at other times action takes place despite the best efforts of management. In these circumstances, outside, independent help is needed.

As a result of the trade union legislation of the 1980s and the entrance to the UK economy of Japanese businesses and their work practices, many businesses started to introduce single union agreements for their workers. A single union agreement means that workers and management will agree on one union that will represent any worker who wishes to belong to a union. Before this, many large businesses often found themselves in situations where change had to be agreed with a number of unions representing different groups of workers, often with different views on the proposed changes. It was sometimes the case that there was more disagreement between different unions than between management and workers. The single union deal makes negotiation easier and reduces the conflict in any situation of change. Toyota in Derby has operated such a scheme since first coming to the area.

Other businesses have moved into different schemes to avoid conflict and confrontation.

No-strike deals

A number of businesses have adopted no-strike deals with their employees in return for certain benefits and guarantees. This sort of system is in place at the Toshiba factory in the UK. For obvious reasons the trade union movement is not happy with these agreements, and complains that they put too much power in the hands of management. On the other hand, it is often the case that they encourage positive discussion and negotiation, rather than forcing groups into conflict situations.

Arbitration

No-strike agreements often use a system of pendulum arbitration. In such a system an independent arbitrator is appointed to help in the negotiation of agreements where the two sides are in conflict. The arbitrator will in the final instance make a straight choice between the different positions. Those who support pendulum arbitration feel that it makes workers and management more realistic and aware of the opposing group's view. Those who oppose it feel that it creates a climate of winners and losers, which is not good for relations between managers and workers.

Acas (Advisory, Conciliation and Arbitration Service)

During an industrial dispute, if employers and employees have reached a stalemate situation or have stopped talking, Acas can be called in to help them in reaching a compromise situation. As its name suggests, the organisation will try to bring the two sides together and mediate in order to reach an acceptable conclusion for both groups. It will try to find common ground and move groups to a closer and more realistic stance, using trained negotiators.

> ### Key Terms
> **Conciliation:** the act of bringing parties together with an independent conciliator to find common ground and a solution to the problem. It differs from arbitration, in that it has no legal standing. Arbitration is a legal process outside the courts where both parties are bound by the decision of the arbitrator.

As well as being involved in resolving disputes, Acas also produces a wide range of resources to help managers avoid the need for their services. They would prefer to be involved by giving assistance before a situation of conflict arises.

New working practices

In the past 20 years there have been a number of changes in the area of employment, some of which have been introduced as a result of pressure from workers and others to satisfy the demands of management. Much of the pressure has come as a result of the changing pattern of family life and particularly the changes in the retail sector. Twenty-four-hour opening and Sunday working have changed the working lives of many people, and such changes require consultation and cooperation to ensure that they can be introduced successfully and operate effectively.

Flexible working is now common in many businesses. This may be a situation where each employee is allowed to vary the hours they work as long as they are in the office for certain core times; for example, an employee may work longer days without taking lunch-hours, but then take time off at the end of the day. This is usually called flexitime. In other cases, workers may be allowed to work from home for some part of the week; this practice is particularly useful for parents with young children, but its use is increasingly widespread, especially in IT-based firms. Reuters, the news agency, have found that allowing some home-working makes it easier for it to retain qualified and experienced staff, because workers enjoy the flexibility. Both of these systems are usually introduced in response to employee pressure, and the change is usually welcome. However, zero hours contracts are less popular with workers. This is a situation where the workload varies throughout the year or week, and workers are only called into work when they are required. The result is uncertainty about earnings in any particular time period. This is rarely a welcome change for the workforce.

Further Sources

www.acas.org.uk
Managing conflict at work (Acas)
www.TUC.org.uk
www.gov.je: The A–Z of work
www.flexibility.co.uk
www.direct.gov.uk/employees

Your Turn

Questions   Time allowed 45 minutes

1. Explain how a business like Toyota might benefit from having a single union at its Derby car plant.
(5 marks)

2. A high street bank decides to introduce flexible working for all staff. What might the costs and benefits of this change be for the business?
(10 marks)

3. A local bus company wants to introduce new working arrangements for drivers that will involve working longer hours for fewer days each week. Suggest ways in which management could introduce this change.
(15 marks)

(30 marks)

Case Study   Time allowed 45 minutes

New strike threat to Royal Mail

During the summer of 2007, Royal Mail workers staged a number of one-day strikes in a dispute over pay and modernisation of the service. Royal Mail workers felt that up to 40,000 jobs were being threatened by the changes and that they were being forced into accepting new working practices.

In September 2007, the union Unite announced that it was about to ballot workers again because it believed that Royal Mail was about to close its final salary pension scheme and raise the retirement age for workers to 65. Royal Mail denied that such a decision had been made, although it confirmed that the pension scheme was going to be closed to new joiners.

A Unite spokesperson said, 'We call upon Royal Mail to honour its commitment to preserve the past service benefits that have been built up and paid for by our members'.

A Royal Mail representative said that it would consult with staff before any pension changes came into effect. He confirmed that consultation was vital in achieving a clear objective of protecting existing workers' pensions in a way that was affordable, while exposing no one to unacceptable risk in the future.

(Adapted from BBC News, 24 September 2007)

1. Explain the problem that Royal Mail management face with regard to the pensions of employees.
(10 marks)

2. Analyse the situation from the point of view of the union and its members.
(10 marks)

3. Evaluate the overall situation and make recommendations to Royal Mail management about how to proceed to minimise disruption to present and future services.
(20 marks)

(40 marks)

INDUSTRIAL RELATIONS AND CHANGE

There is an old tale about a man who loves hiking and goes on holiday abroad. During a particularly long hike across the countryside, he becomes lost. After hours of walking he eventually comes across a farmer and asks him for directions back to his hotel. The farmer thinks for a moment and then says, 'If I were you, I wouldn't start from here'. This was not what the hiker wanted to hear but he had to accept it.

When trying to achieve something, a business or a person must start from where it actually is and not where it would like to be. Change is a fact of business life, and managers must try to ensure that the business is in the right place for change to be successfully implemented. Positive industrial relations (the relationship between management and employees at national or local level) are a significant factor that will help facilitate this.

The process of change is easier in a climate where managers and employees work together with mutual trust and a willingness to compromise and cooperate. Consultation is an important part of the management of change, and is often conducted through a trade union. No manager can be truly effective in helping the business to meet its objectives if there is no consultation with the workforce.

Key Term

Trade union: an organisation of employees that seeks to protect and improve the interests of its members. It does this by negotiating with employers on pay and conditions of work.

The nature and history of trade unions

Many businesses have employees who are members of one or more trade unions. In order to achieve successful change, it is important for a business to communicate and negotiate with the union(s) involved.

A trade union is an organisation of employees that seeks to protect and improve the interests of its members. It does this by negotiating with employers on pay and conditions of work. Members of a union pay a subscription, usually every month. In return, as well as the union negotiating for better pay and conditions, members are entitled to all sorts of support, assistance and benefits. These include free legal advice on redundancy, harassment, dismissal, and pensions as well as special deals on non-work-related matters such as insurance, travel agency services etc.

At national level, unions have full-time salaried employees working at a permanent headquarters. The governing body is called the union executive. At local level (i.e. the workplace), the union representatives (sometimes called 'shop stewards') are elected from the workforce in that business. This person is by law allowed 'reasonable' time off work to take part in trade union activities. Representatives usually attend training courses run by the union to help them perform their role. The full-time union staff are also available for advice and support if needed.

The origins of trade unionism lie back in the late eighteenth century when tradesman began meeting socially in public houses. It is therefore no surprise that so many pubs have names such as 'The Carpenters' Arms'. The nature of these meetings gradually changed when workers realised a basic truth that continues today – unity is strength; an organised group of workers acting together has a better chance of improving their working life than an individual acting on his/her own. The term 'trade union' was born. These early unions sought to limit membership to their craft, as higher wages could be demanded with a limited supply of craftsmen.

The Industrial Revolution brought an upsurge in union activity, particularly among the unskilled and low paid. These people began to realise that not only skilled workers could benefit from membership of a union. The unions sought influence through gathering large numbers of members rather than limiting entrance. To some extent this division between the unions representing skilled workers, and those representing unskilled employees, has persisted to this day. However, whatever the type of employee or union, the basic premise is the same; unity is strength. Employers also realised this, and for over 100 years unions fought a political battle for their legal right to exist and organise. Unions in the UK enjoyed the most power in the 1970s.

rationed. There were regular power cuts and many businesses operated only for a few days a week.

Many trade unions are affiliated to (i.e. are members of) the Trade Union Congress (TUC). This is an organisation that brings Britain's unions together to draw up common policies and lobby the government to implement policies that will benefit employees. In the 1970s the leaders of the most powerful unions in the TUC were household names. Their influence was so important that they were regularly invited for 'tea and talks' with the Prime Minister to discuss economic issues. The Labour government which came into power in 1974 was also to suffer at the hands of the unions during the so-called 'winter of discontent' of 1978. Union after union went on strike for higher pay with vast disruption to the public and businesses. It seemed at the time as if some union leaders saw themselves in a political role – they disliked the whole capitalist system and wanted to use their influence to fight it.

However, such attitudes and influence did not last; the unions' behaviour was not acceptable in a democracy. The incoming Conservative government in 1979 pledged to curb union power through legislation. Union behaviour was severely constrained, especially over matters relating to strikes.

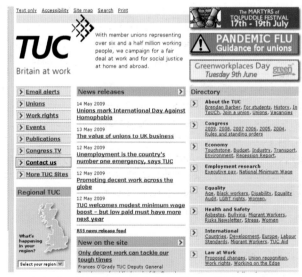

Figure 70.1 Unity is strength

Figure 70.2 The TUC's website offers advice to union members and news of current campaigns

The miners' strike brought down the Conservative government of Prime Minister Ted Heath in 1974. At a time when much of the nation's electricity was generated by coal, the miners' stranglehold over supplies to the power stations meant that electricity had to be

Key Term

Sympathetic strike: where one union strikes 'in sympathy' with another to assist in putting pressure on an employer. This is now illegal.

Trade unionism today

Union membership and influence has fallen considerably since the 1970s. In 1976, around 12 million people belonged to a union, but by 2006 this had declined to around 7.5 million. Union membership is now heavily concentrated in the public sector, where around 60% of the workforce is unionised as opposed to the private sector where the figure is less than 20%.

Like many a product in decline, the majority of unions have rebranded themselves and no longer present an image of being in conflict with management. There is not always harmony and agreement between unions and management, as unions still exist to protect their members' rights; but most union leaders and indeed the TUC today are very different from their counterparts of the 1970s. The TUC now promotes a partnership which it defines as 'employers and trade unions working together to achieve common goals such as fairness and competitiveness'.

To help achieve this it urges businesses to 'recognise' unions. Employers which recognise a union agree to negotiate with it over members' pay and conditions. This negotiation is known as 'collective bargaining'. If an agreement to recognise cannot be reached and the business employs more than 20 people, the union(s) involved may apply to the courts for legal recognition under the Employment Relations Act 1999. To achieve statutory recognition, the union has to demonstrate that more than 50% of the workers in the business are members of the union.

Figure 70.3 The CBI provides information to its members and lobbies the government on business issues

Union recognition may increase costs in the short run but result in benefits in the longer term. On the other hand, if both union representatives and managers are antagonistic towards one another, there may be very few benefits to either group whatever the timeframe.

The counterpart of the TUC is the Confederation of British Industry (CBI), the employers' organisation. The CBI provides information to its members and lobbies the government on policy issues that directly affect business. Relations between the TUC and the CBI can still become rather strained but are usually much more friendly and constructive than they were in the 1970s.

Key Terms

Trade Union Congress (TUC): an organisation that brings Britain's unions together to draw up common policies and lobby the government to implement policies that will benefit employees.

Union recognition: employers who recognise a union agree to negotiate with it over members' pay and conditions.

The benefits to a business of recognising a union

Recognition shows a willingness to engage in discussions with employees and treat them as stakeholders. This can mean:

- better communication between managers and staff. Even if the business has a clear set of objectives and a strategy to achieve them, this cannot guarantee success. The commitment of employees will play a major part in whether the strategy succeeds or fails. Improved communication can mean improved trust, and this can lead to improved commitment.
- assisting managers in identifying employees training needs.
- assisting managers in complying with health and safety procedures.
- early identification and resolution of problems, as union representatives often have considerable experience and training in employment law.

These are all factors that can impact positively on productivity and costs and so, if these benefits actually do occur, they will assist the business in reaching its objectives. The strategic benefits of union recognition could therefore include:

- reduced labour turnover and therefore reduced recruitment costs.
- increased staff motivation and morale and therefore improved productivity and greater efficiency.
- fewer days lost through work-related injuries and illnesses, thus minimising lost output, fines and compensation payouts.
- the ability to manage change more effectively, thus giving the business a competitive advantage in a changing environment.

Trade unions and the management of change

This last point above is particularly important. If it is accepted that consultation is necessary for effective change management, several questions arise - when will any consultation take place and who with? how many employees will be involved? from which sections of the factory/office will they be drawn? how will they be chosen? when will the meetings be held? Any employees involved have the legal right to paid time off work during the working day, but they may not want to attend a meeting before or after work unless they are paid for this as well. Who will 'cover' for the employees while they are being consulted? Also, if the business operates a bonus scheme, how will their bonus be affected by 'absence' due to the consultation process?

One obvious way for the consultation to occur would be with the union representatives. If the union is recognised and the collective bargaining process already established, the arrangements for the timing of the meetings, the pay issues and the personnel involved may already be established. The scope of meetings would be extended beyond simply 'bargaining' and would involve consultation and participation in decision-making.

If there is no union then managers may want to consider recognising one. Indeed, as so much rests on the sincerity of the consultation process when implementing change, it would be difficult for managers to claim to be truly interested in consultation and then refuse to accept a union's existence!

However it would be naïve to assume that a process where union representatives and managers can meet and discuss issues will automatically lead to harmonious industrial relations. Much will depend on:

- whether or not the consultation is genuine; i.e. employees' views are actually listened to as part of the culture of the business. The Acas website states:

'Making pretence of consulting on issues that have already been decided is unproductive and engenders suspicion and mistrust about the process among staff".

Like many business initiatives, the process of consultation must be driven from 'the top'. If junior managers see that senior managers are not really interested or concerned with genuine consultation, they will not devote much time and effort to it either.

- employees accepting that their views will not always be accepted and acted upon; there may be very good reasons for managers not doing so. They also have to accept that they will be involved in decisions that have previously been 'management territory'. Some of these decisions will be difficult, especially in matters such as redundancy.
- whether either side tries to score points off the other and in a 'workers versus management' confrontation.

Decision-making is slower with participation but it is to be hoped that better decisions (i.e. ones which have a measure of agreement and support from all parties) will be made. There will have to be a trade-off between the need to reach a consensus and the speed with which some business decisions are made.

The costs to a business of recognising a union

The reality of recognising a union is that union representatives will press for better wages and conditions for their members, and decision-making will be slower. This is likely to increase costs and reduce the business's profits, at least in the short term. Only if the gains to the employees result in greater productivity and profitability in the long term will recognition be beneficial in financial terms.

It could be argued that recognising a union can make a manager's life more difficult. Issues can also arise when employees who are not members of the union still receive the same terms and conditions negotiated by the union for its members. Union members may understandably become annoyed with those people who benefit without paying the union subscription. Managers will have to deal with any resentment.

Examiner's voice

Careful thought must be given to the business's culture when answering a question about union recognition and employee consultation. A business which has approachable managers who adopt a democratic style will find it relatively easy to accept the idea of union recognition; or, if they have already done so, introduce some sort of formal consultation process. A business which has traditionally been managed in an autocratic manner will find it rather more difficult; the whole culture of the firm will be against it. Changing a business's culture is a complex process: people are used to behaving in a certain way, and cultural change cannot be achieved in a short time.

Industrial action

This is another way in which the union might affect the achievement of a business's objectives. 'Industrial action' refers to the measures that can be taken by a union to put pressure on management in a dispute. Managers are aware that those workers in a union are better placed to do this than an individual employee would be. Failure to resolve a dispute could therefore result in the following:

Strike action

This will severely disrupt the fulfilment of the business's contracts with customers, and as such is a powerful weapon. However, employees who take strike action face financial consequences. As they are not working they are in breach of their contract, although if the strike is legal (see below) they cannot be dismissed for this. Naturally they will not receive any pay, and they are not entitled to any social security benefits while on strike. Any pension contributions due to be made by the employer will not be made for the period on strike.

A work to rule

This can be very effective since employees working to rule are not acting illegally, but are simply doing exactly what is stipulated in their contract of employment; they will start and stop work at exactly the stated time with no 'goodwill' (i.e. a few minutes extra) worked at all.

A refusal to work overtime

If overtime is a normal part of completing the work, a refusal to work any hours in excess of those in the contract can be quite effective as it will impact on the business's ability to meet customer requirements.

Key Term

Industrial action: the measures that a union can take to put pressure on management in a dispute.

Trade unions and the law

Unions cannot however behave exactly as they please, and the law relating to trade unions is complex. The Employment Acts of the 1980s represented a major change in the way in which unions could operate. Until then, a union representative at a plant could call a 'mass meeting' at a few minutes' notice and decide on a show of raised hands whether or not to call a strike. There were no secret ballots and this meant that members could be intimidated into voting for a strike. These 'wildcat' strikes were highly disruptive to businesses. Also, unions could legally have large numbers of members picketing (i.e. blocking) the entrance to the place of work which prevented goods entering or leaving.

Until the 1980s it was also legal for one union to strike 'in sympathy' with another. This meant that the coal miners might themselves go on strike 'in sympathy' with the railway workers' pay claim, even though this pay dispute was nothing to do with them.

The changes to the law were effective:

A union must now ensure that all members can vote in secret if it wants to call a strike

Union members can no longer be intimidated into voting for a strike at a public meeting held on the spur of the moment. The union must send the ballot papers to its members by post and must not interfere with the balloting process. Majority support must be obtained in response to a clearly asked question on the voting paper, which asks if members are prepared to take part in (or continue with) strike action. Secret ballots also apply to other union matters such as the election of executive members.

'Sympathetic' strikes and sympathetic picketing are against the law

The legal status of a union has changed. A union can now be fined in a criminal court for calling a strike without a ballot, and it can also be sued for damages in a civil court by a business if that business loses out as a result of the illegal action. If the miners' union now took sympathetic strike action on behalf of another union, it could be sued for damages.

Picketing is still legal but must be 'peaceful'

The police can restrict the number of pickets if they think it is necessary to prevent a breach of the peace.

The consequences of legislation

These Acts were labelled 'anti-union' by some groups, while others merely saw them as a necessary step to redress the balance between employers and employees. There have been further pieces of legislation since the 1980s which have continued the process of reforming the rights of businesses, employees and their unions. Some of this has weakened union power and some has strengthened it. The Trade Union Reform and Employment Act 1993 introduced new procedures which a union must follow before industrial action can lawfully be called, including giving advance notice to the business. It also restated the right for employees not to belong to a union at work if they did not want to. However, the Employment Relations Act 2004 improved the position of union members by preventing employers from discriminating against employees on the grounds of trade union membership.

Acas

The main way to avoid conflict between management and employees is for unions and managers to follow Acas guidelines. Acas stands for Advisory, Conciliation and Arbitration Service. It gives advice on industrial relations to employees and managers, offers them a service of conciliation (i.e. mediation – trying to reconcile two different positions and persuade one party to see the other's view), and finally (if both parties agree) it will provide arbitration; an independent Acas assessor will decide between two conflicting claims who is right.

Acas is funded by the government which ensures that it is independent. Its website states:

'Our aim is to improve organisations and working life through better employment relations. We provide up-to-date information, independent advice, high quality training and we work with employers and employees to solve problems and improve performance'.

If managers want to set up an effective system of industrial relations with employees (with or without a union), Acas can provide the guidelines to do so.

The website has up-to-date, accessible information and impartial guidelines covering every aspect of workplace life; from appraisal to adoption rights, from recruitment to redundancy.

Acas also has codes of practice in key areas of industrial relations e.g. on dealing with dismissal. These give authoritative advice to which employment tribunals refer. There is a helpline which gives access to an advisor for immediate guidance.

Advice

Acas is however not a kind of emergency service that can be contacted and expected to solve the problem in a matter of hours! Their regional offices are not drop-in centres for angry employees and managers. The first step is for either the employee(s) or employer to call the Acas helpline, where they can speak to someone who can give general advice and refer the party to the relevant guidelines. The information in the guideline can then be presented to the other party. This may help to resolve the dispute since advice has been offered by the organisation best placed to do so.

> ### Key Term
>
> **Acas:** the Advisory, Conciliation and Arbitration Service. It gives impartial advice and support to employees and managers on industrial relations issues.

Mediation

If this does not succeed, Acas offers mediation, which is a way of sorting out disagreements or disputes without having to go to court. A member of Acas will work with those in disagreement to help them sort out their problems. Initially this will be carried out by phone and by considering any relevant documentation. Later on, the mediator will bring both parties together in a meeting and, now in possession of all the facts and opinions, will seek to persuade them to reach an agreement that will sort out their problems. The emphasis is on the two sides reaching a settlement by themselves but if both sides ask, the mediator can recommend a way forward (this is not binding on either side however). The Acas website states:

'the aim is to maintain the employment relationship if at all possible and so mediation is about the future, not the past and who was right or wrong.'

This process has to be voluntary; if a union suggests mediation but the employer does not want to participate, that is the end of the matter. Both parties must willingly have Acas involvement. If not, the dispute will then either end or escalate – possibly to a tribunal. Both of these will result in bad feeling and therefore have a detrimental effect on the business.

Arbitration

If mediation fails, then that is the end of the matter unless both parties wish Acas to arbitrate. Arbitration is final and binding, and is usually only available for serious matters such as unfair dismissal or flexible working disputes. Arbitration is a judgement as to which party is in the wrong, and as such is distinct from mediation. It is sometimes called 'pendulum arbitration' because there must be a distinct judgment; the arbitrator cannot find both parties right or wrong. Those who agree to arbitration need to understand that it is an alternative to going to an industrial tribunal (a special court for hearing matters of employment law, and so if the judgment goes against them, they cannot go back to court.

Hearings usually last less than a day, and the arbitrator will base their judgements and any awards made on the same criteria as a tribunal. In a typical year, three out of four cases referred to an employment tribunal never arrive there, and this is largely because of Acas's help. If employees and managers want to work in harmony and avoid disputes, they should try to abide by the Acas guidelines and codes. The Acas helpline (and guidance from the website) is free, as is conciliation which is often conducted over the telephone. Acas do however charge for mediation and training services.

Business initiatives

Zero-hours contracts

Businesses often face variable levels of demand and so do not need the same number of employees all the time. A zero-hours contract is one under which an employer does not guarantee the employee a fixed number of hours per week; essentially the employee is 'on call' to work according to the business's short-term needs.

It is not hard to see why many unions dislike these contracts; unless the employee is genuinely in a position not to have to be concerned about having regular jobs

(e.g. they have retired early and are financially fairly comfortable), the employee has everything to lose and the employer everything to gain from such an arrangement. The business is showing very little commitment to the employee. Union opposition has only been slightly diminished by the fact that since 1994, the legal requirement that employees have to work a minimum number of hours per week to build up a period of continuity of employment to obtain their statutory employment rights has been abolished. Now, those on zero-hours contracts are treated like any other part-time employee when it comes to protection against dismissal and redundancy. Even so, a union is unlikely to welcome the attempt to introduce a contract of this nature.

Flexible working

'Flexible working' can have several different meanings:

Overtime

A premium rate of pay ('time and a half' or 'double time') is made for hours worked in excess of those contracted. Overtime working is normal among manual workers and unions are unlikely to object to it as long as it is paid at an acceptable rate and is not compulsory. Unions claim that the UK's culture of working long hours is detrimental to health and family life.

Part-time working

Employees are contracted to work for less than the normal full-time hours. When the business is busy, the number of employees can be increased. Part-time employees are now entitled to the same rights as those working full-time, and so there is less union opposition to this than in the past. For the business, the advantages of the flexibility might be somewhat offset by the increased recruitment and training costs.

Flexitime

Employees are contracted to work 'core hours' (e.g. 10 am to 3 pm) and an agreed number of additional hours. These hours can be worked when the employee wishes. The workforce thus becomes more flexible, and flexitime may help retain staff who do not want to work '9 am to 5 pm'. Flexible working could therefore help the business meet its legal requirements with regard to a work–home balance; e.g. the Employment Act 2003 introduced the right for parents of young and disabled children to apply to work flexibly. However there are issues for the business, such as increased recruitment costs and the probability that it will now have to be open for longer than before (higher variable costs). Acas published an important document about flexible working ('Flexible working and work–life balance') in 2007 which outlines the nature of flexible working, the practical issues involved, and how best for a business to introduce it. A copy can be found on the Acas website.

Subcontracting

This is where one business signs a contract to perform part of another business's contracted obligations. It is common in the construction industry where the main contractor (i.e. the builder) signs a contract with another business which agrees to install the plumbing or do the decorating. In recent years, subcontracting has grown and a number of activities that used to be done 'inhouse' (such as the business's payroll) are now performed by other businesses. It is common in the public sector too; councils have a legal duty to ensure that refuse is collected from households and businesses, but this collection is likely to be subcontracted to a private business and not undertaken by the council's own workforce.

The advantage to the main contractor is that it does not have to have such a large workforce or pay employment costs such as National Insurance and pension contributions; the subcontractor has to bear these. Some jobs may be created and others lost, and because redundancy is often associated with subcontracting, it is not always popular with trade unions.

Key Term

Flexitime: employees are contracted to work 'core hours' during the working day and an agreed number of additional hours. These hours can be worked whenever the employee wishes.

'No-strike' deals

This is where a union gives up the right to strike. This is the case with the police, and in the business world, Nissan and Toyota are among those companies in the UK to have such a deal in place. The government has in the past urged employers and unions to sign such a deal; for example, in 2002 it called upon the train operating companies and their unions to do so, in order to prevent disruption.

These deals can be the way to avoid disputes. Some unions are in favour of signing such an agreement on the grounds that it might encourage a business to recognise a union when it would otherwise be hostile to the idea

of doing so. Others are against it, saying that it undermines a very basic trade union principle.

Apart from recognition, a union signing any such deal would normally expect several benefits in return; e.g. regular communication, a system of employee participation and consultation, a commitment from managers to agree to regular workforce training etc. Finally it would seek an agreement to go to some form of arbitration in wage settlements if there is a dispute. The advantages to managers seem to be self evident; employees cannot withdraw their labour and so should be at work unless on holiday or ill. However, even if employees cannot strike, this in itself cannot guarantee good industrial relations; their discontent could easily manifest itself in some other way, e.g. through a work to rule, absenteeism or poor timekeeping.

Summary

Businesses need to be flexible and able to change quickly in a very dynamic globalised economy. Trade unions exist to protect their members' rights but they need to recognise this fact. Initiatives come in and out of fashion but there is no substitute for good industrial relations if managers want to have a productive, committed workforce that will accept change readily. In addition, there are certain principles that will be useful when unions and managers are negotiating and/or bargaining:

- Meetings should be at a convenient time to both parties.
- The personnel attending the meeting should be agreed in advance.
- Both parties should be allowed to submit agenda items for discussion – along with some information/data/figures concerning their current bargaining position.
- The chairman of the meeting must ensure that all agenda items are raised and that no one party dominates the meeting.
- A written statement at the end of the meeting on what (if anything) has been agreed is good practice. The management 'side' will need to report back to the board and the union 'side' will report back to their members.
- Both parties should be prepared to compromise. Perhaps a union wants a 5% rise in pay and management offers 3%. They could both settle for 4%. Where the bargaining is over changes in working practices rather than pay rises, it will be best for each side to set out clearly its objectives in an open manner, in order to identify some common ground and so move forward.

Further Sources

www.acas.org.uk – the Acas website. The motherlode of industrial relations information in the UK. Very informative and extremely easy to navigate. It includes 'movie' clips that can be watched to illustrate the issues.

www.berr.gov.uk – the Department for Business, Enterprise and Regulatory Reform. Very useful for a wide variety of current employment related matters.

www.cbi.org.uk – the Confederation of British Industry. The CBI is 'the employers' organisation' ('the voice of business'). It provides information to its members and lobbies the government on policy issues that directly affect business. Useful for up-to-date responses to government policy and trade union proposals.

www.etuc.org – the European Trade Union Confederation. This organisation's aim is 'to promote the interests of working people at European level and to represent them in the EU institutions'. It is very useful for a straightforward explanation of the many EU directives relating to industrial relations.

www.tuc.org.uk – the TUC's website. Lots of up-to-date information on the TUC itself, an employee's rights at work, labour law, the economy etc.

www.unison.org.uk – Unison is the largest trade union in the UK. Its website is very comprehensive and offers news of its current campaigns and its benefits for members.

Case Study Time allowed 40 minutes

Gregory and Setter Ltd (GSL)

GSL makes a variety of products in moulded plastic. These range from storage shelving for garages to garden furniture. Most employees belong to a union, 80%. The business has always recognised the union but industrial relations have deteriorated recently because of the board's decision to hold wage rises to the rate of inflation. Matters have worsened because of a decision by the board of GSL to introduce some new technology in order to improve productivity and profitability.

For several months there have been rumours of impending job losses. The news became official last week and was communicated to the shop steward Andy Fairclough via email. He was requested to attend a meeting with Dave Nixon, the personnel manager. On arrival at the meeting he was surprised to see that Roger Dennis, the production director was also present. He felt slightly intimidated.

'Last week was the first we've heard of it, officially,' Andy said, 'I should have been informed about this ages ago – and not by email. Why on earth haven't you mentioned it before? I could have consulted my members and then come back to you. A whole load of hassle could have been avoided.'

'Look, Andy,' replied Roger, 'All your members would have done is complain and threaten to take some sort of industrial action. The MD told me to keep it quiet until now.'

'They are not going to be happy with this lack of communication,' replied Andy. 'I would like to point out that you have a legal duty to consult with us on matters of redundancy.'

'Only in certain circumstances,' said Dave hurriedly. 'This is going ahead in six months time as planned. I'll just have to manage any discontent won't I?'

'You certainly will. You mentioned industrial action. Well, the first thing I'm going to do when I leave here is call for a ballot. We'll start with an overtime ban. I know how keen you are to get the current order out; we wouldn't have been offered double-time otherwise. Let's see what happens when you fail to deliver. Yes, let's see what happens to you two when the board learns that it's all your fault.'

'We have to have the new technology in place,' snapped Roger. 'Don't you realise that if we're not competitive, we all lose out. Your members won't have any jobs unless we change.'

'It's the same old thing every time,' said Andy. 'That's the excuse you always give when people are going to be sacked.'

'That's because it happens to be true. And they are not going to be "sacked". But there may have to be redundancies.'

'Same thing,' said Andy. 'So that's it then. No negotiations? We'll just be told who's going, will we?'

'The proper procedures will be followed,' said Dave.

'And they will be with regard to our industrial action,' replied Andy. 'Good luck with explaining to the board what's going to happen.'

1. Define the term 'industrial relations'. (2 marks)

2. Define the term 'industrial action'. Give one example of industrial action. (3 marks)

3. Outline **two** costs to GSL of recognising the trade union. (4 marks)

4. 'I should have been informed about this ages ago.' Analyse two reasons why early consultation with the union could have benefited GSL. (6 marks)

5. Evaluate how Dave Nixon could successfully implement the installation of the new technology. (18 marks)

(33 marks)

Index

Page numbers in **bold** refer to figures and tables